Get the most out of your study time!

This FREE CD-ROM works chapter-by-chapter with Samaha's text

Criminal Law Companion CD-ROM

By Joel Samaha

Let the exercises and activities on this CD-ROM help you improve your chance at success! If you want to master the concepts in your criminal law course, this multimedia tool is the way to study.

Dynamic and interactive, the **Criminal Law Companion CD-ROM** can help you gain a better understanding of the concepts of criminal law.

Throughout each chapter, icons lead you to the CD-ROM, where you'll find:

- updated activities
- flashcards that help you review the principles of criminal law, and the elements of many of the crimes included in the book
- a complete version of the U.S. Constitution
- the full version of all the case excerpts from the book's *Exploring Further* feature, and some important cases discussed in the text, but not excerpted
- links to the *Chapter Summary Outlines*, formatted so that you can add your own notes during class lectures, or later
- links to other features on the *Book Companion Web Site*

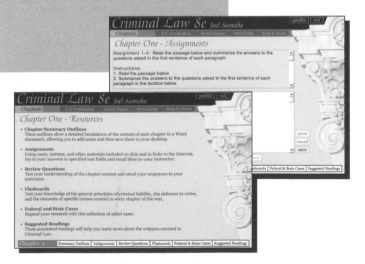

THOMSON
WADSWORTH

www.wadsworth.com

www.wadsworth.com is the World Wide Web site for Thomson Wadsworth and is your direct source to dozens of online resources.

At *www.wadsworth.com* you can find out about supplements, demonstration software, and student resources. You can also send email to many of our authors and preview new publications and exciting new technologies.

www.wadsworth.com
Changing the way the world learns®

Criminal Law

Eighth Edition

JOEL SAMAHA
University of Minnesota

THOMSON
WADSWORTH

Australia • Canada • Mexico • Singapore • Spain • United Kingdom • United States

THOMSON
WADSWORTH

Senior Executive Editor, Criminal Justice: Sabra Horne
Development Editor: Julie Sakaue
Assistant Editor: Jana Davis
Editorial Assistant: Elise Smith
Technology Project Manager: Susan DeVanna
Marketing Manager: Terra Schultz
Marketing Assistant: Annabelle Yang
Advertising Project Manager: Stacey Purviance
Project Manager, Editorial Production: Jennie Redwitz
Art Directors: Vernon Boes, Carolyn Deacy

Print/Media Buyer: Karen Hunt
Permissions Editor: Sommy Ko
Production Service: Ruth Cottrell, Ruth Cottrell Books
Text Designer: Adriane Bosworth
Copy Editor: Lura Harrison
Illustrator: Judith Ogus, Random Arts
Cover Designer: Yvo
Cover Image: Hirsham F. Ibrahim/Getty Images
Compositor: R&S Book Composition
Text and Cover Printer: Quebecor World/Taunton

For more information about our products,
contact us at:
Thomson Learning Academic Resource Center
1-800-423-0563
For permission to use material from this text or product, submit a request online at
http://www.thomsonrights.com.
Any additional questions about permissions can be submitted by email to
thomsonrights@thomson.com.

Library of Congress Control Number: 2004104326

Student Edition: ISBN 0-534-62991-1

Instructor's Edition: ISBN 0-534-62992-X

Image credits: p. 76: Drawing of Kitty Genovese, A. Balz; photo of Winston Moseley, AP/Wide World Photos; p. 201: Photo of Bernard Goetz, AP/Wide World Photos; p. 295: Drawing of Cora Dean, A. Balz; photo of Ray Snowden, Idaho State Historical Society, #79-5-552

Thomson Wadsworth
10 Davis Drive
Belmont, CA 94002-3098
USA

Thomson Learning
5 Shenton Way #01-01
UIC Building
Singapore 068808

Australia/New Zealand
Thomson Learning
102 Dodds Street
Southbank, Victoria 3006
Australia

Canada
Nelson
1120 Birchmount Road
Toronto, Ontario M1K 5G4
Canada

Europe/Middle East/Africa
Thomson Learning
High Holborn House
50/51 Bedford Row
London WC1R 4LR
United Kingdom

Latin America
Thomson Learning
Seneca, 53
Colonia Polanco
11560 Mexico D.F.
Mexico

Spain/Portugal
Paraninfo
Calle Magallanes, 25
28015 Madrid, Spain

For my students, Doug, and Steve

About the Author

Professor Joel Samaha teaches Criminal Law, Criminal Procedure, Introduction to Criminal Justice, and The Supreme Court and the Bill of Rights at the University of Minnesota. He is both a lawyer and an historian whose primary research interest is constitutional and legal history. He received his B.A., J.D., and Ph.D. from Northwestern University. Professor Samaha also studied under the late Sir Geoffrey Elton at Cambridge University, England.

Professor Samaha was admitted to the Illinois Bar in 1962 and practiced law briefly in Chicago. He taught at UCLA before going to the University of Minnesota in 1971. At the University of Minnesota, he served as Chair of the Department of Criminal Justice Studies from 1974 to 1978. He now teaches and writes full time. He has taught both television and radio courses in criminal justice and has co-taught a National Endowment for the Humanities seminar in legal and constitutional history. He was named Distinguished Teacher at the University of Minnesota in 1974.

In addition to *Law and Order in Historical Perspective* (1974), an analysis of law enforcement in pre-industrial English society, Professor Samaha has transcribed and written a scholarly introduction to a set of criminal justice records in the reign of Elizabeth I. He has also written several articles on the history of criminal justice, published in *Historical Journal*, *The American Journal of Legal History*, *Minnesota Law Review*, *William Mitchell Law Review*, and *Journal of Social History*. In addition to *Criminal Law*, he has written two other textbooks, *Criminal Procedure* and *Criminal Justice*, both in their sixth editions.

Brief Contents

Contents

13 Crimes Against the State   462

Elements of Crimes
and Defenses

Go to the Criminal Law 8e Web site at http://cj.wadsworth.com/samaha/crim_law8e, where you'll find the Elements of Crimes and Defenses flash cards. Use these to help you learn all of the elements for the crimes and defenses featured in this list.

Preface

I've loved studying criminal law since I took the Criminal Law course as a first-year law student at Northwestern University Law School in 1958. I've loved teaching it since I came to the University of Minnesota in 1971. I've also loved writing *Criminal Law,* now for the eighth time. And, it's a source of great satisfaction that my modest innovation to the study of criminal law, the **text/case book**—which combines definitions and analysis of general principles with excerpts of cases edited for nonlawyers—has been successful.

Criminal Law 8, like its predecessors, stresses both the **general principles** that apply to all of criminal law and the specific **elements of particular crimes** that prosecutors have to prove beyond a reasonable doubt. Learning the principles of criminal law isn't just a good mental exercise, although it does stimulate students to use their minds. Understanding the general principles is the prerequisite for understanding the elements of specific crimes. The general principles have lasted for centuries. The elements of specific crimes, on the other hand, differ from state to state and over time because they have to meet the varied and changing needs of new times and different places.

That the principles have stood the test of time testifies to their strength as a framework for explaining the elements of crimes as they are defined in fifty states and the U.S. criminal codes. But, there is more to their importance than durability; knowledge of the principles is also practical. The general principles are the bases both of the elements that prosecutors have to prove beyond a reasonable doubt to convict defendants and of the defenses that justify or excuse the guilt of defendants.

So, *Criminal Law* 8 rests on a solid foundation. But, it can't stand still any more than the subject of criminal law can remain frozen in time. The more I teach and write about criminal law, the more I learn and rethink what I've already learned; the more "good" cases I find that I didn't know were there; and, the more I'm able to include cases that weren't decided and reported when *Criminal Law* 7 went to press.

Of course, it's my obligation to incorporate into *Criminal Law* 8 these now decided and reported cases and this new learning, rethinking, and discovery. But, obligation doesn't describe the pleasure that preparing now eight new editions of *Criminal Law* brings me. Finding cases that don't just elaborate on a principle in terms students can understand but that also stimulate students to think critically about subjects worth thinking about is the most exciting part of teaching and writing. Looking for and finding cases with facts that will get students to pay attention to fundamental issues of good and evil, right and wrong, and justifications and excuse and at the same time give them pleasure are among my favorite pastimes.

Criminal Law 8 continues the **interactive approach** to learning that lies at the heart of the text/case method. The text explains general principles. Then, the cases follow, applying the principles explained in the text to specific facts. The text/case approach invites students to participate actively in learning. They can agree or disagree with the application made by the court in its opinion, but they have to understand the principles and definitions to apply them. The text/case approach demonstrates that students not only *understand* what they've learned, that they not only actually *enjoy* what they've learned, but also that they *remember* what they've learned. Perhaps the most gratifying part of teaching criminal law by the text/case method is having students tell me many years after they've taken the course that they remember the cases and the principles the cases stood for.

The case excerpts portray the criminal law in action, because they apply the general principles to real-life events. Students have to think about, to formulate their own interpretations of, and to apply the principles of criminal law to these real-life events. Students in my classes have to act as legislators, prosecutors, defense attorneys, judges, and juries so they can see the principles and rules of criminal law from all perspectives. They have to show that they understand the principles and rules first by stating them as the text presents them and then by applying them to the facts and reasoning of the case excerpts. This close relationship between the principles and rules that appear in the text and the case excerpts remains central to *Criminal Law,* Eighth Edition.

Case excerpts in *Criminal Law* 8 remain tailored to teach students the principles, doctrines, and rules of criminal law but with an eye toward **policy** rather than the technical knowledge needed by lawyers. Also, the case excerpts remain distinct from the text, as they have in previous editions. The text covers all of the main points, so it can stand alone as an analysis of the criminal law. Instructors can choose to omit the cases altogether from assignments; use them as illustrations and elaborations of the points made in the text; use them to test students' grasp of the text; or integrate them fully into the course.

An opening question introduces each case, focusing students' attention on the point that the case excerpt elaborates. Introductions to the case excerpts state the case history, including the outcome of the case, and the sentence imposed if it's known. The excerpts present the facts and the opinion of the case in the actual words of the court. **Case questions** follow the excerpts. The case questions test students' mastery of the facts and their understanding of the principle in the case excerpt. The questions also provoke students to think critically by inviting them to evaluate and propose alternatives to the arguments and the decisions of the court as presented in the case excerpt.

The **Rest of the Story** feature introduced in *Criminal Law* 7 is my effort to put the people back into criminal law cases. The feature demonstrates that the cases involve real people; they don't just decide an impersonal legal principle. Students frequently want to get beyond the confines of the case excerpt; they wonder what happened to criminals and their victims before, during, and after the crime. They even want to know what they looked like. It's difficult to fill in these details, but I've done it for a few where it's possible.

The **Exploring Further** feature—an enhancement of the Note Case feature in previous editions—follows some of the case excerpts. This feature provides brief synopses of cases that illustrate how courts vary in interpreting and applying the principles of criminal law and definitions of crimes involved in the primary case excerpt. Instructors and students have convinced me that the note cases are a valuable tool both in understanding and applying the topics covered in the text.

All the case excerpts and their corresponding features promote and expand *Criminal Law*'s interactive approach to learning.

THE ORGANIZATION OF THE CHAPTERS

The chapters in the text follow a traditional arrangement. The first eight chapters cover the **general part of the criminal law,** which includes the following topics: the nature, origins, structure, and purposes of criminal law; the constitutional limits on the criminal law; the general principles of criminal liability; the doctrines of complicity and inchoate crimes; and the defenses of justification and excuse to criminal liability. The next five chapters cover the **special part of the criminal law:** the major crimes against persons, habitation, property, and public order and morals and crimes against the state. The logic of the arrangement is to first treat the principles and doctrines common to all crimes and then to apply the general principles and doctrines to the crimes against persons, habitation, property, public order, and public morals. For example, Chapters 3 and 4 examine the general principles of criminal liability (*actus reus, mens rea,* concurrence, causation, and resulting harm). Chapter 9 applies these general principles to the rules governing criminal homicide; it examines the *actus reus, mens rea,* concurrence, causation, and resulting harm required to satisfy the requirements of the law of homicide. Similarly, Chapter 10 applies the general principles to the law of criminal sexual conduct, assault, and kidnapping. Chapter 11 applies the principles to crimes against property. Chapter 12 applies the principles to public order and morals crimes, with special emphasis on their application to "quality of life" crimes. It invites debate about the use of criminal law to regulate not only conduct that physically injures people, their homes, and their property but also behavior that creates community disorder by "offending respectable people." Chapter 13 examines the traditional crimes against the state (treason and sedition) and then applies them to the crimes created by the Anti-Terrorism and Effective Death Penalty Act and the USA Patriot Act.

NEW OR ENHANCED IN THIS EDITION

New cases. *Criminal Law,* Eighth Edition, contains over thirty-five new cases and many reedited cases from the previous edition. Why so many? First, the new cases are needed to keep the text current and relevant to students. Second, the discovery of cases that explain the general principles better and apply the facts in clearer and more interesting ways than cases in previous editions requires the addition of new cases. Third, actual use in the classroom makes it necessary to reedit some cases.

New Chapter 13, Crimes Against the State. This chapter reflects the impact of the September 11, 2001, terrorist attacks. But, consistent with the other chapters and all previous editions, the coverage of **terrorist crimes** created by the **Anti-Terrorism and**

Effective Death Penalty Act and the **USA Patriot Act** follows and builds on the ancient and enduring traditional crimes against the state (treason and sedition). So, Chapter 13 begins by examining how these enduring principles have influenced modern laws that are designed to respond to modern-day domestic and foreign terrorist acts.

New Chapter 11, Crimes Against Property. As a result of reviewers' comments, the Seventh Edition's Chapter 11 (Crimes Against Habitation) and Chapter 12 (Crimes Against Property) have been combined into one chapter: Chapter 11, Crimes Against Property. This new chapter also provides expanded coverage of such crimes as identity theft, theft by computers and the Internet, computer trespass, and white-collar crimes.

Expanded Chapter 12, Crimes Against Public Order and Morals. *Criminal Law* 8 expands the coverage of crimes against public order and morals to include such traditional crimes as riot, disorderly conduct, and victimless crimes. The chapter retains its previous sections on the application of the "broken windows" theory to the "quality of life."

New Exploring Further feature. This feature enhances the Note Cases from previous editions, providing examples of how interpretations and applications of the principle of the main case excerpt can vary from state to state and depending on the facts of each case. By exploring such variations in interpretation and application, this feature reinforces and deepens students' understanding of the law while also prompting them to think critically about the practical application of the law to real life.

Chapter Summaries in detailed outline form. Reviewers and students have always praised the summary outline I provided in the chapter on criminal homicide in previous editions. In *Criminal Law* 8, I expanded this concept so that every chapter now contains an outline summary. I have also included the outline in eletronic format on the enclosed CD-ROM. The electronic version is formatted so that students can expand the outline by adding their own notes from class, reading assignments, and so on. Students are thus encouraged to build their own outline that they can then use to study and review.

A new, more accessible design. The design for the Eighth Edition was created with greater accessibility in mind. Thus, it has Web site and CD-ROM references that are more visible throughout the text to guide students to the relevant sections of these helpful resources. These and other design enhancements were made to help focus and guide students through the chapter content more effectively.

Text-case method explanation moved to Chapter 1. The "How to Read, Brief, and Find Cases" section in Chapter 2 has been moved to Chapter 1 (now called the "Text-Case Method"), so that students learn these important skills at the beginning—well before reading their first case excerpt.

Interactive Criminal Law, 8e CD-ROM

The interactive CD-ROM made its debut in *Criminal Law* 7. Based on my own use as well as comments from students at the University of Minnesota and from adopters of *Criminal Law* 7, the CD-ROM now contains the following components for each chapter:

- **Interactive Summary Outline.** This is an interactive copy of the text's Chapter Summary outlines that students can annotate with their lecture notes, notes from reading, and recommendations from their instructors.

- **Assignments.** Instructors may use the assignments either as required work or for extra credit enrichment. Typical topics include comparing a criminal statute in the text with the student's own state code and/or the *Model Penal Code* (for example, comparing the kinds, degrees, and elements of murder discussed in the text with the student's own state criminal code or the *Model Penal Code*) and comparing a case excerpt in the book with another case discussed in the text (for example, *Robinson v. California* and *Powell v. Texas,* which deal with the treatment of "status" as a criminal act [*actus reus*]). Each assignment asks specific questions about the statutes, cases, and other sources and includes specific instructions on how to find these materials.

  Many students and adopters complained that *Criminal Law* 7 had too many assignments requiring them to connect to the Internet—I heard you. Many assignments in the *Criminal Law* 8 CD-ROM don't require connecting to the Internet, and the instructions identify those that don't.

- **Flash cards.** These will help students review the principles of criminal law and the elements of many of the crimes covered in the text.

- **Links to Exploring Further cases.** Full case reports of all case excerpts in the Exploring Further feature are included.

- **Links to Review Questions.** All Review Questions at the end of each chapter are included on the CD-ROM.

- **Suggested Readings.** The Suggested Readings have been revised and updated with annotations summarizing the content and indicating the level of difficulty of each reading. They can be found on the CD-ROM.

- **The U.S. Constitution.** A complete version of the U.S. Constitution is now provided on the CD-ROM, and the full text of the First, Eighth, and Fourteenth Amendments to the U.S. Constitution are included in the text appendix for easy access.

- **Links to many of the features on the Companion Web Site.**

ANCILLARIES

These ancillaries are available to qualified adopters. Please contact your local sales representative for details.

For the Instructor

Instructor's Manual. The manual includes learning objectives, chapter outlines, key terms and concepts, chapter summaries, discussion topics, student activities, and recommended readings. Also included is a test bank that contains multiple-choice, true/false, fill-in-the-blank, and essay questions, with answer keys and rejoinders.

ExamView® Computerized Testing. Create, deliver, and customize tests and study guides (both print and online) in minutes with this easy-to-use assessment and tutorial system. ExamView offers both a Quick Test Wizard and an Online Test Wizard that guide instructors step by step through the process of creating tests, while the unique WYSIWYG capability allows instructors to see the created test on screen exactly as it will print or display online. Instructors can build tests of up to 250 questions using up to 12 question types. With ExamView, instructors can also enter an unlimited number of new questions or edit existing questions.

WebTutor™ ToolBox for Blackboard and WebCT. Preloaded with content and available for free via pincode when packaged with this text, WebTutor Toolbox pairs all the content of this text's rich Companion Web Site with all the sophisticated course management functionality of a WebCT or BlackBoard product. Instructors can assign materials (including online quizzes) and have the results flow automatically to your gradebook. ToolBox is ready to use at log on, or instructors can customize its pre-loaded content by uploading images and other resources, adding Web links, or creating their own practice materials. Students only have access to student resources on the Web site. Instructors enter a pincode for access to password-protected instructor resources.

Criminal Law: A Microsoft® PowerPoint® Presentation Tool. FREE to adopters of this text, this dual platform CD-ROM is designed to work with Power-Point® presentation software and includes detailed outlines that will help you develop your Criminal Law lecture presentations.

Wadsworth Criminal Justice Video Library. Choose from hundreds of videos featuring topics covered in criminal justice courses, from such respected sources as CNN®, Court TV, Films for the Humanities and Sciences, and the American Society of Criminology's Oral History Project. For a complete listing and adoption policies, please contact your local Thomson Wadsworth representative.

For the Student

Study Guide. The guide contains learning objectives, key terms and concepts, and chapter outlines, as well as a practice test bank that includes multiple-choice, true/false, fill-in-the-blank, and essay questions, with an answer key at the end of each chapter.

The Companion Web Site for *Criminal Law*, Eighth Edition.
http://cj.wadsworth.com/samaha/crim_law8e

This unique Web site offers instructors and students alike many exciting resources. It includes electronic versions of the Chapter Summary outlines from the text, formatted so that students can easily annotate them with class and reading notes, as well as flash cards that quiz students on the elements of specific crimes. To assist students in writing case briefs, the Web site also includes an exciting new InfoWrite feature. Standard features for students include flash cards and a glossary of key terms, chapter quizzes, one final exam, 3-Step Concept Builders, Opposing Viewpoints Resource Center term projects with discussion/critical thinking questions, links to state and federal cases, and much more!

Key Cases, Comments, and Questions on Substantive Criminal Law by Henry F. Fradella (The College of New Jersey). This book examines cases with comments, analyses, and discussion questions to help students grasp challenging material and test their knowledge. For more information, contact your Thomson Wadsworth representative.

Careers in Criminal Justice Interactive CD-ROM, Version 3.0. This CD provides students with extensive career profiling information and self-assessment testing and is designed to help them investigate and focus on the criminal justice career choices that are right for them. With links and tools to assist students in finding a professional position, this new version includes ten new "Career Profiles" and two new "Video Interviews," bringing the total number of careers covered to fifty-eight.

Guide to Criminal Law for California; Guide to Criminal Law for Florida; Guide to Criminal Law for Illinois; Guide to Criminal Law for New York; Guide to Criminal Law for Texas. These brief guides explore state-specific laws and cases. They include chapter introductions, overviews of codes and implications, and exercises for state-specific penal codes.

InfoTrac® College Edition Student Guide for Criminal Justice. This twenty-four-page booklet provides detailed user guides for students, illustrating how to use the InfoTrac College Edition database. Special features include log-in help, a complete search tips cheat sheet, and a topic list of suggested keyword search terms for criminal justice.

ACKNOWLEDGMENTS

Criminal Law 8 didn't get here just by my efforts. I had a lot of help. As always I'm indebted to the contributions of the reviewers for this edition:

Jim Beckman, University of Tampa

Frances Coles, California State University, San Bernardino

Daniel Hillyard, Southern Illinois University Carbondale

Tom Hughes, University of Louisville

Thomas Lateano, Kean University

Rick Michelson, Grossmont-Cuyamaca Community College

Criminal Justice Editor Sabra Horne has supported me at every stage of the book. Julie Sakaue developed the manuscript for publication. Susan DeVanna helped to develop the CD-ROM. Elise Smith and Jana Davis helped with the print supplements. Jennie Redwitz facilitated rough spots along the way. Ruth Cottrell's calm efficiency, warm kindness, careful editing, and extraordinary patience were as welcome (and necessary) in this edition as they have been in so many others. Once again, Lura Harrison's superb copyediting definitely improved the text.

Julia Shaw, my former student, compiled a superb index. I'm always turning to the indexes of books I read. Because I believe they're so important, I always used to make my own indexes. In recent years, when I've turned to others to compile the indexes, I've usually been disappointed. But not this time! I knew I could count on Julia, because everything she does is outstanding.

Abbey Baltz has definitely enriched the "Rest of the Stories" with her drawings of Katherine Genovese and Cora Dean. How she could turn the awful original newspaper photos into these excellent drawings is a mystery to me. But, that's why she's an artist and I'm a teacher.

What would I do without Doug and Steve. Doug takes me there and gets me here and everywhere, day in and day out, days that now have stretched into years. And, my old and dear friend Steve, who from the days when he watched over my kids to now decades later, keeps the Irish Wolfhounds, the Siamese cat, the Standard Poodle, me, and a lot more around here in order. And they do it all while putting up with what my old Cambridge mentor Sir Geoffrey Elton called "Joel's mercurial temperament." Only those who really know me can understand how I can try the patience of Job! Friends and associates like these have made *Criminal Law* 8. The blame for its faults is, of course, all mine.

Joel Samaha
Minneapolis

Criminal Law

Eighth Edition

First Things First: The Nature and Limits of Criminal Law

Chapter Main Points

- Criminal law in the U.S. version of constitutional democracy is broad but not unlimited.
- The first limit on criminal law is our democratic form of government; nothing is a crime unless a majority passes a law defining the crime and setting the punishment for committing it.
- Majorities can't make just anything they want a crime because of the U.S. and state constitutional guarantees of due process, equal protection, and individual rights to life, liberty, and privacy.
- Democracy and constitutions set the minimum standards for criminal law. The principles of criminal liability, justification, and excuse raise the minimum to optimum levels.
- Punishment is limited by the U.S. Constitution, the principle of limited methods, and the purposes it's supposed to achieve.
- Punishment has two basic purposes: retribution—looking back to the crime—and prevention—looking forward to deter future crimes and rehabilitating criminals.
- Schemes used to classify and grade crimes help us make sense out of criminal law; criminal codes are designed according to them; and criminal justice professionals think about criminal law in terms of schemes.
- The oldest classification is to divide criminal law into a general part that covers the principles that apply to all crimes and a special part that applies the general part to the elements of specific crimes.
- Dividing crimes into felonies, misdemeanors, and violations classifies and grades crimes according to punishment.
- The schemes of *malum in se* and *malum prohibitum* divide crimes according to their severity.
- Separating crimes into crimes against the state, persons, property, public order and morals, and the administration of justice is a scheme based on the subject matter of the crime.
- Criminal law in a federal system consists of federal, state, and municipal criminal codes and courts.
- Most criminal law is state criminal law, but it includes an expanding federal component.
- Modern criminal law is mainly found in statutes (codes), but it originated in and is still influenced by its common-law origins.
- The purpose of precedent and the doctrine of stare decisis is to give the law stability and predictability.
- Courts aren't absolutely bound by precedent and stare decisis; they can, and sometimes do, get off the beaten path of precedent.

How "Limited" Is Our Criminal Law?

POLICE OFFICER: We should have a billboard at our city limits that reads:
"Welcome to Bloomington, you're under arrest."

PROFESSOR: Why?

POLICE OFFICER: Because everything in Bloomington is a crime.

PROFESSOR: But Bloomington is a city in the freest country in the history of
the world. ◆

We're the freest country in the history of the world, but our criminal law punishes everything from murder to playing loud music. The last time I checked, "harboring overdue library books" can land you in jail for thirty days in Palo Alto, California. Fornicating with a bird is a crime in Minnesota. My own neighbor (not my favorite one) reported me for parking *my* car on *my* lawn (a fineable offense in my suburb). In the suburb next to mine, it's an offense to hang your laundry out in your backyard. In Minneapolis, it's an offense to eat on a bus or hang out in shopping malls.

 Check your town's ordinances or your state's criminal code for silly crimes where you live.

"First things first Joel," my mother reminded every Saturday morning while I was growing up. She meant, first I had to do my chores, then I could play with my friends. In the title to this chapter, "first things first" means you have to learn something about the basic nuts and bolts of U.S. criminal law before you can get the most out of the really interesting and important stuff (like the opening dialogue and the scenarios in the next section and in the rest of the chapters).

LIMITS OF CRIMINAL LAW

Our criminal law may be broad, but it's not unlimited. In fact, the study of criminal law is to a large extent a study of its limits. To introduce you to the limits we'll be examining in the rest of the book, think about the fifteen scenarios listed below. In your opinion, which of the scenarios describe crimes? For the scenarios you believe describe crimes, put them into three categories—most serious, serious, and least serious. Can you explain in words why you put them into the categories you did?

Now, look at the scenarios you didn't call crimes. Even if they're not crimes, do they call for *some* response? Think of these responses:

1. *Private lawsuits.* "Victims" should sue the *actors* (a word for parties in legal cases) who injured them.

2. *Government regulation.* There should be a tax on or a license required for what the actors in the scenarios did.

3. **Social condemnation.** Friends and other people who matter should criticize what the actors did and maybe even cut off their relationship with them for doing it.

4. *Individual conscience.* Leave the control to the individual's guilty conscience.

5. *No action.* Ignore what the actors did.

6. *Social encouragement.* The actors should be praised for what they did.

OK, now classify the fifteen scenarios according to the six listed responses.

1. Sheila hates Rosemary because she's richer and smarter. Sheila goes over the edge when a prestigious medical school accepts Rosemary, while the law school at the same university rejects her. Sheila decides to kill Rosemary. She gets her chance when Rosemary invites her to a celebration party. Sheila poisons Rosemary's drink and gleefully watches her die a slow, agonizing death.

2. Tom's wife suffers excruciating pain from terminal bone cancer. The family has exhausted its insurance coverage and run through its savings to keep her alive. Every time Tom sees her, she pleads, "Tom, please put me out of my misery. I can't take this anymore." Tom loves his wife and can't bear her pain. An avid hunter, he takes one of his guns and shoots her in the head, killing her instantly.

3. Driving down an icy city street, Nathan steps on the gas when he approaches a particularly slick spot, hoping for the thrill of feeling the car spin out. As it does, Nathan sees a frail old man crossing the street in front of him. He tries to swerve away but can't. He hits the old man. "Oh, my God!" cries Nathan. "This is the last thing I wanted to happen." Two days later, the man dies of a heart attack.

4. Scott's drowning in a lake. Scott sees Foy, an Olympic swimmer (but a creep). Scott hollers, "Foy, save me! For God's sake save me!" "Sorry, I don't feel like it," Foy laughingly replies. Scott drowns.

5. Every night when he gets home from work, Frank watches child pornography on his new DVD player. He finds it highly erotic, especially when it involves sex between teenage girls. After getting his "release," Frank falls asleep until it's time to get up for work the next morning.

6. Michael is a demonstrative person who really likes women. He goes into a singles bar, where he's immediately drawn to Marietta. Michael puts his arm around her waist and introduces himself. Marietta, offended by a stranger touching her, says firmly, "Stop that!" Michael doesn't remove his arm, saying, "Don't be such a prude, I'm just trying to be friendly."

7. Adam sees an MP3 player in an electronics store. When the clerk walks away, Adam takes the radio.

8. Bill's addicted to crystal meth.

9. Jessica smokes marijuana on weekends.

10. Michelle cheats on her boyfriend Cameron with his best friend D. J. Cameron comes home from work early and catches them in *his* bed. He falls apart, starts drinking, becomes an alcoholic, and loses his highly successful web page construction business.

11. Monty tells his boyfriend Brad he's HIV negative. It's a lie. Monty's really HIV positive.

12. A major pharmaceutical corporation introduced a drug used to treat high blood pressure. The company knew that—in another country—the drug had been reported to cause death and liver damage. Nevertheless, the corporation labeled the product, "No cause-and-effect relationship exists between this drug and liver damage." After the drug was linked to thirty-six deaths and more than five hundred cases of liver and kidney damage, the corporation withdrew the drug from the U.S. market.

13. Hilary, a gynecologist, recommended a hysterectomy for Jane, who suffers from back pain. After the surgery, the pain continued. Another doctor discovered the source of Jane's pain is the difference in length between her left and right legs. He recommends platform shoes; Jane's pain disappears.

14. Duran burns the American flag while chanting, "I hate America."

15. Matt dances nude in a local tavern. A sign outside the bar reads: "All male strippers. Adults welcome."

You don't know this yet, but the scenarios you've just read deal with most of the limits on our criminal law. Let's briefly identify the limits we'll be examining in *Criminal Law,* 8e, and your instructor will be helping you understand in your criminal law class:

- Democracy
- Constitutions
- Principles of criminal liability
- Defenses to crime
- Principle of limited methods

Democracy

The first limit on criminal law is our democratic government. In democracies, nothing is a crime unless a legislature passes and a mayor, governor, or president signs a law that includes two elements:

1. *Definition of offenses.* This spells out what the law prohibits, like murder, rape, and robbery.

2. *Punishment for the offense.* This spells out the penalty (fines, incarceration, and death) for the offense defined in (1).

So, criminal law is a list of "don'ts" and punishments for doing the "don'ts." As an ancient legal saying puts it: "No crime without law; no punishment without law."

U.S. and State Constitutions

Majorities have lots of power but they can't make just anything they want a crime. Why? We live in a *constitutional* democracy. In the U.S. version of **constitutional democracy,** the U.S. Constitution and state constitutions tell the majority what they can and can't make a crime. Here's the list of constitutional limits we'll cover later (Chapter 2).

1. *Due process of law.* Legislatures have to write criminal laws that are clear enough for individuals and government officials to know in advance exactly what the law bans.

2. *Equal protection of the law.* Legislatures can't define crimes and punishments that apply differently based on inherited characteristics (race, ethnicity, gender, and age).

3. *Individual rights and liberties.* Legislatures can't make crimes that violate the rights to free speech, religion, and privacy.

So, laws passed by representatives elected by a majority of voters are *necessary*, but they're not *enough* to define crimes and punishments. The laws have to satisfy the three constitutional requirements just listed. Sometimes, laws that satisfy these requirements are referred to as laws that "pass constitutional muster."

Principles of Criminal Liability

Laws passed by representatives of majorities of voters may pass constitutional muster, but, as a famous judge once said, "It doesn't pay a law much of a compliment to say it's constitutional." Why? Because they meet only the *minimum* standards of the U.S. version of constitutional democracy. In other words, they're the floor, not the optimum and certainly not the best we can do in defining crimes and punishments.

This is where the **principles of criminal liability** (Chapters 3 and 4) come in. For centuries, and long before there was a U.S. constitutional democracy, the prosecution had to prove three **elements of a crime** beyond a reasonable doubt:

1. A criminal act was committed.

2. Criminal intent existed.

3. Criminal intent triggered the criminal act.

Each of these elements is related to a principle of criminal liability that lies at the heart of our criminal law:

1. *Actus reus (criminal act).* We punish people for what they *do*, not for what they *intend* to do or for who they are.

2. *Mens rea (criminal intent).* Punishment (at least for serious crimes) depends on the blameworthiness of the intent that triggers the criminal act.

3. **Concurrence.** Criminal intent (*mens rea*) has to trigger criminal acts (*actus reus*) and cause criminal harm.

These elements and principles are connected and are more complicated than they look here. Until we discuss them fully (Chapters 3 and 4), it's enough to point out that they limit criminal behavior and punishment to actions punished according to the blameworthiness of the intent that triggered the criminal acts.

Defenses to Crime

Everybody knows that someone who kills an attacker in self-defense or commits a crime while she's insane isn't guilty of a crime. Why? Self-defense is what we call a **defense of justification** (it's not wrong to kill someone who's about to kill you

[Chapter 7]). Insanity is a **defense of excuse** (it's wrong to commit a crime, but you're not responsible if you're insane when you commit it [Chapter 8]). People who can prove they have **alibis** (they weren't at the crime scene) aren't guilty either. So, the reach of criminal liability is limited by three defenses:

1. Justifications
2. Excuses
3. Alibis

CRIMINAL PUNISHMENT: LIMITS AND PURPOSES

By now, you should have firmly in your mind the first of the first things: The U.S. version of criminal law has many limits. Punishment has limits, too. You're not ready to start your study of criminal law unless you know something about the limits on punishment. We briefly touch on two of these limits:

1. The constitutional ban on cruel and unusual punishments (Chapter 2)
2. The principle of limited methods

Cruel and Unusual Punishment

Let's start with the U.S. Constitution, Amendment VIII, which bans **cruel and unusual punishment** (we'll discuss it fully in Chapter 2). Here, we'll only note that the amendment commands that legislatures can't impose

1. Punishment that inflicts needless pain (like torturing an offender to death)
2. Punishment out of proportion to the crime (sending a shoplifter to prison for life without parole)

The Principle of Limited Methods

Criminal law is also limited by the idea that in a rational society, criminal law is the last resort of social control. From that idea stems the **principle of limited methods.** According to this principle, if informal private sanctions work, criminal law has no social control role to play. If informal sanctions fail and civil actions work, then criminal law still has no role to play. If civil actions don't secure obedience, and criminal law becomes necessary, if a lesser penalty is as effective as a greater penalty, the lesser penalty is the rational one.

This is the principle that guides the *Model Penal Code and Commentaries* (1985), which you're going to hear a lot about in this book. The code is the work of the American Law Institute (ALI), a private association of eminent lawyers, judges, law enforcement professionals, and professors that has substantially advanced the cause of an effective, rational criminal law. Based on extensive cooperation among the members, the ALI published the *Model Penal Code and Commentaries* in 1961 and updated it in 1985. By that year, thirty-four states had enacted some of the model provisions and fifteen hundred courts had cited its provisions and referred to its commentary. Although it's now almost twenty years since the revision, it's frequently referred to and highly respected by lawyers, judges, and criminal justice professionals. And, just because states haven't adopted the *Model Penal Code* doesn't mean their criminal codes and court decisions aren't affected by it.

Purposes of Criminal Punishment

Criminal punishment is also limited by its purposes. Billions of words have been written trying to answer the question, "What's the purpose of criminal punishment?" Or, to put it another way, "What's criminal punishment good for?" There's a simple answer. Criminal punishment has two purposes, and it's good for two things: retribution and prevention. **Retribution** (sometimes called "just deserts") looks back to the crime committed, punishing criminals because they deserve it. **Prevention** looks forward, punishing offenders to prevent future crimes. There are four kinds of prevention: general deterrence, special deterrence, incapacitation, and rehabilitation. Let's look at these two purposes of criminal punishment.

Retribution

Striking out to hurt what hurts us (retribution) is a natural impulse. It's why we kick the rock we stubbed our toe on. The Old Testament sums up the idea this way, "Life for life, fracture for fracture, eye for eye, tooth for tooth" (Lev. 24:20, Holy Bible 2000). The words of the famed Victorian judge and historian of the criminal law, Sir James F. Stephen, written in the 1800s don't sound at all strange today:

> The criminal law . . . proceeds upon the principle that it is morally right to hate criminals. . . . I think it highly desirable that criminals should be hated, that the punishments inflicted upon them should be so contrived as to give expression to that hatred, and to justify it so far as the public provision of means for expressing and gratifying a healthy natural sentiment can justify and encourage it. (1883, 81–82)

Retribution is two-edged: It benefits society by retaliation, and it benefits criminals by "paying their debt to society." Retribution assumes that offenders are free to choose between committing and not committing crimes. Because offenders have this choice, society can blame them for making the wrong choice. We call this blameworthiness *culpability*. **Culpability** means offenders are responsible for their actions and have to suffer the consequences if they act irresponsibly.

Retribution has several appealing qualities. First, it assumes we have free will and individual autonomy. We're not mere pawns at the mercy of forces we can't control; we're the masters of our own destinies. Second, retribution accords with human nature. Hating what and who hurts us—especially murderers, rapists, robbers, and other violent criminals—is a natural impulse (Gaylin 1982; Wilson and Herrnstein 1985, ch. 19).

From the Old Testament's philosophy of taking an eye for an eye, to the nineteenth-century Englishman's claim that it's right to hate and hurt criminals, to the modern idea of "three strikes and you're out" and "lock 'em up and throw away the key," the desire for retribution has run strong and deep in religion, in criminal justice, and in society. Retributionists see this long tradition as proof of its worth, as if its sheer tenacity validates its use. The long and strong life of retribution lies mainly in its dependence on the idea of culpability. Simply put, we can't punish those we can't blame; and, we can't blame those who aren't responsible. But justice demands that we *do* punish the blameworthy.

One problem with retribution is the difficulty of translating abstract justice into specific penalties. What are a rapist's just deserts? Is castration justice? How many years in prison is a robbery worth? How much offender suffering will repay the pain of a disfigured assault victim? Critics of retribution answer, "We can't! And, we shouldn't even try." Why? Retributionists can't prove human nature craves vengeance (Weihofen 1960, 116–120).

Many criminologists reject the most basic assumption of retribution—free will. Their research has demonstrated a relationship between social conditions and crime. They call it **determinism.** (Of course, relationship doesn't prove cause and effect.) Some biologists have linked violent crime to an extra Y chromosome (Wilson and Herrnstein 1985, 69–70). Medical doctors have tried to show a link between brain chemistry and violence (Mayer and Wheeler 1982). Still, there's no convincing empirical proof of any of these claims for determinism. (The retributionists haven't convincingly proved their claims of free will either.) In any event, determinism undermines the legitimacy of retribution to the extent that we act according to "forces" either inside or outside our conscious minds instead of choosing our behavior.

Probably the strongest argument against retribution is that the crimes most people commit in real life (like disorderly conduct and public drunkenness) aren't based on moral blameworthiness because they don't require criminal intent (Diamond 1996, 111–131[Chapter 12]).

Prevention

Retribution justifies punishment on the ground that it's right to hurt criminals, whereas *prevention* inflicts pain not for its own sake but to prevent future crimes. **General prevention,** also called **general deterrence,** aims by threat of punishment to prevent criminal "wannabes" from committing crimes. **Special deterrence,** by inflicting pain on individual offenders, aims to deter them from committing future crimes. **Incapacitation** also aims to prevent already convicted criminals from committing future crimes by confining them or, more rarely, altering them surgically, or, at the extreme, executing them. **Rehabilitation** aims to prevent crime by changing individuals so they'll want to (and then do) obey the law. These purposes all have in common the premise that pain is necessary only to prevent future crime. They differ from retribution in this essential respect: Retribution purposely inflicts pain to give criminals their "just deserts" for past criminal conduct.

CLASSIFYING AND GRADING CRIMES

Now that you're clear about the importance of limits in criminal law and punishment, let's look at some schemes for classifying crimes. The urge to make sense of criminal law is ancient. That urge has produced a lot of schemes to classify and grade the content of criminal law. Although I'll be the first to admit it's not the most exciting part of your study of criminal law, I'll also tell you the basics of these schemes are among the first things you need to know right at the beginning of your study. Why? At least three reasons: First, criminal codes are organized according to schemes. Second, scholars and criminal justice professionals organize their thinking about criminal law based on the schemes. Third, they'll help you understand and think critically about what you learn in this book.

The General and Special Parts of Criminal Law

The oldest classification scheme (which is followed in this book) is to divide criminal law into two parts. The **general part of criminal law** covers principles that apply to all crimes: constitutional principles found in the U.S. and state constitutions (Chapter 2); principles of criminal liability included in state statutes and court opinions (Chapters 3–4); principles that define the liability for accomplices and accessories to crime (Chapter 5); liability for the uncompleted crimes of attempt, conspiracy, and solicitation (Chapter 6); and finally the general principles of justification and excuse known as the defenses to crimes, such as self-defense and insanity (Hall 1960, 16–26 [Chapters 7–8]).

The **special part of criminal law** applies the principles in the general part of criminal law to elements of specific crimes (like murder, criminal sexual conduct, burglary, disorderly conduct, and helping terrorists [Chapters 8–13]). For example, the general principle *actus reus* says that criminal liability depends on a criminal act. So, all specific crimes include an action—killing in murder, breaking and entering in burglary, taking someone else's stuff in theft, or giving a terrorist money in aiding and abetting.

Grading Schemes

Not all bad conduct is criminal, nor should it be. A "creep" is not necessarily a criminal! Fairness calls for a measured response, one proportional to the wrong. As the ancient saying goes, "Let the punishment fit the crime." So, the pained conscience of the wrongdoer is enough punishment for some conduct. Other conduct, while reprehensible, still doesn't need a criminal law response; private sanctions are enough. These might include suspending students who cheat on exams; docking the pay of lazy workers; and scorning liars and unfaithful spouses.

All grading schemes include **criminal punishment** enacted by legislatures to punish crimes defined by law. There are several types of grading schemes. One scheme for grading the seriousness of crimes is to classify them according to punishment. Another distinguishes crimes that are inherently evil conduct from merely prohibited conduct. A third classifies crimes according to their general subject matter. We'll take a look at each variation.

Felony, Misdemeanor, and Violation

One scheme for grading the seriousness of crimes is to classify them according to punishment (Table 1.1). From the most severe to the least severe, the penalty categories are

Capital felonies

Felonies

TABLE 1.1	
Grading by Punishment	
Classification	**Punishment**
Capital felony	Death in death penalty state, or life in prison without parole in states without death penalty
Felony	More than one year imprisonment
Gross misdemeanor	6 to 12 months in jail and/or fine
Misdemeanor	3 to 6 months and/or fine
Petty misdemeanor	10 to 30 days and/or fine
Violation (usually traffic)	Fine only, not recorded as a crime

Gross, ordinary, and petty misdemeanors

Violations

In states with capital punishment, **capital felony** means the death penalty; in states without the death penalty, it means life in prison without hope of release before death. Until the mid-1990s, aggravated murder was the only capital felony punishable by death. (Louisiana enacted a statute in 1995 allowing the death penalty for the rape of a child under 12 [Chapter 2].) However, some states have enacted life-without-parole statutes for some drug law violations. Michigan, for example, punishes the possession of more than 650 grams of cocaine with life imprisonment without parole (*Harmelin v. Michigan* 1991). **Felonies** are crimes punishable by incarceration of at least one year in state prisons; **misdemeanors** are punishable by incarceration in local jails for less than one year and/or by fines. **Gross misdemeanors** are punishable for six months to one year in jail and/or a fine; **ordinary misdemeanors** fall into the ninety-day to six-month range and/or a fine; and **petty misdemeanors** fall into the ten- to thirty-day range and/or a fine. **Violations** (usually traffic offenses) are punishable by fines; aren't labeled criminal convictions; and don't become part of your criminal record (American Law Institute 1985 [1], Article 6).

Wrongs *Mala in Se* and *Mala Prohibita*

Another grading scheme divides crimes into inherently evil conduct *(malum in se)* and merely prohibited conduct *(malum prohibitum)*. Murder, rape, robbery, burglary, arson, larceny are *malum in se*, because they would be evil even if the law didn't make them crimes. On the other hand, if you make an illegal left turn or commit most of the long list of offenses that regulate life in the twenty-first century, no one will treat you as a bad person even though you broke the law. The law bans them, but they're not naturally bad like murder and rape.

Grading According to Subject

A variation of the *malum in se/malum prohibitum* scheme of grading is to classify crimes according to their general subject matter. This scheme is at least as old as the 1500s. In the special part of most state criminal codes, you'll still see the sixteenth-century classifications. Here are the subjects, listed as they are in most codes, from most to least serious:

1. *Crimes against the state.* Treason, sabotage, sedition, and now terror (Chapter 13)

2. *Crimes against persons.* Murder, manslaughter, rape, kidnapping, assault, and battery (Chapters 9–10)

3. *Crimes against property.* Larceny, embezzlement, false pretenses, theft, arson, burglary, malicious mischief, and robbery (Chapter 11)

4. *Crimes against public order.* Disorderly conduct, public drunkenness (Chapter 12)

5. *Crimes against public morals.* Prostitution, fornication, and profanity (Chapter 12)

6. *Crimes against the administration of justice.* Obstruction of justice and bribery

 Go to Exercise 1-1 on the Criminal Law 8e CD to learn more about state criminal codes.

CRIMINAL LAW IN A FEDERAL SYSTEM

Up to now we've referred *inaccurately* to "criminal law" in the singular. Why isn't it accurate? Our **federal system** has three levels of government—national, state, and local. They all have criminal codes. So, we have a federal criminal code, fifty state criminal codes, and countless city ordinances. Of course, there are many similarities among these many codes. For example, all state codes include the most serious crimes—murder, rape, robbery, burglary, arson, theft, and assault; all allow the most common defenses—self-defense and insanity; and all punish serious crimes by imprisonment. However, they don't all define a particular crime the same way. For example, in some states, burglary requires unlawful breaking and entering; in others, it requires only entering without breaking; and in still others, it requires merely unlawfully remaining in a building entered lawfully, such as hiding until after closing time in a department store rest room lawfully entered during business hours (Chapter 11).

The defenses to crime also vary from state to state. In some states, insanity requires proof defendants didn't know what they were doing *and* they didn't know that it was wrong to do it. In other states, it's enough to prove that either defendants didn't know what they were doing or they didn't know it was wrong (Chapter 8). Some states permit individuals to use deadly force to protect homes from intruders; others require proof the occupants in the home were in danger of serious bodily harm or death before they can shoot intruders (Chapter 7).

Criminal penalties also differ widely among jurisdictions. Several states prescribe death for some convicted murderers; others, life imprisonment. Hence, where murderers kill can determine whether they will live or die. It also determines how they will die: by electrocution, lethal injection, the gas chamber, hanging, or even the firing squad.

The death penalty is only the most dramatic example of different penalties, and it affects only a few individuals. Other, less dramatic examples affect far more people. Some states subject those who engage in "open and notorious" sexual intercourse to fines; others make the mere fact of living together outside marriage punishable by up to five years of prison. Some states imprison individuals who possess small quantities of marijuana; others have protected private marijuana use as a constitutional right.

SOURCES OF CRIMINAL LAW

Understanding the sources of criminal law is another not very exciting but still very important preliminary you'll need. The main sources of criminal law include:

- U.S. Constitution
- State constitutions
- Common law of England and the United States
- U.S. criminal code
- State criminal codes
- Municipal ordinances
- Judicial decisions interpreting codes and the common law

Most criminal law is state criminal law. But federal criminal law is growing, mainly because of increases in federal drug, weapons, and terrorist-related crimes. Municipal codes in towns and cities throughout the country include long lists of minor offenses, like traffic violations and disorderly conduct on streets, sidewalks, and buses and in parks, stadiums, and other public buildings. State criminal laws, and sometimes municipal ordinances, are the focus of this book because that is where most criminal laws are made and enforced.

 Go to Exercise 1-2 on the Criminal Law 8e CD to learn more about municipal ordinances.

Common-Law Origins

Criminal codes didn't spring full-grown from state legislatures. They evolved from a long history of ancient offenses called the **common-law crimes.** These crimes were created before legislatures existed and when social order depended on obedience to unwritten rules (the *lex non scripta*) based on community customs and tradition. These traditions were passed on from generation to generation and changed from time to time to meet changed conditions. They were eventually incorporated into court decisions. The **common-law felonies** have still familiar names and meanings (murder, manslaughter, burglary, arson, robbery, assault, larceny, rape, and sodomy). The **common-law misdemeanors** do, too (assault, battery, false imprisonment, libel, perjury, corrupting morals, and disturbing the peace [LaFave and Scott 1986, 59]).

Exactly how the common law began is a mystery, but like the traditions it incorporated, it grew and changed to meet new conditions. At first, its growth depended mainly on judicial decisions (Chapter 2). As legislatures became more established, they added crimes to the common law. They did so for a number of reasons: to clarify existing common law; to fill in blanks left by the common law; and to adjust the common law to new conditions. Judicial decisions interpreting the statutes became part of the growing body of precedent making up the common law.

The English colonists brought this common law with them to the New World and incorporated the common-law crimes into their legal systems. Following the American Revolution, the thirteen original states adopted the common law. Almost every state created after that enacted "reception statutes" that adopted the English common law. For example, the Florida reception statute reads: "The Common Law of England in relation to crimes...shall be of full force in this state where there is no existing provision by statute on the subject" (*West's Florida Statutes Annotated* 1991).

Criminal Codes

From time to time in U.S. history, reformers have called for the abolition of the common-law crimes and for their replacement with **criminal codes** (definitions of crimes and punishments defined by elected legislatures). The first appeared in 1648, the work of the New England Puritans. The Laws and Liberties of Massachusetts *codified* (put into writing) the criminal law, defining crimes and spelling out punishments. The authors stated their case for a code this way: "So soon as God had set up political government among his people Israel he gave them a body of laws for judgment in civil and criminal causes.... For a commonwealth without laws is like a ship without rigging and steerage" (Farrand 1929, A2).

Some of the offenses sound odd today (witchcraft, cursing parents, blasphemy, idolatry, and adultery), but others, such as rape—

> If any man shall ravish any maid or single woman, committing carnal copulation with her by force, against her own will, that is above ten years of age he shall be punished either with death or some other grievous punishment (5)—

and murder—

> If any man shall commit any wilful murder, which is manslaughter, committed upon premeditate malice, hatred, or cruelty not in a man's necessary and just defense, nor by mere casualty against his will, he shall be put to death (6)—

sound familiar.

Hostility to English institutions after the American Revolution spawned another call by reformers for written legislative codes to replace the English common law. The eighteenth-century Enlightenment, with its emphasis on reason and natural law, inspired reformers to put aside the piecemeal "irrational" common law scattered throughout judicial decisions and to replace it with criminal codes based on a natural law of crimes. Despite anti-British feelings, Blackstone's *Commentaries* remained popular with reformers who hoped to transform his complete and orderly outline of criminal law into criminal codes.

Reformers contended that judge-made law was not just disorderly and incomplete; it was antidemocratic. They believed legislatures representing the popular will should make laws, not aloof judges out of touch with public opinion. Thomas Jefferson proposed such a penal code for Virginia (Bond 1950). The proposed Virginia code never passed the Virginia legislature, not because it codified the law but because it recommended too many drastic reductions in criminal punishments (Preyer 1983, 53–85).

 Go to Exercise 1-3 on the Criminal Law 8e CD to learn more about the nineteenth-century codification movement.

The codification movement gathered renewed strength during the 1900s. The supported codification, and the earliest drafts of the *Model Penal Code* abolished common-law crimes in § 1.05: "All Offenses Defined by Statute. (1) No conduct constitutes an offense unless it is a crime or violation under this Code or another statute of this State" (American Law Institute 1985 [1], § 1.01 to 2.13).

Common-Law Crimes and Criminal Law Today

Since the American Law Institute adopted § 1.05, twenty-five states have abolished the common-law crimes and ten others have proposed doing so. Several states, however, still recognize the common law of crimes, at least in part. Abolishing the common-law crimes doesn't render the common law useless. Most states that have abolished common-law offenses (these states are called **code jurisdictions**) retain the common-law defenses, such as self-defense and insanity. Furthermore, statutes frequently contain the terms murder, manslaughter, robbery, burglary, rape, and assault without defining them, and courts have to rely on the common-law meanings of those terms. For example, the 1975 Alabama criminal code provides as follows: "Any person who commits...voluntary manslaughter, shall be guilty of a felony. Voluntary manslaughter is punishable as a Class 5 felony" (Code of Alabama 1975, § 13A-1-4).

California, a code jurisdiction, went even further by including all of the common-law felonies in its criminal code (*West's California Penal Code* 1988, § 187(a)). The California Supreme Court reviewed the common law to determine the meaning of its murder statute in *Keeler v. Superior Court* (1970). Robert Keeler's wife Teresa was pregnant with another man's child. Robert kicked the pregnant Teresa in the stomach, causing her to abort the fetus. The California court had to decide whether fetuses were included in the murder statute. The court, in the following passage, reveals the importance of the common law in interpreting present statutes:

> Penal code § 187 provides: "Murder is the unlawful killing of a human being, with malice aforethought." The dispositive question is whether the fetus which petitioner is accused of killing was, on February 23, 1969, a "human being" within the meaning of this statute....
> We therefore undertake a brief review of the origins and development of the common law of abortional homicide.... From that inquiry it appears that by the year 1850—the date with which we are concerned—an infant could not be the subject of homicide at common law unless it had been born alive.... Perhaps the most influential statement of the "born alive" rule is that of Coke, in mid-seventeenth century: "If a woman be quick with childe and by a potion or otherwise killeth it in her wombe, or if a man beat her, whereby the childe dyeth in her body, and she is delivered of a dead childe, this is a great misprision (i.e., misdemeanor), and no murder; but if the childe be born alive and dyeth of the potion, battery, or other cause, this is murder; for in law it is accounted a reasonable creature...when it is born alive." (3 Coke, Institutes 58 [1648])...
> We hold that in adopting the definition of murder in Penal Code § 187 the Legislature intended to exclude from its reach the act of killing an unborn fetus. (*Keeler v. Superior Court* 1970)

As a result of the court's decision, the California legislature changed the criminal homicide statute to include fetuses (Chapter 9).

Courts in jurisdictions that still recognize the common-law crimes (these are called **common-law jurisdictions**) have recognized many offenses besides common-law felonies, even though there are no state statutes making them crimes. These include conspiring, attempting, and soliciting to commit crimes; uttering grossly obscene language in public; burning a body in a furnace; keeping a house of prostitution; maliciously killing a horse; being a common scold; negligently permitting a prisoner to escape; discharging a gun near a sick person; being drunk in public; using libel; committing an indecent assault; and eavesdropping (LaFave and Scott 1986, 68–69).

 Go to Exercise 1-4 on the Criminal Law 8e CD to learn more about common law and modern criminal law.

THE TEXT-CASE METHOD

The "last" first thing you'll need is the method you're going to use to learn and understand criminal law. It's what I call the text-case method. *Criminal Law,* 8e, is what I call a **text-case book** (it's part text and part excerpts from real-life criminal law cases edited for nonlawyers). The text part of the book explains the general principles of criminal law and the definitions of specific crimes. The case excerpts contain real-life crimes so you can apply the general information in the text to real-life situations and think critically about the principles and their application. I believe the best way to test whether you understand a general concept is to apply it to concrete situations. So, although you can learn a lot from the text without reading the case excerpts, you won't get the full benefit of what you've learned without applying and thinking about it by reading the case excerpts.

For most of my students (and many of you who send me e-mails), reading and discussing the case excerpts are their favorite part of the book. That's good. Cases bring criminal law to life by applying the abstract general principles, doctrines, and rules described in the text to real events in the lives of real people. But, keep in mind that *judges* write the reports of the cases the excerpts are taken from. So, don't be surprised to learn they don't all write with college students in mind. So, reading the excerpts may take some getting used to. This section is designed to help you get the most out of the cases.

The cases in this book are all **excerpts**; that is, they're edited versions of the complete reports of the cases. (A little later on in this section, I've included instructions for finding cases either online or in libraries. That way you can read the whole case to find out what I've left out.) When you see the three (...) dots called **ellipses**, you'll know I've cut something out that I don't think you need to know at this point in the text. When you see text inside brackets ([ ]), it's something I've added, usually to define a technical term or explain a concept you need to know to understand the case.

In almost all the case excerpts, you'll be reading reports of the appeals of guilty verdicts, not transcripts of the criminal trial. In other words, the defendant has been convicted already by a trial court and has asked an appeals court to review the conviction. You'll never read a review of a case in which a defendant was acquitted. Why not? In the criminal law of the United States, a "not guilty" verdict is final and not subject to review. (There's an exception, sort of, to this rule, but we'll take it up in the first of the few case excerpts where the exception applies.)

Most states and the federal government have two levels of appeals courts (Figure 1.1), an intermediate court of appeals and a supreme court.

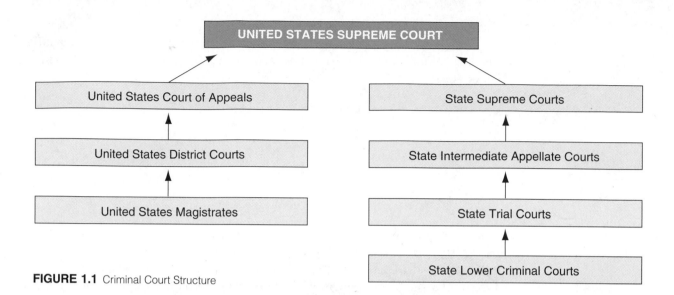

FIGURE 1.1 Criminal Court Structure

The usual procedure is to appeal first to the intermediate court of appeals and then to the state supreme court. In a few cases involving issues about the U.S. Constitution, the case may go to the U.S. Supreme Court. The first case excerpt in the book (Chapter 2), *State v. Metzger* (1982), is an appeal from a Nebraska trial court to the Nebraska intermediate appeals court.

Cases like *State v. Metzger* are called **appellate cases.** The parties who appeal them are called **appellants,** and the parties appealed against are called **appellees.** The case title tells you who the appellant is and who the appellee is. The party who brings the appeal is always the first name in the title (the name before the *"v."* The appellee's name follows the *"v."* So, in *State v. Metzger,* the state of Nebraska is the appellant (you'll see two other names for states, "People" and "Commonwealth"); the *"v."* is the abbreviation for the Latin word "versus," which means "against"; and Metzger is the appellee. (Most of the case excerpts are not like *State v. Metzger.* Instead, they involve convicted defendants appealing against the state to get their convictions overturned, or **reversed.**)

In cases involving constitutional questions (there are only a few in this book), defendants may seek a different kind of review called a **collateral attack.** Collateral attacks are separate legal actions from the criminal proceeding. They're noncriminal (civil) lawsuits that challenge either the authority of a court to hear a case or the legality of a person's detention in a prison or jail. The most common collateral attack is **habeas corpus.** Habeas corpus begins with the habeas corpus petition, in which a prisoner asks for a court order commanding the person in charge of the prison or jail detaining him to show that the agency has the legal authority to incarcerate him. In the few case excerpts in the book involving habeas corpus proceedings, the person challenging his imprisonment is called the petitioner; these petitioners are the defendants in the criminal case. You can tell whether the case is a collateral attack by its title. The title contains two individuals' names—the name of the petitioner and the name of the respondent, who is the warden or the person in charge of the facility holding the petitioner.

Parts of Case Excerpts

Don't worry if reading cases intimidates you at first. Like so many students before you, you'll get the hang of it before long. To help you get the most out of the case excerpts, I've outlined the main parts of each case, the (1) title, (2) citation, (3) procedural history, (4) judge, (5) facts, (6) decision, and (7) opinion. Now we'll take a closer look at all the parts of the case excerpts to guide you through reading and understanding what each contains and what each means.

1. *Title.* The case title consists of the names of the parties, either appellants and appellees or petitioners and respondents.

2. *Citation.* The **citation** is like the footnote or endnote in any text; it tells you where to find the case. (See below on "Finding cases.")

3. *Procedural history.* The **case history** is a brief description of the procedural steps and **judgments** (decisions) made by each court that has heard the case.

4. *Judge.* The name of the judge who wrote the opinion and issued the court's judgment in the case.

5. *Facts.* The facts of the case are the critical starting point in reading and analyzing cases. If you don't know the facts, you can't understand the principle the case is teaching. One of my favorite law professors used to tell us again and again: "Remember cases are stories with a point. You can't get the point if you don't know the story." He also told us something else I think will help you: "Forget you're lawyers. Tell me the story as if you were telling it to your grandmother who doesn't know anything about the law." Take Professor Hill's advice. I do, because it's still good advice.

6. *Judgment (decision).* The court's judgment (sometimes called the court's decision) is how the court disposes of the case. In the trial court, the judgments are almost always guilty or not guilty. In appeals courts, the judgments are affirmed, reversed, or reversed and remanded. This is the most important legal action of the court, because it's what decides what happens to the defendant and the government.

7. *Opinion.* For students of criminal law, the court's opinion is more important than the judgment: it's "the point of the story." In the opinion, the court backs up its judgment by explaining how and why the court applied the law (legal principle, doctrine, or definition) to the facts of the case. The law in the case excerpts includes the constitutional principles in this chapter; the principles of criminal liability in Chapters 3 and 4; the law of parties to crime and incomplete offenses in Chapters 5 and 6; the defenses in Chapters 7 and 8; and the law of crimes against persons, property, and public order in Chapters 9 through 13.
   The opinion contains two essential ingredients:
   a. The court's **holding**—the legal rule the court has decided to apply to the facts of the cases
   b. The court's **reasoning**—the reasons the court gives to support its holding
   In some cases, there are majority *and* dissenting opinions. A **majority opinion,** as its name indicates, is the opinion of the majority of the justices on the court who participated in the case. The majority opinion is the law of the case. Although the majority opinion represents the established law of the case, **dissenting opinions**

present a plausible alternative to the majority opinion. Dissents of former times sometimes become the law of later times. For example, dissents in U.S. Supreme Court opinions of the 1930s became the law in the 1960s; and many of the dissents of the 1960s became the law by the 1990s. Occasionally, you'll see a **concurring opinion.** In concurring opinions, justices agree with the conclusions of either the majority or dissenting opinion, but they have different reasons for reaching the conclusion. Sometimes (mostly in U.S. Supreme Court cases), enough justices agree with the result in the case so there's a majority decision, but not enough justices agree on the reasoning to make up a majority opinion. In these cases, there is a **plurality opinion,** an opinion that represents the reasoning of the greatest number (but less than a majority) of justices. So, there is no majority opinion. All of the differing perspectives in the opinions get you to think about the principles of criminal law. They also clearly demonstrate that there is almost always more than one reasonable way to look at important questions.

Precedent and Stare Decisis

You'll notice court opinions frequently back up their arguments and decisions by referring to past cases. These prior decisions are called **precedent.** The ancient and still entrenched doctrine of **stare decisis** binds judges to follow precedent. But, there are limits to how inflexible stare decisis really is. First, judges only have to follow decisions of courts above them (like state supreme courts) in their own state and the U.S. Supreme Court).

U.S. Supreme Court Justice and respected judicial philosopher Benjamin Cardozo once said this about precedent and the doctrine of stare decisis:

> It is easier to follow the beaten track than it is to clear another. In doing this, I shall be treading in the footsteps of my predecessors, and illustrating the process that I am seeking to describe, since the power of precedent, when analyzed, is the power of the beaten path. (1921, 62)

The idea of precedent isn't special to criminal law, nor is it the basis only of legal reasoning. We're accustomed to the basic notion of precedent in ordinary life. We like to do things the way we've done them in the past. For example, if a professor asks multiple-choice questions covering only material in the text on three exams, you expect multiple-choice questions on the fourth exam. If you get an essay exam instead, you won't like it. Not only won't you like it; you'll probably think it's "unfair." Why? Precedent—the way we've done things before—makes life stable and predictable. Knowing what to expect, and counting on it, guides our actions in the future so we can plan for and meet challenges and solve problems. Changing this without warning is unfair. In ordinary life, then, as in criminal procedure, following past practice gives stability, predictability, and a sense of fairness and justice to decisions.

Of course, doing things the way we've always done them isn't always right or good. When we need to, we change (usually reluctantly) and do things differently. These changes themselves become guides to future action. The same is true of legal precedent. Courts change precedent, but they do it reluctantly. Courts, like individuals in ordinary life, don't like to change, particularly when they have to admit they were wrong. That's why, as you read the case excerpts, you'll rarely find one that comes right out and says, "We were wrong in that earlier case, so we reverse ourselves and overrule our prior decision." Instead, when courts decide to get off the beaten path they do it by **distinguishing cases.** This means that a court decides that a prior decision doesn't apply to the current case because the facts are different. For example, the rule that controls the right to a lawyer in death penalty cases doesn't have to apply to a case punishable by a fine. As the Court has noted, "Death is different" (Chapter 11).

Briefing the Case Excerpts

To get the most from your reading of the case excerpts, you should write out the answers to the following questions about each. This is what we call briefing a case.

1. *What are the facts?* State the facts in simple narrative form in chronological order. As Professor Hill said, "Tell me the story as if you were telling it to your grandmother." Then, select, sort, and arrange the facts into the following categories:
   a. *Actions of the defendant.* List what the defendant did in chronological order. (Remember, there's no criminal case without the criminal acts of the defendant.)
   b. *Intent of the defendant.* If not relevant, say none.
   c. *Harmful result.* If not relevant, say none.
   d. *Causing a harmful result.* If not relevant, say none.
   e. *Justification or excuse (defense).* If not relevant, say none.

2. *Identify the legal issue in the case.* State the principle and/or the rule of criminal law raised by the facts of the case.

3. *Summarize the court's opinion.* List the reasons the court gives for its decision. The court's opinion consists of how and why the court applies the principle, doctrine, and/or rule to the facts of the case.

4. *State the court's judgment (decision).* The most common judgments are
   a. *Affirmed.* Upheld the judgment (decision) of the lower court
   b. *Reversed.* Overturned the judgment (decision) of the lower court
   c. *Reversed and remanded.* Overturned the judgment (decision) of the lower court and sent the case back for further proceedings in accord with the appellate court's decision

You can't answer all these questions in every case. First, the answers depend on the knowledge you'll accumulate as the text and your instructor introduce more principles, doctrines, and rules. Second, courts don't necessarily follow the same procedure in reviewing an appeal as the one outlined here. Third, not all of the questions come up in every case—except for one: What did the defendant do? That's because there's no criminal case without some action by the defendant.

Developing the skills needed to sort out the elements of the case excerpts requires practice, but it's worth the effort. Answering the questions can challenge you to think not only about the basic principles, doctrines, and rules of criminal law but also about your own fundamental values regarding life, property, privacy, and morals.

Finding Cases

Knowing how to read and brief cases is important. So is knowing how to find cases. It will help you complete the Internet exercises on the CD that accompanies the text.

Also, you might want to look up cases on your own, in the library, or in the rapidly expanding cases published on the Internet. These cases might include those your instructor talks about in class or those cited in the excerpts to back up the court's opinion and decision. You may even want to look up a case you read or hear about outside of class.

The case citation consists of the numbers, letters, and punctuation that follow the title of a case in the excerpts or in the bibliography at the end of the book. These letters and numbers tell you where to locate the full case report. For example, in the first case excerpt (*State v. Metzger* [Chapter 2]), just after the title of the case, *State v. Metzger*, you read "319 N.W. 2d 459 (Neb. 1982)." Here's how to interpret this citation:

- 319 = Volume 319
- N.W.2d = *Northwestern Reporter*, Second Series
- 459 = page 459
- (Neb. 1982) = Nebraska Supreme Court in the year 1982

So, if you're looking for the full version of *State v. Metzger*, you'll find it in Volume 319 of the *Northwestern Reporter*, second series, page 459. The *Northwest Reporter*, Second Series, is the second series of a multivolume set of law books that publishes reports of cases decided by the supreme courts and intermediate appellate courts in Nebraska and several other states in the region. There are comparable *Reporters* for other regions, including the Northeast (N.E.), Southern (So.), Southeast (S.W.), and Pacific (P.). Case citations always follow the same order. The volume number always comes before the title of a reporter and the page always comes immediately after the title. The abbreviation of the name of the court and the year the case was decided follow the page number in parentheses. You can tell if the court was the highest or an intermediate appellate court by the abbreviation. For example, in *Metzger* the court is the Nebraska Supreme Court. (If the Nebraska intermediate appeals court had decided the case, you'd see "Neb. App.")

SUMMARY

    I. Limits of criminal law

        A. Criminal law in a constitutional democracy is mainly about limits

        B. A democratic form of government limits crime to crimes and punishments defined by the majority and enacted into specific statutes

        C. U.S. and state constitutions require criminal laws to be consistent with due process, equal protection, and individual rights and liberties to life, liberty, and privacy

        D. Democracy and constitutions set minimum standards; the principles of criminal liability, justification, and excuse aim at the optimum standard:

            1. Principles of liability limit criminal behavior to criminal conduct and criminal conduct causing a criminal harm

            2. Principle of justification makes otherwise criminal behavior right when actors act out of necessity

            3. Principle of excuse excuses criminal behavior if actors are not responsible

II. Criminal punishments: Limits and purposes
   A. Punishment, like crime, is limited in U.S. criminal law
      1. U.S. Constitution, Amendment VIII, bans the infliction of cruel and unusual punishment (punishments that either inflict unnecessary pain or are disproportionate to the crime)
      2. Principle of limited methods
         a. Don't use criminal punishment when noncriminal social control will do the job
         b. Don't use a more severe criminal punishment when a less severe one will accomplish social control
   B. Criminal punishment has two purposes and is good for two things:
      1. Retribution (just deserts) for past crimes
      2. Prevention of future crimes

III. Classifying and grading crimes
   A. A response to an ancient urge to make sense out of banning and punishing antisocial behavior
   B. Three reasons to learn right away the basics of classifying and grading crimes:
      1. States organize their criminal codes according to them
      2. It's the way professionals and scholars think about them
      3. It'll help you organize, understand, and think critically about what you're learning
   C. General and special part of criminal law divide criminal law between the general principles and doctrines of criminal law and the applications of the general information to the definitions of specific crimes
   D. "Felony, misdemeanor, and violation" grades crimes according to punishments:
      1. Capital felonies (death and life without parole)
      2. Ordinary felonies (one year to life in prison)
      3. Gross (6–12 months in jail), ordinary (3–9 months in jail), and petty misdemeanors (10–30 days in jail)
      4. Violations (fine only, with no mark on criminal record)
   E. Wrongs *mala in se* (crimes inherently evil) and *mala prohibita* (crimes only because the law says they're crimes) classify and grade crimes according to their inherent severity
   F. Grading according to subject groups crimes by the subjects they cover:
      1. Crimes against the state
      2. Crimes against persons
      3. Crimes against property
      4. Crimes against public order
      5. Crimes against public morals
      6. Crimes against the administration of justice

IV. Criminal law in a federal system
   A. There are fifty-one (1 U.S. and 50 state) criminal codes because of our federal system of government
   B. All fifty-one codes resemble one another but they differ significantly in both definitions of crimes and severity of punishment

V. Sources of criminal law
   A. Official sources of U.S. criminal law
      1. Constitutions (U.S. and state)
      2. Common law of England and the United States
      3. Criminal codes (U.S., state, and municipal ordinances)
      4. Judicial decisions interpreting codes and the common law
   B. Common-law origins
      1. U.S. twenty-first century criminal law evolved from ancient and unwritten local English customs, which were turned into the common-law crimes (homicide, assault, robbery, burglary, and larceny) by English courts before there were legislatures
      2. As society became more complex, English courts and then English legislatures modified the list of common-law crimes and then added new crimes to the list
      3. English colonists brought the common law with them to the American colonies; after the Revolution, the new states passed "reception statutes" adopting the common law as their own
      4. Many times since the Revolution, reform movements have tried to abolish the court-created common-law crimes and replace them with codes passed by majorities in state legislatures and signed by elected state governors
      5. Today, we have so-called code states and common-law states. That's the formal side of criminal law. Informally, the common-law definitions of crimes and the common-law defenses to crime still have a powerful influence on U.S. state criminal law

VI. The text-case method
   A. Two parts of book
      1. Text defines and explains concepts and principles
      2. Case excerpts test your understanding (and get you to think critically by applying definitions, concepts, and principles to real cases)
   B. Precedent and stare decisis
      1. Judges use prior decisions to decide present cases
      2. Judges are very reluctant to get off the beaten path of precedent
      3. Changing needs and times and prior mistakes encourage judges occasionally to overcome their resistance to stay on the beaten path of precedent

Go to the Criminal Law 8e CD to download this summary outline. The outline has been formatted so that you can add notes to it during class lectures, or later create a customized chapter outline to use while reviewing. Either way, the summary outline will help you understand the "big picture" and fill in the details as you study.

REVIEW QUESTIONS

1. List and give an example of four methods of social control *besides* criminal law.

2. Explain how our democratic form of government limits criminal law.

3. List, describe, and give examples of how U.S. and state constitutions limit criminal law.

4. Describe the relationship between the principles of criminal liability and the elements of crime.

5. Identify, describe, and give an example of four defenses to criminal liability.

6. Explain and give an example of the difference between defenses of justification and defenses of excuse.

7. Explain how the U.S. Constitution limits criminal punishment.

8. Explain how the principle of limited methods limits criminal punishment.

9. Identify, describe, and give an example of the two purposes of criminal punishment.

10. List four kinds of prevention.

11. Describe each of the four schemes used to classify criminal laws.

12. Explain how and why it's inaccurate to refer to U.S. criminal law in the singular.

13. Identify, explain, and give an example of the seven sources of U.S. criminal law.

14. List the main steps in the development of U.S. criminal law from its common-law origins to the twenty-first century.

15. What's the formal difference between U.S. common-law jurisdictions and code jurisdictions, and what's the reality of the difference in the twenty-first century?

16. Explain the importance of precedent and stare decisis.

KEY TERMS

private lawsuits p. 2
government regulation p. 2
social condemnation p. 3
constitutional democracy p. 4
due process of law p. 5
equal protection of the law p. 5
principles of criminal liability
     p. 5
elements of a crime p. 5
actus reus p. 5
mens rea p. 5
concurrence p. 5
defense of justification p. 5
defense of excuse p. 6
alibis p. 6
cruel and unusual punishment
     p. 6
principle of limited methods p. 6
*Model Penal Code and
     Commentaries* p. 6
retribution p. 7

prevention p. 7
culpability p. 7
determinism p. 8
general prevention p. 8
general deterrence p. 8
special deterrence p. 8
incapacitation p. 8
rehabilitation p. 8
general part of criminal law p. 9
special part of criminal law p. 9
criminal punishment p. 9
capital felony p. 10
felony p. 10
misdemeanor p. 10
gross misdemeanor p. 10
ordinary misdemeanor p. 10
petty misdemeanor p. 10
violation p. 10
malum in se p. 10
malum prohibitum p. 10
crimes against the state p. 11

crimes against persons p. 11
crimes against property p. 11
crimes against public order p. 11
crimes against public morals
     p. 11
crimes against the administration
     of justice p. 11
federal system p. 11
common-law crimes p. 12
common-law felonies p. 12
common-law misdemeanors
     p. 12
criminal codes p. 13
code jurisdictions p. 14
common-law jurisdictions p. 14
text-case book p. 15
excerpts p. 15
ellipses p. 15
appellate cases p. 16
appellant p. 16
appellee p. 16

SUGGESTED READINGS

 Go to the Criminal Law 8e CD for Suggested Readings for this chapter.

THE COMPANION WEB SITE FOR *CRIMINAL LAW,* EIGHTH EDITION

http://cj.wadsworth.com/samaha/crim_law8e

 Supplement your review of this chapter by going to the companion Web site to take one of the Tutorial Quizzes, use the flash cards to test your knowledge of the elements of various crimes and defenses, and check out the many other study aids you'll find there. You'll find valuable data and resources at your fingertips to help you study for that big exam or write that important paper.

Constitutional Limits on Criminal Law

2

Chapter Main Points

- The writers of the U.S. Constitution were realists who recognized the threat to individual liberty from an uncontrolled people *and* an uncontrolled government.
- The United States is a *constitutional* democracy, where the desires of the majority are limited by provisions in the U.S. and state constitutions.
- It's very tough to overturn the will of the majority expressed in criminal laws.
- The purposes of banning ex post facto and vague criminal statutes are to give fair warning of what the law prohibits to private individuals and to prevent arbitrary action by public officials.
- The constitutional basis for banning laws so vague that reasonable private individuals and public officials can't understand them is that such laws deprive individuals of life, liberty, or property without due process of law.
- The U.S. Constitution doesn't guarantee that criminal laws treat everybody exactly alike; it does command that the criteria for classifying people or behavior differently be reasonable.
- Classifications based on race and ethnicity are almost never reasonable.
- Under the U.S. Constitution, Amendment I, the guarantee of free speech is a fundamental right.
- According to the U.S. Supreme Court, some kinds of nonverbal expressive conduct are speech; some words aren't "speech"; and some speech isn't protected by the guarantee of free speech.
- The word *privacy* doesn't appear in the U.S. Constitution, but the U.S. Supreme Court has based an implied right to privacy on several amendments to the U.S. Constitution.
- The U.S. Supreme Court has narrowly confined the right to privacy to homes, traditional forms of family life, reproduction, and child rearing.
- The U.S. Supreme Court has interpreted the ban on cruel and unusual punishments to include barbaric punishments and punishments disproportionate to the crimes.

Chapter Outline

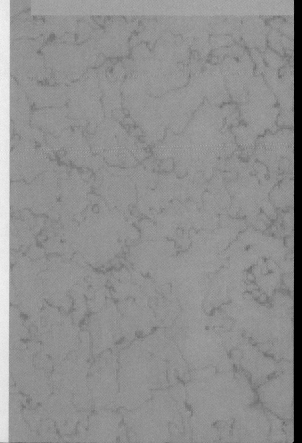

Was the Ordinance Unconstitutionally Vague?

Metzger lived in Lincoln, Nebraska, in a garden-level apartment with a large window facing a parking lot. At about 7:45 A.M., on April 30, 1981, another resident of the building was parking his automobile in a space directly in front of Metzger's apartment window. While doing so, he observed, for a period of 5 seconds, Metzger standing naked in the window with his arms at his sides. The resident testified that he saw Metzger's body from the thighs up. The resident called the police, and two officers arrived at the apartment at about 8 A.M. The officers testified that they observed Metzger standing in front of the window, within a foot of it, eating a bowl of cereal, and that his naked body was visible from the mid-thigh up. A city ordinance made it an offense to "commit any indecent, immodest, or filthy act in the presence of any person, or in such a situation that persons passing might ordinarily see the same." ◆

The authors of the U.S. Constitution were suspicious of power, especially power in the hands of government officers. They were also devoted to the right of individuals to control their own destinies without government interference. But they were realists, too. They knew freedom depends on order, and order depends on social control. So, they created a Constitution that balanced the power of government and the liberty of individuals. No one has expressed the purpose of the Constitution better than James Madison, the fourth president of the United States:

> If men were angels, no government would be necessary. If angels were to govern men, neither external nor internal controls on government would be necessary. In framing a government which is to be administered by men over men, the great difficulty is this: You must first enable the government to control the governed; and in the next place, oblige it to control itself. (1961, 349)

We live in a *constitutional* democracy, not a *pure* democracy. In a pure democracy, the majority can have whatever it wants. In a constitutional democracy, the majority can't make a crime out of what the Constitution protects as a fundamental right. Even if all the people want to make it a crime to say, "God damn the president of the United States," they can't. Why? The First Amendment to the U.S. Constitution guarantees the fundamental right of free speech.

A central feature of criminal law in a constitutional democracy is that limits are placed on the power of government to create crimes (Chapter 1). In this chapter, we focus on the limits imposed by the U.S. and state constitutions. These limits include:

1. The rule of law

2. The prohibition against ex post facto laws

3. The right to "due process of law"

4. The right to "equal protection of the law"

5. The right to free speech, association, press, and religion

6. The right to privacy

7. The right against "cruel and unusual punishment"

THE RULE OF LAW

Deeply embedded in our constitutional democracy is the principle that government can punish people only if there's a specific law that defines a crime and spells out the punishment for committing the crime. We call this principle the **rule of law,** also known as the **principle of legality.**

This is a grand principle, but, in practice, challenging the constitutionality of laws isn't easy. One reason is another principle—that the will of the people should prevail in a democracy. So, courts are extremely reluctant to overturn popular will enacted into law. To make it difficult to overturn the will of the majority, the government doesn't have to prove laws are constitutional; challengers have to prove they're *not.* Put in technical terms, there's a strong presumption in favor of the constitutionality of laws, which means challengers have the burden of proving laws are unconstitutional. This is a heavy burden, sometimes requiring challengers to prove unconstitutionality beyond a reasonable doubt, the heaviest burden known to the law. In fact, it's the same burden the government has to carry to convict defendants of crimes (Chapter 1). So, it's no surprise most defendants don't challenge the constitutionality of laws; when they do, they usually lose.

EX POST FACTO LAWS

Article I, Section 10, of the U.S. Constitution commands: "No state shall . . . pass any **ex post facto law** . . ." (a law that defines crimes after the behavior it defines takes place). Most state constitutions contain similar provisions (Hall 1960, 31–32).

The ex post facto prohibition has two major goals:

1. To give fair warning to private individuals

2. To prevent arbitrary action by government officials

VOID-FOR-VAGUENESS DOCTRINE

Like ex post facto laws, vaguely defined laws fail to warn private individuals of what the law forbids, and they permit arbitrary action by government officials. (**Arbitrary** means without reason or standards.) But what's vague and arbitrary? The key to understanding the meaning of vague and arbitrary is the word *reasonable.* Constitutionally speaking, it's not enough for the defendant to believe honestly that a law is vague.

To be void-for-vagueness, the belief has to be *objective* (namely, the belief of a "reasonable" person). According to the U.S. Supreme Court, laws that are vague to reasonable individuals and officers violate the due process clauses of the U.S. Constitution. The rule that objectively measured vague laws violate due process is called the **void-for-vagueness doctrine.**

The reasoning behind the doctrine goes like this:

1. Criminal punishment deprives individuals of life (capital punishment), liberty (imprisonment), or property (fines).

2. The Fifth and Fourteenth amendments to the U.S. Constitution ban both federal and state governments from taking any person's "life, liberty, or property without due process of law."

3. Failure to adequately warn private persons of what the law forbids and/or allowing officials the chance to arbitrarily define what the law forbids denies individuals life, liberty, and/or property without due process of law.

The Court has adopted a two-pronged test to determine whether laws are void-for-vagueness; they have to

1. Fail to give fair warning to individuals as to what the law prohibits

2. Allow arbitrary and discriminatory criminal justice administration

Notice the first prong is aimed at private individuals, the second at criminal justice officials. In early cases, the Court focused on the fair-warning-to-individuals prong. For example, in 1939, in *Lanzetta v. New Jersey*, the Court struck down a New Jersey statute that made it a crime to be a member of a "gang." After deciding *gang* was too vague to give fair warning, the Court commented:

> No one may be required at peril of life, liberty, or property to speculate as to the meaning of penal statutes. All are entitled to be informed as to what the State commands or forbids. . . . A statute which either forbids or requires the doing of an act in terms so vague that men of common intelligence must necessarily guess at its meaning and differ as to its application violates the first essential of due process of law. (453)

Despite the importance of giving fair warning to individuals, by 1983, in the case of *Kolender v. Lawson*, the Supreme Court decided the

> more important aspect of the vagueness doctrine is not actual notice [to private individuals], but the other principal element of the vagueness doctrine—the requirement that a legislature establish minimal guidelines to govern law enforcement. (357)

 Go to Exercise 2-1 on the Criminal Law 8e CD to learn more about *Kolender v. Lawson*.

Whether the emphasis is on notice to individuals or control of officials, the void-for-vagueness doctrine can never cure the uncertainty in all laws. After all, laws are written in words, not numbers. U.S. Supreme Court Justice Thurgood Marshall expressed this opinion when he wrote, "Condemned to the use of words, we can never expect mathematical certainty from our language." It's not just the natural uncertainty of words that creates problems. It's also because the variety of human behavior and the limits of human imagination make it impossible for lawmakers to predict all the variations that might arise under the provisions of statutes. So, courts allow considerable leeway in the degree of certainty required to pass the two prongs of fair warning and avoidance of arbitrary law enforcement.

Still, the strong presumption of constitutionality (referred to earlier) requires challengers to prove the law is vague. The Ohio Supreme Court summarized the heavy burden of proof challengers have to carry this way:

> The challenger must show that upon examining the statute, an individual of ordinary intelligence would not understand what he is required to do under the law. Thus, to escape responsibility ... [the challenger] must prove that he could not reasonably understand that ... [the statute] prohibited the acts in which he engaged. ... The party alleging that a statute is unconstitutional must prove this assertion beyond a reasonable doubt.
>
> *State v. Anderson* 1991, 1226–1227

State v. Metzger (1982) is a good example of how one court applied the void-for-vagueness doctrine to uncertain words in a Lincoln, Nebraska, city ordinance. (Please make sure you review the "The Text-Case Method" section in Chapter 1 before you read this first excerpt.)

CASE | *Was His Act "Indecent, Immodest, or Filthy"?*

State v. Metzger
319 N.W. 2d 459 (Neb. 1982)

Douglas Metzger was convicted by the municipal court of Lincoln, Nebraska, of violating a Lincoln city ordinance prohibiting any person from committing any indecent, immodest, or filthy act in the presence of any person. The District Court, Lancaster County, affirmed, and he appealed. The Nebraska Supreme Court reversed and dismissed.

KRIVOSHA, CJ.

FACTS

Metzger lived in a garden-level apartment located in Lincoln, Nebraska. A large window in the apartment faces a parking lot, which is situated on the north side of the apartment building. At about 7:45 A.M. on April 30, 1981, another resident of the apartment, while parking his automobile in a space directly in front of Metzger's apartment window, observed Metzger standing naked with his arms at his sides in his apartment window for a period of 5 seconds. The resident testified that he saw Metzger's body from his thighs up.

The resident called the police department, and two officers arrived at the apartment at about 8 A.M. The officers testified that they observed Metzger standing in front of the window eating a bowl of cereal. They testified that Metzger was standing within a foot of the window and his nude body, from the mid-thigh up, was visible.

The pertinent portion of § 9.52.100 of the Lincoln Municipal Code, under which Metzger was charged, provides as follows:

> It shall be unlawful for any person within the City of Lincoln ... to commit any indecent, immodest or filthy act in the presence of any person, or in such a situation that persons passing might ordinarily see the same.

OPINION

... The ... issue presented to us by this appeal is whether the ordinance, as drafted, is so vague as to be unconstitutional. We believe that it is. There is no argument that a violation of the municipal ordinance in question is a criminal act. Since the ordinance in question is criminal in nature, it is a fundamental requirement of due process of law that such criminal ordinance be reasonably clear and definite. ...

A criminal statute cannot rest upon an uncertain foundation. The crime and the elements constituting it must be so clearly expressed that the ordinary person can intelligently choose in advance what course it is lawful for him to pursue. Penal statutes prohibiting the doing of certain things and providing a punishment for their violation should not admit of such a double meaning that the citizen may act upon one conception of its requirements and the courts upon another. A statute which forbids the doing of an act in terms so vague that men of common intelligence must necessarily guess as to its meaning and differ as to its application violates the first essential elements of due process of law. It is not permissible to enact a law which in effect spreads an all-inclusive net for the feet of everybody upon the chance that, while the innocent will surely be entangled in its meshes, some wrongdoers may also be caught....

Several other jurisdictions which have viewed ordinances with the same general intent in mind have reached similar conclusions. In the case of *State v. Sanders*, 245 S.E.2d 397 (1978), the South Carolina Court of Appeals was presented with a statute making it a misdemeanor for members of the opposite sex to occupy the same bedroom at a hotel for "any immoral purpose." In finding the ordinance too vague and indefinite to comply with constitutional due process standards, the court said:

> A criminal statute or ordinance must be sufficiently definite to inform citizens of common intelligence of the particular acts which are forbidden. [The statute] fails to define with sufficient precision exactly what the term "any immoral purpose" may encompass. The word *immoral* is not equivalent to the word *illegal*; hence, enforcement of [the statute] may involve legal acts which, nevertheless, are immoral in the view of many citizens. One must necessarily speculate, therefore, as to what acts are immoral. If the legislative intent of [the statute] is to proscribe illicit sexual intercourse the statute could have specifically so provided. (397)

...The ordinance in question makes it unlawful for anyone to commit any "indecent, immodest or filthy act." We know of no way in which the standards required of a criminal act can be met in those broad, general terms. There may be those few who believe persons of opposite sex holding hands in public are immodest, and certainly more who might believe that kissing in public is immodest. Such acts cannot constitute a crime. Certainly one could find many who would conclude that today's swimming attire found on many beaches or beside many pools is immodest. Yet, the fact that it is immodest does not thereby make it illegal, absent some requirement related to the health, safety, or welfare of the community. The dividing line between what is lawful and what is unlawful in terms of "indecent," "immodest," or "filthy" is simply too broad to satisfy the constitutional requirements of due process. Both lawful and unlawful acts can be embraced within such broad definitions. That cannot be permitted. One is not able to determine in advance what is lawful and what is unlawful.

We do not attempt, in this opinion, to determine whether Metzger's actions in a particular case might not be made unlawful, nor do we intend to encourage such behavior. Indeed, it may be possible that a governmental subdivision using sufficiently definite language could make such an act as committed by Metzger unlawful. We simply do not decide that question at this time because of our determination that the ordinance in question is so vague as to be unconstitutional.

We therefore believe that § 9.52.100 of the Lincoln Municipal Code must be declared invalid. Because the ordinance is therefore declared invalid, the conviction cannot stand.

REVERSED AND DISMISSED.

DISSENT

BOSLAUGH, J, joined by CLINTON
and HASTINGS, JJ.

The ordinance in question prohibits indecent acts, immodest acts, *or* filthy acts in the presence of any person.... The exhibition of his genitals under the circumstances of this case was, clearly, an indecent act. Statutes and ordinances prohibiting indecent exposure generally have been held valid. I do not subscribe to the view that it is only "possible" that such conduct may be prohibited by statute or ordinance.

Questions

1. State the exact words of the offense for which Douglas Metzger was convicted.

2. List all of Metzger's acts and any other facts relevant to deciding whether he violated the ordinance.

3. State the test the court used to decide whether the ordinance was void-for-vagueness.

4. According to the majority, why was the ordinance void-for-vagueness?

5. According to the dissent, why was the ordinance clear enough to pass the void-for-vagueness test?

6. In your opinion, was the statute clear to a reasonable person? Back up your answer with the facts and arguments in the excerpt and information from the void-for-vagueness discussion in the text.

EXPLORING VOID-FOR-VAGUENESS FURTHER

 Go to the Criminal Law 8e CD to read the full text version of the case featured here.

Was the "Noise" Ordinance Void-for-Vagueness?

FACTS

Section 147-1 of the Washington, New Jersey, Township Code states:

> It shall be unlawful for any person to make, continue or cause to be made or continued any loud, unnecessary or unusual noise or any noise which either annoys, disturbs, injures or endangers the comfort, repose, health, peace or safety of others within the limits of the Township of Washington.

Section 147-2, in relevant part, provides:

> The following acts, among others, are declared to be loud, disturbing and unnecessary noises in violation of this chapter, but said enumeration shall not be deemed to be exclusive: . . . Animals, birds, etc. The keeping of any animal or bird which by causing frequent or long-continued noise shall disturb the comfort or repose of any person in the vicinity.

Washington Township issued eight separate summonses to the Friedmans for violation of Washington Township Ordinance 147-2(E) based upon complaints by their neighbor Naomi Theisz that the defendants' dog, a Collie named Whitney, repeatedly woke her up in the early morning hours. After hearing the testimony of the complainant Theisz and the defendants, the municipal court judge found the defendants guilty on all eight summonses.

The defendants appealed to the Law Division and moved to dismiss the Washington Township summonses on the ground that the township's anti-noise ordinance was unconstitutional. The Law Division determined that the ordinance was constitutional and that although the barking complained of was very brief in duration, it occurred with sufficient frequency to sustain a conviction under the ordinance. The Friedmans argued that the anti-noise ordinance is void-for-vagueness.

DECISION AND REASONS

Was the ordinance void-for-vagueness? Yes, according to the New Jersey Superior Court:

> Neither the Law Division Judge nor the Municipal Court Judge considered the reasonableness of the Friedmans' conduct in determining whether their dog's barking violated the anti-noise ordinance. A purely subjective standard of behavior [a standard based on the comfort of *any* person's, not a reasonable person's] was utilized to determine whether the dog's barking constituted a disturbance of the peace; such a standard is unconstitutionally vague.

> Hence, section 147-2(E) of the Washington Township Code is defective because it proscribes noise which disturbs "the comfort or repose of any person in the vicinity." Such a standard does not provide any guidance as to what constitutes a violation of the statute, leaving the determination as to whether a violation has occurred "to any person who feels a dog's frequent or habitual barking is annoying or disturbing." Although the ordinance does provide a relatively detailed list of conduct which violates its proscription, its articulation of the standard of conduct as it applies to animals is extremely vague.

> *State v. Friedman*, 697 A.2d 947 (N.J. Sup. Ct. 1997)

◆   ◆   ◆

EQUAL PROTECTION OF THE LAWS

In addition to the due process guarantee, the Fourteenth Amendment to the U.S. Constitution commands that "no state shall deny to any person within its jurisdiction the equal protection of the laws." Equal protection doesn't require the government to treat everybody exactly alike. Statutes can and often do classify particular groups of people and types of conduct for special treatment. For example, almost every state ranks premeditated killings as more serious than negligent homicides.

Several states punish habitual criminals more harshly than first-time offenders. None of these classifications violates the equal protection clause. Why? Because they make sense. Or, as the courts say, they have a **"rational basis"** (*Buck v. Bell* 1927, 208).

Classifications in criminal codes based on race are another matter. The U.S. Supreme Court subjects all racial classifications to **"strict scrutiny."** Practically speaking, strict scrutiny means race-based classifications are never justified. According to the U.S. Supreme Court, any statute that "invidiously classifies similarly situated people on the basis of the immutable characteristics with which they were born...*always* [emphasis added] violates the Constitution, for the simple reason that, so far as the Constitution is concerned, people of different races are always similarly situated."

Gender classifications stand somewhere between the strict scrutiny applied to race and the rational basis applied to most other classifications. The Supreme Court has had difficulty deciding exactly how carefully to scrutinize gender classifications in criminal statutes. The plurality, but not a majority, of the justices in *Michael M. v. Superior Court of Sonoma County* (1981, 477) agreed that gender classifications deserve **heightened scrutiny,** meaning there has to be a "fair and substantial relationship" between classifications based on gender and "legitimate state ends."

What about classifications based on age? The Alaska Court of Appeals applied the equal protection clauses of both the U.S. and the Alaska constitutions to an age-based possession of marijuana criminal statute in *Allam v. State* (1992).

CASE	*Did the Age Distinction Violate the Equal Protection Clause?*

Allam v. State
830 P.2d 435 (Alaska App. 1992)

Peter Allam pleaded no contest to a charge of possession of marijuana by a person under the age of 19. When he entered his plea, Allam preserved the right to challenge the constitutionality of this statute on appeal. The court imposed a suspended imposition of sentence conditioned on his good behavior for a period of 90 days, his performance of 24 hours of community work, and his being screened by the Alcohol Safety Action Program. The Alaska Court of Appeals affirmed.

MANNHEIMER, J.

FACTS

On May 15, 1990, Allam was 18 years old and a senior at Dimond High School in Anchorage. He and the rest of his high school class were at Kincaid Park, participating in "Senior Fun Day," a school-sponsored event. Allam and three other boys, one of whom was also 18 years old and two of whom were under 18 years of age, left the main group of students and went off by themselves to an area several hundred yards away. A school official found the four of them rolling marijuana cigarettes. The boys were taken back to the high school, where school officials called the police. Allam and the other 18-year-old were arrested.

OPINION

Allam asserts that, under former AS 11.71.060(a), he and all other 18-year-olds were denied the equal protection of the law. He contends that the legislature unreasonably put 18-year-olds in a class by themselves: a person older than 18 who possessed up to four ounces of marijuana committed no crime, an 18-year-old like Allam who possessed the same amount of marijuana would be criminally prosecuted, while persons 17 years old or younger who possessed marijuana would be dealt with under the juvenile justice system. We reject Allam's attack on the statute and affirm his conviction.

The Alaska Supreme Court has recognized that the legislature may restrict minors' freedom in ways that would be unconstitutional if applied to adults. In *Hanby v. State*, 479 P.2d 486, 498 (Alaska 1970), the court upheld a criminal statute that prohibited the distribution or showing of certain sexually oriented material to minors, even though the material did not qualify as "obscene" and thus could not be banned for the general population. Similarly, in *Anderson v. State*, 562 P.2d 351, 358–59 (Alaska 1977), the court upheld criminal prohibitions on consensual sexual activity with minors. Lastly, in *Ravin v. State*, 537 P.2d 494, 511 & n. 69 (Alaska 1977), when the court declared that the Alaska Constitution protected marijuana possession and use in the privacy of one's home, the court emphasized that this rule did not apply to minors. . . .

Allam concedes that he has no fundamental or protected right to smoke or possess marijuana. He argues, however, that if the legislature allows people 19 years of age or older to engage in these activities, then the equal protection clauses of the federal and state constitutions (United States Constitution, Fourteenth Amendment, Section 1; Alaska Constitution, Article I, Section 1) require the legislature to extend the same freedom of action to 18-year-olds. . . .

Under federal equal protection law, when neither a fundamental right nor a suspect or quasi-suspect classification is involved, a statute will satisfy the requirement of equal protection if it is rationally related to furthering a legitimate state interest. Under this test, a statute will not be invalidated unless its "varying treatment of different groups or persons is so unrelated to the achievement of any combination of legitimate purposes that . . . the legislature's actions were irrational.". . .

Former AS 11.71.060(a)(3) established 19 years as the age of majority for the purpose of regulating the possession of marijuana. This statute was passed in 1982, when the general age of majority was 18 years. Nevertheless . . . for purposes of possessing and using marijuana, the legislature intended to set the age of majority at 19 years. . . . While the Alaska legislature has, since 1977, been willing to recognize 18-year-olds as legal adults in most respects, the legislature has consistently affirmed its view that, for purposes of alcohol and drug use, the age of majority should be set higher.

To satisfy the . . . [U.S. Constitution's Fourteenth Amendment equal protection standard], legislation must be rationally related to a valid legislative purpose. The Alaska Supreme Court has repeatedly recognized the protection of minors as a valid legislative purpose. Within our system

of government, subject to constitutional limitations, it is the legislature's prerogative to restrict or forbid the use of dangerous intoxicants and, if a restriction is based on age, to establish the age at which persons can presumably be trusted to handle those intoxicants in a mature and socially acceptable manner. Former AS 11.71.060(a)(3) set the age for marijuana use at 19 years. We conclude that this choice was rational.

Allam concedes that the legislature's current decision to establish the drinking age at 21 years is supported by "years of scientific study and years of conscious legislative debate." If a drinking age of either 19 years (Alaska law until 1983) or 21 years (current Alaska law) is constitutional, then we have no difficulty concluding that reasonable people could also conclude that 19 years should be the minimum age for using marijuana, another intoxicant.

The facts of Allam's particular case demonstrate another rationale for establishing the age of marijuana use at 19 years. Allam and another 18-year-old were found sharing marijuana with two other high school students who were under the age of 18 years. Like Allam, many 18-year-olds attend high school and regularly associate with students under the age of 18 years. Establishment of a minimum age of 19 years for marijuana use is justified by the danger that, if 18-year-olds were allowed to possess and use marijuana, they would share the drug with other younger students or would at least frequently expose those younger students to drug use. . . . We . . . conclude that former AS 11.71.060(a)(3) satisfied the federal equal protection clause.

The final question is whether former AS 11.71.060(a)(3) violated the Alaska Constitution's equal protection guarantee. . . . This court must first identify the individual interest impaired by the statute and evaluate its importance; we then identify the social purposes underlying the statute and evaluate their importance. The level of justification required for the statute rises in proportion to the importance of the individual interest it affects. Depending upon the importance of that individual interest, the government's interest in enacting the statute must fall somewhere on a continuum between "mere legitimacy" to a "compelling interest."

Second, if the government's interest in enacting the statute is sufficiently strong, this court must examine the connection between the social policies underlying the statute and the means adopted in the statute to further those policies. Again, depending upon the importance of the individual interest affected, this nexus between ends and means must fall somewhere on a continuum between "substantial relationship" and "least restrictive alternative."

Here, Allam concedes that he has no protected interest in possessing or using marijuana. Even if Allam had not conceded this point, we would recognize the legislature's legitimate interest in regulating marijuana. Indeed, the Alaska Supreme Court has already held that, except for personal use of marijuana by adults in their own home, the legislature is justified in regulating the possession and use of this drug.

The second prong of the equal protection test is also satisfied. Because Allam has no interest in possessing or using marijuana, the classification drawn by former AS 11.71.060(a)(3) between people at least 19 years old and people younger than 19 years must bear a "substantial relationship" to the policy interests underlying the regulation of marijuana. We conclude that, given the relationship between age and discretion, the establishment of a minimum age of 19 years for marijuana use bears a substantial relationship to the social interests advanced by marijuana regulation....

For these reasons, we conclude that the Alaska legislature acted constitutionally when they enacted former AS 11.71.060(a)(3), establishing 19 years as the minimum age for possession and use of marijuana guarantee, and when they left the maximum age for juvenile jurisdiction at 18 years, so that 18-year-olds who violated former AS 11.71.060(a)(3) would be prosecuted as adults....

The judgment of the district court is affirmed.

Questions

1. List all of Peter Allam's actions and the circumstances surrounding what he did.

2. Summarize the elements of the Alaska statute regarding age and marijuana use.

3. State the elements of the test the court used to determine whether the statute satisfies the U.S. Constitution's Fourteenth Amendment equal protection command.

4. State the elements of the test the court used to decide whether the Alaska statute satisfied the requirements of the Alaska constitution's equal protection clause.

5. Summarize Allam's arguments that the Alaska statute denies him equal protection of the laws under the U.S. and Alaska constitutions.

6. Summarize the Alaska court's answers to Allam's arguments.

7. Do you agree with Allam or the court? Defend your answer.

8. What arguments can you give for making special rules for marijuana use that are different from those governing the drinking age?

EXPLORING EQUAL PROTECTION OF THE LAW FURTHER

Go to the Criminal Law 8e CD to read the full text version of the case featured here.

Did the Inclusion of Marijuana in the Law Deny Him Equal Protection of the Laws?

FACTS

Colorado prohibits the possession, use, and sale of "narcotic drugs." It defines narcotic drugs as "coca leaves, opium, cannabis [i.e., marijuana], isonipecaine, amidone, isoamidone, ketobemidone, and every other substance neither chemically nor physically distinguishable from them, and any other drug to which the federal narcotic laws may apply." David Stark was convicted of possessing marijuana. On appeal, he argued that the classification of cannabis in the same category as addictive narcotic drugs denied him the equal protection of the law.

DECISION AND REASONS

Was he right? No, said the Colorado Supreme Court:

We recognize that differences of opinion exist as to whether cannabis causes physical or psychological addiction. This fact is not material in determining what drugs may be included within the classification of "narcotic drugs" in an exercise of police powers by a state. The important and pivotal consideration is whether the classification bears a reasonable relation "to the public purpose sought to be achieved by the legislation involved." Clearly, the use of marijuana and other drugs identified in the Colorado statute presents a danger to the public safety and welfare of the community since they are clearly related to each other and to the commission of crime.

People v. Stark was decided thirty-nine years ago as I write this. But, according to the most recent survey on the point, the case was still good law in 2003 (*American Jurisprudence* 2nd, 2003, vol. 25, § 36 "Marijuana").

People v. Stark, 400 P.2d 923 (1965)

◆   ◆   ◆

FREE SPEECH

"Congress shall make no law...abridging the freedom of speech," the First Amendment commands. The U.S. Supreme Court has expanded the prohibition beyond this already sweeping scope. First, although the amendment refers only to "speech," the Court has ruled the protection of the amendment "does not end with the spoken or written word." It also includes expressive conduct, meaning actions that communicate ideas and feelings. So, free speech includes wearing black arm bands to protest war, "sitting in" to protest racial segregation, and picketing to support all kinds of causes from abortion to animal rights. It even includes giving money to political candidates. Second, although the amendment directs its prohibition only at the U.S. Congress, the Court has applied the prohibition to the states since 1925 (*Gitlow v. New York* 1925).

A further protection against government limits on free speech and expression is the Court's decision that free speech is a **fundamental right,** one that enjoys preferred status. This means the government has to provide more than a rational basis for restricting speech and other forms of expression. It has the much higher burden of proving that a compelling interest justifies the restrictions.

Despite these broad prohibitions and the heavy burden the government faces in justifying them, the First Amendment doesn't mean you can express yourself anywhere, anytime, anyplace, on any subject. According to the Supreme Court, there are five categories of expression that the amendment does not protect:

1. *Obscenity.* Material whose predominant appeal is to nudity, sex, or excretion
2. *Profanity.* Irreverence toward sacred things, particularly the name of God
3. *Libel and slander.* The former: defamation expressed in print, writing, pictures, or signs; the latter: defamation by the spoken word
4. *Fighting words.* Words that are likely to provoke the average person to retaliation and, thereby, to cause a "breach of the peace"
5. *Clear and present danger.* Expression that creates a *clear and present danger* of an evil that legislatures have the power to prohibit (*Chaplinsky v. New Hampshire* 1942, 574)

Why doesn't the First Amendment protect these forms of expression? Because they're not an "essential element of any exposition of ideas, and are of such slight value as a step to truth that any benefit that may be derived from them is clearly outweighed by the social interest in order and morality" (*Gitlow v. New York* 1925, 572).

These exceptions create the opportunity for the government to make these kinds of expression a crime, depending on the manner, time, and place of expression. For example, under the clear and present danger doctrine the government can punish words "that produce clear and present danger of a serious substantive evil that rises far above public inconvenience, annoyance, or unrest." So, the First Amendment didn't save Walter Chaplinsky from conviction under a New Hampshire statute that made it a crime to call anyone an "offensive or derisive name" in public (*Chaplinsky v. New Hampshire* 1942). Chaplinsky had called the marshal of the City of Rochester, New Hampshire, "a God damned racketeer." In perhaps the most famous reference to the doctrine, U.S. Supreme Court Justice Oliver Wendell Holmes wrote, "The most stringent protection of free speech would not protect a man in falsely shouting fire in a theatre and causing a panic" (*Schenk v. U.S.* 1919, 52).

The most difficult problem in making a crime out of speech and expressive conduct is when they reach so far they include not just expression the Constitution *bans* but also expression it *protects*. According to the **void-for-overbreadth doctrine,** laws that include not only prohibited but also protected expression are void because they deny people freedom of expression without due process of law. Why? Because people will hesitate to express themselves if they fear criminal prosecution. This "chilling effect" on the exercise of the fundamental right to freedom of expression violates the right to liberty guaranteed by the Fifth and Fourteenth amendments to the U.S. Constitution. The Illinois Appellate Court dealt with the problem of free speech and hate crimes in *People v. Rokicki* (1999).

CASE	*Does the Hate Crime Statute Violate Free Speech?*

People v. Rokicki
718 N.E.2d 333 (Ill.App. 1999)

Kenneth Rokicki was charged in a single-count indictment with a hate crime based on the predicate [underlying] offense of disorderly conduct. Before trial, Rokicki moved to dismiss the charges alleging, among other things, that the hate crime statute was unconstitutional. The trial court denied his motion. Rokicki waived his right to a jury, and the matter proceeded to a bench trial [trial without a jury]. Rokicki was convicted, sentenced to two years' probation, and ordered to perform 100 hours of community service and to attend anger management counseling. He appealed, contending that the hate crime statute is unconstitutionally overly broad and chills expression protected by the First Amendment to the United States Constitution. The Illinois Appellate court affirmed the conviction and sentence.

HUTCHINSON, J.

FACTS

Donald Delaney testified that he is the store manager of a Pizza Hut in South Elgin. On October 20, 1995, at approximately 1:30 P.M., defendant entered the restaurant. The victim was a server there and took defendant's order. The victim requested payment, and defendant refused to tender payment to him. Delaney, who was nearby, stepped in and completed the sale. Defendant told Delaney not to let "that faggot" touch his food. When defendant's pizza came out of the oven, Delaney was on the telephone, and the victim began to slice the pizza. Delaney saw defendant approaching the counter with an irritated expression and hung up the telephone. Before Delaney could intervene, defendant leaned over the counter and began yelling at the victim and pounding his fist on the counter. Defendant directed a series of epithets at the victim including "Mary," "faggot," and "Molly Homemaker." Defendant continued yelling for 10 minutes and, when not pounding his fist, shook his finger at the victim. Delaney asked defendant to leave several times and threatened to call the police. However, Delaney did not call the police because he was standing between the victim and defendant and feared that defendant would physically attack the victim if Delaney moved. Eventually, Delaney returned defendant's money and defendant left the establishment.

The victim testified that he was working at the South Elgin Pizza Hut on October 20, 1995. Defendant entered the restaurant and ordered a pizza. When defendant's pizza came out of the oven, the victim began to slice it. Defendant then began yelling at the victim and pounding his fist on the counter. Defendant appeared very angry and seemed very serious. The victim, who is much smaller than defendant, testified that he was terrified by defendant's outburst and remained frightened for several days thereafter. Eventually, the manager gave defendant a refund and defendant left the restaurant. The victim followed defendant into the parking lot, recorded the license number of his car, and called the police.

Christopher Merritt, a sergeant with the South Elgin police department, testified that, at 2:20 P.M. on October 20, 1995, defendant entered the police station and said he wished to report an incident at the Pizza Hut. Defendant told Merritt that he was upset because a homosexual was working at the restaurant, and he wanted someone "normal" to touch his food. Defendant stated that he became angry when the victim touched his food. He called the victim a "Mary," pounded on the counter, and was subsequently kicked out of the restaurant. Merritt asked defendant what he meant by a "Mary," and defendant responded that a "Mary" was a homosexual. Merritt conducted only a brief interview of defendant because shortly after defendant arrived at the police station Merritt was dispatched to the Pizza Hut.

Deborah Hagedorn, an employee at the Pizza Hut in St. Charles, testified that in 1995 defendant came into the restaurant and asked for the address of the district manager for Pizza Hut. When asked why he wanted the address, defendant complained that he had been arrested at the South Elgin restaurant because he did not want a "f_____ faggot" touching his food.

Defendant testified that he was upset because the victim had placed his fingers in his mouth and had not washed his hands before cutting the pizza. Defendant admitted calling the victim "Mary" but denied that he intended to suggest the victim was a homosexual. Defendant stated that he used the term "Mary" because the victim would not stop talking and "it was like arguing with a woman." Defendant denied yelling and denied directing other derogatory terms towards the victim. Defendant admitted giving a statement to Merritt but denied telling him that he pounded his fist on the counter or used homosexual slurs. Defendant testified that he went to the St. Charles Pizza Hut but that Hagedorn was not present during his conversation with the manager. Defendant testified that he complained about the victim's hygiene but did not use any homosexual slurs.

The trial court found defendant guilty of hate crime. In a posttrial motion, defendant again argued that the hate crime statute was unconstitutional. The trial court denied defendant's motion and sentenced him to two years' probation. As part of the probation, the trial court ordered defendant not to enter Pizza Hut restaurants, not to contact the victim, to perform 100 hours' community service, and attend anger management counseling. Defendant timely appeals.

OPINION

On appeal, defendant does not challenge the sufficiency of the evidence against him. Defendant contends only that the hate crime statute is unconstitutional when the predicate offense is disturbing the peace. Defendant argues that the statute is overly broad and impermissibly chills free speech.

…The Illinois hate crime…reads in part as follows:

A person commits hate crime when, by reason of the actual or perceived race, color, creed, religion, ancestry, gender, sexual orientation, physical or mental disability, or national origin of another individual or group of individuals, [she or] he commits assault, battery, aggravated assault, misdemeanor theft, criminal trespass to residence, misdemeanor criminal damage to property, criminal trespass to vehicle, criminal trespass to real property, mob action or disorderly conduct.…720 ILCS 5/12–7.1(a) (West 1994)

…Rokicki's conviction was based on the predicate offense of disorderly conduct. A person commits disorderly conduct when she or he knowingly "does any act in such unreasonable manner as to alarm or disturb another and to provoke a breach of the peace." Disorderly conduct is punishable as a Class C misdemeanor. However, hate crime is punishable as a Class 4 felony for a first offense and a Class 2 felony for a second or subsequent offense.

Rokicki notes that the Appellate Court, Third District, was faced with a similar challenge to the hate crime statute in *People v. Nitz*, 674 N.E.2d 802 (1996). The *Nitz* court held that the hate crime statute, when predicated on disorderly conduct, was constitutional and neither infringed upon a defendant's free speech rights directly nor was overly broad because of its "chilling effect" on free speech. However, Rokicki urges us to reconsider the *Nitz* analysis and hold the hate crime statute overly broad.

Infringement upon Free Speech Rights

The issue presented in this case highlights the limits imposed by the First Amendment on a state's power to regulate its citizens' speech and thought. In a pair of cases decided in 1992 and 1993, the Supreme Court staked out the boundary between a state's unconstitutional regulation of unpopular beliefs in the marketplace of ideas and the permissible regulation of conduct motivated by those beliefs. See *R.A.V. v. City of St. Paul*, 505 U.S. 377 (1992); *Wisconsin v. Mitchell*, 508 U.S. 476 (1993). Our analysis of defendant's claims is controlled by these two cases, and we will begin by examining them.

In *R.A.V.*, the petitioner was alleged to have burned a crudely constructed wooden cross on the lawn of the residence of an African-American family and was charged with violating St. Paul's Bias-Motivated Crime Ordinance. The ordinance declared that anyone who places a burning cross, Nazi swastika, or other symbol on private or public property knowing that the symbol would arouse "'anger, alarm or resentment in others on the basis of race, color, creed, religion, or gender commits disorderly conduct and shall be guilty of a misdemeanor.'" The Minnesota Supreme Court found that the ordinance was constitutional because it could be construed to reach only "fighting words," which are outside the protection of the First Amendment. The United States Supreme Court held that, even when a statute addresses speech that is otherwise proscribable, the state may not discriminate on the basis of the content. The *R.A.V.* Court then found that the St. Paul ordinance violated the First Amendment because it would allow the proponents of racial tolerance and equality to use fighting words to argue in favor of tolerance and equality but would prohibit similar use by those opposed to racial tolerance and equality.

One year later, the United States Supreme Court revisited the issue in *Mitchell*. The defendant in *Mitchell* was convicted of aggravated battery, which carried a maximum term of two years' incarceration. However, Mitchell was sentenced to a term of four years' incarceration under a Wisconsin statute that enhanced the penalty for an offense when the defendant intentionally selected a victim because of his or her "'race, religion, color, disability, sexual orientation, national origin or ancestry.'" The Wisconsin Supreme Court reversed the conviction and held that the statute was unconstitutional under *R.A.V.*, holding that the legislature cannot "criminalize bigoted thought with which it disagrees."

The *Mitchell* Court held that, unlike the ordinance in *R.A.V.*, the Wisconsin statute was aimed solely at conduct unprotected by the First Amendment. The Court noted that, although a defendant may not be punished for his or her abstract beliefs, motive has traditionally been used as a factor in sentencing. The Court also observed that, although the statute punished the defendant for his discriminatory motive, motive played the same role in federal and state antidiscrimination statutes that had withstood First Amendment challenges. The Court further held that a state legislature could reasonably conclude that bias-motivated crimes cause greater societal harm warranting stiffer penalties because such offenses are more likely to provoke retaliatory crimes, inflict distinct emotional harms on their victims, and incite community unrest. Consequently, the Court found that the Wisconsin statute did not infringe upon free speech rights. . . .

The overbreadth doctrine protects the freedom of speech guaranteed by the First Amendment by invalidating laws so broadly written that the fear of prosecution would discourage people from exercising that freedom. A law regulating conduct is facially overly broad if it (1) criminalizes a substantial amount of protected behavior, relative to the law's plainly legitimate sweep, and (2) is not

susceptible to a limiting construction that avoids constitutional problems. A statute should not be invalidated for being overly broad unless its overbreadth is both real and substantial.

Rokicki's argument ignores the long-standing principle that speech alone cannot form the basis for a disorderly conduct charge: "Vulgar language, however distasteful or offensive to one's sensibilities, does not evolve into a crime because people standing nearby stop, look, and listen. The State's concern becomes dominant only when a breach of the peace is provoked by the language." Consequently, the hate crime statute does not reach those who, in defendant's words, simply "express themselves loudly and in a highly-animated, passionate manner" but applies only when their conduct is unreasonable and provokes a breach of the peace.

In this case, Rokicki is not being punished merely because he holds an unpopular view on homosexuality or because he expressed those views loudly or in a passionate manner. Rokicki was charged with hate crime because he allowed those beliefs to motivate unreasonable conduct. Rokicki remains free to believe what he will regarding people who are homosexual, but he may not force his opinions on others by shouting, pounding on a counter, and disrupting a lawful business. Rokicki's conduct exceeded the bounds of spirited debate, and the First Amendment does not give him the right to harass or terrorize anyone. Therefore, because the hate crime statute requires conduct beyond mere expression, we follow *Nitz* and conclude that . . . the Illinois hate crime statute constitutionally regulates conduct without infringing upon free speech.

Content Discrimination

Rokicki cites *R.A.V.* and argues that the hate crime statute is constitutionally impermissible because it discriminates based on the content of an offender's beliefs. Rokicki argues that the statute enhances disorderly conduct to hate crime when the conduct is motivated by, e.g., an offender's views on race or sexual orientation but that it treats identical conduct differently if motivated, e.g., by an offender's beliefs regarding abortion or animal rights. The *R.A.V.* Court invalidated the St. Paul ordinance because it favored some political views over others. . . . However, . . . the Court recognized several limitations to its content discrimination analysis, including statutes directed at conduct rather than speech, which sweep up a particular subset of proscribable speech. . . . We too decide that the legislature was free to determine as a matter of sound public policy that bias-motivated crimes create greater harm than identical conduct not motivated by bias and should be punished more harshly. Consequently, we reject defendant's content discrimination argument.

Chilling Effect

Rokicki also argues that the hate crime statute chills free expression because individuals will be deterred from expressing unpopular views out of fear that such expression will later be used to justify a hate crime charge. We disagree. The overbreadth doctrine should be used sparingly and only when the constitutional infirmity is both real and substantial.... We find Rokicki's argument speculative, and we cannot conclude that individuals will refrain from expressing controversial beliefs simply because they fear that their statements might be used as evidence of motive if they later commit an offense identified in the hate crime statute.

Conclusion

We hold that the hate crime statute is not facially unconstitutional when the predicate offense is disorderly conduct because (1) the statute reaches only conduct and does not punish speech itself; (2) the statute does not impermissibly discriminate based on content; and (3) the statute does not chill the exercise of first amendment rights.

AFFIRMED.

Questions

1. State the elements of the Illinois hate crime statute.

2. List all of the facts relevant to deciding whether Kenneth Rokicki violated the hate crime statute.

3. According to the court, why doesn't the Illinois "hate crime" statute violate Rokicki's right to free speech?

4. In your opinion, does the statute punish speech or nonexpressive conduct?

5. Do you think the purpose of this statute is to prevent disorderly conduct or expression?

6. Does Rokicki have a point when he argues that the statute prohibits only some kinds of hatred—race, ethnic, and sexual orientation—but not other kinds, like hatred for animal rights and abortion? Defend your answer.

EXPLORING FREE SPEECH FURTHER

 Go to the Criminal Law 8e CD to read the full text versions of the cases featured here.

1. *Is Panhandling Speech?*

FACTS

The New York Transit Authority, which has the authority to make rules equivalent to laws, made it unlawful to panhandle or beg in the New York subways. Several homeless people argued that the rule violated their right to free speech.

DECISION AND REASONS

Does it? No, said the U.S. Second Circuit Court of Appeals: "Common sense tells us that begging is much more 'conduct' than it is 'speech.'" The court conceded the conduct had an element of expression in it, but said: "The only message that we are able to espy as common to all acts of begging is that beggars want to exact money from those whom they accost. Such conduct, therefore, is subject to regulation." Research and other experts indicated that panhandlers and beggars frighten passengers. This, the court concluded, provides adequate grounds to regulate them.

Young v. New York City Transit Authority,
903 F.2d 146 (2d Cir. 1990) (Chapter 12)

2. *Is "Nude Dancing" Expressive Speech?*

FACTS

An Indiana statute prohibits nude dancing in public. Glen Theatre, a bar that featured nude dancing, sought an injunction against enforcing the law, arguing it violated the First Amendment. The law permitted erotic dancing, so long as the dancers wore "G-strings" and "pasties." It prohibited only totally nude dancing. The law argued that dancers can express themselves erotically without total nudity. Did the ordinance unduly restrict expressive conduct protected by the right to free speech?

DECISION AND REASONS

No, said the U.S. Supreme Court. Chief Justice Rehnquist, writing for a plurality, admitted that nude dancing is expressive conduct, but he concluded that the public indecency statute is justified because it "furthers a substantial government interest in protecting order and morality." So, the ban on public nudity was not related to the erotic message the dancers wanted to send.

Barnes v. Glen Theatre, Inc. et al., 501 U.S. 560 (1991)

3. *Is Flag Burning Expressive Conduct?*

FACTS

While the Republican National Convention was taking place in Dallas in 1984, Gregory Lee Johnson participated in a political demonstration called the "Republican War Chest Tour." The purpose of this event was to protest the policies of the Reagan administration and of certain Dallas-based corporations. The demonstrators marched through the Dallas streets, chanting political slogans and stopping at several corporate locations to stage "die-ins" intended to dramatize the consequences of nuclear war. On several occasions they spray-painted the walls of buildings and overturned potted plants, but Johnson himself took no part in such activities. He did, however, accept an American flag handed to him by a fellow protestor who had taken it from a flagpole outside one of the targeted buildings.

The demonstration ended in front of Dallas City Hall, where Johnson unfurled the American flag, doused it with kerosene, and set it on fire. While the flag burned, the protestors chanted, "America, the red, white, and blue, we spit on you." After the demonstrators dispersed, a witness to the flag-burning collected the flag's remains and buried them in his backyard. No one was physically injured or threatened with injury, though several witnesses testified that they had been seriously offended by the flag-burning.

Johnson was charged and convicted under Texas's "desecration of a venerated object" statute, sentenced to one year in prison, and fined $2,000. Did the flag burning statute violate Johnson's right to free speech?

DECISION AND REASONS

Yes, said a divided U.S Supreme Court:

The First Amendment literally forbids the abridgment only of "speech," but we have long recognized that its protection does not end at the spoken or written word. While we have rejected "the view that an apparently limitless variety of conduct can be labeled 'speech' whenever the person engaging in the conduct intends thereby to express an idea, we have acknowledged that conduct may be sufficiently imbued with elements of communication to fall within the scope of the First and Fourteenth Amendments.". . .

Texas claims that its interest in preventing breaches of the peace justifies Johnson's conviction for flag desecration. However, no disturbance of the peace actually occurred or threatened to occur because of Johnson's burning of the flag. Although the State stresses the disruptive behavior of the protestors during their march toward City Hall, it admits that "no actual breach of the peace occurred at the time of the flag burning or in response to the flag burning.". . .

Nor does Johnson's expressive conduct fall within that small class of "fighting words" that are "likely to provoke the average person to retaliation, and thereby cause a breach of the peace." No reasonable onlooker would have regarded Johnson's generalized expression of dissatisfaction with the policies of the Federal Government as a direct personal insult or an invitation to exchange fisticuffs.

We thus conclude that the State's interest in maintaining order is not implicated on these facts. The State need not worry that our holding will disable it from preserving the peace. We do not suggest that the First Amendment forbids a State to prevent "imminent lawless action.". . .

If there is a bedrock principle underlying the First Amendment, it is that the Government may not prohibit the expression of an idea simply because society finds the idea itself offensive or disagreeable. We have not recognized an exception to this principle even where our flag has been involved. Justice Jackson described one of our society's defining principles in words deserving of their frequent repetition: "If there is any fixed star in our constitutional constellation, it is that no official, high or petty, can prescribe what shall be orthodox in politics, nationalism, religion, or other matters of opinion or force citizens to confess by word or act their faith therein.". . .

Although Justice Kennedy concurred, the flag burning obviously disturbed him. He wrote:

The hard fact is that sometimes we must make decisions we do not like. We make them because they are right, right in the sense that the law and the Constitution, as we see them, compel the result. And so great is our commitment to the process that, except in the rare case, we do not pause to express distaste for the result, perhaps for fear of undermining a valued principle that dictates the decision. This is one of those rare cases. Our colleagues in dissent advance powerful arguments why respondent may be convicted for his expression, reminding us that among those who will be dismayed by our holding will be some who have had the singular honor of carrying the flag in battle. And I agree that the flag holds a lonely place of honor in an age when absolutes are distrusted and simple truths are burdened by unneeded apologetics. . . . The case here today forces recognition of the costs to which [our] . . . beliefs commit us. It is poignant but fundamental that the flag protects those who hold it in contempt. . . . So I agree with the court that he must go free.

Four justices dissented. Perhaps none of the justices felt more strongly than the World War II naval officer Justice Stevens, who wrote:

The ideas of liberty and equality have been an irresistible force in motivating leaders like Patrick Henry,

Susan B. Anthony, and Abraham Lincoln, schoolteachers like Nathan Hale and Booker T. Washington, the Philippine Scouts who fought at Bataan, and the soldiers who scaled the bluff at Omaha Beach. If those ideas are worth fighting for—and our history demonstrates that they are—it cannot be true that the flag that uniquely symbolizes their power is not itself worthy of protection from unnecessary desecration. I respectfully dissent.

Texas v. Johnson, 491 U.S. 397 (1989)

◆ ◆ ◆

RIGHT TO PRIVACY

Unlike the right to free speech, which is clearly spelled out in the First Amendment, you won't find the word *privacy* in the U.S. Constitution. Nevertheless, the U.S. Supreme Court has decided there *is* a constitutional right to privacy, a right that prohibits "all governmental invasions of the sanctity of a man's home and the privacies of life." And, like free speech, the right to privacy is a fundamental right that requires the government to prove a compelling interest justifies invading it. According to the Court, the fundamental right to privacy originates in six amendments to the U.S. Constitution:

- The First Amendment prohibition against laws that infringe on the right to free expression, association, and belief
- The Third Amendment prohibition against the quartering of soldiers in private homes
- The Fourth Amendment right to be secure in one's "person, house, papers, and effects" from "unreasonable searches"
- The Ninth Amendment provision that "The enumeration in the Constitution, of certain rights, shall not be construed to deny or disparage others retained by the people"
- The Fifth and Fourteenth amendments' prohibition against government denial of "liberty without due process of law" (*Griswold v. Connecticut* 1965)

This cluster of amendments sends the strong (but implied) message that the people have the right to be let alone by the government. In the First Amendment, it's our beliefs and expression of them and our associations with other people that are protected from the government. In the Third and Fourth Amendments, our homes are the object of protection. And, in the Fourth Amendment, it's not only our homes but our bodies, our private papers, and even our "stuff" that fall under its protection. The Ninth, or catch-all, Amendment acknowledges we have rights not named in the Constitution. According to the Court, privacy is one of these rights. Finally, according to the Court, liberty would mean little without a zone of autonomy that promotes individual personality and relationships central to the meaning of life in a free society.

In most cases, the Court has confined the right of privacy to activities that are part of the intimate relationships within the traditional family and home. In the leading case on the point, *Griswold v. Connecticut* (1965), the Court struck down a criminal statute that made it a crime for married couples to use contraceptives. Justice Douglas, writing for the majority, said that the law operates directly on an intimate relation of husband and wife.... The present case ... concerns a relationship lying within the zone of privacy created by several different fundamental constitutional guarantees. And it concerns a law which, in forbidding the use of contraceptives rather than regulating their manufacture or sale, seeks to achieve its goals by means having a maximum destructive impact upon that relationship. Such a law cannot stand.

Four years later, in *Stanley v. Georgia* (1969), it looked like the Court might take a more expanded view of the right to privacy. In *Stanley,* the Court struck down a statute that made it a crime to possess pornography within the privacy of a home. Some supporters of the right to privacy hoped that the Court had permanently locked the criminal law out of private homes, believing that the Court's holding meant that except for committing serious felonies, what people do at home is none of the law's business (Rubenfeld 1989, 737). But, they were disappointed when, in 1986 in *Bowers v. Hardwick,* the Court ruled that consenting adult homosexuals had no right to engage in sodomy in the privacy of their homes.

Then, in 2003, the Court reversed *Bowers v. Hardwick* (a rare occurrence especially when it involved a case decided only eighteen years before; see Chapter 1 on precedent and stare decisis) in *Lawrence v. Texas.* Here's an extended excerpt of that case.

CASE | *Did They Have the Right to Engage in Consensual Sodomy in Their Own Home?*

Lawrence v. Texas
123 S.Ct. 2472 (2003)

John Lawrence and Tyrone Garner, Defendants, were convicted in the Harris County Criminal Court at Law No. 10, of engaging in homosexual conduct. They appealed. On rehearing en banc [the full court], the Texas Court of Criminal Appeals affirmed. Certiorari was granted. The Supreme Court overruled its prior decision in *Bowers v. Hardwick,* 478 U.S. 186, 106 S.Ct. 2841, 92 L.Ed:2d 140 (1986) and reversed and remanded.

KENNEDY, J.

FACTS

In Houston, Texas, officers of the Harris County Police Department were dispatched to a private residence in response to a reported weapons disturbance. They entered an apartment where one of the petitioners, John Geddes Lawrence, resided. The right of the police to enter does not seem to have been questioned. The officers observed Lawrence and another man, Tyrone Garner, engaging in a sexual act. The two petitioners were arrested, held in custody over night, and charged and convicted before a Justice of the Peace.

The complaints described their crime as "deviate sexual intercourse, namely anal sex, with a member of the same sex (man)." The applicable state law is Tex. Penal Code Ann. § 21.06(a) (2003). It provides:

A person commits an offense if he engages in deviate sexual intercourse with another individual of the same sex." The statute defines "[d]eviate sexual intercourse" as follows:
(A) any contact between any part of the genitals of one person and the mouth or anus of another person; or
(B) the penetration of the genitals or the anus of another person with an object." § 21.01(1).

The petitioners exercised their right to a trial *de novo* [new trial] in Harris County Criminal Court. They challenged the statute as a violation of the Equal Protection Clause of the Fourteenth Amendment and of a like provision of the Texas Constitution. Tex. Const., Art. 1, § 3a. Those contentions were rejected. The petitioners, having entered a plea of *nolo contendere* [no contest], were each fined $200 and assessed court costs of $141.25.

The Court of Appeals for the Texas Fourteenth District considered the petitioners' federal constitutional arguments under both the Equal Protection and Due Process Clauses of the Fourteenth Amendment. After hearing the case en banc [all members of the court] the court, in a divided opinion, rejected the constitutional arguments and affirmed the convictions. The majority opinion indicates that the Court of Appeals considered our decision in *Bowers v. Hardwick*, 478 U.S. 186 (1986) to be controlling on the federal due process aspect of the case. *Bowers* then being authoritative, this was proper.

We granted certiorari, to consider three questions:

1. Whether Petitioners' criminal convictions under the Texas "Homosexual Conduct" law—which criminalizes sexual intimacy by same-sex couples, but not identical behavior by different-sex couples—violate the Fourteenth Amendment guarantee of equal protection of laws?

2. Whether Petitioners' criminal convictions for adult consensual sexual intimacy in the home violate their vital interests in liberty and privacy protected by the Due Process Clause of the Fourteenth Amendment?

3. Whether *Bowers v. Hardwick*, 478 U.S. 186, 106 S.Ct. 2841, 92 L.Ed.2d 140 (1986) should be overruled?

The petitioners were adults at the time of the alleged offense. Their conduct was in private and consensual.

OPINION

Liberty protects the person from unwarranted government intrusions into a dwelling or other private places. In our tradition the State is not omnipresent in the home. And there are other spheres of our lives and existence, outside the home, where the State should not be a dominant presence. Freedom extends beyond spatial bounds. Liberty presumes an autonomy of self that includes freedom of thought, belief, expression, and certain intimate conduct. The instant case involves liberty of the person both in its spatial and more transcendent dimensions. The question before the Court is the validity of a Texas statute making it a crime for two persons of the same sex to engage in certain intimate sexual conduct.

We conclude the case should be resolved by determining whether the petitioners were free as adults to engage in the private conduct in the exercise of their liberty under the Due Process Clause of the Fourteenth Amendment to the Constitution. For this inquiry we deem it necessary to reconsider the Court's holding in *Bowers*.

...The most pertinent beginning point is our decision in *Griswold v. Connecticut*, 381 U.S. 479 (1965). In *Griswold* the Court invalidated a state law prohibiting the use of drugs or devices of contraception and counseling or aiding and abetting the use of contraceptives. The Court described the protected interest as a right to privacy and placed emphasis on the marriage relation and the protected space of the marital bedroom.

After *Griswold* it was established that the right to make certain decisions regarding sexual conduct extends beyond the marital relationship. In *Eisenstadt v. Baird*, 405 U.S. 438 (1972), the Court invalidated a law prohibiting the distribution of contraceptives to unmarried persons....The opinions in *Griswold* and *Eisenstadt* were part of the background for the decision in *Roe v. Wade*, 410 U.S. 113 (1973)....Although the Court held the woman's rights were not absolute...the Court cited cases that protect spatial freedom and cases that go well beyond it. *Roe* recognized the right of a woman to make certain fundamental decisions affecting her destiny and confirmed once more that the protection of liberty under the Due Process Clause has a substantive dimension of fundamental significance in defining the rights of the person.

In *Carey v. Population Services Int'l*, 431 U.S. 678 (1977), the Court confronted a New York law forbidding sale or distribution of contraceptive devices to persons under 16 years of age....The law was invalidated [because]...the reasoning of *Griswold* could not be confined to the protection of rights of married adults. This was the state of the law with respect to some of the most relevant cases when the Court considered *Bowers v. Hardwick*.....

The Court began its substantive discussion in *Bowers* as follows: "The issue presented is whether the Federal Constitution confers a fundamental right upon homosexuals to engage in sodomy and hence invalidates the laws of the many States that still make such conduct illegal and have done so for a very long time." That statement, we now conclude, discloses the Court's own failure to appreciate the extent of the liberty at stake. To say that the issue in *Bowers* was simply the right to engage in certain sexual conduct demeans the claim the individual put forward, just as it would demean a married couple were it to be said marriage is simply about the right to have sexual intercourse.

The laws involved in *Bowers* and here are, to be sure, statutes that purport to do no more than prohibit a particular sexual act. Their penalties and purposes, though, have more far-reaching consequences, touching upon the most private human conduct, sexual behavior, and in the most private of places, the home. The statutes do seek to control a personal relationship that, whether or not entitled to formal recognition in the law, is within the liberty of persons to choose without being punished as criminals.

This, as a general rule, should counsel against attempts by the State, or a court, to define the meaning of the relationship or to set its boundaries absent injury to a person or abuse of an institution the law protects. It suffices for us to acknowledge that adults may choose to enter upon this relationship in the confines of their homes and their own private lives and still retain their dignity as free persons. When sexuality finds overt expression in intimate conduct with another person, the conduct can be but one element in a personal bond that is more enduring. The liberty protected by the Constitution allows homosexual persons the right to make this choice.

Having misapprehended the claim of liberty there presented to it, and thus stating the claim to be whether there is a fundamental right to engage in consensual sodomy, the *Bowers* Court said: "Proscriptions against that conduct have ancient roots." In academic writings, and in many of the scholarly *amicus* briefs filed to assist the Court in this case, there are fundamental criticisms of the historical premises relied upon by the majority and concurring opinions in *Bowers*. We need not enter this debate in the attempt to reach a definitive historical judgment, but the following considerations counsel against adopting the definitive conclusions upon which *Bowers* placed such reliance.

At the outset it should be noted that there is no long-standing history in this country of laws directed at homosexual conduct as a distinct matter. Beginning in colonial times... prohibition of sodomy... was understood to include relations between men and women as well as relations between men and men. Nineteenth-century commentators similarly read American sodomy, buggery, and crime-against-nature statutes as criminalizing certain relations between men and women and between men and men.... Thus early American sodomy laws were not directed at homosexuals as such but instead sought to prohibit nonprocreative sexual activity more generally. This does not suggest approval of homosexual conduct. It does tend to show that this particular form of conduct was not thought of as a separate category from like conduct between heterosexual persons.

Laws prohibiting sodomy do not seem to have been enforced against consenting adults acting in private. A substantial number of sodomy prosecutions and convictions for which there are surviving records were for predatory acts against those who could not or did not consent, as in the case of a minor or the victim of an assault.... Thus the model sodomy indictments... addressed the predatory acts of an adult man against a minor girl or minor boy. Instead of targeting relations between consenting adults in private, 19th-century sodomy prosecutions typically involved relations between men and minor girls or minor boys, relations between adults involving force, relations between adults implicating disparity in status, or relations between men and animals....

It was not until the 1970's that any State singled out same-sex relations for criminal prosecution, and only nine States have done so. Post-*Bowers* even some of these States did not adhere to the policy of suppressing homosexual conduct. Over the course of the last decades, States with same-sex prohibitions have moved toward abolishing them.

In summary, the historical grounds relied upon in *Bowers* are more complex than the majority opinion and the concurring opinion by Chief Justice Burger indicate. Their historical premises are not without doubt and, at the very least, are overstated.

It must be acknowledged, of course, that the Court in *Bowers* was making the broader point that for centuries there have been powerful voices to condemn homosexual conduct as immoral. The condemnation has been shaped by religious beliefs, conceptions of right and acceptable behavior, and respect for the traditional family. For many persons these are not trivial concerns but profound and deep convictions accepted as ethical and moral principles to which they aspire and which thus determine the course of their lives.

These considerations do not answer the question before us, however. The issue is whether the majority may use the power of the State to enforce these views on the whole society through operation of the criminal law. "Our obligation is to define the liberty of all, not to mandate our own moral code."

Chief Justice Burger joined the opinion for the Court in *Bowers* and further explained his views as follows: "Decisions of individuals relating to homosexual conduct have been subject to state intervention throughout the history of Western civilization. Condemnation of those practices is firmly rooted in Judeo-Christian moral and ethical standards." As with Justice White's assumptions about history, scholarship casts some doubt on the sweeping nature of the statement by Chief Justice Burger as it pertains to private homosexual conduct between consenting adults.

In all events we think that our laws and traditions in the past half century are of most relevance here. These references show an emerging awareness that liberty gives substantial protection to adult persons in deciding how to conduct their private lives in matters pertaining to sex. "History and tradition are the starting point but not in all cases the ending point of the substantive due process inquiry."

This emerging recognition should have been apparent when *Bowers* was decided. In 1955 the American Law Institute promulgated the *Model Penal Code* and made clear that it did not recommend or provide for "criminal penalties for consensual sexual relations conducted in private." ALI, *Model Penal Code* § 213.2, Comment 2, p. 372 (1980). It justified its decision on three grounds: (1) The prohibitions undermined respect for the law by penalizing conduct many people engaged in; (2) the statutes regulated private conduct not harmful to others; and (3) the laws were arbitrarily enforced and thus invited the danger of blackmail. Other States soon followed....

The sweeping references by Chief Justice Burger to the history of Western civilization and to Judeo-Christian moral and ethical standards did not take account of other authorities pointing in an opposite direction. A committee advising the British Parliament recommended in 1957 repeal of laws punishing homosexual conduct. Of even more importance, almost five years before *Bowers* was decided the European Court of Human Rights considered a case with parallels to *Bowers* and to today's case. An adult male resident in Northern Ireland alleged he was a practicing homosexual who desired to engage in consensual homosexual conduct. The laws of Northern Ireland forbade him that right. He alleged that he had been questioned, his home had been searched, and he feared criminal prosecution. The court held that the laws proscribing the conduct were invalid under the European Convention on Human Rights. Authoritative in all countries that are members of the Council of Europe (21 nations then, 45 nations now), the decision is at odds with the premise in *Bowers* that the claim put forward was insubstantial in our Western civilization.

In our own constitutional system the deficiencies in *Bowers* became even more apparent in the years following its announcement. The 25 States with laws prohibiting the relevant conduct referenced in the *Bowers* decision are reduced now to 13, of which 4 enforce their laws only against homosexual conduct. In those States where sodomy is still proscribed, whether for same-sex or heterosexual conduct, there is a pattern of nonenforcement with respect to consenting adults acting in private. The State of Texas admitted in 1994 that as of that date it had not prosecuted anyone under those circumstances.

Two principal cases decided after *Bowers* cast its holding into even more doubt. In *Planned Parenthood of Southeastern Pa. v. Casey,* 505 U.S. 833 (1992), the Court reaffirmed the substantive force of the liberty protected by the Due Process Clause. The *Casey* decision again confirmed that our laws and tradition afford constitutional protection to personal decisions relating to marriage, procreation, contraception, family relationships, child rearing, and education. In explaining the respect the Constitution demands for the autonomy of the person in making these choices, we stated as follows:

These matters, involving the most intimate and personal choices a person may make in a lifetime, choices central to personal dignity and autonomy, are central to the liberty protected by the Fourteenth Amendment. At the heart of liberty is the right to define one's own concept of existence, of meaning, of the universe, and of the mystery of human life. Beliefs about these matters could not define the attributes of personhood were they formed under compulsion of the State.

Persons in a homosexual relationship may seek autonomy for these purposes, just as heterosexual persons do. The decision in *Bowers* would deny them this right....

When homosexual conduct is made criminal by the law of the State, that declaration in and of itself is an invitation to subject homosexual persons to discrimination both in the public and in the private spheres.... The stigma this criminal statute imposes, moreover, is not trivial. The offense, to be sure, is but a class C misdemeanor, a minor offense in the Texas legal system. Still, it remains a criminal offense with all that imports for the dignity of the persons charged. The petitioners will bear on their record the history of their criminal convictions. Just this Term we rejected various challenges to state laws requiring the registration of sex offenders. We are advised that if Texas convicted an adult for private, consensual homosexual conduct under the statute here in question the convicted person would come within the registration laws of at least four States were he or she to be subject to their jurisdiction. This underscores the consequential nature of the punishment and the state-sponsored condemnation attendant to the criminal prohibition. Furthermore, the Texas criminal conviction carries with it the other collateral consequences always following a conviction, such as notations on job application forms, to mention but one example....

The doctrine of *stare decisis* is essential to the respect accorded to the judgments of the Court and to the stability of the law. It is not, however, an inexorable command..., rather, it is a principle of policy and not a mechanical formula of adherence to the latest decision.... The rationale of *Bowers* does not withstand careful analysis. In his dissenting opinion in Bowers Justice STEVENS came to these conclusions:

Our prior cases make two propositions abundantly clear. First, the fact that the governing majority in a State has traditionally viewed a particular practice as immoral is not a sufficient reason for upholding a law prohibiting the practice; neither history nor tradition could save a law prohibiting miscegenation from constitutional attack. Second, individual decisions by married persons, concerning the intimacies of their physical relationship, even when not intended to produce offspring, are a form of 'liberty' protected by the Due Process Clause of the Fourteenth Amendment. Moreover, this protection extends to intimate choices by unmarried as well as married persons.

Justice STEVENS' analysis, in our view, should have been controlling in *Bowers* and should control here. *Bowers* was not correct when it was decided, and it is not correct today. It ought not to remain binding precedent. *Bowers v. Hardwick* should be and now is overruled.

The present case does not involve minors. It does not involve persons who might be injured or coerced or who are situated in relationships where consent might not easily be refused. It does not involve public conduct or prostitution. It does not involve whether the government must give formal recognition to any relationship that homosexual persons seek to enter. The case does involve two adults who, with full and mutual consent from each other, engaged in sexual practices common to a homosexual lifestyle. The petitioners are entitled to respect for their private lives. The State cannot demean their existence or control their destiny by making their private sexual conduct a crime. Their right to liberty under the Due Process Clause gives them the full right to engage in their conduct without intervention of the government. "It is a promise of the Constitution that there is a realm of personal liberty which the government may not enter." The Texas statute furthers no legitimate state interest which can justify its intrusion into the personal and private life of the individual.

Had those who drew and ratified the Due Process Clauses of the Fifth Amendment or the Fourteenth Amendment known the components of liberty in its manifold possibilities, they might have been more specific. They did not presume to have this insight. They knew times can blind us to certain truths and later generations can see that laws once thought necessary and proper in fact serve only to oppress. As the Constitution endures, persons in every generation can invoke its principles in their own search for greater freedom.

The judgment of the Court of Appeals for the Texas Fourteenth District is reversed, and the case is remanded for further proceedings not inconsistent with this opinion.

DISSENT

SCALIA, J., joined by REHNQUIST CJ., and THOMAS, J. ... Today's opinion is the product of a Court, which is the product of a law-profession culture, that has largely signed on to the so-called homosexual agenda, by which I mean the agenda promoted by some homosexual activists directed at eliminating the moral opprobrium that has traditionally attached to homosexual conduct. I noted in an earlier opinion the fact that the American Association of Law Schools (to which any reputable law school *must* seek to belong) excludes from membership any school that refuses to ban from its job-interview facilities a law firm (no

matter how small) that does not wish to hire as a prospective partner a person who openly engages in homosexual conduct.

One of the most revealing statements in today's opinion is the Court's grim warning that the criminalization of homosexual conduct is "an invitation to subject homosexual persons to discrimination both in the public and in the private spheres." It is clear from this that the Court has taken sides in the culture war, departing from its role of assuring, as neutral observer, that the democratic rules of engagement are observed.

Many Americans do not want persons who openly engage in homosexual conduct as partners in their business, as scoutmasters for their children, as teachers in their children's schools, or as boarders in their home. They view this as protecting themselves and their families from a lifestyle that they believe to be immoral and destructive. The Court views it as "discrimination" which it is the function of our judgments to deter. So imbued is the Court with the law profession's anti-anti-homosexual culture, that it is seemingly unaware that the attitudes of that culture are not obviously "mainstream"; that in most States what the Court calls "discrimination" against those who engage in homosexual acts is perfectly legal; that proposals to ban such "discrimination" under Title VII have repeatedly been rejected by Congress; that in some cases such "discrimination" is *mandated* by federal statute, see 10 U.S.C. § 654(b)(1) (mandating discharge from the armed forces of any service member who engages in or intends to engage in homosexual acts); and that in some cases such "discrimination" is a constitutional right, see *Boy Scouts of America v. Dale*, 530 U.S. 640 (2000).

Let me be clear that I have nothing against homosexuals, or any other group, promoting their agenda through normal democratic means. Social perceptions of sexual and other morality change over time, and every group has the right to persuade its fellow citizens that its view of such matters is the best. That homosexuals have achieved some success in that enterprise is attested to by the fact that Texas is one of the few remaining States that criminalize private, consensual homosexual acts.

But persuading one's fellow citizens is one thing, and imposing one's views in absence of democratic majority will is something else. I would no more *require* a State to criminalize homosexual acts—or, for that matter, display *any* moral disapprobation of them—than I would *forbid* it to do so. What Texas has chosen to do is well within the range of traditional democratic action, and its hand should not be stayed through the invention of a brand-new "constitutional right" by a Court that is impatient of democratic change. It is indeed true that "later generations can see that laws once thought necessary and proper in fact serve only to oppress"; and when that happens, later generations can repeal those laws. But it is the premise of our system that those judgments are to be made by the people, and not imposed by a governing caste that knows best.

One of the benefits of leaving regulation of this matter to the people rather than to the courts is that the people, unlike judges, need not carry things to their logical conclusion. The people may feel that their disapprobation of homosexual conduct is strong enough to disallow homosexual marriage, but not strong enough to criminalize private homosexual acts—and may legislate accordingly. The Court today pretends that it possesses a similar freedom of action, so that that we need not fear judicial imposition of homosexual marriage, as has recently occurred in Canada (in a decision that the Canadian Government has chosen not to appeal).

At the end of its opinion—after having laid waste the foundations of our rational-basis jurisprudence—the Court says that the present case "does not involve whether the government must give formal recognition to any relationship that homosexual persons seek to enter." Do not believe it. More illuminating than this bald, unreasoned disclaimer is the progression of thought displayed by an earlier passage in the Court's opinion, which notes the constitutional protections afforded to "personal decisions relating to *marriage*, procreation, contraception, family relationships, child rearing, and education," and then declares that "persons in a homosexual relationship may seek autonomy for these purposes, just as heterosexual persons do" [emphasis added].

Today's opinion dismantles the structure of constitutional law that has permitted a distinction to be made between heterosexual and homosexual unions, insofar as formal recognition in marriage is concerned. If moral disapproval of homosexual conduct is "no legitimate state interest" for purposes of proscribing that conduct; and if, as the Court does (casting aside all pretense of neutrality), "[w]hen sexuality finds overt expression in intimate conduct with another person, the conduct can be but one element in a personal bond that is more enduring," what justification could there possibly be for denying the benefits of marriage to homosexual couples exercising "[t]he liberty protected by the Constitution?" Surely not the encouragement of procreation, since the sterile and the elderly are allowed to marry. This case "does not involve" the issue of homosexual marriage only if one entertains the belief that principle and logic have nothing to do with the decisions of this Court. Many will hope that, as the Court comfortingly assures us, this is so.

The matters appropriate for this Court's resolution are only three: Texas's prohibition of sodomy neither infringes a "fundamental right" (which the Court does not dispute), nor is unsupported by a rational relation to what the Constitution considers a legitimate state interest, nor denies the equal protection of the laws. I dissent.

THOMAS, J.

I join Justice SCALIA'S dissenting opinion. I write separately to note that the law before the Court today "is . . . uncommonly silly." *Griswold v. Connecticut*, 381 U.S. 479, 527, 85 S.Ct. 1678, 14 L.Ed.2d 510 (1965) (STEWART, J., dissenting). If I were a member of the Texas Legislature, I would vote to repeal it. Punishing someone for expressing his sexual preference through noncommercial consensual conduct with another adult does not appear to be a worthy way to expend valuable law enforcement resources.

Notwithstanding this, I recognize that as a member of this Court I am not empowered to help petitioners and others similarly situated. My duty, rather, is to "decide cases 'agreeably to the Constitution and laws of the United States.'" And, just like Justice Stewart, I "can find [neither in the Bill of Rights nor any other part of the Constitution a] general right of privacy," or as the Court terms it today, the "liberty of the person both in its spatial and more transcendent dimensions."

Questions

1. Summarize the arguments and evidence the majority opinion uses to support the right of privacy generally and the right to engage in homosexual conduct specifically.

2. State the specific limits of the right as identified by the majority of the Court.

3. Summarize the arguments and evidence the dissenting opinions use against a constitutional right of homosexuals to engage in homosexual conduct.

4. How important do you think history should be in defining the right to privacy? Explain your answer.

5. Exactly how far did the Court go in reading the Constitution to protect homosexual rights?

6. Do you think the Court went too far, just about right, or not far enough in extending the right to privacy under the U.S. Constitution? Explain your answer.

7. Exactly how broadly do you think the U.S. Constitution *should* be interpreted to protect the rights of homosexuals beyond consensual sexual behavior in the home? Defend your answer.

Unlike the U.S. Constitution, several state constitutions contain specific provisions guaranteeing the right to privacy. For example, the Florida Declaration of Rights provides: "Every natural person has the right to be let alone and free from governmental intrusion into his private life" (Florida Constitution 1998). Other states have followed the example of the U.S. Supreme Court and implied a state constitutional right to privacy.

CRUEL AND UNUSUAL PUNISHMENTS

The Eighth Amendment commands that "cruel and unusual punishments" shall not be "inflicted." The U.S. Supreme Court has ruled there are two kinds of cruel and unusual punishments:

- "Barbaric" punishments
- Punishments that are disproportionate to the crime committed (*Solem v. Helm* 1983, 284)

Barbaric punishments are punishments considered no longer acceptable to civilized society. At the time of the amendment, these included drawing and quartering, boiling in oil, beheading, and other medieval forms of torture and mutilation.

For more than a hundred years after the adoption of the Bill of Rights, no "cruel and unusual" punishment cases reached the U.S. Supreme Court because these medieval forms of execution weren't used in the United States. But in 1885, the governor of the state of New York in his annual message to the legislature wrote:

> The present mode of executing criminals by hanging has come down to us from the dark ages, and it may well be questioned whether the science of the present day cannot provide a means for taking...life...in a less barbarous manner.
>
> *In re Kemmler* 1890, 444

The legislature appointed a commission to study the matter. The commission reported that electrocution was "the most humane and practical method [of execution] known to modern science (*In re Kemmler* 1890, 444)." In 1888, the legislature replaced the hangman's noose with the electric chair.

Shortly thereafter, William Kemmler, convicted of murdering his wife, and sentenced to die in the electric chair, argued that electrocution was "cruel and unusual punishment." The U.S. Supreme Court disagreed. The Court said that electrocution was certainly unusual but not cruel. For the first time, the Court defined what "cruel" means in the Eighth Amendment. According to the Court, punishment by death isn't cruel as long as it isn't "something more than the mere extinguishment of life." The Court spelled out what it meant by this phrase: First, death has to be both instantaneous and painless. Second, it can't involve unnecessary mutilation of the body. So, according to the Court, beheading is cruel because it mutilates the body. Crucifixion is doubly cruel because it inflicts a "lingering" death and mutilates the body (*In re Kemmler* 1890, 446–447).

The **principle of proportionality**—namely, that punishment should fit the crime—has an ancient history. The Magna Carta, adopted in 1215 before imprisonment was a form of punishment, prohibited "excessive" fines. The English Bill of Rights in 1689 repeated the principle of proportionality in language that later appeared in the Eighth Amendment.

The U.S. Supreme Court first applied proportionality as a principle required by the Eighth Amendment in 1910, in *Weems v. United States.* Weems was convicted of falsifying a public document. The trial court first sentenced him to fifteen years in prison at hard labor in chains and then took away all of his civil rights for life. The Court ruled that the punishment was "cruel and unusual" because it was disproportionate to his crime.

In extending the cruel and unusual punishment ban to state criminal justice in the 1960s, the Court in *Robinson v. California* (1962) reaffirmed its commitment to the proportionality principle. The Court majority ruled that a ninety-day sentence for drug addiction was disproportionate because addiction is an illness, and it is cruel and unusual to punish persons for being sick. "Even one day in prison would be a cruel and unusual punishment for the 'crime' of having a common cold," wrote Justice Marshall for the Court majority. However, cases decided during the 1980s reflected disagreement about whether the principle of proportionality should apply to sentences of imprisonment.

A majority of the Supreme Court has consistently agreed that the proportionality principle applies to death penalty cases. For example, it held that the death penalty for raping an adult woman violated the principle of proportionality (*Coker v. Georgia* 1977). In fact, it looked as if a majority of the Court was committed to the idea that the death penalty is always disproportionate except in some aggravated murders. However, the state of Louisiana has challenged this notion by making child rape a capital offense. In 1996, the Louisiana Supreme Court dealt with the proportionality of capital punishment for child rape in *State v. Wilson.*

CASE | *Is the Death Penalty for Child Rape Cruel and Unusual?*

State v. Anthony Wilson
State v. Dewayne Bethley
685 So.2d 1063 (1996)

Anthony Wilson was charged by grand jury indictment with aggravated rape of a five-year-old girl. Wilson moved to quash indictment. The Criminal District Court, Parish of Orleans, quashed defendant's indictment. The Fourth Judicial District Court, Parish of Ouachita, quashed the indictment of Dewayne Bethey, another defendant charged with raping three girls under age of twelve. The two cases were consolidated. The Louisiana Supreme Court reversed and remanded both cases.

BLEICH, J.

FACTS

On December 21, 1995, Anthony Wilson was charged by grand jury indictment with the aggravated rape of a five-year-old girl.

Patrick Dewayne Bethley was charged with raping three girls, one of whom was his daughter, between December 1, 1995, and January 10, 1996. The ages of the little girls at the time of the rapes were five, seven, and nine. Furthermore, the State alleges that at the time of the alleged crimes, Bethley knew that he was HIV positive. Bethley filed a motion to quash urging the unconstitutionality of La. R.S. 14:42(C). The trial court granted Bethley's motion to quash. Although finding La. R.S. 14:42(C) would pass constitutional muster under the Eighth Amendment and the Equal Protection clause of the United States Constitution and Article I, § 20 of the Louisiana Constitution, the trial court held La. R.S. 14:42(C) unconstitutional because the class of death-eligible defendants was not sufficiently limited. That ruling resulted in an appeal.

OPINION

The thrust of both defendants' arguments is that the imposition of the death penalty for a crime not resulting in a death is "cruel and unusual punishment" and therefore unconstitutional under the Eighth Amendment to the United States Constitution and Article I, § 20 of the Louisiana Constitution of 1974....

A punishment is excessive and unconstitutional if it (1) makes no measurable contribution to acceptable goals of punishment and hence is nothing more than the purposeful and needless imposition of pain and suffering; or (2) is grossly out of proportion to the severity of the crime.

Excessive Punishment

The defendants' primary argument is that death is a disproportionate penalty for the crime of rape. The defendants' contention is based on *Coker v. Georgia*, 433 U.S. 584 (1977) decided by the Supreme Court in a plurality opinion. The *Coker* court rejected capital punishment as a penalty for the rape of an adult woman saying: "Although rape deserves serious punishment, the death penalty, which is unique in its severity and irrevocability, is an excessive penalty for the rapist who, as such and as opposed to the murderer, does not take human life." The plurality took great pains in referring only to the rape of adult women throughout their opinion, leaving open the question of the rape of a child. The defendants argue that the *Coker* findings cannot be limited to the rape of an adult.... The *Coker* plurality further [finds]...rape..."highly reprehensible, both in a moral sense and in its almost total contempt for the personal integrity and autonomy of the female victim. Short of homicide, it is the ultimate violation of self." These scathing descriptions of rape refer to the rape of an adult female. While the rape of an adult female is in itself reprehensible, the legislature has concluded that rape becomes much more detestable when the victim is a child.

La. R.S. 14:42(C) was amended by Acts 1995, No. 397, § 1 to allow for the death penalty when the victim of rape is under the age of twelve. Rape of a child less than twelve years of age is like no other crime. Since children cannot protect themselves, the State is given the responsibility to protect them. Children are a class of people that need special protection; they are particularly vulnerable since they are not mature enough nor capable of defending themselves. A "maturing society," through its legislature has recognized the degradation and devastation of child rape, and the permeation of harm resulting to victims of rape in this age category. The damage a child suffers as a result of rape is devastating to the child as well as to the community....

It has been argued that the death penalty should not be an option when the crime committed produces no death.... Louisiana courts have held that sex offenses against children cause untold psychological harm not only to the victim but also to generations to come.... While the Eighth Amendment bars the death penalty for minor crimes under the concept of disproportionality, the crime of rape when the victim is under the age of twelve is certainly not a minor crime.... "In part, capital punishment is an expression of society's moral outrage at particularly offensive conduct. This function may be unappealing to many, but it is essential in an ordered society that asks its citizens to rely on legal processes rather than self-help to vindicate their wrongs." Thus, we conclude that given the appalling nature of the crime, the severity of the harm inflicted upon the victim, and the harm imposed on society, the death penalty is not an excessive penalty for the crime of rape when the victim is a child under the age of twelve years old....

Goals of Punishment

Two legitimate goals of punishment are retribution and deterrence.... The child is the innocent victim. The offender is responsible for his own actions. The subject punishment is for the legislature to determine, not this Court.

Self-help is not permitted in our society, so there is a need for retribution in our criminal sanctions. The death penalty for rape of a child less than twelve years old would be a deterrence to the commission of that crime. While Louisiana is the only state that permits the death penalty for the rape of a child less than twelve, it is difficult to believe that it will remain alone in punishing rape by death if the years ahead demonstrate a drastic reduction in the incidence of child rape, an increase in cooperation by rape victims in the apprehension and prosecution of rapists, and a greater confidence in the role of law on the part of the people. This experience will be a consideration for this and other states' legislatures.

Our holding today permits the death penalty without a death actually occurring. In reaching this conclusion, we give great deference to our legislature's determination of the appropriateness of the penalty. This is not to say, however, that the legislature has free reign in proscribing penalties. They must still conform to the mandates of the Eighth Amendment and Article I, § 20 of the Louisiana Constitution, and they are still subject to judicial review by the courts. We hold only that in the case of the rape of a child under the age of twelve, the death penalty is not an excessive punishment nor is it susceptible of being applied arbitrarily and capriciously.

REVERSED AND REMANDED.

DISSENT

CALOGERO, CJ.
No other State in the union imposes the death penalty for the aggravated rape of a child under twelve years of age.

The reason for this, in my view, is that the statute fails constitutional scrutiny....I therefore dissent and would hold R.S. 14:42(C) facially unconstitutional under the Eighth Amendment to the United States Constitution.

Questions

1. According to the court, why is death a proportionate penalty for child rape? Do you agree? Explain your reasons.

2. Who should make the decision as to what is the appropriate penalty for crimes? Courts? Legislatures? Juries? Defend your answer.

3. In deciding whether the death penalty for child rape is cruel and unusual, is it relevant that Louisiana is the only state that punishes child rape with death?

4. According to the court, some crimes are worse than death. Do you agree? Is child rape one of them? Why? Why not?

SUMMARY

I. Rule of law—U.S. version of constitutional democracy places limits on government power *and* majority rule

II. Ex post facto laws are banned to
   A. Give fair warning to private individuals
   B. Prevent arbitrary government action

III. Vague laws are also banned (void-for-vagueness); they
   A. Are limited to laws that are vague to *reasonable* individuals and officers, not subjectively unreasonable (specific individuals and officers in the case)
   B. Deprive individuals of life, liberty, and property without due process
   C. Affect all laws to some extent, because words can never have the precise meaning of numbers
   D. Carry a heavy burden of proof for defendants in challenges

IV. U.S. Constitution, Article XIV, equal protection guarantee doesn't compel government to treat all people exactly like
   A. Criminal statutes that reasonably classify people differently don't violate the equal protection guarantee
   B. Classifications in criminal statutes based on race and ethnicity are never reasonable
   C. Gender classifications are suspect but not always unreasonable
   D. Age classifications are examined for reasonableness

V. The First Amendment guarantee of free speech is a preferred right (preferred status)
   A. Free speech includes nonverbal expressive conduct
   B. Speech doesn't include all words and expressive conduct (obscenity, profanity, libel and slander, and fighting words)
   C. Excluded expression can be made a crime, depending on the time, place, and manner of the expression
   D. Hate speech can be made a crime, depending on the circumstances

VI. According to U.S. Supreme Court, the U.S. Constitution guarantees an implied fundamental right to privacy
   A. Right to privacy derives from several amendments to the U.S. Constitution

B. U.S. Supreme Court has strictly limited the right to the home, family life, procreation, and child rearing

VII. U.S. Constitution, Amendment VIII, bans cruel and unusual punishments
    A. Unnecessary infliction of pain
    B. Punishments disproportionate to the crime committed
    C. Death (at least for intentional murder) is not cruel and unusual punishment

 Go to the Criminal Law 8e CD to download this summary outline. The outline has been formatted so that you can add notes to it during class lectures or later create a customized chapter outline to use while reviewing. Either way, the summary outline will help you understand the "big picture" and fill in the details as you study.

REVIEW QUESTIONS

1. Identify what the writers of the Constitution were suspicious of, and describe the effects of their suspicions on the kind of Constitution they wrote.

2. What's the significance of James Madison's "If men were angels ..." comment?

3. What's the difference between the extent of criminal law in a constitutional and a pure democracy?

4. Why is the grand principle of the rule of law not so grand in practice?

5. Identify two goals of the ban on ex post facto laws.

6. Explain the difference between a subjective and objective test of vagueness in the void-for-vagueness doctrine.

7. Explain how laws that are void-for-vagueness violate the due process clause.

8. Identify the two prongs of the test to determine whether laws are void-for-vagueness and the targets of each prong.

9. Why can't the void-for-vagueness test cure the uncertainty in laws?

10. Who has the burden to prove laws are vague, and why do they have it?

11. Discuss the benefits and the costs of precedent and stare decisis.

12. When, if ever, do criminal laws based on race, ethnicity, sex, and age not violate the constitutional guarantee of equal protection of the laws?

13. Identify, and give examples of, conduct protected by the right to free speech.

14. List five types of speech that are not protected by the First Amendment.

15. Explain where in the U.S. Constitution the U.S. Supreme Court "found" the right to privacy.

16. According to the U.S. Supreme Court, what activities does the right to privacy protect from criminal law?

17. Why didn't any cruel and unusual punishment cases get to the U.S. Supreme Court until the 1890s?

18. Identify and briefly describe the two types of punishment the U.S. Supreme Court recognizes as cruel and unusual.

KEY TERMS

rule of law p. 27
principle of legality p. 27
ex post facto law p. 27
arbitrary (law enforcement) p. 27
void-for-vagueness doctrine p. 28
rational basis p. 32
strict scrutiny p. 32

heightened scrutiny p. 32
fundamental right p. 35
obscenity p. 35
profanity p. 35
libel p. 35
slander p. 35
fighting words p. 35

clear and present danger p. 35
void-for-overbreadth doctrine
    p. 36
barbaric punishments p. 48
principle of proportionality p. 48

SUGGESTED READINGS

Go to the Criminal Law 8e CD for Suggested Readings for this chapter.

THE COMPANION WEB SITE
FOR *CRIMINAL LAW,* EIGHTH EDITION

http://cj.wadsworth.com/samaha/crim_law8e

Supplement your review of this chapter by going to the companion Web site to take one of the Tutorial Quizzes, use the flash cards to test your knowledge of the elements of various crimes and defenses, and check out the many other study aids you'll find there. You'll find valuable data and resources at your fingertips to help you study for that big exam or write that important paper.

3

The General Principles of Criminal Liability: *Actus Reus*

Chapter Main Points

- The first principle of criminal liability is the requirement of a criminal act.
- The criminal act (*actus reus*) is one of the elements of criminal liability the prosecution has to prove beyond a reasonable doubt.
- There are two types of crime: crimes of criminal conduct and crimes of criminal conduct causing criminal harms. They are defined as crime based on their elements.
- Intending to commit a crime is not a crime.
- A criminal act has to be voluntary to qualify as *actus reus*.
- *Actus reus* is the only principle of criminal liability that's also a constitutional requirement.
- Status (who we are) can't qualify as *actus reus*.
- Failure to act when there's a legal duty to act qualifies as *actus reus*.
- Possession is a passive state, but it can qualify as a criminal act when the items possessed are dangerous.

Did Mrs. Cogdon Murder Pat?

Mrs. Cogdon went to sleep. She dreamed that "the war was all around the house," that soldiers were in her daughter Pat's room, and that one soldier was on the bed attacking Pat. Mrs. Cogdon, still asleep, got up, left her bed, got an axe from a woodpile outside the house, entered Pat's room, and struck her two accurate forceful blows on the head with the blade of the axe, thus killing her. ◆

Crooking your finger ordinarily doesn't attract anyone's attention. But if you crook it around the trigger of a gun, squeeze the trigger, and kill someone, crooking your finger suddenly takes on great significance—it becomes the criminal act (*actus reus*) of murder. Stripping naked before you take a shower is hardly worth mentioning. But if you do it in your criminal law class, that's a different story—it becomes the *actus reus* of indecent exposure. So, under extraordinary circumstances, ordinary acts can turn into applications of the first principle of criminal liability—the requirement of a criminal act.

THE GENERAL PRINCIPLES OF LIABILITY

In practical terms, the **elements of crime** are what the prosecution has to prove beyond a reasonable doubt to convict defendants. Based on these elements, there are two types of crimes (Holmes 1963, 45–47):

1. *Crimes of criminal conduct.* Criminal conduct means an act was triggered by criminal intent. More technically, criminal conduct is the *concurrence* of criminal intent and action. (Please don't think of *conduct* as just another word for act or bodily movement. That's what it means in daily life, but in criminal law it's a technical term. It means "an act set in motion by an intent.")

2. *Crimes of criminal conduct causing a criminal harm.* Crimes in which criminal conduct (as defined in [1]) produces a criminal harm.

Crimes of criminal conduct consist of three elements:

1. *Actus reus.* A criminal act (the physical element of a crime), sometimes called the objective element because it can be proved without reference to the intent of the actor

2. *Mens rea.* A criminal intent (the mental element of a crime), sometimes called the subjective element because intent resides inside the actor and can't be observed

3. Concurrence. Act and intent are joined in the exact sense that the criminal intent sets the criminal act in motion

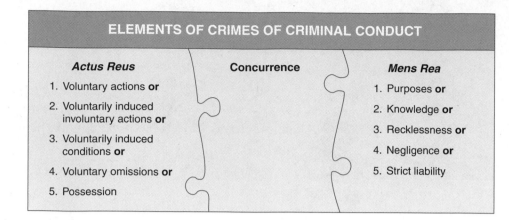

ELEMENTS OF CRIMES OF CRIMINAL CONDUCT

Actus Reus	Concurrence	*Mens Rea*
1. Voluntary actions **or**		1. Purposes **or**
2. Voluntarily induced involuntary actions **or**		2. Knowledge **or**
3. Voluntarily induced conditions **or**		3. Recklessness **or**
4. Voluntary omissions **or**		4. Negligence **or**
5. Possession		5. Strict liability

Let's look at burglary as an example of a crime of criminal conduct. It consists of the *actus reus* (criminal act) of breaking and entering joined with the *mens rea* (the intent to commit a crime), such as stealing an MP3 player once inside the house. The crime of burglary is complete whether or not the intended crime to be committed inside the house (in our example, stealing an MP3 player) is completed. So, the crime of burglary is criminal conduct whether or not it causes any harm beyond the conduct itself.

Crimes of criminal conduct causing a criminal harm consist of five elements:

1. Actus reus. As defined in the elements of crimes of criminal conduct

2. Mens rea. As defined in the elements of crimes of criminal conduct

3. *Concurrence*
   a. *Actus reus* and *mens rea* combine to produce criminal conduct, as defined in the elements of crimes of criminal conduct, and
   b. *Actus reus* and *mens rea* (criminal conduct) result(s) in harm

4. *Causation.* Criminal conduct produces criminal harm as defined in the criminal statute

5. *Resulting harm.* The specific result defined in the criminal statute

In all crimes consisting of criminal conduct causing a criminal harm, the requirement of concurrence applies not only to the union of action and intention but also to

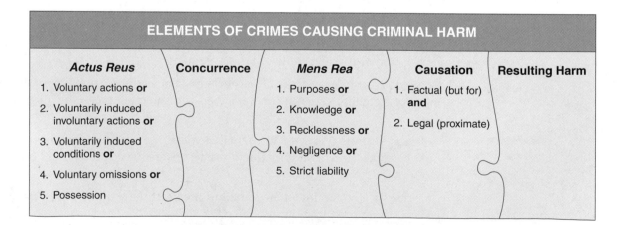

ELEMENTS OF CRIMES CAUSING CRIMINAL HARM

Actus Reus	Concurrence	*Mens Rea*	Causation	Resulting Harm
1. Voluntary actions **or**		1. Purposes **or**	1. Factual (but for) **and**	
2. Voluntarily induced involuntary actions **or**		2. Knowledge **or**	2. Legal (proximate)	
3. Voluntarily induced conditions **or**		3. Recklessness **or**		
4. Voluntary omissions **or**		4. Negligence **or**		
5. Possession		5. Strict liability		

TABLE 3.1	
Elements of Homicide and General Principles of Criminal Liability	
Elements of Homicide	**General Principle of Liability**
Criminal act: shooting a gun	*Actus reus:* the requirement of a voluntary act, omission, or possession
Criminal intent: shooting the gun on purpose	*Mens rea:* acting intentionally, knowingly, recklessly, or negligently
Joining act and intent: the intent to shoot produced the act of shooting the gun	Concurrence: the requirement of a causal relation between act and intent
Causation: shooting caused the victim's death	Causation: that criminal conduct caused the harm specifically prohibited by the law
Harm: the death of the victim	Harmful result: criminal conduct has to produce a harm specifically defined in the law

the union of criminal conduct and the cause of the particular result, such as the conduct of one who intentionally shoots another, causing the other's death (Chapter 9). Other crimes of cause and result are battery, conduct that causes bodily injury (Chapter 10); arson, conduct that causes injury to property (Chapter 11); and false pretenses, conduct that causes the loss of property (Chapter 12).

Each of the five elements of specific crimes relates to a general principle of criminal liability. Table 3.1 uses the example of criminal homicide to show the link between the practical elements of crimes and the general principles of liability, which will be discussed in this chapter and applied to specific offenses in Chapters 9 through 13.

THE CRIMINAL ACT: THE PRINCIPLE OF *ACTUS REUS*

Action is the heart of the **principle of *actus reus*** (the "evil act"). Intention is the heart of the **principle of *mens rea*** (the "evil mind") (Chapter 4). The union of act and intent in the sense that the criminal intent set the criminal act in motion is the **principle of concurrence** (Chapter 4). That the criminal conduct causes a harm prohibited by the law is the **principle of causation** (Chapter 4). Causation is another concurrence, this time between criminal conduct and criminal result. That criminal conduct has to cause a criminal result is the **principle of harmful result.**

These general principles allow us to organize the content of the special part of the criminal law (the part that defines the elements of the specific crimes included in Chapters 9 through 12; see Chapter 1) into a logical, orderly theoretical framework. For example, in murder, the intent to kill unites with the act of killing; in illegal left turn violations, the intent to turn unites with the act of turning. So, the elements of every specific crime have to fit within the bounds of the general principles of *actus reus*, *mens rea*, concurrence, and, where relevant, causation and result.

 Go to Exercise 3-1 on the Criminal Law 8e CD to learn more about general principle of *actus reus* in state codes.

The prestigious American Law Institute, in its widely cited *Model Penal Code*, succinctly summarizes the main aspects of the general principle of *actus reus* in the following provision:

SECTION 2.01 REQUIREMENT OF VOLUNTARY ACT;
OMISSION AS BASIS OF LIABILITY; POSSESSION AS AN ACT.

(1) A person is not guilty of an offense unless his liability is based on conduct that includes a voluntary act or the omission to perform an act of which he is physically capable.
(2) The following are not voluntary acts within the meaning of this section:
(a) a reflex of convulsion;
(b) a bodily movement during unconsciousness or sleep;
(c) conduct during hypnosis or resulting from hypnotic suggestion;
(d) a bodily movement that otherwise is not a product of the effort or determination of the actor, either conscious or habitual.
(3) Liability for the commission of an offense may not be based on an omission unaccompanied by action unless
(a) the omission is expressly made sufficient by the law defining the offense; or
(b) a duty to perform the omitted act is otherwise imposed by law. . . .
(4) Possession is an act, within the meaning of this Section, if the possessor knowingly procured or received the thing possessed or was aware of his control thereof for a sufficient period to have been able to terminate his possession.

Imagine a statute that makes it a crime merely to intend to kill another person. Why does such a statute strike us as absurd? One reason is that intent alone is impossible to prove. In the words of a medieval judge, "The thought of man is not triable, for the devil himself knoweth not the thought of man." Furthermore, intentions by themselves don't harm anyone. Although the *moral* law may condemn those who have immoral thoughts, the *criminal* law demands conduct—intention turned into action. So, punishing the mere *intent* to kill (even if we could prove it) misses the harm the statute aims at—another's death (Morris 1976, ch. 1).

Another problem with punishing intent is that it's terribly hard to separate daydreaming and fantasy from intent. The angry thought, "I'll kill you for that!" rarely turns into actual killing (or for that matter even an attempt to kill), because it's almost always just a blunt way of saying, "I'm really pissed." Punishment has to wait for enough action to prove the speaker really intends to commit a crime (Chapter 6). Punishing thoughts stretches the reach of the criminal law too far when it puts within its grasp a "mental state that the accused might be too irresolute even to begin to translate into action." The bottom line: We don't punish thoughts because it's impractical, inequitable, and unjust (Williams 1961, 1–2).

Now you know why the first principle of criminal liability is the requirement of a voluntary act. This requirement is as old as our law. Long before there was a principle of criminal intent, there was the requirement of a criminal act. The requirement that intentions have to turn into deeds is called **manifest criminality.** The requirement of manifest criminality leaves no doubt about the criminal nature of the act. The modern phrase "caught red-handed" comes from the ancient idea of manifest criminality. Then it meant catching murderers with the blood still on their hands; now, it means catching someone in the act of wrongdoing. For example, if bank customers see several people enter the bank, draw guns, threaten to shoot if the tellers don't hand over money, take the money the tellers give them, and leave the bank with the money, their criminality—the *actus reus* and *mens rea* of robbery—is manifest (Fletcher 1978, 115–116).

The *actus reus* requirement serves several purposes. First, it helps to prove the *mens rea*. We can't observe intentions; we can only infer them from actions. Second, it reserves the harsh sanction of the criminal law for cases of actual danger. Third, it protects the privacy of individuals. The law doesn't have to pry into the thoughts of individuals unless the thinker crosses "the threshold of manifest criminality." Many axioms illustrate the *actus reus* principle: "Thoughts are free." "We're punished for what we do, not for who we are." "Criminal punishment depends on conduct, not status." "We're punished for what we've done, not for what we might do." Although simple to state as a general rule, much in the principle of *actus reus* complicates its apparent simplicity (Fletcher 1978, 117).

Requirement of a Voluntary Act

Only *voluntary* acts qualify as criminal acts. In the words of the great justice and legal philosopher Oliver Wendell Holmes, "An act . . . is a muscular contraction, and something more. . . . The contraction of muscles must be willed" (Holmes 1963, 46–47). So, *actus reus* consists of two requirements: bodily movements and free will. Why? The reasoning goes like this:

1. Criminal law punishes people.
2. We can only punish people we can blame.
3. We can only blame people who are responsible for their actions.
4. People are only responsible for their voluntary actions.

The best example of an involuntary act is a reflex or spasm. So, a spasm that lurches an arm forcefully into someone's face in its path doesn't satisfy the *actus reus* of assault and battery. What about acts that aren't instantaneous spasms and reflexes? Like **automatism** (acts committed when you're unconscious)? Sleepwalking (**somnambulism**), one form of automatism, was involved in *King v. Cogdon*, the bizarre case of a woman who while she was sleepwalking killed her daughter.

CASE	*Was Killing Her Daughter a Voluntary Act?*

King v. Cogdon
(Reported in Morris 1951, 29)

Mrs. Cogdon was charged with the murder of her only child, a daughter called Pat, age 19. The jury found her not guilty.

FACTS

Pat had for some time been receiving psychiatric treatment for a relatively minor neurotic condition of which, in her psychiatrist's opinion, she was now cured. Despite this, Mrs. Cogdon continued to worry unduly about her. Describing the relationship between Pat and her mother, Mr. Cogdon testified: "I don't think a mother could have thought any more of her daughter. I think she absolutely adored her." On the conscious level, at least, there was no reason to doubt Mrs. Cogdon's deep attachment to her daughter. To the charge of murdering Pat, Mrs. Cogdon pleaded not guilty. Her story, though somewhat bizarre, was not seriously challenged by the Crown, and led to her acquittal.

She told how, on the night before her daughter's death, she had dreamt that their house was full of spiders and that these spiders were crawling all over Pat. In her sleep, Mrs. Cogdon left the bed she shared with her husband, went into Pat's room, and awakened to find herself violently brushing at Pat's face, presumably to remove the spiders. This woke Pat. Mrs. Cogdon told her she was just tucking her in. At the trial, she testified that she still believed, as she had been told, that the occupants of a nearby house bred spiders as a hobby, preparing nests for them behind the pictures on their walls. It was these spiders which in her dreams had invaded their home and attacked Pat. There had also been a previous dream in which ghosts had sat at the end of Mrs. Cogdon's bed and she had said to them, "Well, you have come to take Pattie." It does not seem fanciful to accept the psychological explanation of these spiders and ghosts as the projections of Mrs. Cogdon's subconscious hostility towards her daughter; a hostility which was itself rooted in Mrs. Cogdon's own early life and marital relationship.

The morning after the spider dream she told her doctor of it. He gave her a sedative and, because of the dream and certain previous difficulties she had reported, discussed the possibility of psychiatric treatment. That evening Mrs. Cogdon suggested to her husband that he attend his lodge meeting, and she asked Pat to come with her to the cinema. After he had gone Pat looked through the paper, not unusually found no tolerable programme, and said that as she was going out the next evening she thought she would rather go to bed early. Later, while Pat was having a bath preparatory to retiring, Mrs. Cogdon went into her room, put a hot water bottle in the bed, turned back the bedclothes, and placed a glass of hot milk beside the bed ready for Pat. She then went to bed herself. There was some desultory conversation between them about the war in Korea, and just before she put out her light Pat called out to her mother, "Mum, don't be so silly worrying there about the war, it's not on our front doorstep yet."

Mrs. Cogdon went to sleep. She dreamt that "the war was all around the house," that soldiers were in Pat's room, and that one soldier was on the bed attacking Pat. This was all of the dream she could later recapture. Her first "waking" memory was of running from Pat's room, out of the house to the home of her sister who lived next door. When her sister opened the front door Mrs. Cogdon fell into her arms, crying "I think I've hurt Pattie."

In fact Mrs. Cogdon had, in her somnambulistic state, left her bed, fetched an axe from the woodheap, entered Pat's room, and struck her two accurate forceful blows on the head with the blade of the axe, thus killing her.

OPINION

Mrs. Cogdon's story was supported by the evidence of her physician, a psychiatrist, and a psychologist. The jury believed Mrs. Cogdon. The jury concluded that Mrs. Cogdon's account of her mental state at the time of the killing, and the unanimous support given to it by the medical and psychological evidence, completely rebutted the presump-

tion that Mrs. Cogdon intended the natural consequences of her acts. It must be stressed that insanity was not pleaded as a defence because the experts agreed that Mrs. Cogdon was not psychotic [Chapter 8, see "Insanity" section]. The jury acquitted her because the act of killing itself was not, in law, regarded as her act at all.

Questions

1. List all of Mrs. Cogdon's acts resulting in Pat's death.

2. List all the evidence relevant to deciding whether Mrs. Cogdon's acts were involuntary.

3. Could Mrs. Cogdon have done anything to prevent Pat's death? What?

4. Would it matter if she had taken preventive measures? Why or why not?

5. It's commonly believed it's wrong to punish someone we can't blame. Would it be "right" to punish Mrs. Cogdon? Why or why not?

EXPLORING VOLUNTARY ACTS FURTHER

Go to the Criminal Law 8e CD to read the full text versions of the cases featured here.

1. *Were His Acts Committed During an Epileptic Seizure Voluntary?*

FACTS

Emil Decina suffered an epileptic seizure while driving his car. During the seizure, he struck and killed four children. Was the killing an "involuntary act" because it occurred during the seizure?

DECISION AND REASONS

The court said no:

> This defendant knew he was subject to epileptic attacks at any time. He also knew that a moving vehicle uncontrolled on a public highway is a highly dangerous instrumentality capable of unrestrained destruction. With this knowledge, and without anyone accompanying him, he deliberately took a chance by making a conscious choice of a course of action, in disregard of the consequences which he knew might follow from his conscious act, which in this case did ensue.

People v. Decina, 138 N.E.2d 799 (N.Y.1956)

2. Were His Acts Following a Concussion Voluntary?

FACTS

Robert Brian Fulcher got into a fight in a bar, passed out, and was picked up by the police. He was taken to jail, where he brutally stomped on another jail inmate and shouted ethnic slurs at him. Fulcher testified that he remembers nothing after passing out in the bar. At the trial, Doctor LeBegue testified that Fulcher suffered from a concussion incurred during the bar fight and that it caused a brain injury that put him "in a state of traumatic automatism at the time of his attack on Hernandez... the state of mind in which a person does not have conscious and willful control over his actions...." Was Fulcher liable?

DECISION AND REASONS

No, said the court. Unconscious automatism is an affirmative defense because "The rehabilitative value of imprisonment for the automatistic offender who has committed the offense unconsciously is nonexistent. The cause of the act was an uncontrollable physical disorder that may never recur and is not a moral deficiency."

Fulcher v. State, 633 P.2d 142 (Wyo.1981)

3. Were His Acts Following Exposure to Agent Orange Voluntary?

FACTS

Bruce Jerrett terrorized Dallas and Edith Parsons—he robbed them, killed Dallas, and kidnapped Edith. At trial, Jerrett testified that he could remember nothing of what happened until he was arrested, and that he had suffered previous blackouts following exposure to Agent Orange during military service in Vietnam. The trial judge refused to instruct the jury on the defense of automatism. Did he act voluntarily?

DECISION AND REASONS

The North Carolina Supreme Court reversed and ordered a new trial. They wrote:

> The rule in this jurisdiction is that where a person commits an act without being conscious thereof, the act is not a criminal act even though it would be a crime if it had been committed by a person who was conscious....
>
> [In this case,] there was corroborating evidence tending to support the defense of unconsciousness.... Defendant's very peculiar actions in permitting the kid-

napped victim to repeatedly ignore his commands and finally lead him docilely into the presence and custody of a police officer lends credence to his defense of unconsciousness. We therefore hold that the trial judge should have instructed the jury on the defense of unconsciousness.

State v. Jerrett, 307 S.E.2d 339 (1983)

4. Were His Acts Committed While Hypnotized Voluntary?

FACTS

In a Danish case, Bjorn Nielson masterminded a robbery by hypnotizing his friend Palle Hardrup. While in the hypnotic trance, Hardrup held up a Copenhagen bank, shooting and killing a teller and director. Was Hardrup guilty of robbery and murder?

DECISION AND REASONS

The Danish court said no. Nielson was tried and convicted and sentenced to life imprisonment. He was guilty, even though he was nowhere near the scene of the crimes, because he masterminded the holdup and acted through his friend Hardrup to commit it. Hardrup wasn't prosecuted because he acted involuntarily; he was sent to a mental hospital.

Goldstein, Dershowitz, and Schwartz 1974, 766
[not included on the CD]

5. Was the "Slip of the Thumb" Voluntary?

FACTS

Bobby George was convicted of aggravated assault. George put a gun to a friend's head and demanded a dollar. After he cocked the hammer, it "slipped off [his] thumb" and the "gun went off." George did not mean for the gun to go off. He did not intend to hurt his friend; it was an accident. Was his thumb's slipping a voluntary act?

DECISION AND REASONS

Yes, the Texas Court of Criminal Appeals ruled:

> There is no law and defense of accident in the present penal code, but... the Legislature had not jettisoned the notion. The function of the former defense of accident is performed now by the requirement of... § 6.01(a), that, A person commits an offense if he voluntarily

engages in conduct....If the issue is raised by the evidence, a jury may be charged that a defendant should be acquitted if there is a reasonable doubt as to whether he voluntarily engaged in the conduct of which he is accused."...

If the hammer "slipped off [his] thumb," it had to be that the thumb holding the hammer partially back released just enough pressure for the hammer to "slip" forward. However slight, that is "bodily movement" within the meaning of § 1.07(a)(1), and there is no evidence that it was involuntary.

George v. State, 681 S.W.2d 43 (Tex.Crim.App.1984)

6. Were His Acts During Sleep Deprivation Voluntary?

FACTS

On December 20, 1993, David McClain was involved in an altercation with police officers in the Broad Ripple section of Indianapolis. McClain is alleged to have struck several officers before being subdued by police. On December 22, 1993, McClain was charged with aggravated battery, two counts of battery against police officers, and two counts of resisting law enforcement. On March 4, 1994, McClain filed a notice of intent to interpose an insanity defense. The basis for the defense was sleep deprivation allegedly preventing McClain from forming the necessary intent for the crimes charged. Two days before the altercation with police, McClain flew from Japan to Indianapolis and did not sleep on the flight. McClain further claims to have slept just three hours in the forty-eight hours prior to his arrest.

Indiana Code § 35–41–2–1(a) provides that "a person commits an offense only if he voluntarily engages in conduct in violation of the statute defining the offense." McClain argues that his violent behavior toward police was a form of automatism caused by sleep deprivation. He contends that as a result of his condition his acts were not voluntary, and therefore he has no criminal responsibility for them. The state argues that McClain's altercation with police cannot be described as an involuntary act, because his conduct was not a convulsion or reflex. Could McClain's attack on the officer be an involuntary act?

DECISION AND REASONS

Yes, said the Indiana Supreme Court:

Indiana's criminal voluntary act statute codified the axiom that voluntariness is a "general element of crim-

inal behavior" and reflected the premise that criminal responsibility "postulates a free agent confronted with a choice between doing right and doing wrong and choosing freely to do wrong." As the Commission explained: "The term voluntary is used in this Code as meaning behavior that is produced by an act of choice and is capable of being controlled by a human being who is in a conscious state of mind."

The evidence McClain seeks to present on automatism bears on the voluntariness of his actions within the meaning of the statute. In essence McClain claims... [he was in] an automatistic state of mind that precluded voluntary behavior. Although the jury is obviously not required to accept this explanation, permitting McClain to make the argument is consistent with the statute's general purpose that criminal conduct be an "act of choice" by a person in a "conscious state of mind." Accordingly, at trial McClain can call expert witnesses and otherwise present evidence of sleep deprivation and automatism within the confines of the Indiana Rules of Evidence...." Once evidence in the record raises the issue of voluntariness, the state must prove the defendant acted voluntarily beyond a reasonable doubt." If McClain's conduct is found to be involuntary, then the State has not proved every element of its case and the law requires an acquittal....

McClain's argument...is that but for a lack of sleep over the course of several days, he would not have been in this state at the time he allegedly involuntarily struck police officers on December 20, 1993. Automatism is simply a denial of one element—voluntary action—that the Legislature has required for most crimes.

McClain v. State, 678 N.E.2d 104 (Ind. 1997)

Are any of the following voluntary acts?
a. Drowsy drivers who fall asleep while they're driving
b. Drunk drivers who aren't in control
c. Drivers with dangerously high blood pressure who suffer strokes while they're driving

These are what we might call voluntarily induced involuntary acts. Should we stretch the meaning of voluntary to include them within the grasp of the voluntary act requirement because it might deter people whose voluntary acts create risks of involuntarily hurting innocent people?

Status as an Act

Action refers to what we do; **status** (or condition) denotes who we are. Most statuses or conditions don't qualify as *actus reus*. Status can arise in two ways. Sometimes, it results from prior voluntary acts—methamphetamine addicts voluntarily used methamphetamine the first time and alcoholics voluntarily took their first drink. Other conditions result from no act at all. The most obvious examples are the characteristics we're born with: sex, age, race, and ethnicity.

In Samuel Butler's (1927) imaginary land of *Erehwon* ("nowhere" spelled backward), it's a crime to have tuberculosis. Following conviction for tuberculosis, the judge pronounced sentence on one defendant with these words:

> It only remains for me to pass such a sentence on you, as shall satisfy the ends of the law. That sentence must be a very severe one. It pains me much to see one who is yet so young, and whose prospects in life were otherwise so excellent, brought to this distressing condition by a constitution which I can only regard as radically vicious; but yours is no case for compassion: this is not your first offense: you have led a career of crime, and have only profited by the leniency shown you upon past occasions, to offend yet more seriously against the laws and institutions of your country. You were convicted of aggravated bronchitis last year: and I find that though you are but twenty-three years old, you have been imprisoned on no less than fourteen occasions for illnesses of a more or less hateful character; in fact, it is not too much to say that you have spent the greater part of your life in jail.
>
> It is all very well for you to say that you came of unhealthy parents, and had a severe accident in your childhood which permanently undermined your constitution; excuses such as these are the ordinary refuge of the criminal; but they cannot for one moment be listened to by the ear of justice. I am not here to enter upon curious metaphysical questions as to the origins of this or that—questions to which there would be no end were their introduction once tolerated, and which would result in throwing the only guilt on the tissues of the primordial cell, or on the elementary gasses. There is no question of how you came to be wicked, but only this—namely, are you wicked or not? This has been decided in the affirmative, neither can I hesitate for a single moment to say that it has been decided justly. You are a bad and dangerous person. . . .
>
> I do not hesitate to sentence you to imprisonment, with hard labor, for the rest of your miserable existence. (104–111)

Why does it strike us as wrong to sentence someone to life imprisonment for having tuberculosis? Because the voluntary acts of the defendant didn't cause the disease. And why is that so bothersome? The U.S. Supreme Court explained why in *Robinson v. California* (1962), where drug addiction was a crime. Robinson was convicted and sentenced for being a heroin addict. The Court ruled that punishing Robinson for his addiction to heroin was cruel and unusual punishment prohibited by the Eighth Amendment to the U.S. Constitution (Chapter 2). According to the Court, it's cruel and unusual punishment to sentence someone to "even one day" for an illness. Why? For the same reasons only voluntary acts qualify as *actus reus* (pages 57–59). Addiction isn't an act; it's an involuntary condition. And, according to the Court, we can't blame people who aren't responsible for their conditions. And, if we can't blame them, then it's not fair to punish them. (Of course, Robinson differs from the fictional defendant with tuberculosis; Robinson's addiction resulted from a prior voluntary act.)

Go to Exercise 3-2 on the Criminal Law 8e CD to learn more about the oral arguments in *Robinson v. California.*

What about acts that result from conditions? In *Powell v. Texas* (1968), the U.S. Supreme Court had to decide whether to extend the prohibition against punishing the status of drug addiction resulting from the prior voluntary act of drug use to an alcoholic's act of public drunkenness resulting from his alcoholism.

| CASE | *Is Public Drunkenness an Act?* |

Powell v. Texas
392 U.S. 514 (1968)

Leroy Powell was tried, found guilty, and fined $20 in the Corporation Court of Austin, Texas. The County Court of Travis County, Texas affirmed. The U.S. Supreme Court affirmed.

MARSHALL, J. announced the judgment of the Court, joined by WARREN, CJ., and BLACK and HARLAN, JJ.

FACTS

In late December 1966, appellant (Leroy Powell) was arrested and charged with being found in a state of intoxication in a public place, in violation of Vernon's Ann.Texas Penal Code, Art. 477 (1952), which reads as follows: "Whoever shall get drunk or be found in a state of intoxication in any public place, or at any private house except his own, shall be fined not exceeding one hundred dollars." Powell was tried in the Corporation Court of Austin, Texas., found guilty, and fined $20. He appealed to the County Court at Law No. 1 of Travis County, Texas, where a trial de novo [a new trial as if the first had not occurred and no decision was rendered] was held. [At the trial de novo] His counsel urged that appellant was "afflicted with the disease of chronic alcoholism," that "his appearance in public (while drunk was) . . . not of his own volition," and therefore that to punish him criminally for that conduct would be cruel and unusual, in violation of the Eighth and Fourteenth Amendments to the United States Constitution. The trial judge in the county court, sitting without a jury . . . ruled . . . that chronic alcoholism was not a defense to the charge. He found Powell guilty, and fined him $50. There being no further right to appeal within the Texas judicial system, Powell appealed to this Court. . . .

[At the original trial in the Austin Corporation Court] Powell testified concerning the history of his drinking problem. He reviewed his many arrests for drunkenness; testified that he was unable to stop drinking; stated that when he was intoxicated he had no control over his ac-

tions and could not remember them later, but that he did not become violent; and admitted that he did not remember his arrest on the occasion for which he was being tried. On cross-examination, Powell admitted that he had had one drink on the morning of the trial and had been able to discontinue drinking.

. . . Dr. David Wade, a Fellow of the American Medical Association, duly certificated in psychiatry [testified at length at Powell's trial]. . . . Dr. Wade sketched the outlines of the "disease" concept of alcoholism; noted that there is no generally accepted definition of "alcoholism"; alluded to the ongoing debate within the medical profession over whether alcohol is actually physically "addicting" or merely psychologically "habituating"; and concluded that in either case a "chronic alcoholic" is an "involuntary drinker," who is "powerless not to drink," and who "loses his self-control over his drinking." He testified that he had examined Powell, and that Powell is a "chronic alcoholic," who "by the time he has reached (the state of intoxication) . . . is not able to control his behavior, and (who) . . . has reached this point because he has an uncontrollable compulsion to drink."

Dr. Wade also responded in the negative to the question whether Powell has "the willpower to resist the constant excessive consumption of alcohol." He added that in his opinion jailing appellant without medical attention would operate neither to rehabilitate him nor to lessen his desire for alcohol.

On cross-examination, Dr. Wade admitted that when Powell was sober he knew the difference between right and wrong, and he responded affirmatively to the question whether appellant's act in taking the first drink in any given instance when he was sober was a "voluntary exercise of his will." Qualifying his answer, Dr. Wade stated that "these individuals have a compulsion, and this compulsion, while not completely overpowering, is a very strong influence, an exceedingly strong influence, and this compulsion coupled with the firm belief in their mind that they are going to be able to handle it from now on causes their judgment to be somewhat clouded."

Evidence in the case then closed.... The State contented itself with a brief argument that Powell had no defense to the charge because he "is legally sane and knows the difference between right and wrong."

[Powell was found guilty] and fined $20. He appealed to the County Court at Law No. 1 of Travis County, Texas, where a trial de novo [a new trial as if the one just summarized never occurred] was held.

[In the County Court trial de novo] His counsel urged that Powell was "afflicted with the disease of chronic alcoholism," that "his appearance in public [while drunk was]...not of his own volition," and therefore that to punish him criminally for that conduct would be cruel and unusual, in violation of the Eighth and Fourteenth Amendments to the United States Constitution.

Following this abbreviated exposition of the problem before it [by Powell's counsel], the [County Court]...indicated its intention to disallow Powell's claimed defense of chronic alcoholism. Thereupon defense counsel submitted, and the trial court entered, the following findings of fact:

(1) That chronic alcoholism is a disease which destroys the afflicted person's will power to resist the constant, excessive consumption of alcohol.

(2) That a chronic alcoholic does not appear in public by his own volition but under a compulsion symptomatic of the disease of chronic alcoholism.

(3) That Leroy Powell, defendant herein, is a chronic alcoholic who is afflicted with the disease of chronic alcoholism.

PLURALITY OPINION

...Powell seeks to come within the application of the Cruel and Unusual Punishment Clause announced in *Robinson v. California*, 370 U.S. 660 (1962), which involved a state statute making it a crime to "be addicted to the use of narcotics." This Court held there that "a state law which imprisons a person thus afflicted (with narcotic addiction) as a criminal, even though he has never touched any narcotic drug within the State or been guilty of any irregular behavior there, inflicts a cruel and unusual punishment...."

On its face the present case does not fall within that holding, since Powell was convicted, not for being a chronic alcoholic, but for being in public while drunk on a particular occasion. The State of Texas thus has not sought to punish a mere status, as California did in *Robinson*; nor has it attempted to regulate Powell's behavior in the privacy of his own home. Rather, it has imposed upon Powell a criminal sanction for public behavior which may create substantial health and safety hazards, both for Powell and for members of the general public, and which offends the moral and esthetic sensibilities of a large segment of the community. This seems a far cry from convicting one for being an addict, being a chronic alcoholic, being "mentally ill, or a leper...."

Robinson so viewed brings this Court but a very small way into the substantive criminal law.... The entire thrust of *Robinson's* interpretation of the Cruel and Unusual Punishment Clause is that criminal penalties may be inflicted only if the accused has committed some act, has engaged in some behavior, which society has an interest in preventing, or perhaps in historical common-law terms, has committed some *actus reus*....

Traditional common-law concepts of personal accountability and essential considerations of federalism lead us to disagree with Powell. We are unable to conclude, on the state of this record or on the current state of medical knowledge, that chronic alcoholics in general, and Leroy Powell in particular, suffer from such an irresistible compulsion to drink and to get drunk in public that they are utterly unable to control their performance of either or both of these acts and thus cannot be deterred at all from public intoxication. And in any event this Court has never articulated a general constitutional doctrine of *mens rea*.

We cannot cast aside the centuries-long evolution of the collection of interlocking and overlapping concepts which the common law has utilized to assess the moral accountability of an individual for his antisocial deeds. The doctrines of *actus reus, mens rea*, insanity, mistake, justification, and duress have historically provided the tools for a constantly shifting adjustment of the tension between the evolving aims of the criminal law and changing religious, moral, philosophical, and medical views of the nature of man. This process of adjustment has always been thought to be the province of the States....

But formulating a constitutional rule would reduce, if not eliminate...fruitful experimentation, and freeze the developing productive dialogue between law and psychiatry into a rigid constitutional mold. It is simply not yet the time to write the Constitutional formulas cast in terms whose meaning, let alone relevance, is not yet clear either to doctors or to lawyers.

AFFIRMED.

CONCURRING OPINIONS

BLACK, J., joined by HARLAN, J.
...Punishment for a status is particularly obnoxious, and in many instances can reasonably be called cruel and unusual, because it involves punishment for a mere propensity, a

desire to commit an offense; the mental element is not simply one part of the crime but may constitute all of it. This is a situation universally sought to be avoided in our criminal law; the fundamental requirement that some action be proved is solidly established even for offenses most heavily based on propensity, such as attempt, conspiracy, and recidivist crimes. In fact, one eminent authority has found only one isolated instance, in all of Anglo-American jurisprudence, in which criminal responsibility was imposed in the absence of any act at all.

The reasons for this refusal to permit conviction without proof of an act are difficult to spell out, but they are nonetheless perceived and universally expressed in our criminal law. Evidence of propensity can be considered relatively unreliable and more difficult for a defendant to rebut; the requirement of a specific act thus provides some protection against false charges.

Perhaps more fundamental is the difficulty of distinguishing, in the absence of any conduct, between desires of the daydream variety and fixed intentions that may pose a real threat to society; extending the criminal law to cover both types of desire would be unthinkable, since "there can hardly be anyone who has never thought evil. When a desire is inhibited it may find expression in fantasy; but it would be absurd to condemn this natural psychological mechanism as illegal."

In contrast, crimes that require the State to prove that the defendant actually committed some proscribed act involve none of these special problems. In addition, the question whether an act is "involuntary" is . . . an inherently elusive question, and one which the State may, for good reasons, wish to regard as irrelevant. In light of all these considerations, our limitation of our *Robinson* holding to pure status crimes seems to me entirely proper. . . .

. . . I would hold that *Robinson v. California* establishes a firm and impenetrable barrier to the punishment of persons who, whatever their bare desires and propensities, have committed no proscribed wrongful act. But I would refuse to plunge from the concrete and almost universally recognized premises of *Robinson* into the murky problems raised by the insistence that chronic alcoholics cannot be punished for public drunkenness, problems that no person, whether layman or expert, can claim to understand, and with consequences that no one can safely predict. I join in affirmance of this conviction.

WHITE, J. concurring

. . . Unless *Robinson* is to be abandoned, the use of narcotics by an addict must be beyond the reach of the criminal law. Similarly, the chronic alcoholic with an irresistible urge to consume alcohol should not be punishable for drinking or

for being drunk. Powell's conviction was for the different crime of being drunk in a public place. Thus even if Powell was compelled to drink, and so could not constitutionally be convicted for drinking, his conviction in this case can be invalidated only if there is a constitutional basis for saying that he may not be punished for being in public while drunk. The statute involved here, which aims at keeping drunks off the street for their own welfare and that of others, is not challenged on the ground that it interferes unconstitutionally with the right to frequent public places. No question is raised about applying this statute to the nonchronic drunk, who has no compulsion to drink, who need not drink to excess, and who could have arranged to do his drinking in private or, if he began drinking in public, could have removed himself at an appropriate point on the path toward complete inebriation.

DISSENT

FORTAS, J., joined by DOUGLAS, BRENNAN,
and STEWART, JJ.

. . . It is settled that the Federal Constitution places some substantive limitation upon the power of state legislatures to define crimes for which the imposition of punishment is ordered. . . . *Robinson v. California* . . . stands upon a principle which, despite its subtlety, must be simply stated and respectfully applied because it is the foundation of individual liberty and the cornerstone of the relations between a civilized state and its citizens: Criminal penalties may not be inflicted upon a person for being in a condition he is powerless to change. . . .

In the present case, Powell is charged with a crime composed of two elements—being intoxicated and being found in a public place while in that condition. The crime, so defined, differs from that in *Robinson*. The statute covers more than a mere status. But the essential constitutional defect here is the same as in *Robinson*, for in both cases the particular defendant was accused of being in a condition which he had no capacity to change or avoid.

Questions

1. According to the Court, is *actus reus* a general principle of criminal liability *and* a constitutional requirement? Explain.

2. State exactly what Leroy Powell did to land him in criminal court.

3. Does it make sense to punish Powell if he was drunk in public because of his alcoholism? Why or why not?

4. Was his alcoholism a condition?

5. If so, did it result from a voluntary act? What act? When did it take place?

6. Was Powell's alcoholism a "disease"? What's the evidence that it was?

7. Does the public drunkenness statute punish Powell for being "sick"?

8. Which opinion do you agree with, the plurality, the concurring, or the dissenting opinion? Why?

Failure to Act as an Act

We support punishment for people who rape, murder, and rob because their actions caused harm. But what about people who stand by and do nothing while bad things are happening around them? As Professor George Fletcher describes these people, "They get caught in a situation in which they falter. Someone needs help and they cannot bring themselves to render it." Can these failures to act (omissions) satisfy the *actus reus* requirement? Yes, when it's outrageous to fail to do something to help someone in danger.

There are two kinds of failure to act (**criminal omission**). One is the simple failure to act, usually the **failure to report** something required by law, such as reporting an accident or child abuse, filing an income tax return, registering a firearm, or notifying sexual partners of positive HIV status. The other type of omission is the **failure to intervene** to prevent injuries and death to persons or the damage and destruction of property.

Failures to report or intervene are criminal omissions only if defendants had a **legal duty** (a duty enforced by law), not just a moral duty, to act. Legal duty is an example of what's called a **circumstance element** (an element of a crime in addition to *actus reus, mens rea,* concurrence, and causation). As with the other elements of crimes, the prosecution has to prove the circumstance element beyond a reasonable doubt.

Legal duties are created in three ways:

1. Statutes

2. Contracts

3. Special relationships

Statutes are the basis for most legal duties to report—like the duty to file income tax returns, report accidents and child abuse, and register firearms. Individuals can also contract to perform duties; for example, law enforcement officers agree to "protect and serve." Failure to perform those duties can create criminal liability. The main special relationships are the parent-child relationship, the doctor-patient relationship, the employer-employee relationship, the carrier-passenger relationship, and, in some states, the husband-wife relationship.

Failure to perform **moral duties** (enforced by conscience, religion, and social norms) does not qualify as a criminal omission. According to Professors Wayne LaFave and Austin Scott:

> Generally one has no legal duty to aid another person in peril, even when that aid can be rendered without danger or inconvenience to himself. He need not shout a warning to a

blind man headed for a precipice or to an absent-minded one walking into a gunpowder room with a lighted candle in hand. He need not pull a neighbor's baby out of a pool of water or rescue an unconscious person stretched across the railroad tracks, though the baby is drowning or the whistle of the approaching train is heard in the distance. A doctor is not legally bound to answer a desperate call from the frantic parents of a sick child, at least if it is not one of his regular patients. A moral duty to take affirmative action is not enough to impose a legal duty to do so. But there are situations which do give rise to legal duties. (1986, 203)

There are two approaches to defining a *legal duty* to rescue strangers or call for help. One is the **"Good Samaritan" doctrine,** which "imposes a legal duty to render or summon aid for imperiled strangers." Only a few jurisdictions follow the Good Samaritan approach. Nearly all follow the approach of the **American bystander rule** (*State v. Kuntz* 2000, 951). According to the bystander rule, there's no legal duty to rescue or summon help for someone who's in danger, even if the bystander risks nothing by helping. So, it might be a revolting breach of the moral law for an Olympic swimmer to stand by and watch a kid drown, without so much as even placing a 911 call on her cell phone, but the law demands nothing from her.

Limiting criminal omissions to the failure to perform legal duties is based on three assumptions:

1. Individual conscience, peer pressure, and other informal mechanisms condemn and prevent behavior more effectively than criminal prosecution.

2. Prosecuting omissions puts too much of a burden on an already overburdened criminal justice system.

3. Criminal law can't force "Good Samaritans" to help people in need.

The Montana Supreme Court grappled with the problems of special relationship and the legal duty to report and intervene in *State v. Kuntz* (2000).

CASE	*Did She Have a Legal Duty to Report or Intervene?*

State v. Kuntz
995 P.2d 951 (Mont. 2000)

Bonnie Kuntz, the defendant, was accused of negligently causing the death of Warren Becker, a man she lived with, by stabbing him and then failing to call for medical assistance. She moved to strike the portion of the charge pertaining to her failure to summon medical aid. The District Court, Yellowstone County, denied her motion. The Montana Supreme Court remanded.

NELSON, J.

FACTS

Yellowstone County Sheriff's deputies were dispatched on April 19, 1998, to the home of Bonnie Kuntz and Warren Becker to investigate a reported stabbing. When the deputies arrived at the trailer house, Becker was dead from a single stab wound to the chest. Kuntz, who was waiting for medical and law enforcement personnel to arrive, told the deputies she and Becker had argued the morning of April 18, 1998. At some point during the day, both parties left the trailer home. After Kuntz returned that evening, at or before midnight, a physical altercation ensued.

Kuntz and Becker, who had never married but had lived together for approximately six years, were in the process of ending what is described as a stormy relationship. When Kuntz arrived at the mobile home that night, she discovered that many of her personal belongings had been destroyed, the interior of the home "trashed," and the phone ripped from the wall. Kuntz told the deputies that she then went into the kitchen. There, allegedly, Becker physically attacked her, and at one point grabbed her by the hair, shook her, and slammed her into the stove.

Kuntz told the deputies that she could not clearly remember what happened, only that she had pushed Becker away and had then gone outside by the kitchen door to "cool off." When she thought that the fight was over, and that it was safe to go back inside, she returned to the kitchen. She discovered a trail of blood leading from the kitchen through the living room and out onto the front porch where she found Becker collapsed face-down on the porch. She alleges that she rolled him over. Becker was unresponsive.

Kuntz then alleges that she found Becker's car keys in one of his pockets, got in his vehicle, drove to a friend's house several miles away, and called her mother. Kuntz does not allege that she personally contacted medical or law enforcement personnel; rather, authorities were apparently summoned by Kuntz's sister-in-law, who lived next door to Kuntz's mother, sometime within an hour after the stabbing. Kuntz did return, however, to the trailer home where she waited for the deputies and medics to arrive.

On June 23, 1998, Bonnie Kuntz was charged with negligent homicide for causing the death of Warren Becker by stabbing him once in the chest. Although she admitted stabbing Becker and causing his death, Kuntz entered a plea of not guilty based on the defense of justifiable use of force.

On November 6, 1998, shortly before the scheduled trial date, the State filed an amended information [a formal document] charging the same offense but alleging that Kuntz caused the death of Becker by stabbing him once in the chest with a knife *and* by failing to call for medical assistance. Kuntz again entered a plea of not guilty. On December 18, 1998, Kuntz filed a motion to dismiss the amended information or in the alternative to strike the allegation that the failure to seek medical assistance constituted negligent homicide. Following a hearing and briefing, the District Court... [denied] Bonnie Kuntz's motion to dismiss the amended information on January 8, 1999. Kuntz sought [review].... In an order dated March 23, 1999, this Court accepted original jurisdiction at the request of both parties.

OPINION

For criminal liability to be based upon a failure to act, there must be a duty imposed by the law to act, and the person must be physically capable of performing the act.

[A material element of every offense is a voluntary act, which includes an omission to perform a duty which the law imposes on the offender and which he is physically capable of performing.] (See § 45–2-202, MCA]

As a starting point in our analysis, the parties here have identified what is often referred to as "the American bystander rule." This rule imposes no legal duty on a person to rescue or summon aid for another person who is at risk or in danger, even though society recognizes that a moral obligation might exist. This is true even "when that aid can be rendered without danger or inconvenience to" the potential rescuer....

But this rule is far from absolute. Professors LaFave and Scott have identified seven common-law exceptions to the American bystander rule: (1) a duty based on a personal relationship, such as parent-child or husband-wife; (2) a duty based on statute; (3) a duty based on contract; (4) a duty based upon voluntary assumption of care; (5) a duty based on creation of the peril; (6) a duty to control the conduct of others; and (7) a duty based on being a landowner. *See* LaFave & Scott, § 3.3, at 283–289. A breach of one of these legal duties by failing to take action, therefore, may give rise to criminal liability. Our review of the issues presented here can accordingly be narrowed to two of the foregoing exceptions as briefed by the parties and identified by the District Court:

1. a duty based on a personal relationship, and

2. a duty based on creation of the peril.

One of the lead authorities on the personal relationship duty arose in Montana. In the widely cited case of *State v. Mally* (1961), 139 Mont. 599, 366 P.2d 868, this Court held that under certain circumstances a husband has a duty to summon medical aid for his wife and breach of that duty could render him criminally liable. The facts of the case described how Kay Mally, who was suffering from terminal kidney and liver diseases, fell and fractured both her arms on a Tuesday evening. Her husband, Michael Mally, put her to bed and did not summon a doctor until Thursday morning. "During this period of time, as she lay there with only the extended arm of death as a companion, she received but one glass of water." Although his wife ultimately died of kidney failure, Mally was found guilty of involuntary manslaughter, a forerunner of Montana's negligent homicide statute, because his failure to act hastened his wife's death.

In *Mally*, however, we alluded to a limitation of this rule which is a point of contention between the parties here. We cited to *People v. Beardsley* (1907).... [In *Beardsley*,] the

Michigan Supreme Court concluded that the legal duty imposed on the personal relationship of husband and wife could not be extended to a temporary, non-family relationship. The court held that a married defendant had no duty to summon medical help for his mistress, who was staying in his house for the weekend, after she took morphine following a bout of heavy drinking and fell into a "stupor."

We agree with the State, as well as myriad commentators over the years . . . that *Beardsley* is indeed "outmoded." . . . See, for example, Graham Hughes, *Criminal Omissions*, 67 Yale L.J. 590, 624 (1958) (stating that *Beardsley* "proclaims a morality which is smug, ignorant and vindictive"). . . . *See also State v. Miranda* (1998), 715 A.2d 680, 682 (concluding that person who is not a biological or legal parent of a child but who establishes a "familial relationship" with a live-in girlfriend has a duty to protect her child from abuse). . . .

Applying the foregoing to the facts here, we conclude that Kuntz and Becker, having lived together for approximately six years, owed each other the same "personal relationship" duty as found between spouses. . . . This duty, identified as one of "mutual reliance" . . . would include circumstances involving "two people, though not closely related, [who] live together under one roof." To hold otherwise would result in an untenable rule that would not . . . impose a legal duty to summon medial aid on persons in a relationship involving cohabitation. Nevertheless, this holding is far from dispositive in establishing a legal duty under the facts presented.

We agree with the District Court that the duty based on "creation of the peril" is far more closely aligned with the factual circumstances here. Undoubtedly, when a person places another in a position of danger, and then fails to safeguard or rescue that person, and the person subsequently dies as a result of this omission, such an omission may be sufficient to support criminal liability.

This duty may include peril resulting from a defendant's criminal negligence, as alleged here. The legal duty based on creation of the peril has been extended in other jurisdictions to cases involving self-defense. . . .

The legal duty imposed on personal relationships and those who create peril are not absolute; i.e., there are exceptions to these exceptions. The personal relationship legal duty, for example, does not require a person to jeopardize his own life. Furthermore, the duty does not arise unless the spouse "unintentionally entered a helpless state," or was otherwise incompetent to summon medical aid on his or her own behalf.

Similarly, the law does not require that a person, who places another person in a position of peril, risk bodily injury or death in the performance of the legally imposed duty to render assistance. . . . Therefore, where self-preservation is at stake, the law does not require a person to "save the other's life by sacrificing his own," and therefore no crime can be committed by the person who "in saving his own life in the struggle for the only means of safety," causes the death of another. Even states such as Vermont that have adopted a "Good Samaritan Doctrine" which—contrary to the American bystander rule—imposes a legal duty to render or summon aid for imperiled strangers, do not require that the would-be rescuer risk bodily injury or death. Thus, although a person may still be held accountable for the results of the peril into which he or she placed another, the law does not require that he or she risk serious bodily injury or death in order to perform a legal duty.

With these general principles in place, we now turn to the issue. . . . Does one who justifiably uses deadly force in defense of her person nevertheless have a legal duty to summon aid for the mortally wounded attacker? Our analysis of this issue is narrowed to whether the legal duty to summon aid, based on the defendant's personal relationship or creation of peril, extends into circumstances where the defendant's alleged use of justifiable force places his or her aggressor in need of medical attention. The State contends that even if Kuntz's use of force was justified, a proven subsequent failure by her to summon aid could constitute a gross deviation from ordinary care. Thus, the State's amended information charging Kuntz with negligent homicide for stabbing Becker and then failing to immediately call for medical assistance was proper and should not be stricken. Although the use of force may be justified, to not hold such a person criminally accountable for the subsequent omission would, according to the State, "encourage revenge and retaliation."

Whether inflicted in self-defense or accidentally, a wound that causes a loss of blood undoubtedly places a person in some degree of peril, and therefore gives rise to a legal duty to either (1) personally provide assistance; or (2) summon medical assistance. Accordingly . . . we hold that when a person justifiably uses force to fend off an aggressor, that person has no duty to assist her aggressor in any manner that may conceivably create the risk of bodily injury or death to herself, or other persons. This absence of a duty necessarily includes any conduct that would require the person to remain in, or return to, the zone of risk created by the original aggressor. We find no authority that suggests that the law should require a person, who is justified in her use of force, to subsequently check the pulse of her attacker, or immediately dial 9-1-1, before retreating to safety.

Under the general factual circumstances described here, we conclude that the victim has but one duty after fending off an attack, and that is the duty owed to one's self—as a matter of self-preservation—to seek and secure safety away from the place the attack occurred. Thus, the person who justifiably acts in self-defense is temporarily afforded the same status as the innocent bystander under the American rule. LaFave & Scott, § 3.3(a)(5), at 288 (suggesting that "one who innocently creates danger is on principle in the same position as that of a bystander who happens by when a situation of danger has developed").

Finally, we conclude that the duty to summon aid may in fact be "revived" . . . but only after the victim of the aggressor has fully exercised her right to seek and secure safety from personal harm. Then, and only then, may a legal duty be imposed to summon aid for the person placed in peril by an act of self-defense. We further hold that preliminary to imposing this duty, it must be shown that (1) the person had knowledge of the facts indicating a duty to act; and (2) the person was physically capable of performing the act. It must be emphasized, however, that once imposed, a proven breach of this legal duty may still fall far short of negligent homicide . . . which requires a gross deviation from an ordinary or reasonable standard of care. . . . For these reasons, the District Court's order denying Kunz's motion to amend or strike the amended information is affirmed, and this case is remanded for further proceedings consistent with this opinion.

CONCURRING AND DISSENTING OPINIONS

TRIEWEILER, J. concurring and dissenting.
I concur with the majority's conclusion that two people who have cohabited for a prolonged period of time may, under certain circumstances, owe each other the same duties flowing from their personal relationship as would be owed from one married person to his or her spouse. I also concur with the majority's conclusion that when a person justifiably uses force to defend herself against an aggressor she has no duty to assist her aggressor if to do so would create a risk of harm to her.

However, I disagree with, and therefore dissent from the majority's conclusion that at some point, a victim of aggression who has justifiably defended herself has a "revived" obligation to come to the assistance of the person against whom it was necessary for her to defend herself. The majority has concluded that although circumstances occur which are so extreme that a woman is justified in the use of deadly force to defend herself, a jury can, after the fact, in the safe confines of the jury room, conclude that at some subsequent point she was sufficiently free from danger that she should have made an effort to save her assailant and that because she didn't she is still criminally liable for his death even though at some previous point in time she was justified in taking his life. This result is simply unworkable as a practical matter and makes poor public policy. . . .

I conclude that when a person is attacked by another and reasonably believes that deadly force is necessary to prevent imminent death or serious bodily injury to herself and therefore uses deadly force to defend herself, she has no duty, "revived" or otherwise, to summon aid for her assailant. The fact that the use of force by her was justifiable as defined by statute is a complete defense to any charge based on her assailant's death.

Nor, has the majority cited any authority for its conclusion that a person who causes another's death in justifiable defense of herself can be criminally liable for then failing to summon aid for her assailant. There is no authority for good reason. A person driven to the point of having to violently defend herself from a violent attack should not, at the risk of criminal punishment, be required to know that at some undefined point in time she has a duty to save that same person. A normal person under those circumstances is incapable of undertaking such an intellectual process. To require her to do so is inconsistent with the traditional notion that when criminal liability is based on the failure to perform a duty, it must be a plain duty which leaves no doubt as to its obligatory force.

For these reasons I dissent from the majority's conclusion that a person justified in the use of deadly force in self-defense, ever has an obligation to come to the aid of her assailant. . . .

Questions

1. List all the facts relevant to deciding the nature of Bonnie Kuntz's relationship with Warren Becker.

2. Assuming Kuntz was in a qualifying special relationship with Becker, list all the facts relevant to deciding exactly how she carried out her legal duty.

3. Explain and list the "exceptions to the exception" to the personal (special) relationship exception.

4. In your opinion, does Kuntz fit within any of the exceptions to the exception? Back up your answer with facts and arguments from the majority and dissent's opinions.

5. When can a legal duty to act be "revived," according to the majority opinion?

6. In your opinion, was Kuntz's legal duty (if there was one) revived? Back up your answer with the facts and the opinions and arguments of the majority and dissenting opinions.

7. Summarize the dissent's objections to the majority opinion. Do they make sense to you? Defend your answer.

EXPLORING OMISSIONS FURTHER

 Go to the Criminal Law 8e CD to read the full text versions of the cases featured here.

1. *Did She Have a Special Relationship with the Man in Her House?*

FACTS

Carol Ann Oliver met Carlos Cornejo in the afternoon when she was with her boyfriend at a bar. She and her boyfriend purchased jewelry from Cornejo. In the late afternoon, when Oliver was leaving the bar to return home, Cornejo got into the car with her, and she drove him home with her. At the time, he appeared to be extremely drunk. At her house, he asked her for a spoon and went into the bathroom. She went to the kitchen, got a spoon, and brought it to him. She knew he wanted the spoon to take drugs. She remained in the living room while Cornejo "shot up" in the bathroom. He then came out and collapsed onto the floor in the living room. She tried but was unable to rouse him. Oliver then called the bartender at the bar where she had met Cornejo. The bartender advised her to leave him and come back to the bar, which Oliver did.

Oliver's daughter returned home at about 5 P.M. that day with two girlfriends. They found Cornejo unconscious on the living room floor. When the girls were unable to wake him, they searched his pockets and found eight dollars. They did not find any wallet or identification. The daughter then called Oliver on the telephone. Oliver told her to drag Cornejo outside in case he woke up and became violent. The girls dragged Cornejo outside and put him behind a shed so that he would not be in the view of the neighbors. He was snoring when the girls left him there. About a half hour later, Oliver returned home with her boyfriend. She, the boyfriend, and the girls went outside to look at Cornejo. Oliver told the girls that she had watched him "shoot up" with drugs and then pass out.

The girls went out to eat and then returned to check on Cornejo later that evening. He had a pulse and was snoring. In the morning, one of the girls heard Oliver tell her daughter that Cornejo might be dead. Cornejo was purple and had flies around him. Oliver called the bartender at about 6 A.M. and told her she thought Cornejo had died in her backyard. Oliver then told the girls to call the police and she left for work. The police were called.

Oliver was convicted of involuntary manslaughter and appealed. Did Oliver have a "special relationship" with Cornejo that created a legal duty?

DECISION AND REASONS

Yes, said the appeals court:

We conclude that the evidence of the combination of events which occurred between the time appellant left the bar with Cornejo through the time he fell to the floor unconscious, established as a matter of law a relationship which imposed upon appellant a duty to seek medical aid. At the time appellant left the bar with Cornejo, she observed that he was extremely drunk, and drove him to her home. In so doing, she took him from a public place where others might have taken care to prevent him from injuring himself, to a private place—her home—where she alone could provide care. To a certain, if limited, extent, therefore, she took charge of a person unable to prevent harm to himself. She then allowed Cornejo to use her bathroom, without any objection on her part, to inject himself with narcotics, an act involving the definite potential for fatal consequences.

When Cornejo collapsed to the floor, appellant should have known that her conduct had contributed to creating an unreasonable risk of harm for Cornejo—death. At that point, she owed Cornejo a duty to prevent that risk from occurring by summoning aid, even if she had not previously realized that her actions would lead to such risk. Her failure to summon any medical assistance whatsoever and to leave him abandoned outside her house warranted the jury finding a breach of that duty.... The judgment is affirmed.

People v. Oliver, 258 Cal.Rptr. 138 (1989)

3. *Did He Have a Legal Duty to His Girlfriend's Baby?*

FACTS

Santos Miranda started living with his girlfriend and her two children in an apartment in September 1992. On January 27, 1993, Miranda was 21 years old, his girlfriend was 16, her son was 2, and her daughter, the victim in this case, born on September 21, 1992, was 4 months old. Although he was not the biological father of either child, Miranda took care of them and considered himself to be their stepfather.

He represented himself as such to the people at Meriden Veteran's Memorial Hospital where, on January 27, 1993, the victim was taken for treatment of her injuries following a 911 call by Miranda that the child was choking on milk. Upon examination at the hospital, it was determined that the victim had multiple rib fractures that were approximately two to three weeks old, two skull fractures that were approximately seven to ten days old, a brachial plexus injury to her left arm, a rectal tear that was actively "oozing blood," and nasal hemorrhages.

On the basis of extensive medical evidence, the trial court determined that the injuries had been sustained on three or more occasions and that none of the injuries had been the result of an accident, a fall, events that took place at the time of the child's birth, cardiopulmonary resuscitation, a blocked air passageway, or the child choking on milk. Rather, the trial court found that the injuries, many of which created a risk of death, had been caused by great and deliberate force.

The trial court further found in accordance with the medical evidence that, as a result of the nature of these injuries, at the time they were sustained the victim would have screamed inconsolably, and that her injuries would have caused noticeable physical deformities, such as swelling, bruising, and poor mobility, and finally, that her intake of food would have been reduced.

The court also determined that anyone who saw the child would have had to notice these injuries, the consequent deformities, and her reactions. Indeed, the trial court found that Miranda had been aware of the various bruises on her right cheek and the nasal hemorrhages, as well as the swelling of the child's head; that he knew she had suffered a rectal tear, as well as rib fractures posteriorly on the left and right sides; and that he was aware that there existed a substantial and unjustifiable risk that the child was exposed to conduct that created a risk of death.

The trial court concluded that despite this knowledge, the defendant "failed to act to help or aid [the child] by promptly notifying authorities of her injuries, taking her for medical care, removing her from her circumstances and guarding her from future abuses. As a result of his failure to help her, the child was exposed to conduct which created a risk of death to her, and the child suffered subsequent serious physical injuries. . . ."

Did Santos Miranda have a legal duty to "protect health and well-being" of the baby?

DECISION AND REASONS

Yes, said the Connecticut Supreme Court:

We conclude that, based upon the trial court's findings that the defendant had established a familial relationship with the victim's mother and her two children, had assumed responsibility for the welfare of the children, and had taken care of them as though he were their father, the defendant had a legal duty to protect the victim from abuse. . . .

Duty is a legal conclusion about relationships between individuals, made after the fact. . . . The nature of the duty, and the specific persons to whom it is owed, are determined by the circumstances surrounding the conduct of the individual. Although one generally has no legal duty to aid another in peril, even when the aid can be provided without danger or inconvenience to the provider, there are four widely recognized situations in which the failure to act may constitute breach of a legal duty: (1) where one stands in a certain relationship to another; (2) where a statute imposes a duty to help another; (3) where one has assumed a contractual duty; and (4) where one voluntarily has assumed the care of another. . . .

It is undisputed that parents have a duty to provide food, shelter and medical aid for their children and to protect them from harm. . . . Indeed, the status relationship giving rise to a duty to provide and protect that has been before the courts more often than any other relationship and, at the same time, the one relationship that courts most frequently assume to exist without expressly so stating, is the relationship existing between a parent and a minor child.

In addition to biological and adoptive parents and legal guardians, there may be other adults who establish familial relationships with and assume responsibility for the care of a child, thereby creating a legal duty to protect that child from harm. . . . The traditional approach in this country is to restrict the duty to save others from harm to certain very narrow categories of cases. We are not prepared now to adopt a broad general rule covering other circumstances. We conclude only that . . . when Miranda who considered himself the victim's parent, established a familial relationship with the victim's mother and her children and assumed the role of a father, he assumed . . . the same legal duty to protect the victim from the abuse as if he were, in fact, the victim's guardian.

Under these circumstances, to require the defendant as a matter of law to take affirmative action to prevent harm to the victim or be criminally responsible imposes a reasonable duty. . . . We recognize the continuing demographic trend reflecting a significant increase in nontraditional alternative family arrangements. Consequently, more and more children will be living with or may depend upon adults who do not qualify as a natural or adoptive parent. The attachment by children to the adults who care for them does not, however, depend exclusively upon whether the caregiver is the natural or adoptive parent or another person who has assumed the caretaker role. Children become attached to people who care for them, and this attachment is "rooted inevitably in the infant's inability to ensure his own survival. . . ."

We conclude that the defendant had a duty, under the facts and circumstances of this case, to protect the victim and prevent further harm to her, and that for violating that duty to her, he can be found guilty. . . .

State v. Miranda, 715 A.2d 680 (1998)

Only *unreasonable* failures to perform legal duties are punishable as criminal omissions. For example, in one case, a sea captain allowed a crew member who had fallen overboard to drown in order to save other crew members and passengers from a dangerous storm. The court held that failure to try and save the one crew member was not a criminal omission because it was reasonable to allow one crew member to die in order to save many others. Neither is it a criminal omission for a baby-sitter who could not swim to fail to dive into deep water to save the child he was watching.

A famous incident that occurred in New York City, the failure of residents to take action to save Kitty Genovese from a brutal murder at the hands of Winston Moseley, raises both the questions of when a legal duty arises and what acts amount to a reasonable fulfillment of a legal duty, once the duty arises.

CASE | *Did the Bystanders Have a Legal Duty?*

FACTS

For more than half an hour 37 respectable, law-abiding citizens in Queens watched a killer stalk and stab a woman in three separate attacks in Kew Gardens. Twice the sound of their voices and the sudden glow of their bedroom lights interrupted him and frightened him off. Each time he returned, sought her out and stabbed her again. Not one person telephoned the police during the assault; one witness called after the woman was dead. But Assistant Chief Inspector Frederick M. Lussen, in charge of the borough's detectives and a veteran of 25 years of homicide investigations, is still shocked. He can give a matter of fact recitation of many murders. But the Kew Gardens slaying baffles him—not because it is a murder, but because the "good people" failed to call the police. "As we have reconstructed the crime," he said, "the assailant had three chances to kill this woman during a 35-minute period. He returned twice to complete the job. If we had been called when he first attacked, the woman might not be dead now."

She got as far as a street light in front of a bookstore before the man grabbed her. She screamed. Lights went on in the 10-story apartment house at 82–67 Austin Street, which faces the bookstore. Windows slid open and voices punctured the early morning stillness. Miss Genovese screamed: From one of the upper windows in the apartment house, a man called down: "Let that girl alone!"

The assailant looked up at him, shrugged and walked down Austin Street toward a white sedan parked a short distance away. Miss Genovese struggled to her feet. Lights went out. The killer returned to Miss Genovese, now trying to make her way around the side of the building by the parking lot to get to her apartment. The assailant stabbed her again. "I'm dying!" she shrieked. "I'm dying!"

Windows were opened again, and lights went on in many apartments. The assailant got into his car and drove away. Miss Genovese staggered to her feet. A city bus, Q i 10, the Lefferts Boulevard line to Kennedy International Airport, passed. It was 3:35 A.M.

The assailant returned. By then, Miss Genovese had crawled to the back of the building, where the freshly painted brown doors to the apartment house held out hope of safety. The killer tried the first door; she wasn't there. At the second door, 82–62 Austin Street, he saw her slumped on the floor at the foot of the stairs. He stabbed her a third time—fatally.

It was 3:50 by the time the police received their first call, from a man who was a neighbor of Miss Genovese. In two minutes they were at the scene. The neighbor, a 70-year-old woman, and another woman were the only persons on the street. Nobody else came forward.

The man explained that he had called the police after much deliberation. He had phoned a friend in Nassau County for advice and then he had crossed the roof of the building to the apartment of the elderly woman to get her to make the call. "I didn't want to get involved," he sheepishly told the police.

The police stressed how simple it would have been to have gotten in touch with them. "A phone call," said one of the detectives, "would have done it." The police may be reached by dialing "0" for operator or SPring 7–3100. Today, witnesses from the neighborhood, which is made up of one-family homes in the $35,000 to $60,000 range with the exception of the two apartment houses near the railroad station, find it difficult to explain why they didn't call the police.

Lieut. Bernard Jacobs, who handled the investigation by the detectives, said: "It is one of the better neighborhoods. There are few reports of crimes."...

The police said most persons had told them they had been afraid to call, but had given meaningless answers when asked what they had feared. "We can understand the reticence of people to become involved in an area of violence,"

Lieutenant Jacobs said, "but where they are in their homes, near phones, why should they be afraid to call the police?"

Witnesses—some of them unable to believe what they had allowed to happen—told a reporter why. A housewife, knowingly if quite casual, said, "We thought it was a lover's quarrel." A husband and wife both said, "Frankly, we were afraid." They seemed aware of the fact that events might have been different. A distraught woman, wiping her hands in her apron, said, "I didn't want my husband to get involved."...A man peeked out from a slight opening in the doorway to his apartment and rattled off an account of the killer's second attack. Why hadn't he called the police at the time? "I was tired," he said without emotion. I went back to bed." It was 4:25 A.M. when the ambulance arrived for the body of Miss Genovese. It drove off. "Then," a solemn police detective said, "the people came out."

"37 Who Saw Murder Didn't Call...," by M. Gansberg, March 17, 1964. Copyright 2000 by the New York Times Co. Reprinted with permission.

Questions

1. Did the residents have a legal duty to intervene? A moral duty? What is the basis of the duty?

2. Should the "neighborly" relationship give rise to a duty? Why?

3. Should a statute impose a duty of individuals to intervene? Why or why not?

4. Assuming there is a duty, what does it consist of?

5. What, if any, penalty would you impose for failing to intervene?

6. Consider two other incidents.
   a. An assailant raped and beat an 18-year-old switchboard operator. The victim ran naked and bleeding from the building onto the street, screaming for help. A crowd of forty people gathered and watched, in broad daylight, while the rapist tried to drag her back into the building. No onlooker intervened; two police officers happened on the scene and arrested the assailant.
   b. Eleven people watched while an assailant stabbed 17-year-old Andrew Melmille in the stomach on a subway. The assailant left the subway at the next stop. Not one of the eleven people on the train helped Melmille. He bled to death. Was there a legal duty to act in either of these incidents? If so, what was the duty?

7. How, if at all, do these incidents differ from the Genovese incident?

Whatever Happened to Winston Moseley?

(Rosenthal 1999)

A. Balz

AP/Wide World Photos

Winston Moseley appealed his murder conviction because the trial judge refused to permit evidence that mental illness had reduced his ability to control his actions.

1967: The Court of Appeals, New York's highest court, commuted Moseley's death sentence to life imprisonment. Why? Because the trial judge didn't allow into evidence enough information about the mitigating circumstances surrounding the crime, such as Moseley's mental illness.

Moseley cut himself with a bottle in Attica state prison. He was sent to a prison hospital in Buffalo, where he overpowered a guard and escaped. Before he was caught four days later, he tied up a man and his wife and raped the woman while the husband was forced to watch.

1971: Moseley earned a college degree.

1977 (April 16): Letter from Winston Moseley to the *New York Times* from Attica prison.

> More than a decade ago, I committed a crime I genuinely regret. No one should murder or can justify it. Society was rightly outraged. One of its members had been murdered. The murderer should have been speedily apprehended and punished. I've been imprisoned many years now, and I've wished so many times that I could bring Kitty Genovese back to life, back to her family and friends.
>
> My perpetual torment and agony will not resurrect her but if my arrest, conviction, and even execution would have served to deter others, if my death would have somehow balanced the scales of justice, then in accordance with the laws in force in 1964, my life should have been taken. The crime was tragic, but it did serve society, urging it, as it did to come to the aid of its members in distress or danger.
>
> Newspapers, and *The New York Times* specifically, acted conscientiously and responsibly. You informed the public and suggested that it can't in good conscience afford the luxury of being indifferent to the fate of other human beings.
>
> Pre-eminent journalism focused attention on a senseless murder and heightened the public's awareness as to apathy. A salient reminder that all people should care and be concerned about others was long overdue. To help others is both good and right. It is necessary to sometimes get involved.
>
> Those sent to prison are ultimately society's responsibility too. Prison and prisoners involve everyone in one way or another. Prison as it presently stands is an inherently evil place that insidiously and systematically works to destroy imprisoned persons. It should rather be a place that builds better human beings. Men can and do change for the better despite the miasma of imprisonment, however.
>
> I went through a trial of fire and death. The '71 Attica rebellion profoundly affected me. Misunderstanding, suspicion, animosity, hostility, and virulent hate lashed out and killed viciously and indiscriminately. I saw all that and more and was sickened. I vowed then and there that I was going to get on the right track and make amends for my own past wrongdoing. I learned that human life has great value. In the future I would act responsibly.
>
> My life in 1973, however, was still a bit harsh and chaotic, and it was pretty much an empty shell. In that year college courses were offered here, and I availed myself of that positive opportunity. Now, I have earned a B.A. degree in sociology.
>
> One professor, Sister Mary Frances Welch, has been particularly instrumental in helping me remold my character and my way of thinking. Another woman, Dorothy Tishler, came into my life and filled it with goodness and sunshine. She provided me with specific direction and exact guidance. The bright miracle of her faith, deep devotion, and the inspirational, affectionate love she gives that covers all, accounts for the final stages, of my transformation.
>
> Transformation, a new outlook, caused me to get involved. I began applying myself to problems that periodically plague Attica. I've been both president and vice president of the inmate liaison committee here. I've made reasonable suggestions to state officials about prison reform, and I exercised my influence and used my expertise to the utmost in the formulation of the peaceful demonstration that began here Aug. 23. Many prisoners, then as now, felt that they had many legitimate grievances and complaints badly in need of an airing and redress.

I tried and succeeded in doing something good, and it was something that came out right. In striking contrast to the '71 rebellion, intelligent dialogue triumphed over emotional rancor, and a peaceful settlement ensued this time.

The man who killed Kitty Genovese in Queens in 1964 is no more. He was also destroyed in that calamity and its aftermath. Another vastly different individual has emerged, a Winston Moseley intent and determined to do constructive, not destructive, things.

Today I'm a man who wants to be an asset to society, not a liability to it.

"Today I am a man who wants to be an asset to society, not a liability to it," Op-Ed by Winston Moseley, April 16, 1977. Copyright 2000 by the New York Times. Reprinted by permission.

1984: At a parole hearing, a commissioner told Moseley that he sounded like he was suggesting that "it was as difficult…for a person like yourself, as it is for your victim." Moseley responded, "In a sense, yes. For a victim outside, it's a one-time or one-hour or one-minute affair, but for the person who's caught, it's forever." The shocked commissioner responded, "Well, that's one way to look at it….Miss Genovese [is] no longer with us….But, you're here…at least it's debatable that you're as bad off as Miss Genovese."

1990: At a parole hearing, the following exchange took place about the rape of a woman during Moseley's prison escape:

MOSELEY: I wrote to the victims to apologize for the inconvenience I have caused.

COMMISSIONER: That's a good way to say it. They were inconvenienced.

MOSELEY: No one was hurt.

COMMISSIONER: Someone was hurt. You don't rape someone without them being hurt.

MOSELEY: "Physically injured," he corrected the commissioner.

1995: Now 61 years old, Moseley went to the U.S. District Court in Brooklyn, walked to the witness stand, and claimed he should get a new trial because his original lawyer had once represented Genovese (Sexton 1995). The lawyer, now 81 but still practicing law, was in court. The prosecutor was there, too; he said "the only reason Moseley is alive is because of the effective representation of his lawyer who saved him from the electric chair." Genovese's surviving family were there—three brothers, a sister, and two aunts.

[They]…stood in the front row of seats, angry, numb, curious, but together. "It's surreal," said Frank Genovese who was 12 when his sister was killed, with the circumstances of her death and her cries for help provoking a national debate about civic apathy and human indifference to violence. "We have lived with this for 31 years, through movies and books and newspapers," he said. "We had chosen to live it alone, removed. But now, we are here, with the gloves off, because we will not let her be the victim again."

"Reviving Kitty Genovese Case…" by J. Sexton, July 25, 1995. Copyright 2000 by the New York Times. Reprinted by permission.

The judge heard arguments on Moseley's motion for a new trial. The judge denied the motion. The sister and brothers of Catherine Genovese were present. So were Moseley's original lawyer and the prosecutor. They had not attended the original trial. The family was satisfied with the decision. So was the prosecutor, who said that the only reason Moseley is alive is because of the effective representation of his lawyer who saved him from the electric chair.

Possession as an Act

Let's start by making clear one point: *Possession isn't an action; it's a passive state.* Yet, by means of a **legal fiction** (pretending something's a fact when it's not when there's a good reason for pretending), the principle of *actus reus* covers the possession of many things, including weapons, illegal drugs, drug paraphernalia, stolen property, and pornography. The good reason for pretending possession is an act is the powerful pull of the idea "an ounce of prevention is worth a pound of cure." Better to nip the bud of possession before it grows into an act of doing drugs or shooting someone. Also, most people get possession by their voluntary act—like buying marijuana and putting it in their pocket. So their passive possession is caused by their active acquisition. But not always. Maybe a student who got a bad grade "planted" the marijuana in my briefcase when I wasn't looking.

Before we can understand and discuss the passive state of possession as *actus reus*, we need to define two aspects of possession:

1. Control of items and substances
2. Awareness of the control

There are two types of control: actual and constructive possession. **Actual possession** means I've got banned stuff "on me" (marijuana's in my pocket). **Constructive possession** means I control banned stuff, but it's not on me (it's in my car or apartment) (American Law Institute 1985, I:2, 24).

As for the awareness aspect, possession can be either "knowing" or "mere." **Knowing possession** means possessors are aware of what they possess. So, if you buy crystal meth and know it's crystal meth, you have knowing possession. (Knowing doesn't mean you have to know it's a crime to possess crystal meth, only that you know it's crystal meth.) **Mere possession** means you don't know what you possess. So, if you agree to carry your friend's briefcase you don't know is filled with stolen money, you've got mere possession of the money. Most states (except for North Dakota and Washington) require knowing possession. Also, almost all the cases in the court reports are constructive possession cases. One of them is an illegal weapon possession case, *Porter v. State* (2003).

CASE | *Did He Constructively Possess the Ruger .357 Revolver?*

Porter v. State
2003 WL 1919477 (Ark.App. 2003)

ROAF, J.

Appellant Jermaine Porter was found delinquent for being a minor in possession of a handgun and was committed to the Department of Youth Services. Porter appealed. The Arkansas Court of Appeals affirmed.

FACTS

Little Rock Police Officer Beth McNair testified that she stopped a vehicle with no license plate on the evening of May 23, 2002. Porter was a passenger in the vehicle and was sitting in the back seat on the passenger side. Porter's cousin was the driver of the vehicle, and his uncle was in the front passenger seat. As McNair approached the vehicle, she testified that she observed Porter reaching toward the floor with his left hand. McNair told Porter to keep his left hand where she could see it. As McNair shined her flashlight into the vehicle, she testified that she saw a handgun on Porter's left shoe and that the barrel of the gun was pointing toward her. McNair drew her weapon and alerted her assisting officer that there was a gun.

Officer Robert Ball testified that he assisted McNair with the traffic stop. Ball stated that he was standing near the trunk on the driver's side of the vehicle, when he heard McNair yell "Gun." Ball drew his weapon and came to the passenger side of the vehicle, where he saw that Porter had his hand near his shin and that there was a gun lying on top of Porter's foot. Porter was then taken into custody. McNair testified that the gun was a Ruger .357 revolver, which was loaded. Another weapon was found in plain view in the floorboard of the front passenger seat.

Porter testified that his cousin and his uncle had picked him up at a hotel and that they were taking him to his sister's house. Porter stated that he had only been in the car for approximately five minutes when it was stopped, that he did not know that there were any guns inside the vehicle, and that the gun found near his foot was not his. He also denied that he bent over and reached toward the floor, and he testified that there was nothing touching his foot. Porter admitted that the gun may have been found near his foot but explained that it probably "slid back there" from underneath the seat when they were driving up some steep hills.

OPINION

...Porter contends that the State failed to prove that he possessed the gun because the vehicle was also occupied by two other persons. It is not necessary for the State to prove actual physical possession of a firearm; a showing of constructive possession is sufficient. To prove constructive possession, the State must establish beyond a reasonable doubt that the defendant exercised care, control, and management over the contraband and that the defendant knew the matter possessed was contraband.

Although constructive possession can be implied when the contraband is in the joint control of the accused and another, joint occupancy of a vehicle, standing alone, is not sufficient to establish possession. In a joint-occupancy situation, the State must prove some additional factor, which links the accused to the contraband and demonstrates the accused's knowledge and control of the contraband, such as: (1) whether the contraband was in plain view; (2) whether the contraband was found on the accused's person or with his personal effects; (3) whether it was found on the same side of the car seat as the accused was sitting or in near proximity to it; (4) whether the accused is the owner of the vehicle or exercises dominion or control over it; (5) and whether the accused acted suspiciously before or during the arrest.

In making its finding that Porter had possession of the handgun found in the back seat of the vehicle, the trial court stated that almost all of the above factors were present except that Porter was not the owner or driver of the vehicle. Porter, however, contends that all of these factors must be shown to prove that he had constructive possession. Because the trial court did not find there to be any exercise of dominion and control over the vehicle, Porter argues that it was not proven that he exercised dominion and control over the handgun.

Contrary to Porter's argument, it is not necessary that all of the above stated factors be shown in order to find a person in constructive possession of contraband in a case of joint occupancy; rather, there must be "some additional factor linking the accused" to the contraband. For example in *Miller v. State*, 6 S.W.3d 812 (1999), the court found that the defendant Miller had constructive possession of contraband in a jointly-occupied vehicle in which Miller was a passenger, where none of the linking factors were present, but the officer smelled a strong odor of burning marijuana upon approaching the vehicle. The court held that although the contraband was not in plain view, the defendant's knowledge of the contraband could be inferred from the strong smell of the marijuana....

There is substantial evidence in this case supporting the trial court's finding that Porter had possession of the handgun. According to the police officers' testimonies, the handgun was found in plain view on the floorboard of the back seat of the vehicle, the gun was lying on Porter's left foot, it was on the same side of the vehicle as Porter was sitting, and Porter acted suspiciously prior to his arrest by

reaching toward the floor with his left hand. The presence of these factors is sufficient to show Porter's knowledge and control of the handgun. Although Porter testified that the gun was not his, that he did not know that there were guns in the vehicle, and that the gun must have "slid back" near his foot when the vehicle went up a steep hill, the trial court specifically stated that it credited the testimony of the State's witnesses. We defer to the trial court in matters of credibility of witnesses, and the trial court is not required to believe the testimony of the accused, as he is the person most interested in the outcome of the trial.

AFFIRMED.

Questions

1. Identify the two elements of constructive possession identified by the court.

2. List the five factors the court identifies that can prove possession in joint-occupancy cases.

3. Match the facts of the case to the five factors you listed in (2).

4. Assume you're the prosecutor. Argue that Porter actually and constructively possessed the handgun. Back up your arguments with facts in the case.

5. Assume you're the defense attorney. Argue that Porter didn't physically or constructively possess the gun.

EXPLORING POSSESSION FURTHER

 Go the Criminal Law 8e CD to read the full text versions of the cases featured here.

1. *Did He Possess the Marijuana in the Car But Not "on Him"?*

FACTS

Arkansas State Police Officer Tim Land testified that on February 23, 1997, he came into contact with James Luther Miller who was a passenger in a vehicle driven by Michael Alexander. Officer Land became suspicious of the vehicle because it approached him from the rear and would not pass his vehicle although he slowed to thirty miles per hour. Land pulled his car into the median, and, as the car passed, he noticed that it did not have a license plate. He initiated a stop of the vehicle, and upon approaching it he smelled the very strong odor of burned marijuana emanating from inside. Land had the driver exit the vehicle, and after noting the odor of burned marijuana and alcohol on his person, administered field sobriety tests, which Alexander failed. Land called for assistance, and Alexander was transported to the county jail for a breathalyzer. According to Land, there were four occupants in the vehicle: Alexander, who was the driver; James Giles, who was sitting in the right front seat; Damon Albert, who was sitting in the rear seat behind the driver; and Miller, who was seated on the right rear seat.

Trooper Land recovered three rolling papers from three of the vehicle's occupants but could not recall which three. He also stated that he found three rocks of crack cocaine and marijuana in the pouch located on the back of the driver's seat, directly in front of Damon Albert.

The driver of the vehicle, Michael Alexander, testified that on the date in question he asked Miller if he wanted to ride to Hope, Arkansas, with him. He picked up Giles and Albert and took them to a residence in Hope, where they purchased crack cocaine. According to Alexander, Miller did not know that Giles and Albert were purchasing crack, and he did not know about the marijuana until it was smoked. However, Alexander later testified that all of the vehicle's occupants knew that the marijuana was in the vehicle because it was in the car before the group traveled to Hope. Did Miller possess marijuana? Did he possess cocaine?

DECISION AND REASONS

The Arkansas Court of Appeals, relying on the five factors applied in *Porter* (the case excerpt above) decided that Miller possessed marijuana but not cocaine. According to the court:

> Joint occupancy of a vehicle, standing alone, is not sufficient to establish possession or joint possession. There must be some additional factor linking the accused to the drugs. When viewed in the light most favorable to the State, we believe the evidence is sufficient to conclude that the jury had substantial evidence from which it could find that Miller constructively possessed marijuana. By way of analogy, we note that had the officer observed the marijuana in plain view inside of the vehicle, the evidence would be sufficient to compel the conclusion that Miller constructively possessed the marijuana. Here, although the marijuana was not in plain view, we believe that the fact that the police officer smelled marijuana upon approaching the vehicle tends to establish that Miller had knowledge of the presence of the marijuana. It is the knowledge of the existence of the contraband that provides substantial evidence of constructive possession.

> Whether the evidence is sufficient to support the conviction of possession of cocaine presents a more difficult question.... Miller was a rear-seat passenger in his

friend's car when the vehicle was stopped by Trooper Land. The contraband found was not in plain view, was not under Miller's exclusive control, and was not found near the seat in which Miller was seated. There was no testimony that Miller acted suspiciously, and, there was no evidence of any contraband found on Miller's person. There was, however, testimony that Miller did not know that there was cocaine in the car until after the police searched the vehicle.

> Based upon the evidence presented, we hold that the State did not present sufficient evidence of any factor, other than occupancy, to establish Miller's constructive possession of the cocaine. Miller's conviction for possession of cocaine is reversed and dismissed. His conviction for possession of marijuana is affirmed.

Three justices disagreed:

> [This case should be decided according to] the well-established principle that a person in joint occupancy of an automobile who is in close proximity to contraband located within that automobile can be found to be in possession of the contraband.... In this case, if Miller was close enough to the marijuana that the officer smelled to be found guilty of its possession, I fail to see how the majority can say that there was not sufficient evidence to sustain the jury's verdict that appellant was guilty of possession of cocaine that was located in exactly the same place as the marijuana.

> ... Because the appellant was in close proximity to the marijuana and the cocaine, and because appellant could have had dominion and control over both substances from his position in the right rear seat of the automobile, I would affirm Miller's convictions on the marijuana and cocaine possession charges.

> *Miller v. State*, 6 S.W.3d 812, (Ark.App., 1999)

2. *Did He Possess Crack That He Bought in a Reverse Sting?*

FACTS

The Omaha Police Department was engaged in a reverse sting operation. Kevan Barbour, a narcotics officer, sold crack cocaine to parties who approached him. After the purchase, Barbour signaled fellow officers, who arrested the purchasers.

Earl Clark had approached Officer Barbour, asking for a "twenty" ($20 worth of crack cocaine). Barbour handed Clark a sack. After examining it, Clark handed it back, saying it was "too small." Barbour then handed Clark a larger sack. According to Barbour, Clark then handed him $20.

Barbour signaled for the arrest. While being arrested, Clark dropped the crack. In a trial without a jury for possessing crack cocaine, the court believed Barbour's testimony and convicted Clark.

According to Clark's testimony, he handed back the first package because it was too small. But, when given the larger package, he held it for about a minute and a half while trying to decide whether to buy it. Officer Barbour snatched the $20 from him and signaled for the arrest.

Did Clark criminally possess the smaller package? If his story is true, did Clark possess the larger package of crack?

DECISION AND REASONS

Yes, said the Nebraska Supreme Court:

> To sustain a conviction for possession of a controlled substance, all the State must prove is that the defendant "knowingly or intentionally" possessed the substance. . . .
>
> The evidence shows that the defendant drove to an area where he knew he could purchase crack cocaine. He approached an undercover police officer who was posing as a drug dealer and asked to buy 20 dollars' worth of crack cocaine. The undercover officer handed the defendant a $20 package of cocaine. The defendant was unhappy with the size of the cocaine package, so he returned it to the undercover officer. The undercover officer then handed the defendant a larger package of cocaine, which the defendant examined. According to Officer Barbour, the defendant then handed Barbour the $20 and Barbour signaled the other officers to arrest the defendant.
>
> Taking the view of the evidence most favorable to the State, we find that the evidence was more than sufficient for the trial court to find beyond a reasonable doubt that the defendant "knowingly or intentionally" possessed cocaine.
>
> *State v. Clark*, 236 Neb. 475, 461 N.W.2d 576 (1990)

3. *Did He Possess the Drugs He Didn't Know He Was Holding for His Girlfriend?*

FACTS

Leonard Dawkins was convicted of possession of heroin and "controlled paraphernalia." The police testified that when they entered a Baltimore, Maryland, hotel room, Dawkins held a tote bag in his hand. The police searched the bag, finding in it narcotics paraphernalia and a bottle cap containing heroin residue. Dawkins testified that the tote bag belonged to his girlfriend, who had asked him to carry the bag to her hotel room. He testified further that he had arrived only a few minutes before the police and that he did not know what was in the bag. Dawkins's girlfriend produced a receipt for the purchase of the bag and testified that she owned the bag. The trial court refused Dawkins's request that the jury be instructed that knowledge was a requirement of criminal possession. The Maryland statute prohibits "possession of controlled substances." It is silent on intent, but it defines possession as "the exercise of actual or constructive dominion or control over a thing by one or more persons."

Did Dawkins criminally possess heroin and controlled substance paraphernalia, even if he didn't know the bag contained them?

DECISION AND REASONS

No, said the Maryland Supreme Court:

> In accord with the overwhelming majority of other jurisdictions, we hold that "knowledge" is an element of the offenses charged in this case. The accused, in order to be found guilty, must know of both the presence and the general character or illicit nature of the substance. Of course, such knowledge may be proven by circumstantial evidence and by inferences drawn therefrom.
>
> *Dawkins v. State*, 313 Md. 638, 547 A.2d 1041 (1988)

4. *Did She Possess Marijuana in Her Boyfriend's House?*

FACTS

Sometime between 9:30 and 10:00 A.M., officers legally entered an apartment looking for two men who had caused a disturbance earlier that morning. They found Alisha Kimberley lying on the couch, apparently asleep. She did not immediately respond to loud commands but finally responded. Marijuana and drug paraphernalia were observed in plain view on the coffee table approximately 2 feet from where Kimberley was lying. She was handcuffed and informed that she was under arrest. The police then escorted her out of the house and into the back of a patrol car. Other officers finished clearing the residence to be sure no one else was inside. No one else was found. The two men who reportedly were part of the original disturbance were never located. The police recovered a shotgun from the residence. A "bong" used for smoking marijuana was found resting on the floor in a corner of a "computer room" in the apartment.

Kimberley was taken to the police station. She was questioned by an officer. He discovered that Kimberley was a resident of the apartment where the drugs and paraphernalia were found. Kimberley shared the apartment with Paul Hoffman, who had earlier run from the apartment and was apprehended. She was charged with possession of marijuana paraphernalia. Did Kimberley possess marijuana paraphernalia?

DECISION AND REASONS

Yes, said the Missouri Court of Appeals:

> The mere presence of the accused on shared premises where contraband is found is not enough circumstantial evidence to show ownership or possession. Mere presence at a place where contraband is found is not enough to create an inference of control. Additional factors are required to prove conscious possession. Some of those factors are: routine access to an area where contraband is kept; large quantities of the substance at the scene where the accused is arrested; self-incriminating statements or admissions showing consciousness of guilt; commingling of contraband with defendant's personal belongings; and the substance being in public view and easily accessible by the defendant. Inferences drawn from defendant's statements, admissions, conduct, or the situation itself may also be considered. The totality of the circumstances must be considered in determining whether additional incriminating circumstances have been proved.

> Here the issue is the sufficiency of the evidence to convict in view of the evidence that Kimberley *was* a resident of the premises. There were other individuals at the apartment that morning. A neighbor observed several men, apparently Hoffman and his friends, in the backyard early that morning, destroying some furniture. Had the court been bound to believe that Kimberley was asleep when discovered, that fact would have been of assistance to her, in view of the fact that others had been

> in the apartment recently. However, as we have noted, the trial court was not required to believe that she was asleep when officers entered the apartment.

> Also, there were other indications, besides the location of the paraphernalia, that Kimberley was guilty of possession. There was an additional item of paraphernalia, a "yellow glass-colored bong," found in a corner, apparently in plain view, in another room (a computer room) to which she had access. Kimberley acknowledged that it was a "large bong" and that it was a "couple feet tall." Kimberley admitted that she recognized the contraband for what it was, and that she knew that marijuana had previously been smoked in the apartment. Hoffman and Kimberley said that the use of the marijuana in the apartment was against Kimberley's wishes; again, however, the court was not required to believe her testimony.

> Because of the presence of the "dug-out," a ceramic pipe, and marijuana on a television tray in very close proximity to Kimberley (and under her apparent control), just about two feet away from Kimberley as she lay on the couch, with some seeds spilled on the floor near the couch (as though used by a person on the couch), in Kimberley's own apartment, with another large item of paraphernalia accessible to her in another room, we cannot say the trial court was being speculative in concluding (beyond a reasonable doubt) that Kimberley possessed the contraband. The totality of the circumstances was such that a rational fact finder *could* believe beyond a reasonable doubt that Kimberley knowingly possessed the paraphernalia. It was not necessary for the State to eliminate all theoretical possibilities of her innocence. Accordingly, under our standard of review, we must affirm the conviction.

> *State v. Kimberley,* 103 S.W.2d (Mo.App. 2003)

◆ ◆ ◆

SUMMARY

I. The general principles of criminal liability
   A. The Constitution requires a criminal act to prove criminal liability
      1. A criminal act is the basis of the principle of *actus reus*
      2. This is an element the prosecution has to prove beyond a reasonable doubt
   B. Two types of crimes lead to criminal liability
      1. Criminal conduct requires proving three elements of crimes
         a. *Actus reus* (criminal act)
         b. *Mens rea* (criminal intent)
         c. Concurrence (criminal act triggered by criminal intent)

    2. Criminal conduct causing criminal harm requires proving five elements of crimes
      a. *Actus reus*
      b. *Mens rea*
      c. Concurrence
        (1) *Actus reus* and *mens rea* produce criminal conduct
        (2) The criminal conduct results in harm
      d. Causation (must prove the criminal conduct produced criminal harm as defined in the criminal statute)
      e. Resulting harm (the specific result defined in the criminal code)
  C. Each element of crime relates to a general principle of criminal liability

II. The criminal act: The principles of *actus reus*
  A. *Actus reus* (requirement of a criminal act) is the first principle of criminal liability
  B. Two requirements to prove *actus reus*
    1. Bodily movements resulted in criminal act
    2. Bodily movements were voluntary
  C. Reasoning for the voluntary act requirement
    1. Criminal law punishes people
    2. Criminal law can't punish without blame
    3. There is no blame without responsibility
    4. There is no responsibility without a voluntary act (free will)
  D. Status as a criminal act
    1. Act is what we do; status is who we are
    2. Status is created two ways
      a. Voluntary act (first use of alcohol or other drug)
      b. Inherent (race, ethnicity, sex, age)
    3. Punishment for status violates U.S. Constitution, Amendment VIII (cruel and unusual punishment) by the same reasoning a voluntary act is required by the principle of *actus reus*
  E. Failure to act as a criminal act
    1. Two types of criminal omissions
      a. Failure to report (accident, income tax)
      b. Failure to intervene (call for help or rescue)
    2. It's wrong (but not always a crime) to stand by while bad things happen
      a. Moral and legal duties differ
      b. Failure to act is a criminal act only when there's a legal duty to act, created by
        (1) Statute
        (2) Contract
        (3) Special relationship
    3. Criminal liability exists only when both of the following are true:
      a. There's a legal duty to act
      b. The legal duty is performed *unreasonably*
    4. Two approaches to creating and carrying out legal duties toward strangers in trouble
      a. American bystander rule (most states)—no legal duty to rescue or summon help for strangers

   b. Good Samaritan rule—legal duty to help or summon help for strangers in danger

  F. Possession as a criminal act

   1. Possession is a passive state, not a positive act

   2. Legal fiction makes it an act for good policy reasons

    a. Nip crime in the bud

    b. Many times possession is the result of a voluntary act

   3. Two aspects of possession

    a. Control of items and substances

     (1) Actual (substance or item on the person)

     (2) Constructive (control the stuff but not on the person)

    b. Awareness of control

     (1) Knowing possession (you know you possess the stuff)

     (2) Mere possession (the stuff is physically on you, but you don't know it)

   4. Kinds of possession

    a. Control: actual and constructive

    b. Awareness: knowing and mere

Go to the Criminal Law 8e CD to download this summary outline. The outline has been formatted so that you can add notes to it during class lectures, or later create a customized chapter outline to use while reviewing. Either way, the summary outline will help you understand the "big picture" and fill in the details as you study.

REVIEW QUESTIONS

1. How can extraordinary circumstances make ordinary acts significant in criminal law?

2. Identify the three elements of crimes of criminal conduct.

3. Identify the five elements of crimes of criminal conduct causing criminal harm.

4. Identify the two applications of concurrence in crimes of criminal conduct causing criminal harm.

5. Describe the link between the elements of crimes and the principles of criminal liability.

6. List the reasons why the requirement of a criminal act is the first principle of criminal liability.

7. List the purposes for the principle of *actus reus*.

8. Identify the two requirements included in *actus reus*.

9. Why does the criminal act have to be voluntary?

10. Why does punishing drug addiction violate the U.S. Constitution, Amendment VIII?

11. How does Professor Fletcher describe people who stand by and do nothing when they see someone in trouble?

12. Explain the difference between moral and legal duties.

13. Explain the difference between the Good Samaritan and the American bystander definitions of legal duty.

14. Identify the three assumptions the legal duty requirement in omissions is based on.

15. What kinds of failures to perform legal duties are punishable as criminal omissions?

16. How is possession a legal fiction, and why is the use of the fiction a good idea?

17. Identify and explain the two aspects of the definition of possession.

18. Explain the difference between actual and constructive possession.

19. Explain the difference between knowing and mere possession.

KEY TERMS

elements of crime p. 55
crimes of criminal conduct p. 55
crimes of criminal conduct
   causing a criminal harm p. 55
principle of *actus reus* p. 57
principle of *mens rea* p. 57
principle of concurrence p. 57
principle of causation p. 57
principle of harmful result p. 57

manifest criminality p. 58
automatism p. 59
somnambulism p. 59
status p. 63
criminal omission p. 67
failure to report p. 67
failure to intervene p. 67
legal duty p. 67
circumstance element p. 67

moral duty p. 67
"Good Samaritan" doctrine p. 68
American bystander rule p. 68
legal fiction p. 75
actual possession p. 78
constructive possession p. 78
knowing possession p. 78
mere possession p. 78

SUGGESTED READINGS

 Go to the Criminal Law 8e CD for Suggested Readings for this chapter.

THE COMPANION WEB SITE FOR *CRIMINAL LAW,* EIGHTH EDITION

http://cj.wadsworth.com/samaha/crim_law8e

 Supplement your review of this chapter by going to the companion Web site to take one of the Tutorial Quizzes, use the flash cards to test your knowledge of the elements of various crimes and defenses, and check out the many other study aids you'll find there. You'll find valuable data and resources at your fingertips to help you study for that big exam or write that important paper.

4

The General Principles of Criminal Liability: *Mens Rea*, Concurrence, and Causation

Chapter Main Points

- Serious crimes require a criminal act and criminal intent.
- It's right to punish only people we can blame—people who are culpable.
- The principle of *mens rea* consists of four states of mind (levels of culpability).
- The most culpable state of mind is purpose, followed by knowledge, recklessness, and then negligence.
- Most minor offenses don't require *mens rea*; a voluntary act or a voluntary act that causes criminal harm is enough.
- The rationales for dropping the *mens rea* requirement are that there's a strong public interest in public safety and morals and that the punishment for offenses without a *mens rea* is not jail but a fine.
- Coincidences that intervene between a triggering act by defendants and injuries or death break the causal chain unless the coincidences are foreseeable.
- Defendants' acts that provoke reactions by victims, bystanders, and medical professionals break the causal chain only if they're abnormal *and* not foreseeable.

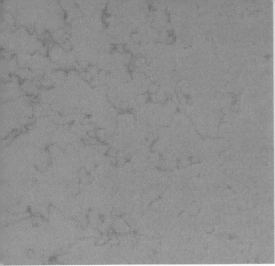

Was He Guilty?

Police officers stopped Steven Loge for speeding. During a routine search of his automobile, the officers found a nearly empty bottle of beer in a brown paper bag underneath the front passenger seat. Based on this finding, they charged Loge with keeping an open bottle containing intoxicating liquor in an automobile. At trial, Loge testified that the car he was driving belonged to his father and that he, as well as others, had driven it for the past two weeks. He also testified that the open bottle did not belong to him and that he did not know it was in the car. ◆

"I didn't mean to" captures a basic idea about criminal liability: a criminal act is necessary but it's not enough to impose criminal liability. At least for serious crimes, there has to be criminal intent (*mens rea*), too. Why? Because it's right to punish only people we can blame. Lawyers call it culpability or **blameworthiness.** Justice Holmes (1963, 4) put it this way, "Even a dog distinguishes between being stumbled over and being kicked."

 Go to Exercise 4-1 on the Criminal Law 8e CD to learn more about *mens rea*.

THE PRINCIPLE OF *MENS REA*

The **principle of *mens rea*** (the mental element or kind of criminal intent the prosecution has to prove beyond a reasonable doubt) is a complex idea. Several things account for this complexity. First, courts and legislatures have used so many definitions of the term. According to the Commentary on *mens rea* accompanying the Alabama Criminal Code:

> It would be impossible to review, much less reconcile and make clear and uniform, the myriad of Alabama statutes and cases that have employed or discussed some term of mental culpability. Such mental terms and concepts, while necessarily difficult to articulate, sometimes have been vaguely or only partly defined, or otherwise seem imprecise or inconclusive, unclear or ambiguous, even confusing or contradictory, or over refined with technical, obscure and often subtle, if not dubious, distinctions. These adverbial terms include, e.g.: "intentionally," "willfully," "purposely," "designedly," "knowingly," "deliberately," "maliciously," "with premeditation," "recklessly," "negligently," "with culpable negligence," "with gross negligence," "with criminal negligence," "without due caution," "wickedly," "unlawfully," "wrongfully" and scores of others.
>
> *Burnett v. State* 1999, 575

Second, *mens rea* consists of four kinds of criminal intent, each with a different degree of blameworthiness. Third, a different kind of intent might apply to each of the elements of a crime. So, it's possible for one kind of intent to apply to *actus reus*, another to causation (see "Principle of Causation"), another to the harm defined in the statute, and still another to circumstance elements. Finally, proving *mens rea* can create difficult practical problems for prosecutors in criminal cases (American Law Institute 1985 I:2, 229–233).

Proving *Mens Rea*

You can't see intent; not even the finest instruments of modern technology can find or measure it (Hall 1960, 106). Electroencephalograms can record brain waves, and X rays can photograph brain tissue, but Chief Justice Brian's words are as true today as they were when he wrote them in 1477: "The thought of man is not triable, for the devil himself knoweth not the thought of man" (Williams 1961, 1). Three hundred years later, Sir William Blackstone put it this way, "A tribunal can't punish what it can't know" (Blackstone 1769, 21).

Confessions are the only direct evidence of *mens rea*. But defendants rarely confess their true intentions, so proof of their intent usually depends on indirect **(circumstantial) evidence.** Action is the overwhelming kind of circumstantial evidence. In everyday experience, we rely on what people *do* to tell us what they *intend.* For example, if I break into a stranger's house at night, it's reasonable to infer I'm up to no good. So, by observing directly what I *do*, you can know indirectly what I *intend.*

Four Kinds of *Mens Rea*

One analysis of the U.S. Criminal Code found seventy-nine separate definitions of criminal intent. Yet, all of them boiled down to four mental states: general, specific, transferred, and constructive intent (Goldstein, Dershowitz, and Schwartz 1974, 777–778).

General intent applies to crimes of criminal conduct, and it means the intent to commit a criminal act. For example, the *actus reus* of burglary is breaking and entering (Chapter 11), of larceny is the taking and carrying away of another's property (Chapter 11), and of rape is the sexual penetration of another person (Chapter 10). **Specific intent** applies to crimes of cause and result. So, in addition to the intent to commit the criminal act, specific intent includes the intent to cause a particular result, such as homicide, which requires the intent to cause death (Chapter 9).

Transferred intent applies to cases in which actors intend to harm one victim but instead harm another. For example, if Nathan shoots at his enemy Doug but hits Michelle when she steps in front of Doug to block the shot, the law transfers Nathan's intent to kill Doug to the intent to kill Michelle. Transferred intent is sometimes called "bad aim intent," because a high number of these cases involve misfired guns. But the law also transfers intent in other situations. If Matt intends to burn down Michael's restaurant but mistakenly burns down Paul's house instead, Matt has still committed arson. However, there's a limit to transferred intent; it only transfers to *similar* crimes. So, the intent to assault a man by throwing a rock at him doesn't transfer to the intent to break a window when the rock intended to hit the man hits the window instead.

Constructive intent applies to cases where actors cause harms greater than they intended or expected. For example, if Laila drives above the speed limit on an icy

TABLE 4.1
Everyday Definitions of *Model Code* Levels of Culpability

Level of Culpability	Definition
Purpose	"You did (or caused) it on purpose."
Knowledge	"OK, so you didn't do it because you *wanted* to hurt me, but you *knew* (or were practically certain) you *were* hurting me."
Recklessness	"OK, so you didn't *want* to hurt her, but you *knew* the odds were very high you *could* hurt her, and you did."
Negligence	"OK, so you didn't *mean* to hurt him, and you didn't even know how high the odds were you would hurt him, but you *should've* known the odds were very high, and he got hurt."

street and her car veers out of control, killing Irmgard, Laila has the constructive intent to kill.

The *Model Penal Code* has refined these four types of intent in its *mens rea* provision (Table 4.1). After enormous effort, and sometimes heated debate, the drafters sorted out, identified, and defined four criminal mental states. From most to least blameworthy, they are

1. Purpose

2. Knowledge

3. Recklessness

4. Negligence

The *Model Code* levels of culpability are roughly equivalent to, but more elaborate and precise than, general, specific, transferred, and constructive intent. The *Model Code* specifies that all crimes requiring a mental element (some do not) must include one of these mental states. They are defined in Section 2.02, reproduced here.

§ 2.02.
GENERAL REQUIREMENTS OF CULPABILITY.

1. *Minimum Requirements of Culpability....* [A] person is not guilty of an offense unless he acted purposely, knowingly, recklessly or negligently . . . with respect to each material element of the offense.

2. *Kinds of Culpability Defined*

a. *Purposely.* A person acts purposely with respect to a material element of an offense when:

i. if the element involves the nature of his conduct [crimes of criminal conduct] or a result thereof [crimes of criminal conduct causing criminal harm], it is his conscious object to engage in conduct of that nature or to cause such a result; . . .

b. *Knowingly.* A person acts knowingly . . . when:

i. if the element involves the nature of his conduct . . . he is aware that his conduct is of that nature . . . and

ii. if the element involves a result of his conduct, he is aware that it is practically certain that his conduct will cause such a result.

c. *Recklessly.* A person acts recklessly with respect to a material element of an offense when he consciously disregards a substantial and unjustifiable risk that the material element exists or will result from his conduct. The risk must be of such a nature and degree that, considering the nature and purpose of the actor's conduct and the circumstances known to him, its disregard involves a gross deviation from the standard of conduct that a law-abiding person would observe in the actor's situation.

d. *Negligently.* A person acts negligently with respect to a material element of an offense when he should be aware of a substantial and unjustifiable risk that the material element exists or will result from his conduct. The risk must be of such a nature and degree that the actor's failure to perceive it, considering the nature and purpose of his conduct and the circumstances known to him, involves a gross deviation from the standard of care that a reasonable person would observe in the actor's situation.... (American Law Institute 1985 I:2, 229)

Purpose

In the *Model Penal Code,* the first (most blameworthy) state of mind, **purpose,** is roughly the same as the idea in the everyday expression, "You hit me on purpose." Technically, it means having the *specific intent* (purpose or "conscious object") either to commit crimes of criminal conduct or to cause criminal harms (in criminal conduct causing criminal harm). For example, in common-law burglary, the burglar has to break into and enter a house for the very purpose (conscious object) of committing a crime after getting inside. In murder, the murderer's purpose (conscious object) has to be to cause the victim's death. The court in *State v. Stark* (1992) examined the mental state of purpose required in the Washington state assault statute.

CASE	*Did He Expose His Victims to HIV on Purpose?*

State v. Stark
832 P.2d 109 (Wash.App.1992)

Calvin Stark was convicted in the Superior Court, Clallam County, Washington, of two counts of second-degree assault for intentionally exposing his sexual partners to the human immunodeficiency virus (HIV), and he appealed. The Washington Court of Appeals affirmed and remanded the case for resentencing.

PETRICH, CJ.

FACTS

On March 25, 1988, Calvin Stark tested positive for HIV, which was confirmed by further tests on June 25 and on June 30, 1988. From June 30, 1988, to October 3, 1989, the staff of the Clallam County Health Department had five meetings with Stark during which Stark went through extensive counseling about his infection. He was taught about "safe sex," the risk of spreading the infection, and the necessity of informing his partners before engaging in sexual activity with them. On October 3, 1989, Dr. Locke, the Clallam County Health Officer, after learning that

Stark had disregarded this advice and was engaging in unprotected sexual activity, issued a cease and desist order as authorized by RCW 70.24.024(3)(b).

Stark did not cease and desist, and, consequently, on March 1, 1990, Dr. Locke went to the County prosecutor's office.... The prosecutor... had Dr. Locke complete a police report. The State then charged Stark with three counts of assault in the second degree under RCW 9A.36.021(1)(e). [RCW 9A.36.021(1)(e) provides:

(1) A person is guilty of assault in the second degree if he or she, under circumstances not amounting to assault in the first degree: ... (e) With intent to inflict bodily harm, exposes or transmits human immunodeficiency virus as defined in chapter 70.24 RCW; ..."]

Each count involved a different victim:

Count One: The victim and Stark engaged in sexual intercourse on October 27 and October 29, 1989. On both occasions, Stark withdrew his penis from the victim prior to ejaculation. The victim, who could not become pregnant because she had previously had her fallopian tubes tied, asked Stark on the second occasion why he withdrew. He then told her that he was HIV positive.

Count Two: The victim and Stark had sexual relations on at least six occasions between October, 1989, and February, 1990. Stark wore a condom on two or three occasions, but on the others, he ejaculated outside of her body. On each occasion, they had vaginal intercourse. On one occasion Stark tried to force her to have anal intercourse. They also engaged in oral sex. When she told Stark that she had heard rumors that he was HIV positive, he admitted that he was and then gave the victim an AZT pill "to slow down the process of the AIDS."

Count Three: The victim and Stark had sexual relations throughout their brief relationship. It was "almost non-stop with him," "almost every night" during August 1989. Stark never wore a condom and never informed the victim he was HIV positive. When pressed, Stark denied rumors about his HIV status. The victim broke off the relationship because of Stark's drinking, after which Stark told her that he carried HIV and explained that if he had told her, she would not have had anything to do with him.

… At the jury trial, the victim in count one testified to her contacts with Stark and the jury received Dr. Locke's deposition testimony regarding the Health Department's contacts with Stark. Stark did not testify. In the bench trial [trial without a jury], Dr. Locke testified. There the State also presented the testimony of one of Stark's neighborhood friends. She testified that one night Stark came to her apartment after drinking and told her and her daughter that he was HIV positive. When she asked him if he knew that he had to protect himself and everybody else, he replied, "I don't care. If I'm going to die, everybody's going to die."

The jury found Stark guilty on count one. A second trial judge found Stark guilty of the second and third counts at a bench trial. On count one, Stark was given an exceptional sentence of 120 months based on his future danger to the community. The standard range for that offense was 13 to 17 months. On counts two and three, Stark was given the low end of the standard range, 43 months each, to be served concurrently, but consecutively to count one.

OPINION

… Stark contends that there is insufficient evidence to prove he "exposed" anyone to HIV or that he acted with intent to inflict bodily harm. Since Stark is undisputedly HIV positive, he necessarily exposed his sexual partners to the virus by engaging in unprotected sexual intercourse. The testimony of the three victims supports this conclusion.

The testimony supporting the element of intent to inflict bodily harm includes Dr. Locke's statements detailing his counseling sessions with Stark. With regard to the first victim, we know that Stark knew he was HIV positive, that he had been counseled to use "safe sex" methods, and that it had been explained to Stark that coitus interruptus will not prevent the spread of the virus. While there is evidence to support Stark's position, all the evidence viewed in a light most favorable to the State supports a finding of intent beyond a reasonable doubt. The existence of non-criminal explanations does not preclude a finding that a defendant intended to harm his sexual partners.

With regard to the later victims, we have, in addition to this same evidence, Stark's neighbor's testimony that Stark, when confronted about his sexual practices, said, "I don't care. If I'm going to die, everybody's going to die." We also have the testimony of the victim in count two that Stark attempted to have anal intercourse with her and did have oral sex, both methods the counselors told Stark he needed to avoid. See also *Commonwealth v. Brown*, 605 A.2d 429 (1992) (Defendant threw his feces into face of prison guard. Court found that there was sufficient evidence to support finding of intent to inflict bodily harm when defendant had been counseled by both a physician and a nurse about being tested HIV positive and that he could transmit the virus through his bodily fluids.); *State v. Haines*, 545 N.E.2d 834 (Ind.App.1989) (sufficient evidence to convict of attempted murder when defendant, knowing he was HIV positive, spit, bit, scratched, and threw blood at officer); *Scroggins v. State*, 401 S.E.2d 13 (1990) (sufficient evidence to convict of aggravated assault with intent to murder when defendant, knowing he was HIV positive, sucked up excess sputum, bit an officer, and laughed about it later).

… Stark also contends that the trial court erred in imposing an exceptional sentence based solely on future dangerousness. [Washington has a guidelines scheme of sentencing. Judges can sentence outside the guidelines if they provide written reasons for doing so. According to Washington law, "the reasons must be substantial and compelling. … Once substantial and compelling factors exist to support an exceptional sentence, the length of the sentence is left to the discretion of the sentencing court."]

… The trial court abused its discretion in imposing a 10-year sentence. In order to commit this crime, a person has to know he or she is HIV positive, know how the virus is transmitted, and engage in activity with intent to cause harm. Although such conduct is by nature very serious and reprehensible, the Legislature fixed the same relatively light standard range term that applies in all other second-degree assault cases. Significantly, since "transmitting" the virus is an alternative means of committing the offense, the standard range remains the same even if the victim acquires the virus.

Here, there was no evidence that as of the date of the trial that any of the victims had contracted the virus, and Stark's conduct does not seem to be the "worst possible" example of this offense. The trial court, therefore, abused its discretion in imposing a 10-year term. Cf. *State v. Farmer*, 116 Wash.2d 414, 431–32, 805 P.2d 200, 812 P.2d 858 (1991) (upholding exceptional 7½-year sentence based on finding of deliberate cruelty where defendant knowingly exposed his two minor victims to HIV). . . .

We affirm the convictions, but remand for resentencing on count one.

Questions

1. Identify all of the facts relevant to determining Stark's *mens rea*.

2. Using the common-law definition of specific intent and the *Model Penal Code* definitions of purposely, knowingly, recklessly, and negligently, and relying on the relevant facts, identify Stark's intention with respect to his acts.

3. Is motive important in this case?

4. Do you agree that the sentence should fall within the standard range, or was it proper to make it more severe, as the trial court did? Defend your answer.

◆   ◆   ◆

Disturbed by what appears to be a trend in church burning, race and ethnic violence, and gay bashing, many state legislatures have passed church burning, hate crime, ethnic intimidation, gay bashing, and similar criminal laws. For example, a commission in California concluded that "minorities had been harassed, intimidated, assaulted, and even murdered in virtually every part of the state, and further found that the rate of such hate crimes was increasing, and that existing laws were inadequate to protect Californians from hate-motivated violence." A statute followed that created heavy criminal penalties aimed at both preventing and punishing "acts of hate violence." The court in *Commonwealth v. Barnette* (1998) applied the Massachusetts hate crime statute to a race and ethnic altercation.

CASE | *Did He Assault for the Purpose of Ethnic Intimidation?*

Commonwealth v. Barnette
699 N.E.2d 1230 (Mass.App. 1998)

Aubrey Barnette was convicted by a jury in the District Court Department, Concord Division, Middlesex County, of two counts of assault and battery for the purpose of intimidation and two counts of threatening to commit a crime. Defendant appealed the convictions and the denial of a motion for a new trial. The Appeals Court affirmed.

LENK, J.

FACTS

In the early evening of September 21, 1995, Maria Acuna (Acuna) was working at her computer on the second floor of her home in Lexington, where she had been living with her son, Israel Rodriguez (Rodriguez), since May 1995. The defendant, Aubrey Barnette, was next door at his sister's house baby-sitting his niece. Acuna heard a loud noise, like someone banging or shaking a wooden fence, looked out her window, and saw Barnette trying to enter her backyard to retrieve his niece's ball. Concerned that Barnette was going to break her fence, Acuna called through the window to Barnette to please not trespass, and that she would come downstairs to help him out.

Barnette shouted, "You b____, I just came to pick up my ball." Acuna went downstairs, walked into her backyard, and observed that the defendant had entered her yard and was turning to leave. As Barnette left her yard, he repeatedly called her a "b____" and told her that she could keep the ball the next time. Acuna walked toward the fence to latch the gate and Barnette said: "You b____. You don't fit here. What are you doing here, you damn Mexican? Why don't you go back to your country? All of you come and get our jobs and our houses. Get out of here. You don't fit here. I'll kill you and your son."

Barnette's tirade continued in the same vein: "I am a black man. I have been living here for seven years. I can go inside your house or anyplace I want to. Because nobody will stop me, you b____, and I will kill you if you say something. Why don't you just go back to your country? Why don't you just go back to Mexico? You don't fit here. . . . By the way, do you speak English? Greasy b____."

While standing next to the fence shouting at Acuna, Barnette thrust his fist towards her face so that she "could almost feel the hit of his fist" in her nose and face. Barnette then threw his fingers in a forking motion towards her, coming to within an inch of her eyes. He was yelling at Acuna so loudly that Rodriguez awoke from his nap and came outside to the backyard. Rodriguez testified that he could hear Barnette shouting "f___," "s__t," and "Mexican," "Get the hell out of the country," "You don't belong here," and "Mexicans don't belong here" at his mother. He pulled his mother away from the fence and demanded to know from Barnette what was going on. Barnette now attempted to hit Rodriguez with his fists, from the other side of the fence, rattling the gate, trying to enter the backyard, and saying: "You little s__t. Come up here. I'm going to take the f____ing s__t out of you and your mother together. I will beat you both to death." Barnette continued saying, "Damn Mexicans. What are you doing here?" Acuna and Rodriguez both testified that they felt afraid and threatened by Barnette's rage and determination to hit them.

At the time of the incident, Barnette's neighbor, Michael Townes, was barbecuing in his backyard, approximately twenty feet away. Townes heard Barnette yell at Acuna and Rodriguez, "You should go back to where you're from," and refer to "whupping" Rodriguez's ass. Townes came over and, smelling alcohol on Barnette's breath, told him to "Let it go" and to go home and "sleep it off." Townes put his hands on Barnette and led him away. Rodriguez went inside and, after calling Townes to express his gratitude, called the police.

Officer Paul Callahan responded to the call and arrived at Acuna's residence to find her and her son visibly upset. Callahan filed an incident report and tried, unsuccessfully, to locate Barnette. The next day, Detective Charles Mercer returned to the neighborhood and interviewed Barnette. In response to the detective's questions, Barnette asserted that he entered the yard to retrieve the ball only after knocking on the fence and not receiving a response, that Acuna had appeared and yelled at him for not going around to ring

the bell, and that he did not swear at or threaten Acuna. Nonetheless, Barnette did admit that he had said that Acuna should "go back to where she came from" but claims to have said it to his neighbor Townes, not directly to Acuna.

OPINION

. . . General Laws c. 265, § 39, as inserted by St.1983, c. 165, § 1, is a so-called "hate crime" statute. It provides that "whoever commits an assault or a battery upon a person . . . for the purpose of intimidation because of said person's race, color, religion, or national origin, shall be punished. . . ." As instructed by the trial judge, the essential elements of the crime are: (1) the commission of an assault or battery (2) with the intent to intimidate (3) because of a person's race, color, religion, or national origin.

In general, a hate crime is "a crime in which the defendant's conduct was motivated by hatred, bias, or prejudice, based on the actual or perceived race, color, religion, national origin, ethnicity, gender, or sexual orientation of another individual or group of individuals." Thus, hate crime laws such as G.L. c. 265, § 39, operate to "enhance the penalty of criminal conduct when it is motivated by racial hatred or bigotry." It is not the conduct but the underlying motivation that distinguishes the crime.

Here, the defendant was convicted of assaulting the victims for the purpose of intimidation. The intent required by G.L. c. 265, § 39 was not only that required to establish . . . the intent either to cause a battery or to cause apprehension of immediate bodily harm, but also the intent to intimidate because of the victim's membership in a protected class. . . .

At trial, Acuna and Rodriguez both testified that, throughout the altercation that gave rise to this case, the defendant repeatedly called them "damn Mexicans," and demanded that they "get out of here." Acuna testified that the defendant verbally attacked her, saying that she should go back to her country and that he would kill her and her son. Rodriguez testified that the defendant told him that he was going to beat up Rodriguez and his "b____y" mother. Both Acuna and Rodriguez also testified that they felt threatened by the defendant's behavior.

The Commonwealth presented ample evidence that the defendant assaulted Acuna and Rodriguez with the intent to intimidate them because of their national origin in violation of c. 265, § 39. A rational trier of fact could find that the defendant's repetition of the phrase "damn Mexican," accompanied by his repeated demand that Acuna and Rodriguez "Get out of here," demonstrated a purpose of intimidation because of the victims' national origin. The trial judge did not err in denying the defendant's motion for a required finding of not guilty.

The defendant contends that his outburst at Acuna and Rodriguez was motivated by his anger at being called a trespasser and was not motivated by any anti-Mexican sentiment. The defendant believes that the fact that his niece is of Puerto Rican descent demonstrates that he lacks any anti-Hispanic bias or prejudice.

The uncontroverted evidence at trial, however, was that the defendant was shouting specifically anti-Mexican slurs at Acuna and Rodriguez, not that he expressed any more generalized anti-Hispanic animus. Moreover, the evidence submitted in conjunction with the defendant's motion for new trial established merely that the defendant's niece was of Puerto Rican descent not that the defendant thought favorably of Puerto Ricans or Hispanics in general. The trial judge found that the fact that the defendant has an Hispanic niece was not necessarily relevant to whether the victims in the instant case were subjected to racial invective and actions on the part of the defendant. . . . The trial judge did not err in denying the defendant's motion for new trial.

Judgments affirmed. Order denying motion for new trial affirmed.

Questions

1. List all of the facts relevant to determining whether the crime was motivated by ethnic hatred.

2. Does the defendant have a point when he argues that the crime was motivated by the trespass and not ethnic hatred? Explain.

3. It was objected in this case, as it is frequently in hate crime cases, that the statutes violate guarantees of free speech. Do you agree? Defend your answer.

4. Which of the following do you think is the best response to acts motivated by group hatred: Punishing them as hate crimes? Increasing the penalty for existing crimes if hate motivated the crime? Keeping the criminal law out of the business of punishing hate, relying instead on informal sanctions against prejudice? Defend your choice.

Knowledge

"Maybe you didn't do it for the very purpose of hurting me, but you *knew* you were hurting me when you did it." This is an example of the second mental state (level of culpability) the law calls **knowledge.** It means you can *know* you're acting or causing harm without doing it on *purpose* or with the *conscious object* of causing the harm. So, a surgeon who removes a cancerous uterus to save a pregnant woman's life knowingly kills the fetus in her womb, but killing the fetus is not the purpose (conscious object) of the removal. Rather, the death of the fetus is an unavoidable side effect of removing the cancerous uterus.

Similarly, treason, the only crime defined in the U.S. Constitution, requires that traitors provide aid and comfort to enemies for the purpose of overthrowing the government. Defendants may provide aid and comfort to enemies of the United States knowing their actions are practically certain to contribute to overthrowing the government. But that isn't enough; they have to provide them for the *purpose* of overthrowing the U.S. government. If their conscious object was to get rich, then they haven't committed treason (*Haupt v. U.S.* 1947). The purpose requirement in treason led to the enactment of other statutes to fill the void, like making it a crime to provide secrets to the enemy, an offense that requires only that defendants purposely provide such secrets. The need to distinguish between knowledge and purpose arises most frequently in attempt, conspiracy, and solicitation (Chapter 6).

In *State v. Barnes* (1997) (and the Exploring Further case following it), the Oregon Court of Appeals grappled with the "knowing" requirement in the state's assault statute. These cases clearly show just how complicated the application of "knowingly" to the facts of specific cases can get.

Did He Knowingly Cause Injury?

State v. Barnes
945 P.2d 627 (Ore.App. 1997)

Edward Forrest Barnes, the defendant, was convicted following jury trial in the Circuit Court, Lincoln County, of resisting arrest and assault in the second degree. Barnes appealed. The Court of Appeals affirmed the conviction for resisting arrest and remanded for resentencing and reversed the conviction for assault in the second degree and remanded for a new trial.

DE MUNIZ, J.

FACTS

The charges arose following an incident at the Newport Seafood and Wine Festival in February 1994. Barnes, the defendant, and his wife Debra were at the marina building with another couple, Dean and Dana Chase. Barnes had had four or five glasses of wine at the festival when, around 6:00 P.M., the incident started. Newport Chief of Police Rivers testified that breaking wine glasses had become "kind of a tradition" at the marina and that the crowd there numbered about 3,500, the limit the security personnel tried to maintain.

Rivers heard glass being broken in the area where Barnes, his wife, and the Chases were. Rivers sent officers Miller and Simpson to the area. Simpson testified that he asked Dana Chase to leave, and she refused. Simpson then physically removed her and outside, after she tried to slap and kick him, Simpson told her that she was under arrest. She tried to run, and when he caught her she continued to fight.

Debra Barnes then jumped on his back, as did the defendant Barnes. Simpson said that Miller took the defendant off his back and, as Simpson rolled over, he saw the defendant throwing punches at Miller.

Paul Rose was working as a security guard. He testified that he saw a police officer coming out with a female who was yelling and screaming, and that he saw her try to slap and kick the officer and try to run. Rose testified that he saw Miller go down and that Rose stepped forward with his hands out, intending to keep the crowd back.

Defendant Barnes struck Rose in the right eye. Rose suffered a "blow-out fracture" of the eye socket—a fracture of a thin layer of bone at the floor of the socket. The injury re-sulted in double vision and required surgery. Rose still has some double vision and a "sunken" eye.

Barnes was indicted for "unlawfully and knowingly causing serious physical injury to Paul Rose" under ORS 163.175(1)(a), which provides: "(1) A person commits the crime of assault in the second degree if the person: (a) Intentionally or knowingly causes serious physical injury to another." In turn, ORS 161.085(8) provides: "'Knowingly' or 'with knowledge,' when used with respect to conduct or to a circumstance described by a statute defining an offense, means that a person acts with an awareness that the conduct of the person is of a nature so described or that a circumstance so described exists."

OPINION

Defendant Barnes first assigns error to the denial of his requested jury instruction on assault in the second degree and to the instruction given. Barnes's requested instruction stated, in part, that, to find the crime of assault in the second degree, the state had to prove:

[Barnes] caused serious physical injury to Paul Rose. Serious physical injury means a physical injury that either (1) creates a substantial risk of death, or (2) causes serious and protracted disfigurement, or (3) causes protracted impairment of health, or (4) causes protracted loss or impairment of the function of any bodily organ; and that the defendant caused said physical injury knowingly. To act knowingly in this case the defendant had to have acted with an awareness that his conduct would cause a serious physical injury. A person achieves a particular result knowingly when he is practically certain that his conduct will cause that result. A person who is aware of and consciously disregards a substantial and unjustifiable risk that a serious physical injury will occur acts recklessly, but not knowingly.

The trial court rejected defendant's instruction, instead instructing the jury that

a person acts "knowingly" if that person acts with an awareness that his or her conduct is of a particular nature. Oregon law provides that a person commits the crime of Assault in the Second Degree if that person knowingly—I've defined the term "knowingly"—causes serious physical injury—and I've defined "serious physical injury"—to another. In this case to establish Assault in the Second Degree, the State must prove beyond a reasonable doubt the following three elements:

. . .

Number three, that [defendant] knowingly caused serious physical injury to Paul Rose.

The court also gave the state's special instruction:

You are instructed when knowingly suffices to establish a culpable mental state, it is also established if a person acts intentionally.

Neither party makes an argument specifically directed to that instruction. However, we note that "intent" and "knowledge" are distinct concepts under the criminal code.

Defendant argues that the statutory definitions of "intentionally," "recklessly" and "criminal negligence," ORS 161.085(7); ORS 161.085(9); ORS 161.085(10), all refer to "a result . . . described by a statute defining an offense," but that "result" is absent from the definition of "knowingly." Defendant contends, however, that assault in the second degree is a "result offense" and requires proof that the person knowingly caused serious physical injury.

Defendant argues that the instructions given did not distinguish between conduct and result. He argues that the instructions must inform the jury that there must be proof beyond a reasonable doubt that he intended a serious physical injury to occur or that he was conscious of the result of the blow and was almost certain that a serious physical injury would occur. He further argues that here the instruction permitted the jury to find him guilty of assault in the second degree if they found that he knowingly struck Rose, even though he did not intend or was not almost certain that Rose would suffer serious physical injury from the blow.

The state responds that the court's elements instruction specifically stated that, to establish second-degree assault, the state had to prove that defendant "knowingly caused serious physical injury to Paul Rose." It argues that the court's instructions "tracked" the uniform jury instructions and relevant statutes and accurately stated the law. It contends that, given the juxtaposition of "knowingly" and "caused" in the instruction, as well as the court's instruction that "a person acts 'knowingly' if that person acts with an awareness that his or her conduct is of a particular nature," the jury could not reasonably have understood the instructions to mean anything but that defendant had to be aware that his act of punching Rose in the face would cause serious physical injury. It argues that, taken as a whole, the instructions could not have been un-

derstood to mean that the state only had to prove that defendant knew he struck Rose in the face.

The drafters of the Oregon Criminal Code sought to restrict the concept of "knowingly" to awareness of the nature of one's conduct or to the existence of specified circumstances. Thus, ORS 161.085(8) specifically provides that the definition of "knowledge" applies "when [knowingly] is used with respect to conduct or to a circumstance described by a statute defining an offense." However, despite that general definition, "knowingly" in ORS 163.175(1)(a) is not used with respect to conduct or a circumstance. It is used instead, as defendant contends, with a result.

. . . Unlike sexual abuse, assault in the second degree under ORS 163.175(1)(a) proscribes a result—causing serious physical injury. The trial court concluded that one who intends the act must live with the consequences, i.e. that "you take the victim as you find them." However, the clear language of ORS 163.175(1)(a) does not proscribe conduct resulting in serious physical injury; it requires intentionally or knowingly causing that injury. Here, the trial court instructed the jury according to the statutory definition of "knowingly" and incorporated that definition in its instructions on the elements of assault in the second degree. However, the statutory definition of "knowingly" is restricted to awareness of conduct; it does not define awareness as to result. It is the result that must be proved for the offense of assault in the second degree, and an instruction using only the statutory definition of "knowingly" does not sufficiently inform the jury of the nexus between conduct and knowledge of the result of the conduct to satisfy the elements of ORS 163.175(1)(a).

. . . Conviction for resisting arrest affirmed and remanded for resentencing; conviction for assault in the second degree reversed and remanded for a new trial.

Questions

1. List all of the facts relevant to determining Barnes's state of mind.

2. According to the court, what *mens rea* does the assault statute require?

3. Explain why it makes a difference whether assault is a crime of criminal conduct or a crime of causing a result.

4. Explain the difference between Barnes's requested instruction and the one the trial court gave.

5. According to the court, what's wrong with the instruction the trial court gave? Should it make a difference? Defend your answer.

EXPLORING THE MENTAL STATE OF KNOWLEDGE FURTHER

 Go to the Criminal Law 8e CD to read the full text version of the case featured here.

Did He "Knowingly" Assault Him with a Knife?

FACTS

Pete Jantzi, the defendant, accompanied Diane Anderson, who shared a house with the defendant and several other people, to the home of her estranged husband, Rex. While Diane was in the house talking with Rex, Jantzi was using the blade of his knife to let the air out of the tires on Rex's van. Another person put sugar in the gas tank of the van. While the Andersons were arguing, Diane apparently threatened damage to Rex's van and indicated that someone might be tampering with the van at that moment. Rex's roommate ran out of the house and saw two men beside the van. He shouted and began to run toward the men. Rex ran from the house and began to chase Jantzi, who ran down a bicycle path. Jantzi, still holding his open knife, jumped into the bushes beside the path and landed in the weeds. He crouched there, hoping that Rex would not see him and would pass by. Rex, however, jumped on top of Jantzi and grabbed his shirt. They rolled over and Rex was stabbed in the abdomen by Jantzi's knife. Jantzi

could not remember making a thrusting or swinging motion with the knife; he did not intend to stab Rex.

An indictment charged that Jantzi "did unlawfully and knowingly cause physical injury to Rex Anderson by means of a deadly weapon, to-wit: knife, by stabbing the said Rex Anderson with said knife." According to the same Oregon assault statute as that in *State. v. Barnes*, "A person commits the crime of assault in the second degree if he intentionally or knowingly causes physical injury to another..." Did Jantzi knowingly assault Rex Anderson?

DECISION AND REASONS

The trial court said yes. But, according to the appellate court:

> Although the trial judge found defendant guilty of "knowingly" causing physical injury to Anderson, what he described in his findings is recklessness. The court found that defendant knew he had a dangerous weapon and that a confrontation was going to occur. The court believed that defendant did not intend to stab Anderson. The court's conclusion seems to be based on the reasoning that because defendant knew it was possible that an injury would occur, he acted "knowingly." However, a person who "is aware of and consciously disregards a substantial and unjustifiable risk" that an injury will occur acts "recklessly," not "knowingly." Recklessly causing physical injury to another is assault in the third degree.

> *State v. Jantzi*, 56 Or.App. 57, 641 P.2d 62 (1982)

◆ ◆ ◆

Recklessness

"OK, so you didn't *want* to hurt her by what you did, but you *knew* the odds were very high you *could* hurt her if you did it; you did it anyway, and it did hurt her." Recklessness is about creating risks either on purpose or knowingly. Reckless people know they're creating risks of harm but they don't intend, or at least don't expect, to cause harm itself. **Recklessness** (conscious risk creation) isn't as blameworthy as acting purposely or knowingly because reckless defendants don't act for the very purpose of doing harm; they don't even act knowing harm is practically certain to follow. Reckless defendants *do* know they're creating risks of harm. So, the blameworthiness of recklessness lies in probabilities—of purpose and knowledge, in certainties.

Recklessness requires more than awareness of *ordinary* risks; it requires awareness of *substantial* and *unjustifiable* risks. The American Law Institute's *Model Penal Code* proposes that fact finders determine recklessness according to a two-pronged test:

1. *Were the defendants aware of how substantial and unjustifiable the risks that they disregarded were?* Under this prong, notice that even a substantial risk isn't by itself reckless. For example, a doctor who performs life-saving surgery has created a substantial risk. But the risk is justifiable because the doctor took it to save the life of the patient. This prong doesn't answer the important questions of how substantial and how unjustifiable the risk amounts to recklessness. So, the second prong gives guidance to juries.

2. *Does the defendants' disregard of risk amount to so "gross a deviation from the standard" that a law-abiding person would observe in that situation?* This prong requires juries to make the judgment whether the risk is substantial and unjustifiable enough to deserve condemnation in the form of criminal liability.

This test has both a subjective and an objective component. The first prong of the test is subjective; it focuses on a defendant's actual awareness. The second prong is objective; it measures conduct according to how it deviates from what reasonable people do.

It should be clear to you by now that actual harm isn't the conscious object of reckless wrongdoers. In fact, most reckless actors probably hope that they don't hurt anyone. Or, at most, they don't care if they hurt anyone. But the heart of their culpability is that in the full knowledge of the risks, they act anyway. For example, in one case, a large drug company knew that a medication it sold to control high blood pressure had caused severe liver damage and even death in some patients; it sold the drug anyway. The company's officers, who made the decision to sell the drug, didn't want to hurt anyone (indeed, they hoped no one would die or suffer liver damage). They sought only profit for the company. But they were prepared to risk the deaths of their customers in order to make a profit (Shenon 1985, A1).

Negligence

Like recklessness, negligence is about risk creation. But recklessness is about *consciously* creating risks; **negligence** is about *negligently* creating risks. Here's an example of a negligent wrongdoer: "OK, so you didn't *mean* to hurt him, and you didn't even know the odds were very high you *could* hurt him, but you *should've* known the odds were high, and you did hurt him." The test for negligence is totally objective—the actors *should* have known, even though in fact they did *not* know, they were creating risks.

For example, a reasonable person should know that driving fifty miles per hour down a crowded street creates a risk of harm, even if in fact the driver doesn't know it. The driver who should know this but doesn't is negligent. The driver who knows it but drives too fast anyway is reckless. Negligent defendants, like reckless defendants, have to create substantial and unjustifiable risks—risks that grossly deviate from the ordinary standards of behavior. The case of *Koppersmith v. State* (1999) wrestled with the difficulty of drawing the line between recklessness and negligence.

Koppersmith v. State
742 So.2d 206 (Ala.App. 1999)

Gregory Koppersmith, the appellant, was charged with the murder of his wife, Cynthia ("Cindy") Michel Koppersmith. He was convicted of reckless manslaughter, a violation of § 13A-6–3(a)(1), Ala.Code 1975, and the trial court sentenced him to 20 years in prison. The Alabama Court of Appeals reversed and remanded.

BASCHAB, J.

FACTS

Gregory Koppersmith (appellant) and his wife were arguing in the yard outside of their residence. Cindy tried to enter the house to end the argument, but the appellant prevented her from going inside. A physical confrontation ensued, and Cindy fell off of a porch into the yard. She died as a result of a skull fracture to the back of her head.

In a statement he made to law enforcement officials after the incident, the appellant gave the following summary of the events leading up to Cindy's death. He and Cindy had been arguing and were on a porch outside of their residence. Cindy had wanted to go inside the house, but he had wanted to resolve the argument first. As she tried to go inside, he stepped in front of her and pushed her back. Cindy punched at him, and he grabbed her. When Cindy tried to go inside again, he wrapped his arms around her from behind to stop her. Cindy bit him on the arm, and he "slung" her to the ground. He then jumped down and straddled her, stating that he "had her by the head" and indicating that he moved her head up and down, as if slamming it into the ground. When Cindy stopped struggling, he rolled her over and found a brick covered with blood under her head. The appellant stated that, although Cindy fell near a flowerbed, he did not know there were bricks in the grass.

At trial, the appellant testified that Cindy had tried to go into the house two or three times, but he had stopped her from doing so. During that time, she punched at him and he pushed her away from him. At one point, he put his arms around her from behind to restrain her, and she turned her head and bit him. When she bit him, he pulled her by her sweater and she tripped. He then "slung" her off of him, and she tripped and fell three to four feet to the ground. He jumped off of the porch and straddled her,

grabbing her by the shoulders and telling her to calm down. When he realized she was not moving, he lifted her head and noticed blood all over his hands.

Koppersmith testified that, when he grabbed Cindy from behind, he did not intend to harm her. He also testified that, when he "slung" her away from him off of the porch, he was not trying to hurt her and did not intend to throw her onto a brick. Rather, he stated that he simply reacted after she bit his arm. He also testified that he did not know there were bricks in the yard, that he had not attempted to throw her in a particular direction, and that he was not aware of any risk or harm his actions might cause. He further testified that, when he grabbed and shook her after she fell, he did not intend to harm her, he did not know there was a brick under her head, and he did not intend to hit her head on a brick or anything else. Instead, he testified that he was trying to get her to calm down.

The medical examiner, Dr. Gregory Wanger, testified that the pattern on the injury to the victim's skull matched the pattern on one of the bricks found at the scene. He stated that, based on the position of the skull fracture and the bruising to the victim's brain, the victim's head was moving when it sustained the injury. He testified that her injuries could have been caused by her falling off of the porch and hitting her head on a brick or from her head being slammed into a brick.

The indictment in this case alleged that the appellant "did, with the intent to cause the death of Cynthia Michel Koppersmith, cause the death of Cynthia Michel Koppersmith, by striking her head against a brick, in violation of § 13A-6–2 of the Code of Alabama. (C.R.11)." Koppersmith requested that the trial court instruct the jury on criminally negligent homicide as a lesser included offense of murder. However, the trial court denied that request, and it instructed the jury only on the offense of reckless manslaughter.

OPINION

The appellant argues that the trial court erred in denying his request that it instruct the jury on criminally negligent homicide. An individual accused of the greater offense has a right to have the court charge on the lesser offenses included in the indictment, when there is a reasonable theory from the evidence supporting his position. . . . Every accused is entitled to have charges given, which would not be misleading, which correctly state the law of his case, and which are supported by any evidence, however, weak, insufficient, or doubtful in credibility.

Section 13A-6-3(a), Ala.Code 1975, provides that a person commits the crime of manslaughter if he recklessly causes the death of another person.

A person acts recklessly with respect to a result or to a circumstance described by a statute defining an offense when he is aware of and consciously disregards a substantial and unjustifiable risk that the result will occur or that the circumstance exists. The risk must be of such nature and degree that disregard thereof constitutes a gross deviation from the standard of conduct that a reasonable person would observe in the situation.

A person who creates a risk but is unaware thereof solely by reason of voluntary intoxication, as defined in subdivision (e)(2) of Section 13A-3-2 acts recklessly with respect thereto. § 13A-2-2(3), Ala.Code 1975. "A person commits the crime of criminally negligent homicide if he causes the death of another person by criminal negligence." §13A-6-4(a), Ala.Code 1975. A person acts with criminal negligence with respect to a result or to a circumstance which is defined by statute as an offense when he fails to perceive a substantial and unjustifiable risk that the result will occur or that the circumstance exists. The risk must be of such nature and degree that the failure to perceive it constitutes a gross deviation from the standard of care that a reasonable person would observe in the situation. A court or jury may consider statutes or ordinances regulating the defendant's conduct as bearing upon the question of criminal negligence.

...The only difference between manslaughter under Section 13A-6-3(a)(1) and criminally negligent homicide is the difference between recklessness and criminal negligence. The reckless offender is aware of the risk and "consciously disregards" it. On the other hand, the criminally negligent offender is not aware of the risk created ("fails to perceive") and, therefore, cannot be guilty of consciously disregarding it. The difference between the terms "recklessly" and "negligently"...is one of kind, rather than degree. Each actor creates a risk or harm. The reckless actor is aware of the risk and disregards it; the negligent actor is not aware of the risk but should have been aware of it....

Thus, we must determine whether there was any evidence before the jury from which it could have concluded that the appellant did not perceive that his wife might die as a result of his actions. We conclude that there was evidence from which the jury could have reasonably believed that his conduct that caused her to fall was unintentional and that he was not aware he was creating a risk to his wife. He testified that, after she bit him, his reaction—which caused her to fall to the ground—was simply reflexive. He also testified that he did not know there were bricks in the yard. Even in his statement to the police in which he said he was slamming her head against the ground, Koppersmith said he did not know at that time that there was a brick under her head. Finally, he stated that he did not intend to throw her onto a brick or harm her in any way when he "slung" her, and that he did not intend to hit her head on a brick or otherwise harm her when he grabbed and shook her after she had fallen.

Because there was a reasonable theory from the evidence that would have supported giving a jury instruction on criminally negligent homicide, the trial court erred in refusing to instruct the jury on criminally negligent homicide. Thus, we must reverse the trial court's judgment and remand this case for a new trial.

REVERSED AND REMANDED.

Questions

1. List all of the facts relevant to determining Koppersmith's mental state with respect both to his acts and the results of his actions.

2. In your opinion, was Koppersmith reckless or negligent? Support your answer with relevant facts.

3. Is it possible to argue that Koppersmith knowingly or even purposely killed his wife? What facts, if any, support these two states of mind?

Liability Without *Mens Rea*: Strict Liability

As you've now learned, criminal liability depends on at least some degree of blameworthiness. That's true when we're talking about *serious* crimes, like the homicides in the last several excerpts. But, there are an enormous number of minor crimes where there's liability without culpability, or **strict liability**. Let's be blunt: Strict liability makes accidental injuries a crime. We call these criminal accidental injuries **strict lia-**

bility offenses. In these cases, the prosecution has to prove only that defendants committed a voluntary criminal act that caused harm. The U.S. Supreme Court has upheld the power of legislatures to create strict liability offenses to protect the "public health and safety," as long as they make clear they're imposing liability without *mens rea*. In other words, the U.S. Constitution doesn't require a *mens rea*. The Court has ruled that the U.S. Constitution *does* require an *actus reus* (Chapter 3).

Supporters of strict liability make two main arguments. First, there is a strong public interest in protecting public health and safety. Strict liability arose during the industrial revolution when manufacturing, mining, and commerce exposed large numbers of the public to death, mutilation, and disease from poisonous fumes, unsafe railroads, workplaces, and adulterated foods, and other products. Second, the penalty for strict liability offenses is almost always mild (fines not jail time).

But strict liability still has its critics. The critics say it's too easy to expand strict liability beyond offenses that seriously endanger the public. They're always wary of making exceptions to blameworthiness, which is central to the *mens rea* principle. It does no good (and probably a lot of harm) to punish people who haven't harmed others purposely, knowingly, recklessly, or at least negligently. At the end of the day, a criminal law without blameworthiness will lose its force as a stern moral code. The court decided whether Minnesota's legislature created a strict liability open bottle offense in *State v. Loge* (2000).

CASE | *Did He Have to "Know" There Was an Open Bottle in the Car?*

State v. Loge
608 N.W.2d 152 (Minn. 2000)

Steven Loge, the defendant, was convicted in the District Court, Freeborn County, of keeping an opened bottle of intoxicating liquor in an automobile while on a public highway, and he appealed. The Court of Appeals affirmed. Granting the defendant's petition for further review, the Supreme Court affirmed.

GILBERT, J.

FACTS

Appellant Steven Mark Loge was cited on September 2, 1997, for a violation of Minn.Stat. § 169.122, subd. 3 (1998), which makes it unlawful for the driver of a motor vehicle, when the owner is not present, "to keep or allow to be kept in a motor vehicle when such vehicle is upon the public highway any bottle or receptacle containing intoxicating liquors or 3.2 percent malt liquors which has been opened." Violation of the statute is a misdemeanor.

After a bench trial, the district court held that subdivision 3 imposed "absolute liability" on the driver/owner. Loge appealed. The court of appeals affirmed the conviction, holding that proof of knowledge that the open container was in the motor vehicle was not required.

On September 2, 1997, Loge borrowed his father's pickup truck to go to his evening job. Driving alone on his way home from work, he was stopped by two Albert Lea city police officers on County Road 18 at approximately 8:15 P.M. because he appeared to be speeding. Loge got out of his truck and stood by the driver's side door. While one officer was talking with Loge, the second officer, who was standing by the passenger side of the truck, observed a bottle, which he believed to be a beer bottle, sticking partially out of a brown paper bag underneath the passenger's side of the seat. He retrieved that bottle, which was open and had foam on the inside. He searched the rest of the truck and found one full, unopened can of beer and one empty beer can. After the second officer found the beer bottle, the first officer asked Loge if he had been drinking. Loge stated that he had two beers while working and was on his way home. Loge passed all standard field sobriety tests. The officers gave Loge a citation... for a violation of the open bottle statute but not for speeding....

The trial on the open bottle charge took place on January 29, 1998. Loge testified that the bottle was not his, he did not know it was in the truck and had said that to one of the officers. That officer did not remember any such statements. At the close of the testimony, the trial court requested memoranda from Loge's counsel and the city attorney on the question of whether knowledge is an element of subdivision 3 of the open bottle statute. Both attorneys came to the same legal conclusion that proof of knowledge was required. The trial court found that one of the police officers "observed the neck of the bottle, which was wrapped in a brown paper sack, under the pickup's seat of the truck being operated by defendant." Based on an analysis of section 169.122 as a whole, the trial court held that subdivision 3 creates "absolute liability" on a driver/owner to "inspect and determine... whether there are any containers" in the motor vehicle in violation of the open bottle law and found Loge guilty. Loge was sentenced to five days in jail, execution stayed, placed on probation for one year, and fined $150 plus costs of $32.50.

Loge appealed the verdict. The city attorney did not file a respondent's brief but sent a letter to the Clerk of Appellate Court stating that he "concurred with the reasoning and rationale in the Appellant's brief and therefore there was no reason for the State of Minnesota to file a Respondent's brief." In a published opinion, the court of appeals affirmed the decision of the trial court finding that the evidence, which establishes that one of the officers saw an open bottle containing intoxicating liquor underneath the passenger seat of the truck Loge was driving on a public highway, was sufficient to support Loge's conviction. The court of appeals held that proof of knowledge that the bottle was in the truck is not required to sustain a conviction.

Loge's petition for further review was granted. The Attorney General then assumed responsibility for this case and filed a respondent's brief in which the Attorney General argues, contrary to the previous position of the state, that there is no knowledge requirement under subdivision 3.

OPINION

Loge is seeking reversal of his conviction because, he argues, the trial court and court of appeals erroneously interpreted subdivision 3 of the open bottle statute not to require proof of knowledge.

FN1. Minnesota Statutes § 169.122 reads in part:

Subdivision 1. No person shall drink or consume intoxicating liquors or 3.2 percent malt liquors in any motor vehicle when such vehicle is upon a public highway.

Subdivision 2. No person shall have in possession while in a private motor vehicle upon a public highway, any bottle or receptacle containing intoxicating liquor or 3.2 percent malt liquor which has been opened, or the seal broken, or the contents of which have been partially removed. For purposes of this section, "possession" means either that the person had actual possession of the bottle or receptacle or that the person consciously exercised dominion and control over the bottle or receptacle. This subdivision does not apply to a bottle or receptacle that is in the trunk of the vehicle if it is equipped with a trunk, or that is in another area of the vehicle not normally occupied by the driver and passengers if the vehicle is not equipped with a trunk.

Subdivision 3. It shall be unlawful for the owner of any private motor vehicle or the driver, if the owner be not then present in the motor vehicle, to keep or allow to be kept in a motor vehicle when such vehicle is upon the public highway any bottle or receptacle containing intoxicating liquors or 3.2 percent malt liquors which has been opened, or the seal broken, or the contents of which have been partially removed except when such bottle or receptacle shall be kept in the trunk of the motor vehicle when such vehicle is equipped with a trunk, or kept in some other area of the vehicle not normally occupied by the driver of passengers, if the motor vehicle is not equipped with a trunk. A utility compartment or glove compartment shall be deemed to be within the area occupied by the driver and passengers.

Loge argues that the words "to keep or allow to be kept" implicitly and unambiguously require a defendant to have knowledge of the open container in the motor vehicle in order for criminal liability to attach. He argues that "keep" means "to maintain, or cause to stay or continue, in a specified condition, position, etc." Loge argues that that definition suggests that a person must purposely choose to continue possession. Further, Loge argues that the word "allow" from the phrase "allow to be kept" means "to permit; to grant license to," suggesting awareness at the minimum.

The state argues that the language of subdivision 3 creates a strict liability offense. The statute was enacted in 1959 and subdivision 3 has not had any substantive change since its enactment.... The state argues that subdivision 3's "keep[s] or allow[s] to be kept" language must mean more than mere possession of alcohol because owners/drivers are already subject to liability under subdivision 2 for mere possession, which applies to all persons in the motor vehicle....

...An analysis of a statute must begin with a careful and close examination of the statutory language. We undertake such a review to ascertain and effectuate legislative intent. If the meaning of the statute is "clear and free from all ambiguity, the letter of the law shall not be disregarded under the pretext of pursuing the spirit.". . . This is the first time we have reviewed this statute since its enactment 40 years ago. We are asked only to interpret this statute under the facts presented. . . . Minn.Stat. § 169.122, subd. 3 . . . establishes liability for . . . a driver when that driver "keep[s] *or* allow[s] to be kept" any open bottle containing intoxicating liquor within the area normally occupied by the driver and passengers [emphasis added]. These two alternate concepts are separated by the disjunctive "or," not "and." Unlike the use of the word "and," "or" signifies the distinction between two factual situations. We have long held that in the absence of some ambiguity surrounding the legislature's use of the word "or," we will read it in the disjunctive and require that only one of the possible factual situations be present in order for the statute to be satisfied. Accordingly, we limit our opinion to the words "to keep."

...In delineating the elements of the crime, we have also held that the legislature is entitled to consider what it deems "expedient and best suited to the prevention of crime and disorder." The Supreme Court has addressed the dichotomy between the opportunity to discover and the difficulty of proof in arranging a statutory scheme establishing criminal liability for an unknowing individual:

> Congress weighed the possible injustice of subjecting an innocent seller to a penalty against the evil of exposing innocent purchasers to danger from the drug, and concluded that the latter was the result preferably to be avoided. Doubtless considerations as to the opportunity of the seller to find out the fact and the *difficulty of proof* of knowledge contributed to this conclusion.

Here, if knowledge was a necessary element of the open container offense, there would be a substantial, if not insurmountable, difficulty of proof. . . . It is therefore reasonable to conclude that the legislature, weighing the significant danger to the public, decided that proof of knowledge under subdivision 3 was not required.

The legislature has made knowledge distinctions within its traffic statutes that also guide our interpretation. For example, with respect to marijuana in a motor vehicle, the Minnesota legislature has used language similar to the language found in section 169.122, subdivision 3 ("keep or allow to be kept") but added a knowledge requirement. An owner, or if the owner is not present, the driver, is guilty of a misdemeanor if he "*knowingly* keeps or allows to be kept" marijuana in a motor vehicle. Minn.Stat. § 152.027, subd. 3 (1998) (emphasis added). . . . If the legislature had in-tended section 169.122 to have a knowledge requirement, it could have added the word "knowingly," as the legislature did in section 152.027. . . .

Lastly, *Loge* argues that an interpretation excluding knowledge as an element could lead to absurd results. While it is true that the legislature does not intend a result that is absurd or unreasonable, we do not believe such a result exists here. Loge's conviction resulted from an officer standing outside the truck observing the open container of beer sticking partially out of a brown bag underneath the seat on the passenger side of the truck Loge was driving. By simply taking control of the truck, Loge took control and charge of the contents of the truck, including the open bottle, even if he did not know the open bottle was in the truck. . . .

The "to keep" an open bottle language of subdivision 3 means more than knowingly continuing possession because such conduct is already made illegal by subdivision 2. Any other interpretation would . . . violate the statutory presumption that the legislature intends an entire statute to be effective and certain. Therefore, we hold that in a prosecution under section 169.122, subdivision 3, the state need not prove that the driver and sole occupant of a motor vehicle on a public highway knew of the existence of the open bottle containing intoxicating liquors in the motor vehicle.

AFFIRMED.

DISSENT

ANDERSON, J. (DISSENTING).

I respectfully dissent. In its effort to reach a correct policy decision, the majority disregards our proper role as interpreters of the law. In doing so, the majority has preempted the legislature's function and assumed the mantle of policymaker. I agree that under certain circumstances the legislature may provide that criminal liability attach without requiring any showing of intent or knowledge on the part of the person charged. Further, in the context of open containers of alcohol in motor vehicles, there is a credible argument that it is good public policy given the social and economic costs that result from the combination of alcohol and motor vehicles. But, all of that said, the majority's analysis simply does not demonstrate the requisite clear statement of legislative intent necessary to create criminal liability in the absence of a showing of knowledge or intent. . . .

We have stated that when the legislature intends to make an act unlawful and to impose criminal sanctions without any requirement of intent or knowledge, it must do so clearly. . . . Historically, our substantive criminal law is based upon a theory of punishing the vicious will. It postulates a free agent confronted with a choice between doing right and doing wrong and choosing freely to do wrong. . . .

The majority's analysis of the language of Minn.Stat. § 169.122 does not demonstrate the level of certainty necessary to allow me to conclude that the statute manifests a clear intent by the legislature to impose criminal liability regardless of intent or knowledge. . . . Minnesota Statutes § 169.122, subd. 3, simply lacks the requisite clarity to support the imposition of criminal liability without any showing of intent or knowledge. . . .

The majority attempts to avoid the implications of the phrase "allow to be kept" by discarding it on the grounds that Loge was the sole occupant of the vehicle. While we may limit the application of law to the facts presented, that does not mean that we may disregard inconvenient language contained in the statute as a whole. The majority cannot avoid the implications of the term "allow" because it is convenient to do so. In other contexts, we have held that the inclusion of words like "permit" (a synonym of "allow") clearly indicates a legislative intent to require some level of knowledge or intent. . . .

While not binding on this court, we do look to the practical construction of a statute by public officials in determining its meaning. The district court judges of Minnesota are divided about the meaning of Minn.Stat. § 169.122, subd. 3. . . .

Note: This division was further demonstrated in this case when both the city attorney and defense counsel agreed that the statute required a showing of knowledge. The city attorney has maintained this position throughout the appellate process. It is the attorney general who now argues that the statute requires no showing of intent or knowledge.

. . . In *In re A.A.E.*, we acknowledged that the legislature may make a person criminally liable for injuries resulting from the discharge of a firearm regardless of whether that person intended to cause injury, but we held that some level of intent, reckless disregard of a known danger, was required. While the actor need not intend to cause injury, he must intend to recklessly discharge a firearm. . . .

Finally, under the majority's holding, we now will impose criminal liability on a person, not simply for an act that the person does not know is criminal, but also for an act the person does not even know he is committing. While the district court and the majority seem to assume that everyone who drives a motor vehicle knows that he or she is obligated to search the entire passenger compartment of the vehicle before driving on the state's roads, the law imposes no such requirement. Most drivers would be surprised to discover that after anyone else used their vehicle—children, friends, spouse—they are criminally liable for any open containers of alcohol that are present, regardless of whether they know the containers are there. This also means that any prudent operator of a motor vehicle must also carefully check any case of packaged alcohol before transport and ensure that each container's seal is not broken. *See* Minn.Stat. § 169.122 (defining an open bottle as a container that is open, has the contents partially removed, or has the seal broken). Under the majority's interpretation, all of these situations would render the driver criminally liable under Minn.Stat. § 169.122. Without a more clear statement by the legislature that this is the law, I cannot agree with such an outcome.

Questions

1. What words, if any, in the statute indicate a *mens rea* requirement?

2. What *mens rea*, if any, do the words in the statute require?

3. Summarize the arguments that the majority of the court gives to support this as a strict liability offense.

4. What arguments did the dissent give in response to the majority's arguments?

5. Do you agree with the majority or the dissent? Defend your answer.

Go to Exercise 4-2 in the Criminal Law 8e CD to learn more about open bottle laws.

◆ ◆ ◆

THE PRINCIPLE OF CONCURRENCE

The principle of concurrence applies to both crimes of criminal conduct and to crimes of criminal conduct causing a criminal harm (see Table 4.2). Suppose you and your friend agree to meet at her house on a cold winter night. She's late because her car won't start. So, she calls you on her cell phone and tells you to break the lock on her front door so you can wait inside safe from the cold. But, once you're inside, you de-

TABLE 4.2	
Concurrence	
Crimes of Criminal Conduct	**Criminal Conduct Causing Criminal Harm**
criminal act (*actus reus*)	criminal conduct (*actus reus* + *mens rea*)
+	+
criminal intent (*mens rea*)	causing criminal harm

cide to steal her new TiVo®. Have you committed burglary? No, because in crimes of criminal conduct, the **principle of concurrence** requires that a criminal intent (*mens rea*) *trigger* a criminal act (*actus reus*). You decided to steal her TiVo *after* you broke into and entered her house. Burglary requires that the intent to steal set in motion the acts of breaking and entering.

That's how concurrence applies to burglary, a crime of criminal conduct. Let's look at an example of murder, a crime of criminal conduct causing a criminal harm. Shafeah hates her sister-in-law Nazirah and plans to kill her by running over her with her Ford Explorer. Coincidentally, just as Shafeah is headed toward Nazirah in her Explorer, a complete stranger in a Humvee® appears out of nowhere and accidentally runs over and kills Nazirah. Shafeah gets out of her Explorer, runs over to Nazirah's dead body, and dances around her with joy. Although definitely a creepy thing to do, Shafeah's not a murderer because her criminal conduct (driving her Explorer with the intent to kill Nazirah) didn't cause Nazirah's death. Concurrence here means the criminal conduct has to produce the criminal harm; the harm can't be a coincidence (Hall 1960, 185–190; Chapter 11).

THE PRINCIPLE OF CAUSATION

The principle of causation applies only to crimes of criminal conduct causing a criminal harm. In practice, causation applies only to criminal homicide and other crimes of bodily harm (Chapter 8). Like all elements, prosecutors have to prove causation beyond a reasonable doubt. Proving causation requires proving two kinds of cause:

1. **Factual cause** (also called **"but for"** cause of death or other bodily harm)
2. **Legal cause** (also called **proximate cause** of death or other bodily harm)

Factual ("But For") Cause

What's the "cause in fact" of death or bodily harm in criminal law? (Cause in fact is frequently called "but for" cause in the cases. I'm going to call it "except for" because it's clearer to nonlawyers.) To understand cause in fact, ask this question, "Except for (or "but for") an act by the defendant that triggered a chain of events that, sooner or later, wound up killing or hurting someone, would this have happened? Put another way, "If it hadn't been for the defendant's original act, would the victim probably be

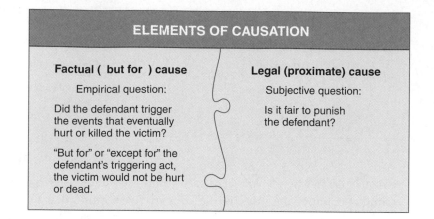

ELEMENTS OF CAUSATION

Factual (but for) cause

Empirical question:

Did the defendant trigger the events that eventually hurt or killed the victim?

"But for" or "except for" the defendant's triggering act, the victim would not be hurt or dead.

Legal (proximate) cause

Subjective question:

Is it fair to punish the defendant?

---

alive and well?" For example, I push a huge smooth round rock down a hill with a crowd at the bottom because I want to see the crowd panic and scatter. The people see the rock and, to my delight, they scatter. Unfortunately, the rock hits and kills two people who couldn't get out of its path. My push is the cause in fact (the "except for") that kills the two people at the bottom. If I hadn't pushed the rock, they'd be alive.

Legal (Proximate) Cause

Proving factual cause is almost always as easy as the no-brainer example of pushing the rock. But proving "except for" cause isn't enough. The prosecution has to prove legal (proximate) cause, too. So, "except for" cause is *necessary,* but it's not enough to prove my push *legally* caused the deaths. "Except for" cause is an objective, empirical question of fact; that's why we call it factual cause. Proximate cause is a subjective question of fairness that appeals to the jury's sense of justice. It asks, "Is it fair to blame the defendant for this death or injury?" If the death or injury is accidental enough or far enough removed from the defendant's triggering act, there's a reasonable doubt about the justice of blaming the defendant, and there's no proximate cause.

Take our pushing the rock example. Change the facts: On the way down the hill, the rock runs into a tree and gets lodged there. ("Damn! I guess that's the end of that fun prank.") A year later, a mild earthquake shakes the rock free and it finishes its roll down the hill, hitting and killing two people at the bottom who didn't see it coming. It's still true that except for my pushing the rock, it wouldn't have broken loose and killed the victims at the bottom.

But now, the no-brainer isn't a no-brainer anymore. Why? Because something else, facts in addition to my pushing, caused the deaths. We call this "something else" an **intervening cause,** and now we've got our proximate cause problem: Is it fair to punish me for something that's not *entirely* my fault? Most legal causation cases don't create problems, but the ones that do are serious crimes involving death, mutilation, injury, and occasionally property destruction and damage. So, we need to make sure you understand the problem.

There are lots of ways to approach the problem of intervening causes. We'll follow the approach of the distinguished Professors LaFave and Scott (1986, 281–282, and 288–294), whose work courts cite more than any other (even though the courts don't always identify and apply the approach as clearly as we'd like). Intervening cause cases arise out of intervening acts from four sources:

1. Victims' acts
2. Defendants' acts
3. Someone besides the defendant and victim
4. Nonhuman sources like the earthquake

Whatever the source of the intervening cause, it's important to distinguish between merely coincidental intervening acts and acts taken in response to defendants' acts (see Figure 4.1). Acts by *defendants* that "merely put the victim in a certain place at a certain time" that made it possible for the intervening cause to kill or hurt the victim are **coincidental intervening acts** (LaFave and Scott 1986, 288). For example, I shoot at Adam; Adam changes course and lightning strikes him. That's a coincidence, and coincidences break the chain of legal cause. There is one big exception: unless the criminal harm was foreseeable. If Joe stabs Lauren (triggering act), leaving her wounded by the side of a country road (coincidental intervening act), and then Abby drives by and runs over her and she dies, Abby has broken the causal link between Joe's stab and Lauren's death. That is, unless Joe could've predicted (foreseen) a car might come along and kill Lauren.

Responsive intervening acts are reactions to conditions created by defendants' triggering acts. These are usually acts by victims trying to avoid harm; bystanders helping to rescue; or medical professionals treating victims. Compared to coincidences, it's harder to break the causal link in responsive intervening act cases. For example, in *Whaley v. State* (1946), William Whaley forced his wife into their car, took her to an isolated spot, and severely beat her. Then he forced her back into the car and drove off toward her mother's house. Soon, according to Whaley's later admission, "I was mad and I guess I was cussing and I drew back like I was going to hit her with my fists and she jumped out of the car." Mrs. Whaley died the next day from injuries she got from hitting the pavement when she jumped (658). Mrs. Whaley's jump (responsive intervening act) didn't break the causal link between the triggering act (Whaley's raised fists) and her death because it was a normal response and Whaley should've foreseen it. According to the law, responsive intervening acts break the link in the causal chain only if they're abnormal *and* not foreseeable.

The California Supreme Court dealt with cause in fact, legal cause, and intervening cause in *People v. Armitage* (1987).

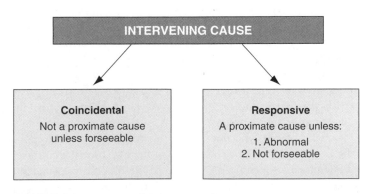

FIGURE 4.1 Intervening Cause

People v. Armitage
239 Cal.Rptr. 515 (Cal.App. 1987)

David James Armitage (defendant) was convicted of the felony of drunk boating causing death in violation of former Harbors and Navigation Code. The Court of Appeal affirmed the judgment.

SPARKS, J.

FACTS

On the evening of May 18, 1985, David Armitage and his friend, Peter Maskovich, were drinking in a bar in the riverside community of Freeport. They were observed leaving the bar around midnight. In the early morning hours, Armitage and Maskovich wound up racing Armitage's boat on the Sacramento River while both of them were intoxicated. The boat did not contain any personal flotation devices.

At about 3 A.M., Gary Bingham, who lived in a houseboat in a speed zone (5 miles per hour, no wake), was disturbed by a large wake. He went out to yell at the boaters and observed a small aluminum boat with two persons in it at the bend in the river. The boaters had the motor wide open, were zigzagging, and had no running lights on at the time. About the same time, Rodney and Susan Logan were fishing on the river near the Freeport Bridge when they observed an aluminum boat with two men in it coming up the river without running lights. The occupants were using loud and vulgar language and were operating the boat very fast and erratically.

James Snook lives near the Sacramento River in Clarksburg. Some time around 3 A.M., Armitage came to his door. Armitage was soaking wet and appeared quite intoxicated. He reported that he had flipped his boat over in the river and had lost his buddy. He said that at first he and his buddy had been hanging onto the overturned boat, but that his buddy swam for shore and he did not know whether he had made it. As it turned out, Maskovich did not make it; he drowned in the river.

Mr. Snook notified the authorities of the accident. Deputy Beddingfield arrived and spent some time with Armitage in attempting to locate the scene of the accident or the victim. Eventually, Deputy Beddingfield took Armitage to the sheriff's boat shed to meet with officers who normally work on the river. At the shed, they were met by Deputy Snyder. Deputy Snyder attempted to question the defendant about the accident, and Armitage stated that he

had been operating the boat at a high rate of speed and zigzagging until it capsized. Armitage also stated that he told the victim to hang onto the boat, but his friend ignored his warning and started swimming for the shore. As he talked to Armitage, the officer formed the opinion that he was intoxicated.

OPINION

...David Armitage (Defendant)...contends his actions were not the proximate cause of the death of the victim. In order to be guilty of felony drunk boating the defendant's act or omission must be the proximate cause of the ensuing injury or death. Armitage asserts that after his boat flipped over he and the victim were holding on to it and the victim, against his advice, decided to abandon the boat and try to swim to shore. According to Armitage, the victim's fatally reckless decision should exonerate him from criminal responsibility for his death.

We reject Armitage's contention. The question whether Armitage's acts or omissions criminally caused the victim's death is to be determined according to the ordinary principles governing proximate causation.... Proximate cause is clearly established where the act is directly connected with the resulting injury, with no intervening force operating. Armitage claims that the victim's attempt to swim ashore...constituted a break in the natural and continuous sequence arising from the unlawful operation of the boat. The claim cannot hold water....

A defendant may be criminally liable for a result directly caused by his act even if there is another contributing cause. "If an intervening cause is a normal and reasonably foreseeable result of defendant's original act the intervening... will not relieve defendant of liability."...An obvious illustration...is the victim's attempt to escape from a deadly attack or other danger in which he is placed by the defendant's wrongful act. Thus, it is only an unforeseeable intervening cause, an extraordinary and abnormal occurrence, which rises to the level of an exonerating...cause.

Consequently, in criminal law a victim's predictable effort to escape a peril created by the defendant is not considered a superseding cause of the ensuing injury or death. As leading commentators have explained it, an unreflective act in response to a peril created by defendant will not break a causal connection. In such a case, the actor has a choice, but his act is nonetheless unconsidered. "When defendant's conduct causes panic an act done under the influence of panic or extreme fear will not negate causal connection unless the reaction is wholly abnormal."

Here Armitage, through his misconduct, placed the intoxicated victim in the middle of a dangerous river in the early morning hours clinging to an overturned boat. The fact that the panic stricken victim recklessly abandoned the boat and tried to swim ashore was not a wholly abnormal reaction to the perceived peril of drowning. Just as "detached reflection cannot be demanded in the presence of an uplifted knife" (*Brown v. United States* (1921) 256 U.S. 335, 343 HOLMES, J.), neither can caution be required of a drowning man. Having placed the inebriated victim in peril, defendant cannot obtain exoneration by claiming the victim should have reacted differently or more prudently. In sum, the evidence establishes that defendant's acts and omissions were the proximate cause of the victim's death.

The judgment is affirmed.

Questions

1. State all of the facts relevant to determining whether Armitage was both the factual and legal cause of his friend Peter Maskovich's death.

2. List the facts that prove Armitage was the *factual* cause of Maskovich's death.

3. List the facts that prove Armitage was the *legal* cause of Maskovich's death.

4. Summarize the court's arguments and the facts it used to back up its conclusion that Maskovich's response was normal and foreseeable to Armitage.

5. Assume you're Armitage's lawyer. Argue that Maskovich's response broke the causal chain. Back up your answer with facts from the case.

EXPLORING PROXIMATE CAUSATION FURTHER

 Go to the Criminal Law 8e CD to read the full text versions of the cases featured here.

1. *Were His Actions in the Drag Race the Legal Cause of Death?*

FACTS

At about 2:30 A.M., Isaac Alejandro Velazquez met the deceased Adalberto Alvarez at a Hardee's restaurant in Hialeah, Florida. The two had never previously met but in the course of their conversation agreed to "drag race" each other with their automobiles. They accordingly left the restaurant and proceeded to set up a quarter-mile drag race course on a nearby public road that ran perpendicular to a canal alongside the Palmetto Expressway in Hialeah; a guardrail and a visible stop sign stood between the end of this road and the canal.

The two men began their drag race at the end of this road and proceeded away from the canal in a westerly direction for a quarter mile. Upon completing the course without incident, the deceased Alvarez suddenly turned his automobile 180 degrees around and proceeded east toward the starting line and the canal; Velazquez did the same and followed. Alvarez led and attained an estimated speed of 123 mph; he was not wearing a seat belt and subsequent investigation revealed that he had a blood alcohol level between .11 and .12. Velazquez, who had not been drinking, trailed Alvarez the entire distance back to the starting line and attained an estimated speed of 98 mph. As both drivers approached the end of the road, they applied their brakes, but neither could stop. Alvarez, who was about a car length ahead of Velazquez, crashed through the guardrail first and was propelled over the entire canal, landing on its far bank; he was thrown from his car upon impact, was pinned under his vehicle when it landed on him, and died instantly from the resulting injuries. Velazquez also crashed through the guardrail but landed in the canal where he was able to escape from his vehicle and swim to safety uninjured. Velazquez was charged with vehicular homicide. Were his actions in participating in the drag race the legal (proximate) cause of Alvarez's death?

DECISION AND REASONS

No, according to the appeals court:

> In unusual cases like this one, whether certain conduct is deemed to be the legal cause of a certain result is ultimately a policy question. The question of legal causation thus blends into the question of whether we are willing to hold a defendant responsible for a prohibited result. Or, stated differently, the issue is not causation; it is responsibility. In my opinion, policy considerations are against imposing responsibility for the death of a participant in a race on the surviving racer when his sole contribution to the death is the participation in the activity mutually agreed upon . . .
>
> It is clear that the defendant's reckless operation of a motor vehicle in participating in the "drag race" with

the deceased was, technically speaking, a cause-in-fact of the deceased's death under the "but for" test. But for the defendant's participation in the subject race, the deceased would not have recklessly raced his vehicle at all and thus would not have been killed. However, . . . the defendant's participation in the subject "drag race" was not a proximate cause of the deceased's death because, simply put, the deceased, in effect, killed himself by his own volitional reckless driving—and, consequently, it would be unjust to hold the defendant criminally responsible for this death. REVERSED AND REMANDED.

Velazquez v. State, 561 So.2d 347 (Fla.App. 1990)

2. *Who Legally Caused His Death?*

FACTS

Barry Kibbe and a companion, Roy Krall, met George Stafford in a bar on a cold winter night. They noticed Stafford had a lot of money and was drunk. When Stafford asked them for a ride, they agreed, having already decided to rob him. "The three men entered Kibbe's automobile and began the trip toward Canandaigua. Krall drove the car while Kibbe demanded that Stafford turn over any money he had. In the course of an exchange, Kibbe slapped Stafford several times, took his money, then compelled him to lower his trousers and to take off his shoes to be certain that Stafford had given up all his money. When they were satisfied that Stafford had no more money on his person, the defendants forced him to exit the Kibbe vehicle.

As he was thrust from the car, Stafford fell onto the shoulder of the rural two-lane highway on which they had been traveling. His trousers were still down around his ankles, his shirt was rolled up toward his chest, he was shoeless, and he had also been stripped of any outer clothing. Before the defendants pulled away, Kibbe placed Stafford's shoes and jacket on the shoulder of the highway. Although Stafford's eyeglasses were in Kibbe's vehicle, the defendants, either through inadvertence or perhaps by specific design, did not give them to him before they drove away.

Michael W. Blake, a college student, was driving at a reasonable speed when he saw Stafford in the middle of the road with his hands in the air. Blake could not stop in time to avoid striking Stafford and killing him. Did Kibbe and his companion or Blake legally cause Stafford's death?

DECISION AND REASONS

Who legally caused Stafford's death? Kibbe and his companion according to the court:

> To be a sufficiently direct cause of death so as to warrant the imposition of a criminal penalty . . . it is not necessary that the ultimate harm be intended by the actor. It will suffice if it can be said beyond a reasonable doubt, as indeed it can be here said, that the ultimate harm is something which should have been foreseen as being reasonably related to the acts of the accused.

> Applying these criteria to the defendants' actions, we conclude that their activities on the evening of December 30, 1970 were a sufficiently . . . proximate . . . cause of the death of George Stafford so as to warrant the imposition of criminal sanctions. In engaging in what may properly be described as a despicable course of action, Kibbe and Krall left a helplessly intoxicated man without his eye-glasses in a position from which, because of these attending circumstances, he could not extricate himself and whose condition was such that he could not even protect himself from the elements. The defendants do not dispute the fact that their conduct evinced a depraved indifference to human life which created a grave risk of death, but rather they argue that it was just as likely that Stafford would be miraculously rescued by a good samaritan. We cannot accept such an argument. There can be little doubt but that Stafford would have frozen to death in his state of undress had he remained on the shoulder of the road. The only alternative left to him was the highway, which in his condition, for one reason or another, clearly foreboded the probability of his resulting death.

> Under the conditions surrounding Blake's operation of his truck (i.e., the fact that he had his low beams on as the two cars approached; that there was no artificial lighting on the highway; and that there was insufficient time in which to react to Stafford's presence in his lane), we do not think it may be said that any . . . intervening wrongful act occurred to relieve the defendants from the directly foreseeable consequences of their actions. In short, we will not disturb the jury's determination that the prosecution proved beyond a reasonable doubt that their actions . . . "caused the death of another person."

> *People v. Kibbe,* 362 N.Y.S.2d 848 (1974)

SUMMARY

I. The principle of *mens rea*
- A. Serious crimes require both a criminal act (*actus reus*) and criminal intent (*mens rea*)
- B. Proof of *mens rea*
  1. We can't see intent or measure it by technological devices
  2. We infer intent from actors' actions (circumstantial evidence)
- C. Four kinds of *mens rea*
  1. *Mens rea* consist of four states of mind with different levels of culpability
  2. The four levels of culpability are
     - a. Purpose—acting on purpose and/or with the conscious object of causing harm
     - b. Knowledge—acting knowingly but without the conscious purpose or object of causing harm
     - c. Recklessness—acting with a conscious creation of a high risk of harm
     - d. Negligence—acting with an unconscious creation of a high risk of harm
- D. Strict liability offenses don't require culpability (i.e., *mens rea*)
  1. Justifications for strict liability
     - a. The offenses are a danger to public health, safety, and morals
     - b. Penalties are limited to fines as the only punishment
  2. Criticisms of strict liability
     - a. It violates the basic idea of punishment for culpability
     - b. It could be expanded to include more serious crimes

II. The principle of concurrence
- A. *Mens rea* triggers (comes before) the criminal act
- B. Criminal conduct causes the criminal harm

III. The principle of causation
- A. Applies only to crimes of criminal conduct causing criminal harm
- B. Two kinds of causation
  1. Factual ("but for" or "except for") cause
     - a. Boils down to an empirical question of fact
     - b. "Except for" or "but for" an act by the defendant that triggered a chain of events, would this criminal harm have occurred?
     - c. A necessary but not sufficient cause for proving causation
  2. Legal (proximate) cause
     - a. Based on a subjective question of fairness: Should the defendant be blamed and punished for this injury or death?
     - b. Two types of intervening acts in the chain between the triggering act of defendants and the end result of criminal harm
       - (1) Coincidental intervening acts break the causal chain unless they're foreseeable (predictable)
       - (2) Responsive intervening acts only break the causal chain if
         - (a) They're abnormal
         - (b) They're not foreseeable

REVIEW QUESTIONS

1. Explain the significance of "I didn't mean to" in the principle of *mens rea*.

2. Identify and explain the reasons why *mens rea* is a complex idea.

3. Identify the usual way prosecutors prove *mens rea*, and explain why prosecutors use this means.

4. List the four mental states that the seventy-nine definitions of criminal intent in the U.S. Criminal Code boiled down to.

5. List and define, from most to least culpable, the four mental states that make up the *Model Code*'s principle of *mens rea*.

6. Explain the difference between purpose and knowledge in the principle of *mens rea*.

7. Explain the difference between recklessness and negligence as they're used in the principle of *mens rea*.

8. Identify and describe the two prongs of the *Model Penal Code*'s test of recklessness.

9. Which prong of the *Model Penal Code*'s test of recklessness is called subjective, and which is called objective? Why are they called subjective and objective?

10. Explain how the test for negligence as it's used in the principle of *mens rea* is totally objective.

11. What kinds of crimes does strict liability apply to?

12. List the arguments for and against strict criminal liability.

13. Explain and give an example of how the principle of concurrence applies to crimes of criminal conduct and to crimes of causing a criminal harm.

14. In practice, what kinds of crimes does the principle of causation apply to?

15. Explain how factual cause is an objective cause and legal cause is a subjective question.

16. Explain the difference between coincidental and responsive intervening acts.

17. Identify and give an example of the one circumstance when a coincidence does *not* break the causal chain between defendants' triggering acts and criminal harm.

18. Identify and give examples of the circumstances when a responsive intervening act *does* break the causal link between defendants' triggering acts and criminal harm.

KEY TERMS

blameworthiness p. 87
principle of *mens rea* p. 87
circumstantial evidence p. 88
general intent p. 88

specific intent p. 88
transferred intent p. 88
constructive intent p. 88
purpose p. 90

knowledge p. 94
recklessness p. 97
negligence p. 98
strict liability p. 100

SUGGESTED READINGS

 Go to the Criminal Law 8e CD for Suggested Readings for this chapter.

THE COMPANION WEB SITE
FOR *CRIMINAL LAW,* EIGHTH EDITION

http://cj.wadsworth.com/samaha/crim_law8e

 Supplement your review of this chapter by going to the companion Web site to take one of the Tutorial Quizzes, use the flash cards to test your knowledge of the elements of various crimes and defenses, and check out the many other study aids you'll find there. You'll find valuable data and resources at your fingertips to help you study for that big exam or write that important paper.

5

Parties to Crime and Vicarious Liability

Chapter Main Points

- The doctrine of complicity (parties to crime) establishes when you can be held criminally liable for someone else's *conduct*.
- The doctrine of vicarious liability establishes what types of *relationships* can create criminal liability.
- Participants *before* and *during* the commission of crimes are guilty of the crime itself.
- Participants *after* the commission of crimes are guilty of a separate, less serious offense.
- The core idea in accomplice *actus reus* is that the accomplice took some positive action to aid in the commission of a crime.
- The *mens rea* of complicity varies; depending on the state it may be purpose, knowledge, recklessness, or negligence.
- The core idea of accessory liability is that it's not as blameworthy to help someone else escape prosecution and punishment as it is to participate in the crime itself.
- *Mens rea* in business crimes is hard to prove because of the complexity of organizations and decision making.
- Vicarious liability raises due process constitutional questions and policy questions about its effectiveness.
- Owners of cars are vicariously liable for operators' parking tickets because of the owner-operator relationship.
- Vicarious liability based on the parent-child relationship grew out of public fear, frustration, and anger over juvenile crime and the "parents who can't control their kids."

Was She Guilty of First-Degree Murder?

When David Hoffman's wife, Carol, refused to make love with him, he lost his temper and choked her to death. He called down to the basement to wake his mother, asking her to come upstairs to sit on the living room couch. From there she would be able to see the kitchen, bathroom, and bedroom doors and could stop his daughter if she awoke and tried to use the bathroom. His mother came upstairs to lie on the couch. In the meantime, David had moved the body to the bathtub. His mother was aware that while she was in the living room her son was dismembering the body, but she turned her head away so that she could not see. After dismembering the body and putting it in bags, Hoffman cleaned the bathroom, took the body to a lake, and disposed of it. On returning home, he told his mother to wash the cloth covers from the bathroom toilet and tank, which she did. David fabricated a story about Carol leaving the house the previous night after an argument, and his mother agreed to corroborate it. David phoned the police with a missing person report and during the ensuing searches and interviews with the police, he and his mother continued to tell the fabricated story. ◆

The principle of *actus reus* stands on the fundamental idea that we punish people for what they *do*, not for who they are. The principle of *mens rea* stands on the fundamental idea that we can only punish people we can blame. This chapter affirms another basic idea of our criminal law: that one person can be liable for someone else's crimes. This liability arises in two ways:

1. When an actor is liable for someone else's *conduct* (**parties to crime** or **complicity**)

2. When the nature of the *relationship* between two people creates liability (**vicarious liability**)

The **doctrine of complicity** (parties to crime) establishes when you can be criminally liable for someone else's *conduct*. The **doctrine of vicarious liability** establishes when you can be criminally liable because of a *relationship*. The most common of these relationships are business relationships, like employer-employee, corporation-manager, buyer-seller, producer-consumer, and service provider–recipient. But vicarious liability can also arise in other situations, such as making the owner of a car liable for the driver's traffic violations and holding parents liable for their minor children's crimes.

PARTIES TO CRIME

At common law, there were four parties to crime:

1. *Principals in the first degree*. Persons who actually commit the crime
2. *Principals in the second degree*. Persons present when the crimes are committed (lookouts and getaway drivers)
3. *Accessories before the fact*. Persons not present when the crimes are committed but who helped before the crimes were committed (for example, someone who provided a weapon used in a murder)
4. *Accessories after the fact*. Persons who help after the crimes are committed (harboring a fugitive)

These distinctions used to be important because of a common-law rule that the government couldn't try accomplices until principals in the first degree were convicted. This ban on trying accomplices before these principals were convicted applied even if there was absolute proof of guilt. Why? Probably, because during that time, all felonies were capital offenses. But, as the number of capital crimes shrank, so did the need for the complicated law of principals and accessories.

Today, there are two parties to crime:

1. *Accomplices.* Participants *before* and *during* the commission of crimes
2. *Accessories.* Participants *after* crimes are committed

Participation *Before* and *During* the Commission of a Crime

All participants before and during the commission of a crime (accomplices) are prosecuted for the crime itself (accomplices to murder are prosecuted as murderers). So, participation before and during a crime (accomplice liability) is a very serious business, because the punishment for being an accomplice is the same as for the person who actually committed the crime. Participation after crimes are committed (accessory liability) is prosecuted for separate, minor offenses (accessory to murder). Accessories are punished for misdemeanors, a much less serious offense because accessories are looked at as obstructors of justice, not as felons.

We need to clear up a problem before we get further into accomplice liability. Accomplices are often confused with co-conspirators (Chapter 6) because both accomplice and conspiracy cases have more than one participant. But, they're two completely different crimes. **Conspiracy** is an agreement to commit some other crime. A conspiracy to commit murder is not murder; it's the lesser offense of agreeing to commit murder (Chapter 6). Participating in a murder is the crime of murder itself. For example, two people agree to commit a murder. They go, buy a gun, and drive together to the victim's house. One acts as a lookout, while the other kills the victim. They drive away together. They've committed conspiracy to commit murder *and* murder itself.

The rule that the crime of conspiracy and the crime the conspirators agree to commit are separate offenses is called the *Pinkerton* **rule.** The name comes from a leading

U.S. Supreme Court case, *Pinkerton v. U.S* (1946). The two Pinkerton brothers conspired to evade taxes. They were found guilty of both conspiracy to evade taxes and tax evasion itself. According to Justice Douglas, who wrote the opinion for the Court, "It has been long and consistently recognized by the Court that the commission of the...offense and a conspiracy to commit it are separate and distinct offenses (643)."

Actus Reus of Accomplice Liability

You'll usually see words borrowed from the old common law of principals and accessories to define **accomplice *actus reus*** in modern accomplice statutes. The use of words like "aid," "abet," "assist," "counsel," procure," "hire," or "induce" is widespread. The meaning of these words boils down to this core idea: The actor took "some positive act in aid of the commission of the offense." How much aid is enough? It's not always easy to decide, but here are a few acts that definitely qualify:

- Providing guns, supplies, or other instruments of crime
- Serving as a lookout
- Driving a getaway car
- Sending the victim to the principal
- Preventing warnings from getting to the victim (American Law Institute 1953, 43)

Words are also acts that can amount to accomplice *actus reus* if they encourage and approve the commission of the crime.

Mere presence at the scene of a crime isn't enough to satisfy the *actus reus* requirement. According to the **mere presence rule,** even presence at the scene of a crime followed by flight is not enough action to satisfy the *actus reus* requirement of accomplice liability. In *Bailey v. U.S.* (1969), Bailey spent most of the afternoon shooting craps with another man. Then, when a man carrying cash walked by, Bailey's craps partner pulled a gun and robbed the man with the cash. Both Bailey and the other man fled the scene. Bailey was caught; the other man never was. The court held that although flight from the scene of a crime can be taken into account, it's not enough to prove accomplice *actus reus*. According to the court:

> We no longer hold tenable the notion that "the wicked flee when no man pursueth, but the righteous are as bold as a lion." The proposition that "one flees shortly after a criminal act is committed or when he is accused of something does so because he feels some guilt concerning the act" is not absolute as a legal doctrine "since it is a matter of common knowledge that men who are entirely innocent do sometimes fly from the scene of a crime through fear of being apprehended as guilty parties or from an unwillingness to appear as witnesses." (1114)

Be aware that there's one major exception to the mere presence rule. When defendants have a legal duty to act, presence alone is enough. In *State v. Walden* (1982), George Hoskins beat Aleen Walden's one-year-old son Lamont "repeatedly over an extended period of time" with a leather belt until he was bloody. Walden "looked on the entire time the beating took place but did not say anything or do anything to stop the 'Bishop' [Hoskins] from beating Lamont or to otherwise deter such conduct (783)." A jury found Walden guilty as an accomplice to assault. On appeal, the court said that

> the trial court properly allowed the jury...to consider a verdict of guilty of assault...upon a theory of aiding and abetting, solely on the ground that the defendant was present when

her child was brutally beaten. . . . A person who so aids or abets under another in the commission of a crime is equally guilty with that other person as a principal. (787)

One final point about accomplice *actus reus:* Actions taken after crimes are committed aren't themselves accomplice *actus reus,* but juries can use participation after the crime to prove defendants participated before or during the commission of the crime. In the grisly murder case, *State v. Ulvinen* (1981), the Minnesota Supreme Court dealt with all these problems connected with Carol Hoffman's murder:

1. Words of encouragement before and during the commission of the crime

2. Accomplices not present when the crime was committed

3. Inferring participation *before* and *during* the commission of the crime from actions to help *after* the commission of the crime

---

CASE | *Was She an Accomplice to Murder?*

State v. Ulvinen
313 N.W.2d 425 (Minn. 1981)

Helen Ulvinen was convicted of first degree murder pursuant to Minn. Stat. § 609.05, subd. 1 (1980), which imposes criminal liability on one who "intentionally aids, advises, hires, counsels, or conspires with or otherwise procures" another to commit a crime. The Minnesota Supreme Court reversed.

OTIS, J.

FACTS

Carol Hoffman, Helen Ulvinen's (appellant's) daughter-in-law, was murdered late on the evening of August 10th or the very early morning of August 11th by her husband, David Hoffman. She and David had spent an amicable evening together playing with their children, and when they went to bed David wanted to make love to his wife. However, when she refused him he lost his temper and began choking her. While he was choking her he began to believe he was "doing the right thing" and that to get "the evil out of her" he had to dismember her body.

After his wife was dead, David called down to the basement to wake his mother, asking her to come upstairs to sit on the living room couch. From there she would be able to see the kitchen, bathroom, and bedroom doors and could stop the older child if she awoke and tried to use the bathroom. Mrs. Ulvinen didn't respond at first but after being called once, possibly twice more, she came upstairs to lie on the couch. In the meantime David had moved the body

to the bathtub. Mrs. Ulvinen was aware that while she was in the living room her son was dismembering the body but she turned her head away so that she could not see.

After dismembering the body and putting it in bags, Hoffman cleaned the bathroom, took the body to Weaver Lake and disposed of it. On returning home he told his mother to wash the cloth covers from the bathroom toilet and tank, which she did. David fabricated a story about Carol leaving the house the previous night after an argument, and Helen agreed to corroborate it. David phoned the police with a missing person report and during the ensuing searches and interviews with the police, he and his mother continued to tell the fabricated story.

On August 19, 1980, David confessed to the police that he had murdered his wife. In his statement he indicated that not only had his mother helped him cover up the crime but she had known of his intent to kill his wife that night. After hearing Hoffman's statement the police arrested Mrs. Ulvinen and questioned her with respect to her part in the cover up. Police typed up a two-page statement which she read and signed. The following day a detective questioned her further regarding events surrounding the crime, including her knowledge that it was planned.

Mrs. Ulvinen's relationship with her daughter-in-law had been a strained one. She moved in with the Hoffmans on July 26, two weeks earlier to act as a live-in babysitter for their two children. Carol was unhappy about having her move in and told friends that she hated Helen, but she told both David and his mother that they could try the arrangement to see how it worked. On the morning of the murder Helen told her son that she was going to move out of the Hoffman residence because "Carol had been so nasty to me." In his statement to the police David reported the conversation that morning as follows:

...Sunday morning I went downstairs and my mom was in the bedroom reading the newspaper and she had tears in her eyes, and she said in a very frustrated voice, "I've got to find another house." She said, "Carol don't want me here," and she said, "I probably shouldn't have moved in here." And I said then, "Don't let what Carol said hurt you. It's going to take a little more period of readjustment for her." Then I told mom that I've got to do it tonight so that there can be peace in this house.

Q: What did you tell your mom that you were going to have to do that night?

A: I told my mom I was going to have to put her to sleep.

Q: Dave, will you tell us exactly what you told your mother that morning, to the best of your recollection?

A: I said I'm going to have to choke her tonight and I'll have to dispose of her body so that it will never be found. That's the best of my knowledge.

Q: What did your mother say when you told her that?

A: She just—she looked at me with very sad eyes and just started to weep. I think she said something like "it will be for the best."

David spent the day fishing with a friend of his. When he got home that afternoon he had another conversation with his mother. She told him at that time about a phone conversation Carol had had in which she discussed taking the children and leaving home. David told the police that during the conversation with his mother that afternoon he told her "Mom, tonight's got to be the night."

Q: When you told your mother, "Tonight's got to be the night," did your mother understand that you were going to kill Carol later that evening?

A: She thought I was just kidding her about doing it. She didn't think I could....

Q: Why didn't your mother think that you could do it?

A: ...Because for some time I had been telling her I was going to take Carol scuba diving and make it look like an accident.

Q: And she said?

A: And she always said, "Oh, you're just kidding me."...

Q: But your mother knew you were going to do it that night?

A: I think my mother sensed that I was really going to do it that night.

Q: Why do you think your mother sensed you were really going to do it that night?

A: Because when I came home and she told me what had happened at the house, and I told her, "Tonight's got to be the night," I think she said, again I'm not certain, that "it would be the best for the kids."

OPINION

...It is well-settled in this state that presence, companionship, and conduct before and after the offense are circumstances from which a person's participation in the criminal intent may be inferred. The evidence is undisputed that appellant was asleep when her son choked his wife. She took no active part in the dismembering of the body but came upstairs to intercept the children, should they awake, and prevent them from going into the bathroom.

She cooperated with her son by cleaning some items from the bathroom and corroborating David's story to prevent anyone from finding out about the murder. She is insulated by statute from guilt as an accomplice after-the-fact for such conduct because of her relation as a parent of the offender. See Minn. Stat. § 609.495, subd. 2 (1980). The jury might well have considered appellant's conduct in sitting by while her son dismembered his wife so shocking that it deserved punishment. Nonetheless, these subsequent actions do not succeed in transforming her behavior prior to the crime to active instigation and encouragement. Minn.Stat. § 609.05, subd. 1 (1980) implies a high level of activity on the part of an aider and abettor in the form of conduct that encourages another to act. Use of terms such as "aids," "advises," and "conspires" requires something more of a person than mere inaction to impose liability as a principal.

The evidence presented to the jury at best supports a finding that appellant passively acquiesced in her son's plan to kill his wife. The jury might have believed that David told his mother of his intent to kill his wife that night and that she neither actively discouraged him nor told anyone in time to prevent the murder. Her response that "it would be the best for the kids" or "it will be the best" was not, however, active encouragement or instigation. There is no evidence that her remark had any influence on her son's decision to kill his wife. Minn.Stat. § 609.05, subd. 1 (1980), imposes liability for actions which affect the principal, encouraging him to take a course of action which he might not otherwise have taken.

The state has not proved beyond a reasonable doubt that appellant was guilty of anything but passive approval.

However morally reprehensible it may be to fail to warn someone of their impending death, our statutes do not make such an omission a criminal offense. We note that mere knowledge of a contemplated crime or failure to disclose such information without evidence of any further involvement in the crime does not make that person liable as a party to the crime under any state's statutes. . . .

David told many people besides appellant of his intent to kill his wife but no one took him seriously. He told a co-worker, approximately three times a week that he was going to murder his wife, and confided two different plans for doing so. Another co-worker heard him tell his plan to cut Carol's air hose while she was scuba diving, making her death look accidental, but did not believe him. Two or three weeks before the murder, David told a friend of his that he and Carol were having problems and he expected Carol "to have an accident sometime." None of these people has a duty imposed by law, to warn the victim of impending danger, whatever their moral obligation may be. . . .

Her conviction must be reversed.

Questions

1. List all the facts (including words) surrounding Mrs. Ulvinen's behavior *before* or *during* the murder that might make her an accomplice.

2. List all the facts *after* the murder that a jury could infer proved Mrs. Ulvinen participated before or during the murder itself.

3. According to the court, why isn't Mrs. Ulvinen guilty of murder?

4. Do you agree with the court that however morally reprehensible her behavior, she nonetheless was not an accomplice? Defend your answer.

EXPLORING ACCOMPLICE *ACTUS REUS* FURTHER

 Go to the Criminal Law 8e CD to read the full text version of the case featured here.

Did He Participate in a "Hate" Crime?

FACTS

In July 1998, Mr. Whitney and three or four others gathered at the home of Mr. Whitney's brother, Anthony. An African-American teenager, Kenneth Green, passed by on the sidewalk, and the men began yelling racial epithets at him. Mr. Green returned a few hours later and knocked on the door to Anthony's house. Mr. Whitney answered the door, and Mr. Green punched him in the face, leaving him with a black eye.

A week later, Mr. Whitney, Anthony, Raymond Roland, and Paul Geiger were gathered at Anthony's house. The men were drinking heavily and discussing the prior incident with Mr. Green. Mr. Green lived in the neighborhood, just down the street from Anthony with an African-American family named the Madkins. At some point during this gathering, the idea arose to burn a cross in the Madkins' yard.

Following the discussion, Anthony, Mr. Roland, and Mr. Geiger proceeded to Anthony's garage and nailed two boards together to form a cross. Mr. Whitney passed in and out of the garage but did not aid in building the cross. Anthony and Mr. Roland then carried the cross down the street toward the Madkins' home. However, there were people outside, so they left the cross in an alley and returned to Anthony's home.

Next, all four men decided to drive to the fairgrounds to watch a demolition derby. Shortly after they arrived, they changed their minds, bought more alcohol, and drove back to Anthony's house. When they arrived back at Anthony's, Mr. Whitney stayed in the house while Anthony, Mr. Roland, and Mr. Geiger retrieved the cross and a gas can. Mr. Geiger watched as Mr. Roland and Anthony stuck the cross in the Madkins' front yard and lit it on fire. The men ran back to the house and informed Mr. Whitney they had burned the cross in the Madkins' yard. Mr. Roland described Mr. Whitney's reaction as, "Just, okay. Cool, it's done."

Later, Mr. Whitney told investigators he was not aware of the cross burning until the following day, when his landlady informed him. However, eventually, Mr. Roland, at the urging of his wife, confessed to the Kansas City Fire Department and gave a statement regarding everything he knew about the incident. The statement implicated all four men. The government charged Mr. Roland, Mr. Whitney, and Anthony Whitney . . . with violating 42 U.S.C. § 3631(a), interference with housing rights on the basis of race. . . . Mr. Roland and Anthony entered into plea agreements. Mr. Whitney went to trial, and Mr. Roland and Anthony testified on behalf of the government pursuant to their plea agreements. A jury convicted Mr. Whitney on both counts. The district court sentenced him to twenty-one month terms of imprisonment on each count to run concurrently. Did Whitney do enough to satisfy the *actus reus* of accomplice liability?

DECISION AND REASONS

Yes, said the 10th Circuit U.S. Court of Appeals.

At trial, defense counsel moved for a judgment of acquittal on the charge of aiding and abetting a violation of § 3631(a), arguing there was no evidence that Mr. Whitney "did anything." The court denied the motion. On appeal, Mr. Whitney contends the government did not prove he "did something to help or to encourage the crime with the intent that it be committed." He emphasizes that "mere presence at the scene of the crime, even with knowledge that a crime is being committed is not enough." In support of his argument that the evidence of aiding and abetting was insufficient, he also points to the fact that the jury asked the court during deliberations to define "encouragement." We are not persuaded by Mr. Whitney's arguments....

To be guilty of aiding and abetting the commission of a crime, the defendant must willfully associate himself with the criminal venture.... Participation in the criminal venture may be established by circumstantial evidence and the level of participation may be of "rela-tively slight moment." Further, "one may become an accomplice ... by words or gestures of encouragement, or by providing others with the plan for the crime." Conduct of the defendant or special circumstances may justify an inference that the defendant has associated himself with the criminal objective."

Here, the government presented evidence that Mr. Whitney used racial epithets when referring to Mr. Green and the Madkins, and discussed cross burning as a symbol of hatred towards African-Americans on the afternoon prior to the crime. A juror could reasonably find these were "words or gestures of encouragement."

There was also testimony from one of the co-defendants ... that Mr. Whitney initiated the idea to burn the cross in the Madkins' yard. Confronted with this testimony, the jury reasonably could have inferred he "provided others with a plan for the crime." Accordingly, there was sufficient evidence to support Mr. Whitney's conviction of aiding and abetting a violation of § 3631(a)....

U.S. v. Whitney, 229 F.3d 1296 (10th Cir. 2000)

Mens Rea of Accomplice Liability

MY FRIEND STEVE: Lend me your gun.

ME: What for?

STEVE: So I can rob the grocery store.

ME: OK. But only if you give me half the take.

My intent is clear in this scenario (as it is in most complicity cases): My purpose in lending Steve my gun is to help him rob the grocery store, and I definitely want the robbery to succeed. So, we can say my state of mind is purposeful; I am committing intentional acts for the very purposes of (1) helping Steve *and* (2) committing robbery.

Cases like this scenario don't give courts much trouble. Others do—like knowingly helping someone but not for the purpose of benefiting from the criminal venture in these examples:

- I lease an apartment to someone I know is going to use it for prostitution.

- A gun dealer sells me a gun she knows I'm going to use to shoot someone.

- A telephone company provides service to a customer it knows is going to use it for illegal gambling.

- A farmer leases 200 acres of farmland to a renter he knows is going to grow marijuana for sale. (American Law Institute 1985 I:2, 316)

Early decisions said that knowingly helping someone was enough to prove the *mens rea* required for accomplice liability. In one Fourth Circuit U.S. Court of Appeals case (*Backun v. U.S.* 1940), Max Backun sold silver he knew was stolen to Zucker. But Backun didn't sell the silver for the purpose of sharing any profits with Zucker. Still, according to the court, knowingly selling the stolen property was good enough:

> Guilt...depends, not on having a stake in the outcome of crime...but on aiding and assisting the perpetrators; and those who make a profit by furnishing to criminals, whether by sale or otherwise, the means to carry on their nefarious undertakings aid them just as truly as if they were actual partners with them, having a stake in the fruits of their enterprise. To say that the sale of goods is a normally lawful transaction is beside the point. The seller may not ignore the purpose for which the purchase is made if he is advised of that purpose, or wash his hands of the aid that he has given the perpetrator of a felony by the plea that he has merely made a sale of merchandise. One who sells a gun to another knowing that he is buying it to commit a murder, would hardly escape conviction as an...[accomplice] to the murder by showing that he received full price for the gun; and no difference in principle can be drawn between such a case and any other case of a seller who knows that the purchaser intends to use the goods which he is purchasing in the commission of felony.... (637)

In another very famous federal case (*U.S. v. Peoni* 1938, 401), decided by the very famous and enormously respected Judge Learned Hand, the outcome was the opposite. In that case, Joseph Peoni sold counterfeit money to Dorsey in the Bronx. Dorsey was caught trying to pass the fake money in Brooklyn. Peoni was indicted as an accomplice to Dorsey. At the trial, the prosecution relied on the words "aids, abets, counsels, commands, induces, or procures" in the U.S. Criminal Code's accomplice statute. The prosecution argued that Peoni knew Dorsey possessed counterfeit money and that knowledge was enough to convict him. The jury convicted Peoni. But, on appeal, Judge Hand didn't buy the argument. According to Judge Hand, if someone were suing Peoni for damages, knowledge was good enough. But, this was a *criminal* case, where all the words in the statute

> demand that he in some sort associate himself with the venture, that he participate in it as in something that he wishes to bring about, that he seek by his action to make it succeed. All the words used—even the most colorless, "abet"—carry an implication of purposive attitude towards it. (402)

U.S. v. Peoni is cited over and over again as defining the *mens rea* of accomplice liability.

If only it were that clear; but it's not. In a 2002 survey of just the cases in federal courts, Assistant U.S. Attorney Baruch Weiss (2002) cites "a few examples" illustrating the confusion:

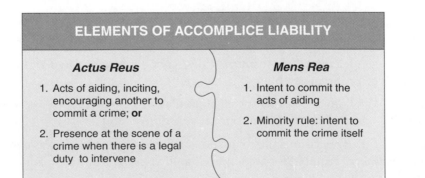

ELEMENTS OF ACCOMPLICE LIABILITY

Actus Reus

1. Acts of aiding, inciting, encouraging another to commit a crime; **or**

2. Presence at the scene of a crime when there is a legal duty to intervene

Mens Rea

1. Intent to commit the acts of aiding

2. Minority rule: intent to commit the crime itself

Is simple knowledge enough? Yes, said the Supreme Court... in 1870; no, said Judge Learned Hand in... 1938; yes, implied the Supreme Court in 1947; no, said the Supreme Court in 1949; yes, if it is accompanied by an act that substantially facilitates the commission of the underlying offense, said the Supreme Court in 1961; usually, said the Second Circuit in 1962; only if knowledge is enough for the underlying offense, said the Second Circuit in another case in 1962; sometimes, said the Seventh Circuit in 1985; always, implied the Seventh Circuit in 1995; no, said the Second Circuit in 1995 and the Seventh Circuit in 1998. (1351–1352)

Further confusion arises because both recklessness and negligence can satisfy the *mens rea* requirement. For example, if participants can predict that aiding and abetting one crime might reasonably lead to another crime, they're guilty of both. The court dealt with this problem in *People v. Poplar* (1970).

CASE | *Did He Have Accomplice Mens Rea?*

People v. Poplar
173 N.W.2d 732 (1970)

Marathon Poplar, the defendant, was charged as an aider and abettor of breaking and entering and of assault with intent to commit murder. He moved for a directed verdict on both charges, claiming that there wasn't enough evidence to submit the case to the jury. The motions were denied. Poplar was found guilty on both counts by a jury in the Circuit Court, Genesee. The Court of Appeals affirmed.

GILLIS, J.

FACTS

Alfred Williams and Clifford Lorrick broke into and entered the Oak Park recreation building in Flint in the early morning of December 3, 1964. When the manager of the building discovered the two men, Williams shot him in the face with a shotgun. Poplar, the defendant, allegedly acted as a lookout. Williams was tried as a codefendant and was convicted, along with this defendant, of breaking and entering and of assault with intent to commit murder. Williams' application for a delayed appeal was denied by this Court on April 18, 1967.

Lorrick pled guilty to breaking and entering on January 25, 1965, and testified for the prosecution at defendant's trial. He stated that he met defendant and Williams in a bar the night before the breaking and entering and left with them and two others. The five men allegedly drove around for a while before stopping to pick up some tools. They then took the tools and placed them in back of the bowling alley. An unsuccessful attempt to enter was made

at that time. The group continued to drive around and during that time a shotgun that was in the car accidentally discharged, blowing a hole in the windshield. Just before the actual breaking and entering, the defendant, after getting out of the car with Lorrick and Williams, proceeded to a house directly across from the bowling alley. Lorrick testified that defendant went to see if anybody was watching.

Poplar took the stand and testified that he was in no way involved in the plans of Lorrick and Williams. He stated that the purpose of his going to the house across the street was to seek a friend who he thought would help him find employment.

OPINION

... It [was not] error for the trial court to deny defendant's motion for directed verdict on the issue of whether defendant (Poplar) aided and abetted in the breaking and entering by acting as a lookout. The circumstances leading up to the offense, coupled with Lorrick's testimony, present sufficient evidence which, if believed by the jury, would support a conviction under the statute.

... A more difficult question is whether Poplar may be found guilty, as an aider and abettor, of assault with intent to commit murder. Where a crime requires the existence of a specific intent, an alleged aider and abettor cannot be held as a principal unless he himself possessed the required intent or unless he aided and abetted in the perpetration of the crime knowing that the actual perpetrator had the required intent.... It is the knowledge of the wrongful purpose of the actor plus the encouragement provided by the aider and abettor that makes the latter equally guilty. Although the guilt of the aider and abettor is dependent upon the actor's crime, the criminal intent of the aider and abettor is presumed from his actions with knowledge of the actor's wrongful purpose.

There was no evidence that Poplar harbored any intent to commit murder. Therefore, knowledge of the intent of Williams to kill the deceased is a necessary element to constitute Poplar a principal. This, however, may be established either by direct or circumstantial evidence from which knowledge of the intent may be inferred.

A typical case of this kind is one where, as here, a crime not specifically within the common intent and purpose is committed during an escape. Convictions for aiding and abetting such crimes have been carefully scrutinized.... Whether the crime committed was fairly within the scope of the common unlawful enterprise is a question of fact for the jury.

In the present case, the evidence tends to show that the gun with which the victim was shot was removed from the trunk of the car to the front seat. It is not clear whether Poplar was present when the gun was moved but he was aware of its presence inside the car. Since the record also fails to reveal whether or not defendant knew that the gun was taken into the bowling alley, the question is whether it was proper for the jury to infer from the circumstantial evidence that the defendant entertained the requisite intent to render him liable as a principal for assault with intent to commit murder.

In our opinion the jury could reasonably infer from the defendant's knowledge of the fact that a shotgun was in the car that he was aware of the fact that his companions might use the gun if they were discovered committing the burglary or in making their escape. If the jury drew that inference, then it could properly conclude that the use of the gun was fairly within the scope of the common unlawful enterprise and that the defendant was criminally responsible for the use by his confederates of the gun in effectuating their escape.

AFFIRMED.

Questions

1. List all of the relevant facts to determine Poplar's mental state.

2. On the basis of these facts, did Poplar intend to kill? Did he do so knowingly? Recklessly? Negligently?

3. According to the Court, what's the *mens rea* required for accomplice liability?

4. In light of Poplar's *mens rea*, does it make sense to hold him criminally liable for breaking and entering and assault with intent to murder? Defend your answer.

EXPLORING ACCOMPLICE *MENS REA* FURTHER

Go to the Criminal Law 8e CD to read the full text versions of the cases featured here.

1. *Did He Have the "Mens Rea" of an Accomplice to Criminal Homicide?*

FACTS

Harry Wren was driving his friend Steve Lewis's car. On the way from Atkins to Morrilton, they purchased twelve cans of beer and drank a considerable amount of beer and gin from 7 P.M. until immediately before colliding head on with another car. Occupants of both automobiles were seriously injured, and Mrs. Pounds, driver of the other car, died from her injuries three days later. Was Lewis guilty of criminal homicide?

DECISION AND REASONS

The court said yes:

> If the owner of a dangerous instrumentality like an automobile knowingly puts that instrumentality in the immediate control of a careless and reckless driver, sits by his side, and permits him without protest so recklessly and negligently to operate the car as to cause the death of another, he is as much responsible as the man at the wheel.
>
> *Lewis et al. v. State*, 251 S.W.2d 490 (Ark. 1952)

2. *Can He Intend to Commit "Negligent" Homicide?*

FACTS

Michael Foster believed Bill had raped Foster's girlfriend. Foster beat Bill up. He, then, handed his friend Otha a knife, telling him to keep Bill from leaving until he returned with his girlfriend to verify the rape. After Foster left, Otha got nervous and stabbed Bill, who died from the stab wounds. Was Foster an accomplice to negligent homicide?

DECISION AND REASONS

Yes, said the court. Even though Foster didn't intend to kill Bill, he was negligent with respect to the death; he should've foreseen that Otha, armed with a knife, might have stabbed Bill.

> *State v. Foster*, 522 A.2d 277 (Conn. 1987)

◆   ◆   ◆

Participation *After* the Commission of a Crime

At common law, accessories after the fact were punished like accomplices; that is, they were treated as if they'd committed the crime itself. So, if you gave a burglar a place to hide after he'd committed burglary, you were guilty of burglary, too. But, accessories aren't really burglars; they don't come on the scene until the burglary's over. That's why they used to be called "accessories after the fact." And (so the thinking goes), it's not as bad to help someone who's already committed a crime as it is to help him commit the crime in the first place. Modern statutes have reduced the punishment to fit this less serious offense. Accessory after the fact (now called simply, *accessory*) is now a separate offense, usually a misdemeanor. Sometimes, it's even got a different name, like obstructing justice, interfering with prosecution, and aiding in escape.

Most accessory-after-the-fact statutes have four elements, one *actus reus*, two *mens rea*, and one circumstance element:

1. The accessory personally aided the person who committed the crime (*actus reus* element).

2. The accessory knew the felony was committed (*mens rea* element).

3. The accessory aided the person who committed the crime for the purpose of hindering the prosecution of that person (*mens rea* element).

4. Someone besides the accessory actually committed a felony (circumstance element).

The Supreme Court of Louisiana dealt with these elements under Louisiana's accessory-after-the-fact statute in the bizarre case of *State v. Chism* (1983).

CASE | *Was He an Accessory After the Fact?*

State v. Chism
436 So.2d 464 (La. 1983)

Brian Chism (Defendant) was convicted before the First Judicial District Court, Caddo Parish, of being an accessory after the fact, and was sentenced to three years in parish prison, with three and one-half years suspended, and defendant appealed. The Supreme Court affirmed the conviction, vacated the sentence, and remanded the case for resentencing.

DENNIS, J.

FACTS

On the evening of August 26, 1981 in Shreveport, Tony Duke gave the defendant, Brian Chism, a ride in his automobile. Brian Chism was impersonating a female, and Duke was apparently unaware of Chism's disguise. After a brief visit at a friend's house the two stopped to pick up some beer at the residence of Chism's grandmother. Chism's one-legged uncle, Ira Lloyd, joined them, and the three continued on their way, drinking as Duke drove the automobile. When Duke expressed a desire to have sexual relations with Chism, Lloyd announced that he wanted to find his ex-wife Gloria for the same purpose. Shortly after midnight, the trio arrived at the St. Vincent Avenue Church of Christ and persuaded Gloria Lloyd to come outside. As Ira Lloyd stood outside the car attempting to persuade Gloria to come with them, Chism and Duke hugged and kissed on the front seat as Duke sat behind the steering wheel.

Gloria and Ira Lloyd got into an argument, and Ira stabbed Gloria with a knife several times in the stomach and once in the neck. Gloria's shouts attracted the attention of two neighbors, who unsuccessfully tried to prevent Ira from pushing Gloria into the front seat of the car alongside Chism and Duke. Ira Lloyd climbed into the front seat also, and Duke drove off. One of the bystanders testified that she could not be sure but she thought she saw Brian's foot on the accelerator as the car left.

Lloyd ordered Duke to drive to Willow Point, near Cross Lake. When they arrived Chism and Duke, under Lloyd's direction, removed Gloria from the vehicle and placed her on some high grass on the side of the roadway, near a wood line. Ira was unable to help the two because his wooden leg had come off. Afterwards, as Lloyd requested, the two drove off, leaving Gloria with him.

There was no evidence that Chism or Duke protested, resisted or attempted to avoid the actions which Lloyd ordered them to take. Although Lloyd was armed with a knife, there was no evidence that he threatened either of his companions with harm.

Duke proceeded to drop Chism off at a friend's house, where he changed to male clothing. He placed the blood-stained women's clothes in a trash bin.

Afterward, Chism went with his mother to the police station at 1:15 A.M. He gave the police a complete statement, and took the officers to the place where Gloria had been left with Ira Lloyd. The police found Gloria's body in some tall grass several feet from that spot.

An autopsy indicated that stab wounds had caused her death. Chism's discarded clothing disappeared before the police arrived at the trash bin.

OPINION

According to Louisiana statute 14:25,

> An accessory after the fact is any person who, after the commission of a felony, shall harbor, conceal, or aid the offender, knowing or having reasonable ground to believe that he has committed the felony, and with the intent that he may avoid or escape from arrest, trial, conviction, or punishment....

> Whoever becomes an accessory after the fact shall be fined not more than five hundred dollars, or imprisoned, with or without hard labor, for not more than five years, or both; provided that in no case shall his punishment be greater than one-half of the maximum provided by law for a principal offender.

La.R.S. 14:25

Chism appealed from his conviction and sentence and argues that the evidence was not sufficient to support the judgment. Consequently, in reviewing the defendant's assigned error, we must determine whether, after viewing the evidence in the light most favorable to the prosecution, any rational trier of fact could have found beyond a reasonable doubt that

(a) a completed felony had been committed by Ira Lloyd before Brian Chism rendered him the assistance described below;

(b) Chism knew or had reasonable grounds to know of the commission of the felony by Lloyd, and

(c) Chism gave aid to Lloyd personally under circumstances that indicate either that he actively desired that the felon avoid or escape arrest, trial conviction, or punishment or that he believed that one of these consequences was substantially certain to result from his assistance.

There was clearly enough evidence to justify the finding that a felony had been completed before any assistance was rendered to Lloyd by the defendant. The record vividly demonstrates that Lloyd fatally stabbed his ex-wife before she was transported to Willow Point and left in the high grass near a wood line. Thus, Lloyd committed the felonies of attempted murder, aggravated battery, and simple kidnapping, before Chism aided him in any way. A person cannot be convicted as an accessory after the fact to a murder because of aid given after the murderer's acts but before the victim's death, but under these circumstances the aider may be found to be an accessory after the fact to the felonious assault....

The evidence overwhelmingly indicates that Chism had reasonable grounds to believe that Lloyd had committed a felony before any assistance was rendered. In his confessions and his testimony Chism indicates that the victim was bleeding profusely when Lloyd pushed her into the vehicle, that she was limp and moaned as they drove to Willow Point, and that he knew Lloyd had inflicted her wounds with a knife. The Louisiana offense of accessory after the fact deviates somewhat from the original common-law offense in that it does not require that the defendant actually know that a completed felony has occurred. Rather, it incorporates an objective standard by requiring only that the defendant render aid "knowing or having reasonable grounds to believe" that a felony has been committed.

The closest question presented is whether any reasonable trier of fact could have found beyond a reasonable doubt that Chism assisted Lloyd under circumstances that indicate that either Chism actively desired that Lloyd would avoid or escape arrest, trial, conviction, or punishment, or that Chism believed that one of these consequences was substantially certain to result from his assistance. After carefully reviewing the record, we conclude that the prosecution satisfied its burden of producing the required quantity of evidence.

...In this case we conclude that the evidence is sufficient to support an ultimate finding that the reasonable findings and inferences permitted by the evidence exclude every reasonable hypothesis of innocence. Despite evidence supporting some contrary inferences, a trier of fact reasonably could have found that Chism acted with at least a general intent to help Lloyd avoid arrest because:

(1) Chism did not protest or attempt to leave the car when his uncle, Lloyd, shoved the mortally wounded victim inside;

(2) he did not attempt to persuade Duke, his would-be lover, exit out the driver's side of the car and flee from his uncle, whom he knew to be one-legged and armed only with a knife;

(3) he did not take any of these actions at any point during the considerable ride to Willow Point;

(4) at their destination, he docilely complied with Lloyd's directions to remove the victim from the car and leave Lloyd with her, despite the fact that Lloyd made no threats and that his wooden leg had become detached;

(5) after leaving Lloyd with the dying victim, he made no immediate effort to report the victim's whereabouts or to obtain emergency medical treatment for her;

(6) before going home or reporting the victim's dire condition he went to a friend's house, changed clothing and discarded his own in a trash bin from which the police were unable to recover them as evidence;

(7) he went home without reporting the victim's condition or location;

(8) and he went to the police station to report the crime only after arriving home and discussing the matter with his mother.

The defendant asserted in his statement given to the police and during trial, that he helped to remove the victim from the car and to carry her to the edge of the bushes be-

cause he feared that his uncle would use the knife on him. The defense of justification can be claimed in any crime, except murder, when it is committed through the compulsion of threats by another of death or great bodily harm and the offender reasonably believes the person making the threats is present and would immediately carry out the threats if the crime were not committed.

However, Chism did not testify that Lloyd threatened him with death, bodily harm or anything. Moreover, fear as a motivation to help his uncle is inconsistent with some of Chism's actions after he left his uncle. Consequently, we conclude that despite Chism's testimony the trier of fact could have reasonably found that he acted voluntarily and not out of fear when he aided Lloyd and that he did so under circumstances indicating that he believed that it was substantially certain to follow from his assistance that Lloyd would avoid arrest, trial, conviction, or punishment.

For the foregoing reasons, it is also clear that the judge's verdict was warranted.... There is evidence in this record from which a reasonable trier of fact could find a defendant guilty beyond a reasonable doubt. We have greater confidence in this conclusion because of our preceding analysis of the evidence....

Therefore, we affirm the defendant's conviction. We note, however, that the sentence imposed by the trial judge is illegal. The judge imposed a sentence of three years. He suspended two and one-half of years of the term. The trial judge has no authority to suspend *part* of a sentence in a felony case. The correct sentence would have been a suspension of all three years of the term, with a six-month term as a condition of two years probation. We therefore vacate the defendant's sentence and remand the case for resentencing.

Conviction AFFIRMED; sentence vacated; REMANDED.

DISSENT

DIXON, CJ.

I respectfully dissent from what appears to be a finding of guilt by association. The majority lists five instances of *inaction*, or failure to act, by defendant:

(1) did not protest or leave the car;

(2) did not attempt to persuade Duke to leave the car;

(3) did neither (1) nor (2) on ride to Willow Point;

(5) made no immediate effort to report crime or get aid for the victim;

(7) failed to report victim's condition or location after changing clothes.

The three instances of defendant's *action* relied on by the majority for conviction were stated to be:

(4) complying with Lloyd's direction to remove the victim from the car and leave the victim and Lloyd at Willow Point;

(6) changing clothes and discarding bloody garments; and

(8) discussing the matter with defendant's mother before going to the police station to report the crime.

None of these actions or failures to act tended to prove defendant's intent, specifically or generally, to aid defendant avoid arrest, trial, conviction or punishment.

Questions

1. Identify the elements of accessory-after-the-fact according to the Louisiana statute.

2. List all the facts stated by the court, and then match them to each of the elements of the statute.

3. Summarize the court's conclusions regarding the evidence of each of the elements.

4. Do you agree with the court that Chism is guilty of being an accessory-after-the-fact? Back up your answer with facts in the case.

5. Summarize the reasons the dissent couldn't go along with the majority. Do you agree with the dissent? Defend your answer.

EXPLORING PARTICIPATION AFTER THE COMMISSION OF A CRIME FURTHER

 Go to the Criminal Law 8e CD to read the full text version of the case featured here.

Was He an Accessory After the Fact to Grand Larceny?

FACTS

On two separate occasions, Charles Lee Dunn was a passenger in a car when two grand larcenies occurred. He claimed he didn't know the others in the car planned to break into cars, and didn't participate in the thefts of stereo equipment and CDs. He admitted that, after the first theft on September 4th, he voluntarily went with the others when they sold the equipment and he received a small piece of crack cocaine from the proceeds. Regarding one of the offenses, he testified that he took no active part in the theft and was taken home immediately thereafter.

The Commonwealth's evidence included testimony from the investigating officer, Detective Ramsey, that appellant (Dunn) told him that he knew the purpose of going to the location of the first offense was "to take equipment belonging to Mr. Roberts. It was known there was equipment in his car." As to the September 7, 1995 offense, Ramsey testified that Dunn said:

> The three of them went to a location near Mr. Jackson's house. Mr. Dunn waited in the car, and Mr. Walker and Mr. Kraegers approached Mr. Jackson's vehicle. They entered the vehicle through an unlocked door and took stereo equipment from the vehicle, brought it back to the car. [Appellant] states that they put the speaker box in the trunk, put the amp and a CD player in the car, and he says, I think they got some CD's. That equipment was also taken to the city and traded for crack cocaine which they all used, and that property has not been recovered.

Ramsey stated that Dunn admitted to participating and taking the property to the city in exchange for crack cocaine. Was Dunn an accessory after the fact?

DECISION AND REASONS

Yes, said the Virginia Court of Appeals:

> While Dunn contends that the evidence failed to establish he did anything other than ride in a car with friends, the trial court was not required to accept his explanation. Dunn admitted to Ramsey that he knew the others intended to steal on both occasions; he smoked crack cocaine purchased with the money received from disposing of the goods; and he went out with the co-defendants three days after the first larceny occurred. Under the facts of this case, the Commonwealth's evidence was sufficient to prove beyond a reasonable doubt that appellant was an accessory after the fact to the two grand larcenies. Affirmed.

Dunn v. Commonwealth, WL 147448 (Va.App. 1997)

Go to Exercise 5-1 on the Criminal Law 8e CD to learn more about the elements of accomplice liability in your state.

◆   ◆   ◆

VICARIOUS LIABILITY

The doctrine of complicity applies criminal liability to accomplices and accessories because they *participate* in crimes. The doctrine of vicarious liability applies criminal liability based on the *relationship* between the person who commits the crime and someone else. Vicarious liability applies mainly to business relationships: employer-employee, manager-corporation, buyer-seller, producer-consumer, and service provider–recipient. But it can also apply to other situations, like making the owner of a car liable for the driver's traffic violations and holding parents liable for their children's crimes.

Vicarious Liability of Corporations

Successfully applying vicarious liability to convict and punish individuals for committing business crimes is difficult. Pinpointing responsibility for corporate crimes is especially difficult because frequently many people are involved in a decision that breaks the law. This problem increases with the complexity of corporate structures. The larger and more spread out the business, the harder it is to identify just who's responsible for actions taken in the name of the corporation. It's also hard (sometimes impossible) to prove intent. Practically speaking, a corporation can't have a *mens rea* because it can't think. So, prosecutors have to rely on two doctrines to prove corporate criminal liability:

1. *Strict liability.* Removes the element of *mens rea*

2. *Vicarious liability.* Attaches the intent of managers and agents to the corporation

Although vicarious and strict liability work together to impose criminal liability, they're very different ideas: strict liability eliminates the *mens rea;* vicarious liability transfers the *actus reus* and *mens rea* of an employee to the corporation (Fisse 1986, 23–54).

Criminal punishment that's based on a relationship, especially when there's no criminal intent, raises constitutional questions. Some courts have ruled that putting someone in jail based on vicarious liability violates the fundamental fairness required by due process (Chapter 2). Some courts have gone so far as to declare that even fining someone based on vicarious liability violates due process if noncriminal measures are enough to control harmful business practices. Fundamental fairness is also

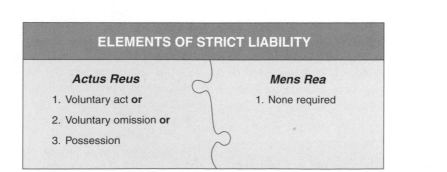

ELEMENTS OF VICARIOUS LIABILITY

Actus Reus

1. Relationship **and**
2. Acts of the other party to the relationship

Mens Rea

1. Relationship **and**
2. Purpose, knowledge, recklessness, negligence of the other party to the relationship

involved because stockholders, "most of whom ordinarily had nothing to do with the offense and were powerless to prevent it," wind up actually paying the fines.

Vicarious liability also raises questions about its effectiveness. Fines probably don't deter officers or other agents who don't have to pay them. Because businesses treat fines as just another business expense, the deterrent effect is further weakened. Finally, officers don't suffer a stigma if their actions are looked at as just violating "regulations" as opposed to committing "real crimes." Quite the contrary: officers can boost their reputation for "shrewd business" practices by breaking the rules to turn a profit.

The Wisconsin Supreme Court dealt with corporate vicarious liability in *State v. Beaudry* (1985).

CASE | *Is She Guilty of Keeping the Bar Open After Hours?*

State v. Beaudry
365 N.W.2d 593 (Wis. 1985)

Janet Beaudry, the designated agent for the corporate holder of a retail alcoholic beverage license, was convicted by a jury and ordered to pay a $200 fine in the Circuit Court, Sheboygan County, of unlawfully remaining open for business after 1:00 A.M. The Wisconsin Court of Appeals affirmed, and Beaudry appealed. The Wisconsin Supreme Court affirmed.

ABRAHAMSON, Justice.

The defendant raises two issues on appeal: (1) whether the statutes impose vicarious criminal liability on the designated agent of a corporate licensee for the conduct of a corporate employee who violates sec. 125.68(4)(c), Stats. 1981–82, and (2) whether there is sufficient evidence to support the verdict in the case. Before we discuss these two issues, we shall set forth the facts.

FACTS

The defendant, Janet Beaudry, and her husband, Wallace Beaudry, are the sole shareholders of Sohn Manufacturing Company, a corporation which has a license to sell alcoholic beverages at the Village Green Tavern in the village of Elkhart Lake, Sheboygan County. Janet Beaudry is the designated agent for the corporate licensee pursuant to sec. 125.04(6)(a), Stats.1981–82.

Janet Beaudry's conviction grew out of events occurring during the early morning hours of February 9, 1983. At approximately 3:45 A.M., a deputy sheriff for the Sheboygan County Sheriff's Department drove past the Village Green Tavern. He stopped to investigate after noticing more lights than usual inside the building and also seeing two individuals seated inside. As he approached the tavern, he heard music, saw an individual standing behind the bar, and saw glasses on the bar. Upon finding the tavern door locked, the deputy sheriff knocked and was admitted by Mark Witkowski, the tavern manager. The tavern manager and two men were the only persons inside the bar. All three were drinking. The deputy sheriff reported the incident to the Sheboygan County district attorney's office for a formal complaint.

At about noon on February 9, the tavern manager reported to Wallace Beaudry about the deputy's stop earlier that morning. After further investigation Wallace Beaudry discharged the tavern manager on February 11.

On March 2, 1983, the Sheboygan County Sheriff's Department served the defendant with a summons and a complaint charging her with the crime of keeping the tavern open after hours contrary to sec. 125.68(4)(c), Stats., and sec. 125.11(1), Stats. The tavern manager was not arrested or charged with an offense arising out of this incident.

Sec. 125.04(6)(a), Stats.1981–82, provides as follows:

(6) Licenses to corporations; appointment of agents. (a) *Agent.* No corporation organized under the laws of this state or of any other state or foreign country may be issued any alcohol beverage license or permit unless: "1. The corporation first appoints an agent in the manner prescribed by the department.

"2. The corporation vests in the agent, by properly authorized and executed written delegation, full authority and control of the premises described in the license or permit of the corporation, and of the conduct of all business on the premises relative to alcohol beverages, that the licensee or permittee could have and exercise if it were a natural person."

Sec. 125.68(4)(c)1., Stats.1981–82, provides as follows:

(c) *"Class B" retailers.* 1. In any county having a population of less than 500,000, except in a 1st class city which is located in more than one county, no premises for which a "Class B" license or permit has been issued may remain open between the hours of 1 A.M. and 8 A.M., except as otherwise provided in this subdivision and subd. 4. On January 1, no premises may remain open between 3 A.M. and 8 A.M. During that portion of each year for which the standard of time is advanced under s. 175.095, no premises may remain open between 2 A.M. and 8 A.M., but the municipality in which the premises is located may establish an earlier closing hour."

Sec. 125.11(1)(a), Stats.1981–82, provides as follows:

125.11 Penalties. (1) Violations of chapter. (a) *First offense.* Any person who violates any provision of this chapter for which a specific penalty is not provided, shall be fined not more than $500 or imprisoned for not more than 90 days or both. Any license or permit issued to the person under this chapter may be revoked by the court."

The case was tried before a jury on May 20, 1983. At trial Janet Beaudry testified that she was not present at the tavern the morning of February 9. Wallace Beaudry testified that Janet Beaudry had delegated to him, as president of Sohn Manufacturing, the responsibilities of business administration associated with the Village Green Tavern; that he had hired Mark Witkowski as manager; that he had in-

formed Witkowski that it was his duty to abide by the liquor laws; and that he never authorized Witkowski to remain open after 1:00 A.M., to throw a private party for his friends, or to give away liquor to friends.

Witkowski testified that he had served drinks after hours to two men. During cross-examination Witkowski confirmed that Wallace Beaudry had never authorized him to stay open after hours; that he had been instructed to close the tavern promptly at the legal closing time; that he knew it was illegal to serve liquor after 1:00 A.M. to anyone, including friends; that his two friends drank at the bar before 1:00 A.M. and had paid for those drinks; that he was having a good time with his friends before closing hours and wanted to continue partying and conversing with them after 1 A.M.; that after closing hours he was simply using the tavern to have a private party for two friends; that he did not charge his friends for any of the liquor they drank after 1:00 A.M.; and that by staying open he was trying to benefit not Wallace Beaudry but himself.

At the close of evidence, the jury was instructed that the law required the premises to be closed for all purposes between 1:00 A.M. and 8:00 A.M. and that if the jury found that there were patrons or customers on the premises after 1:00 A.M., it must find the premises open contrary to statute.

The jury was also instructed regarding Janet Beaudry's liability for the conduct of the tavern manager: As designated agent of the corporation, the defendant had full authority over the business and would be liable for the tavern manager's violation of the closing hour statute if he was acting within the scope of his employment. The instructions, which are pattern instructions Wis.J.I.Cr. 440 (1966), describe what activities are within the scope of employment and what are outside the scope of employment. Specifically, the jury was instructed as follows regarding the defendant's liability for the conduct of the tavern manager:

"It is also the law of the State of Wisconsin that violations of statutes regulating the sale of liquor do not require a showing of a willful or intentional act.

"It is a law that when a corporation is a licensee, the corporation vests in its agent, in this case Janet Beaudry, full control and authority over the premises and of the conduct of all business on the premises relative to alcohol beverages that the licensee could have exercised if it were a natural person.

"Under Wisconsin law if a person employs another to act for him [sic] in the conduct of his [sic] business, and such servant or agent violates the law, as in this case relating to open after hours, then the employer is guilty of that violation as if he [sic] had been present or had done the act himself [*sic*], if such act was within the scope of the employment of the servant or agent. It is no defense to prosecution under the statute that the employer was not upon the premises, did not know of the acts of his [*sic*] servant or agent, had not consented thereto, or even had expressly forbidden such act.

"A servant or agent is within the scope of his employment when he is performing work or rendering services he was hired to perform and render within the time and space limits of his authority and is actuated by a purpose in serving his employer in doing what he is doing. He is within the scope of his employment when he is performing work or rendering services in obedience to the express orders or directions of his master of doing that which is warranted within the terms of his express or implied authority, considering the nature of the services required, the instructions which he has received, and the circumstances under which his work is being done or the services are being rendered.

"A servant or agent is outside the scope of his employment when he deviates or steps aside from the prosecution of his master's business for the purpose of doing an act or rendering a service intended to accomplish an independent purpose of his own, or for some other reason or purpose not related to the business of his employer.

"Such deviation or stepping aside from his employer's business may be momentary and slight, measured in terms of time and space, but if it involves a change of mental attitude in serving his personal interests, or the interests of another instead of his employer's, then his conduct falls outside the scope of his employment.

"If you are satisfied beyond a reasonable doubt from the evidence in this case that Mark Witkowski, the employee of the registered agent, committed the acts charged in the complaint, that Mark Witkowski was the servant or agent of the defendant, and that the acts charged in the complaint were committed by him in the scope of his employment, then you should find the defendant guilty.

"If, however, you are not so satisfied, then you must find the defendant not guilty."

Having been so instructed, the jury returned a verdict of guilty.

OPINION

In light of the facts and these instructions, we consider first the question of whether the statutes impose vicarious criminal liability on a designated agent for the illegal conduct of the tavern manager in this case, *i.e.*, remaining open after 1:00 A.M.

The state's prosecution of the defendant under the criminal laws rests on a theory of vicarious liability, that is respondeat superior. Under this theory of liability, the master (here the designated agent) is liable for the illegal conduct of the servant (here the tavern manager).

> Note: Vicarious liability should be contrasted with liability for one's own acts as a party to a crime: that is, for directly committing the crime, for aiding and abetting the commission of a crime, or for being a party to a conspiracy to commit the crime. Sec. 939.05, Stats.1981–82.

The defendant asserts, contrary to the position of the state, that the statutes do not impose vicarious criminal liability on her as designated agent of the corporation for the tavern manager's illegal conduct.

It is apparently undisputed that the tavern manager violated the closing hour statute and could have been prosecuted as a party to the crime.

While the focus in this case is on the defendant's vicarious criminal liability, it is helpful to an understanding of vicarious liability to compare it with the doctrine of strict liability. Strict liability allows for criminal liability absent the element of *mens rea* found in the definition of most crimes. Thus under strict liability the accused has engaged in the act or omission; the requirement of mental fault, *mens rea*, is eliminated.

This court has construed violations of several statutes regulating the sale of alcoholic beverages which command that an act be done or omitted and which do not include words signifying…[intent] as imposing strict liability on the actor. As early as 1869, this court explained that the legislature imposed strict liability for the sale of spirituous liquors to a minor because protection of the public interest warrants the imposition of liability unhindered by examination of the subjective intent of each accused.

> The act in question is a police regulation, and we have no doubt that the legislature intended to inflict the penalty, irrespective of the knowledge or motives of the person who has violated its provisions. Indeed, if this were not so, it is plain that the statute might be violated times without number, with no possibility of convicting offenders, and so it would become a dead letter on the statute book, and the evil aimed at by the legislature remain almost wholly untouched."

State v. Hartfiel, 24 Wis. 60, 62 (1869)

Note: Whether or not remaining open after hours is a strict liability offense is not squarely before the court. The jury was instructed that "violations of statutes regulating the sale of liquor do not require a showing of a willful or intentional act." The parties do not dispute the illegality of the bar manager's conduct in this case. We discuss the strict liability nature of the several alcoholic beverage sale statutes in order to distinguish strict liability from vicarious liability and to delineate the nature of the offense for which the defendant is determined to be vicariously liable.

Vicarious liability, in contrast to strict liability, dispenses with the requirement of the *actus reus* and imputes the criminal act of one person to another.

Whether the defendant in this case is vicariously liable for the tavern manager's violation of sec. 125.68(4)(c), Stats.1981–82, depends on whether the specific statutes in question impose vicarious liability. We look first at the language of the statutes themselves. The principal statutory provisions are secs. 125.68(4)(c)1., 125.11(1)(a), and 125.02(14).

Sec. 125.68(4)(c), Stats.1981–82, provides that "no premises for which a 'Class B' license or permit has been issued may remain open between the hours of 1 A.M. and 8 A.M. . . ."

Sec. 125.11(1)(a), provides that "[a]ny person who violates any provision of this chapter for which a specific penalty is not provided, shall be fined not more than $500 or imprisoned for not more than 90 days or both."

Sec. 125.02(14), states that "'[p]erson' means a natural person, sole proprietorship, partnership, corporation or association."

It is apparent that no statute expressly imposes criminal liability upon the designated agent for the illegal conduct of the tavern manager. None of the statutes states, for example, that "whoever by herself or by an employee of the corporation for which she is the designated agent keeps the premises open shall be punished by . . ." or "whoever keeps the premises open is punishable by . . . and any act by a corporate employee shall be deemed the act of the designated agent as well as the act of the employee."

The state contends that the defendant's liability as designated agent for the illegal conduct of the tavern manager is predicated on sec. 125.04(6)(a), which requires a corporate licensee selling alcoholic beverages to designate an agent to whom the corporation delegates full authority and control of the premises and of the conduct of the business. Sec. 125.04(6)(a) equates the power and authority of the corporation's designated agent with that of a natural person who is a licensee or permittee. Sec. 125.04(6)(a) provides as follows:

"(6) LICENSES TO CORPORATIONS; APPOINTMENT OF AGENTS. (a) *Agent*. No corporation organized under the laws of this state or of any other state or foreign country may be issued any alcohol beverage license or permit unless:

"1. The corporation first appoints an agent in the manner prescribed by the department. In addition to the qualifications under sub. (5), the agent must, with respect to character, record and reputation, be satisfactory to the department.

"2. The corporation vests in the agent, by properly authorized and executed written delegation, full authority and control of the premises described in the license or permit of the corporation, and of the conduct of all business on the premises relative to alcohol beverages, that the licensee or permittee could have and exercise if it were a natural person."

Relying on sec. 125.04(6)(a), the state reasons that because the designated agent of a corporate licensee has the same authority and control over the premises as a licensee who is a natural person, the criminal liability of a designated agent of a corporate licensee should be the same as that of the licensee who is a natural person. [The court agreed.]

Inasmuch as the natural person licensee is subject to vicarious criminal liability for the conduct of her or his employee who illegally sells alcoholic beverages, it logically follows that a corporation licensee should be similarly liable for the illegal conduct of its employee. But in this case the defendant is not the corporation licensee; the defendant is the designated agent of the corporation. The question for the present case, therefore, is whether a designated corporate agent is subject to vicarious criminal liability for the illegal conduct, *i.e.*, remaining open after closing hours, of the tavern manager who is an employee of the corporation. . . . We agree with the court of appeals that the legislature intended to impose such liability on the designated agent. The court of appeals correctly noted that unless vicarious criminal liability was imposed on the designated agent, a natural person licensee could avoid criminal liability by simply incorporating the business. . . .

We turn now to the question of whether the evidence supports the verdict that the tavern manager was acting within the scope of his employment. As we stated previously, the jury was instructed that the defendant is liable only for the acts of the tavern manager that were within the scope of his employment. Thus the defendant is not liable for all the acts of the tavern manager, only for those acts within the scope of employment. Neither the state nor the defense challenges this statement of the law limiting the designated agent's vicarious criminal liability.

The application of the standard of scope of employment limits liability to illegal conduct which occurred while the offending employee was engaged in some job-related activity and thus limits the accused's vicarious liability to conduct with which the accused has a factual connection and with which the accused has some responsible relation to the public danger envisaged by the legislature.

The defendant argues that...the tavern manager went outside his scope of authority. The state concedes that this is a reasonable view of the evidence and that this is a close case. The state argues, however, that the jury's verdict must be upheld under the standard of review applied to jury verdicts. The test on review, which this court has frequently stated, is not whether this court is convinced of the defendant's guilt beyond a reasonable doubt "but whether this court can conclude that a trier of facts could, acting reasonably, be convinced to the required degree of certitude by the evidence which it had a right to believe and accept as true. On review we view the evidence in the light most favorable to sustaining the conviction."...

We agree with the conclusion reached by the court of appeals. The credibility of the bar manager's testimony was a matter for the jury. The bar manager's testimony which supports the defendant's position that the manager was acting outside the scope of employment was based on a statement the bar manager gave defendant's counsel the night before trial. The jury may not have believed this testimony which was favorable to the defendant. Considering that the conduct occurred on the employer's premises and began immediately after "closing time"; that the employee had access to the tavern after hours only by virtue of his role as an employee of the corporate licensee, which role vested him with the means to keep the tavern open; and that the defendant may anticipate that employees may be tempted to engage in such conduct; the jury could conclude that the tavern manager's conduct was sufficiently similar to the conduct authorized as to be within the scope of employment. The jury could view the tavern manager's conduct as more similar to that of an employee to whom the operation of the business had been entrusted and for whose conduct the defendant should be held criminally liable than to that of an interloper for whose conduct the defendant should not be held liable.

For the reasons set forth, we affirm the decision of the court of appeals affirming the conviction. Decision of the court of appeals is affirmed.

DISSENT

CECI, J.

...I am convinced that, as a matter of law, no trier of fact, acting reasonably, could conclude beyond a reasonable doubt that Mark Witkowski was acting within the scope of his employment when he kept the Village Green tavern open after 1:00 A.M.

We have previously held that a servant is *not* within the scope of his employment if

(a) his acts were different in kind than those authorized by the master,

(b) his acts were far beyond the authorized time or space limits, or

(c) his acts were too little actuated by a purpose to serve the master.

It is important to note that this test is set out in the disjunctive and not the conjunctive, and, thus, not all three elements must be satisfied before there can be a finding that the servant was outside the scope of his authority. Unfortunately, the majority fails to evaluate the uncontroverted facts in this case with respect to these three criteria....In doing so, I conclude that Mark Witkowski was not within the scope of employment when he kept the tavern open after 1:00 A.M.

The first element of the test asks whether Witkowski's acts were different in kind than those authorized by the defendant. Witkowski stated that one of his duties as a manager included closing the tavern at one o'clock. He testified that Wallace Beaudry never authorized him to stay open after the legal closing time. In fact, he was specifically instructed to close promptly at the legal closing time. Additionally, Witkowski testified, "I knew that Wally would not want me to stay open after hours but I decided to do it anyway." Wally Beaudry also testified at the trial. He confirmed Witkowski's testimony by stating that one of Witkowski's duties was to follow all the liquor laws of this state and that he never authorized Witkowski to remain open after 1:00 A.M., throw a private party for his friends, or give away liquor.

A thorough review of the trial transcript reveals that this testimony of Witkowski and Wally Beaudry was in no way impeached by the state. The majority admits that this evidence is undisputed. Slip op. at 2. This testimony was wrongly ignored by the majority. I conclude that Witkowski was not within his scope of employment, because his act of keeping the tavern open until 3:45 A.M. was not authorized by Mr. or Mrs. Beaudry.

The second element of the test...asks whether Witkowski's acts were far beyond the authorized time or space limits. I conclude that Witkowski's acts were beyond the authorized time limit because, as stated above, there was testimony that Witkowski was not hired to stay open after hours, and, at the time the police arrived at the tavern, it was 3:45 A.M. Witkowski testified that he usually was done with his normal cleanup between 1:15 A.M. and 1:30 A.M. Over two hours passed between the time he should have locked up and left the tavern and the time the police arrived. Although there is no testimony to this fact, it can reasonably be inferred that Witkowski did not expect to get paid for these two hours when he was sitting at the bar and drinking with his friends. It is clear that Witkowski was no longer working at 3:45 A.M. and that his acts were far beyond the time limit authorized by Janet or Wally Beaudry.

The third and final factor to be considered is whether Witkowski's acts were too little actuated by a purpose to serve the defendant. Not only the direct testimony of Witkowski, but also the circumstantial evidence, provide support for the finding that Witkowski's acts were in no way intended to further the defendant's business, but were motivated solely for his own enjoyment and convenience. Witkowski testified that after the other patrons left the Village Green tavern, he was not performing any work duties, but was entertaining his "real good friends." Witkowski stated,

> "I was not trying to benefit Wallace Beaudry by staying open after hours. I was simply using Wally's tavern to have a *private party* for my two friends. By staying open for my two friends I was not trying to benefit Wallace Beaudry in any way, rather I was trying to benefit myself by continuing the conversation I had started with my friends." [Emphasis added.]

The undisputed circumstantial evidence also bears out the fact that Witkowski's acts were not serving the purpose of the defendant. Deputy Sheriff Kenneth Van Ess testified that he arrived at the tavern at 3:45 A.M. Loud music was coming from within the tavern. The door was locked to outside patrons. Witkowski and Pethan were sitting at the bar, and Dickman, a nonemployee, was standing behind the bar. Dickman later testified that he went behind the bar to get another bottle of liquor. There were glasses and a bottle of liquor sitting on the bar. Van Ess testified that it was quite apparent that all three men had been drinking. Witkowski was not performing any cleanup or maintenance duties. Finally, Witkowski, Dickman, and Pethan all testified that Witkowski had been charging Dickman and Pethan for drinks before 1:00 A.M. Witkowski testified that he did not charge his friends for drinks after 1:00 A.M. This statement is also confirmed by the testimony of Dickman. Ken Pethan testified that he does not remember if he had anything to drink after 1:00 A.M.

Based on this testimony, I conclude that Witkowski was not acting within the scope of his authority, because his acts were in no way intended to serve the defendant. The fact that Witkowski gave his employer's liquor to his friends without charge after 1:00 A.M., when he knew it was illegal and contrary to his authority as a manager of the tavern to stay open after closing hours, strongly supports the conclusion that Witkowski did not intend to further the defendant's business, but was acting solely for his own enjoyment and convenience. Unfortunately, the majority fails to consider these factors in making its determination....

I conclude that there is nothing in the evidence to sustain a finding that Witkowski was acting within the scope of his employment. The majority's conclusion in this case...unfairly imposes vicarious liability on the defendant simply because Mark Witkowski was an employee and on the premises at the time the two police officers arrived....

In conclusion, I would reverse the judgment of conviction because I conclude that as a matter of law, Mark Witkowski was outside his scope of employment when he kept the Village Green tavern open until 3:45 A.M., and, further, no jury, acting reasonably, could conclude otherwise. It is apparent that the jury did not apply the uncontroverted facts in this case to the law given in the jury instructions.

For the above-stated reasons, I dissent.

Questions

1. State the elements of vicarious liability as they're defined in the relevant sections of the Wisconsin statutes.

2. List all the facts relevant to deciding whether Witkowski was acting within the scope of his employment, as the court defined "scope of employment."

3. List the three elements the dissent identified and applied to the facts of the case to decide whether Witkowski was acting within the scope of his employment.

4. In your opinion, was Witkowski acting within the scope of his employment? Back up your answer with facts and arguments from the majority and dissenting opinions.

5. Now, assuming Witkowski wasn't acting within the scope of his employment, could a reasonable juror believe beyond a reasonable doubt that he was? Defend your answer.

6. Is it "fair" to blame and possibly send Janet Beaudry to jail for a crime she neither intended to commit nor committed? Back up your opinion with information from the excerpt and the section on vicarious liability in the text.

Vicarious Liability of Individuals

Most cases of vicarious liability are like *State v. Beaudry*; they involve employer-employee relationships, and many of these are cases of the vicarious liability of corporations. But not all cases. We'll look at two kinds of individual vicarious liability:

1. Vehicle owners' vicarious liability for traffic tickets
2. Parents' vicarious liability for their children's crimes

Vicarious Liability for Traffic Tickets

You lend your car to a friend who parks it in a "No parking" zone. An officer tickets the car, and under the city's traffic code, which makes owners liable for operators' tickets, you're charged the fine. In the language of vicarious liability, you're guilty because of the owner-driver relationship. The reason why these statutes were created is practical: There's no way we can have enough law enforcement officers on duty to stand near parked cars waiting for operators to come back so the officers can prove they were responsible for the parking violation.

Vicarious liability statutes making owners liable for operators' traffic offenses are often written to give owners a way out of the liability. The statutes create a presumption that owners are operators, and so they're regarded as **prima facie** responsible for the ticket. What does this mean? The owner is presumed responsible for the violation; but, if she can prove someone else was driving the car or that they were driving without her permission, she's not liable.

The Washington Supreme Court dealt with vicarious liability for parking tickets in *Seattle v. Stone* (1966).

| CASE | *Was He Liable for the Parking Tickets?* |

Seattle v. Stone
410 P.2d 583 (Wash. 1966)

Clifford Stone was found guilty of 20 overtime parking violations on the streets of the City of Seattle, and sentenced to pay a fine of $186.00 in the Superior Court, King County, Washington. Stone appealed. The Washington Supreme Court reversed and remanded.

WEAVER, J.

FACTS

Clifford Stone, the defendant, who appears pro se [to defend himself], appeals from a judgment...which finds him guilty of 20 overtime parking violations on the streets of the City of Seattle and sentenced to pay a fine of $186.00. The judgment further provides: "That defendant pay costs in this Court (Superior) to be taxed and stand committed to the City Jail upon his failure fully to comply with this judgment...."

The following is the entire statement of facts before us.... "That the City of Seattle and defendant Clifford A. Stone stipulated as to certain facts recited in the judgment and sentenced dated Nov. 6, 1964. That no witnesses appeared in court and the case was heard on the stipulated facts. That no evidence was introduced."

It is apparent that the statement of facts is meaningless unless read in conjunction with the stipulation contained in the judgment and sentence. The stipulated facts are: "that the defendant owns a (designated vehicle); that this vehicle was issued 20 citations for overtime parking at various times on the streets of the City of Seattle and that the defendant was not present when the car was cited by members of the Seattle Police Department."

OPINION

Stone makes a three-pronged attack upon the judgment and sentence. We first consider his argument that § 21.66.180 of Seattle Ordinance 91910 violates due process of law. The ordinance provides that:

> Every person in whose name a vehicle is registered (licensed) shall be responsible for any parking or angle parking of said vehicle and for all offenses other than moving violations under this code. It shall be no defense that said vehicle was illegally parked or angle parked or used by another, unless it be shown that at such time said vehicle was being used without the consent of the registered (licensed) owner thereof: Provided, that the lessee of a commercially rented or leased vehicle alone shall be responsible for any parking or angle parking of such vehicle and for all violations of this code committed while the vehicle is being leased or rented, if the registered (licensed) owner of such vehicle furnished the Traffic Violations Bureau with a copy of the renting or leasing contract stating the name and address of the renter or lessee.

In its defense, counsel for the city urges that we read into the first sentence of the ordinance the words "prima facie" before the word "responsible," as other courts have done. At this point we cannot do so in view of the unambiguous language of the second sentence which does not allow the defense of authorized use. The ordinance clearly imposes vicarious criminal liability upon the owner of an automobile without allowing him to defend on the ground that one whom he permitted to use the car was actually the offender.

Our review of the authorities discloses that the statutes and ordinances which make automobile owners responsible for parking violations fall into two general classes. First, there are those which Provide that the fact of violation and ownership together raise a Prima facie rebuttable presumption that the owner committed the offense.... [cited cases deleted]. The ordinances and statutes involved in the above cases do not make any inferred fact conclusive. The presumption of vicarious responsibility may be rebutted.

The second class of ordinances and statutes omits any reference to a prima facie presumption. This category declares that whenever an automobile is parked illegally, the registered owner shall be subject to the penalty for the violation. On their face, the ordinances or statutes impose absolute [strict] liability. Courts have, however, construed them to mean that only a prima facie responsibility is established; thus the owner may avoid conviction by showing that he did not in fact commit the violation.

Clearly the Seattle ordinance...is not of the first class mentioned. The second sentence—"It shall be no defense"...removes it from the second category.

This leaves the question whether a conclusive presumption of guilt, upon a showing of ownership and violation, is consistent with due process. Even if the presumption be rebuttable, there must be some rational and reasonable connection between the fact proved and the ultimate fact presumed. Common experience dictates that there is a rational connection between proof of registered ownership of an automobile and a prima facie presumption that it was parked by the owner. The inference is not an arbitrary one....

From an analysis of the reported cases [analysis of cited cases omitted] we conclude that if *Ober* [one of the cited cases] (holding that even an owner whose car had been stolen and parked illegally by the thief would be conclusively guilty)...it is an unfortunate deviation from the generally recognized limits of vicarious criminal liability.

The second sentence of the Seattle ordinance preceding the proviso is patently incompatible with the concept of due process. It purports to make a defendant responsible even though he in fact might not have been responsible for the parking violation. For the reasons indicated, we are forced to strike down as unconstitutional that portion of the second sentence of § 21.66.180 ["It shall be no defense that said vehicle was illegally parked or angle parked or used by another, unless it be shown that at such time said vehicle was being used without the consent of the registered (licensed) owner thereof...."] preceding the proviso, for it deprives an automobile owner of due process of law.

We then interpret the remainder of § 21.66.180, as do the authorities heretofore cited, to establish only a prima facie responsibility upon the registered owner, which he has the right to rebut, if he can. This in nowise interrupts the city's exercise of its police power or its right and power to enforce its parking ordinances.

Next, we find no merit in defendant's contention that his constitutional rights were invaded because the parking tickets were not handed to him or to the driver of the car, but were placed on the automobile. This argument has been rejected by every court that has considered the question. The existence and validity of the ordinance allowing placement of the citation upon the automobile is dictated by the practical and modern necessity of maintaining orderly traffic enforcement.

Finally, defendant argues that he did not receive due process of law because no witnesses appeared at the trial to testify against him. That an accused has the right to be confronted by his accuser and to cross-examine him is so engraved in the law that we cite only our constitutional provision. Art. 1, s 22, Washington Constitution.

> In criminal prosecutions the accused shall have the right to appear and...to meet the witnesses against him face to face, to have compulsory process to compel the attendance of witnesses in his own behalf....

In the instant case we have the rather bizarre situation of an accused being assessed a substantial fine in a judgment which admittedly was entered without the production of witnesses or the introduction of testimony. We are confined to the interpretation and meaning of the bare stipulated facts recited in the judgment and sentence: defendant owned the automobile; he was not present when the car was cited for over-time parking.

In appellate briefs and in oral argument before this court, there is a sharp conflict between defendant and counsel for the city. Defendant contends that he did not waive the necessity of requiring witnesses to testify against him and that no waiver appears in the stipulated facts. The city argues to the contrary and counters that defendant did not present his contention to the trial court; hence, his argument will not be considered by this court on appeal.

In view of (a) the fundamental constitutional nature of defendant's right to be confronted by his accuser and to cross-examine him, (b) the paucity of the record before us, (c) defendant's statement, although equivocal, in oral argument in this court that he believed the trial judge understood his position, and (d) the actual wording of the stipulation, we conclude that defendant did not waive his right to be confronted by his accuser.

The judgment and sentence is reversed and the case is remanded for a new trial. It is so ordered.

Questions

1. Under what specific circumstances does the Seattle ordinance impose vicarious liability for traffic tickets?

2. List the constitutional objections Stone raised to the ordinance.

3. Is this a case of strict liability, vicarious liability, or both? Explain your answer.

4. Assume the role of the attorney for the city in the case. Argue the constitutionality of the ordinances, relying on the opinion and your text.

5. Now, assume the role of Stone's lawyer. Summarize all the arguments made in the case and your text regarding the constitutionality of the ordinances.

6. In your opinion, is the vicarious liability ordinance constitutional? Defend your answer.

EXPLORING VICARIOUS LIABILITY FOR INDIVIDUALS FURTHER

Go to the Criminal Law 8e CD to read the full text version of the case featured here.

Was the Owner Liable for the Clerk Renting "Pornos" to a Minor?

FACTS

Peter Tomaino owns VIP Video, a video sales and rental store in Millville, Ohio. VIP Video's inventory includes only sexually oriented videotapes and materials. On October 13, 1997, Carl Frybarger, age 37, and his son Mark, age 17, decided that Mark should attempt to rent a video from VIP. Mark entered the store, selected a video, and presented it to the clerk along with his father's driver's license and credit card. The purchase was completed, and the Frybargers contacted the Butler County Sheriff's Department.

After interviewing Mark and his father, Sergeant Greg Blankenship, supervisor of the Drug and Vice Unit, determined that Mark should again attempt to purchase videos at VIP Video with marked money while wearing a radio transmitter wire. On October 14, 1997, Mark again entered the store. A different clerk was on duty. Following Sergeant Blankenship's instructions, Mark selected four videos and approached the clerk. He told her that he had been in the store the previous day and that he was 37. Mark told the clerk that he had used a credit card on that occasion and that he was using cash this time and thus did not have his identification with him. The clerk accepted the cash ($100) and did not require any identification or proof of Mark's age. It is this video transaction that constitutes the basis of the indictment.

The clerk, Billie Doan, was then informed by Sergeant Blankenship that she had sold the videos to a juvenile and that she would be arrested. Doan said that she needed to call the appellant and made several unsuccessful attempts to contact him at different locations. The grand jury indicted Tomaino, Doan, and VIP Video on two counts. Count One charged the defendants with recklessly disseminating obscene material to juveniles, and Count Two charged the defendants with disseminating matter that was harmful to juveniles. Was Tomaino vicariously liable for the clerk's illegal sale?

DECISION AND REASONS

No, according to the Ohio Court of Appeals:

The state argued that appellant was reckless by not having a sign saying "no sales to juveniles." Tomaino argued that criminal liability could not be imputed to him based on the actions of the clerk. Vicarious liability for another's criminal conduct or failure to prevent another's criminal conduct can be delineated by statute; it cannot be created by the courts. Statutes defining offenses are to be strictly construed against the state and liberally construed in favor of the accused. The elements of a crime must be gathered wholly from the statute. Where a duty of supervision is specifically enjoined by a statute, a failure to meet such a duty can be the basis for criminal liability. For instance, criminal liability for endangering children can be based on the combination of one's status as a parent, guardian, or person having custody and control of a child with either positive acts such as abuse or allowing the child to act in nudity oriented matter, or by "violating a duty of care, protection or support."

The state posited, and the trial court apparently accepted, that appellant could be criminally liable because he failed to supervise his employees and take affirmative steps to keep juveniles from entering his store and purchasing videos. However, as we have determined, no statute specifically criminalizes this failure. Although such failure may provide circumstantial evidence of appellant's complicity in the clerk's criminal actions, appellant was not indicted or prosecuted and the jury was not instructed under a complicity theory. It is undisputed that the clerk furnished the video to the minor and that appellant was not present. Because we find that a plain reading of the disseminating matter harmful to juveniles statute requires personal action by a defendant unless the issue of aiding and abetting is submitted, and does not by its terms impose vicarious or premises oriented liability, the jury was not correctly instructed in this case.

State v. Tomaino, WL 627370 (OhioApp. 12 Dist. 1999)

◆　　◆　　◆

Vicarious Liability of Parents

In 1995, Salt Lake City enacted an ordinance that made it a crime for parents to fail to "supervise and control their children." As of 1997, seventeen states and cities had adopted one of these **parental responsibility laws.** The idea of holding parents responsible for the crimes of their children is nothing new. Contributing to the delinquency of a minor is an old offense. Contributing-to-the-delinquency-of-minors statutes mandate that the acts of minor children were done at the direction or with the consent of their parents.

So, in one case a father was found guilty for "allowing his child to violate a curfew ordinance," and, in another, a mother was convicted for "knowingly" permitting her children "to go at large in violation of a valid quarantine order." A disturbing case involved the Detroit suburb of St. Clair Shores, which has an ordinance making it a crime to fail to "exercise reasonable control" to prevent children from committing delinquent acts. Alex Provenzino, 16, committed a string of seven burglaries. The local police ordered his parents to "take control" of Alex. When his father tried to discipline him, Alex "punched his father." When he tried to restrain him, Alex escaped by pressing his fingers into his father's eyes. When Alex tried to attack him with a golf club, his father called the police. The parents were acquitted of both vicariously committing the seven burglaries and for failing to supervise their son (Siegel 1996, A1).

Traditional parental responsibility statutes aren't the same as vicarious liability. Parental responsibility statutes are based on *acts* and *omissions;* vicarious liability statutes are based on the parent-child *relationship.* Vicarious liability statutes grew out of public fear, frustration, and anger over juvenile violence *and* parents' failure to control their kids." However, there are only a few cases in the appellate courts based on these vicarious liability statutes that make the crimes of kids the crimes of their parent solely on the basis of the parent-child relationship (DiFonzo 2001). One of these rare cases is *State v. Akers* (1979), where the New Hampshire Supreme Court dealt with a state statute making parents liable for their children's illegal snowmobile driving.

State v. Akers
400 A.2d 38 (N.H. 1979)

Parent defendants were found guilty of violating a snowmobile statute which makes parents vicariously liable for the acts of their children simply because they occupy the status of parents. The parents waived all right to an appeal de novo [new trial] to superior court. The parents objected to the constitutionality of the parent responsibility statute. The New Hampshire Supreme Court sustained the objections.

GRIMES, J.

FACTS

The defendants are fathers whose minor sons were found guilty of driving snowmobiles in violation of RSA 269-C:6-a II (operating on public way) and III (reasonable speed) (Supp.1977). RSA 269-C:24 IV, which pertains to the operation and licensing of off Highway Recreational Vehicles (OHRV), provides that "(t)he parents or guardians or persons assuming responsibility will be responsible for any damage incurred or for any violations of this chapter by any person under the age of 18." Following a verdict of guilty for violating RSA 269-C:24 IV the two defendants waived all right to an appeal de novo to the superior court and all questions of law were reserved and transferred by the District Court to [the New Hampshire Supreme Court].

OPINION

The defendants argue that (1) RSA 269-C:24 IV, the statute under which they were convicted, was not intended by the legislature to impose criminal responsibility, and (2) if in fact the legislative intention was to impose criminal responsibility, then the statute would violate N.H.Const. pt. 1, art. 15 and U.S.Const. amend. XIV, § 1.

... The language of RSA 269-C:24 IV, "parents ... will be responsible ... for any violations of this chapter by any person under the age of 18," clearly indicates the legislature's intention to hold the parents criminally responsible for the OHRV violations of their minor children. It is a general principle of this State's Criminal Code that "(a) person is not guilty of an offense unless his criminal liability is based on conduct that includes a voluntary Act or the voluntary omission to perform an act of which he is physically capable." RSA 269-C:24 IV seeks to impose criminal liability on parents for the acts of their children without basing liability on any voluntary act or omission on the part of the parent. Because the statute makes no reference at all to parental conduct or acts it seeks to impose criminal responsibility solely because of their parental status contrary to the provisions of RSA 626:1.

The legislature has not specified any voluntary acts or omissions for which parents are sought to be made criminally responsible and it is not a judicial function to supply them. It is fundamental to the rule of law and due process that acts or omissions which are to be the basis of criminal liability must be specified in advance and not Ex post facto. N.H.Const. pt. 1, art. 23.

It is argued that liability may be imposed on parents under the provisions of RSA 626:8 II(b), which authorizes imposing criminal liability for conduct of another when "he is made accountable for the conduct of such other person by the law defining the offense." This provision comes from the Model Penal Code s 2.04(2)(b). The illustrations of this type of liability in the comments to the Code all relate to situations involving employees and agents, and no suggestion is made that it was intended to authorize imposing vicarious criminal liability on one merely because of his status as a parent.

Without passing upon the validity of statutes that might seek to impose vicarious criminal liability on the part of an employer for acts of his employees, we have no hesitancy in holding that any attempt to impose such liability on parents simply because they occupy the status of parents, without more, offends the due process clause of our State constitution.

Parenthood lies at the very foundation of our civilization. The continuance of the human race is entirely dependent upon it. It was firmly entrenched in the Judeo-Christian ethic when "in the beginning" man was commanded to "be fruitful and multiply." Genesis I. Considering the nature of parenthood, we are convinced that the status of parenthood cannot be made a crime. This, however, is the effect of RSA 269-C:24 IV. Even if the parent has been as careful as anyone could be, even if the parent has forbidden the conduct, and even if the parent is justifiably unaware of the activities of the child, criminal liability is still imposed under the wording of the present statute. There is no other basis for criminal responsibility other than the fact that a person is the parent of one who violates the law.

One hundred and twenty seven years ago the justices of this court in giving their opinions regarding a proposed law that would have imposed vicarious criminal liability on an employer for acts of his employee stated, "(b)ut this does not seem to be in accordance with the spirit of our Constitution . . ." Because the net effect of the statute is to punish parenthood, the result is forbidden by substantive due process requirements of N.H.Const. pt. 1, art. 15.

Exceptions sustained.

DISSENT

BOIS, J.

The majority read RSA 269-C:24 IV in isolation. They conveniently ignore RSA 626:8 (Criminal Liability for Conduct of Another), which provides in subsection II that "(a) person is legally accountable for the conduct of another person when: (b) he is made accountable for the conduct of such other person by the law defining the offense. . . ." RSA 269-C:24 IV is such a law. Imposing criminal liability based on status for certain violations of a mala prohibitum nature does not offend constitutional requirements.

Even if I were to accept the majority's conclusion that the vicarious imposition of criminal liability on parents of children who have committed an OHRV [Off Highway Recreational Vehicles] violation under RSA ch. 269-C is constitutionally impermissible, I would still uphold the validity of RSA 269-C:24 IV. A closer reading of this State's Criminal Code belies the majority's reasoning that RSA 269-C:24 IV holds parents of minor offenders criminally responsible for their children's offenses solely on the basis of their parental status. RSA 626:1 I, enunciating the fundamental principle of the Criminal Code, states that all criminal liability must be based on a "voluntary act" or "voluntary omission." When RSA 269-C:24 IV is read in conjunction with RSA 626:1 I, a parental conviction can result only when the State shows beyond a reasonable doubt that a minor child has committed a violation under a provision of chapter 269-C, and that his parent voluntarily performed or omitted to perform an act such as participating in the minor's conduct, or entrusting, or negligently allowing his minor child to operate an OHRV.

When RSA 269-C:24 IV is construed to require a voluntary act or voluntary omission in accordance with RSA 626:1 I, there are no due process infirmities, either under N.H.Const. pt. 1, art. 15 or U.S. Const. amend. XIV, § 1. Culpable intent is not required to impose criminal penalties for minor infractions. "It is well settled in this jurisdiction that the Legislature may declare criminal a certain act or omission to act without requiring it to be done with intent."

When the legislature imposes criminal responsibility without requiring intent, we will override it only when such imposition violates concepts of fundamental fairness. In the present case, there is a demonstrable public interest to assure the safe operation of OHRVs, and the minor penalties imposed upon violators of RSA 269-C:24 IV are insubstantial. In such circumstances, we will not second guess the wisdom of the legislature.

Public welfare offenses requiring no criminal intent have also been held consistent with the due process requirements of U.S. Const. amend. XIV, § 1. "There is wide latitude in the lawmakers to declare an offense and to exclude elements of knowledge and diligence from its definition." "In vindicating its public policy . . . a State in punishing particular acts may provide that 'he who shall do them shall do them at his peril. . . .' "

Questions

1. Exactly what does the New Hampshire statute prohibit?

2. Summarize all of the arguments of the majority and dissenting opinions. Which side do you agree with? Defend your answer.

3. Apart from the legal and constitutional arguments, do you think it's good public policy to make parents criminally liable for their children's crimes? Defend your answer.

 Go to Exercise 5-2 on the Criminal Law CD to learn more about vicarious liability of parents for their children's crimes.

SUMMARY

    I. Two types of liability for someone else's crimes
        A. Parties to crime (complicity) establishes when you can be held liable for others' crimes
        B. Vicarious liability establishes which types of relationships can create criminal liability

II. Parties to crime
    A. Four types of parties to crime at common law
        1. Principals in the first degree actually commit the crime
        2. Principles in the second degree are present when the crimes are committed
        3. Accessories before the fact
           a. Help before the crime is committed
           b. Are not present when the crime is committed
        4. Accessories after the fact help after the crime is committed
    B. Participation before and during crime (accomplices)
        1. Are prosecuted for committing the crime itself (helping a murderer is murder)
        2. Accomplice *actus reus*
           a. Core idea—accomplice took some positive act to help commit a crime
           b. Words can be accomplice *actus reus*
           c. Presence at the crime scene isn't enough unless there's a duty (parent to minor child)
           d. Actions after the crime can be relevant to prove *actus reus*
        3. Accomplice *mens rea*
           a. Purposely clearly qualifies
           b. Jurisdictions vary and sometimes are confused as to whether knowledge, recklessness, or negligence qualify
    C. Participation after the commission of a crime (accessory)
        1. Is a separate lesser offense than accomplice liability
        2. Elements of accessory after the fact
           a. Accessory personally helped the person who committed the felony (*actus reus* element)
           b. Accessory knew a felony was committed (*mens rea* element)
           c. Accessory helped for the purpose of hindering prosecution (*mens rea* element)
           d. Someone other than the accessory actually committed a felony (circumstance element)

III. Vicarious liability
    A. Vicarious liability bases liability on a relationship between a person who commits the crime and someone else
    B. Corporate vicarious liability
        1. Pinpointing responsibility is difficult because of the complexity of organizations and the number of people making decisions
        2. Constitutional and policy questions
           a. Due process issues
               (1) Liability is based on relationship and not acts and/or intent
               (2) Fairness to shareholders, who usually pay the fines
           b. Policy question—is there a deterrent effect?
    C. Individual vicarious liability
        1. Traffic violation
           a. Difficulty proving who parked the vehicle
           b. Prima facie case—presumes driver was the operator and is responsible
        2. Parental responsibility

    a. Constitutional question—due process of holding parents responsibility
       solely on the parent-child relationship
    b. Policy goals
       (1) Protect public from violent juveniles
       (2) Get parents to control their kids

 Go to the Criminal Law 8e CD to download this summary outline. The outline has been
formatted so that you can add notes to it during class lectures, or later create a customized
chapter outline to use while reviewing. Either way, the summary outline will help you
understand the "big picture" and fill in the details as you study.

REVIEW QUESTIONS

1. Identify the basic idea of criminal law reflected in the doctrines of complicity
   (parties to crime) and vicarious liability.

2. Identify the two ways criminal liability for someone else's crimes arises.

3. Explain the basic difference between the doctrines of complicity (parties to crime)
   and vicarious liability.

4. Explain the differences between accomplice and accessory liability.

5. What's the thinking behind punishing them differently?

6. Identify and give examples of the core idea of accomplice *actus reus*.

7. When does presence at the scene of a crime satisfy the *actus reus* requirement of
   accomplice liability?

8. What does participation *after* crimes are committed have to do with participation
   before and *during* the commission of crimes?

9. Explain and give examples of the trouble accomplice *mens rea* creates for courts.

10. List the four elements of accessory liability, and identify whether each is an *actus
    reus, mens rea,* or circumstance element.

11. Explain why conviction and punishment on the basis of vicarious liability is diffi-
    cult to obtain in corporate crimes.

12. List and summarize the objections to vicarious liability for corporate crimes.

13. Identify the two doctrines prosecutors rely on to prove corporate liability.

14. Describe and explain why vicarious liability for traffic offenses was created.

15. Identify and explain how vicarious traffic liability statutes are written to give own-
    ers a way out of liability.

16. Explain the difference between traditional parental responsibility statutes and par-
    ents' vicarious liability for their kids' crimes.

17. Identify two reasons for the creation of vicarious liability of parents for their kids'
    crimes.

KEY TERMS

parties to crime p. 115
complicity p. 115
vicarious liability p. 115
doctrine of complicity p. 115
doctrine of vicarious liability
    p. 115
principals in the first degree p. 116

principals in the second degree
    p. 116
accessories before the fact p. 116
accessories after the fact p. 116
accomplices p. 116
accessories p. 116
conspiracy p. 116

Pinkerton rule p. 116
accomplice *actus reus* p. 117
mere presence rule p. 117
prima facie p. 136
parental responsibility laws p. 139

SUGGESTED READINGS

Go to the Criminal Law 8e CD for Suggested Readings for this chapter.

THE COMPANION WEB SITE
FOR *CRIMINAL LAW,* EIGHTH EDITION

http://cj.wadsworth.com/samaha/crim_law8e

Supplement your review of this chapter by going to the companion Web site to take one of the Tutorial Quizzes, use the flash cards to test your knowledge of the elements of various crimes and defenses, and check out the many other study aids you'll find there. You'll find valuable data and resources at your fingertips to help you study for that big exam or write that important paper.

Inchoate Crimes: Attempt, Conspiracy, and Solicitation

6

Chapter Main Points

- Inchoate offenses are about punishing someone for crimes they haven't finished committing.
- Inchoate offenses require *some* action but not enough to finish the crime intended.
- Liability for criminal attempt offenses is based on two rationales: preventing dangerous conduct and neutralizing dangerous people.
- The *mens rea* of inchoate crimes is the specific intent to commit a crime.
- The *actus reus* of attempt is an action that's beyond mere preparation but not completing the crime.
- Legal impossibility is a defense to attempt liability; factual impossibility isn't.
- Voluntary and complete abandonment of an attempt in progress *may* be a defense to attempt liability.
- Criminal conspiracy is the crime of agreeing with one or more persons to commit a crime.
- Criminal solicitation is the crime of trying to get another person or persons to commit a crime.
- Punishing conspiracy and solicitation to commit a crime is based on nipping in the bud, the special danger of group criminality.

Did He Attempt to Murder His Wife?

Ralph Damms and his estranged wife Marjory were parked in a restaurant parking lot. Ralph asked Marjory how much money she had with her, and she said "a couple of dollars." Ralph then requested to see Marjory's checkbook; she refused to give it to him. They quarreled. Marjory opened the car door and started to run around the restaurant building screaming, "Help!" Ralph pursued her with the pistol in his hand. Marjory's cries for help attracted the attention of the persons inside the restaurant, including two officers of the State Traffic Patrol who were eating lunch. One officer rushed out of the front door and the other the rear door. In the meantime, Marjory had run nearly around three sides of the building. In seeking to avoid colliding with a child that was in her path, she turned, slipped, and fell. Ralph crouched down, held the pistol at her head, and pulled the trigger; but nothing happened. He then exclaimed, "It won't fire. It won't fire." ◆

We all know that a man who chases his wife around a restaurant parking lot and shoots her in the head and kills her with the loaded gun in his hand when she trips and falls commits murder. But, what about the same man who does the same thing, but unbeknown to him, the gun's not loaded? When he pulls the trigger and nothing happens, he yells, "It won't fire! It won't fire!" What crime is that? That's what this chapter is about—criminal liability for trying to commit crimes (**criminal attempts**); for making agreements with someone else to commit crimes (**criminal conspiracy**); and for trying to get someone else to commit a crime (**criminal solicitation**). We call these three crimes **inchoate offenses.** (The word *inchoate* comes from the Latin "to begin.") Each inchoate offense has its own elements, but they all share two elements: the *mens rea* of purpose (specific intent [Chapter 4]) and the *actus reus* of taking some steps toward accomplishing the criminal purpose—but not enough steps to complete the crime.

Incomplete criminal conduct poses the dilemma whether to punish someone who's done no harm or to set free someone who's determined to commit a crime. The doctrine of inchoate crimes asks the question: How far should criminal law go to prevent crime by punishing people who haven't accomplished their criminal purpose? Creating criminal liability for uncompleted crimes flies in the face of the notion that free societies punish people for what they've done, not for what they might do. On the other hand, the doctrine of inchoate crimes reflects the widely held belief that "an ounce of prevention is worth a pound of cure." The law of inchoate crimes resolves the dilemma by three means:

1. Requiring a specific intent (purpose) to commit the crime or cause a harm

2. Requiring some action to carry out the purpose

3. Punishing inchoate crimes less severely than completed crimes (American Law Institute 1985 [3], 293–298; Perkins and Boyce 1982, 611–658)

ATTEMPT

Failure is an unwelcome part of everyday life. But, in criminal law, we hope for failure. Criminal attempt is probably the best-known failure in criminal law. So, we're relieved when a wannabe murderer shoots at someone and misses the target, and we're happy when a store detective interrupts an aspiring thief from stealing a CD from a bin in Best Buy®.

In this section, we'll look at how the history of attempt law has evolved over more than one thousand years, rationales for attempt law, the elements of criminal attempt, and how failures to complete crimes because of either impossibility or voluntary abandonment are treated within the law.

History of the Law of Attempt

> [One who] has a purpose and intention to slay another and only wounds him should be regarded as a murderer.
>
> Plato, *Laws*, 360 BC

> For what harm did the attempt cause, since the injury took no effect?
>
> Henry of Bracton (about 1300)

These two quotes, almost a thousand years apart, underscore how long philosophers and judges have struggled with how the criminal law should respond to criminal attempts. By the 1400s, English judges were applying what became a famous common law maxim: "The will shall be taken for the deed." According to the great common-law judge, Justice Shardlowe, "[O]ne who is taken in the act of robbery or burglary, even though he does not carry it out, will be hanged" (Fletcher 1978, 131; Hall 1960, 560–564).

According to the common law, the crime of attempt required more than the bare intent to commit a crime; the early cases required three elements:

1. Purpose (specific intent)

2. Substantial acts to carry out the criminal purpose

3. *Some* injury

Two leading cases illustrate these elements. In the first, a servant, after cutting his master's throat, fled with the master's goods. In the second, a wife's lover attacked and seriously injured her husband, leaving him for dead. Both the servant and the lover were punished for attempted murder because they'd taken substantial steps toward completing the crime *and* also seriously injured their victims (Hall 1960, 560–564).

During the 1500s, English criminal attempt law began to resemble today's attempt law. These beginnings of our modern crime of attempt grew out of threats to peace and safety in a society where everyone was armed and known for hot, short tempers and violent, quarrelsome tendencies. The famous royal court (a special court of the monarch not bound by common-law rules) that met in the Star Chamber started punishing a wide range of potential harms, hoping to nip violence in the bud. Typical cases included lying in wait, threats, challenges, and even words that "tended to challenge." Surviving records are full of efforts to punish budding violence that too often erupted into serious injury and death (Elton 1972, 170–171).

In the early 1600s, the English common-law courts began to develop a doctrine of attempt law. Stressing the need to prevent the serious harms spawned by dueling, Francis Bacon maintained that "all the acts of preparation should be punished." He argued for this criminal attempt principle:

> I take it to be a ground infallible: that wheresoever an offense is capital, or matter of felony, though it be not acted, there the combination or acting tending to the offense is punishable.... Nay, inceptions and preparations in inferior crimes, that are not capital have likewise been condemned.
>
> Samaha 1974; Samaha 1981, 189

By the late 1700s, the English common-law courts had created a full-fledged law of attempt. In 1784, in the great case of *Rex v. Scofield* (1784), a servant put a lighted candle in his master's house, intending to burn the house down. The house didn't burn, but the servant was punished anyway. According to the court, "the intent may make an act, innocent in itself, criminal; nor is the completion of an act, criminal in itself, necessary to constitute criminality."

By the 1800s, common-law attempt was well defined as follows:

> All attempts whatever to commit indictable offenses, whether felonies or misdemeanors... are misdemeanors, unless by some special statutory enactment they are subjected to special punishment.
>
> Stephen 1883, 2:224

Some jurisdictions still follow the common law of attempt. In 1979, a Maryland appeals court judge confidently wrote that "the common law is still alive and well in Maryland," and that the common law of attempt "still prospers on these shores" (*Gray v. State* 1979, 854). As of July 2003, no cases in Maryland have disputed this claim.

Rationales for Criminal Attempt Law

Why do we punish people who haven't hurt anyone? There are two old and firmly entrenched rationales. One focuses on dangerous conduct (*actus reus*), the other on dangerous persons (*mens rea*). The **dangerous conduct rationale** looks at how close defendants came to completing their crimes. The **dangerous person rationale** concentrates on how fully defendants have developed their criminal purpose. Both rationales measure dangerousness according to actions; but they do so for different reasons. The dangerous conduct rationale aims at preventing harm from dangerous acts; so, its concern is how close to completion the crime was. The dangerous person rationale aims at neutralizing dangerous people; so, it looks at how developed the defendant's criminal purpose was (Brodie 1995, 237–238).

The Elements of Criminal Attempt

The crime of attempt boils down to three elements:

1. Intent or purpose to commit a specific crime

2. Act or acts to carry out the intent

3. Failure to complete the crime

ELEMENTS OF ATTEMPT LIABILITY		
Actus Reus	**Mens Rea**	**Result**
1. Substantial steps toward the completion of the crime 2. Minority rules: All but the last act necessary to commit the crime	The specific intent— that is, the purpose, to commit the crime attempted	The failure to complete the attempted crime

There are two types of attempt statutes. Alabama's **general attempt statute** is typical: "A person is guilty of an attempt to commit a crime if, with the intent to commit a specific offense, he does any overt act towards the commission of such offense" (Alabama Criminal Code 1975). **Specific attempt statutes** define attempted murder, attempted robbery, attempted rape, and so on in separate statutes.

We'll look at attempt *mens rea* and attempt *actus reus* to learn what the law requires to prove the first two elements of attempt.

 Go to Exercise 6-1 on the Criminal Law 8e CD to learn more about your state's attempt statute.

Attempt *Mens Rea*

Attempt is a crime of purpose, as its very name tells us. *Attempt* means to try, and you can't try to do something you don't intend to do. As one authority put it:

> To attempt something...necessarily means to seek to do it, to make a deliberate effort in that direction. Intent is inherent in the notion of attempt; it is the essence of the crime. An attempt without intent is unthinkable; it cannot be.
>
> Enker 1977, 847

So, when it comes to **attempt *mens rea*,** you don't have to worry about knowing, reckless, negligent, or strict liability attempts.

But, U.S. Supreme Court Justice and legal philosopher Oliver Wendell Holmes, in his classic essay, *The Common Law*, criticized the view that there can be no attempt without specific intent:

> Acts should be judged by their tendency, under the known circumstances, not by the actual intent which accompanies them. It may be true that in the region of attempts, as elsewhere, the law began with cases of actual intent, as these cases were the most obvious ones. But it cannot stop with them, unless it attaches more importance to the etymological meaning of the word attempt than to the general principles of punishment.
>
> Holmes 1963, 54–55

Despite the weight of Justice Holmes' views, having the purpose to act or to bring about a specific result remains the linchpin of criminal attempt *mens rea*. The Ohio Court of Appeals decided whether Barbara Coulverson intended to commit murder in *State v. Coulverson* (2002).

Did She Specifically Intend to Kill the Victim?

State v. Coulverson
2002 WL 433633 (OhioApp. 10 Dist.)

Barbara Coulverson, Defendant, was convicted by a jury in the Court of Common Pleas, Franklin County, of attempted murder and was sentenced to 10 years in prison. She appealed. The Court of Appeals affirmed.

BRYANT, J.

FACTS

Defendant-appellant, Barbara J. Coulverson aka Caldwell's, . . . appeal arises out of an incident where an assailant struck eighty-one-year-old Emma Lindsley ("the victim") several times on her head with a barbell at the victim's apartment in Columbus, Ohio. The assailant then stole between fifty and eighty dollars from the victim, disconnected her telephone, and left her bleeding profusely. The victim suffered several lacerations to her head, and broken fingers from her efforts to shield her head during the attack.

According to the state's evidence, the victim lived in a government subsidized apartment building that housed senior citizens and handicapped persons capable of independent living. The victim used a walker, had a housekeeper because she could not clean the apartment herself, received Meals on Wheels because she did not cook, and relied on a friend to take her to the grocery store. A church van transported her to church services at Mt. Vernon Baptist Church, which she attended regularly. The victim joined Mt. Vernon Baptist Church because she was unable to manage the steps at her former church. The victim had no family in Columbus, but talked to the pastor of her church several times a week.

On Saturday, December 2, 2000, the victim was sitting in the lobby of her apartment building when defendant unexpectedly appeared at the door. The apartment building had a security door, but the victim let defendant into the building because she knew defendant since: (1) the victim and defendant were members of the same church, where the victim sat behind the defendant at services on Sundays, (2) the victim and defendant occasionally went with a group of church members to restaurants after church services, and (3) on one previous occasion the defendant had been to the victim's apartment to borrow forty dollars, which she repaid.

The victim and defendant chatted in the lobby of the apartment building for some time, during which the victim introduced defendant to some of the building's residents. When the victim mentioned she was hungry for a fish sandwich, the defendant offered to get her one. The victim gave defendant some money from a small pouch she carried, and defendant left to get the food. When defendant returned approximately an hour later, the fish sandwich was cold and they went to the victim's apartment so she could eat the sandwich.

According to the victim, she ate her sandwich while she was sitting in a chair facing a coffee table in the living room; defendant sat at the kitchen table smoking a cigarette. The victim testified that after she asked defendant to pour some orange juice, defendant sneaked up behind her and began hitting her in the head with a barbell defendant had hidden in her jacket. The victim testified she moved into her bedroom where defendant again struck her in the head with the barbell and yelled at the victim to "give me your money." The victim gave defendant the pouch in which she kept her money, and defendant took over fifty dollars from the pouch. Defendant counted the money while the victim was "bleeding like a hog"; defendant pulled the telephone connection out of the wall and left the victim's apartment. While blood ran down her face and all over her clothes, the victim reconnected her telephone and called her pastor, whose number she had near the telephone. The victim told her pastor defendant had attacked and robbed her. The victim identified defendant in court as the person who attacked and robbed her.

Pastor Henry Leftridge immediately drove to the victim's apartment and arrived fifteen to twenty minutes later. Pastor Leftridge testified that upon entering the victim's apartment he "saw the most horrible scene that I have seen in my life." He stated the victim was bleeding profusely and "had blood all over her. She had visible gashes in her head. She had bruises on her arms, on her hands, on her face. And I am amazed that she's still alive." Pastor Leftridge described the scene as "blood everywhere," with blood in the hallway, bedroom, living room and bathroom, and on the carpet, walls, furniture, sink, and the victim's clothing. The pastor called 9-1-1. The following Monday, the pastor spent several hours in the victim's apartment attempting to clean up the blood and throwing away bloodied clothing and other items. Two of the victim's chairs and her bedspread had to be discarded due to bloodstains on them. Bloodstains on the carpet could not be removed.

Paramedics were dispatched at 4:50 P.M. and arrived at the victim's apartment at 4:54 P.M. The paramedics found at least seven one-inch cuts on the victim's scalp, but found her to be alert, oriented and able to answer questions properly. The paramedics dressed the victim's wounds, gave her oxygen and an I.V., and transported her by ambulance to Grant Medical Center, where she remained for over three days. At the hospital, she received stitches in her hand, as well as clamps and stitches in her head where she suffered nine severe lacerations.

Detective Christopher Rond briefly interviewed the victim after her arrival at the hospital. Appearing lucid, the victim told him what happened at her apartment and specifically identified defendant as the person who struck her with a barbell and robbed her. Following the interview, the detective went to the victim's apartment, which he described as having a vast amount of blood throughout it. When the detective again interviewed the victim six days later at her apartment, the victim again named defendant as the person who assaulted her with a barbell, which the victim described as orange-red in color. The victim also identified defendant in a photographic array.

The detective subsequently interviewed defendant, who acknowledged being in the victim's apartment the afternoon the victim was assaulted. The detective and other law enforcement personnel executed a search warrant on defendant's house on January 2, 2001, during which a pair of barbells and another, single, barbell were collected. The single barbell was concealed in an old dusty medical bag covered by other items. The single barbell matched the description of the barbell the victim gave to the detective.

The defense rested without presenting any evidence, and the jury found defendant guilty of attempted murder.... Proceeding directly to sentencing, the court ordered defendant to serve ten years for the attempted murder.... Coulverson appealed....

OPINION

...Coulverson contends her conviction for attempted murder is supported by insufficient evidence and is against the manifest weight of the evidence. Coulverson asserts the prosecution failed to present medical testimony that the cuts to the victim's head, either individually or cumulatively, were life-threatening, and accordingly failed to demonstrate that Coulverson acted purposefully or specifically intended to cause the victim's death.

To the extent Coulverson challenges her conviction as not supported by sufficient evidence, we construe the evidence in favor of the prosecution and determine whether such evidence permits any rational trier of fact to find the essential elements of the offense beyond a reasonable doubt. When presented with a manifest weight argument, we engage in a limited weighing of the evidence to determine whether the jury's verdict is supported by sufficient

competent, credible evidence to permit reasonable minds to find guilt beyond a reasonable doubt. "When a court of appeals reverses a judgment of a trial court on the basis that the verdict is against the weight of the evidence, the appellate court sits as a 'thirteenth juror' and disagrees with the fact finder's resolution of the conflicting testimony" Determinations of credibility and weight of the testimony remain within the province of the trier of fact.

To establish attempted murder...the state must establish that Coulverson "purposely engaged in conduct which, if successful, would have caused [the victim's] death." A person acts purposely when it is his or her specific intention to cause a certain result. A jury may infer an intent to kill where (1) the natural and probable consequence of a defendant's act is to produce death, and (2) all of the surrounding circumstances allow the conclusion that a defendant had an intent to kill. A jury may infer an intent to kill where the victim was vulnerable and was struck in the head with a forceful blow.

Here, the victim was a vulnerable eighty-one-year-old woman who needed a walker to get around, and who was unable to cook meals or clean her apartment without assistance. The evidence at trial allows an inference that Coulverson, who was an acquaintance of the victim, purposely brought a concealed barbell into the victim's apartment for the purpose of assaulting and robbing the victim. The victim was forcefully struck on the head several times with a barbell, causing at least seven severe lacerations and heavy bleeding. Based on evidence that the attacker disconnected the telephone and left the victim weakened and bleeding profusely, the jury rationally could infer and conclude that the attacker intended the victim to bleed to death without being able to summon help. Construed in favor of the prosecution, the evidence supports Coulverson's conviction of attempted murder.

Judgment AFFIRMED.

Questions

1. List all the facts relevant to deciding whether Barbara Coulverson intended to kill her 81-year-old victim.

2. State the Ohio attempt *mens rea*.

3. Assume you're the prosecutor. Relying on the facts in the case and the definition of attempted murder *mens rea*, argue that the evidence proves beyond a reasonable doubt that Coulverson beat the victim for the very purpose of killing her.

4. Now, assume you're Coulverson's lawyer. Relying on the facts of the case and the definition of attempted murder *mens rea*, try to raise a reasonable doubt about Coulverson's purpose in beating the victim with the barbell.

5. In your opinion, did Coulverson have the specific intent to kill the victim? Back up your answer with specific points made in the opinion and with relevant matter from your text.

EXPLORING ATTEMPT MENS REA FURTHER

 Go to the Criminal Law 8e CD to read the full text versions of the cases featured here.

1. *Did He Stab Her for the "Very Purpose" of Killing Her?*

FACTS

In August 1995, Eileen Ridgeway-Taylor got an order of protection prohibiting her sometimes live-in boyfriend, Robert King, from engaging in "illegal conduct" for three years. Although the two continued to see each other, at her request, City of Albany police officers removed him from her apartment in early March 1996. Thereafter, she began a relationship with her future husband. On April 23, 1996, at approximately 1:30 P.M., Ridgeway-Taylor heard her neighbor, Kellie Nadeau, call out that King was approaching the building. King entered Ridgeway-Taylor's apartment and approached her with a large carving knife raised above his head uttering, "I'm going to kill you."

In the presence of her two young daughters, King stabbed her in the head and knee. At some point, Ridgeway-Taylor opened the front door of her apartment. Albany Police Detective Joseph Iwaniec, responding to the scene, observed King on top of Ridgeway-Taylor attempting to stab her. According to Iwaniec, King lunged at him with the knife and he shot King in the arm. King fled the apartment through the rear door and was apprehended a short time later. Did King stab Ridgeway-Taylor for the very purpose of killing her?

DECISION AND REASONS

Yes, said the jury. And, yes, ruled the New York Supreme Court, Appellate Division, Third Department.

Here, the evidence demonstrated that at the outset of the assault defendant stated, "I'm going to kill you." Furthermore, after stabbing her in the head and knee, defendant taunted her by asking "where is your protector now" and saying, "I should just kill you and the kids" while raising the knife up and down and slapping her several times on the leg with the side of the blade. Additionally, Nadeau testified that she heard Ridgeway-Taylor scream for help during the assault and that, as she and her boyfriend tried to lend aid, defendant shouted, "I'll kill you. I'll kill the kids. I'll—Everyone will die in this motherf___er."

We further note that the wound inflicted to Ridgeway-Taylor's head required deep sutures and defendant was still attempting to stab her when Iwaniec intervened. We find that the evidence presented a valid line of reasoning together with a permissible inference of lethal intent from which any rational trier of fact could find defendant guilty beyond a reasonable doubt of all the essential elements of the crime of attempted murder in the second degree.

Furthermore, the verdict is not contrary to the weight of the evidence. Although it may be argued that a different verdict would not have been unreasonable based upon the evidence, upon "weighing the relative probative force of conflicting testimony and the relative strength of conflicting inferences that may be drawn from the testimony" we find that the jury gave the evidence the weight it should be accorded.

State v. King, 293 A.D.2d 815 (N.Y. Supreme Court, 2002)

2. *Did He Intend to Kill or to Injure Her?*

FACTS

At trial, Deputy Joseph Ortego testified that, at approximately 1:55 P.M. on September 12, 1999, he responded to a disturbance call at an apartment on Orange Blossom Lane in Harvey, Louisiana. When he got there, he observed blood splatters on a sports utility vehicle parked in front of the apartment. Deputy Ortego was approached by the Defendant (Thaddeus Harrell) who had blood all over his hands and advised the deputy that he had just "beat up his old lady." After handcuffing Harrell, Deputy Ortego went into the apartment and discovered the victim, lying face down on the ground in a large pool of blood, unconscious, but breathing. The apartment was in disarray, with furniture overturned, things broken and blood splattered everywhere, including the walls.

Deputy Ortego called for an ambulance and the victim was transported to Charity Hospital, where she was treated for massive facial injuries. She had three facial lacerations: a three-centimeter laceration below the right eye involving the corner of the eye and tear duct system, a four-centimeter laceration above the left eye to the forehead with the bone showing, and a two-centimeter laceration on her lower lip. She also sustained massive facial fractures including a blowout fracture of her right eye socket and nasal fractures. Was Harrell guilty of attempted murder?

DECISION AND REASONS

The state said yes. Harrell appealed. In upholding his conviction, the Louisiana Appeals court wrote:

> To prove attempted second degree murder, the State must establish, beyond a reasonable doubt, that the Defendant specifically intended to kill a human being and that he committed an overt act in furtherance of that goal. Specific intent to inflict great bodily harm is sufficient to support a murder conviction, but first or second degree attempted murder requires a specific intent to kill. Specific intent is "that state of mind which exists when the circumstances indicate that the offender actively desired the prescribed criminal consequences to follow his act or failure to act" La.R.S. 14:10(1). Because specific intent is a state of mind, it need not be proven as a fact but may be inferred from the circumstances and actions of the defendant. The intent to kill may be inferred from the extent and severity of the victim's injuries. . . .
>
> In the present case, the Defendant admitted that he hit his wife several times with his fists. Although he testified that he never intended to kill his wife, his specific intent to kill can be inferred from his actions and the extent and severity of the victim's injuries. Defendant first hit his wife outside of the apartment and continued to beat her when they went inside the apartment. There was an obvious struggle during the assault. The apartment furnishings were strewn about and some furniture and other items were broken. Blood was splattered all over the walls and the ceiling, demonstrating the force with which the Defendant struck the victim. The Defendant had blood all over his hands. He continued to beat her until she was unconscious. Although he claimed that he loved her and was concerned after she became unconscious, he nevertheless failed to obtain emergency medical help.
>
> Dr. Lala Dunbar, the attending emergency room physician and director of the Medical Emergency Room at Charity Hospital, testified that the victim's beating was among the worst cases that she had seen in her 16 years in the emergency room at Charity Hospital. She stated that the victim's eyes were swollen shut and that the injuries to the victim's right eye required immediate surgery. In addition, the victim sustained three deep facial

> lacerations, massive facial fractures and massive swelling of her face.
>
> Unquestionably, the victim suffered severe injuries as a result of the beating. We find that the severity of the victim's injuries demonstrates the Defendant's specific intent to kill. Thus, the State proved the essential elements of the charged offense, attempted second degree murder, beyond a reasonable doubt.
>
> *State v. Harrell*, 811 So.2d 1015 (La.App. 2002)

3. *Did She Shoot with the Intent to Kill?*

FACTS

At approximately 10:20 P.M. on May 23, 1999, Mauricio Licea and his wife, Ana, parked their car in the parking lot of a Ralph's grocery store. Mauricio went into the store while Ana waited in the car. Mauricio returned to the car a few minutes later. As he opened the driver's side door to get in the car, the defendant (Lashun Pamela Moreland) approached him. Mauricio got in the car and shut the door. Moreland stood outside next to the car, knocked on the driver's side window, and said something. Mauricio tried to ignore her.

Moreland pulled a gun, pointed it at Mauricio, and motioned for him to open the door. Mauricio did not comply. Moreland then put her hand in the driver's side wing window opening and opened the door. Simultaneously, a man, identified as codefendant Hafez Hakeem, opened the car's rear door and got in the back seat. Hakeem pointed a gun at Ana's head, and Moreland pointed her gun at Mauricio's head.

Hakeem and Moreland took several items from Mauricio and Ana, including Mauricio's watch, Ana's engagement ring, cash, and a receipt from a market named Numero Uno. Moreland yelled at Mauricio, who did not speak English. Still, Mauricio tried to explain to Moreland that he had nothing left for her to take.

Hakeem struck Mauricio in the back of his head with the gun. Mauricio tried to get out of the car, raising his hands to his shoulders. Moreland pulled the trigger of her gun in rapid succession. Her gun did not fire during the first couple of attempts, but it then did so, hitting Mauricio twice in his abdomen and once in a finger. After the shooting, Moreland and Hakeem ran away. . . . Mauricio suffered extensive damage to his intestines as a result of the shooting. He underwent two surgeries, was hospitalized for 20 days, and had to wear colostomy bags for 8 months. . . . Did Moreland shoot Mauricio Licea for the purpose of killing him?

DECISION AND REASONS

Yes, according to the appeals court:

> Moreland and her cohort robbed Mauricio and Ana Licea at gunpoint while they were seated in their car. During the robbery, defendant pointed a gun at Mauricio's head. When Mauricio tried to exit the car, defendant fired point-blank at Mauricio in rapid succession. Although defendant's first few attempts were ineffectual, apparently because her gun misfired, she succeeded in shooting Mauricio twice in his abdomen and once in his finger. A bullet was discovered inside of Mauricio's car. The foregoing reasonably supports a determination that defendant specifically intended to kill Mauricio when she shot him. That the evidence might support a different inference, i.e., that defendant panicked and in her panic she fired the gun without intending to kill Mauricio, is immaterial. On appeal, we are required to determine the legal sufficiency of the evidence and not to reweigh the evidence or second-guess the reasonable inferences reached by the trier of fact.
>
> *People v. Moreland*, WL 459026, (Cal.App. 2 Dist. 2002)

4. *Did He Shoot with the "Intent to Kill"?*

FACTS

Opposing Black and Hispanic gangs co-existed in the Compton area with Rosecrans Boulevard as the boundary between them. Each gang had been involved in murders and shootings against one another. Robert Howell was a member of one of the gangs. On July 11, 1999, Jose Perez, Sr., his wife Juana Gomez, and their sons, Jose Perez, Jr. (Jose) and David Hernandez, were eating outdoors at a restaurant on Rosecrans Boulevard. Serafin Maciel, a brother, and two friends were also eating at a nearby outdoor table. Mr. Maciel saw Howell walk past the restaurant. Approximately five minutes later, Howell fired multiple gunshots from the driveway of the restaurant. Twelve-year-old Jose was shot in the head and died two days later. Howell moved closer to the restaurant, shouted something, fired two more shots, and then left. Mr. Maciel and his companions fled. They drove away from the restaurant in Mr. Maciel's car. Later that day, Mr. Maciel discovered seven bullet holes in the back of his car. . . .

On July 22, 1999, Compton Police Detective Timothy Brennan interviewed Howell. Following his waiver of rights . . . Howell confessed. A videotape of the confession was played for the jury at trial. Howell stated there had been a meeting of his gang prior to July 11, 1999, at a local park. A collection was taken up to buy guns in order "to take care of" the rival gang. Howell stated the rival gang was "constantly shooting at me everyday and shooting at my homeys everyday." Howell said he was at a location known as "the spot" on July 11, 1999. "The spot" was a place where "dope" was sold. Some of those present indicated rival gang members were at the nearby restaurant. Someone asked, "Who gonna put in some work?" Howell said he would do it. Everyone else was scared.

Howell got a nine-millimeter automatic handgun from another gang member at a nearby car wash. One gang member stood as a lookout nearby, while another blocked traffic with his truck. As Howell walked past the restaurant, he saw the rival gang members. He recognized one individual. Howell knew the person as "Woody." This individual had tattoos on his eyebrows. Howell turned around and began firing. Howell told Detective Brennan, "Then I'm trying to get them." Howell admitted trying to hit "Woody." Howell fired approximately 16 times. Howell saw people screaming and ducking. He ran down the street, through someone's backyard. Another gang member picked Howell up. Howell gave the gang member the gun. The gun was in turn given back to another gang member at the car wash. Howell was dropped off at his grandmother's home. . . .

In addition to murder charges for the death of Jose Perez, Jr., Howell was charged with attempting to murder four young men who were shot at but not injured during the shooting. Did Howell shoot at them for the specific purpose of killing them?

DECISION AND REASONS

Yes, said the California Court of Appeals:

> Intent to kill is a necessary element of attempted murder. Howell argues the evidence did not demonstrate he had an intent to kill. Rather, Howell argues, "[T]he fact [that] none of the men at the table were struck supports the inference [Howell] was shooting wildly, with no deliberate intention of hitting anyone, much less killing them." Our colleagues in Division Two of this appellate district have held: "One who intentionally attempts to kill another does not often declare his state of mind either before, at, or after the moment he shoots. Absent such direct evidence, the intent obviously must be derived from all the circumstances of the attempt, including the putative killer's actions and words. Whether Howell possessed the requisite intent to kill is, of course, a question for the trier of fact. . . ." In this case, Howell, by his own admission, fired some 16 shots in

the direction of 4 rival gang members, who were eating at a restaurant patio occupied by other patrons.

There was a history of shootings and killings between Howell's gang and a neighboring Hispanic gang. The members of Howell's gang had: met; collected money for guns; and planned how they would "get" the opposing gang. On the day of the incident, Howell volunteered to "put in some work." Detective Brennan testified that based on his 18 years experience with gangs in the Compton area, he understood the term "put in work" to mean, "It's to go to that gang's neighborhood and shoot at them." Howell deliberately: walked to the car wash to get the gun; walked past the restaurant once to locate the rival gang members; returned; and began shooting. In Howell's words: "Then I start firing. Firing at them. Then they start ducking and stuff. And then I'm trying to get them." Howell also explained: "I was trying to get the [rival gang members]. I wasn't trying to shoot no little kid....And I been shot at too many times. They try to kill me everyday. And I was trying to shoot them, too. I guess I didn't get the person that I wanted." In explaining that one of his gang members stood on the corner as a lookout while another blocked traffic with his truck, Howell stated, "That's when I walked in and start shooting at the person that was trying to shoot me."...

We...agree with the Attorney General that there was substantial evidence to support the jurors' findings the attempted murders were willful, deliberate, and premeditated. Section 664, subdivision (a), provides: "If the crime attempted is willful, deliberate, and premeditated murder...the person guilty of that attempt shall be punished by imprisonment in the state prison for life with the possibility of parole."...

Here...the gang to which Howell belonged had planned their revenge by purchasing guns and conspiring to "get" their rivals. Howell volunteered to do the "work" of the gang. Howell successfully obtained a semiautomatic weapon. Howell made a sweep past the restaurant in order to identify his targets. Once they were located, Howell returned and began firing at them. Howell continued to fire approximately 16 shots in the direction of the 4 young men. Howell had a motive, planned his attack, and intentionally followed through on the plan. During the time that he was carrying out these activities, Howell had ample time to reflect on and to premeditate what he was about to do. Therefore, the jury could reasonably find that the attempted murder of Mr. Maciel and his three companions was willful, deliberate, and premeditated.

People v. Howell, WL 126056 (Cal.App. 2 Dist. 2002)

Attempt *Actus Reus*

You're sitting in your apartment, planning in detail when, how, and where you're going to kill your boyfriend and your best friend for cheating on you with each other. You decide to do it tonight with your roommate's gun. You get up to go to her room and then what you're planning hits you, and you say to yourself, "What's wrong with me? What am I doing? I can't kill them." You go back and turn on the TV. I don't believe anyone would think you committed attempted murder. Why? Because of the basic idea that we don't punish people for their intentions. But, what if you went into her room, took the gun, loaded it, went to your boyfriend's apartment, and, when he answered the door, you took out the gun and were about to pull the trigger when his roommate knocked it out of your hand? I believe everybody would think you *did* commit attempted murder. Why? Because you did everything but the final act of firing the gun.

Most real cases aren't so easy. They fall somewhere between mere intent and "all but the last act" to complete the crime. The toughest question in attempt law is, "How close to completing a crime is close enough to satisfy the criminal act requirement of **attempt** *actus reus*?" The general answer is when a person crosses a critical line—the line between **preparation** (acts amounting to just getting ready to attempt) and acts that signal the beginning of the attempt itself.

Unfortunately, this general answer is *so* general it's useless as a guide for deciding (and for us, understanding) *real* cases. So, courts and attempt statutes have established tests for deciding when the acts of defendants have taken them further than just getting ready to attempt and brought them close enough to completing crimes to qualify as attempt *actus reus*. These tests focus on either or both of the two theories of attempt liability itself: the control of dangerous conduct and the control of dangerous persons. Let's look at the most common of these tests (*U.S. v. Mandujano* 1974, 375–376):

1. The **physical proximity** (nearness to completion) **tests**
2. The **unequivocality** (probable desistance) **test**
3. The *Model Penal Code* **("substantial steps") test**

The *physical proximity tests* are concerned with preventing and punishing dangerous conduct—namely, conduct that is close to turning into a completed crime. The proximity tests pay more attention to what defendants have left to do than to what they've already done. According to the physical proximity doctrine, the criminal law punishes conduct when it gets close to being successful. Of course, "all but the last act" satisfies this test, but the last act excludes dangerous conduct that ought to be included.

The physical proximity test (except in its unacceptable "all but the last act" form) is too general to give much guidance in answering the tough how-close-is-close-enough question. So courts have sharpened the test with a few others. The **indispensable element test** asks whether defendants have gotten control of everything they need to complete the crime. For example, a drug dealer can't attempt to sell "Ecstacy" until she gets some Ecstacy, even if she has a customer right there, ready and waiting to buy it. The **dangerous proximity test** asks whether defendants have come "dangerously close" to completing the crime. There are three ingredients in the test: the seriousness of the offense intended; the closeness to completion of the crime; and the probability the conduct will wind up completing the crime. The more serious the crime, the closer it is to completion, and the higher the probability of completing it, the stronger the case for calling it an attempt.

The unequivocality test contrasts with the proximity tests in important ways. First, it focuses more on what defendants have already done (and what they're likely to continue doing) than on what they have left to do. It asks, "What are the chances the defendant *won't* continue toward completing the crime (this is why the test is sometimes referred to as probable desistance)?" This question points to the second important difference between the proximity and the unequivocality test: proximity looks at dangerous people, not just at dangerous conduct. The test is also called the *res ipsa loquitur* ("the act speaks for itself") **test** because it examines whether an ordinary person who saw the defendants' acts without knowing their intent would guess that they were determined to commit a crime. The problem is the test is too lax; it could catch too many people who we don't want to punish. Why? Because hardly any acts are completely unequivocal (Low 1990, 279).

The *Model Penal Code* test was designed to accomplish three important goals.

1. Replace (or at least drastically reform) the proximity and unequivocality tests with a clearer and easier-to-understand-and-apply test
2. Draw more sharply (and push back further toward preparation) the line between preparation and beginning to attempt the crime

3. Base the law of attempt firmly on the theory of neutralizing dangerous persons, not just on preventing dangerous conduct

In line with these goals, the code's attempt *actus reus* includes two elements:

1. "Substantial steps" toward completing the crime *and*
2. Steps that "strongly corroborate the actor's criminal purpose"

In other words, the code requires that enough acts be taken to complete the crime—not so much to show that a crime is about to occur but to prove that the attempters are determined to commit it.

To sharpen the line between preparation and attempt, push it back closer to preparation, *and* make clear the commitment to neutralizing dangerous people, the code lists seven acts (most of which would qualify as mere preparation in traditional attempt statutes) that *can* amount to "substantial steps" if they strongly corroborate the actor's criminal purpose:

> (a) lying in wait, searching for or following the contemplated victim of the crime;
> (b) enticing or seeking to entice the contemplated victim of the crime to go to the place contemplated for its commission;
> (c) reconnoitering ["casing"] the place contemplated for the commission of the crime;
> (d) unlawful entry of a structure, vehicle or enclosure in which it is contemplated that the crime will be committed;
> (e) possession of materials to be employed in the commission of the crime, that are specially designed for such unlawful use or that can serve no lawful purpose of the actor under the circumstances;
> (f) possession, collection or fabrication of materials to be employed in the commission of the crime, at or near the place contemplated for its commission, if such possession, collection or fabrication serves no lawful purpose of the actor under the circumstances;
> (g) soliciting an innocent agent to engage in conduct constituting an element of the crime (American Law Institute 1985 [3], 296)

Borrowing from indecent liberties statutes (which make it a crime to lure minors into cars or houses for sex), the *Model Penal Code* provides that enticement satisfies the *actus reus* of criminal attempt. The drafters of the code say that enticement clearly demonstrates the intent to commit a crime—so, enticers are dangerous enough to punish. The code provides that reconnoitering—popularly called "casing a joint"—satisfies attempt *actus reus* because "scouting the scene of a contemplated crime" clearly signals the intent to commit the crime. By their unlawful entries, intruders also demonstrate their criminal purpose. The unlawful entry provision is particularly useful in two types of cases: entries to commit sex offenses and entries to steal. In one case (*Bradley v. Ward* 1955), two defendants entered a car intending to steal it, but they got out when the owner unexpectedly came back to the car. According to the court, the defendants hadn't attempted to steal the car. But under the *Model Penal Code* "unlawful entry" provision, they wouldn't have been so lucky.

In most states, collecting, possessing, or preparing materials used to commit crimes is preparation, not attempt. So, courts have found that buying a gun to murder someone, making a bomb to blow up a house, and collecting tools for a burglary are preparations, not attempts. Although these activities aren't criminal attempts, in many criminal codes it's a crime to possess items and substances like burglary tools, illegal drugs, drug paraphernalia, and concealed weapons (Chapter 3). Under the *Model Penal Code* (American Law Institute 1985 [3], 337–346), these possessions can be acts of attempt, but only if they "strongly corroborate" a purpose to commit a crime. Why? Because, say the code's authors, people who carry weapons and burglary tools with them with the clear intent to commit crimes are dangerous enough to punish.

The *Model Penal Code* says bringing weapons, equipment, and other materials to the scene of a crime can qualify as attempt *actus reus*. Examples include bringing guns to a robbery, explosives to an arson, or a ladder to a burglary. But the items have to be plainly instruments of crime. A potential robber who brings a gun to a bank is bringing an instrument of robbery; a would-be forger who brings a ballpoint pen into a bank isn't (American Law Institute 1985 [3], 337).

Preparation isn't criminal attempt. But, some states have created less serious preparation offenses. In Nevada, preparing to commit arson is a crime. Preparing to manufacture illegal substances is an offense in other states. These statutes are aimed at balancing the degree of threatening behavior and the dangerousness of persons against the remoteness in time and place of the intended harm (American Law Institute, 1985 [3], 354–345). *State v. Nesbitt* (2001) tries to answer the tough question, "How close to actually committing a robbery is close enough to satisfy the *actus reus* of attempt to commit robbery?"

CASE | ***Did He Get "Close Enough" to Robbing the Convenience Store?***

State v. Nesbitt

550 S.E.2d 864 (S.C.App. 2001)

Terry Lee Nesbitt, Defendant, was convicted in the Circuit Court, Spartanburg County, of attempted armed robbery. Nesbitt appealed. The Court of Appeals affirmed.

SHULER, J.

FACTS

In the early morning hours of June 10, 1998, Lawrence Brockman, an employee of the Fast Stop convenience store, was taking gas pump readings when he was approached by a man inquiring what time the store would close. After Brockman explained that he was in the process of closing the store, the man turned and walked away. Brockman later described him as a black male approximately five feet, nine inches tall.

Brockman then re-entered the store and went back behind the counter to the register. As Brockman looked up, he saw a man at the front door wearing a mask or goggles and waving a gun. The man did not enter the store, nor did he point the gun at anyone inside the store. Rather, Brockman testified he stopped at the door for approximately two seconds, then turned and fled. In his description to the police, Brockman stated only that the perpetrator was a black male.

Annie Sarratt, Brockman's common-law wife, also witnessed the incident. She testified that before Brockman left the store to check on the gas pumps, she was suspicious of someone in dark clothing loitering in front of the store. When Brockman returned, she asked what had taken so long. Brockman responded that he was attempting to determine who was ducking around the corner of the building. Sarratt then testified:

> I saw Mr. Brockman duck down and I didn't know what was going on. But I looked around. Somebody was in the door, two, two men. One man with dark clothing and I forgot what the other man had on. But [he] was waving something. So I ran to the poker machine and I ducked down and then they left. . . . They didn't come on in the store. But they had the door open and one guy [was] doing something like this [and] saying something. And the guy in the black ran. The other guy was still standing there and I said what was he saying. . . . [H]e wouldn't answer. He left.

Sarratt testified both perpetrators were black males, one of whom wore a hooded piece of clothing and waved something. She also identified one of the perpetrators as the man who had spoken to Brockman outside the store. On cross-examination, Brockman testified the man he spoke to was not the defendant, Terry Nesbitt, whom he knew.

Officer James Powell was the first officer to respond to the reported armed robbery. En route to the scene, Powell observed a black male fitting the description of the suspect and a white male walking side-by-side down railroad tracks near the store. The black male was the defendant, Terry Nesbitt. Powell testified that although he could not identify the object, Nesbitt had something black in his right hand. As Powell swung his patrol car around, Nesbitt fled down the tracks and into the woods. Shortly thereafter, a K-9 officer and his dog tracked Nesbitt and discovered him lying in the woods. Upon discovery, Nesbitt stated, "I threw it down."

The officers handcuffed Nesbitt and placed him in a patrol car. A search of the area along the route Nesbitt had been chased produced a black nylon stocking cap and a pair of goggles. While sitting in the patrol car, Nesbitt waived his *Miranda* rights and gave the following statement:

> Me and Michael and two other guys, black males, were sitting beside the store. . . . Michael said we would do the store. We smoked two rocks and I stayed at the back of the store. Michael had the gun. It looked like a .32 auto. I was going down Druid Street when they went in the store. Michael is a white male about six foot, twenty-six to twenty-seven years old, dark colored clothes, lives on Oak Dale Court. Michael changed clothes at the end of Druid Street and gave me the gun. The other two black males, I, I don't know their names. One lives at the boarding house on Druid Street. The other one I don't know anything about him. They are in their thirties. They always hanging around the store bumming for quarters. Me and Michael were walking down Henry Street. He was going home and I was too. Michael gave me the gun as he took a piss in the street. Then the police came up and I ran.

Nesbitt was subsequently charged with attempted armed robbery. At trial, he moved for a directed verdict based on the insufficiency of the evidence. The trial court denied the motion. Nesbitt was convicted and sentenced to ten years imprisonment. This appeal followed.

OPINION

When reviewing the denial of a motion for directed verdict in a criminal case, the evidence must be viewed in the light most favorable to the State. If there is any direct evidence or any substantial circumstantial evidence reasonably tending to prove the guilt of the accused, an appellate court must find that the case was properly submitted to the jury. This Court is concerned with the existence or non-existence of evidence, not its weight. Accordingly, the trial judge should grant the motion for directed verdict in those cases where the evidence merely raises a suspicion that the defendant is guilty.

Nesbitt argues the trial court erred in failing to grant a directed verdict because the State failed to offer sufficient evidence to prove that an attempted armed robbery occurred or that Nesbitt took part in it. We disagree.

Attempt crimes are . . . ones of specific intent such that the act constituting the attempt must be done with the intent to commit that particular crime. . . . Additionally, the State must prove that the defendant's specific intent was accompanied by some overt act, beyond mere preparation, in furtherance of the intent, and there must be an actual or present ability to complete the crime. "The preparation consists in devising or arranging the means or measures necessary for the commission of the crime; the attempt or overt act is the direct movement toward the commission, after the preparations are made."

In *State v. Quick,* our supreme court stated the following in determining whether a particular defendant's conduct constitutes an overt act:

> It is well settled that the "act" is to be liberally construed, and in numerous cases it is said to be sufficient that the act go far enough toward accomplishment of the crime to amount to the commencement of its consummation. While the efficiency of a particular act depends on the facts of the particular case, the act must always amount to more than mere preparation, and move directly toward the commission of the crime. In any event, it would seem, the act need not be the last proximate step leading to the consummation of the offense.

Nesbitt's statement referring to the perpetrators' agreement to "do the store" constitutes direct evidence that the specific intent to rob the store existed. Therefore, the determinative issue before this Court is whether the perpetrators' conduct as presented by the State was a sufficient overt act to sustain a conviction for attempted armed robbery.

Although we are unaware of any South Carolina cases factually analogous to the situation presented here, other jurisdictions have addressed similar scenarios. In *State v. Ward,* 601 S.W.2d 629 (Mo.Ct.App.1980) three men drove to a motel with the intention of robbing it and its owner. One of the men waited in the getaway car as the other two approached the motel entrance, armed and masked. The motel manager testified he was inside the lobby when he heard a rattling at the outside door and saw the defendant, Ward, pointing a gun at him. As the manager ran from the lobby, he shouted "don't" and "take the money." When he returned with a shotgun, the getaway car was leaving the scene. Although the defendant never entered the building, he admitted he was at the scene but left because he "changed [his] mind." Ward was later convicted of attempted armed robbery.

On appeal, Ward argued his actions amounted to mere preparation. The Missouri Court of Appeals disagreed and affirmed Ward's conviction, stating:

> An overt criminal act is one going beyond mere preparation and done after and in furtherance of a prior plan to commit a crime. We agree with the trial court's conclusion that overt acts were shown by "defendant's act of going up to the door of the motel office, masked, with shotgun in hand, and a getaway car waiting."

In *Young v. State*, 303 Md. 298, 493 A.2d 352 (Md.1985) police set up a surveillance of local banks in an area that had experienced a number of recent robberies. Early one afternoon, the police observed Young driving an automobile in a manner that led them to believe that he was casing the banks. Later that afternoon, Young left his vehicle and proceeded toward the front door of one of the banks. He added a stocking cap, white gloves, and an eye patch to his attire. A bank manager observed Young approaching the door. Young's jacket collar was turned up, his right hand was in his jacket pocket, and his left hand was in front of his face. Unaware that the bank had closed for the day, Young was surprised to discover that the door was locked. He then fled, running past the windows while covering his face.

Police stopped Young as he attempted to drive away and ordered him to exit the vehicle. As he stepped out, the butt of a .22 caliber pistol was sticking out of his right jacket pocket. A pair of white surgical gloves, a black eye patch, a blue knit stocking cap, and a pair of sunglasses were located on the front seat.

In affirming Young's conviction for attempted armed robbery, the court noted that "the determination of the overt act which is beyond mere preparation in furtherance of the commission of the intended crime is a most significant aspect of criminal attempts." The court went on to hold that Young's conduct leading to his apprehension established the necessary overt act toward the commission of armed robbery. The court stated: "Even if we assume that all of Young's conduct before he approached the door . . . was mere preparation, . . . when Young tried to open the bank door . . . that act constituted a 'substantial step' toward the commission of the intended crime."*

---

*In determining the existence of an overt act which is beyond mere preparation, the Maryland Court of Appeals adopted the "substantial step" approach, which posits that a person is guilty of an attempt to commit a crime where he purposely does or omits to do anything which constitutes a substantial step in a course of conduct planned to culminate in his commission of the crime. *See Young*, 493 A.2d at 358.

In *State v. Parker*, 311 S.E.2d 327 (1984) the defendant, Parker, armed with a gun, was lying beside a hedge across the street from a market store. He then crossed the street and got on a bicycle, which he rode a short distance before returning to the area near the hedge. Shortly thereafter, a police officer responding to a complaint from a suspicious employee arrived at the scene. Parker quickly walked away and was arrested while attempting to reach his bicycle. In reversing Parker's conviction for attempted armed robbery, the court found that Parker's actions amounted to no more than mere preparation. The court stated: "Although lurking outside a place of business with a loaded pistol may be unlawful conduct, it does not constitute the sort of overt act which would clearly show that defendant attempted to rob that business."

We believe the facts presented in the instant case more closely resemble those addressed in *Ward* and *Young* than in *Parker*. In *Parker*, the defendant never made any advance toward his intended target. In this case, as in *Ward* and *Young*, the perpetrators approached the entrances of the buildings while armed and disguised and committed an overt act in attempting to gain entrance.

According to Brockman, a black male masking his appearance approached the entrance of the store brandishing a weapon. Sarratt testified that one of two perpetrators opened the door and said something before fleeing the scene. We find that these actions move directly toward the commission of an armed robbery. While the conduct may not have been the last proximate step toward the commission of the offense, the acts committed went beyond mere preparation. In our view, these acts are sufficient to meet the overt act requirement espoused in *Quick*. It should not be necessary to subject victims to a face-to-face confrontation with a lethal weapon in order to find the essential element of an overt act. From the sum of all evidence presented, the jury could infer that an armed robbery was immediately forthcoming, or that the attempt had begun. . . .

AFFIRMED.

Questions

1. State the test the court used to decide whether Terry Lee Nesbitt's actions satisfied the *actus reus* of attempted robbery.

2. List all the facts relevant to deciding whether Nesbitt's actions met the test the court adopted.

3. Summarize how the court applied the facts to the test.

4. In your opinion, did Nesbitt's acts add up to *actus reus* according to the test of the court and according to standards summarized in your text before the case excerpt? Defend your answer.

5. In your opinion, which of the standards for determining attempt *actus reus* discussed in the text is best? Defend your answer.

EXPLORING ATTEMPT *ACTUS REUS* FURTHER

 Go to the Criminal Law 8e CD to read the full text versions of the cases featured here.

1. *Did He Take "Substantial Steps" Toward Escaping?*

FACTS

A guard at Dallas State Correctional Institution discovered that the bars of the window in Richard Gilliam's cell had been cut and were being held in place by sticks and paper. The condition of the bars was such that they could be removed manually at will. The same guard observed that a shelf hook was missing from its place in the cell. A subsequent search revealed vise grips concealed inside the appellant's mattress, and two knotted extension cords attached to a hook were found in a box of clothing. At trial, evidence showed that the hook had been fashioned from the missing shelf hook. The vise grips were capable of cutting barbed wire of the type located along the top of the fence that was the sole barrier between the appellant's cell window and the perimeter of the prison compound. Inspection of the cell immediately before it was assigned to Gilliam as its sole occupant had disclosed bars intact and the shelf hooks in place. Did Gilliam commit the crime of attempted escape?

DECISION AND REASONS

The Pennsylvania Superior court said yes, because Gilliam had taken substantial steps by not only gathering the tools for his escape but also sawing through the bars. According to the court, the substantial step [*Model Penal Code*] test "broadens the scope of attempt liability by concentrating on the acts the defendant has done and does not . . . focus

on the acts remaining to be done before actual commission of the crime."

Commonwealth v. Gilliam, 417 A.2d 1203 (Pa.Sup. 1980)

2. *Did They Get "Very Near" to Robbing the Clerk?*

FACTS

Charles Rizzo, Anthony J. Dorio, Thomas Milo, and John Thomasello were driving through New York City looking for a payroll clerk they intended to rob. While they were still looking for their victim, the police apprehended and arrested them. They were tried and convicted of attempted robbery. Rizzo appealed. Did their acts add up to attempt *actus reus*?

DECISION AND REASONS

The trial court said yes. The New York Court of Appeals (New York's highest court), reversed:

The Penal Law, § 2, prescribes that:

An act, done with intent to commit a crime, and tending but failing to effect its commission, is "an attempt to commit that crime."

The word "tending" is very indefinite. It is perfectly evident that there will arise differences of opinion as to whether an act in a given case is one *tending* to commit a crime. "Tending" means to exert activity in a particular direction. Any act in preparation to commit a crime may be said to have a tendency towards its accomplishment. The procuring of the automobile, searching the streets looking for the desired victim, were in reality acts tending toward the commission of the proposed crime.

The law, however, had recognized that many acts in the way of preparation are too remote to constitute the crime of attempt. The line has been drawn between those acts which are remote and those which are proximate and near to the consummation. The law must be practical, and therefore considers those acts only as tending to the commission of the crime which are so near to its accomplishment that in all reasonable probability the crime itself would have been committed, but for timely interference. The cases which have been before the courts express this idea in different language, but the idea remains the same. The act or acts must come or advance very near to the accomplishment of the intended crime.

People v. Rizzo, 158 N.E. 888 (N.Y.App. 1927)

3. *Did He "Prepare" or Get to "All But the Last Act" to Commit Arson?*

FACTS

Lincoln Peaslee had made and arranged combustibles in a building he owned so they were ready to be lighted and, if lighted, would have set fire to the building and its contents. He got within a quarter of a mile of the building, but his would-be accomplice refused to light the fire. Did Peaslee attempt to commit arson?

DECISION AND REASONS

According to the court, he didn't:

A mere collection and preparation of materials in a room, for the purpose of setting fire to them, unaccompanied by any present intent to set the fire, would be too remote and not all but "the last act" necessary to complete the crime.

Commonwealth v. Peaslee, 59 N.E. 55 (Mass. 1901)

Impossibility of Completing the Crime

To avoid paying customs, a man sneaks an antique book past customs. What he doesn't know is there's an exception in the law for antique books. Has he attempted to evade customs? A woman stabs her battering husband repeatedly, thinking he's asleep. In fact, he's already died of a heart attack two hours before she stabs him. Has she committed attempted murder? The would-be customs evader is *not* guilty; the battered woman *is*. The first scenario is an example of **legal impossibility.** Legal impossibility is where actors intend to commit crimes, and do everything they can to carry out their criminal intent, but the criminal law doesn't ban what they did. So, even though he wanted to evade customs, and did all he could to commit the crime of tax evasion, it's legally impossible to commit a crime that doesn't exist. If the *law* were different he'd be guilty; but it isn't, so legal impossibility is a defense to criminal liability.

Stabbing an already dead victim is an example of **factual impossibility.** Factual impossibility is where actors intend to commit a crime and try to but some fact or circumstance—an **extraneous factor**—interrupts them to prevent the completion of the crime. The woman intended to murder her battering husband. She did all she could to commit it by stabbing him; if the *facts* had been different—that is, if her victim had been alive—she would've murdered him.

Legal impossibility requires a different *law* to make the conduct criminal; factual impossibility requires different *facts* to complete the crime. In most jurisdictions, legal impossibility is a defense to criminal attempt; factual impossibility is not. The principal reason for the difference is that to convict someone for conduct the law doesn't prohibit, no matter what the actor's intentions, violates the **principle of legality**—no crime without a law, no punishment without a crime (see Chapter 2). Factual impossibility, on the other hand, would allow chance to determine criminal liability. A person who's determined to commit a crime, and who does enough to succeed in that determination, shouldn't escape responsibility and punishment because of a stroke of good luck (Dutile and Moore 1979, 181).

The Wisconsin Supreme Court addressed the issue of factual impossibility in *State v. Damms* (1960).

State v. Damms
100 N.W.2d 592 (1960)

A jury convicted Ralph Damms of an attempt to commit murder in the first degree. In the Municipal Court for the Eastern District of Waukesha County, Damms was sentenced to imprisonment for not more than ten years. He appealed. The supreme court of Wisconsin affirmed the conviction.

CURRIE, J.

FACTS

The defendant Ralph Damms was charged by **information** [a document filed by the prosecutor that takes the place of an indictment by a grand jury] with the offense of attempt to commit murder in the first degree.... The jury found the defendant guilty as charged, and the defendant was sentenced to imprisonment in the state prison at Waupun for a term of not more than ten years. The defendant has appealed from the judgment of conviction entered May 1, 1959.

The alleged crime occurred on April 6, 1959, near Menomonee Falls in Waukesha County. Prior to that date Marjory Damms, wife of the defendant, had instituted an action for divorce against him and the parties lived apart. She was thirty-nine years and he thirty-three years of age. Marjory Damms was also estranged from her mother, Mrs. Laura Grant.

That morning, a little before eight o'clock, Damms drove his automobile to the vicinity in Milwaukee where he knew Mrs. Damms would take the bus to go to work. He saw her walking along the sidewalk, stopped, and induced her to enter the car by falsely stating that Mrs. Grant was ill and dying. They drove to Mrs. Grant's home. Mrs. Damms then discovered that her mother was up and about and not seriously ill. Nevertheless, the two Damms remained there nearly two hours conversing and drinking coffee. Apparently it was the intention of Damms to induce a reconciliation between mother and daughter, hoping it would result in one between himself and his wife, but not much progress was achieved in such direction.

At the conclusion of the conversation Mrs. Damms expressed the wish to phone for a taxi-cab to take her to work. Damms insisted on her getting into his car, and said he would drive her to work. They again entered his car but instead of driving south towards her place of employment, he drove in the opposite direction. Some conversation was had in which he stated that it was possible for a person to die quickly and not be able to make amends for anything done in the past, and referred to the possibility of "judgment day" occurring suddenly. Mrs. Damms' testimony as to what then took place is as follows:

> When he was telling me about this being judgment day, he pulled a cardboard box from under the seat of the car and brought it up to the seat and opened it up and took a gun out of a paper bag. [He] aimed it at my side and he said, "This is to show you I'm not kidding." I tried to quiet him down. He said he wasn't fooling. I said if it was just a matter of my saying to my mother that everything was all right, we could go back and I would tell her that.

They did return to Mrs. Grant's home and Mrs. Damms went inside and Damms stayed outside. In a few minutes he went inside and asked Mrs. Damms to leave with him. Mrs. Grant requested that they leave quietly so as not to attract the attention of the neighbors. They again got into the car and this time drove out on Highway 41 towards Menomonee Falls. Damms stated to Mrs. Damms that he was taking her "up North" for a few days, the apparent purpose of which was to effect a reconciliation between them. As they approached a roadside restaurant, he asked her if she would like something to eat. She replied that she wasn't hungry but would drink some coffee. Damms then drove the car off the highway beside the restaurant and parked it with the front facing, and in close proximity to, the restaurant wall.

Damms then asked Mrs. Damms how much money she had with her and she said "a couple of dollars." He then requested to see her checkbook and she refused to give it to him. A quarrel ensued between them. Mrs. Damms opened the car door and started to run around the restaurant building screaming, "Help!" Damms pursued her with the pistol in his hand. Mrs. Damms cries for help attracted the attention of the persons inside the restaurant, including two officers of the State Traffic Patrol who were eating their lunch. One officer rushed out of the front door and the other the rear door. In the meantime, Mrs. Damms had run nearly around three sides of the building. In seeking to avoid colliding with a child, who was in her path, she turned, slipped and fell. Damms crouched down, held the pistol at her head, and pulled the trigger, but nothing happened. He then exclaimed, "It won't fire. It won't fire."

Damms testified that at the time he pulled the trigger the gun was pointing down at the ground and not at Mrs. Damms' head. However, the two traffic patrol officers both testified that Damms had the gun pointed directly at her head when he pulled the trigger. The officers placed Damms under arrest. They found that the pistol was unloaded. The clip holding the cartridges, which is inserted in the butt of the gun to load it, they found in the cardboard box in Damms' car together with a box of cartridges.

That afternoon, Damms was questioned by a deputy sheriff at the Waukesha County jail, and a clerk in the sheriff's office typed out the questions and Damms' answers as they were given. Damms later read over such typed statement of questions and answers, but refused to sign it. In such statement Damms stated that he thought the gun was loaded at the time of the alleged attempt to murder. Both the deputy sheriff and the undersheriff testified that Damms had stated to them that he thought the gun was loaded. On the other hand, Damms testified at the trial that he knew at the time of the alleged attempt that the pistol was not loaded.

OPINION

The two questions raised on this appeal are:

(1) Did the fact, that it was impossible for the accused to have committed the act of murder because the gun was unloaded, preclude his conviction of the offense of attempt to commit murder?

(2) Assuming that the foregoing question is answered in the negative, does the evidence establish the guilt of the accused beyond a reasonable doubt?

Sec. 939.32(2), Stats., provides as follows:

An attempt to commit a crime requires that the actor have an intent to perform acts and attain a result which, if accomplished, would constitute such crime and that he does acts toward the commission of the crime which demonstrate unequivocally, under all the circumstances, that he formed that intent and would commit the crime *except for the intervention of* another person or *some other extraneous factor.* [Italics supplied.]

The issue with respect to the first of the . . . two questions boils down to whether the impossibility of accomplishment due to the gun being unloaded falls within the statutory words, "except for the intervention of . . . some other extraneous factor." We conclude that it does.

Prior to the adoption of the new criminal code by the 1955 legislature the criminal statutes of this state had separate sections making it an offense to assault with intent to do great bodily harm, to murder, to rob, and to rape, etc.

The new code did away with these separate sections by creating sec. 939.32, Stats., covering all attempts to commit a battery or felony, and making the maximum penalty not to exceed one-half the penalty imposed for the completed crime, except that, if the penalty for a completed crime is life imprisonment, the maximum penalty for the attempt is thirty years imprisonment.

In an article in the 1956 *Wisconsin Law Review* by assistant attorney general Platz, who was one of the authors of the new criminal code, explaining such code, he points out that 'attempt' is defined therein in a more intelligible fashion than by using such tests as "beyond mere preparation," "*locus poenitentiae*" (the place at which the actor may repent and withdraw), or "dangerous proximity to success." Quoting the author:

Emphasis upon the dangerous propensities of the actor as shown by his conduct, rather than upon how close he came to succeeding, is more appropriate to the purposes of the criminal law to protect society and reform offenders or render them temporarily harmless.

Robert H. Skilton, in an article entitled, "The Requisite Act in a Criminal Attempt" (1937), 3 *University of Pittsburgh Law Review* 308, 314, advances the view, that impossibility to cause death because of the attempt to fire a defective weapon at a person, does not prevent the conviction of the actor of the crime of attempted murder:

If the defendant does not know that the gun he fires at B is defective, he is guilty of an attempt to kill B, even though his actions under the circumstances given never come near to killing B. . . . The possibility of the success of the defendant's enterprise need only be an apparent possibility to the defendant, and not an actual possibility.

In *State v. Mitchell*, 116 N.W. 808, 810 (1908), the defendant was convicted of assault with intent to do great bodily injury, and, on appeal, complained among other things that the charge in the indictment was insufficient, because it failed to allege that the gun in question was loaded. In sustaining the conviction, the Iowa court held in part as follows:

The specific objection made is that there is no allegation that the gun was loaded; but how could the defendant have intended to shoot the person assaulted unless the gun which he held in his hands, was, *in fact, or, as he believed,* so loaded as that it could be fired? *If he believed that it was loaded and intended to fire it at the person assaulted, he was guilty of an assault with intent to commit great bodily injury, although in fact and contrary to his belief it was not loaded.* The indictment was sufficient, therefore, in charging an intent to do great bodily injury by shooting the person assailed with a gun, although it was not specifically alleged that the gun was in fact loaded. (Emphasis supplied.)

The facts in *Mullen v. State* (Ala. 1871*)* were that the accused pointed a loaded gun at another and pulled the trigger three times, but the gun would not fire because of the absence of a percussion cap. The defendant was convicted of attempt to murder. On appeal, the court upheld a charge to the jury that the absence of the cap would not avail the defendant if he supposed it was on the gun, but the jury must be satisfied beyond all reasonable doubt that the defendant did not know there was no cap on the gun. In its opinion the court quoted from 1 Bishop's *Criminal Law* to the effect that in order to be guilty of the offense of an attempt to commit a felony, such as murder, assuming the necessary intent to exist, the act must have some adaptation to accomplish the result intended, but the adaptation need only be apparent, not perfect. The conviction was reversed on other grounds not here material. . . .

In addition to the authorities . . . cited, it is stated in two recent works on criminal law that pointing an unloaded firearm at another and pulling the trigger is an attempt if the actor believes the gun to be loaded. Perkins, *Criminal Law,* p. 494, and Williams, *Criminal Law,* p. 496, sec. 150. See also 1 Bishop, *Criminal Law* (9th ed.), p. 534, sec. 750, and 1 *Wharton's Criminal Law and Procedure* by Anderson, pp. 164–165, sec. 79.

Sound public policy would seem to support the majority view that impossibility not apparent to the actor should not absolve him from the offense of attempt to commit the crime he intended. An unequivocal act accompanied by intent should be sufficient to constitute a criminal attempt. Insofar as the actor knows, he has done everything necessary to insure the commission of the crime intended, and he should not escape punishment because of the fortuitous circumstance that by reason of some fact unknown to him it was impossible to effectuate the intended result. . . .

It is our considered judgment that the fact, that the gun was unloaded when Damms pointed it at his wife's head and pulled the trigger, did not absolve him of the offense charged, if he actually thought at the time that it was loaded.

We do not believe that the further contention raised in behalf of the accused, that the evidence does not establish his guilt of the crime charged beyond a reasonable doubt, requires extensive consideration on our part.

The jury undoubtedly believed the testimony of the deputy sheriff and undersheriff that Damms told them on the day of the act that he thought the gun was loaded. This is also substantiated by the written statement constituting a transcript of his answers given in his interrogation at the county jail on the same day. The gun itself, which is an exhibit in the record, is the strongest piece of evidence in favor of Damms' present contention that he at all times knew the gun was unloaded. Practically the entire bottom end of the butt of the pistol is open. Such opening is caused by the absence of the clip into which the cartridges must be inserted in order to load the pistol. This readily demonstrates to anyone looking at the gun that it could not be loaded. Because the unloaded gun with this large opening in the butt was an exhibit which went to the jury room, we must assume that the jury examined the gun and duly considered it in arriving at their verdict.

We are not prepared to hold that the jury could not come to the reasonable conclusion that, because of Damms' condition of excitement when he grabbed the gun and pursued his wife, he so grasped it as not to see the opening in the end of the butt which would have unmistakably informed him that the gun was unloaded. Having so concluded, they could rightfully disregard Damms' testimony given at the trial that he knew the pistol was unloaded.

Judgment AFFIRMED.

DISSENT

DIETERICH, J. (dissenting).
Sec. 939.32(2), Stats. provides:

> *An attempt* to commit a crime *requires* that *the actor* have an *intent* to *perform acts* and *attain a result* which, *if accomplished,* would constitute such crime and that *he does acts* toward the commission of the crime which *demonstrate unequivocally,* under all the circumstances, that he *formed* that *intent* and would *commit* the crime *except for the intervention of another person or some other extraneous factor.* [Emphasis supplied.]

In view of the statute, the question arising under sec. 939.32(2) is whether the impossibility of accomplishment due to the pistol being unloaded falls within the statutory words "*except for the intervention of . . . or some other extraneous factor*" it does not.

In interpreting the statute we must look to the ordinary meaning of words. Webster's New International Dictionary defines "extraneous" as not belonging to or dependent upon a thing, originated or coming from without. The plain distinct meaning of the statute is: A person must form an intent to commit a particular crime and this intent must be coupled with sufficient preparation on his part and with overt acts from which it can be determined clearly, surely and absolutely the crime would be committed except for the intervention of some independent thing or something originating or coming from someone or something over which the actor has no control.

As an example,—if the defendant actor had formed an intent to kill someone, had in his possession a loaded pistol, pulled the trigger while his intended victim was within range and the pistol did not fire because the bullet or cartridge in the chamber was defective or because someone unknown to the actor had removed the cartridges or bullets or because of any other thing happening which happening or thing was beyond the control of the actor, the actor could be guilty under sec. 339.32(2), Stats. But when as in the present case (as disclosed by the testimony) the defendant had never loaded the pistol, although having ample opportunity to do so, then he had never completed performance of the act essential to kill someone, through the means of pulling the trigger of the pistol. This act, of loading the pistol, or using a loaded pistol, was dependent on the defendant himself. It was in no way an extraneous factor since by definition an extraneous factor is one which originates or comes from without. . . .

In this case, there is no doubt that the pistol was not loaded. The defendant testified that it had never been loaded or fired. . . . The law judges intent objectively. It is impossible to peer into a man's mind particularly long after the act has been committed.

Viewing objectively the physical salient facts, it was the defendant who put the gun, clip and cartridges under the car seat. It was he, same defendant, who took the pistol out of the box without taking clip or cartridges. It is plain he told the truth,—he knew the gun would not fire,—nobody else knew that so well. In fact his exclamation was "It won't fire. It won't fire." The real intent showed up objectively in those calm moments while driving around the county with his wife for two hours, making two visits with her at her mother's home, and drinking coffee at the home. He could have loaded the pistol while staying on the outside at his mother-in-law's home on his second trip, if he intended to use the pistol to kill, but he did not do this required act.

The majority states:

> The gun itself, which is an exhibit in the record, is the strongest piece of evidence in favor of Damms' present contention that he at all times knew the gun was unloaded. Practically the entire bottom end of the butt of the pistol is open. . . . This readily demonstrates to anyone looking at the gun that it could not be loaded.

They are so correct.

The defendant had the pistol in his hand several times before chasing his wife at the restaurant and it was his pistol. He, no doubt, had examined this pistol at various times during his period of ownership,—unless he was devoid of all sense of touch and feeling in his hands and fingers it would be impossible for him not to be aware or

know that the pistol was unloaded. He could feel the hole in the bottom of the butt, and this on at least two separate occasions for he handled the pistol by taking it out of the box and showing it to his wife before he took her back to her mother's home the second time, and prior to chasing her at the restaurant.

Objective evidence here raises reasonable doubt of intent to attempt murder. It negatives intent to kill. The defendant would have loaded the pistol had he intended to kill or murder or used it as a bludgeon.

It is significant to me in arriving at this decision, that originally the following subsection was a part of that statute which is now sec. 939.32(3). . . .

> It is not a defense to a prosecution under this section that, because of a mistake of fact or law other than criminal law, which does not negative the actor's intent to commit the crime, it would have been impossible for him to commit the crime attempted.

. . . The above-mentioned sec. 339.32(3), was stricken by the criminal code advisory committee, after what is now sec. 939.32(2), was drafted in its present form. This leads me to conclude that impossibility of performance is a defense and that the elimination of this defense was not contemplated to be within the purview of the language in sec. 939.32(2), Stats.

The Assistant Attorney General contends and states in his brief:

> In the instant case, the failure of the attempt was due to lack of bullets in the gun but a loaded magazine was in the car. If defendant had not been prevented by the intervention of the two police officers, or possibly someone else, or conceivably by the flight of his wife from the scene, he could have returned to the car, loaded the gun, and killed her. Under all the circumstances the jury were justified in concluding that that is what he would have done, but for the intervention.

If that conclusion is correct, and juries are allowed to convict persons based on speculation of what *might* have been done, we will have seriously and maybe permanently, curtailed the basic rights of our citizenry to be tried only on the basis of proven facts. I cannot agree with his contention or conclusion.

The total inadequacy of the means (in this case the unloaded gun or pistol) in the manner intended to commit the overt act of murder, precludes a finding of guilty of the crime charged under sec. 939.32(2), Stats.

Questions

1. List all the facts relevant to deciding whether Ralph Damms intended to murder Marjory Damms.

2. List all the facts relevant to deciding whether Damms had taken enough steps to attempt to murder Marjory Damms according to the Wisconsin statute.

3. Summarize the majority's arguments that the unloaded gun was an extraneous factor, a stroke of luck Damms shouldn't benefit from.

4. Summarize the dissent's arguments that the unloaded gun was *not* an extraneous factor but an impossibility that prevents Damms from attempting to murder Marjorie Damms.

5. In your opinion, is the majority or dissent right? Explain your answer in terms of what effect impossibility should have on liability for criminal attempt.

6. Should it matter why the gun was unloaded? Explain your answer.

7. What if Damms *knew* the gun was unloaded? Should he still be guilty of attempted murder? Explain your answer.

8. Is the Wisconsin rule punishing attempts at about half the amount for completed crimes a good idea?

9. Some states punish attempts at the same level as completed crimes because people bent on committing crimes shouldn't benefit *at all* from a stroke of luck. Do you agree? Defend your answer with arguments from the case excerpt and the text.

EXPLORING IMPOSSIBILITY OF COMPLETING THE CRIME FURTHER

 Go to the Criminal Law 8e CD to read the full text versions of the cases featured here.

1. Was It "Legally Impossible" to Commit "Child Enticement"?

FACTS

Beginning on January 31, 2000, Brian Robins, using the screen name "WI4kink," had a series of online conversations with "Benjm13," initially in an Internet chat room known as "Wisconsin M4M." ["M4M" meant either Male For Male or Men For Men.] Unbeknown to Robins, "Benjm13" was Thomas Fassbender, a 42-year-old DOJ agent posing online as a 13-year-old boy named Benjamin living in Little Chute, Wisconsin. The subject of "Benjamin's" age came up within the first twelve minutes of the first online conversation between Robins and Benjm13. Benjamin told Robins that he was 13 years old.

The initial and subsequent online conversations and e-mails between Robins and Benjm13 centered on explicit sexual matters (including, among other things, oral sex, masturbation, ejaculation, and penis size) and were recorded by Fassbender.

Robins, who was 46 years old and lived in Wauwatosa at the time of the offense, suggested that the two meet:

WI4KINK: so you ever get to Milwaukee?

BENJM13: sometimes with my mom

WI4KINK: cool so how would we ever meet?

BENJM13: i dont know u can come here if u want

WI4KINK: ya that is true. you have a place we could go?

BENJM13: just my house but thats scary

WI4KINK: ya it would be, specially [*sic*] if someone comes home :)

BENJM13: wow not cool

WI4KINK: no

BENJM13: i dont know were [*sic*] to go

WI4KINK: could just get a room somewhere

BENJM13: oh that would be cool—like a motel

WI4KINK: yup

Robins acknowledged that what he was proposing to do was illegal:

BENJM13: im getting nervus [*sic*] already

WI4KINK: ok I understand well I am a little to [*sic*] this isn't legal you know

BENJM13: i geus [*sic*] so

The second online conversation between Robins and Benjamin took place the next evening, February 1, 2000. Again it involved mostly sexual topics, and Robins was persistent in setting up a meeting between the two on the following Saturday. The conversation makes clear that Robins was planning to find a motel room:

WI4KINK: what time of the day would be best? . . .

BENJM13: after i get up would be ok

WI4KINK: as far as getting a room that should be like early afternoon

Robins also asked Benjamin for his telephone number. Benjamin appeared to be reluctant to give it to him. After Robins assured Benjamin that he would only use the number to call on Saturday to confirm their meeting, Benjamin replied, "ok."

On February 2 and 3, Robins and Benjamin "missed" each other online and instead exchanged e-mail messages.

In one e-mail, Benjamin informed Robins that he had directions to Little Chute and that they could probably meet at the Burger King® just off the highway. Robins e-mailed Benjamin and asked him to send the directions. He also told Benjamin that he was "still a little nervous" because he "would not want to get scammed." Benjamin sent the directions, together with the message, "i'm a little scared too. u have to promise me not to tell anyone and to be nice ok. my mom would kill me." In another e-mail, Robins advised that he would arrive in Little Chute around noon, but that Benjamin should give Robins his telephone number so that Robins could call on Saturday morning with an exact time. Robins closed the e-mail by saying: "I know we must be very carefull [sic]. I am looking forward to it."

On Friday, February 4, 2000, Robins and Benjamin met online and engaged in another instant message conversation. This conversation confirmed that the two would meet the following day for the purpose of having sex. Robins expressed his hope that Benjamin was "saving" himself for the following day (that is, he hoped Benjamin would not masturbate before their meeting) and that he (Robins) was "getting hard just talking to" him (Benjamin). Robins again asked Benjamin for his telephone number because Robins "want[ed] to make sure that [Benjamin was] serious." Because Benjamin appeared to be nervous about Robins calling his house, they decided to meet online again in the morning before Robins made the telephone call.

At a little after 10 A.M. on Saturday, February 5, 2000, Robins and Benjamin met online for the fourth and final time. Benjamin said he was "exited about goin to a motel." Robins replied that it "should be hot." Benjamin gave Robins his telephone number and they both signed off the Internet.

Soon after they signed off, Robins called the number Benjamin—Fassbender—had given him. Officer Ray Lee of the Fox Valley Metro Police Department posed as Benjamin during the telephone conversation. The conversation was recorded and Fassbender testified at the preliminary hearing that the content of the telephone conversation consisted mainly of setting the final arrangements for the meeting—what Robins would be wearing, what kind of car Robins would be driving, what Benjamin would be wearing, and what he looked like. Fassbender testified that, "Mr. Robins said, we'll have to find a motel when I get up there, something to that effect."

In the meantime, Fassbender had determined through America Online that the screen name "WI4kink" belonged to Robins. The DOJ set up surveillance outside Robins' home in Wauwautosa. Shortly after his telephone conversation with Benjamin on Saturday, February 5, 2000,

Robins left his house. He was surveilled from his home to the Burger King in Little Chute. Robins parked in the Burger King parking lot, got out of his car, and was arrested as he walked toward the restaurant.

Robins admitted in a statement to police that he had met "Benjm13" in an Internet chat room, that Benjm13 told him that he was a 13-year-old boy, that they'd had sexually explicit conversations, and that he had e-mailed sexually explicit materials to Benjm13. Robins further admitted that he had set up the meeting with Benjm13 for the purpose of having sex with him. Robins also stated that he had told Benjm13 that they would go to a motel room for that purpose.

Robins was charged with "Child Enticement." The Wisconsin criminal code defines child enticement as: "Whoever, with intent to cause or attempts to cause any child who has not attained the age of 18 years to go into any vehicle, building, room or secluded place is guilty of a Class B felony...."

According to the Wisconsin criminal code:

An attempt to commit a crime requires that the actor have an intent to perform acts and attain a result which, if accomplished, would constitute such crime and that the actor does acts toward the commission of the crime which demonstrate unequivocally, under all the circumstances, that the actor formed that intent and would commit the crime except for the intervention of another person or some other extraneous factor. Wis. Stat. § 939.32(3).

Robins moved to dismiss the charge because, he argued, he was being charged with a crime that didn't exist because of a legal impossibility—there was no child. Should the motion to dismiss be granted?

DECISION AND REASONS

No, said the trial court and the Wisconsin Supreme Court, which was faced with a bunch of child enticement cases with similar facts involving stings catching both older men looking for boys and those looking for girls:

We reject Robins' argument that the case should be overruled....The extraneous factor that intervened to make the crime an attempted rather than completed child enticement is the fact that "Benjm13" was an adult government agent rather than a 13-year-old boy. That there may be or could have been other intervening factors does not make this an impermissible prosecution for an "attempt to attempt a crime."...

We conclude...that the crime of attempted child enticement contrary to Wis. Stat. § 948.07 may be charged where the extraneous factor that intervenes to make the crime an attempted rather than completed child enticement is the fact that, unbeknownst to the defendant, the "child" is fictitious.

State v. Robins, 646 N.W. 2d (Wis. 2002)

2. Was It "Impossible" to Receive a Stolen Harley-Davidson That Wasn't Stolen?

FACTS

Michael Kordas was charged with buying a Harley-Davidson® motorcycle from an undercover police officer. The police had modified the cycle and made misrepresentations about the cycle to Kordas so that it appeared to be stolen when, in fact, it actually "had been provided to the Milwaukee Police Department for educational purposes." The undercover officer gave Kordas certain information about the motorcycle that signaled that it was stolen. Specifically, the undercover officer represented that the motorcycle in question was a 1988 Harley DynaGlide®, although Harley did not begin making that model until 1991, which Kordas later acknowledged knowing at the time. In addition, the vehicle identification number on the motorcycle had been altered in an obvious way, again a fact that Kordas later acknowledged knowing at the time he examined the motorcycle prior to purchasing it. Kordas bought the motorcycle, was given what purported to be title to it, and took it with him in a van before he was stopped and arrested by backup officers working on the undercover operation. The complaint indicates that Kordas made additional admissions to the police upon his arrest indicating his knowledge that the motorcycle was stolen. In fact, however, the motorcycle was not stolen. Did he attempt to receive a stolen Harley-Davidson?

DECISION AND REASONS

Yes, according to the trial court:

> Here, the allegations are that Kordas had the requisite intent but his actions even after they were fully executed did not constitute the crime and therefore it was an "attempt." But there was no "intervention of another person or some other extraneous factor" which prevented the ultimate commission of the acts which the defendant intended. Instead, the intended acts were completed but the results were not criminal because of the legal status of the property in question.

The Wisconsin Supreme Court disagreed:

> The trial court based its conclusion on the view that "there was no 'intervention of . . . some other extraneous

factor' which prevented the ultimate commission" of receiving stolen property. We disagree. Indeed, an extraneous factor did intervene—the fact, beyond Kordas's knowledge or control, that the motorcycle was *not* stolen property. But for that factor, Kordas allegedly would have committed the crime of receiving stolen property. Because of that factor, Kordas allegedly committed only the attempt to receive stolen property.

> According to the allegations in the amended complaint, Kordas "did in fact possess the necessary criminal intent to commit" the crime of receiving stolen property. The extraneous factor—that the motorcycle was not stolen—was unknown to him and had no impact on his intent. Thus, the legal "impossibility not apparent to [Kordas] should not absolve him from the offense of attempt to commit the crime he intended." Accordingly, we reverse the order dismissing the amended criminal complaint and remand to the trial court for further proceedings.

State v. Kordas, 528 N.W.2d 483 (Wis. 1995)

3. Was the Victim's Escape an "Extraneous Factor"?

FACTS

Anthony Wagner accosted Candace I. on October 24, 1990, in a Laundromat℠ at 3910 North 76th Street in Milwaukee. He approached her from behind, put a gun to her right side, and tried to force her into the bathroom a few feet away. She struggled and escaped. On June 11, 1991, Wagner accosted Megan M. in a Laundromat at 10440 West Silver Spring Drive in Milwaukee. As with Candace I. eight months earlier, he approached her from behind and put a gun to her right side. This time, however, he was able to force his victim into the Laundromat's bathroom. While in the bathroom, Megan M. refused his demand that she remove her clothes. After a struggle, she escaped. Wagner was convicted of attempted kidnapping and sentenced to 72 years in prison. Were Candace I's and Megan M's escapes an extraneous factor, a stroke of luck that prevented Wagner from completing the crimes?

DECISION AND REASONS

Yes, according to the Wisconsin appeals court:

> Section 939.32(3), Stats. provides: An attempt to commit a crime requires that the actor have an intent to perform acts and attain a result which, if accomplished, would constitute such crime and that he does acts

toward the commission of the crime which demonstrate unequivocally, under all the circumstances, that he formed that intent and would commit the crime except for the intervention of another person or some other extraneous factor.

A victim's successful resistance to a kidnapping is an "extraneous factor." In this case, the "extraneous factor" that prevented Wagner from kidnapping Candace I . . . and Megam M. was their escapes.

State v. Wagner, 528 N.W. 2d 85 (Wis.App. 1995)

Voluntary Abandonment of Attempt

We know from the last section that those bent on committing crimes who've taken steps to carry out their criminal plans can't escape criminal liability just because an outside force or person interrupted them. But what about people who clearly intend to commit crimes, take enough steps to carry out their intent, and then change their mind and voluntarily abandon the scheme? Should the law benefit those who themselves are the force that intercepts the crimes they wanted to commit and are marching toward completing? The answer depends on which jurisdiction they're in. A little more than half the states and the U.S. government accept the **affirmative defense of voluntary abandonment** to attempt liability (*People v. Kimball* 1981, 347). Affirmative defense means defendants have to produce some evidence of abandonment, and then the government has to prove beyond a reasonable doubt that the defendants didn't voluntarily abandon.

Michigan has a typical voluntary abandonment provision:

It is an affirmative defense . . . that, under circumstances manifesting a voluntary and complete renunciation of his criminal purpose, the actor avoided the commission of the offense attempted by abandoning his criminal effort. . . .

A renunciation is not "voluntary and complete" within the meaning of this chapter if it is motivated in whole or in part by either of the following:

(a) A circumstance which increases the probability of detection or apprehension of the defendant or another participant in the criminal operation or which makes more difficult the consummation of the crime.

(b) A decision to postpone the criminal conduct until another time or to substitute another victim or another but similar objective.

People v. Kimball, 346–348

According to the *Model Penal Code,* voluntary abandonment means

a change in the actor's purpose not influenced by outside circumstances, what may be termed repentance or change of heart. Lack of resolution or timidity may suffice. A reappraisal by the actor of the criminal sanctions hanging over his conduct would presumably be a motivation of the voluntary type as long as the actor's fear of the law is not related to a particular threat of apprehension or detection.

American Law Institute 1985 (3), 356

Supporters of the voluntary abandonment defense favor it for two reasons. First, those who voluntarily renounce their criminal attempts in progress (especially during the first acts following preparation) aren't the dangerous people the law of attempt is designed to punish; they probably weren't even bent on committing the crime in the first place. Second, at the very end of the progress to completing the crime, it prevents what we most want—the harm the completed crime is about to inflict on victims. This defense encourages would-be criminals to give up their criminal designs by the promise of escaping punishment. Opponents say the defense encourages bad people to take the first steps to commit crimes because they know they can escape punishment. The court in *Le Barron v. State* dealt with the defense of voluntary abandonment (Moriarity 1989, 1).

Did He Voluntarily Abandon His Attempt to Rape?

Le Barron v. State
145 N.W.2d 79 (Wis. 1966)

David Le Barron was convicted of attempted rape and sentenced to not more than fifteen years in prison. He appealed. The Wisconsin Supreme Court affirmed.

CURRIE, J.

FACTS

On March 3, 1965 at 6:55 P.M., the complaining witness, Jodean Randen, a housewife, was walking home across a fairly well-traveled railroad bridge in Eau Claire. She is a slight woman whose normal weight is 95 to 100 pounds. As she approached the opposite side of the bridge she passed a man who was walking in the opposite direction. The man turned and followed her, grabbed her arm and demanded her purse. She surrendered her purse and at the command of the man began walking away as fast as she could. Upon discovering that the purse was empty, he caught up with her again, grabbed her arm and told her that if she did not scream he would not hurt her. He then led her—willingly, she testified, so as to avoid being hurt by him—to the end of the bridge. While walking he shoved her head down and warned her not to look up or do anything and he would not hurt her.

On the other side of the bridge along the railroad tracks there is a coal shack. As they approached the coal shack he grabbed her, put one hand over her mouth, and an arm around her shoulder and told her not to scream or he would kill her. At this time Mrs. Randen thought he had a knife in his hand. He then forced her into the shack and up against the wall. As she struggled for her breath he said, "You know what else I want," unzipped his pants and started pulling up her skirt. She finally succeeded in removing his hand from her mouth, and after reassuring him that she would not scream, told him she was pregnant and pleaded with him to desist or he would hurt her baby. He then felt her stomach and took her over to the door of the shack, where in the better light he was able to ascertain

that, under her coat, she was wearing maternity clothes. He thereafter let her alone and left after warning her not to scream or call the police, or he would kill her.

OPINION

The material portions of the controlling statutes provide:

§ 944.01(1), Stats. Any male who has sexual intercourse with a female he knows is not his wife, by force and against her will, may be imprisoned not more than 30 years.

§ 939.32(2), Stats. An attempt to commit a crime requires that the actor have an intent to perform acts and attain a result which, if accomplished, would constitute such crime and that he does acts toward the commission of the crime which demonstrate unequivocally, under all the circumstances, that he formed that intent and would commit the crime except for the intervention of another person or some other extraneous factor.

The two statutory requirements of intent and overt acts which must concur in order to have attempt to rape are as follows:

(1) The male must have the intent to act so as to have intercourse with the female by overcoming or preventing her utmost resistance by physical violence, or overcoming her will to resist by the use of threats of imminent physical violence likely to cause great bodily harm;

(2) the male must act toward the commission of the rape by overt acts which demonstrate unequivocally, under all the circumstances, that he formed the intent to rape and would have committed the rape except for the intervention of another person or some other extraneous factor.

The thrust of defendant's argument, that the evidence was not sufficient to convict him of the crime of attempted rape, is two-fold: first, defendant desisted from his endeavor to have sexual intercourse with complainant before he had an opportunity to form an intent to accomplish such intercourse by force and against her will; and, second, the factor which caused him to desist, viz., the pregnancy of complainant, was intrinsic and not an 'extraneous factor' within the meaning of sec. 939.32(2), Stats.

It is difficult to consider the factor of intent apart from that of overt acts since the sole evidence of intent in attempted rape cases is almost always confined to the overt acts of the accused, and intent must be inferred therefrom. In fact, the express wording of sec. 939.32(2), Stats. recognizes that this is so.

We consider defendant's overt acts, which support a reasonable inference that he intended to have sexual intercourse with complainant by force and against her will, to be these: (1) He threatened complainant that he would kill her if she refused to cooperate with him; (2) he forced complainant into the shack and against the wall; and (3) he stated, 'You know what else I want, ' unzipped his pants, and started pulling up her skirt. The jury had the right to assume that defendant had the requisite physical strength and weapon (the supposed knife) to carry out the threat over any resistance of complainant.

We conclude that a jury could infer beyond a reasonable doubt from these overt acts of defendant that he intended to have sexual intercourse with defendant by force and against her will. The fact, that he desisted from his attempt to have sexual intercourse as a result of the plea of complainant that she was pregnant, would permit of the opposite inference. However, such desistance did not compel the drawing of such inference nor compel, as a matter of law, the raising of a reasonable doubt to a finding that defendant had previously intended to carry through with having intercourse by force and against complainant's will.

Defendant relies strongly on *Oakley v. State* where this court held that defendant Oakley's acts were so equivocal as to prevent a finding of intent beyond a reasonable doubt to have sexual intercourse by force and against the will of the complainant. The evidence in the case disclosed neither physical violence nor threat of physical violence up to the time Oakley desisted from his attempt to have sexual intercourse with the complainant. He did put his arm around her and attempted to kiss her while entreating her to have intercourse, and also attempted to put his hand in her blouse and to lift up her skirt but did not attempt to renew this endeavor when she brushed his hand away. Thus the facts in Oakley are readily distinguishable from those of the case at bar. To argue that the two cases are analogous because, in the one instance the accused desisted because the complainant was menstruating and in the other because of pregnancy, is an oversimplification. Such an argument overlooks the radical difference in the nature of the overt acts relied upon to prove intent.

The argument, that the pregnancy of the instant complainant which caused defendant's desistance does not qualify as an 'extraneous factor' within the meaning of sec. 939.32, Stats., is in conflict with our holding in *State v. Damms*. There we upheld a conviction of attempt to commit murder where the accused pulled the trigger of an unloaded pistol intending to kill his estranged wife thinking the pistol was loaded. It was held that the impossibility of accomplishment due to the gun being unloaded fell within the statutory words, 'except for the intervention of . . . some other extraneous factor.' Particularly significant is this statement in the opinion:

> An unequivocal act accompanied by intent should be sufficient to constitute a criminal attempt. Insofar as the actor knows, he has done everything necessary to insure the commission of the crime intended, and he should not escape punishment because of the fortuitous circumstance that by reason of some fact unknown to him it was impossible to effectuate the intended result.

The unloaded condition of the gun was every bit as much a part of the intrinsic fact situation in the *Damms* Case as was complainant's pregnancy in the instant case. We determine that such pregnancy constituted the intervention of an "extraneous factor" within the meaning of sec. 939.32(2), Stats.

AFFIRMED.

Questions

1. List all the facts relevant to deciding whether Le Barron had the intent to rape Jodean Randen.

2. At what point, if any, did his acts cross the line from preparation to the *actus reus* of attempt under Wisconsin law?

3. Describe the details surrounding Le Barron's decision to abandon the attempted rape of Randen.

4. Why did Le Barron abandon his attempt to rape Randen? Because he believed it was morally wrong to rape a pregnant woman? Or, did the pregnancy simply repel him sexually? Does it matter? Explain your answer.

5. Is Le Barron equally dangerous, whichever reason led to interrupting the rape? Explain.

6. The court said a jury could have concluded Randen's pregnancy was either an extraneous factor he couldn't benefit from or an intrinsic factor that caused Le Barron to voluntarily renounce his intention to rape. If you were a juror, how would you have voted on whether the pregnancy was an extraneous or an intrinsic factor?

EXPLORING VOLUNTARY ABANDONMENT OF ATTEMPT FURTHER

 Go to the Criminal Law 8e CD to read the full text version of the case featured here.

Did He "Voluntarily Abandon" His Attempt to Commit "Sexual Battery"?

FACTS

On January 18, 1992, at 2:19 A.M., Rodney Herron was stopped in his automobile by the Mechanicsburg, Ohio, Police Department for driving under the influence of alcohol. After processing a DUI charge, the police officer dropped Herron off at his residence at 4:06 A.M. According to Herron, he entered his house, walked into the living room, which was dimly lit by a fluorescent light in the adjacent kitchen, and noticed a person lying on the couch on the opposite wall. Herron testified that he believed the person on the couch to be his wife, since she had been sleeping there on a frequent basis. Additionally, he testified that the person was facing the back of the couch, and had a sheet partially covering her head.

Herron further testified that he unzipped his pants, but left them on, and lay down on the couch behind the person. He testified that he unbuttoned the other person's pants, and pulled them down a little. Herron testified that he then placed the other person's hand upon his penis. Herron also testified that he might have touched the person's butt, and he might have kissed her. According to his testimony, Herron then lay his head down, heard the person "whimpering," and realized that it was not his wife, but his stepdaughter, Trisha. He testified that he immediately jumped up and ended the contact. Herron testified that the lighting in the room was adequate for him to identify the color of the person's shorts, and that had she been facing him, he would have recognized that she was not his wife. Was Herron entitled to have the jury decide whether he was entitled to the defense of voluntary renunciation (abandonment)?

DECISION AND REASONS

Yes, according to the court:

Herron claims that he was entitled to an instruction on abandonment as a defense to the charge of Attempted Sexual Battery. He contends that there was evidence presented that he "abandoned his efforts long before the point of sexual conduct and without the application of any force, ..." He further claims that his abandonment constituted a "complete and voluntary renunciation of his criminal purpose," since it did not arise out of any fear of discovery. The State argues that the defense of abandonment is only available "where the defendant renounces his activity before completing a significant portion of the offense."

An attempt is a failed offense. Any attempt will inevitably reach a point when it either succeeds or fails. If it is successful, it is no longer an attempt, but a completed offense; e.g. a successful rapist is not guilty of the attempt, but of the actual offense of Rape. If the attempt fails, a defendant may or may not be guilty of the attempt, depending upon the reason for the failure. For example, if the attempt is thwarted by someone or something outside of the defendant's control, or if the defendant stops the attempt due to a fear of detection, the defendant will be guilty of an attempt.

However, if the attempt fails because the defendant voluntarily abandons the attempt, the defendant will not be guilty of the attempted offense, although he may be guilty of some lesser offense. Herron is correct in his argument that abandonment is an affirmative defense to an attempt charge. It is an affirmative defense to a charge under this section [DF][the attempt provision] that the actor abandoned his effort to commit the offense or otherwise prevented its commission, under circumstances manifesting a complete and voluntary renunciation of his criminal purpose.

The burden of going forward with the evidence of an affirmative defense, and the burden of proof, by a preponderance of the evidence, for an affirmative defense, is upon the accused." Our review of the record reveals that Herron presented evidence, by way of his own testimony, that he abandoned any alleged attempt to have sexual intercourse with his stepdaughter upon realizing that he had mistaken her identity. If believed, his testimony could lead a jury to find, by a preponderance of the evidence, that Herron did voluntarily and completely renounce his purpose of committing a Sexual Battery.

State v. Herron, 1996 WL 715445 (OhioApp. 2 Dist.)

 Go to Exercise 6-2 on the Criminal Law 8e CD to learn more about the defense of abandonment.

◆ ◆ ◆

CONSPIRACY

Conspiracy, the crime of agreeing to commit a crime, is further removed from actually committing a crime than either attempts or even preparation to commit crimes. There are two public policy justifications for attaching criminal liability to actions further away from completion than attempts and even preparations to commit crimes:

1. Conspiracy works hand in hand with attempt to nip criminal purpose in the bud.

2. Conspiracy strikes at the special danger of group criminal activity. (American Law Institute 1985 [3], 387–378)

In this section, we'll look at what's necessary to prove the *actus reus* and *mens rea* of conspiracy, how the law treats the parties to conspiracies, how large-scale conspiracies differ, and how the law limits the definition of the criminal objective of a conspiracy.

Conspiracy *Actus Reus*

Conspiracy *actus reus* consists of two parts:

1. An agreement to commit a crime (in all states)

2. An overt act in furtherance of the agreement (in about half the states)

The Agreement

The heart of the crime of conspiracy is the act of agreement between two or more people to commit a crime. The agreement doesn't have to be a signed written contract. It's "not necessary to establish that the defendant and his coconspirators signed papers, shook hands, or uttered the words 'we have an agreement'" (*State v. Vargas* 2003, 208–209). Facts and circumstances that point to an unspoken understanding between the conspirators are good enough to prove the conspirators agreed to commit a crime. This rule makes sense because conspirators rarely put their agreements in writing.

Vague definitions of agreement can lead to injustice. In one famous trial during the unhappy period of the Vietnam War, the government tried the famous baby doctor turned war protestor Dr. Benjamin Spock for conspiracy to avoid the draft law. Videotapes showed several hundred spectators clapping while Dr. Spock urged young men to resist the draft. Spurred on by antagonism to anti-war protestors, the prosecu-

---

ELEMENTS OF CONSPIRACY LIABILITY

Actus Reus	*Mens Rea*
1. Agreement	1. Specific intent or purpose to commit an illegal act, **or**
2. Minority Rule: Agreement plus some act in furtherance of the agreement	2. Specific intent or purpose to commit an illegal act by illegal means

tor in the case made the wild assertion that any person seen clapping on the video-tape was a co-conspirator. According to the prosecutor, these people were aiding Spock, and that made them parties to a conspiracy to violate the draft law (Mitford 1969, 70–71).

Overt Act

In about half the states, the agreement itself is the criminal conduct that satisfies the *actus reus* of conspiracy. In the other half, there has to be the act of agreeing to commit a crime *plus* another act to further the agreement; it's called the **overt act.** Why the requirement of an "overt act"? To verify the firmness of the agreement. The overt act doesn't have to amount to much. In the words of the American Law Institute's commentator (1985 [3], 387), it may "be of very small significance." And, according to the U.S. Supreme Court Justice Oliver Wendell Holmes (*Hyde v. U.S.* 1912):

> if the overt act is required, it does not matter how remote the act may be from accomplishing the [criminal] purpose, if done to effect it; that is, I suppose, in furtherance of it in any degree. (388)

The Minnesota Supreme Court dealt with the *actus reus* of conspiracy to manufacture methamphetamines in *State v. Hatfield* (2002).

CASE | *Did He "Agree" to Manufacture Methamphetamines?*

State v. Hatfield
639 N.W.2d 372 (Minn. 2002)

Michael Hatfield (Defendant) was convicted in the Martin County District Court, Robert D. Walker, J., of conspiracy to manufacture methamphetamine. He appealed. The Court of Appeals reversed. The Minnesota Supreme Court affirmed.

BLATZ, CJ.

FACTS

On December 3, 1999, at around 11 P.M., Bobbie Nowak drove Anthony Theobald, her boyfriend, to a house in Fairmont, Minnesota, where Michael Hatfield and his family were temporarily staying. The house was owned by Hatfield's cousin, David Stedman, who had been working out of town for most of the week that the Hatfields stayed in his home. Hatfield had called Theobald earlier that evening and asked him to pick up and bring to him a cooler and propane tank that were in Nowak's neighbor's garage. Theobald did as asked, putting the items in the trunk of Nowak's car before he and Nowak drove to Stedman's house to meet Hatfield.

That same evening, Fairmont police officers had been contacted by the Thomas County, Kansas sheriff's department. At about 11:00 P.M., a Fairmont officer spoke with a Thomas County deputy who requested that Hatfield be arrested under a warrant issued in Thomas County. The Thomas County deputy informed the Fairmont officer that Hatfield was probably staying with Stedman. Based on this information, several Fairmont police officers went to Stedman's house. When the officers arrived, Hatfield was carrying a red cooler from Nowak's car to the garage. A second group of Fairmont police officers, arriving from the rear, saw Hatfield entering the garage through the service entrance. Hatfield soon emerged from the front door of the house and identified himself to officers located at the front of the house who were questioning Theobald and Nowak. He was informed of the warrant for his arrest and taken into custody. Officers searched Hatfield incident to arrest and seized drug paraphernalia, approximately $447 in cash, and razor blades coated with white, powdery residue. Hatfield later told an officer that he received the paraphernalia from "a kid that just got busted for this stuff [and] . . . threw it [my] way."

The officers who saw Hatfield enter the garage detected a smell emanating from the open service entrance. One officer, Sergeant Dale Ellis, noticed a much stronger smell inside the garage. He testified that the odor caused a "metallic taste," a stinging sensation in his eyes, and took his breath away. Sergeant Ellis then entered the house, where he could smell the same odor as that coming from the garage, and found five children, four of whom were Hatfield's. Because Sergeant Ellis believed the odor was caused by anhydrous ammonia, an ingredient used to manufacture methamphetamine, he radioed for Agent James Kotewa, a Fairmont police officer assigned to the Minnesota River Valley Drug Task Force, for additional assistance. Sergeant Ellis also telephoned the Martin County Human Services Department for assistance in removing the children from the house.

Stedman, the owner of the house, returned around midnight and consented to a search of the property. During the search, Officer Ellis and Agent Kotewa found what they believed were the requisite components of an anhydrous-ammonia methamphetamine laboratory.

Hatfield was charged with conspiracy to manufacture methamphetamine. . . . At trial, there was conflicting testimony about the presence of the smell of anhydrous ammonia. Officer Ellis, Agent Kotewa, Officer Kevin Walser, and Officer Michael Hunter testified that they smelled ammonia coming from the garage. Additionally, several officers testified that they smelled an odor, similar to the one in the garage, upon entering the house. In contrast, both Hatfield's wife and Stedman testified that they did not notice an odor in the house.

Agent Kotewa testified that the propane tank had alterations to the handle and a blue-green discoloration around the nozzle, which were typical signs of a propane tank used to transport anhydrous ammonia. He also testified that the red cooler held five mason jars that contained precipitation. Based on the strong smell, Agent Kotewa believed the precipitation to be anhydrous ammonia. Because Agent Kotewa was concerned about the risks posed by the suspected anhydrous ammonia, he directed that the jars and the propane tank be destroyed without being tested.

The state compelled Nowak and Theobald to testify. Nowak testified that she did not bring anything to Hatfield's temporary residence, but stated that Theobald brought a small tank she thought was used for a gas grill. Theobald testified that Hatfield asked him to bring over a cooler and a "propane tank for the grill." He also testified that he did not know the contents of the propane tank and denied discussing any other topic with Hatfield aside from "running out to the Legion and having a drink." When asked who carried the propane tank and red cooler to the garage, Theobald responded that he may have carried one but he was not sure because "at that point, I didn't—you

know, I didn't know if there was a significance." Both Nowak and Theobald testified that they did not smell any odor emanating from the propane tank or the trunk of Nowak's car.

While the state did not present direct evidence showing a criminal agreement between Hatfield and Theobald, Agent Kotewa was allowed to testify, over Hatfield's objection, that there was an "on-going criminal investigation" and that he believed Theobald was involved with Hatfield and would soon be arrested. Agent Kotewa did not explicitly state the basis for such an arrest, but he implied that it involved the same circumstances giving rise to the charges against Hatfield. During the state's case in chief, Agent Kotewa was asked about Theobald:

Q: Was Anthony Theobald present at the scene?

A: I remember seeing—yes. I remember seeing Tony.

Q: Okay. And was Anthony Theobald arrested that evening?

A: No, he was not.

Q: Why wasn't he arrested that night.

A: At that point, there was an on-going inves—Well, at that point, I did not see the probable cause to arrest him. I did not have all the facts at that point.

Q: And why hasn't he been arrested since that time?

A: I anticipate him getting arrested—ongoing criminal investigation.

Q: You believe Anthony Theobald was involved with Michael Hatfield?

A: Yes.

Hatfield was convicted of . . . conspiracy to manufacture methamphetamine. . . . He appealed to the court of appeals . . . , challenging the sufficiency of the evidence supporting . . . [the] verdict. The court of appeals . . . concluded that there was "insufficient evidence in the record from which the jury could reasonably infer that Hatfield entered into an actual agreement with anyone for the purpose of manufacturing methamphetamine."

OPINION

In reviewing a sufficiency of the evidence claim, we are limited to a painstaking analysis of the record to determine whether the evidence, when viewed in a light most favorable to the conviction, was sufficient to permit the jurors to reach their verdict. When weighing the sufficiency of circumstantial evidence, we give it as much weight as any other kind of evidence, as long as the circumstances are both consistent with the hypothesis that the defendant is guilty and inconsistent with any rational hypothesis except that of guilt. Thus, the circumstantial evidence must "'form a complete chain which, in light of the evidence as a whole, leads so directly to the guilt of the accused as to exclude, beyond a reasonable doubt, any reasonable inference other than that of guilt.'"

A conspiracy exists when someone "conspires with another to commit a crime and in furtherance of the conspiracy one or more of the parties does some overt act in furtherance of such conspiracy.... Minn.Stat. § 609.175 (2000). In this case the jury found that Hatfield conspired with another to manufacture methamphetamine. On appeal, Hatfield argued that there was insufficient evidence of an agreement.

Proof of a formal agreement to commit a crime is not required for a conspiracy conviction. In addition, the agreement required for a conspiracy need not be proved through evidence of a subjective meeting of the minds, but must be shown by evidence that objectively indicates an agreement.

The state acknowledges that proof of the agreement in this case was circumstantial. To successfully challenge a conviction based solely on circumstantial evidence, the defendant must establish that the evidence in the record and the reasonable inferences that could be drawn therefrom are consistent with a rational hypothesis other than just the defendant's guilt. Hatfield's theory is that Theobald, as he testified, did not know that anhydrous ammonia was in either the propane tank or the red cooler, and therefore his act of bringing the tank and cooler to Hatfield does not indicate an agreement to manufacture methamphetamine.

In contrast, the state points to three pieces of evidence that could allow the jury to reasonably conclude that Hatfield and Theobald entered into a criminal agreement: evidence that Theobald delivered the propane tank and red cooler to Hatfield at Hatfield's request; testimony that Theobald was under investigation for "drug-related activities"; and testimony that Hatfield associated with known drug users. This evidence, taken in the light most favorable to the verdict, is consistent with a rational hypothesis other than guilt, and not only consistent with Hatfield's guilt.

The state claims that the evidence shows that Theobald knew of the contents of the tank and cooler and argues that a reasonable inference from that knowledge is that Hatfield and Theobald agreed to manufacture methamphetamine. The state must overcome the principle that consorting with an innocent courier does not constitute an agreement necessary for a conspiracy. "Those having no knowledge of the conspiracy are not conspirators ... and one who without more furnishes supplies ... is not guilty of conspiracy even though his sale may have furthered the object of a conspiracy....

We note first that there is no direct evidence that Theobald knew that the tank and cooler contained anhydrous ammonia.*

Moreover, Theobald's *knowledge* of what was in the tank and cooler is simply not particularly probative of an *agreement* to manufacture drugs. That is, Theobald's knowledge of what was in the tank does not make it significantly more likely that Hatfield agreed with him to manufacture methamphetamine. In other cases, an inference of agreement from knowledge may be reasonable. However in this case—where there was no evidence of a common plan, concerted conduct, or prior involvement with the alleged co-conspirator—any inference of an agreement from knowledge, standing alone, is simply not reasonable. We emphasize that the focus of the inquiry is properly on whether there was objective evidence that *Hatfield* agreed with another to produce methamphetamine. For purposes of assessing the sufficiency of this circumstantial evidence, Theobald's knowledge of what was in the tank and red cooler does not "form a complete chain which, in light of the evidence as a whole, leads so directly to the guilt of the accused as to exclude, beyond a reasonable doubt, any reasonable inference other than that of guilt."

The state also argues that Agent Kotewa's statement that Theobald was under investigation for criminal activities is evidence of an agreement between Hatfield and Theobald to manufacture methamphetamine. Over Hatfield's objection Kotewa testified that he believed Theobald would be arrested as a result of an on-going criminal investigation. The officer also testified that he believed Theobald was "involved" with Hatfield. While the admissibility of such evidence is questionable in the first instance, that issue is not before us. The evidence indicates only that Theobald *might be arrested* for criminal activities—the very "activities" that give rise to this appeal. As such, the evidence says nothing about an agreement with Hatfield. In addition, the officer was not asked the basis for his belief that Theobald and Hatfield were "involved," and mere involvement again does not establish an agreement to manufacture methamphetamine. Thus, taking the evidence in the light most favorable to the verdict, the evidence was insufficient to

---

*The state claims Theobald must have known of the contents based on the apparent odor of anhydrous ammonia. However, there was no evidence to indicate that Theobald actually recognized anything suspect about the items, nor was there evidence that an ordinary person would have inferred from the smell of anhydrous ammonia that methamphetamine was being made.

permit the jury to reach a guilty verdict on the conspiracy charge.

Finally, the state argues that the agreement was supported by the presence of drug paraphernalia and methamphetamine on Hatfield's person and in Nowak's trunk, and by Hatfield's statement that he received the drugs from another methamphetamine user. With respect to the conspiracy charge, this evidence goes to Hatfield's knowledge and perhaps an overt act, but says nothing about an agreement with another to manufacture methamphetamine. Thus, the evidence may have supported Hatfield's convictions for possession, but does not lead to the conclusion that there was an agreement with another to manufacture methamphetamine.

To support a conspiracy conviction, the evidence must objectively indicate that at least one person conspired with another to commit a crime and that one or more of those persons performed an overt act in furtherance of the agreement. The conduct proved by the state established at most only that Theobald brought a propane tank and cooler to Hatfield at Hatfield's request, and that Hatfield possessed drugs and drug paraphernalia. The evidence does not "'form a complete chain which, in light of the evidence as a whole, leads so directly to the guilt of the accused as to exclude, beyond a reasonable doubt, any reasonable inference other than that of guilt.'" Specifically, there was simply insufficient evidence, circumstantial or direct, of an agreement between Hatfield and another to manufacture methamphetamine. Therefore, the conspiracy conviction was properly reversed.

AFFIRMED.

Questions

1. State the definition of the agreement part of conspiracy *actus reus* adopted by the court.

2. List all the evidence relevant to deciding whether Michael Hatfield "agreed" to manufacture methamphetamines.

3. Summarize how the court applies the definition of agreement to the facts in the case.

4. Assume you're the prosecutor in the case. Argue there was an agreement to manufacture methamphetamines. Back up your arguments with evidence and arguments made by the state.

Conspiracy *Mens Rea*

Conspiracy *mens rea* wasn't defined clearly at common law, and most modern legislatures haven't made it any clearer. This leaves the courts to define it. The courts in turn have taken imprecise, widely divergent, and inconsistent approaches to the *mens rea* problem. According to former Supreme Court Justice Robert Jackson, "The modern crime of conspiracy is so vague that it almost defies definition" (*Krulewitch v. U.S.* 1949, 445–446).

Authorities frequently call conspiracy a specific intent crime. But what does that mean? Does it mean that conspiracy involves intent to enter an agreement to commit a crime? Or does conspiracy also have to include an intent to attain a *specific* criminal objective? For example, if two men agree to burn down a building, they intend to commit arson. But, if they don't intend to hurt anyone and someone dies, did they also conspire to commit murder? Not if the conspiracy *mens rea* means an intent to achieve a particular criminal objective. This example demonstrates an important distinction between, on one hand, the intent to make agreements and, on the other hand, the intent to achieve a criminal objective. If the objective is to commit a specific crime, it has to satisfy that crime's *mens rea*. So, conspiring to take another's property isn't conspiring to commit larceny unless the conspirators intended to permanently deprive the owner of possession (Chapter 11).

Courts further complicate conspiracy *mens rea* by not clarifying whether it requires purpose. Consider cases involving suppliers of goods and services, such as doctors who order drugs from pharmaceutical companies that they then use or sell illegally. At what point do the suppliers become co-conspirators, even though they haven't agreed specifically to supply drugs for illegal distribution? Do prosecutors have to prove the suppliers agreed specifically to further the buyers' criminal purposes? Most courts say yes, even though that kind of proof is difficult to obtain, because as we've already seen, conspirators aren't foolish enough to put proof of their crimes in writing. So, purpose has to be inferred from circumstances surrounding the agreement, such as quantities of sales, the continuity of the supplier-recipient relationship, the seller's initiative, a failure to keep records, and the relationship's clandestine nature. Some argue that knowing, or conscious, wrongdoing ought to satisfy the conspiracy *mens rea* (*Direct Sales Co. v. U.S.* 1943).

Parties to the Conspiracy

The traditional definition of conspiracy includes the requirement that agreements involve "two or more parties agreeing or combining to commit a crime (American Law Institute 1985 [3], 398). Most modern statutes have replaced this traditional definition with a **unilateral approach** that doesn't require that all conspirators agree—or even know—the other conspirators. For example, if one of two conspirators secretly has no intention to go through with the agreement, the other conspirator is still a party.

When there is more than one party, failure to convict one party doesn't prevent conviction of other parties to conspiracies. Typically, statutes similar to the Illinois Criminal Code (*Illinois Criminal Law and Procedure* 1988), provide:

1. It shall not be a defense to conspiracy that the person or persons with whom the accused is alleged to have conspired

2. Has not been prosecuted or convicted, or

3. Has been convicted of a different offense, or

4. Is not amenable to justice, or

5. Has been acquitted, or

6. Lacked the capacity to commit an offense. (chap. 38, § 8–4)

Large-Scale Conspiracies

The relationship of parties to conspiracies can get intricate, particularly when they involve large operations. Most of these large-scale conspiracies fall into two major patterns: "wheel" and "chain" conspiracies. In **wheel conspiracies,** one or more defendants participate in every transaction. These participants make up the hub of the wheel conspiracy. Others participate in only one transaction; they are the spokes in the wheel. In **chain conspiracies,** participants at one end of the chain may know nothing of those at the other end, but every participant handles the same commodity at different points, such as manufacture, distribution, and sale. Chain conspiracies usually involve the distribution of some commodity, such as illegal drugs. In *U.S. v. Bruno* (1939), for example, smugglers brought narcotics into New York, middlemen purchased the narcotics, and two groups of retailers (one operating in New York and the other in Louisiana) bought narcotics from middlemen.

Criminal Objective of the Conspiracy

Conspiracy is an agreement but an agreement to do what? In the old days, the **criminal objective** was defined extremely broadly. The objective could be as narrow as an agreement to commit a felony or as broad as in

- agreements to commit "any crime";
- to do "anything unlawful";
- to commit "any act injurious to the public health, or for the perversion of or obstruction of justice, or due administration of the laws (American Law Institute [3] 1985, 395);
- or to do even "lawful things by unlawful means."

In most modern statutes, the criminal objective is almost always limited to agreements to commit crimes.

The often vague definitions of the elements in conspiracy offer considerable opportunity for prosecutorial and judicial discretion. At times, this discretion borders on abuse, leading to charges that conspiracy law is unjust. First, a general criticism is that conspiracy law punishes conduct too far remote from the actual crime. Second, labor organizations, civil liberties groups, and large corporations charge that conspiracy is a weapon against their legitimate interests of, respectively, collective bargaining and strikes, dissent from accepted points of view and public policies, and profit making. Critics say that when prosecutors do not have enough evidence to convict for the crime itself, they turn as a last hope to conspiracy. Conspiracy's vague definitions greatly enhance the chance for a guilty verdict.

Not often mentioned, but extremely important, is that intense media attention to conspiracy trials can lead to abuse. This happened in the conspiracy trials of Dr. Benjamin Spock, the Chicago Eight, and others involving radical politics during the 1960s. It also occurred in the Watergate conspiracy trials involving President Nixon's associates during the 1970s and in the alleged conspiracies surrounding the sale of arms to Iran for hostages and the subsequent alleged diversion of funds during the 1980s.

Several states have made efforts to overcome these criticisms by defining conspiracy elements more narrowly. The definitions of agreement or combination (two or more parties combining to commit crimes) are no longer as vague as they once were. The *Model Penal Code* has adopted the overt act requirement (acts in furtherance of the act of agreement), and several states are following that lead. Those states have refined *mens rea* to include only purposeful conduct—that is, a specific intent to carry out the objective of the agreement or combination. Knowledge, recklessness, and negligence are increasingly attacked as insufficient culpability for an offense as remote from completion as conspiracy. Furthermore, most recent legislation restricts conspiratorial objectives to criminal ends. Phrases like "unlawful objects," "lawful objects by unlawful means," and "objectives harmful to public health, morals, trade, and commerce" are increasingly regarded as too broad and, therefore, unacceptable.

On the other hand, the Racketeer Influenced and Corrupt Organizations Act (RICO) demonstrates the continued vitality of conspiracy law. RICO reflects the need for effective means to meet the threat posed by organized crime. It imposes enhanced penalties for "all types of organized criminal behavior, that is, enterprise criminality—from simple political to sophisticated white collar schemes to traditional Mafia-type endeavors" (Blakely and Gettings 1980, 1013–1014).

Racketeering activity includes any act chargeable under state and federal law, including murder, kidnapping, bribery, drug dealing, gambling, theft, extortion, and securities fraud. Among other things, the statute prohibits using income from a "pattern of racketeering activity" to acquire an interest in or establish an enterprise affecting interstate commerce; conducting an enterprise through a pattern of racketeering; or conspiring to violate these provisions.

RICO's drafters intended the statute to "break the back of organized crime." According to conservative columnist William Safire (1989), the racketeers they had in mind were "loansharks, drug kingpins, prostitution overlords, and casino operators who hired murderers and arsonists to enforce and extort—you know, the designated bad guys who presumably did not deserve the rights of due process that should protect all of us (19)." Now, however, aggressive prosecutors use RICO against white-collar crime. Rudolf Giuliani, as a U.S. Attorney, for example, caused Drexel Burnham Lambert to plead guilty to several counts of securities violations in order to avoid RICO prosecution, which would not only have resulted in harsher legal penalties for these white-collar criminals but also attached the label of "racketeer" to them (19).

SOLICITATION

Suppose I want to murder my wife, but I'm afraid to do it. If I ask a friend to kill her and he does, we're both murderers. If he tries to kill her and fails because his gun isn't loaded, then we've committed attempted murder. If he agrees to kill her and buys the gun but doesn't follow through, we've committed conspiracy to commit murder. But what if I try to get my friend to kill her by offering her $5000 to kill my wife and she turns me down? That's a crime, too—**solicitation,** the crime of trying to get someone else to commit a crime.

There's disagreement about whether solicitation to commit a crime is dangerous enough to be a crime. Those in the "not-dangerous-enough" group make two arguments. First, solicitation isn't dangerous enough *conduct* because an independent moral agent (the person solicited) stands between solicitors and their criminal objectives. Second, solicitors aren't dangerous enough *people.* They prove it by trying to get someone else to commit crimes they're too timid to commit themselves. Those on the "dangerous-enough" side have their own arguments. First, they say solicitation is just another form of the danger created by group participation in crime, only more removed from the completed crime than conspiracy—kind of like an attempted conspiracy. Second, solicitors are intelligent, artful masters at manipulating others to do their dirty work.

We'll look at the elements of solicitation—the *actus reus* and *mens rea* required by the law—and the criminal objective of solicitation.

Solicitation *Actus Reus*

Criminal solicitation consists of words, but the law imprecisely tells us what words qualify as **solicitation** *actus reus.* Courts agree that statements that just favor committing a crime aren't enough to qualify as criminal acts. So, someone who says, "I think it'd be great if someone killed that terrorist," hasn't solicited murder. There has to be

ELEMENTS OF SOLICITATION LIABILITY

Actus Reus	Mens Rea
Words commanding, urging, or encouraging a third person to commit a crime	Specific intent—that is, the purpose to induce a third person to commit a crime

some kind of *inducement* to commit a crime. The typical words we see in the statutes and court opinions include advises, commands, counsels, encourages, entices, entreats, importunes, incites, induces, instigates, procures, requests, solicits, and/or urges. In other words, the criminal act in solicitation consists of the *effort* to get another to commit a crime, *whether or not* the solicitation ever ripens into a completed crime (LaFave and Scott 1986, 419).

Does the solicitor have to address the words to precise individuals? Not necessarily. Soliciting audiences is precise enough. One speaker was convicted for urging his audience to commit murder and robbery. Even the inducement that doesn't reach its object qualifies. So, if I send a letter to my hoped-for collaborator, offering her $30,000 to kill my enemy, I've solicited murder even if the letter gets lost in the mail (*State v. Schleifer* 1923).

Solicitation *Mens Rea*

Solicitation is a specific intent crime; that is, it's a crime of purpose. **Solicitation *mens rea*** requires words that convey that their purpose is to get someone to commit a specific crime. If I urge my friend who works in an expensive jewelry shop to take a gold chain for me, I've solicited her to steal the chain. If, on the other hand, I ask another friend who works in a clothing shop to get a coat for me to use for the evening, and I plan to return the coat the next morning before anyone knows it's missing, I haven't solicited her to steal the coat because I don't intend to steal the coat, only to use it for the night (Chapter 11).

Criminal Objective of the Solicitation

Some statutes restrict the criminal objective of solicitation to getting someone to commit felonies—in some cases, to commit violent felonies. In other jurisdictions, it's a crime to solicit another to commit any crime, whether it's a felony, misdemeanor, or violation. Furthermore, solicitation doesn't have to include an inducement to commit an act that is itself a crime. For example, suppose a robber urges a friend to borrow money and lend it to him for a plane ticket to escape from the jurisdiction. The robber has solicited escape, or aiding and abetting a robbery. Although borrowing money isn't a crime, and lending money to a robber isn't by itself a crime, both escape and aiding and abetting robbers are crimes. One who urges another to commit those crimes has committed the crime of solicitation.

The Texas Court of Criminal Appeals dealt with a solicitation to murder for hire in *Ganeson v. State* (2001).

Ganeson v. State
45 S.W.3d 197 (TX 2001)

Apparajan Ganeson, Defendant, was convicted in the District Court, Travis County, 390th Judicial District of two counts of solicitation to commit murder, and sentenced to 10 years in prison. He appealed. The Court of Appeals affirmed in part and reversed in part.

KIDD, J.

A jury convicted appellant Apparajan Ganesan on two counts of solicitation to commit murder. Tex. Penal Code Ann. § § 15.03, 19.02 (West 1994). The jury assessed punishment for each count at imprisonment for ten years, to be served concurrently. We will affirm the conviction on one count, but reverse and render an acquittal on the other.

FACTS

The two counts of the indictment alleged that appellant, with the requisite intent, requested Prier "to engage in specific conduct, to wit: to kill [his wife]" under circumstances that "would have made Reda Sue Prier a party to the commission of murder." It is undisputed that appellant did not ask Prier to kill either Vallabhaneni or Wright. Instead, Prier testified that appellant repeatedly asked her to find someone to kill them. Appellant contends that Prier's testimony does not reflect a criminal solicitation, but merely a noncriminal "solicitation of solicitation." The jury found that Apparajan Ganesan (appellant) solicited Reda Sue Prier to kill Sudha Vallabhaneni, appellant's wife, and Amy Wright, the lawyer representing Vallabhaneni in her divorce action.

OPINION

Appellant contends the State did not prove that he engaged in criminal solicitation as defined in the penal code and alleged in the indictment. The penal code provides that a person commits an offense if, with intent that a capital or first degree felony be committed, he "requests, commands, or attempts to induce another to engage in specific conduct that, under the circumstances surrounding his conduct as the actor believes them to be, would constitute the felony or make the other a party to its commission."

In *Johnson v. State*, 650 S.W.2d 784 (Tex.Crim.App.1983), the indictment alleged that the defendant "attempted to induce Roger Bryant to employ another" to commit a murder. The defendant argued that asking Bryant to employ another to commit murder was a solicitation of a solicitation, and

therefore not an offense under the terms of Tex. Penal Code Ann. § 15.05 (West 1994) (solicitation of a chapter 15 preparatory offense is not an offense). The court rejected this argument. Citing the last phrase in section 15.03(a), the court noted that the act solicited must either constitute the intended felony or make the person solicited a party to its commission. The act solicited by the defendant, Bryant's employment of another to commit murder, would make Bryant a party to the murder. Thus, the defendant's solicitation of Bryant constituted an offense under section 15.03.

If, in the case before us, Prier had arranged for someone else to kill appellant's wife and her attorney as she testified that appellant requested and attempted to induce her to do, Prier would have been a party to the murders. Appellant's contention that Prier's testimony does not show that he committed a criminal solicitation under section 15.03 is without merit.

Appellant further contends that Prier's testimony was not adequately corroborated. A person may not be convicted of criminal solicitation on the uncorroborated testimony of the person allegedly solicited and "unless the solicitation is made under circumstances strongly corroborative of both the solicitation itself and the actor's intent that the other person act on the solicitation." Section 15.03(b) is analogous to the accomplice witness statute, and the same test for evaluating the sufficiency of the corroboration is used. Therefore, we must eliminate Prier's testimony from consideration and determine whether there is other evidence tending to connect appellant to the crime. The corroboration must go to both the solicitation and the alleged intent, but need not be sufficient in itself to establish guilt. We view the corroborating evidence in the light most favorable to the verdict.

Appellant is an engineer who had designed a computer chip that he hoped to market in partnership with a Swiss corporation. In November 1996, one month after Vallabhaneni filed for divorce, appellant liquidated his brokerage account and ordered that the proceeds, over one million dollars, be wired to a Swiss bank account. Before the money could be moved, however, his wife obtained a restraining order and the money was deposited in the registry of the court. In late 1997 or early 1998, appellant filed for bankruptcy. Vallabhaneni, as a claimant to the funds, was scheduled to be deposed in the bankruptcy proceeding in November 1998. The alleged solicitations for the murders of Vallabhaneni and Wright took place in September and October 1998.

The record reflects that appellant believed that his wife's actions were damaging his ability to market the computer chip. During a telephone conversation with Vallabhaneni in January 1997, which she tape recorded on Wright's advice, appellant said that her divorce action was "making sure that this product will die." Appellant went on, "Let me tell you this. I don't care what you do. If this product dies, one of us will be dead, yeah, I promise you that." Vallabhaneni replied, "What do you mean, you'll kill me?" Appellant answered, "I will kill myself or I'll kill you or I'll kill both of us or you will kill yourself. That much I can tell you. If . . . this product dies, one of us will die. I know that. Because I won't be able to live with the shame. Maybe you will be able to live with it."

In *Richardson*, the defendant was convicted of soliciting the murder of a man who was scheduled to testify against him in a prosecution for theft. The court of criminal appeals stated that the "theft charge and [the victim's] actions with respect to it suggest the existence of an agreement [between the defendant and the alleged solicitee]." Applying the reasoning of *Richardson*, appellant's belief that his wife's litigation threatened to derail a potentially lucrative business opportunity was evidence of motive that tends to support Prier's testimony that appellant solicited the murders of his wife and her attorney. While evidence of motive is insufficient in itself to corroborate an accomplice, it may be considered with other evidence to connect the accused with the crime.

Appellant's statement that "one of us will be dead" if the chip design did not succeed adds some additional support to the existence of the solicitation of Vallabhaneni's murder. In his brief, appellant dismisses his remarks during the telephone conversation as nothing more than hyperbole, and notes that the conversation took place twenty months before the alleged solicitation. But viewing the evidence in the light most favorable to the jury's verdict, as we must, we cannot disregard the threat implicit in appellant's statement.

Appellant was arrested in May 1997 for violating a protective order obtained by Vallabhaneni. While in the Travis County Jail, he met James Hammonds, who was awaiting his release on bail following an arrest for theft. Hammonds testified that appellant told him "about how his wife and the system and the judge had destroyed his life and his business and how he was losing everything." According to Hammonds, appellant asked, "Do you know of anyone, or can you take care of my wife for me?" When Hammonds replied, "Excuse me?" appellant said, "You know what I mean." Hammonds said that this "really scared me" and that he thought he was "being set up by the cops." Hammonds refused to give appellant his address but gave appellant a telephone number where he could be reached, not expecting appellant to call.

A few weeks later, however, appellant called Hammonds and asked if he "remember[ed] the conversation in the cell that we had." Appellant added, "I need to talk to you about this again. We need to talk about this." Still fearing that he was being tricked, Hammonds told appellant his upcoming trial date and suggested that they meet at the courthouse. After giving the matter further consideration, Hammonds contacted the police and reported what appellant had said. Subsequently, under the supervision of a Texas Ranger, Hammonds (who had obtained appellant's telephone number by means of caller ID) called appellant while being recorded. When Hammonds attempted to talk about their previous conversations, appellant "started back-peddling. He started trying to get out of the conversation. He didn't want to talk about that." The call ended and the police did not pursue the matter to Hammonds's knowledge.

That appellant solicited Hammonds to kill his wife, albeit sixteen months before the alleged solicitation of Prier, tends to corroborate Prier's testimony both as to the solicitation itself and appellant's intent that Prier act on the solicitation. But Hammonds's testimony corroborates Prier only with respect to the solicitation of Vallabhaneni's murder. It does not tend to connect appellant to the alleged solicitation of Wright's murder.

Prier testified that during the months appellant was asking her to arrange the murders, he instructed her to go to a post office near the Arboretum shopping center and watch who came and went. She also testified that appellant told her to watch an office on Lake Austin Boulevard, which he identified as Wright's husband's law office. The State contends this testimony was corroborated by Vallabhaneni's testimony that she received her mail at the Arboretum post office and by Wright's testimony that her husband's law office was in a building on Lake Austin Boulevard. Standing alone, however, this alleged corroborative evidence does not connect appellant to the criminal solicitations. Vallabhaneni's and Wright's testimony is meaningless except by reference to Prier's testimony. Such "bootstrapping" cannot be used to corroborate an accomplice, and by extension cannot be used to corroborate a solicitee.

The State also contends that Prier's testimony was corroborated by appellant's bankruptcy attorney. This witness testified that in November 1998, following appellant's arrest for the instant offense and at appellant's direction, he retrieved over $100,000 in cash from appellant's house. The State argues that this shows appellant had the financial means to pay for the solicited murders and to flee if necessary. But once again, this evidence has little significance standing alone. Appellant's possession of a large sum of cash is inculpatory, if at all, only when it is considered in light of Prier's testimony regarding the alleged solicitations. We must disregard Prier's testimony in our search for corroborating evidence. . . .

We conclude that the evidence of motive, the veiled threat during the telephone conversation, and the earlier solicitation of Hammonds adequately corroborates Prier's testimony both as to appellant's solicitation of Vallabhaneni's murder and appellant's intent that Prier act on the solicitation. We find, however, insufficient corroboration for Prier's testimony regarding appellant's solicitation of Wright's murder. . . .

Appellant contends the court erred by refusing to instruct the jury on the renunciation defense. It is an affirmative defense to prosecution for criminal solicitation that the defendant countermanded his solicitation under circumstances manifesting a voluntary and complete renunciation of his criminal objective. Appellant urges that Hammonds's testimony that appellant "started back-peddling" during their last telephone conversation raised the renunciation defense. Appellant's trial request was that the court give the renunciation instruction . . . with regard to the solicitation of Hammonds. But appellant was on trial for soliciting Prier. Ham-

monds's testimony did not raise an issue as to whether appellant countermanded his solicitation of Prier. . . .

AFFIRMED in part and REVERSED in part.

Questions

1. State the definition of solicitation to murder for hire as the Texas law defines it.

2. Summarize all the evidence relevant to deciding whether Ganeson solicited Prier to murder his wife and her divorce lawyer.

3. Summarize how the court applied the definition to the evidence in the case, and explain the court's judgment.

4. Assume you're Ganeson's lawer. Relying on the evidence, argue that Ganeson didn't solicit Prier to murder his wife.

5. Assume you're the prosecutor. Argue that Ganeson solicited Prier to murder both his wife and her lawyer. Back up your arguments with the evidence reported in the excerpt.

◆   ◆   ◆

SUMMARY

    I. Inchoate crimes
        A. *Inchoate* comes from the Latin verb "to begin"
        B. Inchoate crimes are separate crimes of starting but not finishing any other crime
        C. Whether to make it a crime to start but not finish committing a crime poses a dilemma
            1. Is the law punishing someone who's done no harm or setting free someone who's determined to do harm?
            2. Dilemma of criminal attempt law is resolved through three requirements
                a. Requiring specific intent
                b. Requiring some action
                c. Punishing inchoate crimes less severely than completed crimes
        D. Inchoate offenses include
            1. Attempt—trying to commit a crime
            2. Conspiracy—agreeing to commit a crime
            3. Solicitation—trying to get someone else to commit a crime
        E. All inchoate offenses are crimes of purpose (specific intent)

    II. Attempt
        A. Attempt is the crime of trying but failing to commit a crime
        B. Rationales for criminal attempt law
            1. Prevent harm from dangerous conduct (focuses on how close to completion the crime is)
            2. Neutralize dangerous people (focuses on how developed the criminal purpose is)

3. Both (1) and (2) look at actions taken to measure the danger

C. *Mens rea* of attempt
   1. Purpose or specific intent always present
   2. No knowing, reckless, or negligent attempts

D. *Actus reus* of attempt
   1. How much action is enough?
      a. Preparation isn't enough to qualify as the *actus reus* of attempt
      b. Toughest problem in criminal attempt: drawing line between preparation and attempt *actus reus*
   2. Tests to help draw the line between preparation and the act of attempt
      a. Physical proximity test
         (1) Focus
            (a) Dangerous conduct, not dangerous people
            (b) What's left to do, not what's already done
         (2) Completion of all but the last act needed to accomplish the crime is surely enough but so are acts falling short of this point, including
            (a) Indispensable element test—defendants who've gotten control of everything they need to complete the crime
            (b) Dangerous proximity test—defendants have gotten dangerously close to completing the crime
      b. Unequivocality (probable desistance) test
         (1) Focus
            (a) Dangerous persons, not dangerous conduct
            (b) What's already done, not what's left to do
         (2) Unequivocality test asks whether an ordinary person observing defendants' actions without knowing their intent would guess they were determined to commit the crime
      c. "Substantial steps" (*Model Penal Code*) test
         (1) Purpose—clarify and simplify other tests
         (2) Focus
            (a) Dangerous persons
            (b) What's already done, not what's left to do
         (3) Definition—substantial steps that "strongly corroborate" defendants' criminal purpose

E. Impossibility of completing the crime
   1. Legal impossibility is a defense to criminal attempt; factual impossibility isn't
   2. Legal impossibility
      a. Defendants intend to commit crimes, do everything they can to complete the crime, but what they intend and do isn't a crime (intending to smuggle antique books into the country without paying customs; they don't know it but there's an exception in the law for antique books)
      b. You can't punish someone for a crime that doesn't exist
   3. Factual impossibility
      a. Defendants' intend to commit a crime and take all the steps necessary to complete it, but a fact makes it impossible (standing over a victim pulling the trigger of a gun the defendant believes is loaded but it's not)
      b. People bent on committing crimes shouldn't benefit from a stroke of luck

F. Abandonment of attempts
   1. Complete and voluntary abandonment of attempts is an affirmative defense in about half the states
   2. Arguments in favor of the abandonment defense
      a. People who voluntarily and completely give up their criminal attempts aren't dangerous
      b. We want to encourage people who are just about to hurt someone or their property to give up their plans
   3. Argument against defense of abandonment—it encourages bad people to take the early steps in committing crimes because they know they won't be punished

III. Conspiracy
   A. Agreeing to commit crimes (criminal conspiracy) is further removed from completed crimes than trying to commit them (criminal attempt)
   B. Justifications for conspiracy law
      1. Works hand in hand with attempt to nip criminal purpose in the bud
      2. Strikes at the special danger of group criminal activity
   C. Conspiracy *actus reus*
      1. Agreement to commit a crime is the heart of the crime of conspiracy
         a. Doesn't have to be in writing
         b. An unspoken understanding inferred from facts and circumstances is good enough to prove agreement
      2. Half the states require an "overt act" in addition to the act of agreement
         a. Purpose—verify the firmness of the agreement
         b. Act doesn't have to amount to much; it can be of "very small significance"
   D. Conspiracy *mens rea*
      1. Crime of purpose (specific intent)
      2. Can mean intent to make the agreement or intent to achieve the criminal objective
   E. Parties to conspiracy
      1. Traditional—two or more individuals agreeing to commit crimes
      2. Unilateral approach—not all the conspirators had to agree to commit a crime as long as the defendant believes they did
   F. Large-scale conspiracies
      1. Wheel conspiracies
         a. Hub—conspirators who participate in all transactions
         b. Spokes—conspirators who only participate in one transaction
      2. Chain conspiracies—participants at one end of the chain don't know anything of participants at the other end, but they all handle the same illegal commodity at different points (manufacture, distribution, sale)
   G. Criminal objective of conspiracy
      1. Traditionally included everything from treason to disturbing the peace
      2. Some effort to limit the reach of conspiracy
         a. Requires an overt act in addition to an act of agreement
         b. Applies to criminal objectives only

IV. Solicitation
   A. Definition—the crime of trying to get someone else to commit a crime

B. Arguments against criminal solicitation law
  1. The act of soliciting isn't dangerous enough to punish because an independent moral force (the person solicited) stands between the solicitation and its objective
  2. Solicitors aren't dangerous enough people, and they prove it by needing someone else to do their dirty work
C. Arguments for criminal solicitation law
  1. Solicitation is another form of the danger of group criminality
  2. Solicitors are smart masters at manipulating others to do their dirty work
D. Solicitation *actus reus* requires words that actually try to get someone to commit a crime (not just approve the commission of the crime)
E. Solicitation *mens rea* requires purpose or specific intent to get someone to commit a specific crime
F. The objective of criminal solicitation varies from limiting it to violent felonies in some jurisdictions to including all crimes in other jurisdictions

 Go to the Criminal Law 8e CD to download this summary outline. The outline has been formatted so that you can add notes to it during class lectures, or later create a customized chapter outline to use while reviewing. Either way, the summary outline will help you understand the "big picture" and fill in the details as you study.

REVIEW QUESTIONS

1. Why are attempt, conspiracy, and solicitation called inchoate offenses?

2. What do all the inchoate crimes have in common?

3. Identify and explain the dilemma caused by the inchoate crimes; then identify the three means by which it is resolved.

4. Explain the significance of the quotes from Plato and Bracton.

5. Briefly summarize the history of criminal attempt law.

6. Explain the difference between the two theories of attempt law.

7. List, define, and give an example of the three elements of criminal attempts.

8. Identify and describe two types of criminal attempt statutes.

9. Identify, define, and give an example of the three most common tests for drawing the line between preparation and the *actus reus* of criminal attempts.

10. What problem are the "indispensable element" and "dangerous proximity" tests supposed to solve in criminal attempt law, and how are they each supposed to solve it?

11. What problems is the "unequivocality test" supposed to correct in criminal attempt law, and how is it supposed to correct them?

12. List the seven examples of "substantial steps" provided in the *Model Penal Code* that can satisfy attempt *actus reus*.

13. Explain the difference between factual and legal impossibility, give an example of each, and explain why they have different consequences in liability for criminal attempt.

14. Summarize the arguments for and against the defense of voluntary abandonment.

15. Identify the two public policy justifications for the crime of conspiracy.

16. Identify, explain, and give an example of the two parts of conspiracy *actus reus.*

17. Explain what specific intent means in conspiracy.

18. State the traditional definition of "parties" to conspiracies, and then identify and state the modern definition that replaced it.

19. Define and give an example of the "objective" in criminal conspiracy.

20. List the criticisms of criminal conspiracy definitions, and describe efforts to overcome these criticisms.

21. Summarize the arguments for and against making it a crime to try and get someone else to commit a crime.

22. Identify and give an example of the elements of criminal solicitation.

KEY TERMS

criminal attempt p. 146
criminal conspiracy p. 146
criminal solicitation p. 146
inchoate offenses p. 146
dangerous conduct rationale p. 148
dangerous person rationale p. 148
general attempt statute p. 149
specific attempt statute p. 149
attempt *mens rea* p. 149
attempt *actus reus* p. 155
preparation p. 155
physical proximity tests p. 156
unequivocality test p. 156

Model penal code test "substantial steps" test p. 156
indispensable element test p. 156
dangerous proximity test p. 156
res ipsa loquitur test p. 156
legal impossibility p. 162
factual impossibility p. 162
extraneous factor p. 162
principle of legality p. 162
information p. 163
affirmative defense of voluntary abandonment p. 170
conspiracy p. 174

conspiracy *actus reus* p. 174
overt act p. 175
conspiracy *mens rea* p. 178
unilateral approach p. 179
wheel conspiracies p. 179
chain conspiracies p. 179
criminal objective p. 180
solicitation p. 181
solicitation *actus reus* p. 181
solicitation *mens rea* p. 182

SUGGESTED READINGS

 Go to the Criminal Law 8e CD for Suggested Readings for this chapter.

THE COMPANION WEB SITE
FOR *CRIMINAL LAW,* EIGHTH EDITION

http://cj.wadsworth.com/samaha/crim_law8e

 Supplement your review of this chapter by going to the companion Web site to take one of the Tutorial Quizzes, use the flash cards to test your knowledge of the elements of various crimes and defenses, and check out the many other study aids you'll find there. You'll find valuable data and resources at your fingertips to help you study for that big exam or write that important paper.

7 Defenses to Criminal Liability: Justifications

Chapter Main Points

- Defenses are based on alibis, justifications, or excuses.
- Defenses of alibi free defendants from criminal liability, because they prove it's *impossible* for the defendants to have committed the crime.
- Justifications free defendants from criminal liability, because they prove the defendants aren't *blameworthy*.
- Excuses free defendants from criminal liability, because they prove the defendants aren't *responsible*.
- All the justification defenses violate the rule of law by allowing individuals to take the law into their own hands.
- Necessity (and sometimes consent) can justify otherwise criminal behavior.
- Self-defense (a grudging concession to necessity) is only justified when the necessity is unprovoked, great, imminent, and for protection only.
- Present danger doesn't justify taking the law into your own hands.
- The retreat rule puts a premium on human life—even the life of an attacker.
- The castle exception and the rules regarding the defense of home clearly demonstrate the ancient doctrine that homes are castles is still alive and well.
- The right to defend others includes everyone from close family members to anyone who needs immediate protection from attack.
- The choice-of-evils defense is based on necessity but is usually more controversial than self-defense, the defense of others, and the defense of home and property.
- The choice-of-evils defense rewards those who make the right choice in deciding to commit a lesser crime to avoid the imminent harm of a greater crime.
- Individual autonomy (not necessity) is the heart of the defense of consent.

Did He Shoot in Self-Defense?

Canty approached Goetz, possibly with Allen beside him, and said to Goetz, "Give me five dollars." Goetz stated that he knew from the smile on Canty's face that they wanted to "play with me." Although he was certain that none of the youths had a gun, he had a fear, based on prior experiences, of being "maimed." Goetz then established "a pattern of fire," deciding specifically to fire from left to right. His stated intention at that point was to "murder [the four youths], to hurt them, to make them suffer as much as possible." When Canty again requested money, Goetz stood up, drew his weapon, and began firing, aiming for the center of the body of each of the four. Goetz recalled that the first two he shot "tried to run through the crowd [but] they had nowhere to run." Goetz then turned to his right to "go after the other two." Cabey "tried pretending that he wasn't with [the others]" by standing still, holding on to one of the subway hand straps, and not looking at Goetz. Goetz nonetheless fired his fourth shot at him. He then ran back to the first two youths to make sure they had been "taken care of." Seeing that they had both been shot, he spun back to check on the other two. Goetz noticed that the youth who had been standing still was now sitting on a bench and seemed unhurt. As Goetz told the police, "I said '[y]ou seem to be all right, here's another,'" and he fired the shot which severed Cabey's spinal cord. Goetz added that "if I was a little more under self-control . . . I would have put the barrel against his forehead and fired." He also admitted that "if I had had more [bullets], I would have shot them again, and again, and again." ◆

The principles of criminal liability (Chapters 3 and 4); accomplice and vicarious liability (Chapter 5); and, criminal attempt, conspiracy, and solicitation (Chapter 6) are all about holding individuals *accountable* for the crimes they commit. The flip side of accountability is *avoiding* accountability. This is where the defenses to criminal liability come into the picture. (Don't confuse *avoiding* accountability with *dodging* it.) Legitimately avoiding criminal liability boils down to three types of defense:

1. *Alibi*. Defendants prove they were in a different place when the crime was committed, so it was impossible for them to have committed it.

2. *Justification* (the subject of this chapter). Defendants accept responsibility for their actions but claim what they did was right under the circumstances.

3. *Excuse* (Chapter 8). Defendants admit what they did was wrong but claim they weren't responsible for what they did. (Fletcher 1978, Chapter 10)

According to the **principle of justification,** under some circumstances, it's right to commit crimes. If so, committing the crime is justified and doesn't deserve punishment. There are two kinds of justification: defenses justified by necessity and defenses justified by consent. In both types, the argument goes like this: "I'm responsible for committing the crime, but under the circumstances it was right to commit it." So, even if the government proves all the elements in the crime beyond a reasonable doubt, the defendant walks because she's not blameworthy. The classic justification is self-defense. ("Kill or be killed.")

Excused conduct doesn't deserve punishment either—but for a different reason. According to the **principle of excuse,** it's wrong to punish someone who's not responsible for his or her conduct. The argument for excuse goes like this: "Committing the crime was wrong, but under the circumstances I wasn't responsible for committing it." So, even if it was wrong to commit the crime, the defendant isn't blameworthy because the government can't prove one of the elements of the crime—for example, that it was a voluntary act or there was criminal intent. The classic excuse is insanity ("I was too insane to know what I was doing" [Chapter 8]). The distinguished professor of criminal law George Fletcher (1978) sums up the difference between justification and excuse this way: "A justification speaks to the rightfulness of the act; an excuse, to whether the actor is accountable for a concededly wrongful act" (759).

Most of the justifications and excuses are what we call **affirmative defenses,** which operate like this: Defendants have to "start matters off by putting in some evidence in support" of their alibi, justification, or excuse (LaFave and Scott, 1986, 52). We call this the **burden of production.** Why put this burden on defendants? Because, according to LaFave and Scott, "We can assume that those who commit crimes are sane, sober, conscious, and acting freely. It makes sense, therefore, to make defendants responsible for injecting these extraordinary circumstances into the proceedings" (52). The amount of evidence required "is not great; some credible evidence" is enough. In some jurisdictions, if defendants meet the burden of production, they also have the **burden of persuasion,** meaning they have to prove their defenses by a **preponderance of the evidence** (more than 50% of the evidence is a preponderance). In other jurisdictions, once defendants meet the burden of production, the burden shifts to the government to prove defendants *don't* have alibis, weren't justified, or weren't excused (Loewy 1987, 192–204).

Most defenses are **perfect defenses.** (Defendants are acquitted in perfect defenses.) The defense of insanity is different. Defendants who successfully plead insanity don't "walk"— at least not right away. Special hearings are held to determine if these defendants are still insane. Most hearings decide they are, and so they're sent to maximum-security hospitals to be confined there until they regain their sanity (Chapter 8).

Evidence that doesn't amount to a perfect defense might amount to an **imperfect defense.** (Defendants are guilty of lesser offenses in imperfect defenses.) For example, an honest but unreasonable belief in the need to kill in self-defense reduces murder to manslaughter. Even if the evidence doesn't add up to a defense, it might still show **mitigating circumstances** that convince judges or juries that defendants don't deserve the maximum penalty for the crime they've committed. For example, words, however insulting, can't reduce murder to manslaughter in most states, but they might mitigate death to life without parole. So, if a black man killed a white man in a rage brought on by the relentless taunting, "nigger, nigger," the killing is still murder but the taunting might mitigate the death penalty to life without parole (Chapter 9).

Motive, the reason why someone commits the crime, can also influence punishment—or sometimes even conviction itself. Suppose a burglar breaks into a store to steal food because he's starving. Mercy killing (killing to end another's suffering) is another example. Juries have refused to convict mercy killers of first-degree murder even though the intent to kill was clearly there (Chapter 9). The murder conviction of Robert Latimer is a good example of this. Latimer could no longer stand the constant pain his 12-year-old daughter, Tracy, was suffering because of her severe and incurable cerebral palsy. She wore diapers, weighed only 38 pounds, and couldn't walk, talk, or feed herself. So, he put Tracy into the cab of his pickup truck on the family farm and pumped exhaust into the cab of the truck. He told the police that he stood by, ready to stop if Tracy started to cry, but that she simply went quietly "to sleep. My priority was to put her out of her pain." He pleaded not guilty to first-degree murder, but the jury found him guilty of second-degree murder. Despite the verdict of guilty on the lesser charge, many people in the town agreed with an 18-year-old high school student who said Latimer "did what he had to do for his daughter's sake. And that's the way a lot of people in town are feeling" (Farnsworth 1994, A6).

In this chapter, we'll look at defenses of justification, including self-defense, the defense of others, the defense of home and property, the choice-of-evils defense, and the defense of consent.

SELF-DEFENSE

If you use force to protect yourself, your home or property, or the people you care about, you've violated the rule of law, which our legal system is deeply committed to (Chapter 1). According to the rule of law, the government has a monopoly on the use of force, and, when you use force, you're "taking the law into your own hands." With that great monopoly on force goes the equally great responsibility of protecting individuals who are banned from using force themselves. But, sometimes, the government isn't or can't be there to protect you when you need it. So, necessity—the heart of the defense of justification—justifies "self-help."

Self-defense is a grudging concession to necessity. It's only good before the law when three circumstances come together: the necessity is great, it's "right now," and it's for prevention only. Preemptive strikes aren't included; so, you can't use force to prevent some *future* attack. Neither is retaliation; so, you can't use it to "pay back" a *past* attack. Preemptive strikes come too soon and retaliation too late; neither is necessary. Individuals have to rely on conventional means to prevent future attacks, and only the state can punish past attacks (Fletcher 1988, 18–19). To learn more about the justification of self-defense, we'll examine the elements of self-defense and whether claims of self-defense can be justifiable when it's possible to retreat to escape harm.

The Elements of Self-Defense

When can we ignore the government's monopoly on force and take the law into our own hands to defend ourselves? The law of self-defense boils down the answer into four elements:

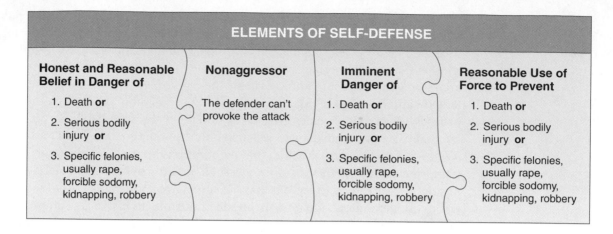

ELEMENTS OF SELF-DEFENSE

Honest and Reasonable Belief in Danger of	Nonaggressor	Imminent Danger of	Reasonable Use of Force to Prevent
1. Death **or**	The defender can't provoke the attack	1. Death **or**	1. Death **or**
2. Serious bodily injury **or**		2. Serious bodily injury **or**	2. Serious bodily injury **or**
3. Specific felonies, usually rape, forcible sodomy, kidnapping, robbery		3. Specific felonies, usually rape, forcible sodomy, kidnapping, robbery	3. Specific felonies, usually rape, forcible sodomy, kidnapping, robbery

1. *Unprovoked attack.* The defender didn't start or provoke the attack.

2. *Imminent danger.* The defender honestly and reasonably believes the time of the attack is "right now."

3. *Necessity.* The defender honestly *and* reasonably believes there's a need to defend against the attack right now.

4. *Reasonable force.* The defender uses only the amount of force reasonably necessary to repel the attack.

Unprovoked Attack

Self-defense is available only against *unprovoked* attacks. So, it's not available to an **initial aggressor**—someone who provokes an attack and then defends herself. But, there's an exception to the initial aggressor requirement. According to the **withdrawal exception,** if attackers completely withdraw from attacks they provoke, they can defend themselves against an attack by their initial victims. In *State v. Good* (1917, 1006) a son threatened to shoot his father with a shotgun. The father went to a neighbor's, borrowed the neighbor's shotgun, and came back. The son told him to "stop." When the father shot, the son turned and ran and the father pursued him. The son then turned and shot his father, killing him. The son pleaded self-defense, but the trial court failed to instruct the jury on the withdrawal exception. The Supreme Court of Missouri reversed because the instruction

> ignores and excludes the defendant's right of self-defense. Although he may have brought on the difficulty with the intent to kill his father, still, if he was attempting to withdraw from the difficulty, and was fleeing from his father in good faith for the purpose of such withdrawal, and if his father, knowing that defendant was endeavoring to withdraw from such conflict, pursued defendant and sought to kill him, or do him some great bodily harm, then the defendant's right of self-defense revived. (1007)

The Connecticut Court of Appeals dealt with the issue of the initial aggressor exception to self-defense in a case involving fight at a Fourth of July party in *State v. Pranckus* (2003).

Was He the Initial Aggressor?

State v. Pranckus
815 A.2d 678 (Conn.App. 2003)

Joseph R. PRANCKUS, III., Defendant, was convicted following a jury trial in the Superior Court, Judicial District of Hartford, of two counts of manslaughter in the first degree, and he appealed. The Appellate Court affirmed.

LAVERY, C.J.

FACTS

On July 4, 1998, a party was held at 69 House Street in Glastonbury. The house belonged to Debra Malcomson, who lived there with her daughter, Samantha Witnauer. Malcomson was vacationing on Cape Cod and had left the defendant (Pranckus) to look after her house and Samantha. Richard Lupacchino, Samantha Witnauer's boyfriend at the time, and Damien McLaughlin organized the party. People first arrived at 69 House Street at about 10 P.M. The greatest number of people at the party at any time was between fifteen and twenty-five. The majority of partygoers were teenagers, with the exception of McLaughlin and the defendant. During the party, many of the participants drank alcohol and some smoked marijuana.

Earlier that day, Karen Witnauer, Samantha Witnauer's sister, and the defendant left 69 House Street to view fireworks. They had no knowledge that the party was taking place, nor had the defendant given permission for a party to occur. Karen Witnauer and the defendant arrived back at 69 House Street in Karen Witnauer's car sometime after 11 P.M. Located in the trunk of the car was the defendant's backpack, which included the defendant's clothes. Samantha Witnauer and Lupacchino approached Karen Witnauer's car to inform them of the party and to see if they had a problem with it continuing. The defendant indicated that he did not have a problem with the party as long as it was not loud and people were out at a reasonable time. The defendant then mingled at the party with others, smoked marijuana, drank alcohol and lit fireworks in the backyard.

By 3 A.M. on July 5, 1998, the majority of people had left the party. The remaining people included the defendant, Karen Witnauer, Samantha Witnauer, Lupacchino, McLaughlin, Gordon Anderson, Peter Doucette and the two victims, Bryan Judd and Paul Potkaj. Anderson, Doucette, Judd and Potkaj were in the kitchen where they continued to drink, arm wrestle and break dance. Shortly thereafter, the defendant entered the kitchen and began yelling and swearing at the boys to leave. Judd approached the defendant in an attempt to calm him.

The defendant then punched Judd in the face. Judd responded by punching the defendant in the face. A brief fight ensued between Judd and the defendant during which a shelf with ceramic mugs fell on the floor and shattered. Doucette, Anderson, and Potkaj attempted to break up the fight. Anderson and Potkaj grabbed Judd by his arms to restrain him while Doucette came up behind the defendant and wrapped his arms around him to stop the fight. The defendant broke free from Doucette and attacked Judd again. Judd freed himself from Potkaj and Anderson in response to the defendant's attack and punched the defendant again. That punch caused the defendant to stumble backward into the kitchen counter. The defendant then picked up a kitchen knife with an eight inch blade from the counter and strode six feet from the counter toward Judd, swinging and stabbing with the knife. As the defendant was stabbing forward with the knife, Potkaj was standing next to Judd. The defendant ultimately stabbed Judd and Potkaj twice apiece.

Judd suffered a seven inch deep stab wound to the left side of his chest and an another wound from the knife to the left side of his back. Potkaj received a seven and one-half inch deep wound to the right side of his chest and a superficial incision wound on the left side of his back around his shoulder blade. Everyone remaining at 69 House Street ran outside, but the defendant remained inside where he called the police. Both Potkaj and Judd collapsed on the ground from their injuries. Potkaj eventually died from the seven and one-half inch stab wound to the right side of his chest, and Judd died from the seven inch stab wound to the left side of his chest. The defendant was arrested on the scene and later treated for a laceration over his left eye and a broken left orbital bone.

OPINION

...The jury reasonably could have concluded from the evidence presented that the defendant was not justified in using deadly force against the victims because he was the initial aggressor. General Statutes § 53a-19 (c)(a)(2) provides in relevant part that "a person is not justified in using physical force when...he is the initial aggressor...." The court defined "initial aggressor" as "the person who acts first in such a manner that creates a reasonable belief in another person's mind that physical force is about to be used upon that other person. The first person to use physical force is not necessarily the initial aggressor."

The defendant argues that Judd threatened the defendant with physical force when he approached the defendant in the kitchen, thus making Judd the initial aggressor. The jury had sufficient evidence before it, however, that Judd was merely trying to calm the defendant down and did not do so in a threatening manner. There was substantial evidence that the defendant was the first person to punch Judd in the face after yelling and swearing at the teens in the kitchen. That evidence was sufficient to permit the jury reasonably to determine beyond a reasonable doubt that the defendant was the initial aggressor and, therefore, not entitled to claim self-defense.

Our standard of review dictates that we construe the evidence in the light most favorable to sustaining the verdict.

Applying that standard, we determine that the jury reasonably could have concluded that the cumulative force of the evidence disproved the defendant's justification defense of use of force in defense of a person beyond a reasonable doubt.

The judgment is AFFIRMED.

Questions

1. Summarize the aggressor exception to the self-defense rule.

2. List the facts relevant to deciding whether Joseph Pranckus is entitled to self-defense.

3. Relying on the facts, do you think that Joseph Pranckus is entitled to self-defense? Do you think he was justified in claiming the initial aggressor defense?

◆　　◆　　◆

Imminent Danger, Necessity, and Reasonable Force

What does imminent danger of attack mean? Simply put, it means, "The time for defense is *now!*" What kind of defense? The kind and the amount of force the imminent danger demands. And, against what kind of attacks? The best-known cases involve individuals who need to kill to save their own lives, but self-defense is broader than that. It also includes killing someone who's about to kill a member of your family, or any innocent person for that matter. And necessity doesn't limit you to killing someone who's going to *kill*. You can also kill anyone you reasonably believe is right now going to *hurt* you or someone else badly enough to send you or them to the hospital for the treatment of serious injury. This is what **serious** (sometimes called **grievous**) **bodily injury** means in most self-defense statutes. Some self-defense statutes go even further. They allow you to kill someone you reasonably believe is about to commit a serious felony against you that doesn't threaten either your life or serious bodily injury. These felonies usually include rape, sodomy, kidnapping, and armed robbery. But, the list also almost always includes home burglary, and even personal property (see "Defense of Home and Property" later).

What kind of belief does self-defense require? Is it enough that you *honestly* believe the imminence of the danger, the need for force, and the amount of force used? No. Almost all statutes require that your belief also be *reasonable;* that is, a reasonable person in the same situation would've believed the imminence of the attack, the need for force, and the amount of force used were necessary to repel an attack. In the 1980s' sensational "New York Subway Vigilante case," the New York Court of Appeals examined these elements as applied to the defense against armed robbery provision in New York's self-defense statute (Fletcher 1988, 18–27).

Did He Shoot in Self-Defense?

People v. Goetz
497 N.E.2d 41 (N.Y. 1986)

Bernhard Goetz, the defendant, was indicted for criminal possession of a weapon, attempted murder, assault and reckless endangerment. The Supreme Court, Trial Term, New York County dismissed the indictment and the People appealed. The Supreme Court, Appellate Division affirmed, and People appealed. The Court of Appeals reversed and dismissed, and the counts of the indictment were reinstated.

WACHTLER, CJ.

A Grand Jury has indicted defendant on attempted murder, assault, and other charges for having shot and wounded four youths on a New York City subway train after one or two of the youths approached him and asked for $5. The lower courts, concluding that the prosecutor's charge to the Grand Jury on the defense of justification was erroneous, have dismissed the attempted murder, assault and weapons possession charges. We now reverse and reinstate all counts of the indictment.

FACTS

On Saturday afternoon, December 22, 1984, Troy Canty, Darryl Cabey, James Ramseur, and Barry Allen boarded an IRT express subway train in The Bronx and headed south toward lower Manhattan. The four youths rode together in the rear portion of the seventh car of the train. Two of the four, Ramseur and Cabey, had screwdrivers inside their coats, which they said were to be used to break into the coin boxes of video machines.

Defendant Bernhard Goetz boarded this subway train at 14th Street in Manhattan and sat down on a bench towards the rear section of the same car occupied by the four youths. Goetz was carrying an unlicensed .38 caliber pistol loaded with five rounds of ammunition in a waistband holster. The train left the 14th Street station and headed towards Chambers Street.

It appears from the evidence before the Grand Jury that Canty approached Goetz, possibly with Allen beside him, and stated, "Give me five dollars." Neither Canty nor any of the other youths displayed a weapon. Goetz responded by standing up, pulling out his handgun and firing four shots in rapid succession. The first shot hit Canty in the chest; the second struck Allen in the back; the third went through Ramseur's arm and into his left side; the fourth

was fired at Cabey, who apparently was then standing in the corner of the car, but missed, deflecting instead off of a wall of the conductor's cab. After Goetz briefly surveyed the scene around him, he fired another shot at Cabey, who then was sitting on the end bench of the car. The bullet entered the rear of Cabey's side and severed his spinal cord.

All but two of the other passengers fled the car when, or immediately after, the shots were fired. The conductor, who had been in the next car, heard the shots and instructed the motorman to radio for emergency assistance. The conductor then went into the car where the shooting occurred and saw Goetz sitting on a bench, the injured youths lying on the floor or slumped against a seat, and two women who had apparently taken cover, also lying on the floor. Goetz told the conductor that the four youths had tried to rob him.

While the conductor was aiding the youths, Goetz headed towards the front of the car. The train had stopped just before the Chambers Street station and Goetz went between two of the cars, jumped onto the tracks and fled. Police and ambulance crews arrived at the scene shortly thereafter. Ramseur and Canty, initially listed in critical condition, have fully recovered. Cabey remains paralyzed, and has suffered some degree of brain damage.

On December 31, 1984, Goetz surrendered to police in Concord, New Hampshire, identifying himself as the gunman being sought for the subway shootings in New York nine days earlier. Later that day, after receiving *Miranda* warnings, he made two lengthy statements, both of which were tape recorded with his permission. In the statements, which are substantially similar, Goetz admitted that he had been illegally carrying a handgun in New York City for three years. He stated that he had first purchased a gun in 1981 after he had been injured in a mugging. Goetz also revealed that twice between 1981 and 1984 he had successfully warded off assailants simply by displaying the pistol.

According to Goetz's statement, the first contact he had with the four youths came when Canty, sitting or lying on the bench across from him, asked, "How are you?" to which he replied, "Fine." Shortly thereafter, Canty, followed by one of the other youths, walked over to the defendant and stood to his left, while the other two youths remained to his right, in the corner of the subway car. Canty then said, "Give me five dollars." Goetz stated that he knew from the smile on Canty's face that they wanted to "play with me." Although he was certain that none of the youths had a gun, he had a fear, based on prior experiences, of being "maimed."

Goetz then established "a pattern of fire," deciding specifically to fire from left to right. His stated intention at that point was to "murder [the four youths], to hurt them, to make them suffer as much as possible." When Canty again requested money, Goetz stood up, drew his weapon, and began firing, aiming for the center of the body of each of the four. Goetz recalled that the first two he shot "tried to run through the crowd [but] they had nowhere to run." Goetz then turned to his right to "go after the other two." One of these two "tried to run through the wall of the train, but...he had nowhere to go." The other youth (Cabey) "tried pretending that he wasn't with [the others]," by standing still, holding on to one of the subway hand straps, and not looking at Goetz. Goetz nonetheless fired his fourth shot at him. He then ran back to the first two youths to make sure they had been "taken care of." Seeing that they had both been shot, he spun back to check on the latter two. Goetz noticed that the youth who had been standing still was now sitting on a bench and seemed unhurt. As Goetz told the police, "I said, 'you seem to be all right, here's another,'" and he then fired the shot which severed Cabey's spinal cord. Goetz added that "if I was a little more under self-control...I would have put the barrel against his forehead and fired." He also admitted that "if I had had more [bullets], I would have shot them again, and again, and again."

After waiving extradition, Goetz was brought back to New York and arraigned on a felony complaint charging him with attempted murder and criminal possession of a weapon. The matter was presented to a Grand Jury in January 1985, with the prosecutor seeking an indictment for attempted murder, assault, reckless endangerment, and criminal possession of a weapon. Neither the defendant nor any of the wounded youths testified before this Grand Jury. On January 25, 1985, the Grand Jury indicted defendant on one count of criminal possession of a weapon in the third degree (Penal Law § 265.02), for possessing the gun used in the subway shootings, and two counts of criminal possession of a weapon in the fourth degree (Penal Law § 265.01), for possessing two other guns in his apartment building. It dismissed, however, the attempted murder and other charges stemming from the shootings themselves.

Several weeks after the Grand Jury's action, the People, asserting that they had newly available evidence, moved for an order authorizing them to resubmit the dismissed charges to a second Grand Jury. Supreme Court, Criminal Term, after conducting an in camera [in the judge's chambers] inquiry, granted the motion. Presentation of the case to the second Grand Jury began on March 14, 1985. Two

of the four youths, Canty and Ramseur, testified. Among the other witnesses were four passengers from the seventh car of the subway who had seen some portions of the incident. Goetz again chose not to testify, though the tapes of his two statements were played for the grand jurors, as had been done with the first Grand Jury.

On March 27, 1985, the second Grand Jury filed a 10-count indictment, containing four charges of attempted murder (Penal Law § § 110.00, 125.25 [1]), four charges of assault in the first degree (Penal Law § 120.10[1]), one charge of reckless endangerment in the first degree (Penal Law § 120.25), and one charge of criminal possession of a weapon in the second degree (Penal Law § 265.03 [possession of loaded firearm with intent to use it unlawfully against another]). Goetz was arraigned on this indictment on March 28, 1985, and it was consolidated with the earlier three-count indictment.

On October 14, 1985, Goetz moved to dismiss the charges contained in the second indictment, alleging, among other things, that the...prosecutor's instructions to that Grand Jury on the defense of justification were erroneous and prejudicial to the defendant so as to render its proceedings defective.

On November 25, 1985, while the motion to dismiss was pending before Criminal Term, a column appeared in the New York Daily News containing an interview which the columnist had conducted with Darryl Cabey the previous day in Cabey's hospital room. The columnist claimed that Cabey had told him in this interview that the other three youths had all approached Goetz with the intention of robbing him.

The day after the column was published, a New York City police officer informed the prosecutor that he had been one of the first police officers to enter the subway car after the shootings, and that Canty had said to him. "We were going to rob [Goetz]." The prosecutor immediately disclosed this information to the court and to defense counsel, adding that this was the first time his office had been told of this alleged statement and that none of the police reports filed on the incident contained any such information....

In an order dated January 21, 1986...the court, after inspection of the Grand Jury minutes...held...that the prosecutor, in a supplemental charge elaborating upon the justification defense, had erroneously introduced an objective element into this defense by instructing the grand jurors to consider whether Goetz's conduct was that of a "reasonable man in [Goetz's] situation." The court, citing prior decisions from both the First and Second Departments [other trial courts] concluded that the statutory test for whether the use of deadly force is justified to protect a person should be wholly subjective, focusing entirely on the defendant's state of mind when he used such force. It concluded that dismissal was required for this error because the justification issue was at the heart of the case.

Criminal Term also concluded that dismissal and resubmission of the charges were required under *People v. Pelchat (supra)* because the *Daily News* column and the statement by the police officer to the prosecution strongly indicated that the testimony of Ramseur and Canty was perjured. Because the additional evidence before the second Grand Jury, as contrasted with that before the first Grand Jury, consisted largely of the testimony of these two youths, the court found that the integrity of the second Grand Jury was "severely undermined" by the apparently perjured testimony.

On appeal by the People, a divided Appellate Division affirmed Criminal Term's dismissal of the charges. The plurality opinion by Justice Kassal, concurred in by Justice Carro, agreed with Criminal Term's reasoning on the justification issue, stating that the grand jurors should have been instructed to consider only the defendant's subjective beliefs as to the need to use deadly force. Justice Kupferman concurred in the result reached by the plurality on the ground that the prosecutor's charge did not adequately apprise the grand jurors of the need to consider Goetz's own background and learning. . . .

Justice Asch, in a dissenting opinion in which Justice Wallach concurred, disagreed with both bases for dismissal relied upon by Criminal Term. On the justification question, he opined that the statute requires consideration of both the defendant's subjective beliefs and whether a reasonable person in defendant's situation would have had such beliefs. Accordingly, he found no error in the prosecutor's introduction of an objective element into the justification defense. . . . In a separate dissenting opinion, Justice Wallach stressed that the plurality's adoption of a purely subjective test effectively eliminated any reasonableness requirement contained in the statute.

. . . We agree with the dissenters that . . . the prosecutor's charge to the Grand Jury on justification . . . [did not] require dismissal of any of the charges in the second indictment.

OPINION

Penal Law article 35 recognizes the defense of justification, which "permits the use of force under certain circumstances." One such set of circumstances pertains to the use of force in defense of a person, encompassing both self-defense and defense of a third person (Penal Law § 35.15). Penal Law § 35.15(1) sets forth the general principles governing all such uses of force:

A person may . . . use physical force upon another person when and to the extent he *reasonably believes* such to

be necessary to defend himself or a third person from what he *reasonably believes* to be the use or imminent use of unlawful physical force by such other person. [emphasis added]

Section 35.15(2) sets forth further limitations on these general principles with respect to the use of "deadly physical force":

A person may not use deadly physical force upon another person under circumstances specified in subdivision one unless

(a) He *reasonably believes* that such other person is using or about to use deadly physical force . . . or

(b) He *reasonably believes* that such other person is committing or attempting to commit a kidnapping, forcible rape, forcible sodomy or robbery. [emphasis added]

Section 35.15(2)(a) further provides, however, that even under these circumstances a person ordinarily must retreat

if he knows that he can with complete safety as to himself and others avoid the necessity of [using deadly physical force] by retreating.

Thus, consistent with most justification provisions, Penal Law § 35.15 permits the use of deadly physical force only where requirements as to triggering conditions and the necessity of a particular response are met. As to the triggering conditions, the statute requires that the actor "reasonably believes" that another person either is using or about to use deadly physical force or is committing or attempting to commit one of certain enumerated felonies, including robbery. As to the need for the use of deadly physical force as a response, the statute requires that the actor "reasonably believes" that such force is necessary to avert the perceived threat. While the portion of section 35.15(2)(b) pertaining to the use of deadly physical force to avert a felony such as robbery does not contain a separate "retreat" requirement, it is clear from reading subdivisions (1) and (2) of section 35.15 together, as the statute requires, that the general "necessity" requirement in subdivision (1) applies to all uses of force under section 35.15, including the use of deadly physical force under subdivision (2)(b).

Because the evidence before the second Grand Jury included statements by Goetz that he acted to protect himself from being maimed or to avert a robbery, the prosecutor correctly chose to charge the justification defense in section 35.15 to the Grand Jury. The prosecutor properly instructed the grand jurors to consider whether the use of deadly physical force was justified to prevent either serious physical injury or a robbery, and, in doing so, to separately analyze the defense with respect to each of the charges. He elaborated upon the prerequisites for the use of deadly physical force essentially by reading or paraphrasing the language in Penal Law § 35.15. The defense does not contend that he committed any error in this portion of the charge.

When the prosecutor had completed his charge, one of the grand jurors asked for clarification of the term "reasonably believes." The prosecutor responded by instructing the grand jurors that they were to consider the circumstances of the incident and determine "whether the defendant's conduct was that of a reasonable man in the defendant's situation." It is this response by the prosecutor—and specifically his use of "a reasonable man"—which is the basis for the dismissal of the charges by the lower courts. As expressed repeatedly in the Appellate Division's plurality opinion, because section 35.15 uses the term "*he* reasonably believes," the appropriate test, according to that court, is whether a defendant's beliefs and reactions were "reasonable *to him.*" Under that reading of the statute, a jury which believed a defendant's testimony that he felt that his own actions were warranted and were reasonable would have to acquit him, regardless of what anyone else in defendant's situation might have concluded. Such an interpretation defies the ordinary meaning and significance of the term "reasonably" in a statute, and misconstrues the clear intent of the Legislature, in enacting section 35.15, to retain an objective element as part of any provision authorizing the use of deadly physical force.

Penal statutes in New York have long codified the right recognized at common law to use deadly physical force, under appropriate circumstances, in self-defense. These provisions have never required that an actor's belief as to the intention of another person to inflict serious injury be correct in order for the use of deadly force to be justified, but they have uniformly required that the belief comport with an objective notion of reasonableness. The 1829 statute, using language which was followed almost in its entirety until the 1965 recodification of the Penal Law, provided that the use of deadly force was justified in self-defense or in the defense of specified third persons "when there shall be a reasonable ground to apprehend a design to commit a felony, or to do some great personal injury, and there shall be imminent danger of such design being accomplished.". . .

The plurality below agreed with defendant's argument that the change in the statutory language from "reasonable ground," used prior to 1965, to "he reasonably believes" in Penal Law § 35.15 evinced a legislative intent to conform to the subjective standard. . . . We cannot lightly impute to the Legislature an intent to fundamentally alter the principles of justification to allow the perpetrator of a serious crime to go free simply because that person believed his actions were reasonable and necessary to prevent some

perceived harm. To completely exonerate such an individual, no matter how aberrational or bizarre his thought patterns, would allow citizens to set their own standards for the permissible use of force. It would also allow a legally competent defendant suffering from delusions to kill or perform acts of violence with impunity, contrary to fundamental principles of justice and criminal law.

We can only conclude that the Legislature retained a reasonableness requirement to avoid giving a license for such actions. . . . Statutes or rules of law requiring a person to act "reasonably" or to have a "reasonable belief" uniformly prescribe conduct meeting an objective standard measured with reference to how "a reasonable person" could have acted. . . .

Goetz . . . argues that the introduction of an objective element will preclude a jury from considering factors such as the prior experiences of a given actor and thus, require it to make a determination of 'reasonableness' without regard to the actual circumstances of a particular incident. This argument, however, falsely presupposes that an objective standard means that the background and other relevant characteristics of a particular actor must be ignored. To the contrary, we have frequently noted that a determination of reasonableness must be based on the "circumstances" facing a defendant or his "situation." Such terms encompass more than the physical movements of the potential assailant. As just discussed, these terms include any relevant knowledge the defendant had about that person. They also necessarily bring in the physical attributes of all persons involved, including the defendant. Furthermore, the defendant's circumstances encompass any prior experiences he had which could provide a reasonable basis for a belief that another person's intentions were to injure or rob him or that the use of deadly force was necessary under the circumstances.

Accordingly, a jury should be instructed to consider this type of evidence in weighing the defendant's actions. The jury must first determine whether the defendant had the requisite beliefs under section 35.15, that is, whether he believed deadly force was necessary to avert the imminent use of deadly force or the commission of one of the felonies enumerated therein. If the People do not prove beyond a reasonable doubt that he did not have such beliefs, then the jury must also consider whether these beliefs were reasonable. The jury would have to determine, in light of all the "circumstances," as explicated above, if a reasonable person could have had these beliefs.

The prosecutor's instruction to the second Grand Jury that it had to determine whether, under the circumstances, Goetz's conduct was that of a reasonable man in his situation was thus essentially an accurate charge. It is true that the prosecutor did not elaborate on the meaning of "circumstances" or "situation" and inform the grand jurors that they could consider, for example, the prior experiences Goetz related in his statement to the police....We have held, however, that a Grand Jury need not be instructed on the law with the same degree of precision as the petit jury. This lesser standard is premised upon the different functions of the Grand Jury and the petit jury: the former determines whether sufficient evidence exists to accuse a person of a crime and thereby subject him to criminal prosecution; the latter ultimately determines the guilt or innocence of the accused, and may convict only where the People have proven his guilt beyond a reasonable doubt....

Accordingly, the order of the Appellate Division should be REVERSED, and the dismissed counts of the indictment reinstated.

Questions

1. Consider the following:
   • New York tried Goetz for attempted murder and assault. The jury acquitted him of both charges. The jury said Goetz "was justified in shooting the four men with a silver-plated .38-caliber revolver he purchased in Florida." They did convict him of illegal possession of a firearm, for which the court sentenced Goetz to one year in jail.

• Following the sentencing, Goetz told the court: "This case is really more about the deterioration of society than it is about me....I believe society needs to be protected from criminals."

• Criminal law professor George Fletcher followed the trial closely. After the acquittal, he commented:

The facts of the Goetz case were relatively clear, but the primary fight was over the moral interpretation of the facts....I am not in the slightest bit convinced that the four young men were about to mug Goetz. If he had said, "Listen buddy, I wish I had $5, but I don't," and walked to the other side of the car the chances are 60–40 nothing would have happened. Street-wise kids like that are more attuned to the costs of their behavior than Goetz was.

If Professor Fletcher is right, was Goetz justified in shooting?

2. Under what circumstances can people use deadly force, according to the New York statutes cited in the opinion?

3. Do you agree with those circumstances?

4. Would you add more? Remove some? Which ones? Why?

5. Were Goetz's shots a preemptive strike? Retaliation? Necessary for self-protection? Explain.

THE REST OF THE STORY

What Happened to Bernhard Goetz?

(Excerpted with permission from the Associated Press)

AP/Wide World Photos

BERNHARD GOETZ'S STORY

1981 Mugging: Goetz called himself a "cold-blooded murderer" and a "monster" during his confession. But, he said, "I wasn't a monster until several years ago in New York."

Several years ago I got jumped...on Canal Street. Two-thirty in the afternoon. I was jumped by three guys. Now, they deliberately went after my knee and they got it. Like I got kicked in the knee and then what hurts you—They didn't have weapons, and people— you don't have to be maimed with a weapon. What— What really hurts you is the sidewalk. They tried to push me through a plate-glass door also, you know? I pushed as hard as I could when I—when I hit that door, with my hands. I still hit that door so hard, the glass hard. The glass didn't break, thank God, you know because I—that would've been it....But the handle—yeah, yeah—the handle hit my chest and it—afterwards, now, I was a wreck.

Incident in Central Park North After the 1981 Mugging but Before the Subway Shootings

By accident I was up there. I got on the wrong train. I was up there and I—I quickly wanted to get back to, uh, a more civilized section, it that's what you want to call it. People use the word "civilized" section. Two fellows, uh… one ran up from behind me and one ran up in front of me. And…the guy in front of me whipped out a cane and shouted, "Okay, motherf___er, give it up." What I did is, I pulled out my gun and I was scared. He was scared. I was so scared I was shaking. I thought I was going to shoot him. He thought I was going to shoot him. I—I just didn't know, but he—his knees buckled. He—He could hardly walk.…And people have said, "Well, showing the gun is enough." But this was an—this was a…

Second Incident After Mugging and Before Subway Shooting

A fellow on the street, this was just a crazy kid on drugs. He…asked me for some money or something, and I just kept walking. He was walking behind me and this was on Sixth Avenue at about 8:00 p.m.…He threatened me okay? He said, "I hope I catch up with you 'cause I'm gonna—you know—…because when I do" and whatever and stuff like that. And I got pissed off and pulled out the gun. And that was stupid because I didn't have to pull the gun, and showing it was enough to make him run away.

"Why did you pull the gun?" one of the interrogating officers asked.

I just—Okay, okay, it's true; I was pissed. But I didn't shoot him. He deserved to die. I—I—I—I told him something like, "I'm gonna blow you away" or something like that. He got scared sh__less and that was that.

The "Subway Shooting": In a videotape made on New Year's Eve, 1984, in the police department in Concord, New Hampshire, where Goetz turned himself in, Goetz explained when and why he decided to shoot. Goetz insisted that "the key was the look Troy Canty gave him when he asked for or demanded five dollars."

GOETZ: The threat, when I was surrounded—At that point pulling the gun would've been enough. But when I saw this one fellow, when I saw the gleam in his eye and the smile on his face…What happened is I snapped. [When Canty first asked] "How're you doing" It wasn't even a warning signal.…These were just kids kidding around.…But then two of them stood up, okay? And they walked over to my left, okay?…The situation, when the two move on my left and the two are on my right—Now that is a real f__king threat. I knew at that point I would have to pull the gun. I'll—I'm gonna say this: At that—At that time I was gonna pull the gun, but I

wasn't gonna kill them.…What my intention was at this time was to follow the situation as closely as I could.

[Although one youth showed a] bulge in his pocket, [Goetz didn't fear that they were armed.] Robbery had nothing to do with it. Canty's exact words were, "Give me five dollars." He said it with a smile and his eyes were bright. The words meant bulls__t. Five dollars to me is bulls__t.…I knew I had to pull the gun, but it was the look and—now, you cannot understand this—it was his eyes were shiny. He had a smile on his face. He'll claim it was all a joke. If you believe that, I accept that. When I saw the the smile on his face and the shine—and the shine in his eyes, that he was enjoying this, I knew what they were going to do. You understand?…And it was at that point I decided I was going to kill 'em all, murder 'em all, do anything.

[ASSISTANT MANHATTAN D.A.] BRAVER: What did you think they were going to do?

GOETZ: How can you ask a question like that? They were going to—They were going to have fun with me, Miss.

BRAVER: What do you mean by that? What is your interpretation of that? I can't get inside your head.

GOETZ: Beat the sh_t out of you.

BRAVER: You thought they were going to beat you up? Is that what you're saying?

GOETZ: You just use such a casual phrase. What are you saying, Miss? Miss, your attitude—your attitude. You are so far removed from reality, and yet they send you here as a professional, as a professional, to investigate this. It's beyond belief. Look, they—what they were going to do is enjoy me for awhile. They were going to beat the f__king sh_t out of me, okay?

BRAVER: Did you feel trapped?

GOETZ: Did I feel—What do you think? Oh, no, no, no. I felt free. I felt—I felt great. I was enjoying Fun City. You know, I was gonna…

BRAVER: I'm trying to see what you felt at the time.

GOETZ: I was just whistling Dixie, okay?

TROY CANTY'S STORY

Troy Canty, a 5 foot, 7 inches tall, 140-pound African American, grew up in a housing project with his mother and brother. He dropped out of school after ninth grade. From then until he was shot he supported himself by stealing cashboxes in video games. "On a good day," he made between $150 and $200. Also, "I used to buy items wholesale and sell them for retail, and occasionally I shoplifted in large department stores." The money he stole went for clothes and drugs.

At the time of Goetz's trial, Canty lived in "Phoenix Academy," a drug rehabilitation center. Since entering the center, he hadn't used drugs, had gone back to school and completed his high school equivalency diploma, and was set to enter a 21-month program at the Culinary Institute of America. He'd worked in the kitchen at the rehab center and wanted to become a cook.

On December 22, 1984, the day Goetz shot him, Troy Canty was 5 feet, 7 inches tall and weighed 140 pounds. He and his friends were on their way to steal from the video games at Pace University. None of them had cash, which they needed to ward off suspicion while they broke open the video cash boxes with screwdrivers. When they saw Goetz, he looked like a good target to get money from. Canty testified that he was three to four feet from Goetz with his hands empty at his sides when he asked Goetz, "Mister, can I have five dollars." Goetz answered, "Yes, you can all have it."

After he was shot, *The National Enquirer* paid Canty $300 (which he split with Barry Allen) for an interview. In the interview, Canty was quoted as saying that in addition to stealing from video cash boxes, they also "learned about taking people's wallets, grabbing gold chains off people's necks and strong-arming people for money." He also was quoted as saying, "The justice system is a joke. If we get caught, we plea-bargain a felony down to a misdemeanor, then walk away."

According to the prosecutor in the Goetz case,

In the first place, you have to bear in mind this group is going downtown for a very specific purpose: to rob video machines. Troy Canty had done this for years. He knew he had a gold mine in this kind of action....Canty knew that breaking into video machines was neat, clean work [that] paid rich dividends with very little risk.

How many times had he done it? Hundreds of times. How many times had he been caught? A handful. Even on those rare occasions when the authorities succeeded in nabbing him, what happened to him? He was charged with a misdemeanor. That's all. He knew that. He got what, the most, thirty days in jail? That was a small price for Troy Canty to pay for the hundreds of dollars that was available to him. But breaking into video machines is one thing. Robbing people is quite another.

Canty may not be the most highly educated person in the world, but he is not dumb. He is shrewd and he is streetwise and Troy Canty knew in December of 1984, as he knows now, that there is a big difference between robbing people and breaking into video machines....

Canty knew that there was a difference between a felony and a misdemeanor, big difference between going upstate to prison with murderers and rapists and spending a few weeks on Rikers Island with the boys.

Canty, I submit, is simply too shrewd to try to rob the defendant in front of a carload of passengers, [that a group] taking care to wear reversible jackets' so they could avoid apprehension [would not have tried to rob someone] in front of a trainload of passengers that they have been riding with for thirty minutes..., conspicuously calling attention to themselves: playing on the bars, pounding on the seats, talking to people, approaching people for matches.

The last published news of Troy Canty is that on August 8, 1996. He was arrested for assaulting Kim Williams, his common-law wife. Canty allegedly punched and choked her when she refused to give him money. Williams suffered a cut lip during the incident. There is no published evidence whether he was convicted.

BARRY ALLEN'S STORY

We piled aboard a subway for a day of hassling passengers for money and this nervous-looking guy got aboard at Fourteenth Street and sat right across from us. One look at him and we could tell he was scared. We thought we had an easy victim. Nudging each other and nodding towards him, we decided to strike. All four of us gathered around him, standing over him threateningly, as he looked up at us from his seat. Troy asked him, "Mister, can we have five dollars?"

A JUROR'S STORY

According to Mark Lesly, an actor and member of the jury, the jury's toughest problem was to decide whether Goetz was justified in shooting Darrell Cabey, especially after Goetz said, "You don't look so bad, here's another." The specific problem was to apply Justice Crane's instruction to that shooting. Justice Crane's instruction was, If you conclude, beyond a reasonable doubt, that any particular shot was an unnecessary or excessive response to whatever the defendant perceived, then you must conclude that he was not legally justified in firing the shot.

Notice that the prosecution had the burden of proving beyond a reasonable doubt that Goetz was not justified—that is, that a reasonable person would not have fired that second shot. Here's how Lesly described and interpreted what Goetz said and did and the jury's deliberations:

For a period of time, I was a cold-blooded murderer; I wanted to kill those guys; I wanted to maim those guys; I wanted to make them suffer in every way I could; if I had more bullets, I would have shot 'em all again and again; were these the comments of a man with a score to settle, a man who held the entire city of New York in contempt, and a man who had decided to take the law into his own hands and deliver his own brutal brand of justice? Or were these the words of a frightened, confused, bitter man who was just coming to terms with the fact that, as a result of what he'd done, his life had been irrevocably changed; and the manifestations of internal turmoil, guilt, self-deprecation, self-directed rage? On the one hand, there really was no way for us to know for certain. And on the other hand it really did not matter, because although it might have made a difference concerning intent, we primarily had to judge Goetz on his actions; not on his words but on his deeds.

...Even as I argued to acquit Goetz for the assault of Canty, Allen, and Ramseur, then, I felt that the Cabey assault was different and made it clear to everyone where I stood. If Cabey had been shot as part of a single burst of gunfire, I believed Goetz had to be found not guilty given the verified threat he faced. If, however, the evidence proved Goetz had shot Cabey in the way he'd described—after a pause that provided him the opportunity to reflect on and to reassess his situation—I was convinced that Goetz should be found guilty of that crime.

This was the big question of the whole trial. Did Cabey get hit by a bullet that paralyzed him while standing in front of his subway seat, then fall backward into the seat as a second bullet fired at him missed, striking the wall of the conductor's cab? Or was he missed by the first volley and then coldbloodedly and unjustifiably shot while cowering in his seat?

...Our ultimate decision rested on the concept of reasonable doubt. Cathy Brody [an uncertain juror] was the final convert, as she had been throughout; but she acquiesced because we agreed we just couldn't be certain of what had happened. Maybe Goetz did shoot at Cabey when he was seated. I still think it is possible that that in fact is what occurred. But neither Goetz's own incriminating statements, the corroborative testimony of Christopher Boucher, nor the two bullet holes in Cabey's jacket was enough to convince me that it had happened. And all the other jurors, ultimately, were unconvinced as well.

After [a lot more]...discussion, we still had to have one final round of discussion to convince Cathy Brody that Goetz faced the threat of deadly force. She was holding out on acquitting Goetz of the assault of Cabey on this issue because Cabey was the last youth shot. We more or less repeated all our previous arguments; and I contended that at the moment when Goetz started firing it was from Cabey that he had the most to fear. I reiter-

ated that when Goetz pulled his gun and turned to face Troy Canty, Cabey had the opportunity to grab Goetz from behind. All Cabey had to do was to have reacted quickly enough, and I argued that the fact that this hadn't happened did not eliminate it as a danger and something that Goetz could have reasonably feared. I urged Brody to accept the threat that the youths represented as one that could have resulted in Goetz's death.

Finally, Brody reluctantly agreed that there was too much reasonable doubt to support a conviction either on the basis of how Goetz shot Darrell Cabey or because of a nagging belief that the shooting of four unarmed youths on a subway train is not a reasonable act, and that somehow Goetz must have overstepped that which the law allows.

Lesly had this to say about critics of the jury's verdict and New York's self-defense law:

To you who...believe in Goetz's guilt on the assault and attempted murder charges, I suggest that the fault in failing to convict him lies not with the jury nor the judge nor the prosecutor, but with a deficiency in the justification laws. The law, I think, is not specific enough about the alternatives Goetz should have been required to seek before being allowed to fire his gun as a legitimate act of self-defense.

According to the law, as explained by Justice Crane, once the implied threat of deadly force is present a person can shoot to defend himself if he cannot retreat "with complete safety to himself." When a person is confronted by two or more persons within the close confines of a moving subway car, a strong argument can always be made that the person's safety is not ensured. I believe that a truly reasonable person with a proper respect for the sanctity of human life should do more than Goetz did to try to avoid shooting preemptively. Nothing more, however, is required by the law....Bernhard Goetz did what the law allows...and I think that the law is flawed.

CABEY V. GOETZ (APRIL 1996)

On April 23, 1996, an eleven-year civil suit in which Darrell Cabey sued Bernhard Goetz came to a close. The jury in the case awarded Darrell Cabey $43,000,000. During the civil trial, Goetz testified that Shirley Cabey, Darrell's mother "should have had an abortion instead of giving birth to Darrell," and that shooting her son was "a public service." Mrs. Cabey, a widow who had to quit her job to take care of Darrell, said that "the Cabey name had been cleared" by the jury's verdict.

Juror Comments: What clinched their verdict was Goetz' testimony that after the 1984 shooting, he admitted he told Cabey: "You don't look so bad, here's another," then fired a final shot that left the youth paralyzed.

Ronald Corley, a chef's assistant from University Heights, said he sympathized with Goetz at first but later changed his mind. "[Darrell Cabey] was scared already. Now you're going to go over there and shoot him?" Corley said.

Juror Sylvester Lewis 3d, 27, a sound engineer who works at the United Nations and Apollo Theatre, agreed. "If Mr. Goetz was to end his shooting on the fourth shot, it might have been a different situation," he said.

"[Cabey] was on the floor, so why did Goetz have anything to be afraid of?" asked Elba Torres, 45, a city worker. Torres said the 4½ hours of deliberations were generally cordial, although sometimes voices including her own were raised as the six jurors grappled with the case.

According to the *New York Daily News,*

From their first vote, the four Hispanics and two blacks on the panel knew they would reach a unanimous decision in Cabey's favor. But there was wrangling over the amount of damages. In the end, the amount totaled just $7 million less than the $50 million Cabey sought.

Much of lawyer Ronald Kuby's case against Goetz centered on race and the gunman's decision to fire on four black teenagers. But, said Torres, "I don't think it was race.... When kids approach you, they approach you with an attitude." Mildred Richardson, an alternate juror, agreed with the verdict but disagreed that race was not a factor. "If you want to be prejudiced, that's your decision but you don't express it the way he did," she said. "That man didn't learn anything. Maybe if he had gone to jail, maybe he would have learned a thing or two," Richardson said, apparently unaware that Goetz had served time for a weapons possession violation. "Maybe he would have learned to say I'm sorry." (Excerpt from R. Olmeda, *The Daily News,* April 24, 1996. © New York Daily News, L.P. Reprinted with permission.)

Professor George Fletcher's Comments: The distinguished professor of criminal law, George Fletcher (1996), had this to say after the civil case trial:

It took two trials to do justice in the serial story of Bernhard Goetz. The first trial, the six-week criminal hearing in 1987, focused on whether Mr. Goetz overreacted after four black teen-agers surrounded him on a downtown No. 2 train and asked him for money. It was Mr. Goetz against the group his lawyers called "the predators" and "the gang of four."

This month's short civil trial brought one of the youths, the paralyzed Darrell Cabey, center stage. In the lens of our time, it pitted a brain-damaged victim in a wheelchair against an eccentric gunman with hate in his heart.

In the first trial, it made sense, given the political atmosphere of the day, that a racially mixed Manhattan jury acquitted Mr. Goetz of attempted murder. It also made sense that a Bronx jury yesterday found him liable to Mr. Cabey to the tune of $43 million. This tendency to split the outcomes is the way justice is now done in the United States.

Our effort to give both sides their due weighs more heavily in these results than does racial politics. Black jurors played an important role in Mr. Goetz's 1987 acquittal. And if this month's civil trial had taken place in Manhattan, instead of the Bronx, my sense is that the judgment would have gone against Mr. Goetz. (21)

WHATEVER HAPPENED TO THE YOUTHS GOETZ SHOT?

Soon after the Goetz case, Barry Allen went to prison for "chain snatching." In 1991, he was released from prison after serving three years for robbery. In 1996, James Ramseur was still serving time for raping, robbing, and sodomizing an 18-year-old woman on a Bronx rooftop. Troy Canty went to Phoenix House to participate in a drug treatment program not related to the Goetz case. He was released in 1989. As of 1996, he had no further criminal record. Darrell Cabey is in a wheelchair, paralyzed for life (Fletcher 1996, 21).

Present Danger

We've talked now about danger from imminent attack. But what about this case: A battered wife who's been beaten repeatedly over a period of years shoots her husband while he's asleep. (She can escape by driving away). The danger of being beaten again, and maybe even killed, is real and it's not going to go away (*People v. Williams* 1969, 753). But, it's not *imminent* because it's not going to happen right now. It's what we call **present danger** (danger you reasonably believe is always hanging over you). In most states, unlike imminent danger, present danger doesn't justify taking the law into your hands. Why? Because you don't have to; you've got time to escape or call the police. The Kansas Supreme Court dealt with the problem of present danger in the battered wife case of *State v. Stewart* (1988).

| CASE | *Was She in "Imminent" Danger?* |

State v. Stewart
763 P.2d 572 (Kans. 1988)

Peggy Stewart, the defendant, was charged with murder in the first degree of her husband, Mike Stewart. The Butler District Court trial jury found Stewart not guilty. The prosecution appealed with a question reserved.* The Supreme Court sustained the appeal.

LOCKETT, J.

FACTS

Following an annulment from her first husband and two subsequent divorces in which she was the petitioner, Peggy Stewart married Mike Stewart in 1974. Evidence at trial disclosed a long history of abuse by Mike against Peggy and her two daughters from one of her prior marriages. Laura, one of Peggy's daughters, testified that early in the marriage Mike hit and kicked Peggy, and that after the first year of the marriage Peggy exhibited signs of severe psychological problems. Subsequently, Peggy was hospitalized and diagnosed as having symptoms of paranoid schizophrenia; she responded to treatment and was soon released. It appeared to Laura, however, that Mike was encouraging Peggy to take more than her prescribed dosage of medication.

In 1977, two social workers informed Peggy that they had received reports that Mike was taking indecent liberties with her daughters. Because the social workers did not want Mike to be left alone with the girls, Peggy quit her job. In 1978, Mike began to taunt Peggy by stating that Carla, her 12-year-old daughter, was "more of a wife" to him than Peggy.

Later, Carla was placed in a detention center, and Mike forbade Peggy and Laura to visit her. When Mike finally al-

lowed Carla to return home in the middle of summer, he forced her to sleep in an un-air conditioned room with the windows nailed shut, to wear a heavy flannel nightgown, and to cover herself with heavy blankets. Mike would then wake Carla at 5:30 A.M. and force her to do all the housework. Peggy and Laura were not allowed to help Carla or speak to her.

When Peggy confronted Mike and demanded that the situation cease, Mike responded by holding a shotgun to Peggy's head and threatening to kill her. Mike once kicked Peggy so violently in the chest and ribs that she required hospitalization. Finally, when Mike ordered Peggy to kill and bury Carla, she filed for divorce. Peggy's attorney in the divorce action testified in the murder trial that Peggy was afraid for both her and her children's lives.

One night, in a fit of anger, Mike threw Carla out of the house. Carla, who was not yet in her teens, was forced out of the home with no money, no coat, and no place to go. When the family heard that Carla was in Colorado, Mike refused to allow Peggy to contact or even talk about Carla.

Mike's intimidation of Peggy continued to escalate. One morning, Laura found her mother hiding on the school bus, terrified and begging the driver to take her to a neighbor's home. That Christmas, Mike threw the turkey dinner to the floor, chased Peggy outside, grabbed her by the hair, rubbed her face in the dirt, and then kicked and beat her.

After Laura moved away, Peggy's life became even more isolated. Once, when Peggy was working at a cafe, Mike came in and ran all the customers off with a gun because he wanted Peggy to go home and have sex with him right that minute. He abused both drugs and alcohol, and amused himself by terrifying Peggy, once waking her from a sound sleep by beating her with a baseball bat. He shot one of Peggy's pet cats, and then held the gun against her head and threatened to pull the trigger. Peggy told friends that Mike would hold a shotgun to her head and threaten to blow it off, and indicated that one day he would probably do it.

In May 1986, Peggy left Mike and ran away to Laura's home in Oklahoma. It was the first time Peggy had left

---

*The state can't appeal an acquittal, because a jury's verdict of not guilty is final. But, the state can appeal questions of law. That's what's happening here. The state is appealing the legal question: What's the definition of "imminent danger"? Whatever the answer is, Peggy Stewart's acquittal stands.

Mike without telling him. Because Peggy was suicidal, Laura had her admitted to a hospital. There, she was diagnosed as having toxic psychosis as a result of an overdose of her medication. On May 30, 1986, Mike called to say he was coming to get her. Peggy agreed to return to Kansas. Peggy told a nurse she felt like she wanted to shoot her husband. At trial, she testified that she decided to return with Mike because she was not able to get the medical help she needed in Oklahoma.

When Mike arrived at the hospital, he told the staff that he "needed his housekeeper." The hospital released Peggy to Mike's care, and he immediately drove her back to Kansas. Mike told Peggy that all her problems were in her head and he would be the one to tell her what was good for her, not the doctors. Peggy testified that Mike threatened to kill her if she ever ran away again. As soon as they arrived at the house, Mike forced Peggy into the house and forced her to have oral sex several times.

The next morning, Peggy discovered a loaded .357 magnum. She testified she was afraid of the gun. She hid the gun under the mattress of the bed in a spare room. Later that morning, as she cleaned house, Mike kept making remarks that she should not bother because she would not be there long, or that she should not bother with her things because she could not take them with her. She testified she was afraid Mike was going to kill her.

Mike's parents visited Mike and Peggy that afternoon. Mike's father testified that Peggy and Mike were affectionate with each other during the visit. Later, after Mike's parents had left, Mike forced Peggy to perform oral sex. After watching television, Mike and Peggy went to bed at 8:00 P.M. As Mike slept, Peggy thought about suicide and heard voices in her head repeating over and over, "kill or be killed." At this time, there were two vehicles in the driveway and Peggy had access to the car keys. About 10:00 P.M., Peggy went to the spare bedroom and removed the gun from under the mattress, walked back to the bedroom, and killed her husband while he slept. She then ran to the home of a neighbor, who called the police.

When the police questioned Peggy regarding the events leading up to the shooting, Peggy stated that things had not gone quite right that day, and that when she got the chance she hid the gun under the mattress. She stated that she shot Mike to "get this over with, this misery and this torment." When asked why she got the gun out, Peggy stated to the police:

"I'm not sure exactly what . . . led up to it . . . and my head started playing games with me and I got to thinking about things and I said I didn't want to be by myself again. . . . I got the gun out because there had been remarks made about me being out there alone. It was as if Mike was going to do something again like had been done before. He had gotten me down here from McPherson one time and he went and told them that I had done something and he had me put out of the house and was taking everything I had. And it was like he was going to pull the same thing over again."

Two expert witnesses testified during the trial. The expert for the defense, psychologist Marilyn Hutchinson, diagnosed Peggy as suffering from "battered woman syndrome," or post-traumatic stress syndrome. Dr. Hutchinson testified that Mike was preparing to escalate the violence in retaliation for Peggy's running away. She testified that loaded guns, veiled threats, and increased sexual demands are indicators of the escalation of the cycle. Dr. Hutchinson believed Peggy had a repressed knowledge that she was in a "really grave lethal situation."

The State's expert, psychiatrist Herbert Modlin, neither subscribed to a belief in the battered woman syndrome nor to a theory of learned helplessness as an explanation for why women do not leave an abusive relationship. Dr. Modlin testified that abuse such as repeated forced oral sex would not be trauma sufficient to trigger a post-traumatic stress disorder. He also believed Peggy was erroneously diagnosed as suffering from toxic psychosis. He stated that Peggy was unable to escape the abuse because she suffered from schizophrenia, rather than the battered woman syndrome.

At defense counsel's request, the trial judge gave an instruction on self-defense to the jury. The jury found Peggy not guilty.

OPINION

. . . K.S.A. 21–3211 . . . provides:

A person is justified in the use of force against an aggressor when and to the extent it appears to him and he reasonably believes that such conduct is necessary to defend himself or another against such aggressor's imminent use of unlawful force.

The traditional concept of self-defense has posited one-time conflicts between persons of somewhat equal size and strength. When the defendant claiming self-defense is a victim of long-term domestic violence, such as a battered spouse, such traditional concepts may not apply. Because of the prior history of abuse, and the difference in strength and size between the abused and the abuser, the accused in such cases may choose to defend during a momentary lull in the abuse, rather than during a conflict. However, in order to warrant the giving of a self-defense instruction, the facts of the case must still show that the spouse was in imminent danger close to the time of the killing.

A person is justified in using force against an aggressor when it appears to that person and he or she reasonably believes such force to be necessary. A reasonable belief implies both an honest belief and the existence of facts which would persuade a reasonable person to that belief. A self-defense instruction must be given if there is any evidence to support a claim of self-defense, even if that evidence consists solely of the defendant's testimony.

Where self-defense is asserted, evidence of the deceased's long-term cruelty and violence towards the defendant is admissible. In cases involving battered spouses, expert evidence of the battered woman syndrome is relevant to a determination of the reasonableness of the defendant's perception of danger....

In order to instruct a jury on self-defense, there must be some showing of an imminent threat or a confrontational circumstance involving an overt act by an aggressor. There is no exception to this requirement where the defendant has suffered long-term domestic abuse and the victim is the abuser. In such cases, the issue is not whether the defendant believes homicide is the solution to past or future problems with the batterer, but rather whether circumstances surrounding the killing were sufficient to create a reasonable belief in the defendant that the use of deadly force was necessary.

In recent Kansas cases where battered women shot their husbands, the women were clearly threatened in the moments prior to the shootings. *State v. Hundley*, 693 P.2d 475, involved a severely abused wife, Betty Hundley.... On the day of the shooting, Carl threatened to kill her. That night he forcibly broke into Betty's motel room, beat and choked her, painfully shaved her pubic hair, and forced her to have intercourse with him. Thereafter, he pounded a beer bottle on the night stand and demanded that Betty get him some cigarettes. Betty testified that he had attacked her with beer bottles before. She pulled a gun from her purse and demanded that Carl leave. When Carl saw the gun he stated: "You are dead, bitch, now." Betty fired the gun and killed Carl.... In *State v. Hodges*, 716 P.2d 563 (1986), on the night of the shooting, the husband attacked Hodges and beat her head against a doorjamb twenty times. He then said he was going to kill her. Hodges was then kicked and beaten before making her way into another room. When her husband said, "God damn you. Get in here now!" she grabbed a gun, ran to the doorway, and shot him.

...Here, however, there is an absence of imminent danger to defendant: Peggy told a nurse at the Oklahoma hospital of her desire to kill Mike. She later voluntarily agreed to return home with Mike when he telephoned her. She stated that after leaving the hospital Mike threatened to kill her if she left him again. Peggy showed no inclination to leave. In fact, immediately after the shooting, Peggy told the police that she was upset because she thought Mike would leave her. Prior to the shooting, Peggy hid the loaded gun. The cars were in the driveway and Peggy had access to the car keys. After being abused, Peggy went to bed with Mike at 8 P.M. Peggy lay there for two hours, then retrieved the gun from where she had hidden it and shot Mike while he slept.

Under these facts, the giving of the self-defense instruction was erroneous. Under such circumstances, a battered woman cannot reasonably fear imminent life-threatening danger from her sleeping spouse. We note that other courts have held that the sole fact that the victim was asleep does not preclude a self-defense instruction. In *State v. Norman*, 366 S.E.2d 586 (1988)... the defendant's evidence disclosed a long history of abuse. Each time defendant attempted to escape, her husband found and beat her. On the day of the shooting, the husband beat defendant continually throughout the day, and threatened either to cut her throat, kill her, or cut off her breast. In the afternoon, defendant shot her husband while he napped. The North Carolina Court of Appeals held it was reversible error to fail to instruct on self-defense. The court found that, although decedent was napping at the time defendant shot him, defendant's unlawful act was closely related in time to an assault and threat of death by decedent against defendant and that the decedent's nap was "but a momentary hiatus in a continuous reign of terror."

There is no doubt that the North Carolina court determined that the sleeping husband was an evil man who deserved the justice he received from his battered wife. Here, similar comparable and compelling facts exist. But, as one court has stated: "To permit capital punishment to be imposed upon the subjective conclusion of the [abused] individual that prior acts and conduct of the deceased justified the killing would amount to a leap into the abyss of anarchy." Finally, our legislature has not provided for capital punishment for even the most heinous crimes. We must, therefore, hold that when a battered woman kills her sleeping spouse when there is no imminent danger, the killing is not reasonably necessary and a self-defense instruction may not be given. To hold otherwise in this case would in effect allow the execution of the abuser for past or future acts and conduct.

One additional issue must be addressed. In its *amicus curiae* brief, the Kansas County and District Attorney Association contends the instruction given by the trial court improperly modified the law of self-defense to be more generous to one suffering from the battered woman syndrome than to any other defendant relying on self-defense. We agree and believe it is necessary to clarify [our prior decisions]. . . .

Here, the trial judge gave the instruction . . . :

> The defendant has claimed her conduct was justified as self-defense. "A person is justified in the use of force against an aggressor when and to the extent it appears to him and he reasonably believes that such conduct is necessary to defend himself or another against such aggressor's imminent use of unlawful force. Such justification requires both a belief on the part of the defendant and the existence of facts that would persuade a reasonable person to that belief."

The trial judge then added the following:

> You must determine, from the viewpoint of the defendant's mental state, whether the defendant's belief in the need to defend herself was reasonable in light of her subjective impressions and the facts and circumstances known to her.

This addition was apparently encouraged by the following language in *State v. Hodges,* 716 P.2d 563:

> Where the battered woman syndrome is an issue in the case, the standard for reasonableness concerning an accused's belief in asserting self-defense is not an objective, but a subjective standard. The jury must determine, from the viewpoint of defendant's mental state, whether defendant's belief in the need to defend herself was reasonable.

The statement that the reasonableness of defendant's belief in asserting self-defense should be measured from the defendant's own individual subjective viewpoint conflicts with prior law. Our test for self-defense is a two-pronged one. We first use a subjective standard to determine whether the defendant sincerely and honestly believed it necessary to kill in order to defend. We then use an objective standard to determine whether defendant's belief was reasonable—specifically, whether a reasonable person in defendant's circumstances would have perceived self-defense as necessary. In *State v. Hundley,* 693 P.2d 475, we stated that, in cases involving battered spouses, "the objective test is how a reasonably prudent battered wife would perceive the aggressor's demeanor."

Hundley makes clear that it was error for the trial court to instruct the jury to employ solely a subjective test in determining the reasonableness of defendant's actions. Insofar as the above-quoted language in *State v. Hodges* can be read to sanction a subjective test, this language is disapproved.

The appeal is sustained.

DISSENT

HERD, J.

The sole issue before us on the question reserved is whether the trial court erred in giving a jury instruction on self-defense. We have a well-established rule that a defendant is entitled to a self-defense instruction if there is any evidence to support it, even though the evidence consists solely of the defendant's testimony. It is for the jury to determine the sincerity of the defendant's belief she needed to act in self-defense, and the reasonableness of that belief in light of all the circumstances.

It is not within the scope of appellate review to weigh the evidence. An appellate court's function is to merely examine the record and determine if there is *any* evidence to support the theory of self-defense. If the record discloses any competent evidence upon which self-defense could be based, then the instruction must be given. In judging the evidence for this purpose, all inferences should be resolved in favor of the defendant.

It is evident . . . [Stewart] met her burden of showing some competent evidence that she acted in self-defense, thus making her defense a jury question. She testified she acted in fear for her life, and Dr. Hutchinson corroborated this testimony. The evidence of Mike's past abuse, the escalation of violence, his threat of killing her should she attempt to leave him, and Dr. Hutchinson's testimony that Peggy was indeed in a "lethal situation" more than met the minimal standard of "any evidence" to allow an instruction to be given to the jury. Peggy introduced much uncontroverted evidence of the violent nature of the deceased and how he had brutalized her throughout their married life. . . .

Psychologist Marilyn Hutchinson qualified as an expert on the battered woman syndrome and analyzed the uncontroverted facts for the jury. She concluded Peggy was a victim of the syndrome and reasonably believed she was in imminent danger. In *State v. Hodges,* 716 P.2d 563 (1986), we held it appropriate to permit expert testimony on the battered woman syndrome to prove the reasonableness of the defendant's belief she was in imminent danger. . . .

The majority implies its decision is necessary to keep the battered woman syndrome from operating as a defense in and of itself. It has always been clear the syndrome is not a defense itself. Evidence of the syndrome is admissible only because of its relevance to the issue of self-defense. The majority of jurisdictions have held it beyond the ordinary jury's understanding why a battered woman may feel she cannot escape, and have held evidence of the battered woman syndrome proper to explain it. The expert testimony explains how people react to circumstances in which the average juror has not been involved. It assists the jury in evaluating the sincerity of the defendant's belief she was in imminent danger requiring self-defense and whether she was in fact in imminent danger.

Dr. Hutchinson explained to the jury at Peggy's trial the "cycle of violence" which induces a state of "learned helplessness" and keeps a battered woman in the relationship. She testified Peggy was caught in such a cycle. The cycle begins with an initial building of tension and violence, culminates in an explosion, and ends with a "honeymoon." The woman becomes conditioned to trying to make it through one more violent explosion with its battering in order to be rewarded by the "honeymoon phase," with its expressions of remorse and eternal love and the standard promise of "never again." After all promises are broken time after time and she is beaten again and again, the battered woman falls into a state of learned helplessness where she gives up trying to extract herself from the cycle of violence. She learns fighting back only delays the honeymoon and escalates the violence. If she tries to leave the relationship, she is located and returned and the violence increases. She is a captive. She begins to believe her husband is omnipotent, and resistance will be futile at best.

It is a jury question to determine if the battered woman who kills her husband as he sleeps fears he will find and kill her if she leaves, as is usually claimed. Under such circumstances the battered woman is not under actual physical attack when she kills but such attack is imminent, and as a result she believes her life is in imminent danger. She may kill during the tension-building stage when the abuse is apparently not as severe as it sometimes has been, but nevertheless has escalated so that she is afraid the acute stage to come will be fatal to her. She only acts on such fear if she has some survival instinct remaining after the husband-induced "learned helplessness."...

It was Dr. Hutchinson's opinion Mike was planning to escalate his violence in retaliation against Peggy for running away. She testified that Mike's threats against Peggy's life, his brutal sexual acts, and Peggy's discovery of the loaded gun were all indicators to Peggy the violence had escalated and she was in danger. Dr. Hutchinson believed Peggy had a repressed knowledge she was in what was really a gravely lethal situation. She testified Peggy was convinced she must "kill or be killed."

The majority claims permitting a jury to consider self-defense under these facts would permit anarchy. This underestimates the jury's ability to recognize an invalid claim of self-defense....

The majority bases its opinion on its conclusion Peggy was not in imminent danger, usurping the right of the jury to make that determination of fact. The majority believes a person could not be in imminent danger from an aggres-

sor merely because the aggressor dropped off to sleep. This is a fallacious conclusion. For instance, picture a hostage situation where the armed guard inadvertently drops off to sleep and the hostage grabs his gun and shoots him. The majority opinion would preclude the use of self-defense in such a case.

The majority attempts to buttress its conclusion Peggy was not in imminent danger by citing 19th Century law. The old requirement of "immediate" danger is not in accord with our statute on self-defense, and has been emphatically overruled by case law. Yet this standard permeates the majority's reasoning. A review of the law in this state on the requirement of imminent rather than immediate danger to justify self-defense is therefore required....*

In *State v. Hundley*, 693 P.2d 475, we joined other enlightened jurisdictions in recognizing that the jury in homicide cases where a battered woman ultimately kills her batterer is entitled to all the facts about the battering relationship in rendering its verdict. The jury also needs to know about the nature of the cumulative terror under which a battered woman exists and that a batterer's threats and brutality can make life-threatening danger imminent to the victim of that brutality even though, at the moment, the batterer is passive. Where a person believes she must kill or be killed, and there is the slightest basis in fact for this belief, it is a question for the jury as to whether the danger was imminent. I confess I am an advocate for the constitutional principle that in a criminal prosecution determination of the facts is a function of the jury, not the appellate court.

Questions

1. How does the court define *imminent*?

2. Can battered women ever be in imminent danger when their husbands are sleeping?

3. Should we have a special battered woman's defense of justification?

4. Or should we expand the definition of imminent? Or change the requirement from imminent to present, or continuing, danger?

5. Why does the court talk about putting the power of capital punishment into the hands of battered wives?

6. Consider the following comment:

Retaliation, as opposed to defense, is a common problem in cases arising from wife battering and domestic violence. The injured wife waits for the first possibility of striking against a distracted or unarmed husband.

---

*A review of these cases is omitted.

The man may even be asleep when the wife finally reacts. . . . Retaliation is the standard case of "taking the law into your own hands." There is no way, under the law, to justify killing a wife batterer or a rapist in retaliation or revenge, however much sympathy there may be for the wife wreaking retaliation. Private citizens cannot act as judge and jury toward each other. They have no authority to pass judgment and to punish each other for past wrongs. (Fletcher 1988, 21–22)

Do you agree with the statement? Explain your answer.

7. In your opinion, was Peggy Stewart's act one of self-defense, a preemptive strike, or retaliation? Back up your answer with facts in the case.

◆   ◆   ◆

In 1993, seven years after the Kansas Supreme Court decided the state's appeal in Peggy Stewart's case, the same court had to decide two other difficult questions regarding battered women who kill: Can evidence of the battered woman's violence toward other people disprove the claim she suffers from battered woman's syndrome? And, what is a fair penalty for battered women who don't suffer from the syndrome who kill their husbands after years of abuse? The court answered the questions in *State v. Cramer* (1993).

| CASE | ***Can a Woman with a History of Violence Use the Battered Woman's Syndrome Defense?*** |

State v. Cramer

841 P.2d 1111 (Kans.App. 1993)

Janette Cramer, the defendant, was convicted in the Finney District Court of involuntary manslaughter and sentenced to from three to five years in prison. She appealed. The Court of Appeals affirmed.

LEWIS, J.

FACTS

Janette and William Cramer were married in July 1987. The record indicates that William first began to beat defendant nine days prior to their wedding and that he continued to beat her on a regular basis up to the time of his death. It would serve little good to recite the details of all of the beatings inflicted by William on defendant. The record shows that there were many, that they were regular, and that they were accompanied by verbal abuse as well. Some of these beatings were so violent that defendant was hospitalized as a result. On one occasion, William picked defendant up and attempted to "hang" her on a nail protruding from a wall. The nail punctured her back and left a scar running up to her shoulder. Frequently, both parties were drinking when these violent episodes took place.

Finally, defendant sued William for divorce. She obtained a restraining order, which did not restrain William, who continued to beat and threaten her. After one of these beatings put defendant in the hospital, a friend gave her a handgun for protection. It is noted that, on the night of William's death, defendant placed the handgun in a strategic position in her house.

On the evening of William's death, he came to defendant's home with her permission. He came to discuss their divorce and brought along a supply of beer and liquor. The two parties apparently sat down at the table and began to drink and discuss the terms of their divorce. As the evening wore on, William became more angry and, finally, began to pound on the table. He started to verbally abuse defendant and stood up and stepped towards her. According to defendant, she got up and retrieved the handgun from where she had placed it. She pointed the gun at William and said, "[You're not] going to beat on me again." William apparently laughed, took one step forward, and defendant shot him in the chest. William was either dead on arrival at the hospital or died shortly thereafter. According to the post-mortem reports, the bullet wound was not necessarily fatal but, as a result of that gunshot, William bled to death.

Defendant was charged with second-degree murder. Her defense was self-defense, based on the battered woman's syndrome. After a three-day trial, the jury returned a verdict, finding her guilty of involuntary manslaughter. At her sentencing, defendant argued that to deny her probation amounted to "manifest injustice" under K.S.A.1991 Supp. 21-4618(3). After listening to defendant's arguments, the trial court denied her probation because of her use of a firearm and the provisions of K.S.A. 21-4618(1) and (2). She appeals her conviction and sentence. After careful consideration, we affirm on both counts.

OPINION

Defendant argues that the trial court erred in admitting evidence of specific instances of past conduct between defendant and third parties. This evidence was not complimentary to defendant and may have been prejudicial. The trial court determined that, despite its potential prejudice, the evidence was admissible. We agree with that conclusion.

In order to prove her battered woman's syndrome defense, defendant introduced the expert testimony of Dr. Stephen E. Peterson, a psychiatrist at the Menninger Clinic. He testified that, in his opinion, defendant was suffering from the battered woman's syndrome. He reached this diagnosis after a two-day examination of defendant. As a result of that examination, Dr. Peterson prepared an extensive report that gave specific details about defendant's past life and experiences. A portion of this report described several instances of violent conduct between defendant and other parties.

The State of Kansas countered Dr. Peterson's testimony by introducing testimony of Dr. Alice Brill. Dr. Brill is also a psychiatrist, and she testified that, in her opinion, defendant did not suffer from the battered woman's syndrome. Dr. Brill's opinion was based in large part on the evidence of specific instances of past conduct, to which defendant objects.

Defendant's argument is that the evidence was so prejudicial that it should not have been admitted. The State argues that the evidence was probative and admissible. It points out that much of the evidence came in as a result of the cross-examination of Dr. Peterson. Basically, the State argues that this testimony was admissible to rebut the diagnosis of the battered woman's syndrome testified to by Dr. Peterson.

Defendant is particularly aggrieved by the testimony of Melvin Fox. A recounting of his testimony will serve to illustrate the type of evidence to which defendant objects. Fox was called as a rebuttal witness by the State of Kansas. He testified that he had had a relationship of sorts with defendant. He described in graphic detail one occasion when he was in the bathroom, throwing up after a drink-ing spree. He testified that, while he was in this rather vulnerable state, defendant entered the bathroom wearing only steel-toed biker boots and proceeded to kick him several times.

Dr. Brill referred to the incident described by Fox in support of her opinion that defendant was not suffering from the battered woman's syndrome. Dr. Brill used other instances involving defendant and third parties in stating that defendant did not suffer from the battered woman's syndrome. Defendant insists that the testimony of Fox and the use of other instances of her past conduct were intended to prejudice the jury against her.

. . . In this instance, we find no abuse of discretion in admitting the evidence under discussion. Testimony concerning the specific instances complained of by defendant was elicited by the State in an effort to cast doubt upon Dr. Peterson's diagnosis of the battered woman's syndrome. On cross-examination, Dr. Peterson was cross-examined about an incident at a wedding party where defendant physically fought with another woman. Another incident concerned an altercation between defendant and a male bouncer at a tavern. Dr. Brill, the State's expert witness, referred to these incidents as inconsistent with those characteristics associated with the battered woman's syndrome. . . .

In the final analysis, the trial court determined that the probative value of the evidence outweighed the prejudicial effect of that evidence. This was a proper decision for the trial court, and we will not substitute our judgment for that of the trial court on this issue. . . .

The defense in this lawsuit was self-defense. This was based on the contention that defendant suffered from the battered woman's syndrome and perceived that she was protecting herself from imminent danger in shooting William. The trial court gave a self-defense instruction. . . . After the jury had retired and begun its deliberation, it submitted a question. This question bracketed the following language from the self-defense instruction: "Such justification requires both a belief on the part of the defendant and the existence of facts that would persuade a reasonable person to that belief." The jury then asked the following question:

"Does this mean:
(1) That a reasonable person, in the same situation, would choose the same.

or

(2) That a reasonable person, would believe that she believed that was her only option.
"Need last part clarified please.

"/s/ Gilbert Widows"

After receiving the question, the trial court adjourned the trial and retired to chambers with all parties and counsel present to formulate an answer to the question. . . . Defendant argues that the trial court should have advised the jury that the objective test is whether a "reasonably prudent battered woman would have perceived self-defense as necessary." We disagree. . . .

The defense in this case was self-defense, based on the battered woman's syndrome. The record is replete with evidence of repeated beatings inflicted upon defendant by William. Both expert witnesses agreed that defendant was a battered woman. To advise the jury that the objective test was "whether a reasonable person in defendant's circumstances would have perceived self-defense as necessary" was to advise the jury to judge defendant's conduct as that of a battered spouse. We see no other way the jury could have perceived the court's instructions and the use of the term "in defendant's circumstances." Defendant's circumstances in this case were those of a battered woman being advanced upon by her battering spouse. The instruction sufficiently advised the jury that it should consider whether a person in defendant's circumstances would perceive self-defense as necessary. We consider that to have been a proper answer to the question and one which could not possibly have confused the jury.

We have reviewed the most recent [Kansas] Supreme Court holdings concerning instructions where a battered spouse is defending against a charge of homicide. . . . Our reading of the Supreme Court decisions concerning battered women reveals no requirement that a jury be advised that it must employ an objective test based on how a "reasonably prudent battered woman" would react to a threat. Indeed, to employ such language would modify the law of self-defense to be more generous to one suffering from the battered woman's syndrome than to any other defendant relying on self-defense. The Supreme Court in *State v. Stewart* expressly disavowed any such interpretation of the law. Under the facts shown, the trial court's answer to the jury's question correctly stated the law and was not confusing or misleading. . . .

The defendant in this case was convicted of the crime of involuntary manslaughter, as defined by K.S.A. 21-3404. This crime was committed with the use of a firearm. Under these circumstances, the mandatory sentencing provisions of K.S.A.1991 Supp. 21-4618 are applicable. This statute requires mandatory imprisonment under the circumstances shown. The trial court sentenced defendant under K.S.A.1991 Supp. 21-4618(1) and (2) and denied her application for probation or assignment to a community corrections program. Defendant argued that the trial court erred in sentencing her in this manner.

Defendant argues that K.S.A.1991 Supp. 21-4618(3) applied and that her sentencing amounts to manifest injustice. K.S.A.1991 Supp. 21-4618(3) reads as follows: "The provisions of this section shall not apply to any crime committed by a person where such application would result in a manifest injustice." It is defendant's position that, in her case, imposition of mandatory imprisonment constitutes manifest injustice.

In a very recent decision, we dealt with a similar question. Although we concluded that the term "manifest injustice" as used in the statute was not possible of exact definition, we said: "A sentence which is 'obviously unfair' or 'shocking to the conscience' accurately and permissibly characterizes one which would result in manifest injustice." In *State v. Turley*, 840 P.2d 529 (1992), we concluded that a sentence which "shocks the conscience of the court" is manifestly unjust. This is similar to saying that, while it is difficult to define "pornography," one will most certainly know it when he or she sees it. While this may not be an entirely satisfactory definition, we believe it to be the only definition possible.

In the first instance, the sentencing court in this state is the trial court. "A sentence imposed will not be disturbed on appeal if it is within the limits prescribed by law and the realm of trial court discretion and not a result of partiality, prejudice, oppression, or corrupt motive." Our standard of review in the ordinary sentencing case is abuse of discretion. We conclude that this is the standard of review to be applied in a case of this nature together with the use of the "shocking to the conscience" philosophy. . . .

We have reviewed the record carefully in the instant matter. We conclude that the trial court considered all of the necessary sentencing factors required by statute in making its decision. . . . It is not our position to second-guess the trial court in matters of sentencing. The trial judge heard all of the testimony, observed the witnesses, and had the opportunity to evaluate their credibility based on personal observance. We do not have that same opportunity. The trial court is in the best position to evaluate the sentencing factors involved, and we respect the trial court's superior knowledge and its primary responsibility in pronouncing sentence. . . .

AFFIRMED.

Questions

1. List all the facts relevant to deciding whether Janette Cramer was in imminent danger when she shot her husband.

2. According to the court, was she in imminent danger? Explain the court's answer.

3. State exactly why the court admitted evidence of Janette Cramer's history of violence.

4. Do you believe the evidence of her violence against other people proves she didn't suffer from battered woman's syndrome? Defend your answer.

5. Do you believe the evidence of her violent history should play a part in sentencing her? Defend your answer.

6. Did the sentence "shock your conscience"? Would you sentence her to probation? Defend your answer.

◆   ◆   ◆

The Retreat Doctrine

What if you can avoid an attack by escaping? Do you have to retreat? Or, can you stand your ground and fight back? The **retreat rule** says you have to retreat, but only if you reasonably believe that backing off won't unreasonably put you in danger of death or serious bodily harm. The **stand-your-ground rule** says that if you didn't start the fight, you can stand your ground and kill. Of course, you have to reasonably believe you're in danger of death or serious bodily harm. Different values underlie these rules. The retreat rule puts a premium on human life and discourages injuring or killing another person (even an assailant). The stand-your-ground rule (we used to call it the "true man rule"; *State v. Kennamore* 1980, 858) is based on the belief that retreat forces innocent people to take a cowardly or humiliating position. Most states follow the stand-your-ground rule.

States that require retreat have carved out an exception to the retreat doctrine. According to this **castle exception,** when you're attacked in your home, you can stand your ground and use deadly force to fend off an unprovoked attack, but, again, only if you reasonably believe the attack threatens death or serious bodily injury. The Second Circuit U.S. District Court of Appeals dealt with retreat and the castle exception in *U.S. v. Peterson* (1973).

CASE	*Did He Have to Retreat?*

U.S. v. Peterson
483 F.2d 1222 (2nd Cir. 1973)

Bennie Peterson, the defendant, was convicted before the United States District Court for the District of Columbia of manslaughter, and he appealed. The District of Columbia Court of Appeals affirmed.

ROBINSON III, J.

FACTS

Charles Keitt, the deceased, and two friends drove in Keitt's car to the alley in the rear of Peterson's house to remove the windshield wipers from Peterson's wrecked car. (The car was characterized by some witnesses as "wrecked" and by others as "abandoned." The testimony left it clear that its condition was such that it could not be operated.) While Keitt was doing so, Peterson came out of the house into the back yard to protest. After a verbal exchange, Peterson went back into the house, obtained a pistol, and very shortly returned to the yard. In the meantime, Keitt had reseated himself in his car, and he and his companions were about to leave.

Upon his reappearance in the yard, Peterson paused briefly to load the pistol. "If you move," he shouted to Keitt, "I will shoot." He walked to a point in the yard slightly inside a gate in the rear fence and, pistol in hand, said, "If you come in here I will kill you." Keitt alighted from his car, took a few steps toward Peterson and exclaimed, "What the hell do you think you are going to do with that?" (There was abundant evidence that Keitt was intoxicated or nearly so. His companions readily admitted to a considerable amount of drinking earlier that day, and an autopsy disclosed that he had a .29% blood-alcohol content.)

Keitt then made an about-face, walked back to his car and got a lug wrench. With the wrench in a raised position, Keitt advanced toward Peterson, who stood with the pistol pointed toward him. Peterson warned Keitt not to "take another step" and, when Keitt continued onward shot him in the face from a distance of about ten feet. Death was apparently instantaneous. Shortly thereafter, Peterson left home and was apprehended 20-odd blocks away.

This description of the fatal episode was furnished at Peterson's trial by four witnesses for the Government. Peterson did not testify or offer any evidence, but the Government introduced a statement which he had given the police after his arrest, in which he related a somewhat different version. Keitt had removed objects from his car before, and on the day of the shooting he had told Keitt not to do so. After the initial verbal altercation, Keitt went to his car for the lug wrench, so he, Peterson, went into his house for his pistol. When Keitt was about ten feet away, he pointed the pistol "away of his right shoulder"; adding that Keitt was running toward him, Peterson said he "got scared and fired the gun. He ran right into the bullet." "I did not mean to shoot him," Peterson insisted, "I just wanted to scare him."

At trial, Peterson moved for a judgment of acquittal on the ground that . . . the evidence was insufficient to support a conviction. The trial judge denied the motion. After receiving instructions . . . the jury returned a verdict finding Peterson guilty of manslaughter. Judgment was entered conformably with the verdict, and this appeal followed.

OPINION

. . . Peterson's . . . position is that . . . his act was one of self-preservation. . . . The Government, on the other hand, has contended from the beginning that Keitt's slaying fell outside the bounds of lawful self-defense. The questions remaining for our decision inevitably track back to this basic dispute. . . .

Necessity is the pervasive theme of the . . . conditions which the law imposes on the right to kill or maim in self-defense. There must have been a threat, actual or apparent, of the use of deadly force against the defender. The threat must have been unlawful and immediate. The defender must have believed that he was in imminent peril of death or serious bodily harm, and that his response was necessary to save himself therefrom. These beliefs must not only have been honestly entertained, but also objectively rea-sonable in light of the surrounding circumstances. It is clear that no less than a concurrence of these elements will suffice.

Here the parties' opposing contentions focus on . . . the defendant's failure to utilize a safe route for retreat from the confrontation. . . . At no time did Peterson endeavor to retreat from Keitt's approach with the lug wrench. The judge instructed the jury that if Peterson had reasonable grounds to believe and did believe that he was in imminent danger of death or serious injury, and that deadly force was necessary to repel the danger . . . Peterson was entitled to stand his ground and use such force as was reasonably necessary under the circumstances to save his life and his person from pernicious bodily harm.

But, the judge continued, if Peterson could have safely retreated but did not do so, that failure was a circumstance which the jury might consider, together with all others, in determining whether he went further in repelling the danger, real or apparent, than he was justified in going.

Peterson contends that this imputation of an obligation to retreat was error, even if he could safely have done so. He points out that at the time of the shooting he was standing in his own yard, and argues he was under no duty to move. We are persuaded . . . that in the circumstances presented here, the trial judge did not err in giving the instruction challenged.

Within the common law of self-defense there developed the rule of "retreat to the wall," which ordinarily forbade the use of deadly force by one to whom an avenue for safe retreat was open. This doctrine was but an application of the requirement of strict necessity to excuse the taking of human life. . . . Even the innocent victim of a vicious assault had to elect a safe retreat if available, rather than resort to defensive force which might kill or seriously injure.

In a majority of American jurisdictions, contrarily to the common law rule, one may stand his ground and use deadly force whenever it seems reasonably necessary to save himself. While the law of the District of Columbia on this point is not entirely clear, it seems allied with the strong minority adhering to the common law. In 1856, the District of Columbia Criminal Court ruled that a participant in an affray "must endeavor to retreat, . . . that is, he is obliged to retreat, if he can safely." . . . In a much later era this court, adverting to necessity as the soul of homicidal self-defense, declared that "no necessity for killing an assailant can exist, so long as there is a safe way open to escape the conflict." . . . We accept these precedents as ample indication that the doctrine of retreat persists.

That is not to say that the retreat rule is without exceptions. Even at common law it was recognized that it was not completely suited to all situations. Today it is the more so that its precept must be adjusted to modern conditions nonexistent during the early development of the common law of self-defense. One restriction on its operation comes to the fore when the circumstances apparently foreclose a withdrawal with safety. The doctrine of retreat was never intended to enhance the risk to the innocent; its proper application has never required a faultless victim to increase his assailant's safety at the expense of his own.

A slight variant of the same consideration is the principle that there is no duty to retreat from an assault producing an imminent danger of death or grievous bodily harm. "Detached reflection cannot be demanded in the presence of an uplifted knife," nor is it "a condition of immunity that one in that situation should pause to consider whether a reasonable man might not think it possible to fly with safety or to disable his assailant rather than to kill him."

The trial judge's charge to the jury incorporated each of these limitations on the retreat rule. Peterson, however, invokes another, the so-called "castle" doctrine. It is well settled that one who through no fault of his own is attacked in his home is under no duty to retreat. The oft-repeated expression that "a man's home is his castle" reflected the belief in olden days that there were few if any safer sanctuaries than the home. The "castle" exception, moreover, has been extended by some courts to encompass the occupant's presence within the curtilage outside his dwelling. Peterson reminds us that when he shot to halt Keitt's advance, he was standing in his yard and so, he argues, he had no duty to endeavor to retreat.

Despite the practically universal acceptance of the "castle" doctrine . . . it is clear . . . it was inapplicable here. The right of self-defense . . . cannot be claimed by the aggressor in an affray so long as he retains that unmitigated role. . . . Any rule of no-retreat which may protect an innocent victim of the affray would . . . [is] unavailable to the party who provokes or stimulates the conflict. Accordingly, the law is well settled that the "castle" doctrine can be invoked only by one who is without fault in bringing the conflict on. That, we think, is the critical consideration here.

. . . By no interpretation of the evidence could it be said that Peterson was blameless in the affair. And while, of course, it was for the jury to assess the degree of fault, the evidence well nigh dictated the conclusion that it was substantial.

The only reference in the trial judge's charge intimating an affirmative duty to retreat was the instruction that a failure to do so, when it could have been done safely, was a factor in the totality of the circumstances which the jury might consider in determining whether the force which he employed was excessive. We cannot believe that any jury was at all likely to view Peterson's conduct as irreproachable. We conclude that for one who, like Peterson, was hardly entitled to fall back on the "castle" doctrine of no retreat, that instruction cannot be just cause for complaint. . . .

The judgment of conviction appealed from
is accordingly AFFIRMED.

Questions

1. List all of the facts relevant to deciding whether Bennie Peterson shot and killed Charles Keitt in self-defense.

2. Apply both the retreat and stand-your-ground rules to the facts of the case. Is Peterson guilty under both, one, or neither? Defend your answer.

3. Does the castle exception apply to the facts of the case? Rely on the specific facts in the case to back up your answer.

4. Do you favor the retreat or the stand-your-ground rule of self-defense? Why?

5. Exactly where would you draw the line in the castle exception? Or would you abolish the exception? Explain your answer.

EXPLORING THE RETREAT DOCTRINE FURTHER

 Go to the Criminal Law 8e CD to read the full text version of the case featured here.

Did He Have to Retreat from His Own Apartment?

FACTS

After eating dinner at home with Pinto, Ronald Quarles went to a union meeting, planning to meet Pinto at a local barroom after the meeting ended. Upon entering the bar, Quarles saw Pinto talking with a man he didn't recognize. At first he felt angry because he thought Pinto was "trying to sneak around behind my back" with another man, but his anger quickly subsided. As the night wore on, Quarles and Pinto drank and shot some pool. Several arguments erupted over Pinto's refusals to go home with Quarles; finally he walked back to their common residence in Newport. About ten minutes later Pinto walked into the house and informed Quarles that he had one week to find another place to live. Quarles agreed to leave in a week and went upstairs to their bedroom and began to undress. Pinto followed him upstairs and started to choke him. He punched her to get her to release him. Infuriated, she told him to get out "tonight." Quarles called her a "tramp" and indicated that he wouldn't put up with her antics any longer. Pinto went downstairs into the kitchen. After Quarles dressed, he followed her downstairs. When he entered the kitchen, Pinto swung a 9-inch kitchen knife at him. He stepped back and wrestled the knife out of her hands. Quarles conceded that at this point he could have left the house with the knife under his control. Did he have to retreat from his co-occupant?

DECISION AND REASONS

According to the appeals court in Rhode Island, yes:

> Rhode Island permits persons who believe that they are in imminent peril of bodily harm to use nondeadly force such as is reasonably necessary in the circumstances to protect themselves. Before resorting to the use of deadly force, the person attacked must attempt retreat if he or she is consciously aware of an open, safe, and available avenue of escape.

> Quarles attempts to persuade us to create a new exception to the retreat requirement by adopting the common-law castle doctrine. He asserts that this "universally recognized" doctrine exempts the person as-

sailed from the obligation of attempting retreat when the attack occurs in the defendant's dwelling. Quarles contends that the castle doctrine, which embodies the notion that a person's authority is paramount in his own home and need not be compromised in the face of an unlawful attack, should be adhered to even when, as in the instant case, the assailant is a cohabitant.

> We are of the opinion that a person assailed in his or her own residence by a co-occupant is not entitled under the guise of self-defense to employ deadly force and kill his or her assailant. The person attacked is obligated to attempt retreat if he or she is aware of a safe and available avenue of retreat.

> The right of self-defense is born of necessity and should terminate when the necessity is no more. Thus, the obligation to attempt retreat exists where one is assaulted in his or her own living quarters by his or her co-occupant. Therefore, the trial justice did not err in refusing to instruct the jury in the manner requested by Quarles.

> *State v. Quarles*, 504 A.2d 473 (R.I. 1986)

Go to Exercise 7-1 on the Criminal Law 8e CD to learn more about self-defense in your state.

◆   ◆   ◆

THE DEFENSE OF OTHERS

Historically, self-defense meant protecting yourself and the members of your immediate family. Although several states still require a special relationship, the trend is in the opposite direction. Many states have abandoned the special-relationship requirement altogether, replacing it with anyone who needs immediate protection from attack. Several states that still have the requirement have expanded it to include lovers and friends.

The "others" have to have the right to defend themselves before someone else can claim the defense. This is important in cases involving abortion rights protestors. In *State v. Aguillard* (1990, 674), protestors argued they had the right to prevent abortions by violating the law because they were defending the right of unborn children to live. In rejecting the defense of others, the court said:

> The "defense of others" specifically limits the use of force or violence in protection of others to situations where the person attacked would have been justified in using such force or violence to protect himself. In view of *Roe v. Wade* . . . and the provisions of the Louisiana abortion statute, defense of others as justification for the defendants' otherwise criminal conduct is not available in these cases. Since abortion is legal in Louisiana, the defendants had no legal right to protect the unborn by means not even available to the unborn themselves. (676)

THE DEFENSE OF HOME AND PROPERTY

The right to defend your home is an extension of the right of self-defense. The law regarding the defense of homes is deeply rooted in the common-law idea that "a man's home is his castle." As early as 1604, Sir Edward Coke, the great common-law judge, in his report of Semayne's Case, wrote:

> The house of everyone is to him his castle and fortress, as well for his defense against injury and violence, as for his repose; and although the life of a man is a thing precious and favored in law ... if thieves come to a man's house to rob him, or murder, and the owner or his servants kill any of the thieves in defense of himself and his house, it is not felony and he shall lose nothing. (*State v. Mitcheson* 1977, 1122)

The most impassioned statement of the supreme value placed on the sanctity of homes came from the Earl of Chatham during a debate in the British Parliament in 1764:

> The poorest man may in his cottage bid defiance to all the forces of the Crown. It may be frail; its roof may shake; the wind may blow through it; the storm may enter; the rain may enter; but the King of England may not enter; all his force dares not cross the threshold of the ruined tenement. (Hall 1993, 2:4)

Don't let the Earl of Chatham's moving words lure you into thinking you can *automatically* kill to defend the sanctity of your home. Sir William Blackstone (1769), in his eighteenth-century *Commentaries* (the best-known—and often the only law book known—to American lawyers at that time), argues the right is broad but limited. He writes:

> If any person attempts ... to break open a house in the nighttime (which extends also to an attempt to burn it) and shall be killed in such attempt, the slayer shall be acquitted and discharged. This reaches not to ... the breaking open of any house in the daytime, unless it carries with it an attempt of robbery. (180)

So, we see the defense was limited to nighttime invasions, except for breaking into homes to commit daytime robberies. Many modern statutes limit the use of deadly force to cases where it's reasonable to believe intruders intend to commit crimes of violence (like homicide, assault, rape, and robbery) against occupants. Some go further and include all felonies. A few include all offenses. The most extreme is the Colorado "make my day law" which provides:

USE OF DEADLY PHYSICAL FORCE AGAINST AN INTRUDER.

(1) The general assembly hereby recognizes that the citizens of Colorado have a right to expect absolute safety within their own homes.

(2) ... Any occupant of a dwelling is justified in using any degree of physical force, including deadly physical force, against another person when that other person has made *an unlawful entry into the dwelling,* and when the occupant has a reasonable belief that such other person has committed a crime in the dwelling *in addition to the uninvited entry,* or is committing or intends to commit a crime against a person or property *in addition to the uninvited entry,* and when the occupant reasonably believes that such other person might use any physical force, no matter how slight, against any occupant.

(3) Any occupant of a dwelling using physical force, including deadly physical force, in accordance with the provisions of subsection (2) of this section shall be immune from criminal prosecution for the use of such force.

(4) Any occupant of a dwelling using physical force, including deadly physical force, in accordance with the provisions of subsection (2) of this section shall be immune from any civil liability for injuries or death resulting from the use of such force (Section 18-1-704.5). [Emphasis added.]

Statutes also vary as to the area the use of deadly force covers. Most require entry into the home itself. This doesn't include the **curtilage,** the area immediately surrounding the home. Many require entry into an occupied home. This means you can't set some automatic device to shoot whomever trips the switch when you're not home.

The Maryland Court of Appeals dealt with the limits on the use of deadly force to protect your home in the tragic case of *Law v. State* (1974).

| CASE | *Was He Justified in Killing to Protect His Home?* |

Law v. State
318 A.2d 859 (Md.App. 1974)

James Law, the defendant, was convicted in the Circuit Court, Charles County, of murder and assault with intent to murder and he appealed. He was sentenced to 10 years in prison. The Court of Special Appeals reversed and remanded.

LOWE, J.

FACTS

When James Cecil Law, Jr., purchased a thirty-nine dollar shotgun for "house protection," he could not possibly have conceived of the ordeal it would cause him to undergo. Mr. Law, a 32-year-old black man, had recently married and moved to a predominantly white middle-class neighborhood. Within two weeks his home was broken into and a substantial amount of clothing and personal property was taken. The investigating officer testified that Mr. Law was highly agitated following the burglary and indicated that he would take the matter in his own hands. The officer quoted Mr. Law as saying: "I will take care of the job. I know who it is." The officer went on to say that Law told him "...he knew somebody he could get a gun from in D.C. and he was going to kill the man and he was going to take care of it." Two days later he purchased a 12-gauge shotgun and several "double ought" shells.

The intruder entered the Laws' home between 6:30 and 9:00 in the evening by breaking a windowpane in the kitchen door which opened onto a screened back porch. The intruder then apparently reached in and unlocked the door. Law later installed "double locks" which required the use of a key both inside and outside. He replaced the glass in the door window in a temporary manner by holding it in place with a few pieces of molding, without using the customary glazing compound to seal it in.

One week after the break-in a well-meaning neighbor saw a flickering light in the Laws' otherwise darkened house and became suspicious. Aware of the previous burglary, he reported to the police that someone was breaking into the Laws' home. Although the hour was 8:00 P.M., Mr. Law and his bride had retired for the evening. When the police arrived, a fuse of circumstances ignited by fear exploded into a tragedy of errors.

The police did not report to or question the calling neighbor. Instead they went about routinely checking the house seeking the possible illegal point of entry. They raised storm windows where they could reach them and shook the inside windows to see if they were locked. They shined flashlights upon the windows out of reach, still seeking evidence of unlawful entry. Finding none, two officers entered the back screened porch to check the back door, whereupon they saw the windowpane which appeared to have been temporarily put in place with a few pieces of molding. These officers apparently had not known of the repair or the cause of damage.

Upstairs Mr. and Mrs. Law heard what sounded like attempts to enter their home. Keenly aware of the recent occurrence, Mr. Law went downstairs, obtained and loaded his newly acquired shotgun and, apparently facing the rear door of the house, listened for more sounds.

In the meantime, the uniformed officers found what they thought to be the point of entry of a burglar, and were examining the recently replaced glass. While Officer Adams held the flashlight on the recently replaced pane of glass, Officer Garrison removed the molding and the glass, laid them down and stated that he was going to reach in and unlock the door from the inside to see if entry could be gained. Officer Adams testified that they "were talking in a tone a little lower than normal at this point." Officer Adams stated that Officer Garrison then tested the inside lock, discovered it was a deadlock and decided no one could have gotten in the door without a key. A law enforcement student, riding with Officer Garrison that evening, testified that he then heard a rattling noise and someone saying "if there was somebody here, he's still in there."

As Officer Garrison removed his hand from the window he was hit by a shotgun blast which Law fired through the door. Officer Garrison was dead on arrival at the hospital. Officer Potts, the officer next to arrive at the scene, saw Officer Adams running to his car to call for reinforcements. He heard another shot and Officer Adams yell "they just shot at me."

The tragedy of errors had only begun. The officers, having obtained reinforcements and apparently believing they had cornered a burglar, subjected the house to a fusillade of gun fire evidenced by over forty bullet holes in the bottom of the kitchen door and the police department transcription of a telephone conversation during the ensuing period of incomprehensible terror.

Mr. Law testified that while he stood listening to the sounds and voices at the door, fearful that someone was about to come in "…the gun went off, like that, and when it went off like that it scared me and I was so scared because I had never shot a shotgun before and then I heard a voice on the outside say that someone had been shot." Mr. Law was not able to hear who had been shot but he then "…hollered up to my wife, call a police officer, I think I shot a burglar." His wife called the police and most of her conversation was recorded.

The appellant, James Cecil Law, Jr. was found guilty of murder in the second degree and of assault with intent to murder. He was convicted by a jury in the Circuit Court for Charles County following removal from Prince George's County. Judge James C. Mitchell sentenced him to concurrent ten year terms.

OPINION

…There is a dearth of Maryland authority upon the question of what constitutes justifiable homicide in the defense of one's home. We hasten to note, however, that the single case directly meeting the question does so concisely and clearly. In 1962, the Court of Appeals in *Crawford v. State*, 90 A.2d 538, reversed a conviction of manslaughter against a 42-year-old man, suffering from a nervous condition and ulcers, whose home was being broken into by a 23-year-old man and a partner. The decedent had knocked out a piece of masonite replacing one of four glass panes in the door. Crawford fired a shotgun through the door killing the attacker before he was able to enter. Certain of the circumstances of that case coincide remarkably with the case at bar. It is as remarkably distinguished, however, by the character and purpose of the decedent, who had previously beaten Crawford and was returning to rob and beat him again after threatening to do so….

The defense of habitation is explained by text writers and treated in *Crawford* as an extension of the right of self-defense. The distinction between the defense of home and the defense of person is primarily that in the former there is no duty to retreat. "A man in his own house was treated as 'at the wall' and could not, by another's assault, be put under any duty to flee therefrom."

The regal aphorism that a man's home is his castle has obscured the limitations on the right to preserve one's home as a sanctuary from fear of force or violence. *Crawford* articulates the rule well, distilling it from a review of cases in many jurisdictions:

> Most American jurisdictions in which the question has been decided have taken the view that if an assault on a dwelling and an attempted forcible entry are made under circumstances which would create a reasonable apprehension that it is the design of the assailant to commit a felony or to inflict on the inhabitants injury which may result in loss of life or great bodily harm, and that the danger that the design will be carried into effect is imminent, a lawful occupant of the dwelling may prevent the entry even by the taking of the intruder's life.

The felonies the prevention of which justifies the taking of a life "are such and only such as are committed by forcible means, violence, and surprise such as murder, robbery, burglary, rape or arson."…It is "essential that killing is necessary to prevent the commission of the felony in question. If other methods would prevent its commission, a homicide is not justified; all other means of preventing the crime must first be exhausted."

The right thus rests upon real or apparent necessity. It is this need for caution in exercising the right that has been relegated to obscurity. The position espoused by appellant typifies the misunderstanding of the extent of the right to defend one's home against intrusion. He says:

The defendant is not required to act as a reasonable, prudent and cautious individual, nor was he required to limit his force to only that that was required under the circumstances—not when the defendant was in his own home, and believed he was being set upon, or about to be set upon by would be robbers or burglars who were in the act of breaking into his home at the time.

The judgment which must usually be made precipitously under frightening conditions nevertheless demands a certain presence of mind and reasonableness of judgment. Although one is "not obliged to retreat...but...may even pursue the assailant until he finds himself or his property out of danger..., this will not justify a person's firing upon everyone who forceably enters his house, even at night.".... The taking of life is not justified "unless unavoidable...Beyond this the law does not authorize the sacrifice of human life or the infliction of serious bodily injury."

In 1894 Mr. Justice Harlan redefined the scope of the rule within its permissible limits:

> In East's Pleas of the Crown, the author, considering what sort of an attack it was lawful and justifiable to resist, even by the death of the assailant, says: "A man may repel force by force in defense of his person, habitation, or property against one who manifestly intends and endeavors, by violence or surprise, to commit a known felony, such as murder, rape, robbery, arson, burglary, and the like, upon either. In these cases he is not obliged to retreat, but may pursue his adversary until he has secured himself from all danger; and if he kill him in so doing it is called justifiable self-defense; as, on the other hand, the killing by such felon of any person so lawfully defending himself will be murder. *But a bare fear of any of these offenses, however well grounded, as that another lies in wait to take away the party's life, unaccompanied with any overt act indicative of such an intention, will not warrant in killing that other by way of prevention....*" [My italics.] Beard v. U.S., 158 U.S. 550, 563.

Judgments REVERSED; case REMANDED for a new trial.*

Questions

1. Exactly how does the court define the defense of habitation?

2. List all of the facts relevant to deciding whether James Cecil Law is entitled to the defense.

---

*The court reversed and remanded the case because the conviction was based on a coerced confession that violated *Miranda v. Arizona.*

3. Assume that you're the prosecutor. Argue that Law was not justified in killing the officer. Rely on the court's definition and the facts of the case to back up your arguments.

4. Now, assume that you're the defense lawyer. Argue that Law was justified in killing the officer. Rely on the court's definition and the facts of the case to back up your arguments.

5. When the case was remanded and the court on remand rejected Law's defense of home defense, the court commented on the mitigating circumstances that might reduce his punishment:

> We think the evidence...fairly generated an issue of mitigation. At the time of the homicide, appellant and his bride of a few weeks were alone in the bedroom in their darkened house. Two weeks before the homicide their house had been burglarized. They heard noises outside. Appellant got out of bed, nude, and went downstairs to investigate the matter. He continued to hear noises like someone was "trying to get in." He obtained from the living room his shotgun, purchased for "home protection" after his house had been burglarized two weeks before. He heard a noise on his back porch, "a fiddling around with the door." There were curtains on the back door and he could see no figures on the darkened back porch. He felt that there were burglars on his porch, and "then I heard the scraping of a window pane." He next heard a voice say, "lets go in." At that time he was in the living room, "standing there with my shotgun shaking..." because he was scared. In appellant's words, "at that time the gun went off." He said he didn't know how the gun went off; he could have pulled the trigger intentionally or accidentally; he didn't know. When the gun went off, it was held about waist high pointed toward the back door. The single shotgun blast went through the door killing police officer Garrison, who at that time was attempting to gain entrance to the house. The blast narrowly missed police officer Adams who was standing beside officer Garrison. The two officers had gone to the house in response to a call from appellant's next door neighbor who, unknown to appellant or his wife, had earlier called the police to report a suspected burglary attempt at appellant's house. The State conceded in closing argument that appellant did not knowingly shoot a police officer and that "he probably thought he shot a burglar or whatever that was outside."
>
> Although by far the most common form of mitigation is that of a hot-blooded response to legally adequate provocation, this is not the only form of mitigation that will negate malice and will reduce what

might otherwise be murder to manslaughter.... For example, if one man kills another intentionally, under circumstances beyond the scope of innocent homicide, the facts may come so close to justification or excuse that the killing will be classed as voluntary manslaughter rather than murder. (*Law v. State*, 349 A.2d 295 [Md.App. 1975])

Do you think that this is evidence of mitigation or of justifiable homicide in the defense of home? Explain your answer.

EXPLORING IN DEFENSE OF HOME AND PROPERTY FURTHER

 Go to the Criminal Law 8e CD to read the full text version of the case featured here.

Was "Outside the Front Door" Part of the "Home"?

FACTS

When neighbors pounded on David and Pam Guenther's door, and Pam went outside and got into a struggle with one of the neighbors, David shot and killed two neighbors standing outside the front door with four shots from a Smith and Wesson .357 Magnum six-inch revolver. The Guenthers lived in Colorado after the state passed its "make my day" law quoted on pp. 218–219. Was David Guenther justified in shooting his neighbors standing outside his front door?

DECISION AND REASONS

No, said the Colorado Supreme Court:

Section 18-1-704.5(3) states that any occupant of a dwelling who uses physical force in accordance with the provisions of subsection (2) of the statute *"shall be immune from criminal prosecution* for the use of such force" [emphasis added]. In our view, this language is susceptible of only one interpretation. The word "shall," when used in a statute, involves a "mandatory connotation" and hence is the antithesis of discretion or choice. "Immunity" means "freedom from duty or penalty." The word "prosecution" is defined as "a proceeding instituted and carried on by due process of law, before a competent tribunal, for the purpose of

determining the guilt or innocence of a person charged with crime." In accordance with the plain meaning of these terms, the phrase "shall be immune from criminal prosecution" can only be construed to mean that the statute was intended to bar criminal proceedings against a person for the use of force under the circumstances set forth in subsection (2) of section 18-1-704.5.

It must be presumed that the legislature has knowledge of the legal import of the words it uses, and that it intends each part of a statute to be given effect. We may properly conclude, therefore, that the legislative choice of the immunity language in section 18-1-704.5(3) was a deliberate one calculated to obtain the result dictated by the plain meaning of the words—that is, to create a bar to criminal prosecution and not merely an affirmative defense.... The immunity created by section 18-1-704.5 is a conditional immunity in the sense that it applies only if certain factual elements are established.

We next consider the scope of the statutory immunity.... Subsection (2) of the statute states that an occupant of a dwelling is justified in using physical force "against *another person* when *that other person* has made an unlawful entry into the dwelling" (emphasis added) and when the additional statutory requirements are met. Subsection (3) provides immunity from criminal prosecution for an occupant using physical force "in accordance with the provisions of subsection (2) of this section."... In accordance with the explicit terms of the statute, we hold that section 18-1-704.5 provides the home occupant with immunity from prosecution only for force used against one who has made an unlawful entry into the dwelling, and that this immunity does not extend to force used against non-entrants....

The district court...erred in concluding that section 18-1-704.5(3) immunizes from criminal prosecution an occupant of a dwelling who uses force against persons who did not actually enter the dwelling. If on remand the district court concludes that the immunity criteria of section 18-1-704.5(2) are established, then the defendant would be entitled to immunity from prosecution for any force used against any person or persons who actually entered his dwelling, but would not be immune from prosecution for any force used against non-entrants.

People v. Guenther, 740 P.2d 971 (Colo. 1987)

◆   ◆   ◆

Homes are special places; they're not in the same category as our "stuff." Can you use force to protect your "stuff"? Not *deadly* force. But, you can use the amount of less-than-deadly force you reasonably believe is necessary to prevent someone from taking your stuff. You also can run after and take back what someone's just taken from you. But, like all the justifications based on necessity, you can't use force if there's time to call the police.

 Go to Exercise 7-2 on the Criminal Law CD to learn more about the defense of home in your state.

THE CHOICE-OF-EVILS DEFENSE

At the heart of the choice-of-evils defense is necessity to prevent imminent danger; so, it's like all the defenses we've discussed up to now. The justifications based on the necessity of defending yourself, other people, and your home aren't controversial. Why? Because we see the attackers as evil and the defenders as good. (But, don't forget—legally, it's *always* evil to take the law into our own hands, even if it's a necessary lesser evil and therefore justified.) However, as you're about to find out in the general choice-of-evils defense, the line between good and evil isn't always drawn as clearly as it is in self-defense and defense of home.

First, a little history. The **choice-of-evils defense** (also known as the **general principle of necessity**) has a long history in the law of Europe and the Americas. And, throughout that history, the defense has generated heated controversy. The great thirteenth-century jurist of English and Roman law Bracton declared that what "is not otherwise lawful, necessity makes lawful." Other famous English commentators, such as Sir Francis Bacon, Sir Edward Coke, and Sir Matthew Hale in the sixteenth and seventeenth centuries, agreed with Bracton. The influential seventeenth-century English judge Hobart expressed the argument this way: "All laws admit certain cases of just excuse, when they are offended in letter, and where the offender is under necessity, either of compulsion or inconvenience."

On the other side of the debate, the distinguished nineteenth-century English historian of criminal law Judge Sir James F. Stephen believed that the defense of necessity was so vague that judges could interpret it to mean anything they wanted. In the mid-1950s, the distinguished professor of criminal law Glanville Williams (1961) wrote: "It is just possible to imagine cases in which the expediency of breaking the law is so overwhelmingly great that people may be justified in breaking it, but these cases cannot be defined beforehand" (724–725).

Early cases record occasional instances of defendants who successfully pleaded the necessity defense. In 1500, a prisoner successfully pleaded necessity to a charge of prison break; he was trying to escape a fire that burned down the jail. The most common example in the older cases is destroying houses in order to stop fires from spreading. In 1912, a man was acquitted on the defense of necessity when he burned a strip of the owner's heather in order to prevent a fire from spreading to his house (Hall 1960, 425).

The most famous case of imminent necessity is *The Queen v. Dudley and Stephens* (1884). Dudley and Stephens, two adults with families, and Brooks, an 18-year-old man without any family responsibilities, were lost in a lifeboat on the high seas. They had no food or water, except for two cans of turnips and a turtle they caught in the sea on the fourth day. After twenty days (the last eight without food), perhaps a thousand miles from land and with virtually no hope of rescue, Dudley and Stephens—after failing to get Brooks to cast lots—told him that, if no rescue vessel appeared by the next day, they were going to kill him for food. They explained to Brooks that his life was the most expendable because they each had family responsibilities and he didn't. The following day, no vessel appeared. After saying a prayer for him, Dudley and Stephens killed Brooks, who was too weak to resist. They survived on his flesh and blood for four days, when they were finally rescued. Dudley and Stephens were prosecuted, convicted, and sentenced to death for murder. They appealed, pleading the defense of necessity.

The judge, Lord Coleridge, in this famous passage, rejected the defense of necessity:

> The temptation to act…here was not what the law ever called necessity. Nor is this to be regretted. Though law and morality are not the same, and many things may be immoral which are not necessarily illegal, yet the absolute divorce of law from morality would be of fatal consequence; and such divorce would follow if the temptation to murder in this case were to be held by law an absolute defense of it. It is not so….
>
> To preserve one's life is generally speaking a duty, but it may be the plainest and the highest duty to sacrifice it. War is full of instances in which it is a man's duty not to live, but to die. The duty, in case of shipwreck, of a captain to his crew, of the crew to the passengers, of soldiers to women and children…; these duties impose on men the moral necessity, not of the preservation, but of the sacrifice of their lives for others….It is not correct, therefore, to say that there is any absolute or unqualified necessity to preserve one's own life….
>
> It is not needful to point out the awful danger of admitting the principle contended for. Who is to be the judge of this sort of necessity? By what measure of the comparative value of lives to be measured? Is it to be strength, or intellect, or what? It is plain that the principle leaves to him who is to profit by it to determine the necessity which will justify him in deliberately taking another's life to save his own. In this case, the weakest, the youngest, the most unresisting, was chosen. Was it more necessary to kill him than one of the grown men? The answer must be "No"—
>
> "So spake the Fiend, and with necessity,
> The tyrant's plea, executed his devilish deeds."
>
> It is not suggested that in this particular case, the deeds were "devilish," but it is quite plain that such a principle once admitted might be made the legal cloak for unbridled passion and atrocious crime.

Lord Coleridge sentenced them to death but expressed his hope that Queen Victoria would pardon them. The queen didn't pardon them, but she almost did—she commuted their death penalty to six months in prison.

The crux of the choice-of-evils defense is proving the defendant made the right choice, the only choice—namely, the necessity of choosing *now* to do a lesser evil to avoid a greater evil. The *Model Penal Code* choice-of-evils provision contains three elements laid out in three steps: (1) identify the evils, (2) rank the evils, and (3) choose the lesser evil to avoid the greater evil that's on the verge of happening (American Law Institute 1985, 1:2, 8–22).

ELEMENTS OF THE CHOICE-OF-EVILS DEFENSE

Identify the Evils	Rank the Evils	Choose Correctly
1. Evil committed **and**	1. Greater evil **and**	1. Avoid greater evil **and**
2. Evil avoided	2. Lesser evil	2. Commit lesser evil in order to avoid greater

Simply put, the choice-of-evils defense justifies choosing to commit a lesser crime to avoid the harm of a greater crime. The choice of the lesser evil has to be both imminent and necessary. Those who choose to do the lesser evil have to reasonably believe their *only* choice is to cause the lesser evil right now.

The *Model Penal Code* (American Law Institute 1985, 1:2, 8) lists all of the following choices of evils:

1. destroying property to prevent spreading fire;

2. violating a speed limit to get a dying person to a hospital;

3. throwing cargo overboard to save a sinking vessel and its crew;

4. dispensing drugs without a prescription in an emergency; and

5. breaking and entering a mountain cabin to avoid freezing to death.

The *right* choice is life, safety, and health over property. Why? Because according to our values, life, safety, and health always trump property interests (American Law Institute 1985, 12).

The *Model Penal Code* doesn't leave the ranking of evils to individuals; it charges legislatures or judges and juries at trial with the task. Once an individual has made the "right" choice, she either walks or it is a mitigating circumstance that can lessen the punishment. The Oregon Court of Appeals applied the Oregon choice-of-evils defense to the medical use of marijuana in *State v. Ownbey* (2000).

CASE | *Was Using Marijuana a Lesser Evil?*

State v. Ownbey
996 P.2d 510 (Ore.App. 2000)

Jack Ownbey, the defendant, was convicted, in the Circuit Court, Multnomah County, of manufacture of a controlled substance, marijuana, and possession of a controlled substance, marijuana. Defendant appealed. The Court of Appeals affirmed.

DEITS, C.J.

FACTS

Jack Ownbey, the defendant, was convicted of manufacture of a controlled substance, marijuana, and possession of a controlled substance, marijuana. Ownbey is a veteran of the Vietnam war. He has been diagnosed with Post-Traumatic Stress Syndrome (PTSD). In his defense to the charges against him, Ownbey intended to show that "his actions in growing marijuana and possessing marijuana were as a result of medical necessity or choice of evils."

Before trial, Ownbey requested jury instructions on the choice-of-evils defense. In response to that request, the state made its motion, asking the trial court to exclude any evidence pertaining to the choice-of-evils defense. ORS 161.200, codifies that defense in Oregon. It provides:

(1) *Unless inconsistent with...some other provision of law,* conduct which would otherwise constitute an offense is justifiable and not criminal when:
   (a) That conduct is necessary as an emergency measure to avoid an imminent public or private injury; and
   (b) The threatened injury is of such gravity that, according to ordinary standards of intelligence and morality, the desirability and urgency of avoiding the injury clearly outweigh the desirability of avoiding the injury sought to be prevented by the statute defining the offense in issue.

(2) The necessity and justifiability of conduct under subsection (1) of this section shall not rest upon considerations pertaining only to the morality and advisability of the statute, either in its general application or with respect to its application to a particular class of cases arising thereunder. [Emphasis added.]

At the hearing on the state's motion that Ownbey not be allowed to present evidence that would support a choice-of-evils defense, Ownbey argued that he should be allowed to present evidence to show that he has suffered from this disorder for some time and that, although he has sought traditional medical treatment, the only substance that alleviates his symptoms is marijuana. The trial court granted the state's motion on the ground that, under ORS 161.200, the choice-of-evils defense was not available to Ownbey because it was inconsistent with other provisions of law. The court explained:

> In our case the Legislature has anticipated the choice of evils and determined the balance to be struck between competing values. And the Ownbeys and the Court are precluded from reassessing those values to determine whether certain conduct is justified when we have a statutory construct such as we do.

We agree with the trial court's conclusion. In *State v. Clowes,* 310 Or. 686, 801 P.2d 789 (1990), the Supreme Court articulated the analysis necessary to determine whether a choice-of-evils defense is available to a defendant. Under that analysis, we must first determine "if allowing the defense would be inconsistent with some other provision of law." If so, "it may not be asserted." Although the phrase "inconsistent with some other provision of law" is not defined in ORS 161.200, the court in *Clowes* ex-

plained that that language means "that the legislature's decision prevails if and when it makes specific value choices," and that "competing values which have been foreclosed by deliberate legislative choice are excluded from the general defense of justification."

Therefore, the critical question here is whether the legislature has made deliberate choices that would exclude the choice-of-evils defense that defendant wishes to assert in this case. Ownbey argues that he should be allowed the choice-of-evils defense here because his use of marijuana was medically necessary to treat a diagnosed illness and, consequently, his choice to use marijuana to treat his PTSD was a lesser evil than letting his condition remain untreated. This is an issue that the legislature has confronted several times and has made a deliberate choice. The legislature and the voters of this state have considered the use of marijuana for medical purposes and, at the time of Ownbey's offense, the legislature had concluded that the use of marijuana for medical treatment under these circumstances should not be allowed. In 1979, the Oregon legislature enacted ORS 475.505 *et seq.* allowing physicians to prescribe marijuana to patients undergoing chemotherapy and for the treatment of glaucoma. The legislature repealed ORS 475.505 in 1987. The Oregon legislature again considered legalizing marijuana for medical use in 1993 and 1997, but did not do so.

The voters of the State of Oregon have also addressed this issue. In fact, since this case was briefed and argued, the 1999 legislature again addressed this issue in response to a measure passed by voters in 1998. The measure itself, the Oregon Medical Marijuana Act, allows the use of marijuana for medical purposes within specified limits. The 1999 legislature subsequently amended portions of that act to "clarify" it. Because the act establishes a defense that expressly applies only to acts or offenses committed on or after December 3, 1998, it does not affect the outcome of this case.

To allow Ownbey to present a choice-of-evils defense in this case would be inconsistent with the law in existence at the time of Ownbey's offense.

Ownbey argues that if "inconsistent...with some other provision of law" means that the legislature has considered a matter and made it illegal, that effectively does away with a choice-of-evils defense because the defense necessarily involves committing an illegal act. However, what Ownbey fails to recognize is that the defense of necessity is available only in situations wherein the legislature has not itself, in its criminal statute, made a determination of values. If the legislature has not made such a value judgment, the defense would be available. However, when, as here, the legislature has already balanced the competing values that would be presented in a choice-of-evils defense and made a choice, the court is precluded from reassessing that judgment.

Finally, Ownbey relies on *State v. Cole*, 874 P.2d 878 (1994)... from the State of Washington in which the defendant... [was] allowed to use the medical necessity defense in response to charges of marijuana possession. Of course, we are not bound by Washington case law, although we occasionally seek guidance from the reasoning of courts of other states. In any event, a more recent case from Washington, reached the opposite result from that desired by Ownbey. The Washington court articulated its reasoning as follows:

> The decision of whether there is an accepted medical use for particular drugs has been vested in the Legislature by the Washington Constitution. The Legislature has determined that marijuana has no accepted medical use. Williams has no fundamental right to have marijuana as his preferred treatment over the State's objections. Further, if the debate over medical treatment belongs in the political arena, it makes no sense for the courts to fashion a defense whereby jurors weigh experts' testimony on the medical uses of a Schedule I drug. Otherwise, each trial would become a battlefield of experts. But the Legislature has designated the battlefield as the Board of Pharmacy. The Washington Constitution has not enabled each individual to be the final arbiter of the medicine he is entitled to take—it is the Legislature that has been authorized to make laws to regulate the sale of medicines and drugs. Thus, our holding is that with respect to Schedule I drugs, there is not a defense of medical necessity.

We conclude that the trial court here properly excluded evidence of a choice-of-evils defense.

AFFIRMED.

Questions

1. State the elements of the choice-of-evils defense as Oregon defines them.

2. Summarize Ownbey's arguments as to why he's entitled to the choice-of-evils defense. Exactly what is the court's reason for denying Jack Ownbey the necessity defense?

3. Do you agree with the court that medical use of marijuana is not available in Oregon? Should it be? Defend your answer.

EXPLORING THE CHOICE-OF-EVILS DEFENSE FURTHER

Go to the Criminal Law 8e CD to read the full text versions of the cases featured here.

1. *Was Speeding the Lesser Evil?*

FACTS

The prosecution proved beyond a reasonable doubt by the use of radar readings that James Dover was driving 80 miles per hour in a 55 mile-per-hour zone. However, the court also found that the defendant, who is a lawyer, was not guilty on the grounds that his speeding violation was justified because he was late for a court hearing in Denver as a result of a late hearing in Summit County, Colorado.

A Colorado statute, § 42–4-1001(8)(a) provides:

> The conduct of a driver of a vehicle which would otherwise constitute a violation of this section is justifiable and not unlawful when:

> It is necessary as an emergency measure to avoid an imminent public or private injury which is about to occur by reason of a situation occasioned or developed through no conduct of said driver and which is of sufficient gravity that, according to ordinary standards of intelligence and morality, the desirability and urgency of avoiding the injury clearly outweigh the desirability of avoiding the consequences sought to be prevented by this section.

Was Dover justified in speeding because of necessity?

DECISION AND REASONS

No, said the Colorado Supreme Court:

> In this case, the defendant did not meet the foundational requirements of § 42-4-1001(8)(a). He merely testified that he was driving to Denver for a "court matter" and that he was late because of the length of a hearing in Summit County. No other evidence as to the existence of emergency as a justification for speeding was presented. The defendant did not present evidence as to the type or extent of the injury that he would suffer if he did not violate § 42-4-1001(1). He also failed to establish that he did not cause the situation or that his injuries would outweigh the consequences of his conduct. The record does not include evidence to establish a sufficient foundation to invoke the emergency justification

defense provided by § 42-4-1001(8)(a). Since the defendant did not lay a proper foundation as to the existence of the defense, the prosecution was not required to prove beyond a reasonable doubt that the defendant was not justified in violating § 42-4-1001(1). § 18-1-407(2). The county court erred by finding the defendant not guilty because the defendant's speeding was justified because of an emergency. § 42-4-1001(8)(a). Accordingly, we reverse the district court and disapprove the ruling of the county court.

People v. Dover, 790 P.2d 834 (Colo.1990)

2. Was Burglary the Lesser Evil?

On a cold winter day, William Celli and his friend, Glynis Brooks, left Deadwood, South Dakota, hoping to hitchhike to Newcastle, Wyoming, to look for work. The weather turned colder, they were afraid of frostbite, and there was no place of business open for them to get warm. Their feet were so stiff from the cold that it was difficult for them to walk.

They broke the lock on the front door, and entered the only structure around, a cabin. Celli immediately crawled into a bed to warm up, and Brooks tried to light a fire in the fireplace. They rummaged through drawers to look for matches, which they finally located, and started a fire. Finally, Celli came out of the bedroom, took off his wet moccasins, socks, and coat; placed them near the fire; and sat down to warm himself. After warming up somewhat they checked the kitchen for edible food. That morning, they had shared a can of beans but had not eaten since. All they found was dry macaroni, which they could not cook because there was no water.

A neighbor noticed the smoke from the fireplace and called the police. When the police entered the cabin, Celli and Brooks were warming themselves in front of the fireplace. The police searched them but turned up nothing belonging to the cabin owners. Did Celli and his friend choose the lesser of two evils?

DECISION AND REASONS

The trial court convicted Celli and Brooks of fourth-degree burglary. The appellate court reversed on other grounds, so the court never got to the issue of the defense of necessity.

State v. Celli, 263 N.W.2d 145 (S.D. 1978)

Go to Exercise 7-3 on the Criminal Law 8e CD to learn more about the choice-of-evils-defense in your state.

◆   ◆   ◆

THE DEFENSE OF CONSENT

Now we turn to a justification that has nothing to do with necessity. At the heart of the defense of consent is the high value placed on individual autonomy in a free society. If mentally competent adults want to be crime victims, so the argument for the justification of consent goes, no paternalistic government should get in their way. Consent may make sense in the larger context of individual freedom and responsibility, but the criminal law is hostile to consent as a justification for committing crimes. Individuals can take their own lives and inflict injuries on themselves, but in most states they can't authorize others to kill them or beat them. Some states' consent statutes are, however, exceptions:

ALABAMA CRIMINAL CODE
SECTION 13A-2-7

(a) In general. The consent of the victim to conduct charged to constitute an offense or to the result thereof is a defense if such consent negatives a required element of the offense or precludes the infliction of the harm or evil sought to be prevented by the law defining the offense.
(b) Consent to bodily harm. When conduct is charged to constitute an offense because it causes or threatens bodily harm, consent to such conduct or to the infliction of such harm is a defense only if:

(1) The bodily harm consented to or threatened by the conduct consented to is not serious; or

(2) The conduct and the harm are reasonably foreseeable hazards of joint participation in a lawful athletic contest or competitive sport; or

(3) The consent establishes a justification for the conduct under Article 2 of Chapter 3 of this title.

(c) Ineffective consent. Unless otherwise provided by this Criminal Code or by the law defining the offense, assent does not constitute consent if:

(1) It is given by a person who is legally incompetent to authorize the conduct; or

(2) It is given by a person who by reason of immaturity, mental disease or defect, or intoxication is manifestly unable and known by the actor to be unable to make a reasonable judgment as to the nature or harmfulness of the conduct; or

(3) It is given by a person whose consent is sought to be prevented by the law defining the offense; or

(4) It is induced by force, duress or deception.

NORTH DAKOTA
12.1-17-08. CONSENT AS A DEFENSE.

1. When conduct is an offense because it causes or threatens bodily injury, consent to such conduct or to the infliction of such injury by all persons injured or threatened by the conduct is a defense if:

a. Neither the injury inflicted nor the injury threatened is such as to jeopardize life or seriously impair health;

b. The conduct and the injury are reasonably foreseeable hazards of joint participation in a lawful athletic contest or competitive sport; or

c. The conduct and the injury are reasonably foreseeable hazards of an occupation or profession or of medical or scientific experimentation conducted by recognized methods, and the persons subjected to such conduct or injury, having been made aware of the risks involved, consent to the performance of the conduct or the infliction of the injury.

2. Assent does not constitute consent, within the meaning of this section, if:

a. It is given by a person who is legally incompetent to authorize the conduct charged to constitute the offense and such incompetence is manifest or known to the actor;

b. It is given by a person who by reason of youth, mental disease or defect, or intoxication is manifestly unable or known by the actor to be unable to make a reasonable judgment as to the nature or harmfulness of the conduct charged to constitute the offense; or

c. It is induced by force, duress, or deception.

MONTANA
45-2-211. CONSENT AS A DEFENSE.

(1) The consent of the victim to conduct charged to constitute an offense or to the result thereof is a defense.

(2) Consent is ineffective if:

(a) it is given by a person who is legally incompetent to authorize the conduct charged to constitute the offense;

(b) it is given by a person who by reason of youth, mental disease or defect, or intoxication is unable to make a reasonable judgment as to the nature or harmfulness of the conduct charged to constitute the offense;

(c) it is induced by force, duress, or deception; or

(d) it is against public policy to permit the conduct or the resulting harm, even though consented to.

In most states, the law recognizes only three exceptions that allow the defense of consent as a justification:

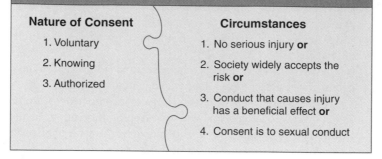

ELEMENTS OF THE CONSENT DEFENSE

Nature of Consent
1. Voluntary
2. Knowing
3. Authorized

Circumstances
1. No serious injury **or**
2. Society widely accepts the risk **or**
3. Conduct that causes injury has a beneficial effect **or**
4. Consent is to sexual conduct

1. No serious injury results from the consensual crime.

2. The injury happens during a sporting event.

3. The conduct benefits the consenting person, such as when a doctor performs surgery.

4. The consent is to sexual conduct. (Fletcher 1978, 770)

Still, fitting into one of these four exceptions is necessary but not enough to entitle defendants to the defense. They also have to prove the consent was voluntary, knowing, and authorized. **Voluntary consent** means consent was the product of free will, not of force, threat of force, promise, or trickery. Forgiveness after the commission of a crime doesn't qualify as voluntary consent. **Knowing consent** means the person consenting understands what she's consenting to; she's not too young or insane to understand. **Authorized consent** means the person consenting has the authority to give consent; I can't give consent for someone else whom I'm not legally responsible for. The court dealt with the sporting event exception in *State v. Shelley* (1997).

CASE | *Did He Consent to the Attack?*

State v. Shelley
929 P.2d 489 (Wash.App. 1997)

Jason Shelley was convicted in the Superior Court, King County, of second-degree assault, arising out of an incident in which Shelley intentionally punched another basketball player during a game. Shelley appealed. The Court of Appeals affirmed the conviction.

GROSSE, J.

FACTS

On March 31, 1993, Jason Shelley and Mario Gonzalez played "pickup" basketball on opposing teams at the University of Washington Intramural Activities Building (the

IMA). Pickup games are not refereed by an official; rather, the players take responsibility for calling their own fouls. During the course of three games, Gonzalez fouled Shelley several times. Gonzalez had a reputation for playing overly aggressive defense at the IMA. Toward the end of the evening, after trying to hit the ball away from Shelley, he scratched Shelley's face, and drew blood. After getting scratched, Shelley briefly left the game and then returned.

Shelley and Gonzalez have differing versions of what occurred after Shelley returned to the game. According to Gonzalez, while he was waiting for play in the game to return to Gonzalez's side of the court, Shelley suddenly hit him. Gonzalez did not see Shelley punch him. According to Shelley's version of events, when Shelley rejoined the game, he was running down the court and he saw Gonzalez make "a move towards me as if he was maybe going to prevent me from getting the ball." The move was with his hand up "across my vision." Angry, he "just reacted" and swung. He said he hit him because he was afraid of being hurt, like the previous scratch. He testified that Gonzalez continually beat him up during the game by fouling him hard.

A week after the incident, a school police detective interviewed Shelley and prepared a statement for Shelley to sign based on the interview. Shelley reported to the police that Gonzalez had been "continually slapping and scratching him" during the game. Shelley "had been getting mad" at Gonzalez and the scratch on Shelley's face was the "final straw." As the two were running down the court side by side, "I swung my right hand around and hit him with my fist on the right side of his face." Shelley asserted that he also told the detective that Gonzalez waved a hand at him just before Shelley threw the punch and that he told the detective that he was afraid of being injured. Gonzalez required emergency surgery to repair his jaw. Broken in three places, it was wired shut for six weeks. His treating physician believed that a "significant" blow caused the damage.

During the course of the trial, defense counsel told the court he intended to propose a jury instruction that: "A person legally consents to conduct that causes or threatens bodily harm if the conduct and the harm are reasonably foreseeable hazards of joint participation in a lawful, athletic contest or competitive sport." Although the trial court agreed that there were risks involved in sports, it stated that "the risk of being intentionally punched by another player is one that I don't think we ever do assume."

The court noted, "In basketball . . . you consent to a certain amount of rough contact. If they were both going for a rebound and Mr. Shelley's elbow or even his fist hit Mr. Gonzalez as they were both jumping for the rebound and Mr. Gonzalez's jaw was fractured in exactly the same way . . . then you would have an issue." Reasoning that "our laws are intended to uphold the public peace and regulate behavior of individuals," the court ruled "that as a matter of law, consent cannot be a defense to an assault." The court indicated that Shelley could not claim consent because his conduct "exceeded what is considered within the rules of that particular sport:

> Consent is a contact that is contemplated within the rules of the game and that is incidental to the furtherance of the goals of that particular game.
>
> If you can show me any rule book for basketball at any level that says an intentional punch to the face in some way is a part of the game, then I would take another . . . look at your argument. I don't believe any such rule book exists.

Later Shelley proposed jury instructions on the subject of consent:

> An act is not an assault, if it is done with the consent of the person alleged to be assaulted. It is a defense to a charge of second degree assault occurring in the course of an athletic contest if the conduct and the harm are reasonably foreseeable hazards of joint participation in a lawful athletic contest or competitive sport.

The trial court rejected these and Shelley excepted. The trial court did instruct the jury about self-defense.

OPINION

First, we hold that consent is a defense to an assault occurring during an athletic contest. This is consistent with the law of assault as it has developed in Washington. A person is guilty of second degree assault if he or she "intentionally assaults another and thereby recklessly inflicts substantial bodily harm." One common law definition of assault recognized in Washington is "an unlawful touching with criminal intent." At the common law, a touching is unlawful when the person touched did not give consent to it, and [it] was either harmful or offensive. As our Supreme Court stated in *State v. Simmons*, "where there is consent, there is no assault." The State argues that because Simmons was a sexual assault case, the defense of consent should be limited to that realm. We decline to apply the defense so narrowly. Logically, consent must be an issue in sporting events because a person participates in a game knowing that it will involve potentially offensive contact and with this consent the "touchings" involved are not "unlawful."

The rationale that courts offer in limiting [consent as a defense] is that society has an interest in punishing assaults as breaches of the public peace and order, so that an individual cannot consent to a wrong that is committed against the public peace. Urging us to reject the defense of consent because an assault violates the public peace, the State argues that this principle precludes Shelley from being entitled to argue the consent defense on the facts of his case. In making this argument, the State ignores the factual contexts that dictated the results in the cases it cites in support.

When faced with the question of whether to accept a school child's consent to hazing or consent to a fight, *People v. Lenti*, 253 N.Y.S.2d 9 (1964), or a gang member's consent to a beating, *Helton v. State*, 624 N.E.2d 499, 514 (Ind.Ct.App.1993), courts have declined to apply the defense. Obviously, these cases present "touchings" factually distinct from "touchings" occurring in athletic competitions.

If consent cannot be a defense to assault, then most athletic contests would need to be banned because many involve "invasions of one's physical integrity." Because society has chosen to foster sports competitions, players necessarily must be able to consent to physical contact and other players must be able to rely on that consent when playing the game. This is the view adopted by the drafters of the *Model Penal Code:*

> There are, however, situations in which consent to bodily injury should be recognized as a defense to crime.... There is...the obvious case of participation in an athletic contest or competitive sport, where the nature of the enterprise often involves risk of serious injury. Here, the social judgment that permits the contest to flourish necessarily involves the companion judgment that reasonably foreseeable hazards can be consented to by virtue of participation.

The more difficult question is the proper standard by which to judge whether a person consented to the particular conduct at issue. The State argues that "when the conduct in question is not within the rules of a given sport, a victim cannot be deemed to have consented to this act." The trial court apparently agreed with this approach. Although we recognize that there is authority supporting this approach, we reject a reliance on the rules of the games as too limiting. Rollin M. Perkins in *Criminal Law* explains:

> The test is not necessarily whether the blow exceeds the conduct allowed by the rules of the game. Certain excesses and inconveniences are to be expected beyond the formal rules of the game. It may be ordinary and expected conduct for minor assaults to occur. However, intentional excesses beyond those reasonably contemplated in the sport are not justified.

Instead, we adopt the approach of the *Model Penal Code* which provides:

> (2) Consent to Bodily Injury. When conduct is charged to constitute an offense because it causes or threatens bodily injury, consent to such conduct or to the infliction of such injury is a defense if: ...
>
> (b) the conduct and the injury are reasonably foreseeable hazards of joint participation in a lawful athletic contest or competitive sport or other concerted activity not forbidden by law.

The State argues the law does not allow "the victim to 'consent' to a broken jaw simply by participating in an unrefereed, informal basketball game." This argument presupposes that the harm suffered dictates whether the defense is available or not. This is not the correct inquiry. The correct inquiry is whether the conduct of defendant constituted foreseeable behavior in the play of the game.

Additionally, the injury must have occurred as a byproduct of the game itself. In construing a similar statutory defense, the Iowa court required a "nexus between defendant's acts and playing the game of basketball." In *State v. Floyd*, a fight broke out during a basketball game and the defendant, who was on the sidelines, punched and severely injured several opposing team members. Because neither defendant nor his victims were voluntarily participating in the game, the defense did not apply because the statute "contemplated a person who commits acts during the course of play, and the exception seeks to protect those whose acts otherwise subject to prosecution are committed in furtherance of the object of the sport."

As the court noted in *Floyd*, there is a "continuum, or sliding scale, grounded in the circumstances under which voluntary participants engage in sport...which governs the type of incidents in which an individual volunteers (i.e., consents) to participate." *State v. Floyd*, 466 N.W.2d 919, 922 (Iowa.Ct.App.1990)

The New York courts provide another example. In a football game, while tackling the defendant, the victim hit the defendant. After the play was over and all of the players got off the defendant, the defendant punched the victim in the eye. The court in *People v. Freer* held that this act was not consented to:

> Initially it may be assumed that the very first punch thrown by the complainant in the course of the tackle was consented to by defendant. The act of tackling an opponent in the course of a football game may often involve "contact" that could easily be interpreted to be a "punch." Defendant's response after the pileup to complainant's initial act of "aggression" cannot be mistaken. Clearly, defendant intended to punch complainant. This was not a consented to act. *People v. Freer*, 381 N.Y.S.2d 976, 978 (1976).

As a corollary to the consent defense, the State may argue that the defendant's conduct exceeded behavior foreseeable in the game. Although in "all sports players consent to many risks, hazards and blows," there is "a limit to the magnitude and dangerousness of a blow to which another is deemed to consent." This limit, like the foreseeability of the risks, is determined by presenting evidence to the jury about the nature of the game, the participants' expectations, the location where the game has been played, as well as the rules of the game.

Here, taking Shelley's version of the events as true, the magnitude and dangerousness of Shelley's actions were beyond the limit. There is no question that Shelley lashed out at Gonzalez with sufficient force to land a substantial blow to the jaw, and there is no question but that Shelley intended to hit Gonzalez. There is nothing in the game of basketball, or even rugby or hockey, that would permit consent as a defense to such conduct. Shelley admitted to an assault and was not precluded from arguing that the assault justified self-defense; but justification and consent are not the same inquiry....

We AFFIRM.

Questions

1. According to the court, why can participants in a sport consent to conduct that would otherwise be a crime?

2. Why should they be allowed to consent to such conduct when in other situations, such as those enumerated in the Exploring Further cases that follow, they can't consent?

3. Should individuals be allowed to knowingly and voluntarily consent to the commission of crimes against themselves? Why or why not?

4. Why was Shelley not allowed the defense of consent in this case?

5. Do you agree with the court's decision? Relying on the relevant facts in the case, defend your answer.

EXPLORING THE DEFENSE OF CONSENT FURTHER

Go to the Criminal Law 8e CD to read the full text versions of the cases featured here.

1. *Is Shooting BB Guns a Sport?*

FACTS

Richard Hiott and his friend Jose were playing a game of shooting at each other with BB guns. During the game, Jose was hit in the eye and lost his eye as a result. Richard was charged with third-degree assault. His defense was consent. Was he entitled to the defense?

DECISION AND REASONS

No, said the Washington Court of Appeals:

> Consent can be a defense to a criminal assault.... State v. Shelley [excerpted before this note] held that consent can be a defense to an assault occurring during an athletic contest.... Under Shelley...consent is a defense only if the game is a lawful athletic contest, competitive sport, or other concerted activity not forbidden by law....
>
> Hiott argues that...the game they were playing "is within the limits of games for which society permits consent." Hiott compares the boys' shooting of BB guns

at each other to dodgeball, football, rugby, hockey, boxing, wrestling, "ultimate fighting," fencing, and "paintball." We disagree.

> The games Hiott uses for comparison, although capable of producing injuries, have been generally accepted by society as lawful athletic contests, competitive sports, or concerted activities not forbidden by law. And these games carry with them generally accepted rules, at least some of which are intended to prevent or minimize injuries. In addition, such games commonly prescribe the use of protective devices or clothing to prevent injuries. Shooting BB guns at each other is not a generally accepted game or athletic contest; the activity has no generally accepted rules; and the activity is not characterized by the common use of protective devices or clothing.
>
> Moreover, consent is not a valid defense if the activity consented to is against public policy. Thus, a child cannot consent to hazing, a gang member cannot consent to an initiation beating, and an individual cannot consent to being shot with a pistol. In *Fransua*, the New Mexico court held that consent was not a defense to aggravated battery, recognizing that criminal statutes are enacted to protect citizens and to prevent breaches of the public peace. Assaults in general are breaches of the public peace. And we consider shooting at another person with a BB gun a breach of the public peace and therefore, against public policy. We conclude that the trial court did not err in refusing to consider Jose's consent as a defense.

State v. Hiott, 987 P.2d 135 (Wash.App. 1999)

2. *Can She Consent to Being Assaulted?*

FACTS

Mrs. Brown was an alcoholic. On the day of the alleged crime she had been drinking, apparently to her husband Reginald Brown's displeasure. Acting according to the terms of an agreement between the defendant Reginald Brown and his wife, he punished her by beating her severely with his hands and other objects.

Brown was charged with atrocious assault and battery. He argued he wasn't guilty of atrocious assault and battery because he and Mrs. Brown, the victim, had an understanding to the effect that if she consumed any alcoholic beverages (and/or became intoxicated), he would punish her by physically assaulting her. The trial court refused the defense of consent. Was Mr. Brown justified because of Mrs. Brown's consent?

DECISION AND REASONS

No, said the New Jersey appellate court:

> The laws...are simply and unequivocally clear that the defense of consent cannot be available to a defendant charged with any type of physical assault that causes appreciable injury. If the law were otherwise, it would not be conducive to a peaceful, orderly and healthy society....
>
> This court concludes that, as a matter of law, no one has the right to beat another even though that person may ask for it. Assault and battery cannot be consented to by a victim, for the State makes it unlawful and is not a party to any such agreement between the victim and perpetrator. To allow an otherwise criminal act to go unpunished because of the victim's consent would not only threaten the security of our society but also might tend to detract from the force of the moral principles underlying the criminal law....
>
> Thus, for the reasons given, the State has an interest in protecting those persons who invite, consent to and permit others to assault and batter them. Not to enforce these laws which are geared to protect such people would seriously threaten the dignity, peace, health and security of our society.

State v. Brown, 364 A.2d 27 (N.J. 1976)

3. Can He Consent to Being Shot?

FACTS

Daniel Fransua and the victim were in a bar in Albuquerque. Fransua had been drinking heavily that day and the previous day. Sometime around 3:00 P.M., after an argument, Fransua told the victim he'd shoot him if he had a gun. The victim got up, walked out of the bar, went to his car, took out a loaded pistol, and went back in the bar. He came up to Fransua, laid the pistol on the bar, and said, "There's the gun. If you want to shoot me, go ahead." Fransua picked up the pistol, put the barrel next to the victim's head, and pulled the trigger, wounding him seriously.

Was the victim's consent a justification that meant Fransua wasn't guilty of aggravated battery?

DECISION AND REASONS

No, said the New Mexico Court of Appeals:

> It is generally conceded that a state enacts criminal statutes making certain violent acts crimes for at least two reasons: One reason is to protect the persons of its citizens; the second, however, is to prevent a breach of the public peace. While we entertain little sympathy for either the victim's absurd actions or the defendant's equally unjustified act of pulling the trigger, we will not permit the defense of consent to be raised in such cases. Whether or not the victims of crimes have so little regard for their own safety as to request injury, the public has a stronger and overriding interest in preventing and prohibiting acts such as these. We hold that consent is not a defense to the crime of aggravated battery, irrespective of whether the victim invites the act and consents to the battery.

State v. Fransua, 510 P.2d 106 (N.Mex.App. 1973)

Go to Exercise 7-4 on the Criminal Law 8e CD to learn more about the defense of consent in your state.

◆   ◆   ◆

SUMMARY

I. Defenses to criminal liability
- A. Three legitimate types
  1. Alibi—individual proves it was impossible for him to have committed the crime
  2. Justification—she's responsible, but the act was justified
  3. Excuse—he committed the wrong but isn't responsible for his action
- B. Affirmative defense
  1. Defendants have some responsibility to prove their defenses
  2. Government has some responsibility to disprove defenses
- C. Results of defendants' successful proof of defense
  1. Perfect defenses—an acquittal results
  2. Imperfect defenses—reduce the crime to a lesser offense

3. Mitigating circumstances—reduce the penalty for the crime

    D. Motive can influence punishment and sometimes liability

II. Justifications based on necessity

    A. Necessity and the rule of law

        1. Government has the monopoly on force under the rule of law

        2. Necessity justifies violating the rule of law by allowing individuals to take the law into their own hands

        3. Strictly limited to situations that meet three conditions

            a. The necessity is great

            b. The danger of harm is imminent

            c. For prevention only

    B. Five types of justification defenses

        1. Self-defense

        2. Defense of others

        3. Defense of home and property

        4. Choice-of-evils defense

        5. Defense of consent

III. Self-defense

    A. The elements of self-defense

        1. Unprovoked attack (total withdrawal by attackers an exception)

        2. Honest and reasonable belief in imminent (not present) danger of death or serious bodily injury

        3. Honest and reasonable belief in the need to defend against attack right now—present danger

        4. Reasonable (not excessive) force to repel attack

    B. The retreat doctrine

        1. Two rules

            a. You have to retreat if escape is reasonable (most states)

            b. If you didn't start the fight, you can stand your ground even if you could escape by retreating (a few states)

        2. Castle exception—retreat from home not required; you can stand your ground

IV. The defense of others

    A. Who's included

        1. Most states include individuals in a "special relationship"

        2. Some states include anyone in imminent danger of harm

    B. Defense applies only to those who can claim the right to defend themselves

V. The defense of home and property

    A. Rooted in ancient idea that our homes are our castles

    B. Extension of the right of self-defense

    C. Limits to using deadly force vary by state

        1. Must have reasonable belief intruders intend to commit

            a. Violent felonies against occupants

            b. Any felony

            c. Any offense

        2. Area covered

            a. Entry into occupied home

            b. Entry into curtilage

VI. The choice-of-evils defense
    A. Basic idea—immediate necessity justifies choosing to commit a lesser crime to avoid the harm of a greater crime
    B. Elements
        1. Identify evils (usually in legislation)
        2. Rank evils (usually in legislation)
        3. Choose the lesser evil to avoid imminent harm from the greater evil

VII. The defense of consent
    A. Justification—the value of individual autonomy in a free society
    B. Consent is not a defense, but there are four exceptions
        1. No serious injury results from consent
        2. Injury occurs during sporting events
        3. Consent benefits the person who consents (patient consents to surgery)
        4. Consent is to sexual conduct (Chapter 9)
    C. Exceptions are necessary to the defense but not enough unless consent is also voluntary and knowing

 Go to the Criminal Law 8e CD to download this summary outline. The outline has been formatted so that you can add notes to it during class lectures, or later create a customized chapter outline to use while reviewing. Either way, the summary outline will help you understand the "big picture" and fill in the details as you study.

REVIEW QUESTIONS

1. Explain the differences between alibi, justification, and excuse. Give an example of each.

2. Explain how affirmative defenses work.

3. What's the significance of motive in criminal law? Give an example.

4. Explain how the defenses of justification violate the rule of law.

5. Identify the "heart" of self-defense, and explain why it's the heart.

6. Identify the three circumstances that have to come together to make good a claim of self-defense.

7. Explain why preemptive strikes and retaliation are not acceptable reasons for self-defense.

8. Identify and define the four elements of self-defense.

9. Identify the difference between imminent and present danger, give an example of each, and explain why present danger doesn't satisfy the danger element of self-defense.

10. Identify the values underlying the "retreat doctrine" and the "stand-your-ground rule."

11. Who's included in the defense of others?

12. Identify and give examples of the various limits that states impose on the use of deadly force in the defense of home.

13. Identify the three elements in the choice-of-evils defense.

14. Explain how the three elements work as steps in deciding whether the defendant can claim the choice-of-evils defense.

15. List the examples of evils and their rank in the *Model Penal Code.*

16. What do we mean by "the *right* choice" in the choice-of-evils defense?

17. How is the rank of evils determined in the choice-of-evils defense?

18. How does the justification of consent differ from the other defenses discussed in the chapter?

19. Identify four exceptions to the rule that consent of the victim doesn't qualify as a defense of justification.

20. The exceptions are necessary but not enough to qualify for the defense of consent. What, in addition to the exceptions, is enough to qualify?

KEY TERMS

alibi p. 191
principle of justification p. 191
principle of excuse p. 192
affirmative defenses p. 192
burden of production p. 192
burden of persuasion p. 192
preponderance of the evidence
    p. 192
perfect defenses p. 192
imperfect defenses p. 192

mitigating circumstances p. 192
motive p. 193
unprovoked attack p. 194
imminent danger p. 194
necessity p. 194
reasonable force p. 194
initial aggressor p. 194
withdrawal exception p. 194
serious (grievous) bodily injury
    p. 196

present danger p. 205
retreat rule p. 214
stand-your-ground rule p. 214
castle exception p. 214
curtilage p. 219
choice-of-evils defense p. 223
general principle of necessity p. 223
voluntary consent p. 230
knowing consent p. 230
authorized consent p. 230

SUGGESTED READINGS

 Go to the Criminal Law 8e CD for Suggested Readings for this chapter.

THE COMPANION WEB SITE
FOR *CRIMINAL LAW,* EIGHTH EDITION

http://cj.wadsworth.com/samaha/crim_law8e

 Supplement your review of this chapter by going to the companion Web site to take one of the Tutorial Quizzes, use the flash cards to test your knowledge of the elements of various crimes and defenses, and check out the many other study aids you'll find there. You'll find valuable data and resources at your fingertips to help you study for that big exam or write that important paper.

8   Defenses to Criminal Liability: Excuses

Chapter Main Points

- Defendants who plead excuses admit what they did was wrong but claim they weren't responsible.
- The excuse of insanity is rarely pleaded, is rarely successful, and almost always leads to confinement.
- The defense of insanity stands for the proposition that we can't blame people who aren't responsible because of mental diseases or defects that impair their reason or will.
- Insanity is not the equivalent of mental disease or defect.
- The right-wrong test focuses on defects in reason.
- The product-of-mental illness test focuses on criminal acts resulting from mental disease.
- The irresistible impulse test focuses on defects in self-control.
- The substantial capacity test focuses on reason *and* self-control.
- Insanity is an affirmative defense in which the actual burden of proof varies, depending on the jurisdiction.
- Diminished capacity may reduce the degree of a crime, because it impairs the capacity to form specific intent.
- Age can excuse criminal liability; it can also increase it.
- Duress can be an excuse when individuals are threatened and forced to commit a crime or be killed.
- Voluntary intoxication is not an excuse; involuntary intoxication is.
- Entrapment—when law enforcement officers actively persuade individuals to commit crimes they otherwise wouldn't commit—is an excuse.

Was He Too Young to Commit Burglary?

In July 1990, K.R.L., who was then 8 years and 2 months old, was playing with a friend behind a business building in Sequim. Catherine Alder, who lived near the business, heard the boys playing, and she instructed them to leave because she believed the area was dangerous. Alder said that K.R.L.'s response was belligerent, the child indicating that he would leave "in a minute." Losing patience with the boys, Alder said, "No, not in a minute, now, get out of there now." The boys then ran off. Three days later, during daylight hours, K.R.L. entered Alder's home without her permission. He proceeded to pull a live goldfish from her fishbowl, chopped it into several pieces with a steak knife, and "smeared it all over the counter." He then went into Alder's bathroom and clamped a "plugged in" hair curling iron onto a towel. ◆

Defendants who plead justification accept responsibility for their actions but claim that under the circumstances (necessity and consent) they were right. Defendants who plead excuse admit what they did was wrong but claim that under the circumstances they weren't responsible for what they did. These "circumstances" raise a reasonable doubt about either the *actus reus* (the act wasn't voluntary) or the *mens rea* (they couldn't form criminal intent). These circumstances also stem from either something **abnormal** about the person claiming the defense (mental disease or defect and age) or about the situation the person is in (duress, intoxication, entrapment, or a syndrome). Let's be clear about what we mean by "abnormal." The criminal law presumes defendants are adults with normal intelligence and healthy minds; defendants have to overcome that presumption by proof of the abnormality.

The best-known excuse is insanity, but there's a long list of others. We'll look first at the excuses based on something abnormal about defendants: insanity, diminished capacity, and age. Then, we'll look at excuses based on situations defendants find themselves in: duress, intoxication, entrapment, and the so-called syndrome defenses.

Two cautions: First, this business of classifying excuses according to abnormal circumstances about defendants and the situations they find themselves in isn't as logical as it might sound. Here are a few wise words from Professor Markus Dubber (2002), "Excuses . . . are a disparate lot . . . in criminal law, and are best treated one at a time" (251). That's what we'll do here. So, although the classification I've followed should help you begin to make sense of the excuses, you'll still have to do as Professor Dubber says and learn them one at a time. Second, excuses in criminal law (as in ordinary life) aren't popular. So, although the list of excuses is long, in practice most defendants fail when they try to escape criminal liability by pleading them as a defense.

INSANITY

Thanks to CNN, in 1994, the whole world knew that Lorena Bobbitt walked out of a mental hospital after she successfully pleaded "not guilty by reason of insanity" for cutting off her husband's penis with a kitchen knife. By contrast, no one knew that John Smith, who drove a Greyhound bus out of the New York City Port Authority bus terminal in 1980, crashed, and was acquitted "by reason of insanity," is still locked up in the Manhattan Psychiatric Center on Ward's Island in New York City. CNN may have made Lorena Bobbitt a household word throughout the world whereas no one but the lawyers, doctors, and hospital staff may know of John Smith, but Smith's case is hands-down the more typical insanity defense case; Bobbitt's is extremely rare (Sherman 1994, 24).

The insanity defense attracts a lot of public and scholarly attention. But the public grossly misunderstands the way the defense works. Keep in mind that **insanity** is a legal concept, not a medical term. What psychiatry calls mental illness may or may not be legal insanity. Mental disease is legal insanity only when the disease affects a person's reason and/or will. Insanity excuses criminal liability only when it seriously damages the person's capacity to act and/or reason and understand. This means that if defendants were so mentally diseased they couldn't form a criminal intent and/or control their actions, then we can't blame them for what they did. Psychiatrists testify in courts to help juries decide whether defendants are legally insane, not to prove defendants are mentally ill. The verdict "guilty but mentally ill" makes this point clear. In this verdict, used in some states, juries can find that defendants weren't insane but were mentally ill when they committed crimes. These defendants receive criminal sentences and go to prison, where they're treated while they're punished.

Contrary to widespread belief, few defendants plead the insanity defense (only a few thousand a year. The few who do plead insanity—nearly all murderers sentenced either to death or life without parole—hardly ever succeed. According to a 1991 eight-state study funded by the National Institute of Mental Health (American Psychiatric Association 2003):

> The insanity defense was used in less than one percent of the cases in a representative sampling of cases before those states' county courts. The study showed that only 26 percent of those insanity pleas were argued successfully. Most studies show that in approximately 80 percent of the cases where a defendant is acquitted on a "not guilty by reason of insanity" finding, it is because the prosecution and defense have agreed on the appropriateness of the plea before trial. That agreement occurred because both the defense and prosecution agreed that the defendant was mentally ill and met the jurisdiction's test for insanity.

The few who succeed don't go free. In a noncriminal proceeding, called **civil commitment,** courts have to decide if defendants who were insane when they committed their crimes are still insane. If they are—and they almost always are—they're locked up in maximum-security prisons called hospitals. And like John Smith, and unlike Lorena Bobbitt, they stay there for a long time—until they're no longer "mentally ill and dangerous"—often for the rest of their lives.

It might be used only rarely, but the insanity defense stands for the important proposition (which we have referred to often) that we can only blame people who are responsible. For those who are not responsible, retribution is out of order. But, what tools do we have for determining who is genuinely responsible? There are four insanity tests:

1. Right-wrong test
2. Product (of mental illness) test
3. Right-wrong-supplemented-by-irresistible-impulse test
4. Substantial capacity test

All four tests look at defendants' mental capacity, but they differ in what they're looking for. The right-wrong test focuses on reason—specifically, on the capacity to tell right from wrong. Psychologists call reason **cognition.** The other two tests focus on both reason and will (defendants' power to control their actions). Psychologists call will **volition;** most people call it "willpower."

The Right-Wrong Test

The **right-wrong test** (also known as the *M'Naghten* **rule**) focuses on **reason**—the capacity to distinguish right from wrong. In 1843, Daniel M'Naghten suffered the paranoid delusion that the prime minister, Sir Robert Peel, had masterminded a conspiracy to kill him. M'Naghten shot at Peel in a delusion of self-defense but killed Peel's secretary, Edward Drummond, by mistake. Following his trial for murder, the jury returned a verdict of "not guilty by reason of insanity." On appeal, in *M'Naghten's Case* (1843) England's highest court, the House of Lords, created the two-pronged right-wrong test, or the M'Naghten rule of insanity. The test requires proof of two elements:

1. The defendant had a mental disease or defect at the time of the crime, and
2. The disease or defect caused the defendant not to know either
   a. The nature and the quality of his or her actions, or
   b. That what he or she was doing is wrong.

Several terms in the test need defining. **Mental disease** means psychosis, like the paranoia from which M'Naghten suffered, and schizophrenia. It doesn't include

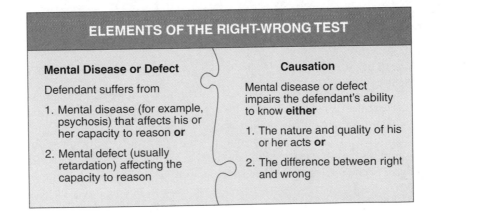

ELEMENTS OF THE RIGHT-WRONG TEST

Mental Disease or Defect

Defendant suffers from

1. Mental disease (for example, psychosis) that affects his or her capacity to reason **or**
2. Mental defect (usually retardation) affecting the capacity to reason

Causation

Mental disease or defect impairs the defendant's ability to know **either**

1. The nature and quality of his or her acts **or**
2. The difference between right and wrong

personality disorders like psychopathic and sociopathic personalities that lead to criminal or antisocial conduct. **Mental defect** refers to mental retardation severe enough to make it impossible to know what you're doing, or to know that it's wrong. In most states, *know* means simple awareness: cognition. Some states require more— that defendants understand or appreciate (grasp the true significance of) their actions. Some states don't define the term, leaving juries to define it by applying it to the facts of specific cases. The **nature and quality of the act** means you don't know what you're doing (American Law Institute 1985 1:2, 174–176). (To use an old law school example, "If a man believes he's squeezing lemons when in fact he's strangling his wife," he doesn't know the nature and quality of his act.)

The meaning of **wrong** has created problems. Some states require that defendants didn't know their conduct was legally wrong; others say it means morally wrong. In *People v. Schmidt* (1915), Schmidt confessed to killing Anna Aumuller by slitting her throat. He pleaded insanity, telling physicians

> who examined him that he had heard the voice of God calling upon him to kill the woman as a sacrifice and atonement. He confessed to a life of unspeakable excesses and hideous crimes, broken, he said, by spells of religious ecstacy and exaltation. In one of these moments, believing himself, he tells us, in the visible presence of God, he committed this fearful crime. (325)

The trial judge instructed the jury that Schmidt had to know that slitting Aumuller's throat was *legally* wrong. The New York Court of Appeals disagreed: "We are unable to accept the view that the word 'wrong'... is to receive such a narrow construction." The court recommended this as a suitable instruction:

> [K]nowledge of the nature and quality of the act has reference to its physical nature and quality, and that knowledge that it is wrong refers to its moral side; that to know that the act is wrong, the defendant must know that it is "contrary to law, and contrary to the accepted standards of morality, and then he added... that it must be known to be contrary to the laws of God and man. (336)

The court applied the right-wrong test in *Serritt v. State* (2003).

Did He Have the Mental Capacity to Distinguish Between Right and Wrong?

Serritt v. State
WL 21182608 (Ga.App. 2003)

Charles Bradley Serritt (Defendant) was found guilty, but mentally ill, in the trial court, of attempting to enter an auto, four counts of entering an auto, two counts of burglary, one count of financial transaction card theft, and two counts of theft by taking. Defendant appealed. The Court of Appeals affirmed.

BARNES, J.

FACTS

The State indicted Serritt on ten counts: attempting to enter an auto; four counts of entering an auto; two counts of burglary; one count of financial transaction card theft; and two counts of theft by taking. Several church employees testified that Serritt attempted to break the window of a car in their parking lot with a rubber mallet, then used the mallet handle to pry open the window of a truck and got inside. When one of the witnesses began to walk toward the truck, Serritt got out and began walking away. All of the witnesses agreed that Serritt did not seem to care if he got caught, that he seemed to be "in his own world" as if nothing mattered anymore.

The director of treatment services at a north Georgia mental health center testified that she was home in bed sick one afternoon when she looked up and saw Serritt standing in her bedroom with a beer in his hand. She put her glasses on and asked him what he was doing; when he did not respond, she jumped out of bed and told him to move down the hall, down the stairs, and out of the house. He obeyed, and when they got to the living room, the witness saw that Serritt had kicked in the screen on the door and crawled through. She told him to unlatch the door and leave, and he did, driving away in her Lincoln Town Car. The witness discovered that Serritt had stolen her wallet with her credit cards, a picture of herself, and a box of coins.

The witness, who was qualified as an expert due to her extensive clinical experience with the mentally ill, testified that Serritt appeared to be impaired from drinking alcohol but did not appear to be delusional. Delusional people, she said, do not respond to immediate direction and do not possess the capability to go through a house in a short time and look through things in a methodical, well-thought-out way as Serritt had. She testified that he had a blunted affect, consistent with substance abuse, depression, or psychiatric medication, but evinced no symptoms of psychosis. She determined later that he had been admitted to two programs she had supervised, a detoxification and crisis stabilization program and a partial hospitalization program, although she did not remember him and had not treated him individually.

A Chattanooga patrol officer testified that he was dispatched to an accident at a hotel parking deck, where he found Serritt in the seat of a Lincoln Town Car. Serritt appeared to be extremely intoxicated, although his blood alcohol level was below the limit, and had no valid I.D., although he offered several items as identification, such as the picture I.D. of a child and a credit card. He said the car belonged to him, but could not confirm the owner's name after the police discovered who the owner was. The officer testified that Serritt displayed no delusional behavior, appeared to know right from wrong, and knew who the officer was and what he was doing. A Dalton police detective testified that the Lincoln Town Car that Serritt was driving contained silver, wine, and a check taken from a household that had been burglarized while the owner was out of town. That homeowner testified in more detail about other items missing from his house in addition to the silver, wine, and check.

Finally, the director of forensic services at Northwest Georgia Regional Hospital testified that he examined Serritt in response to a court order to evaluate his competency to stand trial and degree of criminal responsibility. In his opinion Serritt would have no difficulty assisting his attorney at trial, understanding the charges and basic courtroom procedures, and controlling his behavior in court. Even though he was mentally ill, diagnosed with major depression with psychotic features, Serritt did not meet the criteria to be found not responsible for his actions, because he was . . . able to distinguish right from wrong. . . . Serritt's actions indicated he was capable of organized thinking, and he admitted that he did not pay any attention to right or wrong when he began drinking.

Before the jury heard evidence in this case, the trial court charged them regarding Serritt's insanity defense, noting that [the state's insanity statute] provides:

> A person shall not be found guilty of a crime if, at the time of the act, omission, or negligence constituting the crime, the person did not have mental capacity to distinguish between right and wrong in relation to such act, omission, or negligence.

The court then further charged them . . . regarding the mental status of guilty but mentally ill under [the statute], directing the jury that

> The term mentally ill means having a disorder of thought or mood which significantly impairs judgment, behavior, capacity to recognize reality, or ability to cope with the ordinary demands of life. The term mentally ill does not include a mental state shown only by repeated unlawful or antisocial conduct.

The trial court recharged the jury on those definitions before the testimony of the doctor who examined Serritt for the State.

Serritt's sister testified for the defense, describing her brother's long history of mental problems following his return from serving in the Army in Vietnam. He had tried to return to college and worked at various jobs but rarely stayed long, and until 1994 he would not leave the house. He had lived with his mother since his father died in 1984 and received disability payments from Social Security and the Veteran's Administration. He talked to voices and had flashbacks to the war, and his sister testified that he had stayed at the VA hospital several times and she had him involuntarily committed once.

Three employees from the Whitfield County clerk's office testified that, for a period of six to eight weeks before his arrest on these charges, Serritt came in several times a week, sometimes several times a day, seeking copies of certain records. He always sought the exact same records and never seemed to understand that he was getting the same thing every time. One of the clerks testified that she just made multiple copies of the records ahead of time and handed him a new copy each time he asked, at least 20 times and maybe as many as 50 times. Serritt would become agitated or frustrated if he did not think he was getting what he wanted but never looked anyone in the eyes while he was communicating. He was always in the same mode, "totally out of it."

OPINION

Insanity is an affirmative defense which the defendant must prove by a preponderance of the evidence. The appropriate standard of appellate review of the sufficiency of the evidence with regard to a jury's finding of sanity in a criminal case is whether after reviewing the evidence in the light most favorable to the state, a rational trier of fact could have found that the defendant failed to prove by a preponderance of the evidence that he was insane at the time of the crime. Applying that standard to this case, the evidence is clearly sufficient to support the jury's finding that Serritt was sane when he committed the offenses.

Judgment AFFIRMED.

Questions

1. State the right-wrong test as the Georgia statute defines it.

2. List all the facts supporting the defense of insanity as Georgia defines it.

3. List all the facts supporting the state's argument that Serritt was sane according to the Georgia statute.

4. Now, apply the right-wrong test to the facts of the case as if *you* were the judge. Make sure that you refer to both the meaning of "disease" and "wrong" as they are used in the case and in the text preceding the excerpt.

5. If you were defining the right-wrong test, how would you define "disease" and "wrong"? Would Serritt be guilty under your test? Explain your answer.

The Product-of-Mental-Illness Test

The right-wrong test has generated much argument. One line of criticism began in the 1950s when many social reformers thought that Freudian psychology could cure individual and social "diseases." A widely cited case from that era, *Durham v. U.S.* (1954), reflects the influence of Freud. According to the court:

> The science of psychiatry now recognizes that a man is an integrated personality and that reason, which is only one element in that personality, is not the sole determinant of his conduct. The right-wrong test, which considers knowledge or reason alone, is therefore an inadequate guide to mental responsibility for criminal behavior. (871)

Based on these insights, the court replaced the right-wrong test with the **product test** of insanity, also known as the ***Durham*** **rule.** According to this "new" test, acts that are the products of mental disease or defect excuse criminal liability. So, with this test, the court stretched the concept of insanity beyond the purely intellectual knowledge examined by the right-wrong test into deeper areas of cognition and will. However, only New Hampshire (where the test originated in 1871), the federal court of appeals for the District of Columbia (which decided *Durham*), and Maine ever adopted the product test. (The federal court and Maine later abandoned the test, leaving it in effect only in New Hampshire.)

One reason the product test never took hold is because critics say it misses the point of mental illness in the defense of insanity. They maintain that the product test makes insanity the equivalent of mental illness. But, in the eyes of the criminal law defense, mental illness is only a *tool* to help juries decide whether the illness has impaired *mens rea* enough to relieve persons of criminal responsibility. Two articulate defenders of the right-wrong test (Livermore and Meehl 1967) put their criticism of the product test this way:

It is always necessary to start any discussion of *M'Naghten* by stressing that the case does not state a test of psychosis or mental illness. Rather, it lists conditions under which those who are mentally diseased will be relieved from criminal responsibility. Thus, criticism of *M'Naghten* based on the proposition that the case is premised on an outdated view of mental disease is inappropriate. The case can only be criticized justly if it is based on an outdated view of the mental conditions that ought to preclude application of criminal sanction. (800)

The Irresistible Impulse Test

Just because you *know* something is wrong (even if you fully appreciate its wrongfulness) doesn't mean you can stop yourself from doing it. I used to be fat. I knew and fully appreciated the wrongfulness of overeating. I can remember so many times knowing those french fries were really bad for me, but I just couldn't stop myself from shoving them in. According to the criticism, we can neither blame nor deter people who because of a mental disease or defect lose their self-control and can't bring their actions into line with what the law requires.

Several jurisdictions have responded to the criticism that the insanity defense should look at will as well as reason by supplementing the right-wrong test with what we call the **irresistible impulse test.** According to the test, even if defendants know what they're doing and know it's wrong, they can qualify for a verdict of not guilty by reason of insanity *if* they suffer from a mental disease that damages their volition (willpower). In 1877, the court in *Parsons v. State* (1877) spelled out the application of the right-wrong test with its irresistible impulse supplement:

1. At the time of the crime was the defendant afflicted with "a disease of the mind"?

2. If so, did the defendant know right from wrong with respect to the act charged? If not, the law excuses the defendant.

3. If the defendant did have such knowledge, the law will still excuse the defendant if two conditions concur:
   a. If the mental disease caused the defendant to so far lose the power to choose between right and wrong and to avoid doing the alleged act that the disease destroyed the defendant's free will, and
   b. if the mental disease was the sole cause of the act.

Some critics say the irresistible impulse supplement doesn't go far enough. First, they argue that it should include not just sudden impulses but also conduct "characterized by brooding and reflection." Second, they claim the irresistible requirement implies defendants have to lack total control over their actions. In practice, however,

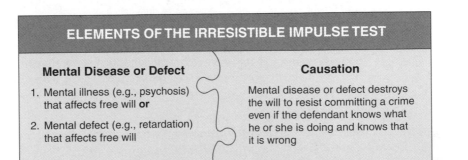

ELEMENTS OF THE IRRESISTIBLE IMPULSE TEST

Mental Disease or Defect	Causation
1. Mental illness (e.g., psychosis) that affects free will **or** 2. Mental defect (e.g., retardation) that affects free will	Mental disease or defect destroys the will to resist committing a crime even if the defendant knows what he or she is doing and knows that it is wrong

juries do acquit defendants who have some control; rarely do juries demand an utter lack of control.

But more critics say the test goes *too* far. By allowing people who lack self-control to escape punishment, the test cripples both retribution and deterrence. They point to the high-profile case of John Hinckley, Jr., acquitted because the jury found him insane when he attempted to assassinate President Ronald Reagan to get actress Jodie Foster's attention. Shortly after Hinckley's trial, Harvard criminal law professor Charles Nesson (1982) wrote:

> To many Mr. Hinckley seems like a kid who had a rough life and who lacked the moral fiber to deal with it. This is not to deny that Mr. Hinckley is crazy but to recognize that there is a capacity for craziness in all of us. Lots of people have tough lives, many tougher than Mr. Hinckley's, and manage to cope. The Hinckley verdict let those people down. For anyone who experiences life as a struggle to act responsibly in the face of various temptations to let go, the Hinckley verdict is demoralizing, an example of someone who let himself go and who has been exonerated because of it. (29)

Since the attempted murder of former President Reagan in 1981, several jurisdictions have abolished the irresistible impulse defense on the ground that juries can't distinguish between irresistible impulses beyond the power to control and those that aren't. The federal statute (U.S. Code 2003) abolishing the irresistible impulse test in federal cases provides as follows:

> It is an affirmative defense to a prosecution under any Federal statute that, at the time of the commission of the acts constituting the offense, the defendant, as a result of a severe mental disease or defect, was unable to appreciate the nature and quality or the wrongfulness of his acts. Mental disease or defect does not otherwise constitute a defense.

The Substantial Capacity Test

The right-wrong test, either supplemented by the irresistible impulse test or not, was the rule in most states until the 1960s, after which the **substantial capacity test** became the majority rule. The substantial capacity test is supposed to remove the objections to both the right-wrong test and its irresistible impulse supplement, while preserving the legal nature of both tests. It emphasizes both the qualities in insanity that affect culpability: reason and will (Schlopp 1988).

As the name of the test indicates, defendants have to lack *substantial*, not *complete*, mental capacity. Both the right-wrong and irresistible impulse tests are ambiguous on this point, leading some courts to conclude they require total lack of knowledge and/or control. So, people who can *modestly* tell right from wrong and/or who have only a *feeble* will to resist are insane. Most substantial capacity test states follow the *Model Penal Code*'s (American Law Institute 1985 [3]) definition of substantial capacity:

> A person is not responsible for criminal conduct if at the time of such conduct as a result of mental disease or defect he lacks substantial capacity either to appreciate the criminality [wrongfulness] of his conduct or to conform his conduct to the requirements of law. (163)

The use of "appreciate" instead of "know" makes clear that intellectual awareness isn't enough to create culpability; affective or emotional components of understanding are required. The phrase "conform his conduct" removes the requirement of a

ELEMENTS OF SUBSTANTIAL CAPACITY TEST

Mental Disease or Defect

Defendant suffers from

1. Mental disease or defect that

2. *Substantially* affects his or her mental *capacity*

Reason or Will

Mental disease or defect causes the defendant to lack the substantial capacity to **either**

1. Appreciate the wrongfulness of his or her conduct **or**

2. Conform his or her conduct to obey the law

"sudden" lack of control. In other words, the code provision eliminates the suggestion that losing control means losing it on the spur of the moment, as the irresistible impulse test can be read to mean. The code's definition of "mental disease or defect" excludes psychopathic personalities, habitual criminals, and antisocial personalities from the defense. The Connecticut Supreme Court reviewed the application of the substantial capacity test to the facts of *State v. Quinet* (2000).

CASE | *Did He Lack "Substantial Capacity" of Reason and Will?*

State v. Quinet
752 A.2d 490 (Conn. 2000)

Corey Quinet was convicted of attempted murder and attempted sexual assault after a bench trial in the Superior Court, Judicial District of Fairfield. He was sentenced to a total effective term of imprisonment of forty years, suspended after twenty years, and five years probation. He appealed. On transfer from the Appellate Court, the Supreme Court affirmed.

PALMER, J.

FACTS

After a trial to the court, the defendant, Corey Quinet, was convicted of two counts of attempted murder and one count of attempted sexual assault in the first degree. On appeal, the defendant claims that the trial court improperly...rejected his affirmative defense of insanity under General Statutes § 53a-13. General Statutes § 53a-3 provides in relevant part:

(a) In any prosecution for an offense, it shall be an affirmative defense that the defendant, at the time he committed the proscribed act or acts, lacked substan-

tial capacity, as a result of mental disease or defect, either to appreciate the wrongfulness of his conduct or to control his conduct within the requirements of the law....

General Statutes § 53a-12 (b) provides that a defendant has the burden of establishing an affirmative defense by a preponderance of the evidence.

On Friday, April 29, 1994, the defendant, then a 19-year-old 1993 graduate of the Hopkins School (Hopkins) in New Haven (a private, coeducational school), conceived a plan to rape and murder twenty seven of his former female classmates and, thereafter, to flee to Australia, where he intended to commit suicide. One of these former classmates, hereinafter referred to as the victim, was a seventeen year old senior at Hopkins with whom the defendant was acquainted (defendant and the victim had worked on the school newspaper together and had attended several of the same classes) and who once had rejected the defendant's request for a date. The defendant decided that she would be his first victim.

On Saturday, April 30, 1994, the defendant purchased a number of items that he intended to use to rape, torture and murder the victim, including a knife, a glue gun, duct tape, rope, and metal and bamboo skewers. On Monday,

May 2, the defendant rented three films containing graphic violence to "get [himself] in the mood" to rape and kill the victim that day. These videotapes are entitled "Faces of Death," "Death Faces," and "Slaughter High."

At approximately 5 P.M. on May 2, the defendant drove to the vicinity of the victim's home and observed the residence from a distance. The defendant did not approach the home immediately because he believed that a car parked in the driveway belonged to the victim's brother and, in addition, because he was not certain that the victim was inside. At about 7:15 P.M., the defendant drove to a nearby pay telephone and called the victim to determine whether she was home. Upon learning that the victim was there, the defendant drove back to the victim's home, walked up to the front door and rang the doorbell. The victim's father answered the door, and the defendant explained that his car had broken down and asked the victim's father if he could use a telephone to call for assistance. The victim's father agreed and, when the defendant entered the house, she recognized him as a former classmate who had graduated from Hopkins the previous year.

The defendant then pretended to use the telephone to call for assistance. The victim's father offered the defendant some food and a drink, which the defendant accepted. The defendant and the victim then engaged in conversation.

The defendant had been at the victim's home for approximately one-half hour when he suddenly pulled out a gun and placed it against the victim's head. It subsequently was determined that the weapon was an unloaded pellet gun. The defendant ordered the victim to lie on the floor and, when the victim's father walked into the room, demanded that he do the same. Both the victim and her father complied with the defendant's command. As the defendant was removing some duct tape from a duffel bag that he had brought with him into the victim's home, the victim's father jumped up from the floor, wrested the gun from the defendant and subdued him. The victim's father then ordered the defendant to lie facedown on the floor and the defendant complied. The defendant remained in that position, motionless and silent, until the police arrived.*

---

*The duffel bag also contained some torn sheets, two packages of metal skewers, two packages of bamboo skewers, moisturizing cream, a glue gun, two glue sticks, two rolls of duct tape, lubricating lotion, rope and a knife with an eight-inch blade. The defendant told the police that he had purchased the items and had brought them with him to the victim's home to use in the rape, torture and murder of the victim. In particular, the defendant stated that he intended to use the knife, rather than a gun, to kill the victim in order to inflict more pain. The defendant further explained that, after raping the victim, he had planned to insert the skewers and the glue into the victim's vagina to cause her additional pain and suffering.

After the police had advised the defendant of his rights, he readily admitted that his purpose in going to the victim's home was to torture, rape and kill her. He further stated that he intended to kill the victim's father and her brother, who also were home at the time, because they would have been able to identify the defendant as the victim's assailant. The defendant also confessed that he had planned to rape and murder twenty-six other female students at Hopkins. Additional facts will be set forth as necessary.

The defendant was charged with three counts of attempted murder for allegedly attempting to kill the victim, her father and her brother, two counts of kidnapping in the first degree in violation of General Statutes § 53a-92 (a)(2), for allegedly abducting the victim and her father and restraining them with the intent to sexually assault the victim, and one count of attempted sexual assault in the first degree for allegedly attempting to compel the victim to engage in sexual intercourse with him by the use or threat of use of force. The defendant, who elected to be tried by the court, raised the affirmative defense of insanity. At the conclusion of the trial, the court rejected the defendant's insanity defense and found him guilty of two counts of attempted murder and one count of attempted sexual assault in the first degree. The trial court rendered judgment sentencing the defendant to a total effective term of imprisonment of forty years, suspended after twenty years, and five years probation. This appeal followed.

OPINION

The defendant first contends that the evidence he adduced at trial established, as a matter of law, that, due to a mental disease or defect, he lacked substantial capacity to control his conduct within the requirements of the law. We reject the defendant's claim.

The following additional facts are relevant to our resolution of this issue. At trial, the defendant did not deny committing the acts alleged by the state. He claimed, rather, that, as a result of his mental disease or defect, he was unable to conform his conduct to the requirements of the law when he engaged in the proscribed conduct. In support of his affirmative defense, the defendant presented the testimony of Madelene Baranoski, a clinical psychologist, and Paul Amble, a psychiatrist. The defendant also adduced evidence tending to establish that he had suffered from a progressively more serious mental illness that culminated in his unsuccessful effort to rape and kill the victim on May 2, 1994.

Baranoski conducted a psychological evaluation of the defendant that consisted of a number of psychological tests, a clinical interview and a review of the defendant's psychiatric history. On the basis of her inquiry into the defendant's mental condition on May 2, 1994, Baranoski opined that the defendant was suffering from paranoid schizophrenia at that time. Baranoski also stated that the behavior of a person suffering from that mental illness "would be more likely to be impulsive when the disease is not under good control either by medication or close psychiatric observation."

Baranoski further opined that the defendant "was having difficulty with rational thought" and had "an impairment of judgment and . . . difficulty controlling his behavior" between April 30 and May 2, 1994. According to Baranoski, the defendant also had frequent delusions that an external entity was controlling his mind, another common trait of individuals suffering from paranoid schizophrenia. Among other examples of the defendant's delusional ideation, Baranoski testified that the defendant, during a psychiatric hospitalization in the fall of 1993, had stated that an "evil entity" was "controlling his mind by putting in . . . rape fantasies. . . ." Finally, Baranoski stated that the ability to plan and organize also was a recognized characteristic associated with paranoid schizophrenia.

Amble conducted a psychiatric examination of the defendant and, in addition, reviewed his mental health history and the results of the psychological tests that Baranoski had administered to the defendant. Amble concluded that the defendant suffered from a "psychotic disorder not otherwise specified," a mental illness that, according to Amble, is characterized by bizarre delusions, a separation from reality and a deterioration in functioning. Amble testified that, although he could not make a definitive diagnosis of paranoid schizophrenia because, in his view, the defendant's disorder was continuing to evolve, his evaluation of the defendant did "seem to strongly point towards . . . chronic paranoid schizophrenia." Amble also testified that the defendant suffered from sexual sadism and, further, that he did not believe that the defendant was malingering. Finally, Amble opined that from April 29 through May 2, 1994, the defendant lacked the ability to control his behavior and that the defendant believed that he was under the influence of an outside force.

The defendant also adduced evidence regarding his treatment and hospitalization for mental problems during the six month period prior to May 2, 1994. Specifically, the defendant, while attending Vassar College (Vassar) in Poughkeepsie, New York, in 1993, after graduating from Hopkins, became obsessed with a young woman that he had met at Vassar. The defendant, distraught because the woman refused his request for a date, decided to fly to Belgium to commit suicide. The defendant purchased an airline ticket to Belgium and boarded the plane, but when the flight was canceled due to a mechanical problem, he contacted his therapist at Vassar and returned to Poughkeepsie. Several days later, however, the woman again rejected the defendant's overture, and the defendant devised a plan to rape and kill her. The defendant had invited the young woman to a campus classroom, ostensibly to show her a computer program. She arrived, accompanied by a friend, and observed that the defendant was talking to himself and appeared to be confused. The defendant told her that he had a knife in his bag with which he planned to injure her but that he then decided to use on himself. Campus and local police were called, and the defendant was transported and involuntarily committed to St. Francis Hospital (St. Francis) in Poughkeepsie on November 20, 1993. Upon his admission to the hospital, he was diagnosed with major depression and borderline personality disorder.

The defendant was discharged from St. Francis on November 24, 1993, and, on that very same day, was admitted to Silver Hill Hospital (Silver Hill) in New Canaan. The defendant remained there as an inpatient until December 20, when he was discharged to outpatient care. He was readmitted to Silver Hill as an inpatient on December 29, however, because he could not control his suicidal ideation. The defendant was discharged from Silver Hill on January 24, 1994, but, because he still was unable to control his suicidal impulses, he was admitted to Four Winds Hospital (Four Winds) in Katonah, New York, on January 28, where he remained until his discharge on February 22. The defendant continued to receive treatment at Four Winds on an outpatient basis until March 11, when he entered an outpatient program at Greenwich Hospital. The defendant remained a participant in that program until his arrest on May 2, 1994.

In rebuttal to the defendant's insanity defense, the state relied primarily on its cross-examination of the defendant's two experts, and on the conduct and statements of the defendant before, during and after the events of May 2, 1994. The state also relied on the notes and records of the various institutions at which the defendant had received treatment or counseling, and on the observations of several persons familiar with the defendant's activities and conduct immediately prior to May 2. Finally, the state emphasized the uncontroverted fact that many of the mental health professionals who had examined the defendant offered differing diagnoses of the defendant's psychiatric condition, including the defendant's own experts, Baranoski and Amble.

In particular, Baranoski acknowledged on cross-examination that she did not have enough information to render an opinion as to whether the defendant was unable to control his conduct at any time between April 29 and May 2, 1994. Baranoski also conceded that her diagnosis of the defendant differed from those of a number of other mental health professionals, including Amble, and, further, that she disagreed with some of those diagnoses. Finally, Baranoski noted that the defendant had told her that, upon executing his plan to kill twenty-seven people, he would become famous.

Amble stated on cross-examination that he had not previously testified concerning the sanity of a person accused of a crime. Amble further stated that he was not board certified in psychiatry, that, as of the time of trial, he had been engaged in the practice of forensic psychiatry only for about two years, and that he never had treated the defendant. Amble also conceded that he was the only mental health professional to have diagnosed the defendant as suffering from sexual sadism, and that the other examining psychiatrists and psychologists, including Baranoski, had offered diagnoses of the defendant that differed from his own.

In addition, Amble acknowledged that the defendant had felt the need to rent several violent films to "get in the mood" to rape and kill the victim. Amble also acknowledged that the defendant initially had not planned to kill the victim's father and brother, but later decided to do so, not out of any compulsion to harm them, but because they would have been able to identify him as the victim's assailant. Amble further acknowledged that the defendant originally had planned to kill only himself, but, thereafter, decided that, if he was going to commit suicide, he would fulfill some of his violent sexual fantasies before doing so.

Moreover, because the defendant had demonstrated a measure of self-control in executing his criminal plan, Amble could not say that the defendant would have been compelled to proceed in accordance with his plan if, for example, there had been a law enforcement officer at the victim's home when the defendant arrived there on the evening of May 2, 1994.

Amble also conceded that the defendant knew that what he was doing was wrong, and that he was not suffering from any hallucinations, or otherwise out of touch with reality, during the several days leading up to and including May 2. Finally, during closing arguments, the prosecutor noted that Amble agreed that a mental disease or illness can result in a lowering of a person's inhibitions without causing that person to lose control over his or her conduct.

The state also relied on other evidence to support its contention that the defendant was able to control his conduct within the requirements of the law. For example, during several interviews with the police immediately after his arrest, the defendant answered all questions calmly and responsively. In one of these interviews, the defendant, when asked why he had attempted to rape and murder the victim, explained that he "had the will to do it" and, further, that he "has a criminal mind." In this interview, the defen-

dant also stated that, if he had been able to execute his plan to rape and murder the victim, he would have felt "fulfilled in a sense. My brain would have been fulfilled because I feel that was what I . . . intended to do. It was intended for me to do that." In addition, the defendant indicated that he had the desire to act out his violent sexual fantasies because, according to him, "nature made my brain a certain way."

Subsequent to his arrest, the defendant also told the police that he had rented the three videotapes on May 2 to "expose [himself] to violence" for the purpose of "get[ting] [himself] in the mood" to assault and kill the victim. The defendant further explained that, in light of his previous struggles with such thoughts, it was "time to cross the line." The defendant indicated that he had become impatient waiting to have his first sexual relationship with a woman, and that he had "tried to cross the line twice and . . . failed," referring to the incidents involving the victim and the young woman at Vassar.

Finally, the state maintained that Amble's opinion regarding the defendant's inability to control himself lacked support in the evidence. In particular, the state noted that the defendant had exhibited self-control by waiting from Friday until Monday to execute his plan to rape and kill the victim and also noted that the defendant, again, demonstrated self-restraint on Monday by postponing his entry into the victim's home for several hours. In addition, the records of the defendant's treatment at Greenwich Hospital during the period preceding the May 2 incident, and those of the Bridgeport correctional center for the period immediately thereafter, contain nothing to indicate that the defendant believed that he was being controlled by an outside force or forces.

Furthermore, the defendant, in responding to a psychological test administered to him while an inpatient at Four Winds in February, 1994, denied that he was possessed by evil spirits; had very peculiar and strange experiences; has something wrong with his mind; often feels as if things are not real; has never seen a vision; and wishes that he were not bothered by thoughts about sex. The state also introduced a letter that had been retrieved from the defendant's laptop computer, in which the defendant, presumably writing to a friend sometime prior to his arrest, indicates that he is doing fine and learning to cope with his problems. The letter, addressed to "Jay," reads as follows:

Oh boy, does it feel good to be out of the hospital and back home where I can take this opportunity to write you. Things are going just fine here, Jay. I got to tell you I feel like a new man. At my last stay in the hospital I really thought over a lot of things. First, it was a big mistake to call [to apologize to the young woman from Vassar]. I knew I would get in trouble for it and I did but what's done is done and we've got to move on. In group therapy I really opened up and talked about my problems. I talked about the loss of my dad and how I really miss him. It was surprising how well I handled it.

The state, moreover, adduced evidence indicating that the defendant had been able to sleep and work normally, and enjoy dinner with his friends, in the days immediately prior to May 2. For example, the defendant, who was employed by the Darien YMCA as a swimming instructor and lifeguard until his arrest, worked there on Sunday, May 1, 1994, without incident....

In light of the totality of the evidence, the court reasonably could have rejected the opinion of Amble, the lone witness to testify that the defendant, due to his mental illness, was unable to control his conduct within the requirements of the law on May 2, 1994.

In addition, the court reasonably could have concluded that, even though the evidence indicated that the defendant was suffering from a mental illness, he nevertheless had the capacity to refrain from acting on his desire to commit rape and murder. In particular, that conclusion is supported by the fact that the defendant felt the need to "get [himself] in the mood" in advance of attempting to commit those crimes by viewing videotapes depicting graphic violence.

That conclusion is further supported by evidence indicating that the defendant decided to act out his sadistic sexual fantasies only after he had resolved to accomplish his primary objective, namely, to kill himself. The assistant state's attorney made the following remarks regarding this point in his rebuttal closing argument:

As [the defendant] thought about [committing suicide] more and planned it more thoroughly, he had the idea that, if he were going to die anyway, he would fulfill some of his sexual fantasies. The sexual fantasies no longer have to be controlled, because he's not going to be around to be apprehended. That doesn't indicate that he lacks... control. It indicates that he doesn't wish to put it off any longer and there's a distinction. His focus is to commit suicide and, as long as he's going to do that, there's no reason to control [himself] any longer with regard to the fantasies.

The defendant also asserts that the trial court, in rejecting his affirmative defense, placed undue emphasis on the fact that the defendant was able carefully to plan his attack on the victim over a period of several days. In particular,

the defendant contends that his ability to plan cannot be viewed as inconsistent with his claim that, due to the particular nature of his mental illness, he could not control his conduct within the requirements of the law. In support of his claim, the defendant relies on the following portion of the trial court's statement explaining its verdict:

The defendant, by the evidence, the court can so find, carefully planned his course of conduct. He made deliberate preparations to seek out [the victim] and other classmates by use of the Hopkins yearbook and handbook, whereby he obtained their addresses and used maps and atlases to determine their locations. He purchased all of the items he felt he needed to carry out his plan. That includes... the rope, the duct tape, skewers, lubricants and, of course, the knife, which he indicated was the intended fatal weapon. "He prepared an escape plan by making a plane reservation for Australia four days hence. He concocted a ruse... to gain entrance to the [the victim's] home. He surveyed that home and made the conscious decision not to immediately go up to the house, because he saw a car and believed that the victim's brother may be at home. He thereupon, called from the railroad station to verify that [the victim] was at home. He proceeded to the house. He entered by deceit and eventually attempted to carry out his planned mayhem, which was thwarted by [the]... actions [of the victim's father].

Surely, one can perceive this type of conduct as unusual and even bizarre, but the court, taking into account the calculated and precise planning and movements of the defendant and his acknowledgement in the statement to the police that he was a criminal and was escaping to Australia and [the trial court quotes], "because I wanted to get far away from here, I would be a criminal and I wanted to be as far away as possible from this country," and also that he would [have killed the victim's father and brother] because, again quot[ing the defendant] "they would have seen me," all suggest... to the court that the defendant appreciated the wrongfulness of his actions and was able to conform his conduct to the requirements of the law even though he suffered from some mental illness.

Of course, an accused who suffers from a mental disease or illness may be able to establish that he was unable to control his conduct according to law even though he had the capacity to plan that illegal conduct. Whether the capacity to plan a course of criminal conduct is probative of an accused's ability to control his behavior within legal requirements necessarily depends upon the specific facts and circumstances of the case, and ultimately is a determination for the trier of fact. Indeed, we previously have indicated that an accused's ability to formulate a plan to kill is relevant to a determination of whether the accused has the capability of conforming his conduct to the requirements of the law. We see no persuasive reason why the court was prohibited from drawing such an inference in this case.

The judgment is AFFIRMED.

Questions

1. State the "substantial capacity" test as the court defines it in the case.

2. List all of the facts relevant to deciding whether Corey Quinet was insane when he committed the crimes.

3. Relying on the facts, did Corey Quinet at the time he committed the crimes, "lack substantial capacity, as a result of mental disease or defect, either to appreciate the wrongfulness of his conduct or to control his conduct within the requirements of the law..."?

 Go to Exercise 8-1 on the Criminal Law 8e CD to learn more about the defense of insanity.

The Burden of Proof

The defense of insanity not only poses definition problems but also gives rise to difficulties in application. States vary as to whom has to prove insanity and how convincingly they have to do so. The Hinckley trial made these questions the subject of heated debate and considerable legislative reform in the 1980s. Federal law required the government to prove Hinckley's sanity beyond a reasonable doubt. So, if Hinckley's lawyers could raise a doubt in jurors' minds about his sanity, the jury had to acquit him. That means that even though the jury thought Hinckley was sane, if they weren't convinced beyond a reasonable doubt that he was, they had to acquit him. And that's just what happened: They thought he was sane but had their doubts, so they acquitted him. In 1984, the federal Comprehensive Crime Control Act (*Federal Criminal Code and Rules* 1988, § 17[b]) shifted the **burden of proof** from the government's having to prove sanity beyond a reasonable doubt to defendants' having to prove they were insane by clear and convincing evidence.

Most states don't follow the federal standard; they call insanity an affirmative defense. As an affirmative defense, sanity and responsibility are presumed. The defense has the burden to offer some evidence of insanity. If they do, the burden shifts to the government to prove sanity. States differ as to how heavy the government's burden to prove sanity is. Some states require proof beyond a reasonable doubt; some require clear and convincing evidence; and some require a preponderance of the evidence. There is a trend in favor of shifting the burden to defendants and making that burden heavier. This is both because Hinckley's trial generated antagonism toward the insanity defense and because of growing hostility toward rules that the public believes coddle criminals (American Law Institute 1985 [3], 226).

DIMINISHED CAPACITY

Some defendants suffer from mental diseases or defects that diminish their mental capacity but not enough to make them insane. Can they claim their **diminished capacity** as a defense of excuse? Most states say no. California (*California Penal Code* 2003,

§25) allowed the defense at one time but abolished it because of public hostility to mental excuses:

> The defense of diminished capacity is hereby abolished. In a criminal action...evidence concerning an accused person's...mental illness, disease, or defect shall not be admissible to show or negate capacity to form the particular purpose, intent, motive, malice aforethought, knowledge, or other mental state required for the commission of the crime charged....Evidence of diminished capacity or of a mental disorder may be considered by the court at the time of sentencing....

The few jurisdictions that allow the defense restrict it, as the state of Washington did in the case of *Dial v. State* (2003). In that case, Greg Dial held his girlfriend and their four children prisoners in an apartment for several days.

> We couldn't leave the room. He was preaching to the kids nonstop. They couldn't go outside and play. He did not want anybody to eat because we needed to fast, and we needed to get the devil out of us. On Monday, Dial took off all his clothes and made the children take off theirs. From Monday to Wednesday, he did not let the others get any regular sleep or eat anything. He did not let D'Orazio use the telephone. (1)

His girlfriend was eventually able to call the police. When the officers got to the apartment they found Dial "cooperative but naked." Several of the children were naked, too. Dial pleaded diminished capacity to the charge of fourth-degree assault. The Washington state trial court refused to instruct the jury on diminished capacity because:

> [O]ur Supreme Court has clearly defined the evidence necessary to support instructing the jury on this statutory defense: "To maintain a diminished capacity defense, a defendant must produce expert testimony demonstrating that a mental disorder, not amounting to insanity, impaired the defendant's ability to form the specific intent to commit the crime charged." Dial did not present expert testimony that he suffered from a disease or defect that impaired his ability to form the mens rea necessary to commit the offense charged. Thus, the trial court did not err in declining to instruct the jury on the statutory defense of diminished capacity. (2)

AGE

A 4-year-old boy stabs a 2-year-old girl in a murderous rage. Is this a criminal assault? What if the boy is 8? 12? 16? 18? At the other end of the age spectrum, what if the person is 85? At how early an age are people liable for criminal conduct? And when, if ever, does someone become too old for criminal responsibility? Age—both old and young—does affect criminal liability, sometimes to excuse it, sometimes to mitigate it, and sometimes even to aggravate it.

Ever since the early days of the English common law, immaturity has excused criminal liability. A rigid but sensible scheme for administering the defense was developed in the sixteenth century. The law divided people into three age groups—under 7 years, 7 to 14 years, and over 14 years. Children under 7 couldn't form criminal intent; that is, there was an **irrebuttable presumption** that they lacked the mental capacity to commit crimes. Between 7 and 14, the presumption became a rebuttable

AGE ◆ 253

presumption; that is, children were presumed to lack the capacity to form criminal intent. The prosecution could rebut the presumption by proving that the individual defendant between 7 and 14 had in fact formed *mens rea*. The presumption of incapacity was strong at age 7 but gradually weakened until it disappeared at age 14. At 14, children were conclusively presumed to have the mental capacity to commit crimes.

About half the states adopted the common-law approach but altered the specific ages within it. Some states excluded serious crimes—usually offenses carrying the death penalty or life imprisonment. States have integrated the age of criminal responsibility with the jurisdiction of the juvenile courts. Some grant the juvenile court exclusive jurisdiction up to a specific age, usually between 15 and 16. Then, from 16 to 18 (although occasionally up to 21), juvenile court judges can transfer, or certify, cases to adult criminal courts. The number of cases certified has increased with the public recognition that youths can and do commit serious felonies (American Law Institute 1985 1:2, 273–279). In *State v. K.R.L.* (1992), the Washington State Supreme Court grappled with the capacity of an 8-year-old boy to form *mens rea*.

CASE	*Was He Too Young to Commit Burglary?*

State v. K.R.L.
840 P.2d 210 (Wash.App. 1992)

K.R.L., an eight-year-old boy, was convicted of residential burglary by the Superior Court, Clallam County, and he appealed. The Court of Appeals reversed.

ALEXANDER, J.

FACTS

In July 1990, K.R.L., who was then 8 years and 2 months old, was playing with a friend behind a business building in Sequim. Catherine Alder, who lived near the business, heard the boys playing and she instructed them to leave because she believed the area was dangerous. Alder said that K.R.L.'s response was belligerent, the child indicating that he would leave "in a minute." Losing patience with the boys, Alder said "no, not in a minute, now, get out of there now." The boys then ran off. Three days later, during daylight hours, K.R.L. entered Alder's home without her permission. He proceeded to pull a live goldfish from her fishbowl, chopped it into several pieces with a steak knife and "smeared it all over the counter. He then went into Alder's bathroom and clamped a "plugged in" hair curling iron onto a towel.

Upon discovering what had taken place, Alder called the Sequim police on the telephone and reported the incident. A Sequim police officer contacted K.R.L.'s mother and told her that he suspected that K.R.L. was the perpe-

trator of the offense against Alder. K.R.L.'s mother confronted the child with the accusation and he admitted to her that he had entered the house. She then took K.R.L. to the Sequim Police Department where the child was advised of his constitutional rights by a Sequim police officer. This took place in the presence of K.R.L.'s mother who indicated that she did not believe "he really understood." K.R.L. told the police officer that he knew it was wrong to enter Alder's home.* K.R.L. was charged in Clallam County Juvenile Court with residential burglary, a class B felony. At trial, considerable testimony was devoted to the issue of whether K.R.L. possessed sufficient capacity to commit that crime. The juvenile court judge heard testimony in that regard from K.R.L.'s mother, Catherine Alder, two school officials, a Sequim policeman who had dealt with K.R.L. on two prior occasions as well as the incident leading to the charge, one of K.R.L.'s neighbors and the neighbor's son.

K.R.L.'s mother, the neighbor, the neighbor's son and the police officer testified to an incident that had occurred

---

*The statement given by K.R.L. to the officer was not offered by the State to prove guilt. Initially, the State took the position that K.R.L. fully understood those rights and that he had made a free and voluntary waiver of rights. Defense counsel objected to the admission of the statements and eventually the State withdrew its offer of the evidence, concluding that the evidence was cumulative in that K.R.L.'s admissions were already in evidence through the testimony of his mother.

several months before the alleged residential burglary. This incident was referred to by the police officer as the "Easter Candy Episode." Their testimony revealed that K.R.L. had taken some Easter candy from a neighbor's house without permission. As a consequence, the Sequim police were called to investigate. K.R.L. responded to a question by the investigating officer, saying to him that he "knew it was wrong and he wouldn't like it if somebody took his candy." The same officer testified to another incident involving K.R.L. This was described as the "joyriding incident," and it occurred prior to the "Easter Candy Episode." It involved K.R.L. riding the bicycles of two neighbor children without having their permission to do so. K.R.L. told the police officer that he "knew it was wrong" to ride the bicycles.

The assistant principal of K.R.L.'s elementary school testified about K.R.L.'s development. He said that K.R.L. was of "very normal" intelligence. K.R.L.'s first grade teacher said that K.R.L. had "some difficulty" in school. He said that he would put K.R.L. in the "lower age academically." K.R.L.'s mother testified at some length about her son and, in particular, about the admissions he made to her regarding his entry into Alder's home. Speaking of that incident, she said that he admitted to her that what he did was wrong "after I beat him with a belt, black and blue." She also said that her son told her "that the Devil was making him do bad things."

The juvenile court rejected the argument of K.R.L.'s counsel that the State had not presented sufficient evidence to show that K.R.L. was capable of committing a crime. It found him guilty, saying:

> From my experience in my eight, nine years on the bench, it's my belief that the so-called juvenile criminal system is a paper tiger and it's not going to be much of a threat to Mr. [K.R.L.], so I don't think that for that reason there is a whole lot to protect him from.

OPINION

There is only one issue—did the trial court err in concluding that K.R.L. had the capacity to commit the crime of residential burglary?* RCW 9A.04.050 speaks to the capability of children to commit crimes and, in pertinent part, provides:

> Children under the age of eight years are incapable of committing crime. Children of eight and under twelve

years of age are presumed to be incapable of committing crime, but this presumption may be removed by proof that they have sufficient capacity to understand the act or neglect, and to know that it was wrong.

This statute applies in juvenile proceedings.

Because K.R.L. was 8 years old at the time he is alleged to have committed residential burglary, he was presumed incapable of committing that offense. The burden was, therefore, on the State to overcome that presumption and that burden could only be removed by evidence that was "clear and convincing." Thus, on review we must determine if there is evidence from which a rational trier of fact could find capacity by clear and convincing evidence.

There are no reported cases in Washington dealing with the capacity of 8-year-old children to commit crimes. That is not too surprising in light of the fact that up to age 8, children are deemed incapable of committing crimes. Two cases involving older children are, however, instructional. In *State v. Q.D.* . . . our Supreme Court looked at a case involving a child who was charged with committing indecent liberties. In concluding that there was clear and convincing circumstantial evidence that the child understood the act of indecent liberties and knew it to be wrong, the court stressed the fact that the child was only 3 months shy of age 12, the age at which capacity is presumed to exist. The court also placed stock in the fact that the defendant used stealth in committing the offense as well as the fact that she had admonished the victim, a 4½-year-old child whom she had been babysitting, not to tell what happened.

In another case, *State v. S.P.*, 746 P.2d 813 (1987), Division One of this court upheld a trial judge's finding that a child, S.P., had sufficient capacity to commit the crime of indecent liberties. In so ruling, the court noted that (1) S.P. was 10 years of age at the time of the alleged acts; (2) S.P. had had sexual contact with two younger boys during the prior year; (3) in treatment for the earlier incident, S.P. acknowledged that sexual behavior was wrong; (4) S.P. was aware that if convicted on the present charge, detention could result; and (5) experts concluded that S.P. had an extensive knowledge of sexual terms and understood the wrongfulness of his conduct toward the victims.

None of the factors that the courts highlighted in the two aforementioned cases is present here. Most notably, K.R.L. is considerably younger than either of the children in the other two cases. In addition, we know almost nothing about what occurred when K.R.L. went into Alder's home. Furthermore, there was no showing that he used "stealth" in entering Alder's home. We know only that he entered her home in daylight hours and that while he was there he committed the act. Neither was there any showing

---

*Residential burglary is defined in RCW 9A.52.025 as: "A person is guilty of residential burglary if, with intent to commit a crime against a person or property therein, the person enters or remains unlawfully in a dwelling. . . ."

that K.R.L. had been previously treated for his behavior, as was the case in *State v. S.P.*

The State emphasizes the fact that K.R.L. appeared to appreciate that what he did at Alder's home and on prior occasions was wrong. When K.R.L. was being beaten "black and blue" by his mother, he undoubtedly came to the realization that what he had done was wrong. We are certain that this conditioned the child, after the fact, to know that what he did was wrong. That is a far different thing than one appreciating the quality of his or her acts at the time the act is being committed.

In arguing that it met its burden, the State placed great reliance on the fact that K.R.L. had exhibited bad conduct several months before during the so-called "Easter Candy" and "Joyriding" incidents. Again, we do not know much about these incidents, but it seems clear that neither of them involved serious misconduct and they shed little light on whether this child understood the elements of the act of burglary or knew that it was wrong. . . .

Here, we have a child of very tender years—only two months over 8 years. While the State made a valiant effort to show prior bad acts on the part of the child, an objective observer would have to conclude that these were examples of behavior not uncommon to many young children. Fur-

thermore, there was no expert testimony in this case from a psychologist or other expert who told the court anything about the ability of K.R.L. to know and appreciate the gravity of his conduct. Although two school officials testified, one of them said K.R.L. was of an age lower than 8, "academically." In short, there is simply not enough here so that we can say that in light of the State's significant burden, there is sufficient evidence to support a finding of capacity.

REVERSED.

Questions

1. Was the trial judge or the supreme court of Washington right in the ruling on the capacity of K.R.L. to form criminal intent? Back up your answer with facts from the case.

2. Did K.R.L. know what he was doing intellectually yet not sufficiently appreciate what he was doing? What facts support this conclusion?

3. Should it matter whether he appreciated what he did as long as he knew what he did? Explain your answer.

Youth doesn't always *excuse* criminal conduct; it can also make it worse. For example, 17-year-old Miguel Muñoz (*People v. Muñoz* 1960) was convicted of possessing a switchblade under a New York City ordinance that prohibited youths under 21 from carrying such knives. Had Muñoz been over 21, what he did wouldn't have been a crime. The Florida Court of Appeals examined the constitutionality of a Dade County, Florida, ordinance that made carrying "jumbo markers" a crime when juveniles carried them but not when adults did so in *D.P. v. State* (1998).

CASE	*Can He Be Punished for Carrying a "Jumbo Marker"?*

D.P. v. State
705 So.2d 593 (Fla.App. 1998)

D.P. was adjudicated a delinquent by the Circuit Court, Dade County and he appealed. The District Court of Appeal affirmed.

COPE, J.

FACTS

Dade County passed a comprehensive anti-graffiti ordinance, which forbids the sale to minors of spray paint cans and broadtipped markers ("jumbo markers"). A broadtipped marker is an indelible felt tip marker having a writing surface of one-half inch or greater. . . . The ordinance does not prohibit the possession of ordinary-sized felt tip markers. The ordinance provides that minors can possess spray paint or jumbo markers on public property only if accompanied by a responsible adult. On private property, the minor must have the consent of the property owner, but need not be accompanied by an adult. It is a misdemeanor for a minor to possess spray paint or a jumbo marker without the required supervision or consent.

D.P. challenges the facial constitutionality of the provisions of the anti-graffiti ordinance that restrict minors' possession of spray paint or jumbo markers. We conclude that the ordinance is constitutional and affirm the adjudication of delinquency.

The ordinance prohibits the sale of spray paint or broad-tipped markers to minors. See id. § 21-30.01(f)(1). The ordinance makes it a misdemeanor to possess spray paint or jumbo markers with intent to make graffiti.

The ordinance then sets forth special provisions pertaining to minors. Subdivision (e)(2) of the ordinance addresses possession of spray paint and jumbo markers by minors on public property, while subdivision (e)(3) addresses possession on private property: (e) Possession of Spray Paint and Markers...

(2) Possession of spray paint and markers by minors on public property prohibited. No person under the age of eighteen (18) shall have in his or her possession any aerosol container or spray paint or broad-tipped indelible marker while on any public property, highway, street, alley or way except in the company of a supervising adult.

(3) Possession of spray paint and markers by minors on private property prohibited without consent of owner. No person under the age of eighteen (18) shall have in his or her possession any aerosol container of spray paint or broad-tipped indelible marker while on any private property unless the owner, agent, or manager, or person in possession of the property knows of the minor's possession of the aerosol container or marker and has consented to the minor's possession while on his or her property.

A petition for delinquency was filed against D.P., alleging violations of subdivisions (e)(2) and (3). D.P. entered a plea of no contest, reserving the right to appeal the trial court order holding the ordinance constitutional.

OPINION

...D.P. suggests that it is impermissible to treat minors differently than adults. That suggestion is clearly incorrect. There are many activities that are legal for adults but prohibited to minors: drinking, and driving under legal age, being the most obvious examples. Some supervisory requirements apply to minors that do not apply to adults, such as compulsory school attendance and the curfew ordinance....

No fundamental right is implicated in the possession of spray paint and jumbo markers. Nor is youth a suspect classification. *White Egret Condominium, Inc. v. Franklin*, 379 So.2d 346, 351 (Fla.1979) ("The law is now clear that restriction of individual rights on the basis of age need not pass the strict scrutiny test, and therefore age is not a suspect class."); *Metropolitan Dade County v. Pred*, 665 So.2d 252 (Fla. 3d DCA 1995).* ("Under both the Florida and United States Constitution, children, due to their special nature and vulnerabilities, do not enjoy the same quantum or quality of rights as adults.").

The Court's review is therefore limited to the rational basis test. The rational basis test does not turn on whether this Court agrees or disagrees with the legislation at issue, and this Court will not attempt to impose on a duly-elected legislative body his reservations about the wisdom of the subject ordinance. Instead, the rational basis test focuses narrowly on whether a legislative body could rationally believe that the legislation could achieve a legitimate government end. The end of controlling the blight of graffiti is obviously legitimate and the Juvenile does not challenge this fact.

In addition, a legislative body could rationally conclude that the subject prohibition of possession by minors of spray paint and jumbo markers without supervision on public property or permission of the private-property owner would serve to control and limit incidences of graffiti. Indeed, the prohibition at issue is less restrictive than the prohibitions on spray paint and jumbo markers upheld in National Paint. The Court notes that juveniles can avoid the restrictions at issue by using markers less than one-half inch in [writing surface] or markers that contain water-soluble ink.

For the above reasons, the Court finds that the challenged graffiti ordinance does not offend the due process or equal protection provisions of either the Florida or Federal Constitutions. Accordingly, the Juvenile's Motion to Dismiss is denied. We concur with the trial court's ruling that the statute is constitutional.

AFFIRMED.

DISSENT

GREEN, J.
...The majority points out that it is not constitutionally impermissible to treat minors differently from adults. While

---

*Review denied, 676 So.2d 413 (Fla.1996).

that is certainly true, it is true only in some delineated areas. Our United States Supreme Court has recognized as a general proposition, that "a child, merely on account of his [or her] minority, is not beyond the protection of the Constitution." For example, in criminal juvenile proceedings, juveniles are afforded the constitutional safeguards of proof beyond a reasonable doubt, notice of the charges, right to counsel, rights of confrontation and examination and the privilege against self-incrimination. Notwithstanding these general principles, the constitutional rights of minors are still not co-equal with those of adults. The Court cited three reasons for not equating the constitutional rights of children with those of adults, namely, "the peculiar vulnerability of children; their inability to make critical decisions in an informed, mature manner; and the importance of the parental role in child rearing."

The central rationale for finding diminished constitutional rights of minors, in limited circumstances, appears to be for the personal protection of the child or the personal protection of others from the acts of minors. For example, in . . . *Metropolitan Dade County v. Pred*, 665 So.2d 252, 253 (Fla. 3d DCA 1995), we . . . upheld the power of the county to impose a curfew for minors, for the personal well-being of minors. Likewise, the laws which prohibit minors from drinking and driving under the legal age limit are constitutionally permissible because they are for the purpose of protecting minors from inherently dangerous activities.

Thus, although the constitutional rights of minors are not co-equal with those of adults under certain circumstances, I must conclude that those factors which generally tend to support a reduction of the rights of minors are simply not present in this case. The purpose of the challenged subsections of the graffiti ordinance is wholly unrelated to the personal protection of minors or others. The county's sole aim is to protect property from graffiti artists. While that is certainly a legitimate and laudable objective, I do not believe that it can be pursued by the county at the expense and deprivation of fundamental due process rights which both adults and minors share. . . .

Questions

1. List the majority's arguments in favor of making age an aggravating circumstance under the graffiti ordinance.

2. List the dissent's arguments against making age an aggravating circumstance under the ordinance.

3. Review *Allam v. State* in the "Equal Protection" section of Chapter 2. Then assume you're the judge, and based on the decision in *Allam*, write an opinion deciding whether the spray paint ordinance in this case is constitutional.

EXPLORING AGE FURTHER

Was He Too Old to Be Responsible?

FACTS

A prosecutor was faced with the question of whether the other end of the age spectrum, old age, should affect the capacity to commit crimes:

> You have this married couple, married for over 50 years, living in a retirement home. The guy sends his wife out for bagels and while the wife can still get around she forgets and brings back onion rolls. Not a capital offense, right? Anyway, the guy goes berserk and he axes his wife; he kills the poor woman with a Boy Scout-type axe! What do we do now? Set a high bail? Prosecute? Get a conviction and send the fellow to prison? You tell me! We did nothing. The media dropped it quickly and, I hope, that's it. (Cohen 1985, 9)

Do you agree? Explain your answer based on the discussion of age.

DURESS

"Sometimes people are forced to do what they do," writes Professor Hyman Gross (1978). What if what they're forced to do is a crime? Should they be excused? Answering these questions is what the defense of **duress** is about. According to Professor Gross, "It seems that the compulsion ought to count in their favor. After all, we say, such a person wasn't free to do otherwise—he couldn't help himself" (276). On the other hand, he continues:

> There are times...when we ought to stand firm and run the risk of harm to ourselves instead of taking a way out that means harm to others. In such a situation we must expect to pay the price if we cause harm when we prefer ourselves, for then the harm is our fault even though we did not mean it and deeply regret it. (276)

Let's take a closer look at the problem of duress and its elements.

The Problem of Duress

Professor Gross's comments strike at the heart of the problem of duress: It's hard to blame someone who's forced to commit a crime, but should we excuse people who harm innocent people to save themselves? The positions taken by three of the last two centuries' great authorities on criminal law show how different the answers can be. At one extreme is a historian of the criminal law and judge, Sir James Stephen (1883 [1], 108), who maintained duress is never an excuse for crime. (Stephen did say duress should mitigate the punishment.) At the other extreme is Professor Glanville Williams (1961, 755). Author of a highly respected treatise on criminal law, he says the law should excuse individuals if they are so "in thrall[ed] to some power" the law can't control their choice. Professor Jerome Hall (1960, 448), author of yet another distinguished treatise, took the middle position that duress shouldn't excuse the most serious crimes, but it should be an excuse when the choice is either commit a minor crime or face imminent death.

The Elements of Duress

There are four elements in the defense of duress. The definitions of the elements vary from state to state.

1. *Threats amounting to duress.* Death threats are required in some states. Threats of "serious bodily injury" qualify in several states. Others don't specify what threats qualify.

2. *Immediacy of the threats.* In some states, the harm has to be "instant." In others "imminent" harm is required. In Louisiana, duress is an excuse only if the defendant reasonably believed the person making the threats would "immediately carry out the threats if the crime were not committed."

3. *Crimes defense applies to.* In the majority of states, duress isn't a defense to murder. In other states it's a defense to all crimes. Some states are silent on the point.

4. *Standard of belief regarding the threat.* Most states require a reasonable belief the threat is real. Others demand the threat actually be real. Some say nothing on the point.

Excerpts from duress statutes in three states follow:

NEW YORK PENAL CODE, § 40.00

In any prosecution for an offense, it is an affirmative defense that the defendant engaged in the proscribed conduct because he was coerced to do so by the use or threatened imminent use of unlawful physical force upon him or a third person, which force or threatened force a person of reasonable firmness in his situation would have been unable to resist.

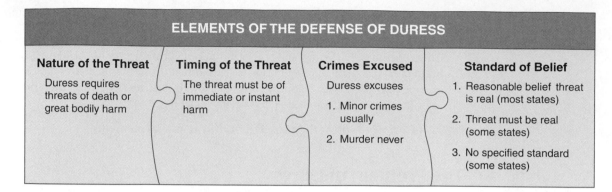

ELEMENTS OF THE DEFENSE OF DURESS

Nature of the Threat	Timing of the Threat	Crimes Excused	Standard of Belief
Duress requires threats of death or great bodily harm	The threat must be of immediate or instant harm	Duress excuses 1. Minor crimes usually 2. Murder never	1. Reasonable belief threat is real (most states) 2. Threat must be real (some states) 3. No specified standard (some states)

ALABAMA PENAL CODE, SECTION 13A-3-30

(a) It is a defense to prosecution that the actor engaged in the proscribed conduct because he was compelled to do so by the threat of imminent death or serious physical injury to himself or another. . . .

(d) The defense provided by this section is unavailable in a prosecution for:

(1) murder; or

(2) any killing of another under aggravated circumstances.

MINNESOTA CRIMINAL CODE, § 609.08

(3) when any crime is committed or participated in by two or more persons, any one of whom participates only under compulsion by another engaged therein, who by threats creates a reasonable apprehension in the mind of such participator that in case of refusal that participator is liable to instant death, such threats and apprehension constitute duress which will excuse such participator from criminal liability.

The court, in *People v. Bowie* (2002), dealt with the element of immediacy in the defense of duress.

CASE | *Was He Threatened with Instant Death?*

People v. Bowie
WL 1072088 (Cal.App. 4 Dist. 2002)

Michael Eugene Bowie, Defendant, was convicted in the Superior Court, San Diego County, of robbery. Defendant appealed. The Court of Appeal affirmed.

KREMER, P.J.

FACTS

Bowie concedes he robbed a Carl's Jr. just before closing time on March 5, 2000. During the robbery, he had his hand in his pocket, acting as if he had a gun; he threatened to shoot people if they did not comply with his demands. . . .

Bowie testified that about three weeks before the robbery, he had returned to San Diego (after an absence of 20 years) at the urging of his family because of drug problems

he was having where he was living in northern California. However, almost immediately upon his return to San Diego, he met friends from high school and prison, some of whom were members of the Emerald Hills street gang, and he began using and selling drugs; his friends gave him $6,000 worth of crack cocaine to sell. Bowie was given a percentage of the sales.

Bowie had about a month to repay the $6,000. The deadline had not been reached at the time of the robbery. By the time of the robbery, Bowie had repaid about $1,500-$2,500, but he had smoked or given away the remaining amount of drugs. He was still repaying the money by selling other crack cocaine for his friends. About five to seven days after he had been given the drugs, his friends started threatening to harm him if he failed to return the rest of the $6,000.

Bowie spent the day of the robbery at a friend's "crack house," smoking and selling crack cocaine. He was part of a "crew" that sold drugs, and some of the money was going toward his $6,000 debt. About 8:00 or 9:00 P.M., he got a call from "Howard" who said he was going to pick up Bowie at the crack house. At trial, Bowie initially testified that he did not remember Howard's name, although he had grown up with Howard and spent time in prison with him. Bowie then gave Howard's first name, but refused to give his last name because he was "not going to be a rat and get killed and my family killed." Bowie knew Howard wanted him to commit a robbery. About 9:30 P.M., Howard and "Tony" picked up Bowie and drove to a shopping center where they met another person who was driving his own car. They told Bowie that he was going to rob a business. Bowie initially refused because he was "a Three-Strike candidate" but they showed him weapons and threatened to "shoot at [his] brother's house and family."

Because Bowie had done time in prison with these people, knew they were active gang members and had heard about murders committed by these people, he believed they would hurt his brother and his brother's family if he did not commit the robbery. He also felt he himself was in danger and might be harmed if he refused. Bowie expected that Howard would wait while he robbed the Carl's Jr. and would give him a ride after the robbery.

Bowie testified that if he had refused to commit the robbery, it was uncertain when these people would have harmed him, his brother or his brother's family. It might take a day, a week or occur at some later time in the future; "you will never know." He testified that if he had not been arrested, he might have committed other robberies. He also testified that he knew selling drugs was illegal and that if he was caught, he would receive the same sentence as for robbery, but he was willing to sell drugs.

A police officer testified that based on his experience with criminal street gangs, a person would have reason to fear being shot or killed if they stole drugs from a gang; he had also heard of people being killed for giving "up a gang member's name to [the] police."

OPINION

Bowie contends the court erred in refusing to instruct the jury on the defense of duress pursuant to [California Jury Instructions]. CALJIC No. 4.40. CALJIC No. 4.40 provides:

A person is not guilty of a crime . . . when he engages in conduct, otherwise criminal, when acting under threats and menaces under the following circumstances:

1. Where the threats and menaces are such that they would cause a reasonable person to fear that his life would be in immediate danger if he did not engage in the conduct charged, and

2. If this person then believed that his life was so endangered.

This rule does not apply to threats, menaces, and fear of future danger to his life. . . .

The duress defense, through its immediacy requirement, negates an element of the crime—the intent to commit the act. The defendant does not have the time to form criminal intent because of immediacy and imminency of the threatened harm and need only raise a reasonable doubt as to the existence or nonexistence of this fact. A fear of future harm to one's life does not relieve one of responsibility for the crimes he commits. In contrast, the defense of . . . duress (which was presented to the jury here) contemplates a threat in the immediate future. The defendant has the time, however limited, to consider alternative courses of conduct. The defendant has the burden of proving necessity by a preponderance of the evidence."

Here, Bowie's testimony indicated that his fear was of a future, not immediate, harm to the life of himself, his brother and his brother's family if he did not commit the robbery. He testified that if he refused to commit the robbery, the harm to himself, his brother or his brother's family might occur later that night, but also that it might occur at a later time; he did not know when they might act, only that he believed they would eventually harm him, his brother or his brother's family. Additionally, Bowie admitted that he had time to consider alternative courses of conduct; indeed, he testified that while at the Carl's Jr., he considered walking out the back door instead of committing the robbery. Bowie testified that he did not do so because it would not solve his problem; he still would have owed these people money. Additionally, if he had reported these people to the police, he and his family would not have been safe because these people could arrange to have others harmed while in they were in jail.

The court properly refused to instruct on the defense of duress because it is not available when, as here, the threat is of future, rather than immediate, harm.

The judgment is AFFIRMED.

Questions

1. List all the facts relevant to deciding whether Michael Bowie is entitled to the defense of duress.

2. State the elements of the duress defense as they're defined in the California jury instructions.

3. According to the court, why was Bowie not entitled to the defense of duress?

INTOXICATION

Johnny James went quietly to his death by lethal injection...inside the Texas prison system's Huntsville Unit. His crimes? Abducting two women, forcing them to have sex with each other, and then shooting them both in the head. One died, the other lived to identify him at trial. The Texas courts turned a deaf ear to James's plea that he was too drunk to know what he was doing when he abducted, raped, and shot his victims.

According to Professor George Fletcher (1978), the defense of intoxication is "buffeted between two conflicting principles":

1. *Accountability.* Those who get drunk should take the consequences of their actions. Someone who gets drunk is liable for the violent consequences.

2. *Culpability.* Criminal liability and punishment depend on blameworthiness. (846)

The common-law approach focused on the first principle:

> As to artificial, voluntarily contracted madness, by drunkenness or intoxication, which, depriving men of their reason, puts them in a temporary frenzy; our law looks upon this as an aggravation of the offense, rather than as an excuse for any criminal misbehavior.
>
> Blackstone 1769, 25–26

The Johnny James case is only one dramatic example that the common-law principle is alive and well today. John Gibeaut, who wrote about the James case in an article entitled "Sobering Thoughts," notes the contemporary emphasis on accountability in the subtitle: "Legislatures and courts increasingly are just saying no to intoxication as a defense or mitigating factor." Section §13-03 of the Arizona Criminal Code (2003) is a typical accountability statute:

> Temporary intoxication resulting from the voluntary ingestion, consumption, inhalation or injection of alcohol, an illegal substance under chapter 34 of this title or other psychoactive substances or the abuse of prescribed medications does not constitute insanity and is not a defense for any criminal act or requisite state of mind.

Between November 1996 and May 1997, at least ten states introduced bills similar to the Arizona statute. According to a member of the Prosecution Function Committee of the American Bar Association's Criminal Justice Section, "The fight goes back to the ancient struggle over just how much free will one has" (Gibeaut 1997, 57).

What we have said so far applies only to voluntary intoxication. Involuntary intoxication is an excuse to criminal liability in all states. **Involuntary intoxication** includes cases in which defendants don't know they are taking intoxicants, or know but are forced to take them. In *People v. Penman* (1915), a man took what his friend told him were "breath perfumer" pills; in fact, they were cocaine tablets. While under their influence, he killed someone. The court allowed the defense of intoxication. Involuntary intoxication applies only under extreme conditions. According to one authority (Hall 1960), "a person would need to be bound hand and foot and the liquor literally poured down his throat, or...would have to be threatened with immediate serious injury" (540). In another case, *Burrows. v. State* (1931), where the defendant claimed involuntary intoxication, an 18-year-old man was traveling with an older man across the desert. The older man insisted that the young man drink some whiskey with him.

ELEMENTS OF THE INTOXICATION DEFENSE

Voluntary Intoxication

1. Voluntary intoxication is not a defense **but**
2. Can negate specific intent
3. Can reduce the degree of the crime

Involuntary Intoxication

1. Involuntary intoxication is an excuse **if**
2. Intoxication is induced by extreme duress

When he said no, the older man got abusive. Afraid that the older man would throw him out of the car in the middle of the desert without any money, he drank the whiskey, got drunk, and killed the older man. The court rejected his defense of involuntary intoxication, because the older man had not compelled the youth "to drink against his will and consent."

So, the reason why the law excuses involuntary intoxication and not voluntary intoxication is that we can blame voluntarily intoxicated persons and hold them accountable for their actions. Why? They *chose* to put themselves in a state where they either didn't know or couldn't control what they were doing. We can't blame involuntarily intoxicated persons for their actions. Why not? Because people forced or tricked into an intoxicated state didn't choose to put themselves out of control. (Review Chapter 3 where we discussed voluntarily induced involuntary conditions or acts qualifying as *actus reus*.)

Alcohol is the main but not the only intoxicant covered by the defense of intoxication. In most states, it includes all "substances" that disturb mental and physical capacities. In *State v. Hall* (1974), Hall's friend gave him a pill, telling him it was only a "little sunshine" to make him feel "groovy." In fact, the pill contained LSD (lysergic acid diethylamide). A car picked up Hall while he was hitchhiking. The drug caused Hall to hallucinate that the driver was a rabid dog, and, under this sad delusion, Hall shot and killed the driver. The court said that criminal responsibility recognizes no difference between alcohol and other intoxicants. An appeals court in California dealt with intoxication by means of a mixture of marijuana and PCP in *People v. Velez* (1986).

CASE | *Was He Involuntarily Intoxicated?*

People v. Velez
221 Cal.Rptr. 631 (Cal.App. 1986)

Alfredo Velez, Defendant, was convicted in the Superior Court, San Joaquin County of assault with a deadly weapon, and he appealed. The Court of Appeal affirmed.

SIMS, J.

FACTS

On November 4, 1983, the victim, a 64-year-old man, was sitting in the living room of his home watching television with his wife. Defendant, who was unknown to the victim, suddenly crashed into the house by kicking open a locked wooden door. According to the victim, defendant was angry and looked like an animal.

Defendant attacked the victim with a screwdriver, stabbing him all over his body, including his eyes. Defendant also stomped on him. The victim's wife ran outside and begged her neighbor to call the police.

Stockton police officers Smallie and Manley arrived at the victim's house shortly after midnight. Smallie saw defendant trying to stab his bloodied victim as he and his wife struggled in defense. Smallie pointed his gun at defendant and told him to drop his weapon. Defendant apparently ignored Smallie and continued to try to stab the victim. The officers started hitting defendant with their clubs, pulled him away from the victim, and handcuffed him while he jumped on the victim's legs. Defendant then became limp and the officers dragged him outside. Both officers thought defendant was under the influence of PCP.

A neighbor saw defendant before the stabbing and thought defendant acted as if drunk. Defendant had been walking in the middle of the street in a zigzag fashion without regard for traffic. As the police dragged defendant from the victim's house, the neighbor stated that defendant still acted drunk and insulted the police.

Two defense witnesses familiar with the use and influence of PCP, a psychologist and a psychiatrist, testified defendant's behavior on the night of the assault was consistent with PCP ingestion.

Defendant testified that on the night in question, he was going around with some people who were new acquaintances, i.e., people defendant had seen but did not really know. The group went to the house of the brother-in-law of one of the group. Defendant sat down, had a beer, and began to watch television.

Some of the other members of the group were in the kitchen, smoking marijuana. They called defendant into the kitchen and offered him a marijuana cigarette. Defendant smoked marijuana "maybe three times a month" and knew what it looked like. Defendant took a puff on the cigarette and passed it back. Defendant then took a second puff on the cigarette.

The people in the room began to look like devils. After that, defendant remembered only running and crawling. Nobody mentioned to defendant that the cigarette might contain PCP. Defendant had never before experienced such an effect when he smoked marijuana.

Jose Hernandez was with defendant on the evening of the assault. Hernandez testified he saw defendant smoke a marijuana "joint" that was being passed around. Hernandez knew it was a "K.J." (a cigarette containing PCP) judging from the behavior of others who had also smoked the same marijuana cigarette. Hernandez claimed no one told him or any of the others it was a "K.J."

Others who were with defendant in the house before the assault testified defendant appeared to be under the influence of PCP though none of them had any that night. They testified they smoked marijuana but were unaware of any PCP in the house.

As a result of defendant's attack, the victim is partially blind, his hearing is impaired, his legs are stiff, and he has no feeling in his left palm.

OPINION

Defendant contends the trial court erred in instructing the jury to the effect that unconsciousness caused by voluntary intoxication is not a defense to a charge of assault with a deadly weapon. Defendant asserts that unconsciousness, however caused, is a complete defense even to a general intent crime. We must disagree.

Assault with a deadly weapon is a general intent crime. In ordinary circumstances, in order to commit the crime of assault with a deadly weapon a defendant must have the general intent willfully to commit an act the direct, natural and probable consequences of which if successfully completed would be injury to another.

Section 26 provides in pertinent part: "All persons are capable of committing crimes except those belonging to the following classes:

. . .

"Four—Persons who committed the act charged without being conscious thereof."

This statute obviously suggests that one who is unconscious for any reason is incapable of committing a crime. However, section 22 provides in pertinent part:

(a) No act committed by a person while in a state of voluntary intoxication is less criminal by reason of his having been in such condition. Evidence of voluntary intoxication shall not be admitted to negate the capacity to form any mental states for the crimes charged, including, but not limited to, purpose, intent, knowledge, premeditation, deliberation or malice aforethought, with which the accused committed the act.

(b) Evidence of voluntary intoxication is admissible solely on the issue of whether or not the defendant actually formed a required specific intent, premeditated, deliberated, or harbored malice aforethought, when a specific intent crime is charged.

(c) Voluntary intoxication includes the voluntary ingestion . . . of any intoxicating . . . drug. . . ."

Section 22 says no act committed by a person who is voluntarily intoxicated is less criminal but the statute does not mention unconsciousness. But what if unconsciousness is precisely the condition caused by voluntary intoxication? Which statute controls, section 22 or section 26? The answer to this dilemma was provided nearly 20 years ago by Chief Justice Traynor:

> Unconsciousness is ordinarily a complete defense to a criminal charge. If the state of unconsciousness is caused by voluntary intoxication, however, it is not a complete defense. Intoxication can so diminish a person's mental capacity that he is unable to achieve a specific state of mind requisite to a crime, but, even if it is sufficient to destroy volition, it cannot excuse homicide. *Unconsciousness caused by voluntary intoxication is governed by Penal Code section 22, rather than section 26, and it is not a defense when a crime requires only a general intent. The union or joint operation of act and intent or criminal negligence must exist in every crime . . . and is deemed to exist irrespective of unconsciousness arising from voluntary intoxication. An instruction that does not distinguish unconsciousness caused by voluntary intoxication from that induced by other causes is erroneous.*

Section 22 provides that unconsciousness caused by voluntary intoxication is available only as a partial defense to an offense requiring a specific intent; it is not a defense to a general intent crime such as assault with a deadly weapon. . . . The trial court did not err in giving the subject instructions. . . .

Defendant's contention that he was entitled to instructions wholly excusing him from criminal responsibility in this case is premised on his previously recounted testimony that he was offered and smoked a marijuana cigarette which, unbeknownst to him, contained PCP. However, if this conduct falls within the definition of voluntary intoxication under section 22 as a matter of law, then defendant was not entitled to instructions on unconsciousness caused by involuntary intoxication. We therefore examine whether defendant's intoxication was voluntary as a matter of law.

We begin by noting that the drug defendant admitted he knowingly consumed—marijuana—is a controlled substance classified as a hallucinogen in California. . . . It is unlawful in this state to possess, transport, sell, furnish, administer or give away marijuana. Consequently, when defendant possessed the marijuana he consumed, and when he gave or furnished it to others, he broke the law.

A plausible argument could be made that, as a matter of policy, defendant should not be wholly excused from criminal responsibility for harm caused others, and arising out of his consumption of an unlawful drug, on the ground that allowance of such an excuse would sanction consumption of unlawful drugs. Moreover, the allowance of an absolute defense in the circumstances presented here would result in an anomalous allocation of criminal responsibility. Thus, had defendant legally purchased alcohol and had he become voluntarily but lawfully drunk in a private place, and had he committed the subject offenses in the same private place, he would be held fully responsible under section 22 for assault with a deadly weapon even though he had committed no crime at all in becoming intoxicated. Given the legal prohibitions placed on marijuana it is hard to rationalize why the law should treat those who knowingly smoke marijuana more leniently than those who knowingly get drunk.

However, the instant case need not be decided on such broad policy grounds. Section 22 codified the common law rule that voluntary intoxication does not excuse the commission of a crime. It is therefore appropriate to construe the statute in "the spirit of the common law" and, indeed, our Supreme Court has done just that.

The preclusion of voluntary intoxication as an absolute defense at common law has been justified on the theory that "when a crime is committed by a party while in a fit of intoxication, the law will not allow him to avail himself of the excuse of his own gross vice and misconduct to shelter himself from the legal consequences of such crime." Also, "It is a duty which every one owes to his fellow-men, and to society . . . to preserve, so far as lies in his power, the inestimable gift of reason. If it is perverted or destroyed by fixed disease, though brought on by his own vices, the law holds him not accountable. But if, by a voluntary act, he temporarily casts off the restraints of reason and conscience, no wrong is done him if he is considered answerable for any injury which, in that state, he may do to others or to society."

Clearly, then, one who becomes voluntarily intoxicated to the point of unconsciousness can have no actual intent to commit a crime; rather, criminal responsibility is justified on the theory that having chosen to breach one's duty to others of acting with reason and conscience, one may not entirely avoid criminal harm caused by one's breach of duty. It is therefore apparent the imposition of criminal responsibility for acts committed while voluntarily intoxicated is predicated on a theory of criminal negligence. In California, whether one is criminally negligent is ascertained by applying an objective test: whether *a reasonable person* in defendant's circumstances has engaged in criminally negligent behavior. We shall apply such a test here to ascertain whether defendant was voluntarily intoxicated as a matter of law.

Boiled down to its essentials, defendant's defense was that he smoked marijuana given to him at a social gathering by others, but he did not in fact know it contained PCP, which produced an unexpected intoxicating effect. This defense depends on the validity of defendant's assumptions that the cigarette did not contain PCP and would produce a predictable intoxicating effect.

However, for reasons previously discussed, these assumptions are tested not by defendant's subjective belief but rather by the standard of a reasonable person. In this regard, it is common knowledge that unlawful street drugs do not come with warranties of purity or quality associated with lawfully acquired drugs such as alcohol. Thus, unlike alcohol, unlawful street drugs are frequently not the substance they purport to be or are contaminated with other substances not apparent to the naked eye. In particular, marijuana is frequently contaminated with PCP or other psychoactive drugs. Indeed, the reported decisions of the California appellate courts provide a ready compilation of cases involving "lacing" or "dusting" of marijuana with PCP.

The instant case simply reflects this well-established knowledge. Marijuana cigarettes laced with PCP were sufficiently common among defendant's acquaintances that they were given a nickname: "K.J.'s." Indeed, one of defendant's own experts, psychologist Dr. Steven Edwin Lerner, testified that PCP was commonly concealed in hand-rolled cigarettes containing various leaf materials including marijuana, and that the most common method of PCP intoxication involved smoking "joints."

Putting aside the question whether a defendant may be precluded in all circumstances from invoking the absolute defense of involuntary intoxication where he has consumed an unlawful drug, we hold a reasonable person has no right to assume that a marijuana cigarette furnished to him by others at a social gathering will not contain PCP; nor may such a person assume such a marijuana cigarette will produce any predictable intoxicating effect. Absent these assumptions, defendant cannot contend he was involuntarily intoxicated, because he had no right to expect the substance he consumed was other than it was nor that it would produce an intoxicating effect different from the one it did. We therefore conclude defendant was voluntarily intoxicated as a matter of law within the meaning of section 22.

The result we reach is consistent with the law of other American jurisdictions. Thus, involuntary intoxication is sometimes referred to as "innocent" intoxication. The defense is allowed where the defendant has been without fault. "Involuntary intoxication, it appears, was first recognized as that caused by the unskillfulness of a physician or by the contrivance of one's enemies. Today, where the intoxication is induced through the fault of another *and*

without any fault on the part of the accused, it is generally treated as involuntary. Intoxication caused by the force, duress, fraud, or contrivance of another, for whatever purpose, without any fault on the part of the accused, is uniformly recognized as involuntary intoxication."

In accordance with this view, courts have allowed the defense of involuntary intoxication based on the ingestion of an unlawful drug where the defendant reasonably believed he was consuming a lawful substance or where the unlawful drug was placed without defendant's knowledge *in a lawful substance*. (See *People v. Scott*, supra, 146 Cal.App.3d at pp. 826–827, 194 Cal.Rptr. 633 [PCP surreptitiously placed in punch at family reunion-type party]; *People v. Carlo* (1974), 361 N.Y.S.2d 168 [defendant took hallucigenic pill in reasonable belief it was aspirin or lawful tranquilizer]; *Commonwealth v. McAlister* (1974), 365 Mass. 454, 313 N.E.2d 113 [coffee spiked with drug that produced reaction consistent with LSD]; *People v. White* (1970), 264 N.E.2d 228 [drug put in defendant's beer without his knowledge]; *People v. Penman* (1915), 271 Ill. 82, 110 N.E. 894 [intoxicating pills reasonably believed to be breath perfume].

Conversely, in *State v. Hall* (Iowa 1974), 214 N.W.2d 205, defendant voluntarily took a pill that casual acquaintances had given him, telling him it was a "little sunshine" and would make him feel "groovy." After taking the pill, defendant began to experience strange perceptions and shot his companion because he thought he was a scary dog. Holding instructions on involuntary intoxication were properly refused because defendant knew the pill was a mind-affecting drug, the Iowa Supreme Court impliedly rejected defendant's theory that his intoxication was involuntary because the intoxicating effect of the pill was different from what he expected.

Returning to the contention at issue—the asserted error of the trial court in instructing on the defense of unconsciousness—such instructions are required only where there is evidence sufficient to deserve consideration by the jury. Since we have concluded defendant's own evidence showed he was voluntarily intoxicated as a matter of law, he was not entitled to instructions on the absolute defense of unconsciousness. And, since the defense instructions at issue were erroneously given in the first place, any error in those instructions did not prejudice defendant and was necessarily harmless.

We caution that we deal here only with the assertion of unconsciousness due to voluntary intoxication as an absolute defense to a general intent crime. Had the victim in this case died, and had defendant been charged with murder, defendant would have been entitled to instructions based on his voluntary intoxication as a partial defense precluding specific intent, such as premeditation, deliberation, or malice.

The judgment is AFFIRMED.

Questions

1. Define involuntary and involuntary intoxication as the court defines them.

2. List all the evidence supporting the conclusion that Velez was *voluntarily* intoxicated.

3. List all the evidence supporting the conclusion that Velez was *involuntarily* intoxicated.

4. Summarize the court's reasons for its decision.

5. Do you agree? Back up your answer with facts and arguments from the court's opinion and from the text in this section.

ENTRAPMENT

Ancient tyrants and modern dictators have relied on secret agents as a law enforcement tool. From the days of Henry VIII to the era of Hitler and Stalin, to Saddam Hussein and Slobodan Milosevic in our own time, the world's police states have relied on persuading people to commit crimes, so they could catch and then crush their opponents. But government persuasion isn't only a tool used by dictators. All societies rely on it even though it violates a basic purpose of government in free societies. The great Victorian British Prime Minister William Gladstone was referring to this purpose when he advised government to make it easy to do right and difficult to do wrong. Persuading people to commit crimes also flies in the face of the entreaty of the Lord's Prayer to "lead us not into temptation, but deliver us from evil" (Carlson 1987).

For a long time, U.S. courts rejected the idea that **entrapment** (government agents getting people to commit crimes they wouldn't otherwise commit) excused criminal liability. In *Board of Commissioners v. Backus* (1864), the New York Supreme Court explained why:

> Even if inducements to commit crime could be assumed to exist in this case, the allegation of the defendant would be but the repetition of the pleas as ancient as the world, and first interposed in Paradise: "The serpent beguiled me and I did eat." That defense was overruled by the great Lawgiver, and whatever estimate we may form, or whatever judgment pass upon the character or conduct of the tempter, this plea has never since availed to shield crime or give indemnity to the culprit, and it is safe to say that under any code of civilized, not to say Christian ethics, it never will. (42)

In *People v. Mills* (1904), another court summed up the acceptance of entrapment this way:

> We are asked to protect the defendant, not because he is innocent, but because a zealous public officer exceeded his powers and held out a bait. The courts do not look to see who held out the bait, but to see who took it. (791)

The earlier attitude was based on indifference to government encouragement to commit crimes. After all, "once the crime is committed, why should it matter what particular incentives were involved and who offered them?" However, attitudes have shifted from indifference to both a "limited sympathy" toward entrapped defendants and a growing intolerance of government inducements to entrap otherwise law-abiding people (Marcus 1986).

The practice of entrapment arose because of the difficulty in enforcing laws against consensual crimes like drug offenses, pornography, official wrongdoing, and prostitution. There's no constitutional right not to be entrapped. Entrapment is an affirmative defense created by statutes; that is, defendants have to show some evidence they were entrapped. If they do this, the burden shifts to the prosecution to prove defendants were not entrapped. The jury—or the judge in trials without juries—decides whether officers in fact entrapped defendants. The courts have adopted two types of tests for entrapment; one is subjective and the other objective.

The Subjective Test

The majority of state and all federal courts have adopted a **subjective test of entrapment.** The subjective test focuses on the predisposition of defendants to commit crimes. According to the test, the defense has to prove the government pressured the defendants to commit crimes they wouldn't have committed without the pressure. The crucial question in the subjective test is, "Where did the criminal intent originate?" If it originated with the defendant, then the government didn't entrap the defendant. If it originated with the government, then the government did entrap the defendant. For example, in the leading case of *Sherman v. U.S.* (1958), Kalchinian, a government informant and undercover agent, met Sherman in a drug treatment center. He struck up a friendship with Sherman and eventually asked Sherman to get him some heroin. Sherman (a heroin addict) refused. Following weeks of persistent begging and pleading, Sherman finally gave in and got Kalchinian some heroin. The police arrested Sherman. The U.S. Supreme Court found that the intent originated with the government. According to the Court, Sherman was hardly predisposed to commit a drug offense since he was seriously committed to a drug treatment program to cure his addiction.

After defendants present some evidence the government persuaded them to commit crimes they wouldn't have committed otherwise, the government can prove disposition to commit the crimes in one of the following ways:

1. Defendants' prior convictions for similar offenses
2. Defendants' willingness to commit similar offenses
3. Defendants' display of criminal expertise in carrying out the offense
4. Defendants' readiness to commit the crime

Consensual crimes, especially drug offenses, are the usual target of law enforcement inducement tactics, but some police departments have also used it to combat street muggings. In *Oliver v. State* (1985), the Nevada Supreme Court dealt with two street mugging decoy cases operating in an area of Las Vegas with a high population of "street people."

Oliver v. State
703 P.2d 869 (Nev. 1985)

Ernest Oliver was convicted of larceny from the person in the Eighth Judicial District Court and sentenced to 10 years in prison. He appealed. The Supreme Court reversed.

GUNDERSON, J.

FACTS

On the night of Oliver's arrest, three policemen undertook to conduct a "decoy operation" near the intersection of Main and Ogden in Las Vegas. That corner is in a downtown area frequented by substantial numbers of persons commonly characterized as "street people," "vagrants," and "derelicts." It appears Oliver, a black man, is one of these.

Disguised as a vagrant in an old Marine Corps jacket, the decoy officer slumped against a palm tree, pretending to be intoxicated and asleep. His associates concealed themselves nearby. The decoy prominently displayed a ten-dollar bill, positioning it to protrude from the left breast pocket of his jacket. This was done, the decoy later testified, "to provide an opportunity for a dishonest person to prove himself."

Oliver, who had the misfortune to come walking down the street, saw the decoy and evidently felt moved to assist him. Shaking and nudging the decoy with his foot, Oliver attempted to warn the decoy that the police would arrest him if he did not move on. The decoy did not respond, and Oliver stepped away. Up to this point, Oliver had shown no predisposition whatever to commit any criminal act.

Then, Oliver saw the ten-dollar bill protruding from the decoy's pocket. He reached down and took it. "Thanks, home boy," he said. Thereupon, he was arrested by the decoy and the two other officers. Following the trial, a jury convicted Oliver of larceny from the person, and he has been sentenced to ten years imprisonment. This appeal followed.

OPINION

Oliver's counsel contends he was entrapped into committing the offense in question. We agree.... Government agents or officers may not employ extraordinary tempta-

tions or inducements. They may not manufacture crime. We have repeatedly endorsed the following concept:

> Entrapment is the seduction or improper inducement to commit a crime for the purpose of instituting a criminal prosecution, but if a person in good faith and for the purpose of detecting or discovering a crime or offense, furnishes the opportunity for the commission thereof by one who has the requisite criminal intent, it is not entrapment.

Thus, because we discern several facts which we believe combined to create an extraordinary temptation, which was inappropriate to apprehending merely those bent on criminal activity, we feel constrained to reverse Oliver's conviction. We note, first of all, that the decoy portrayed himself as completely susceptible and vulnerable. He did not respond when Oliver attempted to wake him, urging him to avoid arrest by moving to another location. Moreover, the decoy displayed his ten dollar-bill in a manner calculated to tempt any needy person in the area, whether immediately disposed to crime or not. In the case of Oliver, the police succeeded in tempting a man who apparently did not approach the decoy with larceny in mind, but rather to help him. Even after being lured into petty theft by the decoy's open display of currency and apparent helplessness, Oliver did not go on to search the decoy's pockets or to remove his wallet.

On this record, then, we think the activities of the officers, however well intentioned, accomplished an impermissible entrapment. The Florida court's comments in *State v. Holliday*, 431 So.2d 309 (Fla.Dist.Ct.App.1983) ... are noteworthy:

> There is no evidence of any prior conduct of the defendant that would have shown predisposition. There is no evidence that he was engaging in criminal activity before he took the money from the decoy. [Citations omitted.] No ready acquiescence is shown; on the contrary, the defendant's acts ... demonstrate only that he succumbed to temptation. The record, as such, reveals that the decoy did not detect or discover, nor could he reasonably be intended to discover, the type of crime the police were attempting to prevent by the use of the decoy, i.e., robberies and purse snatchings. Indeed, lifting some money protruding from the pocket of a seemingly unconscious, drunken bum is just not sufficiently similar to either robbery or purse snatchings.

Upon these facts, the decoy simply provided the opportunity to commit a crime to anyone who succumbed to the lure of the bait.

Similarly, in the instant case, through the state's own witnesses at trial, Oliver's counsel established a prima facie showing that Oliver's criminal act was instigated by the state. There was no countervailing evidence whatever. Accordingly, on this record, we must conclude as a matter of law that Oliver was entrapped, and we reverse his conviction.

◆   ◆   ◆

DePasquale v. State
757 P.2d 367 (1988)

Vincent DePasquale was convicted of larceny from person in the Eighth Judicial District Court, Clark County and sentenced to ten years in prison. He appealed and the Nevada Supreme Court affirmed.

YOUNG, J.

FACTS

Four officers on the LVMPD's S.C.A.T. Unit (Street Crime Attack Team) were performing a decoy operation near the intersection of Fremont Street and Casino Center Blvd. in Las Vegas on April 30, 1983, at 11:45 P.M. Officer Debbie Gautwier was the decoy, and Officers Shalhoob, Young, and Harkness were assigned to "back-up."

Officer Gautwier was dressed in plain clothes and was carrying a tan shoulder bag draped over her left shoulder. Within one of the side, zippered pockets of the bag, she had placed a $5 bill and $1 bill wrapped with a simulated $100 bill. The money, including the numbers of the simulated $100 bill, were exposed so as to be visible to persons near by; however, the zipper was pulled tight against the money so as to require a concentrated effort to remove it.

Officer Young, also in plain clothes, was standing approximately six to seven feet away from Officer Gautwier (the decoy), near the entrance of the Horseshoe Club, when Randall DeBelloy approached Officer Gautwier from behind and asked if he could borrow a pen. Officer Gautwier stated that she did not have a pen, and DeBelloy retreated eight to ten feet. Within a few seconds he approached a second time, asking for a piece of paper. Again the response was "no." During these approaches Officer Young observed DeBelloy reach around Officer Gautwier toward the exposed cash.

DeBelloy again retreated eight to ten feet from Officer Gautwier. He then motioned with his hand to two men who were another eight to ten feet away, and the trio huddled together for 15 to 30 seconds. As DeBelloy talked with the two men, he looked up and over in the direction of Officer Gautwier. Vincent DePasquale was one of the two men who joined DeBelloy in this huddle.

While this trio was conversing, Officer Gautwier had been waiting for the walk signal at the intersection. When the light changed, she crossed Fremont Street and proceeded southbound on the west sidewalk of Casino Center Blvd. DePasquale and DeBelloy followed her, 15 to 20 feet behind. After crossing the street, Officer Gautwier looked back briefly and saw DeBelloy following her. DePasquale was four to seven feet behind DeBelloy and to his right.

As they walked in this formation, DePasquale yelled out, "Wait lady, can I talk to you for a minute." As Officer Gautwier turned to her right in response—seeing DePasquale whom she identified in court—DeBelloy took a few quick steps to her left side, took the money with his right hand and ran. DeBelloy was arrested, with the marked money in his possession, by Officers Harkness and Shalhoob. DePasquale was arrested by Officers Gautwier and Young. Both were charged with larceny from the person and convicted by a jury.

OPINION

DePasquale argues that he was entrapped, that the district court erred in its instruction to the jury on the law of entrapment, that the evidence fails to support the verdict, and that the sentence of ten years is disproportionate and, therefore, cruel and unusual.

In *Shrader v. State*, 706 P.2d 834, 837 (1985), we stated that "entrapment encompasses two elements:

(1) an opportunity to commit a crime is presented by the state

(2) to a person not predisposed to commit the act." Thus, this subjective approach focuses upon the defendant's predisposition to commit the crime.

In contrast,* in the present case, the cash, although exposed, was zipped tightly to the edge of a zippered pocket, not hanging temptingly from the pocket of an unconscious derelict. Admittedly, the money was exposed; however, that attraction alone fails to cast a pall over the defendant's predisposition. The exposed valuables (money) were presented in a realistic situation, an alert and well-dressed woman walking on the open sidewalks in the casino area. The fact that the money was exposed simply presented a generally identified social predator with a logical target. These facts suggest that DePasquale was predisposed to commit this crime. Furthermore, the fact that DePasquale had no contact with the decoy but rather succumbed to the apparent temptation of his co-defendant to systematically stalk their target, evidences his predisposition....

Lastly, DePasquale complains that his sentence was disproportionate to the crime and, therefore, cruel and unusual punishment. In *Schmidt v. State*, 584 P.2d 695, 697 (1978), we stated...a sentence is unconstitutional "if it is so disproportionate to the crime for which it is inflicted that it shocks the conscience and offends fundamental notions of human dignity...." While the punishment authorized in Nevada is strict, it is not cruel and unusual....

Accordingly, we AFFIRM the judgment of conviction.

---

*Contrast with *Oliver v. State*, excerpted on p. 269.

Questions

1. State the test for entrapment according to Nevada law.

2. What facts led the court to conclude that Oliver was entrapped but DePasquale wasn't?

EXPLORING ENTRAPMENT FURTHER

 Go to the Criminal Law 8e CD to read the full text version of the case featured here.

Was the Use of a Sexual Relationship Entrapment?

FACTS

An undercover agent for the FBI, with the knowledge of other federal agents, developed a sexual relationship with a target. After developing the relationship, she asked the target to sell drugs to some "friends" who, unknown to the target, were also FBI agents. Was the target entrapped?

DECISION AND REASONS

No, said the Ninth Circuit Court of Appeals. It saw

...no principled way to identify a fixed point along the continuum from casual physical contact to intense physical bonding beyond which the relationship becomes 'shocking' when entertained by an informant.

U.S. v. Simpson 1987

◆　　◆　　◆

The Objective Test

A minority of courts follow an **objective test of entrapment.** The objective test of entrapment focuses not on the predisposition of defendants but instead on the actions that government agents take to induce individuals to commit crimes. According to the objective test, if the intent originates with the government and their actions would tempt an "ordinarily law-abiding" person to commit the crime, the court should dismiss the case even if the defendant was predisposed to commit the crime. This test is a prophylactic rule aimed to deter "unsavory police methods" (American Law Institute 1985 1:2, 406–407).

ELEMENTS OF SUBJECTIVE VS. OBJECTIVE TESTS	
Subjective	**Objective**
1. Government creates intent +	1. Government creates intent +
2. Defendant not predisposed to commit crime =	2. Their actions would tempt an "ordinarily law-abiding" person to commit the crime =
3. Subjective entrapment	3. Objective entrapment

SYNDROMES

Since the 1970s, a range of **syndromes,** describing affected mental states, has led to novel defenses in criminal law. *Webster's* defines a *syndrome* as "a group of symptoms or signs typical of a disease, disturbance, condition...." Law professor and famous defense attorney Alan Dershowitz (1994) has written a book about these novel defenses. And its title, *The Abuse Excuse and Other Cop-Outs, Sob Stories, and Evasions of Responsibility,* makes clear his opinion of them. Dershowitz's book includes discussions of the policeman's, love, fear, chronic brain, and holocaust syndromes. He worries these excuses are "quickly becoming a license to kill and maim" (3). His is probably a needless worry because defendants rarely plead these excuses, and except for a few notorious cases picked up by television and the newspapers, defendants rarely succeed when they do plead syndromes and other "abuse excuses."

However, some syndromes are (and should be) taken seriously as excuses. For example, some women have relied on the battered woman's syndrome to justify killing spouses in self-defense, even though they weren't in imminent danger (Chapter 7). Occasionally, women also have used premenstrual syndrome (PMS) to excuse their crimes. In a New York case (*Newsweek* 1982), Shirley Santos called the police, telling them, "My little girl is sick." The medical team in the hospital emergency room diagnosed the welts on her little girl's legs and the blood in her urine as the results of child abuse. The police arrested Santos, who explained, "I don't remember what happened.... I would never hurt my baby.... I just got my period" (111).

At a preliminary hearing, Santos asserted PMS as a complete defense to assault and endangering the welfare of a child, both felonies. She admitted beating her child but argued that she had blacked out because of PMS; hence, she couldn't have formed the intent to assault or endanger her child's welfare. After lengthy plea bargaining, the prosecutor dropped the felony charges, and Santos pleaded guilty to the misdemeanor of harassment. She received no sentence, not even probation or a fine, even though her daughter spent two weeks in the hospital from the injuries. The plea bargaining prevented a legal test of the PMS defense in this case. Nevertheless, the judge's leniency suggests that PMS affected the outcome informally.

Still, there are three obstacles to proving the PMS defense (Carney and Williams 1983):

1. Defendants have to prove that PMS is a disease; little medical research exists to prove that it is.

2. The defendant has to suffer from PMS; rarely do medical records document the condition.

3. The PMS has to cause the mental impairment that excuses the conduct; too much skepticism still surrounds PMS to expect ready acceptance that it excuses criminal conduct.

The Vietnam War led to another syndrome defense, Post-Traumatic Stress Syndrome. Many of the war's combat soldiers suffered emotional and mental casualties that were often more lasting and serious than their physical wounds. The Tennessee Court of Criminal Appeals dealt with Post-Traumatic Stress Syndrome and a Gulf War veteran who killed his wife's boyfriend in *State v. Phipps* (1994).

CASE | ***Could Post-Traumatic Stress Syndrome Be an Excuse?***

State v. Phipps
883 S.W.2d 138 (Tenn.App. 1994)

David Phipps, Defendant, was convicted of first-degree murder of his wife's paramour following trial in the Circuit Court, Henry County. Defendant appealed. The Court of Criminal Appeals reversed and remanded for new trial.

WHITE, J.

FACTS

In the fall of 1990, the appellant, David Phipps, a career soldier, was sent to Saudi Arabia as part of the forces in Desert Shield and Desert Storm. His military occupational specialty was that of a nuclear-chemical/biological-chemical warfare coordinator with an emphasis on decontamination. He was responsible for providing appropriate chemical measures and counter-measures and served in a front line unit that was one of the first to enter Iraq. Appellant received a bronze star for his exemplary service in Desert Storm.

While appellant was in Saudi Arabia, his wife, Marcie Ann, entered into a relationship with Michael Presson. Throughout the course of their twelve-year marriage, the appellant had been aware of Marcie's numerous relationships with other men. He was, however, unaware of the existence of Michael Presson until he returned to the United States in April, 1991. Although Marcie Phipps corresponded with her husband while he was overseas and spoke with him by telephone, she did not reveal that she was involved with another man.

Within a month of appellant's return to the States, his wife informed him that she had been living with Presson while he was overseas and that she wanted a divorce. She then moved her possessions out of their home. Marcie Phipps continued to communicate with appellant, visited him occasionally to discuss financial matters, shared meals, and had sexual relations with him. Appellant accompanied her to a trial in which she was a plaintiff. Appellant implored her to move back home, but she refused. Approximately a week after his wife left him, appellant attempted suicide.

On Friday, May 31, 1991, Marcie Phipps and appellant met at their home to work on some bills. She gave the appellant a check for her portion of the bills. They had lunch together and shared a bottle of wine. Marcie Phipps left about 3:00 P.M., returned to the home she shared with the victim, prepared his supper, and laid down until 10:00 P.M. when she left for work. Marcie Phipps' work schedule, known to the appellant, was 11:00 P.M. to 7:00 A.M. During her shift that evening the victim visited on her break around 2:55 A.M. and stayed until 4:00 A.M.

At approximately 4:45 A.M. on June 1st, several of the victim's neighbors were awakened by the sounds of a struggle. At trial, they described repeated thuds that sounded as though someone were hitting a tree or the pavement with a board. The neighbors heard cries for help, grunting, and moaning. In the dark, one neighbor saw "something" being dragged across the yard to a vehicle.

In response to a disturbance call at 4:51 A.M., Officer Damon Lowe, a Henry County deputy sheriff, went to the scene. He found a white Oldsmobile Cutlass parked in the driveway and a white male, the appellant, sitting on the driver's side. The keys were in the ignition. The victim, who was still alive, was lying on the back seat of the car. He appeared to have been brutally and savagely beaten. He was wearing only black underwear and was covered with blood. Lying on top of the victim was a blood-covered wooden stick, probably an ax handle, and one black glove. A second black glove was found on the floor of the back seat. The ax handle had a price tag on it. Testing revealed no fingerprints. The gloves were standard issue military work gloves.

When the deputy found appellant in the car, his pants, shirt, and shoes were covered with blood, he was sweating profusely, and he appeared to be very exhausted. He was wearing a knife in a sheath. At first, the appellant said that as he was driving down the road he saw a fight and had stopped to take the injured man to the emergency room. A few minutes later, he told the officer that he thought the man's name was David Presson and that his wife had been living with Presson.

Appellant's truck was located in a gravel lot across the street from the victim's home and was parked behind some school buses. The truck could not be seen from the victim's house but the view from the truck was of the highway on which Marcie Phipps would return home from work. In the back of the truck were a shovel, a gas can, a tool box, a face shield, and a pair of work gloves. A knapsack propped against the front steps of the house contained a weight bar, nylon rope, garbage bags, and duct tape.

The appellant did not deny beating Presson to death. He testified that he went to the house to wait for his wife to return from work in the hope that he could convince her to leave Presson and come back to him. However, at some point, he approached the house carrying the knapsack. [Appellant testified that the items in the knapsack were for his own suicide which he intended to threaten if his wife refused to return to him.] According to the appellant, Presson was watching television. The appellant knocked on the screen door and entered. Presson jumped up, threw a glass at the appellant, and ran out a side door. Presson went to his car and Phipps thought he was going to leave. However, Presson returned to the house with a stick in his hand. Presson told Phipps that Marcie was no longer his and to leave. According to Phipps, Presson threatened him with the stick. Phipps grabbed the stick and a struggle ensued. Although Phipps said that he had no clear memory of the events that followed, he had no doubt that he struck many blows to the body and head of Presson. He remembered moving the body and being in the car with the body.

On cross-examination, Richard Hixson testified that two weeks before the murder, he, the appellant and a third party had discussed a murder in which the body was hidden in the woods and burned.

Four experts testified as to the appellant's mental state. Dr. Samuel Craddock and Dr. Jackson B. White testified for the state and Dr. William D. Kenner and Dr. Patricia Auble testified for the appellant. All four experts agreed that David Phipps was competent to stand trial and that he was not legally insane at the time of the murder. However, all four experts also agreed that the appellant was suffering from major depression and post-traumatic stress syndrome.

The appellant testified to his experiences during Operation Desert Storm which included his killing a young Iraqi soldier outside the camp and the suicide of an officer. Soldiers who served with the defendant testified to the constant tension created by being on the front line and the anxiety caused by Iraqi scud attacks. They also recounted two incidents in which the appellant had behaved in an unusual manner. In addition to failing to report to his superiors the incident with the young Iraqi, appellant threw his gun into the sand when ordered to remain in Iraq after the rest of his unit moved out. Witnesses viewed those actions as totally out of character for the appellant who was considered an outstanding soldier with an exemplary military record.

Dr. Craddock testified that appellant's depression was "of a sufficient level to significantly affect his thinking, reasoning, judgment, and emotional well-being," and that the "components of his post-traumatic stress disorder may have lessened his threshold or made him more sensitive to defending himself and protecting himself and increased the likelihood of him over-reacting to a real or perceived threat."

Dr. White, the other state expert, agreed that appellant's anxiety was sufficient to significantly affect his thinking and reasoning.

Dr. Kenner, testifying for the defense, stated that while the defendant was not insane, he was unable to make a calculated decision to murder someone.

While Dr. Auble, a psychologist, expressed no opinion on appellant's ability to formulate intent, she agreed with the other three experts that the appellant was suffering from major depression, severe anxiety, and post-traumatic stress syndrome.

All experts expressed the opinion that the appellant was truthful and that he was not dissembling or faking any symptoms.

OPINION

...At trial, the appellant did not deny committing the murder, nor did he plead insanity. His theory of defense was that at the time of the killing he could not and did not formulate the specific intent required to commit first-degree murder.

The trial court rejected appellant's request for a jury instruction based on his theory of the case.*

After giving the pattern instructions on the elements of first-degree murder, including premeditation and deliberation, second-degree murder, and voluntary manslaughter, [the court] issued the following instruction:

> The defendant contends that he was suffering from mental conditions known as post traumatic stress disorder, and major depression at the time of the commission of the criminal offense giving rise to this case. I charge you that post traumatic stress disorder and major depression are not defenses to a criminal charge. Insanity may be a defense, however, the defendant makes no claim that he was insane at the time of the killing giving rise to this case.

Immediately following the above-quoted instruction, the court instructed the jury that:

> The state must have proven beyond a reasonable doubt the required culpable mental state of the defendant before finding him guilty of the offense of first degree murder, or either of the two lesser included offenses earlier set out for you in this charge. As you were earlier

---

*Defendant's Requested Jury Instruction No. 1, which was rejected by the trial court, read as follows:

The jury is further instructed that the defense has submitted evidence that the Defendant was suffering from a mental condition known as post-traumatic stress disorder. This evidence should be considered by you, specifically in reference to whether or not the Defendant possessed the necessary premeditation or malice necessary for him to be convicted of Murder in the First or Second Degree.

The jury is further instructed that you should consider this condition and the expert testimony thereto in relation to the crime of Voluntary Manslaughter as it relates to whether or not the mental condition of the Defendant further obscured his reasoning at the time of the offense and also affected his ability to be reasonably and adequately provoked.

While this evidence may not establish a defense wherein the Defendant would be found not guilty of any offense, it may be considered by you in deliberating upon the necessary elements of Murder in the First Degree, Murder in the Second Degree, and Voluntary Manslaughter, as are herein explained to you.

As I have further instructed you, should you find that the necessary elements of any of these grades of homicide are not present, the Defendant must be acquitted as to that charge and you may consider evidence of post-traumatic stress disorder, along with other relevant evidence in arriving at your verdict.

instructed the killing must have been an intentional, deliberate act done with premeditation for the defendant to be guilty of first degree murder. As to either of the two lesser included offenses, the state must have proven beyond a reasonable doubt that the act was either intentionally or knowingly committed, again as you were earlier instructed.

The essence of appellant's defense was that at the time of the killing he lacked the requisite mental state for first-degree murder. In support of that defense he offered expert and lay testimony which, without contradiction, indicated that he was suffering from post-traumatic stress syndrome and major depression. The court instructed the jury that the evidence offered did not constitute a defense and refused to instruct the jury, as appellant requested, that the evidence could be considered on the issue of proof of requisite mental state. While the court's statement was technically accurate, we are called upon to determine whether the instruction, taken as a whole, fairly advised the jury.

In order to resolve this issue, we must answer two questions: first, whether under Tennessee law the jury is permitted to consider this type of testimony on the issue of intent; and secondly, if so, whether the jury instructions, taken as a whole, had the probable effect of excluding evidence of appellant's mental state from the jury's consideration of the element of specific intent?

For the reasons discussed below, we are compelled to answer both questions in the affirmative. Consequently, we reverse and remand for a new trial but offer no opinion on the substance of appellant's defense....

Evidence of the condition of the mind of the accused at the time of the crime, together with the surrounding circumstances, may be introduced...to prove that the situation was such that a specific intent was not entertained—that is, to show absence of any deliberate or premeditated design....It is clear that the vast majority of jurisdictions that have addressed the issue, allow evidence of a defendant's mental state to negate the existence of *mens rea*....

To find otherwise would deprive a criminal defendant of the right to defend against one of the essential elements of every criminal case. In effect, then, such a finding would deprive the defendant of the means to challenge an aspect of the prosecution's case and remove the burden of proof on that element in contravention of constitutional and statutory law.

While the law presumes sanity it does not presume *mens rea*. Due process requires that the government prove every element of an offense beyond a reasonable doubt. Defendants have a right to present competent and reliable evidence in support of their defenses....The weight of precedent in Tennessee as well as the well-reasoned opinions of the federal circuit courts and of our sister states lead us to conclude that evidence, including expert testimony, on an accused's mental state, is admissible in Tennessee to negate the elements of specific intent, including premeditation and deliberation in a first-degree murder case....

Appellant contends that the jury instruction given by the trial court which stated that post-traumatic stress syndrome and major depression were not defenses to a criminal offense in effect precluded the jury from considering the expert testimony relating to his mental state on the element of intent. We agree.

In this case, the instructions as a whole did not give a clear and distinct exposition of the law in Tennessee. Although the trial court correctly instructed the jury on the elements of first-degree murder, second-degree murder, and voluntary manslaughter, the comment on the nonexistence of the "defense" of post-traumatic stress disorder did not clearly reflect the state of the law in Tennessee. Moreover, it suggested that the evidence was impertinent. As such it served to exclude from jury consideration defendant's theory of the case.

Appellant did not rely on an insanity defense or on any affirmative defense. The cornerstone of appellant's case was that he did not have the requisite intent to commit first-degree murder. Virtually all of his testimony was directed toward negating the specific intent element of first-degree murder. While those schooled in the law may be able to discern the difference between considering expert testimony on defendant's mental condition as a complete defense to the charge and considering it to determine whether the requisite mental state has been proved, that subtlety would be lost on most jurors absent clear instructions.

DISSENT

CORNELIUS, SJ.

In my opinion the direct evidence overwhelmingly established a most brutal and atrocious homicide. The evidence points unerringly to this having been an intentional, deliberately premeditated killing of another human being.

From my review of the record, I find that the evidence, both direct and circumstantial, is overwhelmingly sufficient for any rational trier of fact to find beyond a reasonable doubt that this defendant is guilty of an intentional, deliberately premeditated murder in the first degree for the crime charged. He did not plead insanity, nor did any of the experts find him entitled to such a defense....

Questions

1. State the exact rule the court adopts regarding post-traumatic stress.

2. Summarize the court's arguments for admitting evidence of Post-Traumatic Stress Syndrome.

3. List all the evidence supporting the claim that David Phipps suffered from Post-Traumatic Stress Syndrome.

4. Assume you're the prosecutor, and argue Phipps had the specific intent to kill his wife's boyfriend.

5. Assume you're the defense attorney, and argue Phipps didn't have the specific intent to kill his wife's boyfriend.

6. Now, assume you're a juror. Would you vote to convict or acquit? Defend your answer.

SUMMARY

I. Excuses
    A. Difference between justification and excuse
        1. Justification—"I am responsible, but, under the circumstances, I did the right thing"
        2. Excuse—"I did wrong, but, under the circumstances, I'm not responsible"
    B. Circumstances affecting responsibility
        1. *Actus reus*—the act was involuntary
        2. *Mens rea*—a mental disease or defect left him unable to form criminal intent
    C. Origins of circumstances
        1. Abnormal people—have a mental disease or defect or their age impairs their reasoning skills

a. Insanity

b. Diminished capacity

c. Age

2. Abnormal situations

a. Duress

b. Intoxication

c. Entrapment

d. Syndrome

II. Insanity

A. Definition—defendant was so mentally diseased, he couldn't form intent or control his actions

B. A legal, but not a medical, concept

C. Rationale—can't blame people who aren't responsible

D. Consequence—commitment, not freedom

E. Tests

1. Right-wrong elements

a. Mental disease (psychosis) or defect (retardation) damaged reason at the time of the crime

b. Defendant didn't know (simple awareness)

(1) Nature of her actions

(2) Right or wrong

(a) Legal wrong

(b) Moral wrong

2. Product-of-mental illness elements

a. Checks for both reason and will

b. Acts that are a product of mental illness excuse criminal liability

3. Irresistible impulse elements

a. Defendant had a mental disease or defect at the time of the crime

b. Defendant knew the nature of act and knew it was wrong

c. The mental disease or defect caused an impulse he couldn't control

4. Substantial capacity elements

a. The mental disease or defect damages either or both reason and will

b. The mental disease or defect causes

(1) Substantial (not complete) lack of reason and control

(2) Failure to appreciate (not just purely intellectual awareness of) nature or wrongfulness

(3) Failure to conform behavior to law

F. Burden of proof

1. Federal standard

a. Government has to prove sanity beyond a reasonable doubt

b. Defense has only to raise a reasonable doubt about sanity

2. Most states—affirmative defense

a. Defendant must show some evidence of insanity

b. Government then has to prove sanity (in varying levels, depending on the state)

(1) Beyond a reasonable doubt

(2) With clear and convincing evidence

(3) By a preponderance of the evidence

III. Diminished capacity
   A. Mental disease or defect diminishes capacity but not enough to qualify as insanity
   B. Limited to diseases or defects that make it impossible to form the specific intent required to commit the crime

IV. Age
   A. Immaturity excuses criminal liability
   B. Age of maturity varies, but three stages
      1. Early childhood—can't form criminal intent
      2. Middle childhood—rebuttable presumption against capacity to form intent
      3. Adult—conclusive presumption of capacity to form intent
   C. Age can aggravate as well as excuse criminal responsibility

V. Duress
   A. Definition—individuals who commit crimes because they're threatened with harm if they don't
   B. Three grounds for the defense
      1. No *actus reus*
      2. No *mens rea*
      3. Sound public policy
   C. Elements
      1. Qualifying crimes vary from minor to serious (never for homicide)
      2. Kinds of threats vary from kill to do serious bodily harm
      3. From instant to imminent threat
      4. Measurement of belief regarding threats varies as to objective or subjective

VI. Intoxication
   A. Voluntary is no excuse
   B. Involuntary is an excuse

VII. Entrapment
   A. Definition—persuading someone to commit a crime she wouldn't otherwise commit
   B. Defense of entrapment is not a constitutional right
   C. Subjective test (majority rule)
      1. Did criminal intent originate with the government?
      2. Was the defendant predisposed to commit the crime?
   D. Objective test (minority rule)
      1. Did criminal intent originate with the government?
      2. Would ordinary law-abiding people be tempted to commit the crime?
      3. Dismiss even if the defendant is predisposed

VIII. Syndrome elements
   A. Groups of symptoms impair mental capacity
   B. Affects defendant's capacity to form specific intent
   C. Expert testimony is used to inform the jury of the syndrome

Go to the Criminal Law 8e CD to download this summary outline. The outline has been formatted so that you can add notes to it during class lectures, or later create a customized chapter outline to use while reviewing. Either way, the summary outline will help you understand the "big picture" and fill in the details as you study.

REVIEW QUESTIONS

1. Describe and explain the public misunderstanding about how the insanity defense works.

2. What important proposition does the insanity defense stand for?

3. What do we mean by saying insanity is a legal not a medical term?

4. Identify the four tests of the insanity defense, and contrast the views of mental capacity in each.

5. State and explain the elements of the right-wrong test of insanity.

6. Describe the origins of the irresistible impulse test of insanity, and explain the elements of the test.

7. State and explain the elements of the substantial capacity test.

8. Summarize the arguments for and against each of the four tests of insanity.

9. Identify and explain the various approaches to who has to prove insanity and by how convincingly they have to prove it.

10. Explain the difference between "diminished capacity" and insanity. Give an example of the limits each has as an excuse.

11. Identify, describe, and explain the legal significance of and the reasons for dividing ages into groups for purposes of excusing criminal liability.

12. Identify the four elements of the defense of duress and summarize the different definitions adopted by the states on each.

13. What two conflicting principles is the defense of intoxication buffeted between?

14. For purposes of excuse, what's the significance of the difference between voluntary and involuntary intoxication?

15. Summarize the arguments for and against the defense of entrapment.

16. Identify and explain the elements in the subjective and objective tests of entrapment.

17. Define *syndromes,* and explain their significance as excuses to criminal liability.

18. List three obstacles to proving PMS (premenstrual syndrome) as an excuse.

KEY TERMS

abnormal p. 239
insanity p. 240
civil commitment p. 240
cognition p. 241
volition p. 241
right-wrong test (M'Naghten rule) p. 241

reason p. 241
mental disease p. 241
mental defect p. 242
nature and quality of the act p. 242
wrong (in insanity defense) p. 242
product test p. 244

Durham rule p. 244
irresistible impulse test p. 245
substantial capacity test p. 246
burden of proof p. 252
diminished capacity p. 252
irrebuttable presumption p. 253
duress (defense of) p. 258

SUGGESTED READINGS

Go to the Criminal Law 8e CD for Suggested Readings for this chapter.

THE COMPANION WEB SITE
FOR *CRIMINAL LAW,* EIGHTH EDITION

http://cj.wadsworth.com/samaha/crim_law8e

Supplement your review of this chapter by going to the companion Web site to take one of the Tutorial Quizzes, use the flash cards to test your knowledge of the elements of various crimes and defenses, and check out the many other study aids you'll find there. You'll find valuable data and resources at your fingertips to help you study for that big exam or write that important paper.

Crimes Against Persons I: Criminal Homicide

9

Chapter Main Points

- Criminal homicide is different from all other crimes against persons because of the finality of its result: the death of the victim.
- Most of the law of criminal homicide is about grading the seriousness of the offense according to the elements of *mens rea, actus reus,* or special mitigating or aggravating circumstances.
- Grading murder into first and second degree is important because only first-degree murders qualify for the death penalty (or prison for life without parole in states without the death penalty).
- The intent to commit a qualifying felony substitutes for the intent to kill in felony murder.
- Most murder statutes apply to corporations, but, in practice, liability doesn't extend beyond the rare prosecution for involuntary manslaughter in outrageous cases.
- The heart of voluntary manslaughter is an intentional, sudden killing triggered by an adequate provocation.
- Provocation isn't an excuse for criminal homicide; it only reduces the punishment to allow for human frailty.
- Involuntary manslaughter is unintentional (reckless or negligent) killing.

Did He Murder His Wife?

Schnopps and his wife were having marital problems. Among the problems was that his wife was having an affair with a man at work. Schnopps found out about the affair. Mrs. Schnopps moved out of the house, taking their children with her. Schnopps asked his wife to come to their home and talk over their marital difficulties. Schnopps told his wife that he wanted his children at home, and that he wanted the family to remain intact. Schnopps cried during the conversation and begged his wife to let the children live with him and to keep their family together. His wife replied, "No, I am going to court, you are going to give me all the furniture, you are going to have to get the Hell out of here, you won't have nothing." Then, pointing to her crotch, she said, "You will never touch this again, because I have got something bigger and better for it."

On hearing those words, Schnopps claims that his mind went blank, and that he went "berserk." He went to a cabinet and got out a pistol he had bought and loaded the day before, and he shot his wife and himself. Schnopps survived the shooting, but his wife died. ◆

"Death is different," the U.S. Supreme Court said about capital punishment (Schauer 1987, 571). Killing is different, too—it's the most serious of all crimes. In 1769, Blackstone, the great eighteenth-century commentator on the criminal law, introduced his chapter on homicide with words that are pretty close to describing the crimes you'll be learning about in this chapter:

> Of crimes injurious to . . . persons . . . the most . . . important is the offence of taking away that life, which is the immediate gift of the great creator; and which therefore no man can be entitled to deprive . . . another of. . . . The subject therefore of the present chapter will be, the offense of homicide or destroying the life of man, in its several stages of guilt, arising from the particular circumstances of mitigation or aggravation. (177)

Of course, raping, assaulting, and kidnapping harm people, too; but however awful they may be, they leave their victims alive (Chapter 10). And, crimes against homes and property (Chapter 11)—crimes against public order and morals—also hurt their victims and society (Chapter 12), but these are injuries to worldly things. According to the distinguished professor of criminal law George P. Fletcher (1978):

> Killing another human being is not only a worldly deprivation; in the Western conception of homicide, killing is an assault on the sacred, natural order. In the Biblical view, the person who slays another was thought to acquire control over the blood—the life force—of the victim. The only way that this life force could be returned to God, the origin of all life, was to execute the slayer himself. In this conception of crime and punishment, capital execution for homicide served to expiate the desecration of the natural order. (235–236)

Most of the law of homicide is devoted to answering questions like: Is this murder first or second degree? Is that killing murder or manslaughter? Is this manslaughter voluntary or involuntary? Students ask: "Does it really matter?" Certainly not to the victim—who's already and always dead! But it does make a big practical difference. The punishment for criminal homicide depends on the degree of murder or the type of manslaughter committed. Three elements of criminal homicide—*actus reus, mens rea,* and special mitigating and aggravating circumstances—are used to grade the seriousness of each these crimes.

In this chapter, we'll look at the history of criminal homicide law, the *actus reus* and the *mens rea* elements of criminal homicide, and how they affect the way the degrees of murder and types of manslaughter are classified.

THE HISTORY OF CRIMINAL HOMICIDE LAW

Our modern law of criminal homicide took centuries to develop. By 1700, it recognized three kinds of homicide:

1. *Justifiable homicide.* Self-defense, capital punishment, and police use of deadly force (Chapter 7)

2. *Excusable homicide.* Killings while insane and accidental killings (Chapter 8)

3. *Criminal homicide.* All homicides that are neither justified nor excused (Chapter 8)

Eventually, criminal homicide was further divided into murder and manslaughter. This division was based entirely on the type of *mens rea* involved. **Murder** was killing someone "with malice aforethought." **Malice** referred to intentional killing without excuse or justification. **Aforethought** referred to planning in advance to kill (for example, poisoning or lying in wait to kill). **Manslaughter** was intentionally killing in a sudden heat of passion provoked by the victim.

As time went by, murder came to include not just premeditated killing but all intentional, "deliberate" (meaning not in the sudden heat of passion) killing. Gradually added to the list of criminal homicides were some kinds of *unintentional* killing, like deaths during the commission of felonies and extremely reckless and negligent killings (called **depraved-heart murders**). Last in the development from its "malice aforethought" beginning, the intent to inflict "serious bodily harm" was included among the crimes that satisfy the *mens rea* of criminal homicide.

Today, most states recognize four separate types of criminal homicide (which often are separated further into yet more criminal homicides), ranked according to their seriousness:

1. First-degree murder

2. Second-degree murder

3. Voluntary manslaughter

4. Involuntary manslaughter

 Go to Exercise 9-1 on the Criminal Law 8e CD to learn more about the way states classify criminal homicide.

THE ELEMENTS OF CRIMINAL HOMICIDE

As with other crimes of criminal conduct causing a criminal harm (Chapter 3), proving criminal homicide requires proof of four elements: *actus reus, mens rea,* causation, and a criminal harm result. Let's examine more closely the details of the first two elements.

The *Actus Reus* of Criminal Homicide

Homicide *actus reus* is defined in most states as "killing another live human being," "causing the death of another person," or some variation of these terms. "Killing" or "causing death" is the heart of the criminal homicide *actus reus,* and it's easy to define. We can't improve much on Blackstone's (1769) words here: "The killing may be by poisoning, striking, starving, drowning, and a thousand other forms by which human nature can be overcome" (196). In most cases, how the actor kills another doesn't matter, but, it can become very important if, as Blackstone teaches us (and modern statutes and opinions verify), "one beats another in a cruel and unusual manner" (199):

> As when a park keeper tied a boy, that was stealing wood, to a horse's tail and dragged him along the park; when a master corrected his servant with an iron bar; and a school master stomped on his scholar's belly, so that each of the sufferers died. These were justly held to be murders because, the correction being excessive.... (199–200)

Killing another "person" or "live human being" is quite another story. What's a "person"? What's a "live human being"? Some acts that result in "death" raise questions about whether a life really has been taken. In these cases, how the law defines the beginning and end of life can determine whether the act was a "killing." According to common-law criminal homicide, life begins when fetuses are "born alive" and ends when the heart and breathing stop. These definitions are still in effect in most states—but not in all. Let's look at these two ends of the spectrum covered by the *actus reus* of criminal homicide.

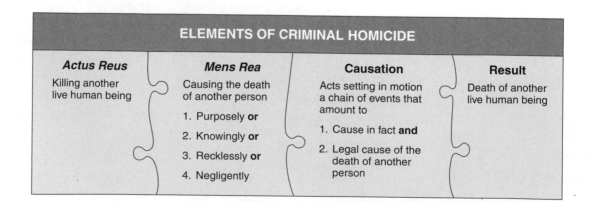

ELEMENTS OF CRIMINAL HOMICIDE

Actus Reus	*Mens Rea*	Causation	Result
Killing another live human being	Causing the death of another person 1. Purposely **or** 2. Knowingly **or** 3. Recklessly **or** 4. Negligently	Acts setting in motion a chain of events that amount to 1. Cause in fact **and** 2. Legal cause of the death of another person	Death of another live human being

When Life Begins

Some statutes define the *actus reus* as killing a "person or a fetus." Other states have specific **fetal death statutes** (laws defining when life begins for purposes of the law of criminal homicide). These statutes are highly controversial because they've gotten mixed up with the controversy over abortion. But, the crime of killing fetuses and abortion differ fundamentally: Abortion is the termination of pregnancy by a medical professional with the woman's consent. Fetal death statutes deal with killing a fetus without the woman's consent. Many who oppose making abortion a form of criminal homicide support fetal death statutes because of these differences. One more point: It would violate the Constitution to make it a crime to either perform or have a medically performed consensual abortion because, in *Roe v. Wade* (1973), the U.S. Supreme Court upheld the right of women to terminate their pregnancies under some conditions.

At the end of the day, the definition of when life begins for purposes of criminal homicide is a tough public policy question—too important to be left to lawyers and doctors. And that's as it should be. Public policy requires that *legislators* (the people's representatives) decide when life in its earliest—and latest—stages is valuable enough that taking it is the major felony of criminal homicide. No amount of medical knowledge or skill in the techniques of law can answer this question. One art student captured the dilemma in a poster. Under a drawing of a just-fertilized egg inside a happy, laughing 14-year-old girl is a caption that reads, "Which life is worth more?"

The California Supreme Court grappled with the problem of when life begins for purposes of the *actus reus* of criminal homicide in *People v. Davis* (1994).

CASE | *Did He Murder a Fetus?*

People v. Davis
872 P.2d 591 (Cal. 1994)

Robert Davis, Defendant, was convicted of murder of a fetus and he appealed. The Court of Appeal affirmed in part, reversed in part, and remanded. The Supreme Court granted review, superseding opinion of the Court of Appeal. The Supreme Court affirmed the judgment of Court of Appeal.

LUCAS, CJ.

Penal Code section 187, subdivision (a), provides that "Murder is the unlawful killing of a human being, or a fetus, with malice aforethought." In this case, we consider and reject the argument that viability of a fetus is an element of fetal murder under the statute. As will appear, however, we also conclude that this holding should not apply to defendant herein. Accordingly, we will affirm the judgment of the Court of Appeal.

FACTS

On March 1, 1991, Maria Flores, who was between 23 and 25 weeks pregnant, and her 20-month-old son, Hector, went to a check-cashing store to cash her welfare check. As Flores left the store, defendant pulled a gun from the waistband of his pants and demanded the money ($378) in her purse. When she refused to hand over the purse, defendant shot her in the chest. Flores dropped Hector as she fell to the floor and defendant fled the scene.

Flores underwent surgery to save her life. Although doctors sutured small holes in the uterine wall to prevent further bleeding, no further obstetrical surgery was undertaken because of the immaturity of the fetus. The next day, the fetus was stillborn as a direct result of its mother's blood loss, low blood pressure and state of shock. Defendant was soon apprehended and charged with assaulting and robbing Flores, as well as murdering her fetus. The prosecution charged a special circumstance of robbery-murder. (§ 190.2, subd. (a).)

At trial, the prosecution's medical experts testified the fetus's statistical chances of survival outside the womb were between 7 and 47 percent. The defense medical expert testified it was "possible for the fetus to have survived, but its chances were only 2 or 3 percent." None of the medical experts testified that survival of the fetus was "probable."

Although section 187, subdivision (a), does not expressly require a fetus be medically viable before the statute's provisions can be applied to a criminal defendant, the trial court followed several Court of Appeal decisions and instructed the jury that it must find the fetus was viable before it could find defendant guilty of murder under the statute. The trial court did not, however, give the standard viability instruction, CALJIC No. 8.10, which states that:

> A viable human fetus is one who has attained such form and development of organs as to be normally capable of living outside of the uterus.

The jury, however, was given an instruction that allowed it to convict defendant of murder if it found the fetus had a possibility of survival:

> A fetus is viable when it has achieved the capability for independent existence; that is, when it is *possible* for it to survive the trauma of birth, although with artificial medical aid. (Italics added.)

The jury convicted defendant of murder of a fetus.... Because the prosecutor did not seek the death penalty, defendant was sentenced to life without possibility of parole, plus five years for the firearm use....

OPINION

We agree with the People and the Court of Appeal that viability is not an element of fetal murder under section 187, subdivision (a), and conclude therefore that the statute does not require an instruction on viability as a prerequisite to a murder conviction. In addition, because every prior decision that had addressed the viability issue had determined that viability of the fetus was prerequisite to a murder conviction under section 187, subdivision (a), we also agree with the Court of Appeal that application of our construction of the statute to defendant would violate due process and ex post facto principles.

Accordingly, we address the instructional issue raised by defendant and agree with the Court of Appeal that the trial court prejudicially erred when it instructed the jury contrary to then-existing law, pursuant to a modified version of CALJIC No. 8.10. Thus, we conclude we should affirm the Court of Appeal judgment in its entirety (affirming the assault and robbery counts and reversing the judgment of murder).

In 1970, section 187, subdivision (a), provided: "Murder is the unlawful killing of a human being, with malice aforethought." In *Keeler v. Superior Court* (1970) 470 P.2d 617, a majority of the court held that a man who had killed a fetus carried by his estranged wife could not be prosecuted for murder because the Legislature (consistent with the common law view) probably intended the phrase "human being" to mean a person who had been born alive.

The Legislature reacted to the *Keeler* decision by amending the murder statute, section 187, subdivision (a), to include within its proscription the killing of a fetus. (Stats.1970, ch. 1311, § 1, p. 2440.) The amended statute reads: "Murder is the unlawful killing of a human being, or a fetus, with malice aforethought." (§ 187, subd. (a).) The amended statute specifically provides that it does not apply to abortions complying with the Therapeutic Abortion Act, performed by a doctor when the death of the mother was substantially certain in the absence of an abortion, or whenever the mother solicited, aided, and otherwise chose to abort the fetus. (§ 187, subd. (b).)

The legislative history of the amendment suggests the term "fetus" was deliberately left undefined after the Legislature debated whether to limit the scope of statutory application to a viable fetus. The Legislature was clearly aware that it could have limited the term "fetus" to "viable fetus," for it specifically rejected a proposed amendment that required the fetus be at least 20 weeks in gestation before the statute would apply.

In 1973, the United States Supreme Court issued a decision that balanced a mother's constitutional privacy interest in her body against a state's interest in protecting fetal life, and determined that in the context of a mother's abortion decision, the state had no legitimate interest in protecting a fetus until it reached the point of viability, or when it reached the "capability of meaningful life outside the mother's womb." (*Roe v. Wade*, 410 U.S. at p. 163) The court explained that "viability is usually placed at about seven months (28 weeks) but may occur earlier, even at 24 weeks." At the point of viability, the court determined, the state may restrict abortion.

Thereafter, in *People v. Smith (Karl Andrew)* (1976) 129 Cal.Rptr. 498 (hereafter *K. A. Smith*) the Court of Appeal construed the term "fetus" in section 187, subdivision (a), to mean a "viable fetus" as defined by *Roe v. Wade*. In *K. A. Smith*, the defendant had beaten his wife, who was 12 to 15 weeks pregnant, saying he did not want the baby to live. The wife miscarried the fetus as a direct result of the beating. At trial, the parties stipulated that the fetus was not viable at the time of the miscarriage....

Defendant asserts that section 187, subdivision (a), has no application to a fetus not meeting *Roe v. Wade*'s definition of viability. Essentially, defendant claims that because the fetus could have been legally aborted under *Roe v. Wade*, 410 U.S. at page 163, at the time it was killed, it did not attain the protection of section 187, subdivision (a). Defendant relies on *K. A. Smith* . . . to assert that if a fetus has not attained "independent human life" status under *Roe v. Wade*, it has not achieved "viability," . . . and he therefore cannot be prosecuted under section 187, subdivision (a), for its murder.

But *Roe v. Wade* does not hold that the state has no legitimate interest in protecting the fetus until viability. . . . The *Roe* decision . . . forbids the state's protection of the unborn's interests only when these interests conflict with the constitutional rights of the prospective parent. The Court did not rule that the unborn's interests could not be recognized in situations where there was no conflict." . . . The *Roe* opinion was correct in recognizing a state's legitimate interest in protecting the previable fetus. In . . . criminal law, when that interest does not oppose a protected interest of the mature mother, the state should not hesitate to vindicate it." . . . Thus, when the state's interest in protecting the life of a developing fetus is not counterbalanced against a mother's privacy right to an abortion, or other equivalent interest, the state's interest should prevail.

. . . We conclude, therefore, that when the mother's privacy interests are not at stake, the Legislature may determine whether, and at what point, it should protect life inside a mother's womb from homicide. Here, the Legislature determined that the offense of murder includes the murder of a fetus with malice aforethought. (§ 187, subd. (a).) Legislative history suggests "fetus" was left undefined in the face of divided legislative views about its meaning. Generally, however, a fetus is defined as "the unborn offspring in the postembryonic period, after major structures have been outlined." This period occurs in humans "seven or eight weeks after fertilization," and is a determination to be made by the trier of fact. Thus, we agree . . . that the Legislature could criminalize murder of the postembryonic product without the imposition of a viability requirement. . . . Accordingly, we now consider whether the trial court prejudicially erred by instructing the jury pursuant to a modified instruction on viability.

Defendant requested the jury be instructed pursuant to CALJIC No. 8.10, which defines fetal murder as follows:

> Every person who unlawfully kills a fetus with malice aforethought is guilty of the crime of murder in violation of Section 187 of the Penal Code. . . .
>
> In order to prove such crime, each of the following elements must be proved:

> 1. A viable human fetus was killed.
> 2. The killing was unlawful, and
> 3. The killing was done with malice aforethought. . . .

> A viable human fetus is one who has attained such form and development of organs as to be normally capable of living outside the uterus.

The comment to the instruction states: "The term 'fetus' as used in Penal Code, § 187, means a viable unborn child."

As noted above, the trial court gave instead the following modified version of CALJIC No. 8.10:

> Within the meaning of Penal Code section 187, subdivision (a), as charged in Count One, a fetus is viable when it has achieved the capability for independent existence; that is, when it is *possible* for it to survive the trauma of birth, although with artificial medical aid. (Italics added.)

. . . As the Court of Appeal below observed, the wording of CALJIC No. 8.10, defining viability as "normally capable of living outside of the uterus," while not a model of clarity, suggests a better than even chance—a probability—that a fetus will survive if born at that particular point in time. By contrast, the instruction given below suggests a "possibility" of survival, and essentially amounts to a finding that a fetus incapable of survival outside the womb for any discernible time would nonetheless be considered "viable" within the meaning of section 187, subdivision (a). Because the instruction given by the trial court substantially lowered the viability threshold as commonly understood and accepted, we conclude that the trial court erred in instructing the jury pursuant to a modified version of CALJIC No. 8.10.

The question then is whether it is reasonably probable a result more favorable to defendant would have been reached absent the instructional error. The record shows the weight of the medical testimony was against the probability of the fetus being viable at the point it was killed. Defendant's medical expert opined that it was "possible" for the fetus to have survived the trauma of an early birth, but that its chances for survival were about 2 or 3 percent. . . . None of the medical experts who testified at defendant's trial believed that the fetus had a "probable" chance of survival. Accordingly, because the evidence on the issue of viability erroneously supported the concept of the "possibility" of survival, and the jury was then instructed that viability means "possible survival," the jury was misinformed that it could find the fetus was viable before it "'attained such form and development of organs as to be normally capable of living outside the uterus." Had the jury been given CALJIC No. 8.10, it is reasonably probable it would have found the fetus not viable. We conclude, therefore, that defendant was prejudiced by the instructional error and the conviction of fetal murder must be reversed.

We conclude that viability is not an element of fetal homicide under section 187, subdivision (a). The third party killing of a fetus with malice aforethought is murder under section 187, subdivision (a), as long as the state can show that the fetus has progressed beyond the embryonic stage of seven to eight weeks.

We also conclude that our holding should not apply to defendant and that the trial court committed prejudicial error by instructing the jury pursuant to a modified version of CALJIC No. 8.10. We therefore affirm the judgment of the Court of Appeal. Because of the multiple opinions in this case, we believe it appropriate to observe that a majority of the court concurs in our determinations that (1) viability of a fetus is not an element of fetal murder under section 187, subdivision (a), (2) the instruction defining viability in terms of mere "possibility" of survival amounted to prejudicial error under ex post facto principles, and (3) the Court of Appeal judgment reversing the conviction of murder must be affirmed.

DISSENT

MOSK, J.

I dissent. I believe the Legislature intended the term "fetus" in its 1970 amendment to Penal Code section 187 to mean a *viable* fetus. I rest this belief on a number of grounds.

First, the fundamental purpose of statutory construction is to ascertain the intent of the lawmakers so as to effectuate the purpose of the law. . . . Here the legislative history of the 1970 amendment to Penal Code section 187 was unusual, even dramatic. On Friday, June 12, 1970, we filed our decision in *Keeler v. Superior Court* (1970) 470 P.2d 617, holding that the Legislature did not intend that a viable fetus be deemed a "human being" within the meaning of section 187. On the very next working day—Monday, June 15—the decision was publicly denounced by the majority floor leader of the Assembly. Although the legislative session was more than halfway over and the deadline for introducing new bills had long since passed, the majority leader nevertheless took immediate action to permit the Legislature to overrule *Keeler*: . . . The bill was passed in both houses . . . in the space of barely eight weeks. And the effort had been successful: despite the evolution of its wording, the bill's author "was convinced that it would accomplish his original intent, that is, to make Robert Keeler's actions susceptible to a charge of murder."

To determine the Legislature's intent, therefore, we need to understand precisely what were (1) "Robert Keeler's actions" and (2) this court's response to them. . . .

The material facts of *Keeler* were essentially undisputed. When Robert and Teresa Keeler were granted an interlocutory decree of divorce on September 27, 1968, Teresa was already pregnant by one Ernest Vogt. She began living with Vogt in a different city and concealed the fact from Robert. Under the decree of divorce Robert had custody of their two daughters, but Teresa had the right to take the girls on alternate weekends. Five months later, on February 23, 1969, Robert encountered Teresa driving on a rural road after delivering the girls to their home. He said to her, "I hear you're pregnant. If you are you had better stay away from the girls and from here." When Teresa got out of her car Robert looked at her abdomen and became "extremely upset." Saying, "You sure are. I'm going to stomp it out of you," he struck her in the face and pushed his knee into her abdomen. When doctors subsequently performed a Caesarean section on Teresa the fetus was delivered still-born. The pathologist was of the opinion that the fetus's fatal injury—a skull fracture—could have been caused by a blow to Teresa's abdomen.

At the time of delivery the fetus weighed five pounds and was eighteen inches in length. In light of these facts Teresa's obstetrician estimated the fetus was 35 weeks old. An attending pediatrician likewise estimated the age of the fetus as between $34\frac{1}{2}$ and 36 weeks. The expert testimony thus "concluded 'with reasonable medical certainty' that the fetus had developed to the stage of viability, i.e., that in the event of premature birth on the date in question it would have had a 75 percent to 96 percent chance of survival."

The majority opinion in *Keeler*, which I authored for the court, demonstrates the materiality of the fact that the fetus was viable by repeatedly incorporating that fact into its legal analyses and conclusions. At the outset we stated that the issue before the court was "whether an unborn but *viable* fetus is a 'human being' within the meaning of [§ 187]," and concluded that "the Legislature did not intend such a meaning" because the common law had always required a live birth to support a charge of murder. . . .

It was thus obvious to any reader of *Keeler* in 1970, as it is obvious today, that the case held that the Legislature did not intend that Robert Keeler's act of maliciously killing an "unborn but viable" fetus be prosecuted as murder under section 187. That was the holding that motivated the Legislature to act with such unusual speed upon publication of the *Keeler* opinions. . . . It follows that by enacting the 1970 amendment to section 187 the Legislature extended the crime of murder, as *Keeler* refused to do, to include the malicious killing of a *viable* fetus. To read that amendment as further extending murder to include the killing of even a *nonviable* fetus, as the lead opinion does now, is to ignore the facts and holding of *Keeler* and the direct legislative response they so plainly triggered. . . .

Yet that is the least of the problems with the lead opinion's new definition of "fetus" in section 187. Because liability after seven weeks necessarily includes liability after eight weeks, we may fairly assume that prosecutors faced with the lead opinion's imprecise definition will opt for the more inclusive figure and charge murder when the fetal death occurs at seven weeks. Do my colleagues have any idea what a seven-week-old product of conception looks like?

To begin with, it is tiny. At seven weeks its "crown-rump length"—the only dimension that can be accurately measured—is approximately 17 millimeters, or slightly over half an inch. It weighs approximately three grams, or about one-tenth of an ounce. (Eichler, *Atlas of Comparative Embryology* (1978) p. 186.) In more familiar terms, it is roughly the size and weight of a peanut. Even at eight weeks the product of conception measures only one inch and weighs only three-quarters of an ounce. It is then the size of a peanut in its shell.

If this tiny creature is examined under a magnifying glass, moreover, its appearance remains less than human. Its bulbous head takes up almost half of its body and is bent sharply downward; its eye sockets are widely spaced; its pug-like nostrils open forward; its paddle-like hands and feet are still webbed; and it retains a vestigial tail. As Professor Cynthia R. Daniels aptly put it in her recent book, *At Women's Expense, supra*, page 20, "In fact, at eight weeks most features of the fetus are so ill defined that it would be difficult for an uninformed observer to recognize it, viewed in its entirety, as distinctly human." And ... "A being so alien to what we know to be human beings seems hardly worth being made the subject of murder" (Comment, *Killing of an Unborn Child, supra*, 2 Pacific L.J. at p. 185).

The contrast between such a tiny, alien creature and the fully formed "5-pound, 18-inch, 34-week-old, living, viable child" is too obvious to be ignored. I can believe that by enacting the 1970 amendment the Legislature intended to make it murder to kill a fully viable fetus like Teresa Keeler's baby. But I cannot believe the Legislature intended to make it murder—indeed, capital murder—to cause the death of an object the size of a peanut.

It is even more unlikely that the Legislature intended many of the consequences of the lead opinion's new definition of "fetus" in section 187. ... First, ... a person may be subject to a conviction of capital murder for causing the death of an object that was literally invisible to everyone, and hence that the person had no reason to know even existed. A woman whose reproductive system contains an immature fetus a fraction of an inch long and weighing a fraction of an ounce does not, of course, appear pregnant. In fact, if she is one of many women with some irregularity in her menstrual cycle, she herself may not know she is pregnant: "quickening" does not occur until two or three months later. Unless such a woman knows she is pregnant and has disclosed that fact to the defendant, the defendant has no way of knowing she is carrying a fetus.

Nor is this problem limited to fetuses that are "seven or eight" weeks old. Although the length of time that a woman can be pregnant without her condition becoming noticeable varies according to such factors as her height and weight, the size of her fetus, and even the style of her clothing, the case at bar demonstrates that it can extend well into her pregnancy. Here Flores testified that in her opinion her pregnancy "showed" on the date of the shooting, March 1, 1991; but defendant testified to the contrary, and there was persuasive evidence to support him. It was undisputed that Flores was only an inch over five feet in height, yet on February 5, 1991, at her last visit to her obstetrician, she weighed 191 pounds. While she was not weighed again on the date of the shooting, at that stage of her pregnancy she would have gained still more weight in the intervening three and one half weeks. On this record Thomas Moore, M.D., an experienced perinatologist, testified that in his opinion it is "not likely" that on the date of the shooting a woman of Flores's stature would have showed her pregnancy when clothed and standing upright. ...

Yet the expert testimony agreed that Flores was between 23 and 25 weeks—approximately 6 months—pregnant on the date of the shooting. This is the very threshold of viability: an expert witness reported on a recent study showing that at 23 weeks the survival rate of the fetus is approximately 7 percent, at 24 weeks 35 percent, and at 25 weeks 47 percent. The case at bar thus demonstrates how long the risk of liability for fetal murder may run under the lead opinion's view before the actor either knows or has reason to know that the victim of the offense even exists. I cannot believe the Legislature intended such an enlargement of liability for the crime of capital murder. ...

Finally, the lead opinion's construction of the 1970 amendment will make our murder law unique in the nation in its severity: it appears that in no other state is it a capital offense to cause the death of a nonviable and invisible fetus that the actor neither knew nor had reason to know existed. To begin with, in the majority of states the killing of a fetus is not a homicide in any degree: "The majority of jurisdictions which have confronted the issue has followed *Keeler*, ... in holding the term 'fetus' does not fall within the definition of a human being under criminal statutes unless the term is so defined by the legislature." In those jurisdictions a live birth remains a prerequisite to a conviction of homicide.

There are, of course, jurisdictions that have enacted statutes criminalizing the killing of a fetus. ... My research has turned up at least 22, with 2 additional jurisdictions so holding as a matter of common law. For convenience I have grouped these jurisdictions into three distinct categories.

First, in at least 13 jurisdictions the killing of a fetus is not criminal unless the fetus is viable or has reached a gestational age significantly more advanced than the "seven or eight weeks" prescribed by the lead opinion....*

The second category of jurisdictions is composed of those in which the legislature has expressly declared that the killing of a product of conception is criminal regardless of its gestational age; contrary to our section 187, therefore, these statutes purport to apply to both viable and nonviable fetuses and to embryos—even to zygotes. There are at least six states in this category. In three the crime is not murder but a lesser offense.... In Arkansas [for example] the offense is deemed first degree battery and is punishable by imprisonment for not less than five nor more than twenty years; in New Mexico the offense is called "injury to [a] pregnant woman" and is punishable by imprisonment for three years with a possible fine of $5,000. Three other states have enacted special statutes making the killing of a fetus homicide under various circumstances, but none punishes fetal murder as severely as our section 187....

The third and last category of jurisdictions is composed of those in which the statute neither prescribes a minimum gestational age for a conviction of fetal murder nor expressly declares that it applies regardless of gestational age; rather, the statute is facially silent on the matter. California is such a jurisdiction, and there are at least five others.... In the remaining four states the offense is given special treatment and is punished much less severely than in California. In two of these states the offense is deemed "feticide." Thus in Indiana one who "knowingly or intentionally" terminates a pregnancy commits feticide, punishable by imprisonment for four years with a possible fine of not more than $10,000. In Louisiana one who kills an unborn child intentionally or in the commission of a listed felony commits first degree feticide punishable by imprisonment for not more than 15 years. In South Dakota one who "intentionally kills a human fetus by causing an injury to its mother" commits a felony punishable by imprisonment for 10 years with a possible fine of $10,000 (id., § 22-6-1). [FN20] And in New Hampshire one who "Purposely or knowingly causes injury to another resulting in miscarriage or stillbirth" commits first degree assault, punishable by imprisonment for not more than 15 years with a possible fine not to exceed $4,000.

---

*In seven of these states, the crime is manslaughter not murder.

Robert Keeler's act of assaulting his estranged wife for the express purpose of terminating her pregnancy by knowingly and intentionally killing her fully viable fetus would have been a crime in all the jurisdictions discussed above that have abrogated the common law rule. It would certainly be a crime in California today. But I cannot believe that in amending section 187 to make that act a crime the Legislature also intended to make California the only state in the Union in which it is a capital offense to cause the death of a nonviable and invisible fetus that the actor neither knew nor had reason to know existed. Yet this, again, is where the lead opinion's construction of the 1970 amendment inexorably takes us. I dissent from that construction....

The prosecution thus took its best shot at proving viability, and on the facts of this case was wholly unable to do so. In a retrial the medical facts will not change: a nonviable fetus will remain nonviable. Given this reality, it is highly unlikely that the prosecution will be able to make a better case for viability, let alone prove that element beyond a reasonable doubt. In these circumstances no purpose will be served by compelling the physician witnesses to repeat their lengthy testimony or by putting the survivors—Mrs. Flores and her family—through the ordeal of once again reliving the events in public. Rather, we should exercise our discretion to end this litigation so that the defendant may serve the multiple and consecutive terms of imprisonment to which he was sentenced for the crimes he actually committed.

Questions

1. State and summarize the definitions of fetus given by the trial court, the majority (called the "lead") opinion, and the dissent in the case.

2. Summarize the arguments of the court for defining fetus differently in abortion and criminal cases.

3. List all the evidence supporting each of the definitions of fetus you summarized in (1).

4. Assume you're the prosecutor, and argue Robert Davis satisfied the *actus reus* under each of the definitions.

5. Assume you're the defense attorney, and argue there's a reasonable doubt about the *actus reus* under each of the definitions.

6. In your opinion, does the evidence show Davis satisfied the *actus reus* requirement? Under which definitions? Back up your answers with the evidence and arguments of the court lead and dissenting opinions.

◆   ◆   ◆

When Life Ends

It used to be easy to define death: when the heart and breathing stop. Not any more. Determining when life ends has become increasingly complex as organ transplants and sophisticated artificial life support mechanisms make it possible to maintain vital life signs. Still, to kill a dying person, to accelerate a person's death, or to kill a "worthless" person is clearly homicide under current law. So, in *State v. Fiero* (1979, 77–78) a doctor who removed a vital organ too soon committed criminal homicide. And anyone who kills another by purposely disconnecting a respirator has also committed criminal homicide.

The concept of **brain death** has complicated the simple definition of as when the heart and breathing stop. This complication has implications not just for medicine and morals but also for criminal law. If artificial supports alone maintain breathing and the heartbeat while brain waves remain minimal or flat, brain death has occurred. The Uniform Brain Death Act provides that an individual who has suffered irreversible cessation of all brain functions, including those of the brain stem, is dead (American Law Institute 1985 [2:1], 10–11).

More difficult are cases involving individuals with enough brain functions to sustain breathing and a heartbeat but nothing more, such as patients in a **deep coma.** They may breathe and their hearts may beat on their own, but are they alive according to the criminal law? Troubling cases arise in which patients in a deep coma have been described by medical specialists as "vegetables" but regain consciousness and live for a considerable time afterward, such as the Minneapolis police officer who was shot and written off for dead after more than a year in a deep coma. He regained consciousness and lived for several more years.

As was true for defining when life begins, defining death doesn't have to be fastened to traditional legal doctrine or medical practice. Definitions of when life ends should depend on the values that homicide statutes are meant to preserve. So, it should be up to policy makers and legislators to decide the tough question: When is it criminal homicide (and how serious a degree is it?) to end the life (or allow life to end) of the critically and hopelessly injured, the gravely mentally ill, and other victims of advanced disease.

The *Mens Rea* of Criminal Homicide

Criminal homicide *mens rea* can include every state of mind we've already learned. So, there are purposeful, knowing, reckless, and negligent criminal homicides (Chapters 3–4). There are even strict liability criminal homicides (see Felony Murder and "misdemeanor manslaughter" later in this chapter). In every state and the federal government, how criminal homicide is classified and graded into degrees depends on the particular *mens rea* involved. We're all familiar with the language of some of this grading: for example, "first-degree murder," and "voluntary manslaughter." We'll learn more about the details of criminal homicide *mens rea* as we examine the degrees of murder and the types of manslaughter.

MURDER

Murder is the crime of killing a person with malice aforethought. The law defines four types of murder:

1. First-degree murder

2. Second-degree murder

3. Felony murder

4. Corporation murder

We'll look at each, in turn, and study the *actus reus, mens rea,* and other elements needed to prove these crimes. But first, we'll look briefly at the legacy of "murder" as it was defined under the common law.

Common-Law Murder

The English judge, and leading authority on the common law, Sir Edward Coke, defined common-law murder as it existed in 1600 this way:

> When a man of sound memory and of the age of discretion unlawfully kills any reasonable creature in being, and under the King's peace, *with malice aforethought, either express or implied by law,* the death taking place within a year and a day. (Italics added)
>
> American Law Institute 1985 [2:1], 14

The critical words are in italics: "with malice aforethought, either express or implied by law." These words point directly to *mens rea,* even though they don't at first look anything like what you learned in Chapter 4.

Express or implied malice aforethought was a broad term in those days, and still affects modern statutes, most of which don't define logically and clearly this vague and broad statement of murder *mens rea.* Common-law murder *mens rea* included (and some common-law states today still include) five very different mental states with very different levels of blameworthiness:

1. Intent to kill

2. Intent to inflict serious bodily harm

3. Intent to commit dangerous felonies

4. Intent to resist arrest by force

5. Creation of a greater than reckless risk of death or serious bodily harm (sometimes called depraved-heart murder, such as shooting into a crowd of people)

First-Degree Murder

As you can see from the last section, the common law didn't recognize degrees of murder; all murders were capital felonies. Pennsylvania was the first state to depart from the common law, enacting a statute in 1794 that divided murder into first and second degrees. The Pennsylvania statute provided

> all murder, which shall be perpetrated by means of poison, lying in wait, or by any other kind of willful, deliberate or premeditated killing, or which shall be committed in the perpetration, or attempt to perpetrate any arson, rape, robbery or burglary shall be deemed murder in the first degree; and all other kinds of murder shall be deemed murder in the second degree.
>
> *Pennsylvania Laws* 1794, ch. 257, §§ 1–2

First-degree murder was limited to *premeditated* (planned in advance) killings. All murders not planned in advance became murder in the second degree. The penalty for murder in the first degree was death; for second degree it was life imprisonment. Most states quickly followed Pennsylvania's example. Behind this quick adoption of the statutes was the first of many waves of opposition to the death penalty throughout U.S. history. Today, the situation is more complicated. Even first-degree murders that *qualify* (not all do) for the death penalty have to be reviewed to decide whether the death penalty should *actually be imposed*. This is because the U.S. Supreme Court has ruled that the Eighth Amendment ban on cruel and unusual punishment (Chapter 2) requires consideration in each case where there are aggravating or mitigating circumstances before a state can impose the death penalty.

The *Mens Rea* of First-Degree Murder

Notice the seriousness of first-degree murder was based on refining the *mens rea* of purpose to include two kinds: killings planned in advance (the worst kind, or most "evil" in the language of the day) and intentional killings without advance planning. The idea was (and still is) that planning ahead to kill is particularly evil; it's the "grand criterion" in Blackstone's (1769) words, "the dictate of a wicked, depraved, and malignant heart" (199). Unfortunately, modern courts don't require **premeditation** to include enough time to concoct a well-laid plan to kill. One court (*Goodman v. State* 1977) that did require real advance planning put it nicely:

> A verdict of murder in the first degree . . . is proper only if the slayer killed "as a result of careful thought and weighing of considerations; as a deliberate judgment or plan; carried on coolly and steadily, according to a preconceived design."

Most courts, in practice, reduce to meaningless the element of advanced planning by including murders that take place instantly after forming the intent to kill. According to the Arizona Supreme Court in *Macias v. State* (1929):

> There need be no appreciable space of time between the intention to kill and the act of killing. They may be as instantaneous as successive thoughts of the mind. It is only necessary that the act of killing be preceded by a concurrence of will, deliberation, and premeditation on the part of the slayer, and, if such is the case, the killing is murder in the first degree. (715)

In *State v. Hall* (1932), another judge put it this way: a defendant premeditated deliberately when his intent to kill arose "at the very moment the fatal shot was fired."

The Idaho Supreme Court dealt with the meaning of premeditated murder in the capital murder case of *State v. Snowden* (1957).

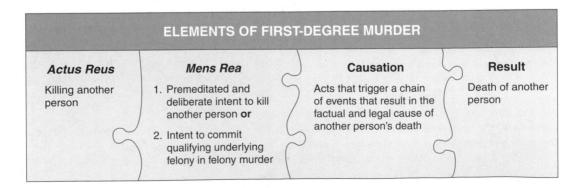

ELEMENTS OF FIRST-DEGREE MURDER			
Actus Reus	*Mens Rea*	Causation	Result
Killing another person	1. Premeditated and deliberate intent to kill another person **or** 2. Intent to commit qualifying underlying felony in felony murder	Acts that trigger a chain of events that result in the factual and legal cause of another person's death	Death of another person

State v. Snowden
313 P.2d 706 (Idaho 1957)

Ray Snowden pleaded guilty to first-degree murder. The trial judge sentenced him to death. He appealed to the Idaho supreme court. The supreme court affirmed.

MCQUADE, J.

FACTS

Ray Snowden had been playing pool and drinking in a Boise pool room early in the evening. With a companion, one Carrier, he visited a club near Boise, then went to nearby Garden City. There the two men visited a number of bars, and defendant had several drinks. Their last stop was the HiHo Club. Witnesses related that while defendant was in the HiHo Club he met and talked to Cora Lucyle Dean. The defendant himself said he hadn't been acquainted with Mrs. Dean prior to that time, but he had "seen her in a couple of the joints up town." He danced with Mrs. Dean while at the HiHo Club. Upon departing from the tavern, the two left together.

In statements to police officers, that were admitted in evidence, defendant Snowden said after they left the club Mrs. Dean wanted him to find a cab and take her back to Boise, and he refused because he didn't feel he should pay her fare. After some words, he related: "She got mad at me so I got pretty hot and I don't know whether I back handed her there or not. And, we got calmed down and decided to walk across to the gas station and call a cab."

They crossed the street, and began arguing again. Defendant said: "She swung and at the same time she kneed me again. I blew my top." Defendant said he pushed the woman over beside a pickup truck which was standing near a business building. There he pulled his knife—a pocket knife with a two-inch blade—and cut her throat.

The body, which was found the next morning, was viciously and sadistically cut and mutilated. An autopsy surgeon testified the voice box had been cut, and that this would have prevented the victim from making any intelligible outcry. There were other wounds inflicted while she was still alive—one in her neck, one in her abdomen, two in the face, and two on the back of the neck. The second neck wound severed the spinal cord and caused death. There were other wounds all over her body, and her clothing had been cut away. The nipple of the right breast was missing. There was no evidence of a sexual attack on the victim; however, some of the lacerations were around the breasts and vagina of the deceased. A blood test showed Mrs. Dean was intoxicated at the time of her death.

Defendant took the dead woman's wallet. He hailed a passing motorist and rode back to Boise with him. There he went to a bowling alley and changed clothes. He dropped his knife into a sewer, and threw the wallet away. Then he went to his hotel and cleaned up again. He put the clothes he had worn that evening into a trash barrel.

OPINION

By statute, murder is defined as the unlawful killing of a human being with malice aforethought. Degrees of murder are defined by statute as follows:

All murder which is perpetrated by means of poison, or lying in wait, torture, or by any other kind of willful, deliberate and premeditated killing...is murder of the first degree. All other murders are of the second degree.

The defendant admitted taking the life of the deceased. The principal argument of the defendant pertaining to... [premeditation] is that the defendant did not have sufficient time to develop a desire to take the life of the deceased, but rather this action was instantaneous and a normal reaction to the physical injury which she had dealt him....

The test to determine if the killing was willful, deliberate, and premeditated has been set out in *State v. Shuff*...:

The unlawful killing must be accompanied with a deliberate and clear intent to take life, in order to constitute murder of the first degree. The intent to kill must be the result of deliberate premeditation. It must be formed upon the pre-existing reflection, and not upon a sudden heat of passion sufficient to preclude the idea of deliberation....

The Supreme Court of Arizona held in the case of *Macias v. State*:

There need be no appreciable space of time between the intention to kill and the act of killing. They may be as instantaneous as successive thoughts of the mind. It is only necessary that the act of killing be preceded by a concurrence of will, deliberation, and premeditation on the part of the slayer, and, if such is the case, the killing is murder in the first degree.

In the present case, the trial court had no other alternative than to find the defendant guilty of willful, deliberate, and premeditated killing with malice aforethought in view of the defendant's acts in deliberately opening up a pocket knife, next cutting the victim's throat, and then hacking and cutting until he had killed Cora Lucyle Dean and expended himself. The full purpose and design of defendant's conduct was to take the life of the deceased. . . .*

Every person guilty of murder in the first degree shall suffer death or be punished by imprisonment in the state prison for life, and the jury may decide which punishment shall be inflicted. . . .

The trial court could have imposed life imprisonment, or, as in the instant case, sentenced the defendant to death. It is abuse of discretion we are dealing with, and in particular the alleged abuse of discretion in prescribing the punishment for murder in the first degree as committed by the defendant. To choose between the punishments of life imprisonment and death there must be some distinction between one homicide and another. This case exemplifies an abandoned and malignant heart and sadistic mind, bent upon taking human life. It is our considered conclusion, from all the facts and circumstances, the imposition of the death sentence was not an abuse of discretion by the trial court.

The judgment is AFFIRMED.

_____

*Snowden objected to the imposition of the death penalty. Idaho provides the following punishment for murder.

Questions

1. The Idaho Supreme Court upheld the trial court's finding that Snowden premeditated Dean's death. In fact, in a part of the opinion not included here, the court approved the trial judge's death sentence over life imprisonment because it was satisfied that Snowden clearly premeditated Dean's murder. Do you agree? Back up your answers with facts in the excerpt and from "The Rest of the Story" that follows these questions.

2. If you were defining premeditation in a criminal statute, would you say it's enough that the deed followed instantly upon the intention? Defend your answer.

3. What practical meaning does premeditation have according to that definition?

4. Do you think the court used premeditation as an "excuse" to make it possible to sentence Snowden to death for the especially brutal way he murdered Dean? (When you read about second-degree murder, rethink how you defined premeditation in first-degree murder.)

5. As for the sentence, do you find any mitigating circumstances, such as Snowden's intoxication, Dean's provocation, and Snowden's quick response to Dean's provocation?

THE REST OF THE STORY

Ray Snowden's Story

Idaho Historical Society, Snowden File

A. Balz

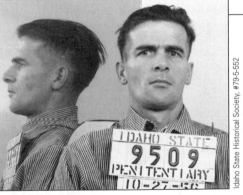

Idaho State Historical Society, #79-5-552

LIFE BEFORE THE MURDER

Raymond Allen Snowden was born on October 22, 1921, in Middleboro, Massachusetts. He was beaten as a boy; the scars were still visible when he was 36 years old in prison waiting to be executed. "He was in the principal's office a good deal of his school life." He quit school in his first year in high school to go to work. He had many jobs as "a general laborer, but he never stayed with one job more than six months." He "smoked and drank to excess." In his own words, he "fights easily and is very touchy," and "has a tendency to tear things up." He admitted to stabbing two women before he murdered Cora Dean.

March 24, 1941: Snowden joined the U.S. Army.

December 15, 1942: Snowden was dishonorably discharged from the army for assaulting and breaking his staff sergeant's jaw.

Tuesday evening, September 10, 1956: Boise police officer Frank Boor got a call from a woman six months pregnant. She said she had been accosted by a man in an alley outside a downtown bar. She said he had "held a knife to the back of her neck and threatened to cut out her unborn child unless she submitted to him." She identified the man as Raymond Snowden, 36, and said he lived at the Milner Hotel. Two detectives went to the hotel. Snowden denied the charge.

Later in the evening the hotel night clerk called police to report a disturbance in Snowden's apartment. The officers went back and found Snowden lying on the bed, holding a hand over his eye, in pain, and the woman's husband standing over him. "Snowden got to his feet, crying like a child," Officer Boor reported. Snowden threatened to have the man arrested, but neither the woman's husband nor Snowden was arrested. The woman and her husband said they'd be in the next morning to file a complaint against Snowden, but they never reappeared.

September 10–September 21, 1956: Snowden drank heavily for the next 10 days. A hotel guest encountered him in the lobby a few evenings later and inquired casually what had become of Marcy. Marcy was Snowden's girlfriend who had run off a few months before. The question triggered an emotional reaction. His eyes blazing, Snowden replied: "I know where she is, but I wouldn't spend two dollars to get her back."

FROM CORA DEAN'S MURDER TO PRISON

Saturday night, September 21, 1956: Snowden spent the morning and afternoon shooting pool and drinking beer. In the early evening he and a friend named Red climbed into the latter's car, a "souped up" Ford. He'd heard that Marcy was back in town. They went to the Collister Club, then to the Pink Elephant in Garden City, then to the Alpine Club, then to Don & Dell's, then to another place, then to the Hi-Ho Club. "I'm looking for a girl," Snowden told Red. "And if I find her I'm going to cut her heart out."

Snowden was looking for Marcy, but he found Cora Lucyle Dean instead. Dean was a recently divorced 48-year-old alcoholic. She was currently engaged to marry a Boise man, but they had fought that evening when he had returned home and found her drunk. She took a taxi to the Garden City nightclub strip, vowing she "would have herself a good time."

Snowden and Dean's encounter began "as a chance meeting of two drunks." He didn't even know her name until after he murdered her. Later, he couldn't remember whether he'd bought her a drink. They talked idly for a while. Then Snowden, noticing that Red had disappeared, asked the bartender to call a cab to take him to town. The bartender didn't hear him, so Snowden left, hoping to hail one himself. Mrs. Dean followed him out of the club.

During the course of a seven-hour interrogation, Snowden told the police that, "She asked if I was going to catch a cab to town. I said I was going to see if I could find one. And then we got to arguing about going to town, and she got mad. She said she wanted to go up town and drink, and we had a bit of an argument." The interrogation also exposed the awful details of the murder and the mutilation that followed it:

Q: What was the argument about, Ray?

A: Well, it was about whether I should pay the cab fare up town and buy drinks for her all night. I figured her boyfriend might be in town, and I didn't figure I should go up there and set up her whiskey all night. So she said something about I should for a lady and I told her that was all the more reason why I shouldn't.

So, she got mad at me so I got pretty hot and I don't know whether I back-handed her there or not. We got calmed down and decided to walk across to the gas station to call a cab.... We got across the street and started arguing some more and I said, "The hell with it," or something like that. I would take her back to the Hi-Ho. I am going back to town the best I could. We started walking back to the Hi-Ho. She swung, and at the same time she kneed me again. I blew my top.

Q: And then what happened?

A: I pushed her over by the pickup and pulled my knife out and cut her throat...She let out a squeal and fell over backwards....She was moaning and groaning so I wanted to stop the noise so I cut her throat again.

Q: What did you do then?

A: After that I don't remember much of anything.... When I became aware of what I had done I began to realize what...what I'd done, so I went on. I don't, know how to put it in words....I must have cut her up because there was blood all over the place.

Q: Do you remember how many times you cut her?

A: I don't know.

Q: Do you remember cutting her nipple from her... breast?

A: Yes.

Q: Can you tell us what you did with that nipple?

A: I ate it.

Q: You ate it, you say?

A: Yes.

Q: Did you have in mind when you cut it off you were going to eat it?

A. No.

Q: What caused you to eat it?

A: I don't know.

Outside of court, a Boise lawyer asked Snowden why he killed Dean. Snowden answered, "She kicked me in the nuts, and so I killed her."

Early Sunday morning, September 22, 1956: A young boy, out looking for empty bottles to return for deposit, found Dean's mutilated body in the alley where Snowden left her.

September 24, 1956: Snowden was arrested and charged with first-degree murder.

October 5, 1956: Snowden pleaded not guilty.

October 18, 1956: Snowden, against the advice of his court-appointed attorney, "sabotaged his own defense" by changing his initial "not guilty" plea to "guilty."

October 26, 1956: Snowden was convicted and sentenced to death.

November 18, 1956: Snowden's attorney filed a notice of appeal in the Idaho Supreme Court.

July 24, 1957: The Idaho Supreme Court affirmed the trial court's judgment of conviction and his sentence of death.

September 18, 1957: The Ada County trial court re-sentenced Snowden to death.

WAITING TO DIE

None of the prison officials who came in contact with Snowden while he was on death row remembers him as troublesome or vicious. Lew Clapp, who left the penitentiary in 1966 after serving twenty years as warden, recalls him as "a quiet man who said little. Unlike many serving lesser sentences, he appeared to be resigned to his lot."

Snowden spoke little to the guards who took turns on the 24-hour "death watch" outside his cell, which was across a hallway from the execution chamber on death row, on the second floor of the maximum-security building.

Following a lifetime habit, he read voraciously. Within a few months he had exhausted the meager stock of the prison library. He had few visitors, but those who had occasion to call brought him books. An attorney once scooped up an armful of paperbacks at random in a Boise drugstore and took them to Snowden's cell. The prisoner's eye fell on one of the titles, and he looked up with a sarcastic scowl. "You son of a bitch," he said. The title was *The First One Hundred Years.*

Time hung heavily on Snowden's hands as the weeks stretched into months while the State Supreme Court pondered his appeal.

The man who came to know him best as a prisoner was Orvil Stiles, who was then the prison chaplain and since 1967 has been the warden of the penitentiary. Snowden said little to Stiles in the first few weeks, but one day he asked the chaplain to bring him a book of crossword puzzles. Stiles brought the book on his next visit and then watched open-mouthed as Snowden snapped it open and began filling in the blanks. "I have never seen anything like it in my life," Stiles recalled much later. "He worked those puzzles as fast as a man can write and never glanced at a dictionary. He had a phenomenal mind."

It was just one of several feats of intellect that Snowden exhibited to Stiles. The chaplain brought him a Bible correspondence course. He passed it and asked for something tougher. He took a Bible memory course and learned 120 verses in less than a week. "My lord, what a memory that man had! One day I told him I was going to Nebraska for my vacation. He told me the names and locations of all the businesses in Ogallala. I guess he'd been there as a truck driver."

A brother, one of Snowden's seven siblings, came out from Massachusetts and visited him in his prison cell. The brother told Stiles that Snowden recounted the details of a fishing trip the two had taken ten years earlier, a trip that he himself had long forgotten.

As spring gave way to summer, a bond grew between the prisoner and the chaplain. They chatted cagily about inconsequential things. But Snowden was unusually somber and quiet on the day the news reached him that the Supreme Court had upheld his conviction and sentence.

"I asked him, 'Do you think your crime was so bad that not even God can find it in his heart to forgive you?' He looked at me, and for the first time we weren't talking about crossword puzzles or things like that. All he said was, 'Yes.' I saw him every day after that." Snowden was determined to get the conviction over with.

As the final days slipped by on death row he lay quietly on his bunk, reading the Bible.

October 17, 1957: Warden Clapp summoned Stiles to his office and asked him if the prisoner was ready. "Warden," said Stiles, "this man is as well prepared as any man I know."

Snowden ate his last meal in his cell, only 60 feet from the gallows where he would be hanged. The meal:

- Boiled lobster with drawn butter
- Sweet potatoes, asparagus, tossed combination salad with French dressing
- Cranberry sauce
- Hot rolls
- Tea
- Strawberry shortcake

October 18, 1957, a few minutes after midnight:

- 12:05 A.M. Snowden entered the death chamber.
- 12:05:45 seconds A.M. Twelve people watched Snowden drop through the trap door in the execution chamber of the Idaho State Penitentiary.
- 12:25:25 seconds A.M. Neither the twelve official witnesses nor anyone else who watched the hanging has ever described the nearly twenty minutes it took to kill Snowden. Nor has anyone explained why it took that long.

Not everyone agrees that premeditated killings are the worst murders. According to the nineteenth-century English judge and criminal law reformer James F. Stephen (1883):

> As much cruelty, as much indifference to the life of others, a disposition at least as dangerous to society, probably even more dangerous, is shown by sudden as by premeditated murders. The following cases appear to me to set this in a clear light. A man, passing along the road, sees a boy sitting on a bridge over a deep river and, out of mere wanton barbarity, pushes him into it and so drowns him. A man makes advances to a girl who repels him. He deliberately but instantly cuts her throat. A man civilly asked to pay a just debt pretends to get the money, loads a rifle and blows out his creditor's brains. In none of these cases is there premeditation unless the word is used in a sense as unnatural as "aforethought" in "malice aforethought," but each represents even more diabolical cruelty and ferocity than that which is involved in murders premeditated in the natural sense of the word. (94)

The *Actus Reus* of First-Degree Murder

The *actus reus* of first-degree murder also can be critical when it comes to deciding whether to sentence a person convicted of first-degree murder to death (or prison for life without parole in states without the death penalty). Killing by means of "heinous, atrocious, or cruel" acts, meaning especially brutal murders or **torture murders** intended to cause lingering death, is an aggravating factor that qualifies a murder for the death penalty. The Florida Supreme Court applied the state's "heinous, atrocious, or cruel" aggravating circumstance provision to determine whether Richard Henyard should receive the death penalty for committing murder in *Henyard v. State* (1996).

Henyard v. State
689 So.2d 239 (Fla. 1996)

Richard Henyard, Defendant, was convicted in the Circuit Court, Lake County, of sexual battery, kidnapping, and murder. Defendant appealed. The Supreme Court affirmed.

PER CURIAM.*

We have on appeal the judgment and sentence of the trial court imposing the death penalty upon Richard Henyard. We have jurisdiction, art. V, § 3(b)(1), Fla. Const., and affirm the convictions and sentence.

FACTS

Around 10 P.M. on January 30, Lynette Tschida went to the Winn Dixie store in Eustis. She saw Richard Henyard and a younger man sitting on a bench near the entrance of the store. When she left, Henyard and his companion got up from the bench; one of them walked ahead of her and the other behind her. As she approached her car, the one ahead of her went to the end of the bumper, turned around, and stood. Ms. Tschida quickly got into the car and locked the doors. As she drove away, she saw Henyard and the younger man walking back towards the store.

At the same time, the eventual survivor and victims in this case, Ms. Lewis and her daughters, Jasmine, age 3, and Jamilya, age 7, drove to the Winn Dixie store. Ms. Lewis noticed a few people sitting on a bench near the doors as she and her daughters entered the store. When Ms. Lewis left the store, she went to her car and put her daughters in the front passenger seat. As she walked behind the car to the driver's side, Ms. Lewis noticed Alfonza Smalls coming towards her. As Smalls approached, he pulled up his shirt and revealed a gun in his waistband. Smalls ordered Ms. Lewis and her daughters into the back seat of the car, and then called to Henyard. Henyard drove the Lewis car out of town as Smalls gave him directions.

The Lewis girls were crying and upset, and Smalls repeatedly demanded that Ms. Lewis "shut the girls up." As they continued to drive out of town, Ms. Lewis beseeched Jesus for help, to which Henyard replied, "this ain't Jesus, this is Satan." Later, Henyard stopped the car at a deserted

---

*A very brief, usually unanimous, decision rendered without elaborate discussion.

location and ordered Ms. Lewis out of the car. Henyard raped Ms. Lewis on the trunk of the car while her daughters remained in the back seat. Ms. Lewis attempted to reach for the gun that was lying nearby on the trunk. Smalls grabbed the gun from her and shouted, "you're not going to get the gun, bitch." Smalls also raped Ms. Lewis on the trunk of the car. Henyard then ordered her to sit on the ground near the edge of the road. When she hesitated, Henyard pushed her to the ground and shot her in the leg. Henyard shot her at close range three more times, wounding her in the neck, mouth, and the middle of the forehead between her eyes. Henyard and Smalls rolled Ms. Lewis's unconscious body off to the side of the road, and got back into the car. The last thing Ms. Lewis remembers before losing consciousness is a gun aimed at her face. Miraculously, Ms. Lewis survived and, upon regaining consciousness a few hours later, made her way to a nearby house for help. The occupants called the police and Ms. Lewis, who was covered in blood, collapsed on the front porch and waited for the officers to arrive.

As Henyard and Smalls drove the Lewis girls away from the scene where their mother had been shot and abandoned, Jasmine and Jamilya continued to cry and plead: "I want my Mommy," "Mommy," "Mommy." Shortly thereafter, Henyard stopped the car on the side of the road, got out, and lifted Jasmine out of the back seat while Jamilya got out on her own. The Lewis girls were then taken into a grassy area along the roadside where they were each killed by a single bullet fired into the head. Henyard and Smalls threw the bodies of Jasmine and Jamilya Lewis over a nearby fence into some underbrush.

Later that evening, Bryant Smith, a friend of Smalls, was at his home when Smalls, Henyard, and another individual appeared in a blue car. Henyard bragged about the rape, showed the gun to Smith, and said he had to "burn the bitch" because she tried to go for his gun. Shortly before midnight, Henyard also stopped at the Smalls' house. While he was there, Colinda Smalls, Alfonza's sister, noticed blood on his hands. When she asked Henyard about the blood, he explained that he had cut himself with a knife. The following morning, Sunday, January 31, Henyard had his "auntie," Linda Miller, drive him to the Smalls' home because he wanted to talk with Alfonza Smalls. Colinda Smalls saw Henyard shaking his finger at Smalls while they spoke, but she did not overhear their conversation....

Henyard was found guilty by the jury of three counts of armed kidnapping in violation of section 787.01, Florida Statutes (1995), one count of sexual battery with the use of a firearm in violation of section 794.011(3), Florida Statutes (1995), one count of attempted first-degree murder in violation of sections 782.04(1)(a)(1) and 777.04(1), Florida Statutes (1995), one count of robbery with a firearm in violation of section 812.13(2)(a), Florida Statutes (1995), and two counts of first-degree murder in violation of section 782.04(1)(a), Florida Statutes (1995).

After a penalty phase hearing, the jury recommended the death sentence for each murder by a vote of 12 to 0. The trial court followed this recommendation and sentenced Henyard to death. The court found in aggravation: (1) the defendant had been convicted of a prior violent felony; (2) the murder was committed in the course of a felony; (3) the murder was committed for pecuniary gain; the murder was especially heinous, atrocious or cruel, *see* section 921.141(5)(h).

The court found Henyard's age of eighteen at the time of the crime as a statutory mitigating circumstance, and accorded it "some weight." The trial court also found that the defendant was acting under an extreme emotional disturbance and his capacity to conform his conduct to the requirements of law was impaired, and accorded these mental mitigators "very little weight." As for nonstatutory mitigating circumstances, the trial court found the following circumstances but accorded them "little weight":

(1) the defendant functions at the emotional level of a thirteen year old and is of low intelligence;

(2) the defendant had an impoverished upbringing;

(3) the defendant was born into a dysfunctional family;

(4) the defendant can adjust to prison life; and

(5) the defendant could have received eight consecutive life sentences with a minimum mandatory fifty years.

Finally, the trial court accorded "some weight" to the nonstatutory mitigating circumstance that Henyard's codefendant, Alfonza Smalls, could not receive the death penalty as a matter of law. The court concluded that the mitigating circumstances did not offset the aggravating circumstances.

OPINION

. . . Henyard contends that the trial court erred in allowing Ms. Lewis to testify during the penalty phase that Henyard, upon hearing Ms. Lewis' prayers to Jesus, stated, "You might as well stop calling Jesus, this ain't Jesus this is Satan." Henyard claims his statement is not relevant to prove the existence of any aggravating circumstance. We disagree.

Under Florida law, the heinous, atrocious, or cruel aggravating circumstance may be proven in part by evidence of the infliction of "mental anguish" which the victim suffered prior to the fatal shot. In this case, Ms. Lewis testified that she was sitting in the back seat between her daughters, that her girls were quiet at the time Henyard made the statement at issue, and that Henyard spoke loudly enough for all to hear. Ms. Lewis explained that neither child had trouble hearing and she believed her daughters heard Henyard's statement. Thus, Henyard's statement, which the trial court characterized as the "harbinger" of the agonizing events to come, was relevant to show the mental anguish inflicted upon the Lewis girls before they were killed, and as evidence of the heinous, atrocious and cruel aggravating circumstance. Consequently, we find that the trial court properly admitted the statement into evidence during the penalty phase of Henyard's trial. . . .

Henyard contends that the trial court erred in finding the heinous, atrocious, or cruel aggravating circumstance in this case because each child was killed with a single gunshot, and "if the victims were adults, heinous, atrocious, [or] cruel would not be present on this record." We disagree.

We have previously upheld the application of the heinous, atrocious, or cruel aggravating factor based, in part, upon the intentional infliction of substantial mental anguish upon the victim. Moreover, "fear and emotional strain may be considered as contributing to the heinous nature of the murder, even where the victim's death was almost instantaneous." In this case, the trial court found the heinous, atrocious or cruel aggravating factor to be present based upon the entire sequence of events, including the fear and emotional trauma the children suffered during the episode culminating in their deaths and, contrary to Henyard's assertion, not merely because they were young children. Thus, we find the trial court properly found that the heinous, atrocious, or cruel aggravating factor was proved beyond a reasonable doubt in this case.

The sentencing order reads in pertinent part:

After shooting Ms. Lewis, Henyard and Smalls rolled Ms. Lewis' unconscious body off to the side of the road. Henyard got back into Ms. Lewis' car and drove a short distance down the deserted road, whereupon Henyard stopped the car.

Jasmine and Jamilya, who had been in continual close approximation and earshot of the rapes and shooting of their mother, were continuing to plead for their mother; "I want my Mommy," "Mommy," "Mommy."

After stopping the car, Henyard got out of Ms. Lewis' vehicle and proceeded to lift Jasmine out of the back seat of the car, Jamilya got out without help. Then both of the pleading and sobbing sisters, were taken a short distance from the car, where they were then executed, each with a single bullet to the head.

...Accordingly, we affirm Henyard's convictions and the imposition of the sentences of death in this case.

Questions

1. How does the court define "heinous, atrocious, and cruel"?

2. List the facts in the case that are relevant to deciding whether this was a "heinous, atrocious, and cruel" murder.

3. Summarize the arguments in favor of and against classifying this as a "heinous, cruel, and atrocious" murder.

EXPLORING THE *ACTUS REUS* OF FIRST-DEGREE MURDER FURTHER

 Go to the Criminal Law 8e CD to read the full text versions of the cases featured here.

1. Was Beating Him to Death with a Baseball Bat Atrocious First-Degree Murder?

FACTS

About 2 P.M. on Sunday, August 24, 1975, a white man about 34 years old came out of a store and walked toward his car. Siegfried Golston, a 19-year-old African American man, tiptoed up behind the victim and hit him on the head with a baseball bat. A witness testified to the sound made by Golston's blow to the victim's head: "Just like you hit a wet, you know, like a bat hit a wet baseball; that's how it sounded." Golston then went into a building, changed his clothes, and crossed the street to the store, where he worked. When asked why he had hit the man, Golston replied, "For kicks." The victim later died. Was this "atrocious murder," a form of first-degree murder that qualified Golston for the death penalty?

DECISION AND REASONS

According to the court, it was:

There was evidence of great and unusual violence in the blow, which caused a four-inch cut on the side of the

skull....There was also evidence that after he was struck the victim fell to the street, and that five minutes later he tried to get up, staggered to his feet and fell again to the ground. He was breathing very hard and a neighbor wiped vomit from his nose and mouth. Later, according to the testimony, the defendant said he did it, "For kicks."

There is no requirement that the defendant know that his act was extremely atrocious or cruel, and no requirement of deliberate premeditation. A murder may be committed with extreme atrocity or cruelty even though death results from a single blow. Indifference to the victim's pain, as well as actual knowledge of it and taking pleasure in it, is cruelty; and extreme cruelty is only a higher degree of cruelty.

Commonwealth v. Golston, 249, 366 N.E.2d 744 (Mass. 1977)

2. Was Killing Him by Multiple Stabbings Heinous First-Degree Murder?

FACTS

On February 15, 1982, Lloyd Duest, carrying a knife in the waistband of his pants, boasted that he was going to a gay bar to "roll a fag." Duest was later seen at a predominantly gay bar with John Pope. Pope and Duest left the bar and drove off in Pope's gold Camaro. Several hours later, Pope's roommate returned home and found the house unlocked, the lights on, the stereo on loud, and blood on the bed. The sheriff was contacted. Upon arrival, the deputy sheriff found Pope on the bathroom floor in a pool of blood with multiple stab wounds. Duest was found and arrested on April 18, 1982. He was tried and found guilty of first-degree murder. In accordance with the jury's advisory recommendation, the trial judge imposed the death sentence. Duest argued that this was not a particularly heinous or atrocious killing. Was it?

DECISION AND REASONS

The court wrote:

We disagree with the defendant. The evidence presented at trial shows that the victim received eleven stab wounds, some of which were inflicted in the bedroom and some inflicted in the bathroom. The medical examiner's testimony revealed that the victim lived some few minutes before dying.

Duest v. State, 462 So.2d 446 (Fla.1985)

Second-Degree Murder

Most **second-degree murder** statutes include all deaths caused by intentional killings that aren't premeditated, justified, or excused. For example, Washington State's second-degree murder provision reads, "A person is guilty of murder in the second degree when... with intent to cause the death of another person but without premeditation, he causes the death of such person...." But, most second-degree murder statutes go further than this; for example, Arizona's second-degree murder statute (Arizona Criminal Code 2003, §13-1104) includes the following types of second-degree murder:

A person commits second degree murder if without premeditation:
1. Such person intentionally causes the death of another person; or
2. Knowing that his conduct will cause death or serious physical injury, such person causes the death of another person; or
3. Under circumstances manifesting extreme indifference to human life, such person recklessly engages in conduct which creates a grave risk of death and thereby causes the death of another person.

Alaska's second-degree murder statute (Alaska Criminal Code 2003, 11.41.110) provides:

(a) A person commits the crime of murder in the second degree if
(1) with intent to cause serious physical injury to another person or knowing that the conduct is substantially certain to cause death or serious physical injury to another person, the person causes the death of any person;
(2) the person knowingly engages in conduct that results in the death of another person under circumstances manifesting an extreme indifference to the value of human life;
(3) under circumstances not amounting to murder in the first degree... while acting either alone or with one or more persons, the person commits or attempts to commit arson in the first degree, kidnapping, sexual assault in the first degree, sexual assault in the second degree, sexual abuse of a minor in the first degree, sexual abuse of a minor in the second degree, burglary in the first degree, escape in the first or second degree, robbery in any degree, or misconduct involving a controlled substance... and, in the course of or in furtherance of that crime or in immediate flight from that crime, any person causes the death of a person other than one of the participants;
(4) acting with a criminal street gang, the person commits or attempts to commit a crime that is a felony and, in the course of or in furtherance of that crime or in immediate flight from that crime, any person causes the death of a person other than one of the participants; or
(5) the person with criminal negligence causes the death of a child under the age of 16...

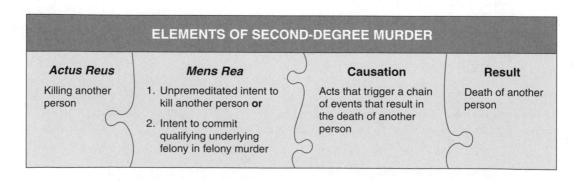

ELEMENTS OF SECOND-DEGREE MURDER			
Actus Reus	*Mens Rea*	Causation	Result
Killing another person	1. Unpremeditated intent to kill another person **or** 2. Intent to commit qualifying underlying felony in felony murder	Acts that trigger a chain of events that result in the death of another person	Death of another person

Michigan's statute (Michigan Criminal Code 2003, § 750.317) has a catchall provision: All murders that aren't first-degree are second-degree murders: "All other kinds of murder shall be murder of the second degree, and shall be punished by imprisonment in the state prison for life, or any term of years, in the discretion of the court trying the same." The Michigan Court of Appeals applied Michigan's murder provisions in *People v. Thomas* (1978).

CASE | *Did He Intend to Kill?*

People v. Thomas
85 Mich.App. 618, 272 N.W.2d 157 (1978)

Daniel Thomas was charged with second-degree murder. The jury convicted him of involuntary manslaughter. The trial judge sentenced Thomas to five to fifteen years in prison. Thomas appealed. The Michigan Court of Appeals affirmed.

HOLBROOK, JR. J.

FACTS

The victim, a 19-year-old male "catatonic schizophrenic," was at the time of his death a resident of Oak Haven, a religious practical training school. When it appeared he was not properly responding to ordinary treatment, defendant, the work coordinator at Oak Haven, obtained permission from the victim's parents to discipline him if such seemed necessary. Thereafter defendant, together with another supervisor at Oak Haven, took decedent to the edge of the campus, whereupon decedent's pants were taken down, following which he was spanked with a rubber hose. Such disciplinary session lasted approximately 15 to 30 minutes. During a portion thereof decedent's hands were tied behind his back for failure to cooperate.

Following the disciplinary session, defendant testified that the young man improved for awhile but then commenced to backslide. Defendant again received permission from decedent's parents to subject him to further discipline. On September 30, 1976, defendant again took decedent to the approximate same location, removed his pants, bound his hands behind him with a rope looped over a tree limb and proceeded to beat him with a doubled-over rubber hose. This beating lasted approximately 45 minutes to an hour. While the evidence conflicted, it appears that the victim was struck between 30 to 100 times. The beating resulted in severe bruises ranging from the victim's waist to his feet. Decedent's roommate testified that decedent had open bleeding sores on his thighs. . . .

OPINION

. . . Appellant claims that the prosecution failed to establish the malice element of second-degree murder. We disagree. Malice or intent to kill may be inferred from the acts of the defendant. In *People v. Morrin,* . . . Justice Levin stated that the intent to kill may be implied where the actor actually intends to inflict great bodily harm or the natural tendency of his behavior is to cause death or great bodily harm. In the instant case defendant's savage and brutal beating of the decedent is amply sufficient to establish malice. He clearly intended to beat the victim and the natural tendency of defendant's behavior was to cause great bodily harm. . . .

AFFIRMED.

Questions

1. Michigan Penal Code Section 750.316 defines first-degree murder this way:

> A person who commits any of the following is guilty of first degree murder and shall be punished by imprisonment for life: (a) Murder perpetrated by means of poison, lying in wait, or any other willful, deliberate, and premeditated killing.

Section 750.317 defines second-degree murder as

> All other kinds of murder shall be murder of the second degree, and shall be punished by imprisonment in the state prison for life, or any term of years, in the discretion of the court trying the same.

Although the jury found Thomas guilty of involuntary manslaughter, the Michigan court of appeals ruled that the jury could've found him guilty of second-degree murder because the facts supported the conclusion that he intended to "inflict great bodily harm" on the deceased. Do the provisions mean this? Or, do they require the specific intent to kill? Should the intent "to beat someone within an inch of his or her life" satisfy the *mens rea* of murder? Defend your answer.

2. How would you define Thomas's state of mind with respect to the student's death? Knowing? Reckless? Negligent? An accident? List the evidence that supports your answer.

3. Does this case mean that reckless homicide is murder? Should it be? Explain.

Felony Murder

Unintentional deaths that occur during the commission of some felonies are called **felony murder** in most states. What felonies? States vary widely, but the most common are criminal sexual conduct, kidnapping, robbery, arson, and burglary. What degree of murder is this? Here, too, states vary. In some states, it's first degree; in others, it's second degree. Alabama's felony murder provisions are representative:

ALABAMA CRIMINAL CODE
SECTION 13A-6-2

(a) A person commits... murder if...
He commits or attempts to commit arson in the first degree, burglary in the first or second degree, escape in the first degree, kidnapping in the first degree, rape in the first degree, robbery in any degree, sodomy in the first degree or any other felony clearly dangerous to human life and, in the course of and in furtherance of the crime that he is committing or attempting to commit, or in immediate flight therefrom, he, or another participant if there be any, causes the death of any person....
(c) Murder is a Class A felony; provided, that the punishment for murder or any offense committed under aggravated circumstances, as provided by Article 2 of Chapter 5 of this title, is death or life imprisonment without parole, which punishment shall be determined and fixed as provided by Article 2 of Chapter 5 of this title or any amendments thereto.

CHAPTER 5, ARTICLE 2, SECTION 13A-5-40

a) The following are capital offenses:
(1) Murder by the defendant during a kidnapping in the first degree or an attempt thereof committed by the defendant.
(2) Murder by the defendant during a robbery in the first degree or an attempt thereof committed by the defendant.
(3) Murder by the defendant during a rape in the first or second degree or an attempt thereof committed by the defendant; or murder by the defendant during sodomy in the first or second degree or an attempt thereof committed by the defendant.
(4) Murder by the defendant during a burglary in the first or second degree or an attempt thereof committed by the defendant....

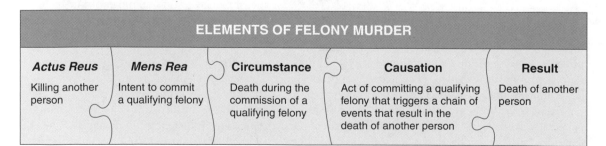

ELEMENTS OF FELONY MURDER				
Actus Reus	***Mens Rea***	**Circumstance**	**Causation**	**Result**
Killing another person	Intent to commit a qualifying felony	Death during the commission of a qualifying felony	Act of committing a qualifying felony that triggers a chain of events that result in the death of another person	Death of another person

(12) Murder by the defendant during the act of unlawfully assuming control of any aircraft by use of threats or force with intent to obtain any valuable consideration for the release of said aircraft or any passenger or crewmen thereon or to direct the route or movement of said aircraft, or otherwise exert control over said aircraft. . . .

Remember: Felony murder doesn't require the intent either to kill or to inflict serious bodily harm. In fact, most felony murderers don't want to kill or injure their victims. Then, how can these unintended deaths be murder? In felony murder, the specific intent to commit the felony substitutes for the intent to kill. Why? Take this example. If a robber fires a gun during the robbery and kills a convenience store clerk without the intent to kill, the intent to rob is blameworthy enough to satisfy the *mens rea* of felony murder.

Felony murder laws have three goals:

1. *Deter offenders.* The added threat of a murder conviction is intended to prevent would-be felons from committing felonies that can lead to death.

2. *Reduce violence.* The threat of a murder conviction is intended to curtail the use of violence during the commission of felonies by inducing felons to act more carefully during robberies and other felonies with risks of injury and death.

3. *Punish wrongdoers.* People who intentionally commit felonies connected with high risks of death or injury deserve the most punishment available.

Research hasn't shown that the rule either deters dangerous felons or reduces the number of deaths during the commission of felonies. Four states—Ohio, Hawaii, Michigan, and Kentucky—have abolished felony murder. Other states have restricted felony murder to deaths that were foreseeable during the commission of the underlying felony. In *State v. Noren* (1985), during a robbery, Monte Noren punched his victim three times in the head so hard that Noren's knuckles bled. The victim was extremely drunk, which Noren knew. The court decided that the victim's death was foreseeable. In the course of its opinion, the court explained why felony murder is limited to foreseeable deaths:

> The statutory requirement that death be a probable consequence of a felony is intended to limit felony-murder liability to situations where the defendant's conduct creates some measure of foreseeable risk of death. Under the predecessor felony-murder statute, a defendant committed murder when death resulted from the commission of any felony. This rule was modified because it imposed severe criminal sanctions without considering the moral culpability of the defendant. . . . [Therefore,] the acts causing death must be inherently dangerous to life. We apply this test to felony-murder because it requires a high degree of foreseeability, thereby implicitly requiring greater culpability than lesser grades of homicide. Our supreme court applied this standard under the predecessor felony-murder statute when it stated that the act constituting the felony must be in itself dangerous to life.

What if someone besides the felon—say the victim, police officers, a co-felon, or a bystander—causes someone's death during a felony? Some states have a **third-party exception** to the felony murder rule. In *State v. Crane* (1981), a resisting victim shot and killed one of two burglars. The court applied the third-party exception and ruled the surviving burglar couldn't be found guilty of felony murder. Similarly, in *Campbell v. State* (1982), a cabdriver and a police officer shot and killed one of two men attempting to rob the driver. The court held the robber couldn't be found guilty of felony murder under the third-party exception. However, some of these states have created a **resisting-victim exception** to the third-party exception. In *State v. O'Dell* (1984), a felony assault victim shot and killed one of his attackers. The court ruled the surviving attacker could be found guilty of felony murder under the resisting-victim exception.

Felony murder applies only to deaths that happen during the commission of *dangerous* felonies. For example, in *People v. Phillips* (1966), the California Supreme Court held that a chiropractor couldn't be found guilty of felony murder when he fraudulently treated a cancer patient and the patient died. The court ruled that fraud wasn't a "dangerous" felony. The Rhode Island Supreme Court examined the meaning of "dangerous felonies" in *State v. Stewart* (1995).

| CASE | *Did She Commit an "Inherently Dangerous" Felony?* |

State v. Stewart
663 A.2d 912 (R.I. 1995)

Twenty-year-old Tracy Stewart was convicted in the Superior Court, Providence County, of second-degree felony murder. She appealed. The Supreme Court affirmed the conviction.

WEISBERGER, CJ.

FACTS

On August 31, 1988, twenty-year-old Tracy Stewart gave birth to a son, Travis Young (Travis). Travis's father was Edward Young, Sr. (Young). Stewart and Young, who had two other children together, were not married at the time of Travis's birth. Travis lived for only fifty-two days, dying on October 21, 1988, from dehydration.

During the week prior to Travis's death, Stewart, Young, and a friend, Patricia McMasters (McMasters), continually and repeatedly ingested cocaine over a two-to three-consecutive-day period at the apartment shared by Stewart and Young. The baby, Travis, was also present at the apartment while Stewart, Young, and McMasters engaged in this cocaine marathon. Young and McMasters injected cocaine intravenously and also smoked it while Stewart ingested the cocaine only by smoking it. The smoked cocaine was in its strongest or base form, commonly referred to as "crack."

When the three exhausted an existing supply of cocaine, they would pool their money and Young and McMasters would go out and buy more with the accumulated funds. The primary source of funds from which the three obtained money for this cocaine spree was Stewart's and McMasters's Aid to Families with Dependent Children

(AFDC) checks. Stewart and McMasters had each just received the second of their semimonthly AFDC checks. They both cashed their AFDC checks and gave money to Young, which he then used to purchase more cocaine. After all the AFDC funds had been spent on cocaine and the group had run out of money, McMasters and Young committed a robbery to obtain additional money to purchase more cocaine.

The cocaine binge continued uninterrupted for two to three days. McMasters testified that during this time neither McMasters nor Stewart slept at all. McMasters testified that defendant was never far from her during this entire two-to three-day period except for the occasions when McMasters left the apartment to buy more cocaine. During this entire time, McMasters saw defendant feed Travis only once. Travis was in a walker, and defendant propped a bottle of formula up on the walker, using a blanket, for the baby to feed himself. McMasters testified that she did not see defendant hold the baby to feed him nor did she see defendant change Travis's diaper or clothes during this period.

Ten months after Travis's death defendant (Stewart) was indicted on charges of second-degree murder, wrongfully causing or permitting a child under the age of eighteen to be a habitual sufferer for want of food and proper care (hereinafter sometimes referred to as "wrongfully permitting a child to be a habitual sufferer"), and manslaughter. The second-degree-murder charge was based on a theory of felony murder. The prosecution did not allege that defendant intentionally killed her son but rather that he had been killed during the commission of an inherently dangerous felony, specifically, wrongfully permitting a child to be a habitual sufferer. Moreover, the prosecution did not allege that defendant intentionally withheld food or care from her son. Rather the state alleged that because of defendant's chronic state of cocaine intoxication, she may have realized what her responsibilities were but simply could not remember whether she had fed her son, when in fact she had not.

At defendant's trial both the prosecution and the defense presented expert medical witnesses who testified concerning what they believed to be the cause of Travis's death. The experts for both sides agreed that the cause of death was dehydration, but they strongly disagreed regarding what caused the dehydration. The prosecution expert witnesses believed that the dehydration was caused by insufficient intake of food and water, that is, malnutrition. The defense expert witnesses, conversely, believed that the dehydration was caused by a gastrointestinal virus known as gastroenteritis which manifested itself in an overwhelming expulsion of fluid from the baby's body.

The defendant was found guilty of both second-degree murder and wrongfully permitting a child to be a habitual sufferer. A subsequent motion for new trial was denied. This appeal followed. . . .

OPINION

. . . Rhode Island's murder statute, § 11231, enumerates certain crimes that may serve as predicate felonies [felonies murder can be based on] to a charge of first-degree murder. A felony that is not enumerated in § 11231 can, however, serve as a predicate felony to a charge of second-degree murder. Thus the fact that the crime of wrongfully permitting a child to be a habitual sufferer is not specified in § 11231 as a predicate felony to support a charge of first-degree murder does not preclude such crime from serving as a predicate to support a charge of second-degree murder.

In Rhode Island, second-degree murder has been equated with common-law murder. At common law, where the rule is unchanged by statute, "homicide is murder if the death results from the perpetration or attempted perpetration of an inherently dangerous felony." To serve as a predicate felony to a charge of second-degree murder, a felony that is not specifically enumerated in § 11231 must therefore be an inherently dangerous felony.

The defendant contends that wrongfully permitting a child to be a habitual sufferer is not an inherently dangerous felony and cannot therefore serve as the predicate felony to a charge of second-degree murder. In advancing her argument, defendant urges this court to adopt the approach used by California courts to determine if a felony is inherently dangerous. This approach requires that the court consider the elements of the felony "in the abstract" rather than look at the particular facts of the case under consideration. With such an approach, if a statute can be

violated in a manner that does not endanger human life, then the felony is not inherently dangerous to human life. Moreover, the California Supreme Court has defined an act as "inherently dangerous to human life when there is 'a high probability that it will result in death.'"

In *People v. Caffero*, 255 Cal.Rptr. 22, 25 (1989) . . . a two-and-one-half-week-old baby died of a massive bacterial infection caused by lack of proper hygiene that was due to parental neglect. The parents were charged with second-degree felony murder and felony-child-abuse, with the felony-child-abuse charge serving as the predicate felony to the second-degree-murder charge. Examining California's felony-child-abuse statute in the abstract, instead of looking at the particular facts of the case, the court held that because the statute could be violated in ways that did not endanger human life, felony-child abuse was not inherently dangerous to human life. By way of example, the court noted that a fractured limb, which comes within the ambit of the felony-child-abuse statute, is unlikely to endanger the life of an infant, much less of a seventeen-year-old. . . . Because felony-child-abuse was not inherently dangerous to human life, it could not properly serve as a predicate felony to a charge of second-degree felony murder.

The defendant urges this court to adopt the method of analysis employed by California courts to determine if a felony is inherently dangerous to life. . . . We decline defendant's invitation to adopt the California approach in determining whether a felony is inherently dangerous to life and thus capable of serving as a predicate to a charge of second-degree felony murder. We believe that the better approach is for the trier of fact to consider the facts and circumstances of the particular case to determine if such felony was inherently dangerous in the manner and the circumstances in which it was committed, rather than have a court make the determination by viewing the elements of a felony in the abstract. We now join a number of states that have adopted this approach. . . .

The proper procedure for making such a determination is to present the facts and circumstances of the particular case to the trier of fact and for the trier of fact to determine if a felony is inherently dangerous in the manner and the circumstances in which it was committed. This is exactly what happened in the case at bar. The trial justice instructed the jury that before it could find defendant guilty of second-degree murder, it must first find that wrongfully causing or permitting a child to be a habitual sufferer for want of food or proper care was inherently dangerous to human life "in its manner of commission." This was a proper charge. By its guilty verdict on the charge of second-degree murder, the jury obviously found that wrongfully permitting a child to be a habitual sufferer for want of food or proper care was indeed a felony inherently dangerous to human life in the circumstances of this particular case....

...We are of the opinion that the evidence offered by the state was sufficient to prove beyond a reasonable doubt each of the elements of second-degree felony murder, including that the crime of wrongfully permitting a child to be a habitual sufferer was an inherently dangerous felony in its manner of commission. The defendant's motions for judgment of acquittal on the felony-murder charge on the ground that wrongfully permitting a child to be a habitual sufferer is not an inherently dangerous felony were properly denied.

The theory of felony murder is that a defendant does not have to have intended to kill one who dies during the course of certain statutorily enumerated felonies, or other inherently dangerous felonies, in order to be charged with murder. The intent to commit the underlying felony will be imputed to the homicide, and a defendant may thus be charged with murder on the basis of the intent to commit the underlying felony.

The defendant claims that the evidence presented at trial failed to establish that she intentionally committed the crime of wrongfully permitting a child to be a habitual sufferer. She claims that absent an intent to commit this felony, it cannot serve as a predicate to support a charge of second-degree felony murder because there would then be no intent to be imputed from the underlying felony to the homicide. We agree with defendant that intent to commit the underlying felony is a necessary element of felony murder. However, we believe the circumstances surrounding the events preceding Travis's death support a finding that defendant did indeed intentionally permit her son to be a habitual sufferer for want of food or proper care.

The defendant's addiction to and compulsion to have cocaine were the overriding factors that controlled virtually every aspect of her life. She referred to the extended periods that she was high on cocaine as "going on a mission." Although she was receiving public assistance and did not have much disposable income, she nevertheless spent a great deal of money on cocaine, including her AFDC money. She shoplifted and traded the stolen merchandise for cocaine. She stole food because she had used the money that she should have been using to purchase food to purchase cocaine. The compulsion to have cocaine at any cost took precedence over every facet of defendant's life including caring for her children.

Although defendant did not testify at trial, she did testify before the grand jury. A redacted tape of her grand jury testimony was admitted into evidence and played for the jury at trial. During the days preceding Travis's death, defendant had been on a two-to three-day cocaine binge, a "mission," as she referred to it. Her grand jury testimony indicated that she knew that during such periods she was unable to care for her children properly.

The defendant testified that whenever she would go on a mission, her mother, who lived only a few houses away, would take and care for the children. This testimony evinced a knowledge on the part of defendant that she was incapable of properly caring for her children during these periods of extended cocaine intoxication.

In addition, defendant was prone to petit mal seizures, which were exacerbated by her cocaine use. During such seizures she would "black out" or "go into a coma state." She testified before the grand jury that she was aware that taking cocaine brought on more seizures and that the weekend before Travis died she had in fact blacked out and "went into a coma state."

Despite her grand jury testimony to the contrary, Travis remained with defendant at her apartment during the entire two- to three-day binge. He died two or three days later. The defendant's repeated voluntary and intentional ingestion of crack cocaine while her seven-week-old son was in her care, in addition to her testimony that she knew that she was incapable of properly caring for her children during these extended periods of cocaine intoxication, support a finding that she intentionally permitted her son to be a habitual sufferer for want of food and proper care.

We make the distinction between a finding that defendant intentionally deprived her son of food and proper care, which even the state does not allege, and a finding that defendant intentionally permitted her son to be a habitual sufferer for want of food or proper care, which we find to be supported by the evidence adduced at trial....

Two or three days after the cocaine binge had ended, defendant went to McMasters's apartment and informed her that Travis had died that morning. The defendant was carrying a bag containing cans of baby formula and asked McMasters if she knew where she (defendant) could exchange the unused formula for cocaine. McMasters told defendant that she did not know where the formula could be exchanged for cocaine but suggested that she take it to a local supermarket to get a cash refund.

McMasters then accompanied defendant to a supermarket in Pawtucket where they attempted to return the formula for cash. They were unsuccessful in this attempt, however, because they did not have a receipt for the formula and store policy dictated that no cash refunds be given for returns without a receipt for the merchandise. The defendant told the assistant store manager that her baby had just died, and the manager gave defendant $20 out of his own pocket because he felt sorry for her. The defendant used this $20 to purchase cocaine. The defendant and McMasters then went to McMasters's apartment and smoked cocaine....

In order for the crime of wrongfully permitting a child to be a habitual sufferer to serve as a predicate felony to a charge of second-degree felony murder, the accused must have had the intent to commit the underlying felony. Although it is true that the trial justice did not specifically instruct the jury that in order to find defendant guilty of second-degree murder, it must find as one of the elements of the crime that she intentionally caused or permitted her son to be a habitual sufferer for want of food or proper care, we believe that the instructions given were substantially equivalent.

The trial justice instructed the jury that it must find that defendant wrongfully, that is, without legal justification or without legal excuse, caused or permitted Travis to be a habitual sufferer. She also instructed that it must find that defendant knew or was aware beforehand that there was a likelihood that Travis's life would be endangered as a result of permitting or causing him to be a habitual sufferer for want of food or proper care.

We believe that these two instructions in combination, requiring that the jury find that defendant had no legal justification or no legal excuse for causing her son to be a habitual sufferer and also requiring that the jury find that defendant knew or was aware beforehand that causing or permitting her son to be a habitual sufferer for want of food or proper care was likely to endanger his life, were the functional equivalent to an instruction requiring the jury to find that defendant intentionally caused or permitted her son to be a habitual sufferer.

"This failure to distinguish between intent . . . and knowledge is probably of little consequence in many areas of the law, as often there is good reason for imposing liability whether the defendant desired or merely knew of the practical certainty of the results." LaFave and Scott, Substantive Criminal Law, § 3.5(b) at 305 (1986); see also Model Penal Code § 2.02 cmt. 2 at 234 (1985) (the "distinction [between acting purposely and knowingly] is inconsequential for most purposes of liability; acting knowingly is ordinarily sufficient"). The trial justice committed no error in refusing to give the requested instruction.

For the foregoing reasons the defendant's appeal is denied and dismissed, and the judgment of conviction is AFFIRMED. The papers in the case may be REMANDED to the Superior Court.

Questions

1. Explain California's approach of determining an "inherently dangerous felony" in the abstract.

2. Why did the Rhode Island court reject the California approach?

3. What test did the Rhode Island court use in determining whether the felony of wrongfully permitting a child to suffer is inherently dangerous?

4. In your opinion, which is the better test? Why?

5. List all of the evidence in this case relevant to determining whether Tracy Stewart was guilty of felony murder.

6. Assume you're a defense attorney in California. Relying on the relevant evidence you listed in (5), argue that Stewart is not guilty of felony murder.

7. Assume you're a prosecutor in Rhode Island. Relying on the evidence in (5), argue that Stewart is guilty of felony murder.

8. Assume you're a defense attorney in Rhode Island. Relying on the evidence in (5), argue there's a reasonable doubt as to Stewart's guilt as to felony murder.

EXPLORING FELONY MURDER FURTHER

 Go to the Criminal Law 8e CD to read the full text version of the case featured here.

Was Fraud a Felony "Inherently Dangerous to Human Life"?

FACTS

Linda Epping died on December 29, 1961, at the age of 8, from a rare and fast-growing form of eye cancer. Linda's mother first observed a swelling over the girl's left eye in June of that year. The doctor whom she consulted recommended that Linda be taken to Dr. Straatsma, an ophthalmologist at the UCLA Medical Center. On July 10th Dr. Straatsma first saw Linda; on July 17th the girl, suffering great pain, was admitted to the center. Dr. Straatsma performed an exploratory operation and the resulting biopsy established the nature of the child's affliction.

Dr. Straatsma advised Linda's parents that her only hope for survival lay in immediate surgical removal of the affected eye. The Eppings were loath to permit such surgery, but on the morning of July 21st Mr. Epping called the hospital and gave his oral consent. The Eppings arrived at the hospital that afternoon to consult with the surgeon. While waiting they encountered a Mrs. Eaton who told them that defendant had cured her son of a brain tumor without surgery.

Mrs. Epping called defendant at his office. According to the Eppings, defendant repeatedly assured them that he could cure Linda without surgery. They testified that defendant urged them to take Linda out of the hospital, claiming that the hospital was "an experimental place," that the doctors there would use Linda as "a human guinea pig" and would relieve the Eppings of their money as well.

The Eppings testified that in reliance upon defendant's statements they took Linda out of the hospital and placed her under defendant's care. They stated that if defendant had not represented to them that he could cure the child without surgery and that the UCLA doctors were only interested in experimentation, they would have proceeded with the scheduled operation. The prosecution introduced medical testimony which tended to prove that if Linda had undergone surgery on July 21st her life would have been prolonged or she would have been completely cured.

Defendant treated Linda from July 22 to August 12, 1961. He charged an advance fee of $500 for three months' care as well as a sum exceeding $200 for pills and medicines. On August 13th Linda's condition had not improved; the Eppings dismissed defendant.

Later the Eppings sought to cure Linda by means of a Mexican herbal drug known as yerba mansa and, about the 1st of September, they placed her under the care of the Christian Science movement. They did not take her back to the hospital for treatment....

Was Phillips guilty of felony murder?

DECISION AND REASONS

The jury said yes. No, ruled the California Supreme Court:

> Only such felonies as are in themselves 'inherently dangerous to human life' can support the application of the felony murder rule. We have ruled that in assessing such peril to human life inherent in any given felony 'we look to the elements of the felony in the abstract, not the particular 'facts' of the case.
>
> We have thus recognized that the felony murder doctrine expresses a highly artificial concept that deserves no extension beyond its required application. Indeed the rule itself has been abandoned by the courts of England, where it had its inception. It has been subjected to severe and sweeping criticism. No case to our knowledge in any jurisdiction has held that because death results from a course of conduct involving a felonious perpetration of a fraud, the felony murder doctrine can be invoked....

People v. Phillips, 414 P.2d 353 (Cal. 1966)

 Go to Exercise 9-2 on the Criminal Law 8e CD to learn more about murder.

◆   ◆   ◆

Corporation Murder

Can corporations commit murder? Yes, according to a few prosecutors who have prosecuted corporations for murder (Cullen, Maakestad, and Cavender 1987). Probably the most publicized corporate murder case involved the deaths of three young women who were killed on an Indiana highway when their Ford Pinto exploded after being struck from behind by another vehicle. The explosion followed several other similar incidents involving Pintos that led to grisly deaths. Published evidence revealed that Ford may have known that the Pinto gas tanks were not safe but took the risk that they would not explode and injure or kill anyone. Following the three young women's deaths, the state of Indiana indicted Ford Motor Company for reckless homicide, charging that Ford had recklessly authorized, approved, designed, and manufactured the Pinto and allowed the car to remain in use with defectively designed fuel tanks. These tanks, the indictment charged, killed the three young women in Indiana. For a number of reasons not related directly to whether corporations can commit murder, the case was later dismissed.

In another case that drew wide public attention during the 1980s, Autumn Hills Convalescent Centers, a corporation that operated nursing homes, went on trial for charges that it had murdered an 87-year-old woman by neglect. David Marks, a Texas assistant attorney general, said, "From the first day until her last breath, she was unattended to and allowed to lie day and night in her own urine and waste." The case attracted attention because of allegations that as many as sixty elderly people had died from substandard care at the Autumn Hills nursing home near Galveston, Texas. The indictment charged that the company had failed to provide nutrients, fluids, and incontinent care for the woman, Mrs. Breed, and neglected to turn and reposition her regularly to combat bedsores. One prosecution witness testified that Mrs. Breed's bed was wet constantly and the staff seldom cleaned her. The corporation defended against the charges, claiming that Mrs. Breed had died from colon cancer, not improper care (Reinhold 1985, 17).

Most state criminal codes apply to corporate criminal homicide in the same way that they apply to other crimes committed for the corporation's benefit. Specifically, both corporations and high corporate officers acting within the scope of their authority and for the benefit of a corporation can commit murder. Practically speaking, however, prosecutors rarely charge corporations or their officers with criminal homicide, and convictions rarely follow.

The reluctance to prosecute corporations for murder, or for any homicide requiring the intent to kill or inflict serious bodily injury, is due largely to the hesitation to view corporations as persons. Although theoretically the law clearly makes that possible, in practice, prosecutors and courts have drawn the line at involuntary manslaughter, a crime whose *mens rea* is negligence and occasionally recklessness. As for corporate executives, the reluctance to prosecute stems from vicarious liability and the questions it raises about culpability (see Chapter 4). It has been difficult to attribute deaths linked with corporate benefit to corporate officers who were in charge generally but didn't order or authorize a killing, didn't know about it, or even didn't want it to happen.

Only in outrageous cases that receive widespread public attention, such as the Pinto and nursing home cases, do prosecutors risk acquittal by trying corporations and their officers for criminal homicide. In these cases, prosecutors aren't hoping to win the case in traditional terms, meaning to secure convictions. Business law professor William J. Maakestad says, "At this point, success of this type of corporate criminal prosecution is defined by establishing the legitimacy of the case. If you can get the case to trial, you have really achieved success" (Lewin 1985, D2).

People v. O'Neil (1990) involved one of the few prosecutions of a corporation and its officers for murder.

| CASE | *Did They "Murder" Their Employee?* |

People v. O'Neil
550 N.E.2d 1090 (Ill.App. 1990)

Following a joint bench trial,* Steven O'Neil, Charles Kirschbaum, and Daniel Rodriguez, agents of Film Recov-

---
*A trial without a jury.

ery Systems, Inc. (Film Recovery), were convicted of the murder of Stefan Golab, a Film Recovery employee, from cyanide poisoning stemming from conditions in Film Recovery's plant in Elk Grove Village, Illinois. Corporate defendants Film Recovery and its sister corporation Metallic Marketing Systems, Inc. (Metallic Marketing), were convicted of involuntary manslaughter in the same death.

O'Neil, Kirschbaum, and Rodriguez each received sentences of 25 years' imprisonment for murder. O'Neil and Kirschbaum were also each fined $10,000 with respect to the murder convictions. Corporate defendants Film Recovery and Metallic Marketing were each fined $10,000 with respect to the convictions for involuntary manslaughter. The defendants appealed, and the appellate court reversed the convictions.

LORENZ, J.

FACTS

... In 1982, Film Recovery occupied premises at 1855 and 1875 Greenleaf Avenue in Elk Grove Village. Film Recovery was there engaged in the business of extracting, for resale, silver from used x-ray and photographic film. Metallic Marketing operated out of the same premises on Greenleaf Avenue and owned 50% of the stock of Film Recovery. The recovery process was performed at Film Recovery's plant located at the 1855 address and involved "chipping" the film product and soaking the granulated pieces in large open bubbling vats containing a solution of water and sodium cyanide. The cyanide solution caused silver contained in the film to be released. A continuous flow system pumped the silver laden solution into polyurethane tanks which contained electrically charged stainless steel plates to which the separated silver adhered. The plates were removed from the tanks to another room where the accumulated silver was scraped off. The remaining solution was pumped out of the tanks and the granulated film, devoid of silver, shoveled out.

On the morning of February 10, 1983, shortly after he disconnected a pump on one of the tanks and began to stir the contents of the tank with a rake, Stefan Golab became dizzy and faint. He left the production area to go rest in the lunchroom area of the plant. Plant workers present on that day testified Golab's body had trembled and he had foamed at the mouth. Golab eventually lost consciousness and was taken outside of the plant. Paramedics summoned to the plant were unable to revive him. Golab was pronounced dead upon arrival at Alexian Brothers Hospital.

The Cook County medical examiner performed an autopsy on Golab the following day. Although the medical examiner initially indicated Golab could have died from cardiac arrest, he reserved final determination of death pending examination of results of toxicological laboratory tests on Golab's blood and other body specimens. After receiving the toxicological report, the medical examiner determined Golab died from acute cyanide poisoning through the inhalation of cyanide fumes in the plant air.

Defendants were subsequently indicted by a Cook County grand jury. The grand jury charged defendants

O'Neil, Kirschbaum, Rodriguez, Pett, and Mackay with murder, stating that, as individuals and as officers and high managerial agents of Film Recovery, they had, on February 10, 1983, knowingly created a strong probability of Golab's death. Generally, the indictment stated the individual defendants failed to disclose to Golab that he was working with substances containing cyanide and failed to advise him about, train him to anticipate, and provide adequate equipment to protect him from, attendant dangers involved. The grand jury charged Film Recovery and Metallic Marketing with involuntary manslaughter stating that, through the reckless acts of their officers, directors, agents, and others, all acting within the scope of their employment, the corporate entities had, on February 10, 1983, unintentionally killed Golab. Finally, the grand jury charged both individual and corporate defendants with reckless conduct as to 20 other Film Recovery employees based on the same conduct alleged in the murder indictment, but expanding the time of that conduct to "on or about March 1982 through March 1983."

Proceedings commenced in the circuit court in January 1985 and continued through the conclusion of trial in June of that year. In the course of the 24-day trial, evidence from 59 witnesses was presented, either directly or through stipulation of the parties. That testimony is contained in over 2,300 pages of trial transcript. The parties also presented numerous exhibits including photographs, corporate documents and correspondence, as well as physical evidence.

On June 14, 1985, the trial judge pronounced his judgment of defendants' guilt. The trial judge found that "the mind and mental state of a corporation is the mind and mental state of the directors, officers and high managerial personnel because they act on behalf of the corporation for both the benefit of the corporation and for themselves." Further, "if the corporation's officers, directors and high managerial personnel act within the scope of their corporate responsibilities and employment for their benefit and for the benefit of the profits of the corporation, the corporation must be held liable for what occurred in the work place."

Defendants filed timely notices of appeal, the matters were consolidated for review, and arguments were had before this court in July 1987....

OPINION

... We find it helpful to set out the pertinent statutory language of the offenses for which the defendants were convicted. The Criminal Code of 1961 defines murder as follows:

A person who kills an individual without lawful justification commits murder if, in performing the acts which cause the death: He knows that such acts create a strong probability of death or great bodily harm to that individual. (Ill.Rev.Stat.1981, ch. 38, par.9-1(a)(2).)

Involuntary manslaughter is defined as:

A person who unintentionally kills an individual without lawful justification commits involuntary manslaughter if his acts whether lawful or unlawful which cause the death are such as are likely to cause death or great bodily harm to some individual, and he performs them recklessly. (Ill.Rev.Stat.1981, ch. 38, par. 9-3(a).)

Reckless conduct is defined as:

A person who causes bodily harm to or endangers the bodily safety of an individual by any means, commits reckless conduct if he performs recklessly the acts which cause the harm or endanger safety, whether they otherwise are lawful or unlawful. (Ill.Rev.Stat.1981, ch. 38, par. 12-5(a)).

...In Illinois, a corporation is criminally responsible for offenses "authorized, requested, commanded, or performed by the board of directors or by a high managerial agent acting within the scope of his employment." A high managerial agent is defined as "an officer of the corporation, or any other agent who has a position of comparable authority for the formulation of corporate policy or the supervision of subordinate employees in a managerial capacity." (Ill.Rev.Stat. 1981, ch. 38, par. 5-4(c)(2).) Thus, a corporation is criminally responsible whenever any of its high managerial agents possess the requisite mental state and is responsible for a criminal offense while acting within the scope of his employment....

Evidence at trial indicated Golab died after inhaling poisonous cyanide fumes while working in a plant operated by Film Recovery and its sister corporation Metallic Marketing where such fumes resulted from a process employed to remove silver from used x-ray and photographic film. The record contains substantial evidence regarding the nature of working conditions inside the plant. Testimony established that air inside the plant was foul smelling and made breathing difficult and painful. Plant workers experienced dizziness, nausea, headaches, and bouts of vomiting.

There is evidence that plant workers were not informed they were working with cyanide. Nor were they informed of the presence of, or danger of breathing, cyanide gas. Ventilation in the plant was poor. Plant workers were given neither safety instruction nor adequate protective clothing.

Finally, testimony established that defendants O'Neil, Kirschbaum, and Rodriguez were responsible for operating the plant under those conditions. For purposes of our disposition, we find further elaboration on the evidence un-

necessary. Moreover, although we have determined evidence in the record is not so insufficient as to bar retrial, our determination of the sufficiency of the evidence should not be in any way interpreted as a finding as to defendants' guilt that would be binding on the court on retrial.

REVERSED and REMANDED.

Questions

1. List the all the evidence for and against the corporation's and the individuals' liability for murder and involuntary manslaughter.

2. Why did the court reverse and remand the case?

3. On remand, would you find the defendants guilty of murder? Explain your answer.

4. Do you agree that it is inconsistent to find that the corporation had one state of mind and the individuals another?

5. Consider the following remarks made after the convictions in the original trial (Greenhouse 1985, 1):

a. Following the conviction in the original trial, then attorney Richard M. Daley said the verdicts meant that employers who knowingly expose their workers to dangerous conditions leading to injury or even death can be held criminally responsible for the results of their actions.

b. Ralph Nader, consumer advocate lawyer, said:

The public is pretty upset with dangerously defective products, bribery, toxic waste, and job hazards. The polls all show it. The verdict today will encourage other prosecutors and judges to take more seriously the need to have the criminal law catch up with corporate crime.

c. Professor John Coffee, Columbia University Law School, said, "When you threaten the principal adequately, he will monitor the behavior of his agent."

d. A California deputy district attorney put it more bluntly: "A person facing a jail sentence is the best deterrent against wrongdoing."

e. Joseph E. Hadley, Jr., a corporate lawyer who specializes in health and safety issues, said the decision would not send shock waves through the corporate community:

I don't think corporate America should be viewed as in the ballpark with these folks. This was a highly unusual situation, but now people see that where the egregious situation occurs, there could be a criminal remedy.

f. Robert Stephenson, a lawyer defending another corporation, said, "I don't believe these statutes [murder and aggravated battery] were ever meant to be used in this way."

g. Utah's governor, Scott M. Matheson, refused to extradite Michael T. McKay, a former Film Recovery vice-president then living in Utah, because he was an "exemplary citizen who should not be subjected to the sensational charges in Illinois."

Which of the statements best describes what you think is proper policy regarding corporate executive murder prosecutions? Defend your answer.

MANSLAUGHTER

Manslaughter, like murder, is an ancient common-law crime created by judges, not by legislators. According to the eighteenth-century commentator Blackstone (1769):

> Manslaughter is . . . the unlawful killing of another . . . which may be either voluntarily upon a sudden heat, or involuntarily . . . where one had no intent to do another any personal mischief. (191–192)

Blackstone's definition is more than three centuries old, but it goes straight to *mens rea*, the heart of manslaughter—as it is in most murder classifications: intentional (voluntary) and unintentional (involuntary).

Voluntary Manslaughter

> If upon a sudden quarrel two persons fight, and one of them kills the other, this is [voluntary] manslaughter. And, so it is, if they upon such an occasion go out and fight in a field, for this is one continued act of passion and the law pays that regard to human frailty, as not to put a hasty and a deliberate act upon the same footing with regard to guilt. So also a man be greatly provoked, as by pulling his nose, or other great indignity, and immediately kills the aggressor, though this is not excusable, since there is no absolute necessity for doing so to preserve himself, yet neither is it murder for there is no previous malice.
>
> Blackstone 1769, 191

Blackstone's description of voluntary manslaughter in the late 1700s is an excellent way to begin our discussion of voluntary manslaughter.

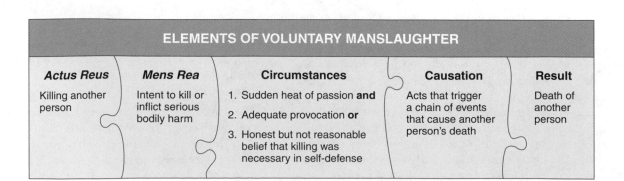

ELEMENTS OF VOLUNTARY MANSLAUGHTER				
Actus Reus	***Mens Rea***	**Circumstances**	**Causation**	**Result**
Killing another person	Intent to kill or inflict serious bodily harm	1. Sudden heat of passion **and** 2. Adequate provocation **or** 3. Honest but not reasonable belief that killing was necessary in self-defense	Acts that trigger a chain of events that cause another person's death	Death of another person

Voluntary manslaughter is about letting your anger get the better of you in the worst possible way—killing another person. Criminal law aims to bridle passions and build self-control, but it also recognizes the frailty of human nature. The law of voluntary manslaughter takes into account both the seriousness of this felony and human frailty. So, while a sudden intentional killing in anger is a very serious felony, it's not the most serious; that's reserved for murder. Let's be clear that the effect of the law of voluntary manslaughter doesn't *reward* individuals who give in to their rages by letting them walk; it punishes them severely, but it punishes them less than they'd get for murder.

Voluntary manslaughter (like all criminal homicides) consists of the elements *actus reus, mens rea,* causation, and death. But, it has one element not present in murder, and one we haven't discussed; this is the circumstance element of **adequate provocation.** In voluntary manslaughter, adequate provocation is the trigger that sets off the sudden killing of another person. But, not everyone who flies into a rage and suddenly kills someone has committed voluntary manslaughter instead of murder. The law of voluntary manslaughter recognizes only specific provocations as adequate. These include:

1. Mutual combat (fighting)

2. Assault and battery (Chapter 10)

3. Trespass (Chapter 11)

4. Adultery

So, only serious fights are adequate provocation; scuffles aren't. Some batteries—but not all offensive touching (see Chapter 10)—are adequate provocation. Being pistol-whipped on the head, being struck hard in the face by fists, or enduring "staggering" body blows qualify. Being slapped or shoved doesn't.

Assault without body contact is sometimes adequate provocation. In *Beasley v. State* (1886), a man shot at Beasley and missed him. Beasley was so enraged he shot his attacker in the back as the assailant ran away. The court ruled the shot in the back wasn't justified as self-defense, but the initial incident was provocative enough to reduce murder to manslaughter.

Insulting gestures by themselves aren't adequate provocation, but, if they indicate an intent to attack with deadly force, they are. So, "flipping someone the bird" isn't adequate provocation, but waving a gun around in a threatening manner can be. Trespassing is adequate provocation only if the trespassers invade the home and threaten someone with death.

To better understand what the law considers adequate provocation (and what it doesn't), we'll look at sudden provocation, provocation and death caused by passion, provocation by words, provocation by paramour, and reasonable provocation.

Sudden Provocation

Voluntary manslaughter requires killing in the "sudden heat of passion" with no "cooling off" period (Perkins and Boyce 1982, 95–96). Whether the actual time between the provocation and the killing—seconds, hours, or even days—qualifies as the "sudden heat of passion" depends upon the facts of the individual case. Courts usually apply an **objective test of cooling-off time**; that is, would a reasonable person under the same circumstances have had time to cool off? If defendants had a reasonable time for their murderous rages to subside, the law views their killings as murders even if the provocations were adequate to reduce those killings to manslaughter had they taken place immediately following the provocations.

Blackstone (1769, 191) applied the objective test to his example (given earlier): If two persons "upon a sudden quarrel" start fighting indoors, it's voluntary manslaughter "if they upon such an occasion go out and fight in a field, for this is one continued act of passion and the law pays that regard to human frailty, as not to put a hasty and a deliberate act upon the same footing with regard to guilt."

Using the same objective test, the time for cooling off may be considerable. In *State v. Flory* (1929), Flory's wife told him her father had raped her. The court ruled that Flory's passion hadn't reasonably cooled even after he walked all night to his father-in-law's house and killed him the next day! The court said the heinous combination of incest and rape was more than enough to keep a reasonable person in a murderous rage for at least several days.

Provocation and Death Caused by Passion

To prove voluntary manslaughter, the prosecution has to prove the provocation caused the passion and the killing. Suppose Sonny intends to kill his wife Carly because she lied to him. He goes to her bedroom, finds her in bed with his worst enemy, and shoots her to death. Is it voluntary manslaughter or murder? Murder, because Carly's lie, not her adultery, provoked Sonny to kill her.

Provocation by Words

One kind of provocation the law of homicide has *never* recognized as adequate is words. However enraging, words can never reduce murder to manslaughter. In *State v. Watson* (1975), the North Carolina Supreme Court examined this ancient rule that words are never adequate provocation (Perkins and Boyce 1982, 95–96).

| CASE | *Were the Racial Slurs Adequate Provocation?* |

State v. Watson
214 S.E.2d 85 (N.C. 1975)

Rufus Watson, Jr. was convicted of second-degree murder and was sentenced to life imprisonment. He appealed, arguing that he was legally provoked. The conviction was affirmed.

COPELAND, J.

FACTS

At the time of this incident, Rufus Watson (defendant), a black, was twenty-years-old. He was serving a twenty-five year prison sentence on judgment imposed at the October, 1972, Session of Rockingham County Superior Court upon his plea of guilty to second-degree murder. The decedent Samples, was white. Neither Samples' age nor the basis for his incarceration appears from the record. The defendant was called "Duck" by his fellow prisoners in I-Dorm. Samples, the decedent, was known as "Pee Wee." Although Samples was referred to as "Pee Wee," there appeared to be no relation between this nickname and his physical size. In fact, he was a strong man who worked out daily with weights.

The "hearsay" among the residents of I-Dorm was to the effect that Watson and Samples were "swapping-out." "Swapping-out" is a prison term that means two inmates are engaging in homosexual practices. Generally, prisoners that are "swapping-out" try to hide the practice from their fellow inmates. In particular, they try to hide it from any "home-boys" that may be in their particular unit. A "home-boy," in the prison vernacular, is a fellow inmate from one's own hometown or community. One of the State's witnesses, Johnny Lee Wilson, a resident of I-Dorm on the date of the offense, was Samples' "home-boy."

It appears that Watson and Samples had been "swapping-out" for several months. Approximately a month or so prior to the date of the killing, Watson and Samples had engaged in a "scuffle" while working in the prison kitchen. This appears to have been nothing more than a fist-fight. Samples was the winner. Although it is by no means clear from the record, it appears that this "scuffle" arose out of Samples' suspicion that Watson had been "swapping-out" with another prisoner.

At approximately 4:30 P.M. on the afternoon of the killing, Johnny Lee Wilson, Samples' "home-boy," saw Watson and Samples sitting together on a bunk in the back of I-Dorm. At this time, "they were close talking, they were close." Apparently, assuming that they were about to "swap-out," and not wanting to embarrass Samples, Wilson quickly turned around and left the dorm.

Shortly before the lights were to be dimmed (10:00 P.M.), Watson and Samples began to argue. After several minutes, Watson got up and walked across the aisle, a distance of approximately seven feet, to his bunk. Samples subsequently followed him and renewed the dispute. At this time, both parties were seated on Watson's bottom bunk. During the course of the renewed argument, Samples was verbally abusing Watson and challenging him to fight. At one point, he said: "Nigger, nigger, you're just like the rest of them." He also told Watson that he was too scared to fight him and that all he was going to do was tremble and stay in his bunk. Finally, Samples made several derogatory and obscene references to Watson's mother. The prisoners refer to this as "shooting the dove." Generally, when a prisoner "shoots the dove," he expects the other party to fight. At this point, Watson told Johnny Lee Wilson, whose bunk was nearby on Watson's side of the room: "You better get your home-boy straightened out before I f— him up." Responding to this statement, Samples said: "Why don't you f— me up if that's what you want to do. All you're gonna do is tremble, nigger."

As Samples was making the above quoted statement, he was walking over to Wilson's bunk. Samples borrowed a cigarette from Wilson and then proceeded to his own bed. He got up in his bunk (top) and was more or less half sitting up with his back propped up against the wall. At this point, he renewed the argument with Watson, who was still in his bottom bunk on the opposite side of the room.

He called Watson a "nigger" and "a black mother f—." While this was going on, Watson, without saying a word, either walked or ran across the aisle between the two rows of bunks and violently and repeatedly stabbed Samples with a kitchen-type paring knife. According to the State's witnesses, this occurred approximately two (2) to ten (10) minutes after Samples had left Watson's bed.

After summarizing the evidence, and prior to fully instructing on first-degree murder, the court stated: "Let me say here, that mere words will not form a justification or excuse for a crime of this sort." In instructing the jury on voluntary manslaughter, the court stated:

> The defendant must satisfy you that this passion was produced by acts of Samples which the law regards as adequate provocation. This may consist of anything which has a natural tendency to produce such passion in a person of average mind and disposition. However, words and gestures alone, where no assault is made or threatened, regardless of how insulting or inflammatory those words or gestures may be, does not constitute adequate provocation for the taking of a human life.

OPINION

[After reviewing several voluntary manslaughter decisions, the court wrote:] These decisions establish the following rules as to the legal effect of abusive language:

(1) Mere words, however abusive, are never sufficient legal provocation to mitigate a homicide to a lesser degree; and

(2) A defendant, prosecuted for a homicide in a difficulty that he has provoked by the use of language "calculated and intended" to bring on the encounter, cannot maintain the position of perfect self-defense unless, at a time prior to the killing, he withdrew from the encounter within the meaning of the law.

These two rules are logically consistent and demonstrate that abusive language will not serve as a legally sufficient provocation for a homicide in this State.

These well-settled rules are clearly controlling in the instant case. Hence, if defendant had provoked an assault by the deceased through the use of abusive language and had thereafter killed the deceased, then it would have been for the jury to determine if the language used by defendant, given the relationship of the parties, the circumstances surrounding the verbal assertions, etc., was "calculated and intended" to bring on the assault. If the jury had found this to be the case, then defendant would not have had the benefit of the doctrine of perfect self-defense, even though the deceased instigated the actual physical attack. But, here there was no evidence that defendant killed the deceased in self-defense. In fact, all of the evidence tends to show that the fatal attack was brought on by the continued verbal abuses directed toward defendant by the deceased. Under these circumstances, there was no basis for a jury determination of whether any of the words were "calculated and intended" to bring on the difficulty.

At this point, we note that in those few jurisdictions that permit abusive language to mitigate the degree of homicide, the majority hold that the words are only deemed sufficient to negate premeditation, thereby reducing the degree of homicide from first to second. Most of these courts reason that since the deceased had made no attempt to endanger the life of the accused, the action of the latter in meeting the insulting remarks with sufficient force (deadly or otherwise) to cause the death of the former, was beyond the bounds of sufficient retaliation to constitute sufficient provocation to reduce the homicide to manslaughter. Although we expressly decline to adopt this minority view, we note that the jury in the instant case apparently applied the same reasoning and found defendant guilty of second-degree murder. Thus, even if the minority rule applied in this State, defendant would not be entitled to a new trial as a result of the instructions here given.

Defendant contends that the trial court committed prejudicial error in charging the jury as follows:

> Now, ladies and gentlemen of the jury, this case is to be tried by you under the laws of the State of North Carolina, and not upon the rules and regulations and customs and unwritten code that exists within the walls of the North Carolina Department of Correction. I can't charge you on that law because I don't know that law. I think I know this one, and this is the law that you are trying this case under.

Defendant argues that this instruction "tends to discount as a matter of law all of the factual information" that the jury was "entitled to consider, not as law, but as a part of the factual background situation within which the incident took place." We find nothing in the charge to support such an inference. During the course of the trial, several of the State's witnesses (either present or former prison inmates) testified about a "prison code," i.e., a set of unwritten rules developed by the prisoners themselves. For example, one of the State's witnesses made the following statements on cross-examination:

> In the prison system, if Watson had not fought after Samples had called him nigger, nigger, and talked about his mother, I guess, you know, everybody else probably would be jugging at him. What I mean by "jugging at him," I mean, messing with him, you know. Taking advantage of the fact that he won't stand up for himself. It is important that you stand up for yourself in the system because if you don't, somebody might get you down in the shower, you know. You might get dead-ended. It means if you don't take up for yourself, everybody picks on you.

Apparently, standing up for oneself was a vital part of this so-called "prison code." In this context, the import of the above instruction was clearly to inform the jurors that the case—like all other criminal cases tried in the North Carolina General Courts of Justice—had to be tried under the laws of this State and not upon any unwritten prisoners' code that existed within the walls of North Carolina's prisons. It is certainly not error for a trial judge to so instruct a jury. Furthermore, it appears that defendant's conduct even constituted a violation of the prisoners' code. We refer to the following redirect testimony of the same witness previously quoted above:

> Standing up for yourself in the prison system would not necessarily include using a knife. He could have run over there and fought with bare fists, that would have been standing up for himself.

Defendant's contention under this assignment is without merit. Therefore, it is overruled.

AFFIRMED.

Questions

1. List all the evidence of provocation you can find in the case excerpt.

2. The court states flatly that words are never adequate provocation to reduce murder to manslaughter, although they may be adequate to reduce murder from first to second degree. Do you think this is a good rule for this case?

3. Identify the informal prison code provisions the defendant wanted the court to admit. Why did the court reject them as evidence? Do you think the code should've been admitted? Explain your answer.

4. If the unwritten prison code does call for him to stand up for himself, was it the words or fears for his personal safety that provoked him?

5. If you were the judge, would you have interpreted the provocation rule differently? If so, how and why?

◆   ◆   ◆

Provocation by Paramour

According to the **common-law paramour rule,** a husband who caught his wife in the act of adultery had adequate provocation to kill: "There could be no greater provocation than this." Many cases have held it's voluntary manslaughter for a husband to kill his wife, her paramour, or both in the first heat of passion following the sight of the wife's adultery. Some statutes went further than the common-law rule and called paramour killings justifiable homicide. Notice this important point: Wives couldn't claim the paramour rule; only husbands could. If the paramour rule applies at all in modern statutes, it applies to both spouses.

In early cases, the rule applied only when husbands caught their wives in the act of adultery and flew into a murderous rage. Husbands who killed when someone told them their wives had committed adultery couldn't claim the benefit of the rule. However, a few modern courts have created an exception to the words-can-never-provoke rule: information that the defendant's spouse has committed adultery. The case of *Commonwealth v. Schnopps* (1983) deals with a husband who killed his wife when she bragged about her adultery.

CASE	*Did He Commit First-Degree Murder?*

Commonwealth v. Schnopps
459 N.E.2d 98 (Mass. 1983)

George Schnopps, the defendant, was convicted before the Superior Court, Berkshire County, Massachusetts, of first-degree murder of his estranged wife and of unlawfully carrying a firearm. At a retrial, the defendant, Schnopps, again was convicted of first-degree murder, and he appealed again. The Massachusetts Supreme Judicial Court affirmed.

ABRAMS, J.

FACTS

On October 13, 1979, George Schnopps fatally shot his wife of fourteen years. The victim and Schnopps began having marital problems approximately six months earlier when Schnopps became suspicious that his wife was seeing another man. Schnopps and his wife argued during this period over his suspicion that she had a relationship with a particular man, whom Schnopps regarded as a "bum." On a few occasions Schnopps threatened to harm his wife with scissors, with a knife, with a shotgun, and with a plastic pistol. A few days prior to the slaying, Schnopps threatened to make his wife suffer as "she had never suffered before." However, there is no evidence that Schnopps physically harmed the victim prior to October 13.

On October 12, 1979, while at work, Schnopps asked a coworker to buy him a gun. He told the coworker he had been receiving threatening telephone calls. After work, Schnopps and the coworker went to Pownal, Vermont, where the coworker purchased a .22 caliber pistol and a box of ammunition for the defendant. Schnopps purchased a starter pistol to scare the caller if there was an attempted break-in. Schnopps stated he wanted to protect himself and his son, who had moved back with him.

Schnopps and his coworker had some drinks at a Vermont bar. The coworker instructed Schnopps in the use of the .22 caliber pistol. Schnopps paid his coworker for the gun and the ammunition. While at the bar Schnopps told the coworker that he was "mad enough to kill." The coworker asked Schnopps "if he was going to get in any trouble with the gun." Schnopps replied that "a bullet was too good for her, he would choke her to death."

Schnopps testified that his wife had left him three weeks prior to the slaying. He claims that he first became aware of problems in his fourteen-year marriage at a point about six months before the slaying. According to Schnopps, on that occasion he took his wife to a club to dance, and she spent the evening dancing with a coworker. On arriving home, Schnopps and his wife argued over her conduct. She told him that she no longer loved him and that she wanted a divorce. Schnopps became very upset.

He admitted that he took out his shotgun during the course of this argument, but he denied that he intended to use it.

During the next few months, Schnopps argued frequently with his wife. Schnopps accused her of seeing another man, but she steadfastly denied the accusations. On more than one occasion Schnopps threatened his wife with physical harm. He testified he never intended to hurt his wife but only wanted to scare her so that she would end the relationship with her coworker.

One day in September, 1979, Schnopps became aware that the suspected boyfriend used a "signal" in telephoning Schnopps' wife. Schnopps used the signal, and his wife answered the phone with "Hi, Lover." She hung up immediately when she recognized Schnopps' voice. That afternoon she did not return home. Later that evening, she informed Schnopps by telephone that she had moved to her mother's house and that she had the children with her. On that day she moved to her mother's home and took their three children with her. (The children were two daughters, age thirteen and age four, and a son, age eleven. On October 6, the son returned to his father's home.) She told Schnopps she would not return to their home. Thereafter she "froze [him] out," and would not talk to him. During this period, Schnopps spoke with a lawyer about a divorce and was told that he had a good chance of getting custody of the children, due to his wife's "desertion and adultery."

On the day of the slaying, Schnopps told a neighbor he was going to call his wife and have her come down to pick up some things. He said he was thinking of letting his wife have the apartment. This was the first time Schnopps indicated he might leave the apartment. He asked the neighbor to keep the youngest child with her if his wife brought her so he could talk with his wife. Schnopps had asked his wife to come to their home and talk over their marital difficulties. Schnopps told his wife that he wanted his children at home, and that he wanted the family to remain intact. Schnopps cried during the conversation, and begged his wife to let the children live with him and to keep their family together. His wife replied, "No, I am going to court, you are going to give me all the furniture, you are going to have to get the Hell out of here, you won't have nothing." Then, pointing to her crotch, she said, "You will never touch this again, because I have got something bigger and better for it."

Schnopps said that these words "cracked" him. He explained that everything went "around" in his head, that he saw "stars." He went "toward the guns in the dining room." He asked his wife, "Why don't you try" (to salvage the marriage). He told her, "I have nothing more to live for," but she replied, "Never, I am never coming back to you." The victim jumped up to leave and Schnopps shot her. He was seated at that time. He told her she would never love anyone else. After shooting the victim, Schnopps said, "I want to go with you," and he shot himself.

Shortly before 3 P.M., Schnopps called a neighbor and said he had shot his wife and also had tried to kill himself. Schnopps told the first person to arrive at his apartment that he shot his wife "because of what she had done to him." Neighbors notified the police of the slaying. On their arrival, Schnopps asked an officer to check to see if his wife had died. The officer told him that she had, and he replied, "Good." A police officer took Schnopps to a hospital for treatment of his wounds. The officer had known Schnopps for twenty-nine years. Schnopps said to the officer that he would not hurt a fly. The officer advised Schnopps not to say anything until he spoke with a lawyer. Schnopps then said, "The devil made me do it." The officer repeated his warning at least three times. Schnopps said that he "loved [his] wife and [his] children." He added, "Just between you and I, . . . I did it because she was cheating on me."

The victim died of three gunshot wounds, to the heart and lungs. Ballistic evidence indicated that the gun was fired within two to four feet of the victim. The evidence also indicated that one shot had been fired while the victim was on the floor.

The defense offered evidence from friends and coworkers who noticed a deterioration in Schnopps's physical and emotional health after the victim had left Schnopps. Schnopps wept at work and at home; he did not eat or sleep well; he was distracted and agitated. On two occasions, he was taken home early by supervisors because of emotional upset and agitation. He was drinking. Schnopps was diagnosed at a local hospital as suffering from a "severe anxiety state." He was given Valium. Schnopps claimed he was receiving threatening telephone calls.

Schnopps and the Commonwealth each offered expert testimony on the issue of criminal responsibility. Schnopps's expert claimed Schnopps was suffering from a "major affective disorder, a major depression," a "psychotic condition," at the time of the slaying. The expert was of the opinion Schnopps was not criminally responsible. The Commonwealth's expert claimed that Schnopps's depression was a grief reaction, a reaction generally associated with death. The expert was of the opinion Schnopps was grieving, over the breakup of his marriage, but that he was criminally responsible.

The judge instructed the jurors on every possible verdict available on the evidence. The jurors were told they could return a verdict of murder in the first degree on the ground of deliberately premeditated malice aforethought; murder in the second degree; manslaughter; not guilty by reason of insanity; or not guilty.

OPINION

On appeal, Schnopps "does not now quarrel with that range of possible verdicts nor with the instruction which the trial court gave to the jury.... [Nor] does...[Schnopps] now dispute that there may be some view of...some of the evidence which might support the verdict returned in this matter." Rather, Schnopps claims that his case is "not of the nature that judges and juries, in weighing evidence, ordinarily equate with murder in the first degree." Schnopps therefore concludes that this is an appropriate case in which to exercise our power under G.L. c. 278, § 33E. We do not agree.

Pursuant to G.L. c. 278, § 33E, we consider whether the verdict of murder in the first degree was against the weight of the evidence, considered in a large or nontechnical sense. Our power under § 33E is to be used with restraint. Moreover, "we do not sit as a second jury to pass anew on the question of Schnopps's guilt."

Schnopps argues that the evidence as a whole demonstrates that his wife was the emotional aggressor, and that her conduct shattered him and destroyed him as a husband and a father. Schnopps points to the fact that he was not a hoodlum or gangster, that he had no prior criminal record, and that he had a "good relationship" with his wife prior to the last six months of their marriage. Schnopps concludes these factors should be sufficient to entitle him to a new trial or the entry of a verdict of a lesser degree of guilt.

The Commonwealth argues that the evidence is more than ample to sustain the verdict. The Commonwealth points out that at the time of the killing there was not a good relationship between the parties; that Schnopps had threatened to harm his wife physically on several occasions; and that he had threatened to kill his wife. Schnopps obtained a gun and ammunition the day before the killing. Schnopps arranged to have his younger child cared for by a neighbor when his wife came to see him. The jury could have found that Schnopps lured his wife to the apartment by suggesting that he might leave and let her live in it with the children. The evidence permits a finding that the killing occurred within a few minutes of the victim's arrival at Schnopps's apartment and before she had time to take off her jacket. From the facts, the jury could infer that Schnopps had planned to kill his wife on October 13, and that the killing was not the spontaneous result of the quarrel but was the result of a deliberately premeditated plan to murder his wife almost as soon as she arrived.

Ballistic evidence indicated that as the victim was lying on the floor, a third bullet was fired into her. From the number of wounds, the type of weapon used, as well as the effort made to procure the weapon, the jurors could find that Schnopps had "a conscious and fixed purpose to kill continuing for a length of time."

If conflicting inferences are possible, "it is for the jury to determine where the truth lies." There was ample evidence which suggested the jurors' conclusion that Schnopps acted with deliberately premeditated malice aforethought. On appeal, Schnopps complains that the prosecutor's summation, which stressed that premeditated murder requires "a thought and an act," could have confused the jurors by suggesting that if "at any time earlier [Schnopps] merely thought about killing that person," that was sufficient to constitute deliberately "premeditated malice aforethought." We do not read the prosecutor's argument as suggesting that conclusion. The prosecutor focused on the Commonwealth's evidence of deliberately premeditated malice aforethought throughout his argument. There was no error. In any event, the argument, read as a whole, does not create a "substantial likelihood of a miscarriage of justice."

Schnopps's domestic difficulties were fully explored before the jury. The jurors rejected Schnopps's claim that his domestic difficulties were an adequate ground to return a verdict of a lesser degree of guilt. The degree of guilt, of course, is a jury determination. The evidence supports a conclusion that Schnopps, angered by his wife's conduct, shot her with deliberately premeditated malice aforethought. The jurors were in the best position to determine whether the domestic difficulties were so egregious as to require a verdict of a lesser degree of guilt. We conclude, on review of the record as a whole, that there is no reason for us to order a new trial or direct the entry of a lesser verdict.

Judgment AFFIRMED.

Questions

1. The paramour rule was adopted to cover cases where husbands found their wives in bed with other men. The provocation was the sight of the adultery itself; so, the passion was immediately connected to the adulterous act. If you were a juror, could you in good conscience say that Schnopps was adequately provoked?

2. If so, was it the adultery that provoked him or the provocative words his wife used to describe her adulterous relationship?

3. Do you think the prohibition against provocative words makes sense?

4. If you were writing a manslaughter law, how would you treat cases like Schnopps?

EXPLORING ADEQUATE PROVOCATION FURTHER

Go to the Criminal Law 8e CD to read the full text version of the case featured here.

Was Cheating on a Former Boyfriend Adequate Provocation?

FACTS

Jerry Elder and Lynn Mallas had an intimate relationship but were never married. Mallas broke off the relationship and moved out of Elder's apartment some time in March or April 1990. On June 2, 1990, Elder saw Mallas, her 2-year-old daughter Angela, and her fiance, Tom Wicks, in an automobile. Elder, in a rented car, followed them to Wicks' apartment. Elder blocked Mallas's exit from the car, and they exchanged words. As Mallas tried to get past him, Elder shot her twice in the back, killing her in front of her 2-year-old daughter.

After seeing that Mallas was shot, Wicks fled on foot. Elder chased after Wicks and caught up to him when Wicks tripped and fell in a nearby field. Elder then shot Wicks in the chest. Wicks rolled onto his stomach, and Elder shot him again in the back. After Elder fled the scene, Wicks managed to return to his apartment and tell a neighbor to call the police. Wicks was seriously injured, but he survived.

Elder was convicted of first-degree murder and of attempted first-degree murder and sentenced to 60 years in prison. Elder claims that he was entitled to a second-degree murder conviction (second-degree murder has replaced manslaughter in Illinois) because of adequate provocation. Was he adequately provoked?

DECISION AND REASONS

According to the Illinois Supreme Court:

In Illinois, only four categories of provocation have been recognized as sufficiently serious to reduce the crime of first degree murder to second degree murder. They are: (1) substantial physical injury or assault; (2) mutual quarrel or combat; (3) illegal arrest; and (4) adultery with the offender's spouse. The defendant has the burden of establishing some evidence of serious provocation, or the trial court may properly deny a second-degree murder instruction.

The facts of this case do not fall under any of the four categories of serious provocation recognized in Illinois. The first three categories clearly do not apply. Under the fourth category, there is obviously no evidence of adultery with the offender's spouse since Elder and the victim were not married.

Elder argues that this last category should be expanded to include the "special relationship" between the defendant and the victim. . . . Although Mallas and the defendant had previously enjoyed an intimate relationship, that relationship had ended two months before the homicide occurred. Additionally, there is no evidence in this case to suggest that the defendant was acting under a "sudden and intense passion." In fact, the evidence here suggests that the defendant literally stalked the murder victim. The defendant carried a loaded gun and followed Mallas in a rented car. This conduct suggests that he was not suddenly provoked when he shot Mallas, but rather that he was completing a contemplated plan. The trial court's decision not to instruct the jury on second-degree murder was proper.

State v. Elder, 579 N.E.2d 420 (Ill.App. 1991)

Reasonable Provocation

Adequate provocation means real provocation; it has to actually drive the defendant into a murderous rage. But this **subjective provocation** isn't enough; the provocation also has to be **reasonable provocation.** But reasonable to whom? Reasonableness can mean how "ordinary people" would react under similar circumstances. Put another way, reasonable means how the defendants *should've* reacted, not how they did react.

But, some defendants in special circumstances argue their provocation should be measured by whether the circumstances would've provoked a reasonable person in their special category. In *People v. Washington* (1976), for example, Merle Francis Washington shot his gay partner following a lover's quarrel brought on by the victim's unfaithfulness. The court instructed the jury on provocation as follows:

The jury was instructed that to reduce the homicide from murder to manslaughter upon the ground of sudden quarrel or heat of passion, the conduct must be tested by the ordinarily reasonable man test. Defendant argues without precedent that to so instruct was error because, "Homosexuals are not at present a curiosity or a rare commodity. They are a distinct third sexual class between that of male and female, are present in almost every field of endeavor, and are fast achieving a guarded recognition not formerly accorded them. The heat of their passions in dealing with one another should not be tested by standards applicable to the average man or the average woman, since they are aberrant hybrids, with an obvious diminished capacity."

Defendant submits that since the evidence disclosed that "he was acting as a servient homosexual during the period of his relationship with the victim, that his heat of passion should have been tested, either by a standard applicable to a female, or a standard applicable to the average homosexual, and that it was prejudicial error to instruct the jury to determine his heat of passion defense by standards applicable to the average male."

We do not agree. In the present condition of our law it is left to the jurors to say whether or not the facts and circumstances in evidence are sufficient to lead them to believe that the defendant did, or to create a reasonable doubt in their minds as to whether or not he did, commit his offense under a heat of passion.

The jury is further to be admonished and advised by the court that this heat of passion must be such a passion as would naturally be aroused in the mind of an ordinarily reasonable person under the given facts and circumstances, and that, consequently, no defendant may set up his own standard of conduct and justify or excuse himself because in fact his passions were aroused, unless further the jury believe that the facts and circumstances were sufficient to arouse the passions of the ordinarily reasonable man.

Thus no man of extremely violent passion could so justify or excuse himself if the exciting cause be not adequate, nor could an excessively cowardly man justify himself unless the circumstances were such as to arouse the fears of the ordinarily courageous man. Still further, while the conduct of the defendant is to be measured by that of the ordinarily reasonable man placed in identical circumstances, the jury is properly to be told that the exciting cause must be such as would naturally tend to arouse the passion of the ordinarily reasonable man. (99)

 Go to Exercise 9-3 on the Criminal Law 8e CD to learn more about voluntary manslaughter.

Involuntary Manslaughter

The central elements in involuntary manslaughter are its *actus reus* (voluntary act or omission) and its *mens rea* (unintentional killing). Of course, as in all crimes of criminal conduct causing criminal harm, involuntary manslaughter also includes the elements of causation and resulting harm (death). We won't repeat our discussion of causation from Chapter 4 here.

There are three kinds of **involuntary manslaughter**:

1. **Reckless manslaughter**

2. **Negligent manslaughter**

3. **Unlawful act manslaughter** (also called **misdemeanor manslaughter**)

Reckless and Negligent Manslaughter

Criminal recklessness (Chapter 4) means the *conscious* creation of a *substantial* and *unjustifiable* risk. **Criminal negligence** (also called **gross criminal negligence** [Chapter 4]) means creating a *substantial* and *unjustifiable* risk the defendant *should've* been, but

ELEMENTS OF INVOLUNTARY MANSLAUGHTER

Actus Reus	Mens Rea	Circumstance	Causation	Result
Killing another person	Creating the risk of killing or seriously injuring another person 1. Recklessly **or** 2. Negligently	Death during the commission of an unlawful act	Acts that trigger a chain of events that lead to another person's death	Death of another person

in fact wasn't, aware of. In criminal reckless and negligent manslaughter, the *mens rea* is creating the risk of death or serious bodily injury.

Reckless and negligent manslaughter statutes cover a wide field, including unintentional deaths caused by using firearms, handling explosives, operating vehicles, practicing medicine, and even allowing vicious animals to run free. The Ohio Court of Appeals dealt with an unusual case of involuntary manslaughter under its vehicular homicide statute in *State v. Mays* (2000).

CASE | *Did He Commit Aggravated Vehicular Homicide?*

State v. Mays

WL 1033098 (Ohio App. Dist. 1, 2000)

Nicholas A. Mays was convicted of aggravated vehicular homicide and tampering with evidence, both felonies of the third degree, in Hamilton County Court of Common Pleas. He was sentenced to consecutive terms of incarceration. He appealed. The Ohio Court of Appeals, First District, reversed the sentences in part and remanded the case to the Court of Common Pleas for resentencing.

DOAN, J.

FACTS

On August 19, 1999, nineteen-year-old Nicholas Mays was operating an automobile in which his cousin was a passenger. At approximately 1:45 A.M., they saw a pedestrian, later identified as Michael Boumer, in a grocery-store parking lot. According to Mays, Boumer appeared to be intoxicated, and the two young men decided that they would "mess with" Boumer by appearing to offer him a ride. Mays intended to nudge Boumer with the vehicle and then drive away.

Investigating officers confirmed that Boumer had consumed some alcohol. However, the record also indicates that Boumer was mentally handicapped. Mays did drive

the vehicle in the direction of Boumer, but instead of merely nudging him, he inadvertently ran over him, causing him fatal injuries. Upon seeing that Boumer was injured, Mays drove to another location and called for emergency aid. He then went to a car wash, where he cleaned the vehicle to remove evidence of the fatal collision.

On the day after the incident, Mays took a planned trip to Florida, during which his mother convinced him that he should report his involvement in the crime. Mays did so, returning to Cincinnati and giving a full confession to the police. In October 1999, Mays entered guilty pleas to one count each of aggravated vehicular homicide and tampering with evidence. The trial court sentenced him to five years' incarceration for the aggravated vehicular homicide and to four years' incarceration for tampering with evidence, with the terms to run consecutively.

OPINION

[The Ohio Revised Code vehicular homicide statute (Section 2903.06) reads in part:

(A) No person, while operating or participating in the operation of a motor vehicle, motorcycle, snowmobile, locomotive, watercraft, or aircraft, shall cause the death of another or the unlawful termination of another's pregnancy in any of the following ways:

(2) Recklessly;

(3) Negligently;

(B)(1) Whoever violates division (A)...(2) of this section is guilty of aggravated vehicular homicide and shall be punished as provided in divisions (B)(1)...(b) of this section....

(b) Except as otherwise provided in this division, aggravated vehicular homicide committed in violation of division (A)(2) of this section is a felony of the third degree....In addition to any other sanctions imposed, the court shall suspend the offender's driver's license, commercial driver's license, temporary instruction permit, probationary license, or nonresident operating privilege for a definite period of three years to life....

(2) Whoever violates division (A)(3) of this section is guilty of vehicular homicide. Except as otherwise provided in this division, vehicular homicide is a misdemeanor of the first degree....

...The sole issue posed in the assignment of error, therefore, is whether the record supports the trial court's findings.

Mays first argues that the court erred in imposing terms of incarceration greater than the minimum....We hold that the trial court's finding with respect to the seriousness of the offenses is supported by the record. Mays conceded that his intention was to "mess with" a person whom he perceived to be impaired in some way, and in doing so, he deprived the thirty-nine-year-old victim of his life. Mays did not immediately seek help for Boumer, but instead thought first of his own interest in evading detection for the crime. His concealment of the crime was compounded when he washed the car and left the jurisdiction....

In his second argument, Mays claims that the trial court erred in imposing the maximum sentence for aggravated vehicular homicide. Before imposing the maximum term of incarceration for an offense, the court must find that the offender has committed the worst form of the offense... [T]he [trial] court found that Mays had committed the worst form of aggravated vehicular homicide. We disagree.

...Though the evidence certainly indicates that Mays exercised extremely poor judgment in carrying out his wish to "mess with" Boumer, there is no indication that he harbored any malice toward the victim. Instead, the record indicates that Mays's conduct started as a reckless, poorly conceived prank and ended in tragedy. And while we in no way wish to minimize the loss of a human life or to condone Mays's actions, this is not the type of conduct for which the legislature has reserved the maximum sentence.

Furthermore, although he admittedly thought of his own interests before seeking help for Boumer, Mays did take steps to ensure that emergency personnel were notified promptly. His actions therefore did not reflect an utter lack of concern for Boumer or otherwise demonstrate a perversity of character that would justify the imposition of the maximum sentence. Further, there is no indication that the victim suffered for a prolonged period of time before he died or suffered to a greater degree than any other victim of a vehicular homicide. Finally, Mays surrendered to authorities and confessed to the crimes. Under these circumstances, we cannot say that Mays committed the worst form of the offense....We therefore hold that the trial court erred in imposing the maximum term for that offense.

Having held that the trial court erred in imposing the maximum sentence for the aggravated vehicular homicide..., we hereby reverse those parts of the trial court's judgment and remand the cause for resentencing in accordance with law.

Judgment AFFIRMED in part and REVERSED in part, and cause REMANDED.

DISSENT

HILDEBRANDT, P.J., concurring in part
and dissenting in part.

...Mays senselessly took the life of the victim because he wished to "mess with" him. The wantonness of that conduct alone could have justified the trial court in imposing the maximum sentence. However, Mays compounded his misconduct by leaving the scene of the collision, thereby making it clear that he valued his own interest in evading detection above the life of Boumer. The majority concedes as much, yet persists in holding that Mays did not commit the worst form of the offense. His eventual call for emergency aid and his subsequent remorse for his actions did not erase the fact that his conduct was egregious and deserving of the greatest punishment.

Questions

1. How does the Ohio statute define vehicular homicide?

2. Relying on the evidence in the case and referring to the Ohio provision, explain why Nicholas Mays was guilty of aggravated vehicular homicide.

3. How would *you* define vehicular homicide? Defend your definition.

4. Do you agree with the majority opinion's reasons for reversing the sentence? Or, do the dissent and the trial court have the better arguments? Back up your answer.

Unlawful Act Manslaughter

In 1260, long before the division between murder and manslaughter was created by the common-law judges, the great jurist Bracton wrote that unintended deaths during unlawful acts are criminal homicides. Some time after the judges created the offense of manslaughter, unlawful act homicides became involuntary manslaughter. In modern times, statutes have restricted unlawful act manslaughter because it's considered too harsh. In fact, there's a trend to abolish unlawful act manslaughter, leaving reckless and negligent manslaughter as the only forms of involuntary manslaughter. Michigan has resisted the trend to abolish, choosing instead to restrict the reach of unlawful act manslaughter to deaths following assaults (LaFave and Scott 1986, 675). The Michigan Supreme Court debated the merits of abolition in *People v. Datema* (1995).

CASE	*Was Her Death Unlawful Act Manslaughter?*

People v. Datema
533 N.W.2d 272 (Mich. 1995)

Gregory Datema, the defendant, was convicted in the Circuit Court, Kent County, of involuntary manslaughter. Datema appealed. The Court of Appeals affirmed. The Michigan Supreme Court affirmed.

BOYLE, J.

FACTS

In the early morning hours of December 22, 1988, defendant and his wife, Pamela Datema, were sitting in their living room with two friends. All four had been smoking marijuana and both defendant and his wife had been drinking throughout the evening.

As the evening wore on, the conversation turned to the topic of previous romances, and the defendant and his wife began to argue about various paramours with whom they had slept. During the argument, Mrs. Datema started to rise from her chair, claiming to have had sexual intercourse with other men in front of defendant's sons. As she rose, defendant slapped her once across the face with an open hand. Mrs. Datema slumped back into her chair, screamed that she hoped defendant would "go to Florida and stay there," then slipped from the chair onto the floor.

Initially, defendant and the two others present in the room thought that Mrs. Datema had passed out from drinking too much but, after five to ten minutes, they became concerned and tried to wake her. When they were unable to do so, they called an ambulance. Mrs. Datema never regained consciousness and died soon after.

The medical examiner testified that Mrs. Datema had a blood-alcohol level between 0.03 and 0.05 percent. He stated that death was caused by a tear in an artery in the head that occurred as a result of defendant's blow. (Most people, when slapped, reflexively stiffen their necks and avoid serious injury. Occasionally, however, when a person is intoxicated, the reflexes do not react quickly enough, and a blow could result in a tearing. Generally, a higher blood-alcohol level is necessary, but the ingested marijuana, which was not able to be tested, was undoubtedly a contributing factor.)

Although the three eyewitnesses called by the prosecution testified that defendant had slapped his wife once with an open hand and that the slap was not a hard one, the medical examiner testified that to cause death, even under the circumstances, the blow had to have been a powerful one and "would have to be with probably all the force that one could muster."

...The jury convicted defendant of involuntary manslaughter. Defendant was convicted as a second-felony offender (Defendant's prior felony conviction was for malicious destruction of property in a building.) and sentenced to 7 to 22½ years in prison. Defendant filed an appeal, contending that, if the unlawful act that results in death is not committed recklessly or with gross negligence, the crime should no longer be recognized as a form of common-law involuntary manslaughter. The Court of Appeals disagreed and affirmed the decision of the trial court in an unpublished opinion. On June 30, 1994, we granted leave to appeal.

OPINION

...The law of manslaughter as it exists today has been adopted from the old English common law. Common-law manslaughter has two broad categories: voluntary and involuntary. These two categories entail distinct elements and apply in different circumstances, but are often misapplied. Confusion is present because Michigan courts, ours included, have been less than precise in the use of language denoting voluntary or involuntary manslaughter.

...Involuntary manslaughter is a catch-all concept including all manslaughter not characterized as voluntary: Every unintentional killing of a human being is involuntary manslaughter if it is neither murder nor voluntary manslaughter nor within the scope of some recognized justification or excuse. To this...statement must be added the caveat [warning] that led to our grant of leave in this case. At common law, if an unlawful act was *malum in se,* inherently wrong, the only *mens rea* required was the *mens rea* of the underlying act....* We conclude that if an assault and battery is committed with a specific intent to inflict injury and causes unintended death, the actor may be found guilty of (at least) involuntary manslaughter. We express no opinion with regard to the merits of the misdemeanor-manslaughter rule in contexts other than assault and battery....

We reject the suggestion that progressive notions of jurisprudence require absolution for an unintended death under circumstances from which the fact finder may infer from a powerful blow an intent to injure that factually causes death. While we agree with the dissent that "Misdemeanors are crimes, and defendants who commit them are subject to punishment under the law," when one strikes another with "probably all the force that one can muster," the proper charge is manslaughter and not assault.

DISSENT

CAVANAGH, J.

....In *State v. Aaron,*** we recognized that it is inherently unjust to presume the existence of the *mens rea* for murder merely on a showing of the *mens rea* required for an underlying felony. Specifically, our holdings in *Aaron* were premised on the following principle of criminal jurisprudence: "If one had to choose the most basic principle of criminal law...it would be that criminal liability for causing a particular result is not justified in the absence of some culpable mental state in respect to that result...."

The unlawful-act misdemeanor-manslaughter rule violates the principle set forth in *Aaron,* and it too should be abrogated. Pursuant to the unlawful-act misdemeanor-manslaughter rule, a defendant may be convicted of involuntary manslaughter where it has been shown that the defendant committed the unlawful act that proximately caused death. Proof of the *mens rea* for manslaughter is presumed to exist on the basis of a showing of the *mens rea* required for the underlying misdemeanor.

Contrary to the principle that we endorsed in *Aaron,* liability for a homicide is imposed without an independent showing of a *mens rea* with regard to the homicide. To eliminate the perpetuation of such an injustice, this Court should abolish the unlawful-act misdemeanor-manslaughter rule....

The instant case is another example of a situation in which it could be shown that the defendant had a specific intent to injure, but perhaps [it] could not be shown that the defendant willfully disregarded a high risk of death or serious bodily injury. The prosecutor's medical expert testified that the cause of death in this case was "very rare," and "very unusual," and that people could receive "similar blows frequently and [not] die and perhaps [not even be] severely injured." (Specifically, Dr. Stephen Cohle testified: I can say this is a very rare cause of death. It is very unusual....And I will say, early on, I can't prove beyond a reasonable doubt all of the reasons why she did die from this blow, because it is very unusual. And I'm sure people receive similar blows frequently and don't die and perhaps aren't even severely injured....) This testimony strongly suggests that a high risk of death or serious bodily injury was not created when the "defendant slapped [his wife] once across the face with an open hand." Notably, the prosecutor characterizes the victim's death in this case as "entirely unexpected."

...The principle embraced by this Court in *Aaron* dictates the elimination of the unlawful-act misdemeanor-manslaughter rule. After *Aaron,* culpability for homicide may not be presumed from the commission of another crime. The majority's special category is unacceptable because it equates a specific intent to injure—to whatever degree and kind—with a willful disregard of a high risk of death or serious bodily injury, and, in effect, violates the principles of *Aaron.* This case provides the Court with an excellent opportunity to abolish the unlawful-act

---

*The caveat is a statement of the misdemeanor-manslaughter rule. The court concluded that assault is inherently wrong, and that the misdemeanor-manslaughter rule applies to this case.

**The case in which the Michigan Supreme Court abolished the felony-murder rule.

misdemeanor-manslaughter rule once and for all. I would do so now, and thereby ensure that common-law liability for homicide will only be imposed where culpability for death has been proven.

Questions

1. List all evidence relevant to deciding Gregory Datema's state of mind when he hit his wife.

2. How would you characterize Datema's state of mind with respect to injuring his wife? Intentional? Knowing? Reckless? Grossly negligent? Negligent? Back up your answer with facts that you listed in (1).

3. How would you characterize Datema's state of mind with respect to his wife's death? Intentional? Knowing?

Reckless? Grossly negligent? Negligent? Back up your answer with facts that you listed in (1).

4. Summarize the reasons that the majority declined to abolish the misdemeanor manslaughter rule.

5. Summarize the dissent's arguments for extending the court's abolition of the felony murder rule to misdemeanor manslaughter.

6. Do you agree with the majority or with the dissent? Back up your answer with the majority and/or dissent's arguments.

 Go to Exercise 9-4 on the Criminal Law 8e CD to learn more about involuntary manslaughter.

◆   ◆   ◆

SUMMARY

I. The history of criminal homicide law
  A. Since the eighteenth century, the law has recognized three kinds of homicide: justifiable, excusable, and criminal
  B. Criminal homicide is the most serious of all felonies known to our law
  C. Criminal homicide is divided into two categories: murder and manslaughter

II. The elements of criminal homicide
  A. *Actus reus*—taking the life of or causing the death of another person (live human being)
    1. Depends on how the law defines
      a. When life begins
      b. When life ends
    2. Defining the beginning and end of life is controversial and differs among jurisdictions
  B. *Mens rea*—causing the death of another
    1. Purposely
    2. Knowingly
    3. Recklessly
    4. Negligently
  C. Causation—acts that set in motion a chain of events that amount to cause in fact or legal cause of the death of another
  D. Criminal harm resulting in the death of another

III. Murder
  A. Murder is the unlawful killing of another with malice aforethought
  B. Historically, "malice aforethought" consisted of five mental states—the specific intent to do one of the following:

1. Kill another person
2. Seriously injure another person
3. Commit specified dangerous felonies
4. Forcibly resist a lawful arrest
5. Create a higher than criminally reckless risk of death or serious bodily injury (depraved-heart murder)

C. The law defines four types of murder
   1. First-degree murder
      a. Premeditated, deliberate killings
      b. Atrocious, brutal, or cruel murders (in capital cases)
   2. Second-degree murder
      a. Intentional killing without premeditation
      b. Killings resulting from the intent to do serious bodily injury
      c. Killings resulting from the resisting of lawful arrest
      d. Killings that occur during the commission of felonies
   3. Felony murders—unintentional deaths that occur while committing dangerous felonies
      a. Intent to commit the underlying crime satisfies the *mens rea* of felony murder
      b. Felony murder has three goals
         (1) Deter offenders
         (2) Reduce violence
         (3) Punish wrongdoers
      c. Four states have abolished it
      d. When someone besides the defendant caused the death
         (1) Third-party exception prevents felony murder conviction
         (2) Resisting victim exception allows felony murder conviction
   4. Corporation murder
      a. Corporations can legally commit murder
      b. Practically, prosecutions of corporations for criminal homicide don't exceed involuntary manslaughter charges

IV. Manslaughter
   A. Can be either voluntary or involuntary
   B. Elements of voluntary manslaughter
      1. *Actus reus*—taking the life or causing the death of another person
      2. *Mens rea*—intent to kill or cause serious bodily harm
      3. Adequate provocation
         a. Is a circumstance element
         b. Occurs in the sudden heat of passion before there was a reasonable time for the passion to cool off
         c. Caused both the passion and the killing
         d. Is specified by law
            (1) Fighting (mutual combat)
            (2) Assault and battery
            (3) Trespass
            (4) Adultery (paramour rule)
         e. Response must be reasonable to ordinary people
         f. Never consists of words

4. Causation—the acts that triggered the chain of events that led to the death
5. Result—the death of another
C. Involuntary manslaughter is the killing of another person unintentionally
   1. Requires the *mens rea* of either criminal recklessness or criminal negligence
   2. Occurs during the commission of unlawful acts (like reckless or negligent driving)

 Go to the Criminal Law 8e CD to download this summary outline. The outline has been formatted so that you can add notes to it during class lectures, or later create a customized chapter outline to use while reviewing. Either way, the summary outline will help you understand the "big picture" and fill in the details as you study.

REVIEW QUESTIONS

1. Briefly trace the history of criminal homicide from its common-law origins to the four present divisions.

2. Identify the various definitions of when life begins and ends for purposes of the *actus reus* of criminal homicide.

3. Identify the four states of mind that can qualify as the *mens rea* of criminal homicide.

4. How have modern courts changed the original meaning of *premeditation*?

5. Define and explain the significance of "heinous, atrocious, and cruel" in first-degree murder *actus reus.*

6. Identify the difference between the *mens rea* of first- and second-degree murder.

7. Identify all the elements among the second-degree murder statutes reproduced on pages 302–303.

8. List the felonies that might turn into a murder any death that occurs while the felony is being committed.

9. List the three goals of felony murder laws, and summarize the research on whether the laws achieve their goals.

10. Summarize the practical importance of the fact that corporations can commit murder.

11. Identify the essential difference between voluntary and involuntary manslaughter.

12. What's human frailty got to do with the law of voluntary manslaughter?

13. Identify and explain the five elements of voluntary manslaughter.

14. Identify and briefly expand on the four provocations recognized by the law as adequate.

15. When can words as provocation be used as a defense to criminal homicide?

16. Explain the difference between subjective and reasonable provocation.

17. Describe and give an example of how "sudden provocation" is measured.

18. Identify the link between provocation, passion, and death in voluntary manslaughter.

19. Identify and explain the differences between the three kinds of involuntary manslaughter.

20. Explain how and why modern laws have changed "unlawful act manslaughter."

KEY TERMS

justifiable homicide p. 283
excusable homicide p. 283
criminal homicide p. 283
murder p. 283
malice p. 283
aforethought p. 283
manslaughter p. 283
depraved-heart murder p. 283
homicide *actus reus* p. 284
fetal death statute p. 285
brain death p. 291
deep coma p. 291
criminal homicide *mens rea* p. 291

express or implied malice
    aforethought p. 292
first-degree murder p. 292
premeditation p. 293
torture murder p. 298
second-degree murder p. 302
felony murder p. 304
third-party exception p. 305
resisting-victim exception p. 306
voluntary manslaughter p. 315
adequate provocation p. 315
objective test of cooling-off time
    p. 315

common-law paramour rule
    p. 319
subjective provocation p. 322
reasonable provocation p. 322
involuntary manslaughter p. 323
reckless manslaughter p. 323
negligent manslaughter p. 323
unlawful act manslaughter p. 323
misdemeanor manslaughter
    p. 323
criminal recklessness p. 323
criminal negligence p. 323
gross criminal negligence p. 323

SUGGESTED READINGS

 Go the Criminal Law 8e CD for Suggested Readings for this chapter.

THE COMPANION WEB SITE
FOR *CRIMINAL LAW,* EIGHTH EDITION

http://cj.wadsworth.com/samaha/crim_law8e

 Supplement your review of this chapter by going to the companion Web site to take one of the Tutorial Quizzes, use the flash cards to test your knowledge of the elements of various crimes and defenses, and check out the many other study aids you'll find there. You'll find valuable data and resources at your fingertips to help you study for that big exam or write that important paper.

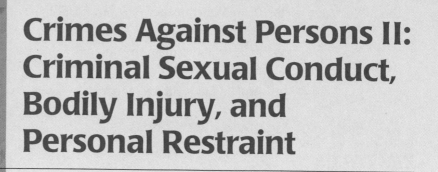

10 Crimes Against Persons II: Criminal Sexual Conduct, Bodily Injury, and Personal Restraint

Chapter Main Points

- Crimes against persons boil down to four types: taking a life; unwanted sexual invasions, bodily injury; and personal restraint.

- Sex offenses are serious crimes even if there's no *physical* injury, because they violate intimacy in a way physical injuries can't.

- The criminal justice system handles rapes by strangers and men with weapons capably, but it doesn't do as well with the overwhelming number of rapes by men who know their victims.

- The old rape law defined a crime of forcible sexual penetration that only men could commit against women who weren't their wives.

- Modern statutes have expanded criminal sexual conduct to include a list of gender-neutral sex offenses, involving unwanted sexual penetrations and contacts.

- Modern rape law has shifted the emphasis from the resistance of victims to unwanted sexual penetrations by perpetrators.

- The emphasis on physical violence to satisfy the element of force in the *actus reus* of rape is shifting in modern rape law to the sufficiency of nonconsent to unwanted sexual advances.

- According to formal law, the prosecution has to prove nonconsent by the victim beyond a reasonable doubt; in practice, defendants claim victim consent as a defense.

- Bodily injury crimes include unlawful nonsexual contacts (battery) or threats of them (assault).

- Kidnappings and false imprisonment are crimes against the right to come and go as we please.

Did He Rape Her?

A college student left her class, went to her dormitory room where she drank a martini, and then went to a lounge to wait for her boyfriend. When her boyfriend didn't show up, she went to another dormitory to find a friend, Earl Hassel. She knocked on the door, but no one answered. She tried the doorknob and, finding it unlocked, went in and found a man sleeping on the bed. At first, she thought the man was Hassel, but he turned out to be Hassel's roommate, Robert Berkowitz. Berkowitz asked her to stay for a while and she agreed. He asked for a backrub and she turned him down. He suggested that she sit on the bed, but she said no and sat on the floor instead.

Berkowitz moved to the floor beside her, lifted up her shirt and bra and massaged her breasts. He then unfastened his pants and unsuccessfully attempted to put his penis in her mouth. They both stood up, and he locked the door. He came back, pushed her onto the bed, and removed her undergarments from one leg. He then penetrated her vagina with his penis. After withdrawing and ejaculating on her stomach, he stated, "Wow, I guess we just got carried away," to which she responded, "No, we didn't get carried away, you got carried away." ◆

This chapter examines three kinds of crimes against persons: sexual violations (rape and related sex offenses); bodily injury (assault and battery); and restraints on liberty (kidnapping and false imprisonment). Sex offenses stand only slightly below murder (Chapter 9) as the most serious crimes against a person. Sex offenses are serious crimes even if victims suffer no *physical* injury, because they violate intimacy in a way that physical injuries can't (Medea and Thompson 1974; Russell 1975). Even offensive sexual *touching*, such as pinching buttocks or fondling breasts, bears the mark of a special violation. These offensive sexual contacts are universally regarded by the law and society as serious felonies, whereas nonsexual **battery**—the unwanted and unjustified offensive touching of another person (unless a batterer seriously injures the victim)— is a misdemeanor. So, the criminal sexual battery in an unwanted erotic caress is treated more seriously than the nonsexual battery of an insulting spit in the face.

In this chapter, we'll continue our look at crimes against persons by examining sex offenses, bodily injury crimes, and personal restraint crimes.

SEX OFFENSES

Originally, the criminal law recognized only two sex offenses—rape and sodomy. **Common-law rape** was strictly limited to intentional forced heterosexual vaginal penetration. It was aimed at the traditional view of rape: a male stranger leaps from the shadows at night and sexually attacks a defenseless woman. **Common-law sodomy** meant anal intercourse between two males. Modern court opinions have relaxed the strict definitions of rape, and **criminal sexual conduct statutes** enacted in the 1970s and the 1980s (discussed below) have expanded the definition of sex offenses to embrace a wide range of nonconsensual penetrations and contacts, even if they fall far short of violent.

These reforms in sex offense law were brought about because a secret was made public: The vast majority of rape victims are raped by men they *know*. In this chapter, we'll distinguish between two kinds of rape: **aggravated rape**—rape by strangers or men with weapons who physically injure their victims—and **unarmed acquaintance rape**—nonconsensual sex between "dates, lovers, neighbors, co-workers, employers, and so on" (Bryden 2000, 318).

The criminal justice system deals fairly well with aggravated rapes, but it hasn't done so well with unarmed acquaintance rapes. Why? For several reasons. Victims aren't likely to report them, or they don't recognize them as rapes. When victims do report them, the police are less likely to believe them than the victims of aggravated rape. Prosecutors are less likely to charge unarmed acquaintance rapists, and juries are less likely to convict them. Appeals court decisions are more likely to cause controversy. Finally, unarmed acquaintance rapists are most likely to escape punishment if their victims don't follow the rules of middle-class morality. According to Professor David P. Bryden (2000):

> An acquaintance rapist is most likely to escape justice if his victim violated traditional norms of female morality and prudence: for example, by engaging in casual sex, drinking heavily, or hitchhiking. When the victim is a norm-violating woman, people often blame her rather than the rapist. (318)

The criminal justice system's poor performance in dealing with unarmed acquaintance rapes would be a serious problem in any case, but it's made worse because they're the overwhelming number of rapes. In one survey of women who didn't report rapes to the police, more than 80 percent said they were raped by men they knew (Williams 1984). In three separate surveys of college women, one in five reported being "physically forced" to have sexual intercourse by her date (Foreman 1986, 27).

Another aspect of the social reality of rape is the substantial number of rapes committed against men (McMullen 1990). It's almost impossible to get details about male rape victims. The most widely cited crime statistic doesn't break down rape victims by gender. The most thorough government victimization survey reports the gender of victims (about 8% are males) but nothing more. A few scattered numbers from rape counseling and rape crisis centers report between 8 and 10 percent of their clients are men (Rochman n.d.)

To learn more about how the law treats rape crimes, in this section, we'll study the history of rape law; the elements of modern rape law, statutory rape; and how the law determines, or grades, the degrees of seriousness of various sex offenses.

The History of Rape Law

As early as 800, rape was a capital offense in Anglo-Saxon England. The common law defined rape as the carnal knowledge (sexual intercourse) by a man of a woman who was not his wife with force and without her consent (Blackstone 1769, 215). This definition boiled down to four elements:

1. Intentional vaginal intercourse

2. Between a man and a woman who was not his wife

3. Achieved by force or a threat of severe bodily harm

4. Without the woman's consent

The common law required proof beyond a reasonable doubt of all four elements because, as Lord Hale, the highly regarded seventeenth-century lawyer and legal scholar of the criminal law, noted:

> It must be remembered, that it is an accusation to make, hard to be proved, and harder to be defended by the party accused, though innocent.... The heinousness of the offence many times transporting the judge and jury with so much indignation, that they are over-hastily carried to the conviction of the person accused thereof, by the confident testimony of sometimes false and malicious witnesses.
>
> Blackstone 1769, 210

Notice there were no causation or criminal harm requirements in common-law rape (or as we'll see in modern criminal sexual conduct crimes either). Why not? In Chapter 3 we distinguished between two kinds of crimes: crimes of criminal conduct and crimes causing a criminal harm. Criminal homicide (Chapter 9) is one of the crimes of causing a criminal harm, as are assault and battery (we'll discuss them later in this chapter). Rape is one of the many crimes of criminal conduct where causation and criminal harm aren't elements. So, there's no need to prove a harm beyond the conduct itself. While physical injury to the victim can be a circumstance element of aggravated rape, it's not required as an element of simple rape or other criminal sexual penetrations and contacts.

In common-law trials, rape victims were allowed to testify against accused rapists; it was up to the jury to decide whether to believe them. But the victim's credibility depended on three conditions, always difficult (and often impossible) to satisfy:

1. Her chastity

2. Whether she reported the rape promptly

3. Whether the rape was corroborated by other witnesses

Blackstone (1769), the leading eighteenth-century authority on the common law in both England and the American colonies, talked tough enough when he asserted that even prostitutes could be of good fame but undermined his words when he added this warning about victim witnesses:

> If the ravished be of evil fame, and stand unsupported by others; if she concealed the injury for any considerable time after she had opportunity to complain; if the place where the fact was alleged to be committed, was where it was possible she might have been heard, and she made no outcry; these and the like circumstances carry a strong, but not conclusive, presumption that her testimony is false or feigned. (213–214)

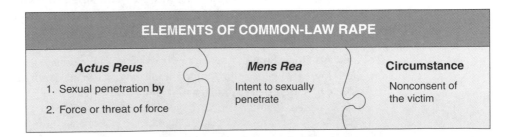

ELEMENTS OF COMMON-LAW RAPE

Actus Reus	*Mens Rea*	Circumstance
1. Sexual penetration **by** 2. Force or threat of force	Intent to sexually penetrate	Nonconsent of the victim

Next, we'll look at how the emphasis on demonstrated nonconsent by victims has evolved over time and other changes to modern criminal sexual conduct statutes.

The "Force and Resistance" Standard

From seventeenth-century England to the 1970s in the United States, the law of rape concentrated on the **element of consent.** Women had to prove by their resistance that they didn't consent to the unwanted sexual advances by the rapists. According to an early frequently cited case, *Reynolds v. State* (1889):

> Voluntary submission by the woman, while she has power to resist, no matter how reluctantly yielded, removes from the act an essential element of the crime of rape . . . if the carnal knowledge was with the consent of the woman, no matter how tardily given, or how much force had theretofore been employed, it is not rape. (904)

Proof of nonconsent by resistance is peculiar to the law of rape. In no other crime where lack of consent is an element of the crime does the law treat passive acceptance as consent. Robbery requires taking someone's property by force or threat of force, but it's outrageous even to think that the element of force puts the burden on victims to prove they resisted. Entering an unlocked apartment house without consent to commit a crime is burglary, but it would be absurd to demand that renters prove they didn't consent to the entry. The same is true of theft. According to Lani Anne Remick (1993):

> A common defense to a charge of auto theft . . . is that the car's owner consented to the defendant's use of the vehicle. A mere showing that the owner never gave the defendant permission to take the car is enough to defeat this defense; no showing that the owner actually told the defendant not to take the car is necessary.
>
> In rape law, however, the "default" position is consent. Proof of the absence of affirmative indications by the victim is not enough to defeat a consent defense; instead, the prosecution must show that the alleged victim indicated to the defendant through her overt actions and/or words that she did not wish to participate in sexual activity with him.
>
> Thus, "the law presumes that one will not give away that which is his to a robber, but makes no similar presumption as to the conduct of women and rapists." In fact, quite the opposite is true: in the context of sexual activity the law presumes consent. For example, proving both that a woman did not verbally consent and that her actions consist of lying still and not moving does not raise a presumption of nonconsent but of consent. Only through evidence of some sort of overt behavior such as a verbal "no" or an attempt to push away the defendant can the prosecution meet its burden of proving nonconsent. (1111)

The amount of resistance required to prove lack of consent has changed over time. From the 1800s until the 1950s, the **utmost resistance standard** prevailed. According to the standard, to show they didn't consent, victims had to resist with all the physical power they possessed. In *Brown v. State* (1906), a 16-year-old virgin testified that her neighbor grabbed her, tripped her to the ground, and forced himself on her.

> I tried as hard as I could to get away. I was trying all the time to get away just as hard as I could. I was trying to get up; I pulled at the grass; I screamed as hard as I could, and he told me to shut up, and I didn't, and then he held his hand on my mouth until I was almost strangled. (538)

The jury convicted the neighbor of rape, but, on appeal, the Wisconsin Supreme Court reversed, deciding the victim hadn't resisted enough:

> Not only must there be entire absence of mental consent or assent, but there must be the most vehement exercise of every physical means or faculty within the woman's power to resist the penetration of her person, and this must be shown to persist until the offense is consummated. (538)

In *Casico v. State* (1947), the Nebraska Supreme Court made the standard even tougher:

> The general rule is that a mentally competent woman must in good faith resist to the utmost with the most vehement exercise of every physical means or faculty naturally within her power to prevent carnal knowledge, and she must persist in such resistance as long as she has the power to do so until the offense is consummated. (900)

Although a tough standard to meet, as was the utmost resistance standard, the law didn't require physical resistance in all cases. No resistance was required to prove nonconsent if victims were incapacitated by intoxication, mental deficiency, or insanity. Sexual penetration obtained by fraud wasn't rape either, but the fraud had to relate to getting the victim's consent, not to the nature of the act (*State v. Ely* 1921). In *Moran v. People* (1872), a doctor told a woman he needed to insert an instrument into her vagina for treatment. She consented. In fact, the doctor was engaging in intercourse. The law didn't recognize her consent. On the other hand, if a woman consented to sexual intercourse because a doctor convinced her that it was good for her health, the law recognized this consent because the woman was defrauded about the benefits, not the act of sexual intercourse (see Chapter 11, fraud in the inducement). Finally, sexual intercourse with a minor who consented was defined as rape, because the law didn't (and still doesn't) recognize the consent of minors.

In the 1950s, courts relaxed the utmost resistance test with the **reasonable resistance standard.** According to the standard, the amount of required victim resistance depends on the totality of circumstances in each case. For example, the Virginia Supreme Court ruled in *Satterwhite v. Commonwealth* (1960) that a "woman is not required to resist to the utmost of her physical strength if she reasonably believes that resistance would be useless and result in serious bodily injury."

Criminal Sexual Conduct Statutes

The 1970s and 1980s were a time of major reform in the law of sex offenses. First came changes in rape prosecution procedures left over from the 1600s. Many states abolished the **corroboration rule** that required the prosecution to back up rape victims' testimony with that of other witnesses (rarely possible to get). Also, most states passed **rape shield statutes,** which banned introducing evidence of victims' past sexual conduct. Many states also relaxed the **prompt reporting rule** that banned prosecution unless women promptly reported rapes.

States have also made changes in the definition of rape. For example, a few states have abolished the **marital rape exception,** the old common-law rule that husbands couldn't rape their wives. Criminal sexual conduct statutes have also shifted the emphasis away from consent by the victim to the unwanted advances by the perpetrator.

For example, the Pennsylvania Superior Court, in *Commonwealth v. Mlinarich* (1985), ruled that the common-law emphasis on lack of consent had "worked to the unfair disadvantage of the woman who, when threatened with violence, chose quite rationally to submit to her assailant's advances rather than risk death or serious bodily injury."

The *Model Penal Code* (American Law Institute 1985 [2:1], 279–281) provision eliminated consent as an element in rape because of its "disproportionate emphasis upon objective manifestations by the woman." But, the drafters of the code also recognized that a complex relationship exists between force and consent. Unlike the acts in all other criminal assaults, under *ordinary circumstances* victims may desire the physical act in rape—sexual intercourse:

> This unique feature of the offense requires drawing a line between forcible rape on the one hand and reluctant submission on the other, between true aggression and desired intimacy. The difficulty in drawing this line is compounded by the fact that there will often be no witness to the event other than the participants and that their perceptions may change over time. The trial may turn as much on an assessment of the motives of the victim as of the actor. (281)

The most far-reaching reforms are included in the criminal sexual conduct statutes of the '70s and the '80s, which consolidated and expanded the definition of rape and a number of other sex offenses to include all **sexual** *penetrations:* vaginal, anal, and oral. They also created offenses of **criminal sexual** *contacts*—like offensive touching of breasts and buttocks. Finally, sex offenses now are gender-neutral; men can sexually assault men or women, and women can sexually assault women or men (Minnesota Criminal Code 2003, §341).

The seriousness of the sex offenses is graded according to several criteria:

1. Penetrations are more serious than contacts.

2. Forcible penetrations and contacts are more serious than simple nonconsensual penetrations and contacts.

3. Physical injury to the victim aggravates the offense.

One of the earliest and best known of the criminal sexual conduct laws is Michigan's 1974 statute (Michigan Criminal Code, § 750.520), which provides:

1st degree: This consists of "sexual penetration," defined as sexual intercourse, cunnilingus, fellatio, anal intercourse, "or any other intrusion, however slight, of any part of a person's body or of any object into the genital or anal openings of another person's body." In addition one of the following must have occurred:
    1. the defendant must have been armed with a weapon;
    2. force or coercion was used and the defendant was aided by another person; or
    3. force or coercion was used and personal injury to the victim was caused.
2nd degree: This consists of "sexual contact," defined as the intentional touching of the victim's or actor's personal parts or the intentional touching of the clothing covering the immediate area of the victim's intimate parts, for purposes of sexual arousal or gratification. "Intimate parts" is defined as including the primary genital area, groin, inner thigh, buttock, or breast. In addition, one of the circumstances required for 1st degree criminal sexual conduct must have existed.
3rd degree: This consists of sexual penetration accomplished by force or coercion.
4th degree: This consists of sexual contact accomplished by force or coercion.

Despite these advances in the rape *law,* keep in mind Professor David Bryden's (2000) assessment of the *reality* of current sexual assault law:

> Most legislatures and courts still define rape narrowly. In acquaintance rape cases, in most states, nonconsensual sex is not rape unless the perpetrator employs force or a threat of force, or the victim is unconscious, badly drunk, underage, or otherwise incapacitated. Even if the victim verbally declines sex, the encounter is not rape in most states unless the man employs "force." Sex obtained by nonviolent threats ("you'll lose your job," etc.), or by deception, usually is not a crime. (321)

 Go to Exercise 10-1 on the Criminal Law 8e CD to learn more about David Bryden's research.

The Elements of Modern Rape Law

Most traditional statutes define rape (and modern criminal sexual conduct statute provisions define criminal sexual penetration) as intentional sexual penetration of another person by force without the other person's consent. So, rape in most jurisdictions boils down to four elements:

1. The *actus reus* of sexual penetration between the perpetrator and the victim
2. The *actus reus* of force, or threat of force, to accomplish sexual penetration
3. The *mens rea* of intentional sexual penetration
4. The circumstance of the victim's nonconsent

To deepen your understanding of the requirements of modern rape law, we'll look at each of these elements.

Rape *Actus Reus*

The **rape** *actus reus* consists of two parts:

1. Sexual penetration
2. By force or the threat of force

Sexual penetration has never meant full sexual intercourse to emission, and it still doesn't. The common-law phrase "penetration however slight" also describes the modern requirement. So, a defendant who "put his fingers between folds of skin over his victim's vagina, but didn't insert his fingers" satisfied the penetration requirement (*State v. Shamp* 1988, 523).

Courts have adopted two standards to determine whether penetration was accomplished by an act of force (Fried 1996, 123–127):

1. Extrinsic force standard
2. Intrinsic force standard

The **extrinsic force standard** requires some act of force in addition to the physical effort needed to accomplish the penetration. The amount of force required varies according to the circumstances of particular cases. The **intrinsic force standard** requires only the amount of physical effort necessary to accomplish the penetration. The following two case excerpts apply the extrinsic and intrinsic force requirements. We look first at the Pennsylvania Supreme Court's application of the extrinsic force standard to the facts of *Commonwealth v. Berkowitz* (1994).

Commonwealth v. Berkowitz

641 A.2d 1161 (Pa. 1994)

Robert Berkowitz, the defendant, was convicted in the Court of Common Pleas, Monroe County, of rape and indecent assault and he appealed. The Superior Court, Philadelphia, 1990, reversed the rape conviction. The Pennsylvania Supreme Court affirmed the Superior Court's reversal of the conviction.

CAPPY, J.

FACTS

The complainant, a female college student, left her class, went to her dormitory room where she drank a martini, and then went to a lounge to await her boyfriend. When her boyfriend failed to appear, she went to another dormitory to find a friend, Earl Hassel. She knocked on the door, but received no answer. She tried the doorknob and, finding it unlocked, entered the room and discovered a man sleeping on the bed. The complainant originally believed the man to be Hassel, but it turned out to be Hassel's roommate, Robert Berkowitz, the appellee. Berkowitz asked her to stay for a while and she agreed. He requested a backrub and she declined. He suggested that she sit on the bed, but she declined and sat on the floor.

Berkowitz then moved to the floor beside her, lifted up her shirt and bra and massaged her breasts. He then unfastened his pants and unsuccessfully attempted to put his penis in her mouth. They both stood up, and he locked the door. He returned to push her onto the bed, and removed her undergarments from one leg. He then penetrated her vagina with his penis. After withdrawing and ejaculating on her stomach, he stated, "Wow, I guess we just got carried away," to which she responded, "No, we didn't get carried away, you got carried away."

OPINION

In reviewing the sufficiency of the evidence, this Court must view the evidence in the light most favorable to the Commonwealth as verdict winner, and accept as true all evidence and reasonable inferences that may be reasonably drawn therefrom, upon which, if believed, the jury could have relied in reaching its verdict. If, upon such review, the Court concludes that the jury could not have determined from the evidence adduced that all of the necessary elements of the crime were established, then the evidence will be deemed insufficient to support the verdict.

The crime of rape is defined as follows:

§ 3121. Rape

A person commits a felony of the first degree when he engages in sexual intercourse with another person not one's spouse:

(1) by forcible compulsion;
(2) by threat of forcible compulsion that would prevent resistance by a person of reasonable resolution;
(3) who is unconscious; or
(4) who is so mentally deranged or deficient that such person is incapable of consent.

The victim of a rape need not resist. "The force necessary to support a conviction of rape . . . need only be such as to establish lack of consent and to induce the [victim] to submit without additional resistance. . . . The degree of force required to constitute rape is relative and depends on the facts and particular circumstance of the case."

In regard to the critical issue of forcible compulsion, the complainant's testimony is devoid of any statement which clearly or adequately describes the use of force or the threat of force against her. In response to defense counsel's question, "Is it possible that [when Appellee lifted your bra and shirt] you took no physical action to discourage him," the complainant replied, "It's possible." When asked, "Is it possible that [Berkowitz] was not making any physical contact with you . . . aside from attempting to untie the knot [in the drawstrings of complainant's sweatpants]," she answered, "It's possible." She testified that "He put me down on the bed. It was kind of like—He didn't throw me on the bed. It's hard to explain. It was kind of like a push but not—I can't explain what I'm trying to say." She concluded that "it wasn't much" in reference to whether she bounced on the bed, and further detailed that their movement to the bed "wasn't slow like a romantic kind of thing, but it wasn't a fast shove either. It was kind of in the middle." She agreed that Appellee's hands were not restraining her in any manner during the actual penetration, and that the weight of his body on top of her was the only force applied.

She testified that at no time did Berkowitz verbally threaten her. The complainant did testify that she sought to leave the room, and said "no" throughout the encounter. As to the complainant's desire to leave the room, the record clearly demonstrates that the door could be unlocked easily from the inside, that she was aware of this fact, but that she never attempted to go to the door or unlock it.

As to the complainant's testimony that she stated "no" throughout the encounter with Berkowitz, we point out that, while such an allegation of fact would be relevant to the issue of consent, it is not relevant to the issue of force. In *Commonwealth v. Mlinarich*, 542 A.2d 1335 (1988) (plurality opinion), this Court sustained the reversal of a defendant's conviction of rape where the alleged victim, a minor, repeatedly stated that she did not want to engage in sexual intercourse, but offered no physical resistance and was compelled to engage in sexual intercourse under threat of being recommitted to a juvenile detention center.

The Opinion in Support of Affirmance acknowledged that physical force, a threat of force, or psychological coercion may be sufficient to support the element of "forcible compulsion," if found to be enough to "prevent resistance by a person of reasonable resolution." However, under the facts of *Mlinarich*, neither physical force, the threat of physical force, nor psychological coercion were found to have been proven, and this Court held that the conviction was properly reversed by the Superior Court.

Accordingly, the ruling in *Mlinarich* implicitly dictates that where there is a lack of consent, but no showing of either physical force, a threat of physical force, or psychological coercion, the "forcible compulsion" requirement under 18 Pa.C.S. § 3121 is not met. The Opinion in Support of Reversal in *Mlinarich* did not take issue with the implicit holding of the Opinion in Support of Affirmance that something more than a lack of consent is required to prove "forcible compulsion." The Opinion in Support of Reversal acknowledged a general legislative intent to introduce an objective standard regarding the degree of physical force, threat of physical force, or psychological coercion required under 18 Pa.C.S. § 3121, in that it must be sufficient to "prevent resistance by a person of reasonable resolution," but argued that the "peculiar situation" of the victim and other subjective factors should be considered by the court in determining "resistance," "assent," and "consent," and that under the specific circumstances in Mlinarich sufficient facts were set forth to allow a finding of the requisite degree of psychological coercion to support the forcible compulsion element of 18 Pa.C.S. § 3121.

Moreover, we find it instructive that in defining the related but distinct crime of "indecent assault" under 18 Pa.C.S. § 3126, the Legislature did not employ the phrase "forcible compulsion" but rather chose to define indecent assault as "indecent contact with another . . . without the consent of the other person." The phrase "forcible compulsion" is explicitly set forth in the definition of rape under 18 Pa.C.S. § 3121, but the phrase "without the consent of the other person," is conspicuously absent. The choice by the Legislature to define the crime of indecent assault utilizing the phrase "without the consent of the other" and to not so define the crime of rape indicates a legislative intent that the term "forcible compulsion" under 18 Pa.C.S. § 3121, be interpreted as something more than a lack of consent. Moreover, we note that penal statutes must be strictly construed to provide fair warning to the defendant of the nature of the proscribed conduct.

Reviewed in light of the above described standard, the complainant's testimony simply fails to establish that the Appellee forcibly compelled her to engage in sexual intercourse as required under 18 Pa.C.S. § 3121. Thus, even if all of the complainant's testimony was believed, the jury, as a matter of law, could not have found Appellee guilty of rape. Accordingly, we hold that the Superior Court did not err in reversing Appellee's conviction of rape. . . .

Accordingly, the order of the Superior Court reversing the rape conviction is

AFFIRMED.

Questions

1. Explain how the court came to the conclusion that the Pennsylvania rape statute required extrinsic force.

2. List the facts that the court used to conclude that Robert Berkowitz's actions didn't satisfy the extrinsic force requirement.

3. Assume you are the prosecution, and argue that Robert Berkowitz did use extrinsic force to achieve sexual penetration.

◆   ◆   ◆

The New Jersey Supreme Court applied the intrinsic force standard in *State in the Interest of M.T.S* (1992).

State in the Interest of M.T.S.
609 A.2d 1266 (N.J. 1992)

The trial court determined that M.T.S., a juvenile, was delinquent for committing a sexual assault. The Appellate Division reversed. The New Jersey Supreme Court granted the State's petition for certification to review the law regarding the element of force in rape, and reversed.

HANDLER, J.

FACTS

On Monday, May 21, 1990, fifteen-year-old C.G. was living with her mother, her three siblings, and several other people, including M.T.S. and his girlfriend. A total of ten people resided in the three-bedroom town home at the time of the incident. M.T.S., then age seventeen, was temporarily residing at the home with the permission of C.G.'s mother; he slept downstairs on a couch. C.G. had her own room on the second floor. At approximately 11:30 P.M. on May 21, C.G. went upstairs to sleep after having watched television with her mother, M.T.S., and his girlfriend. When C.G. went to bed, she was wearing underpants, a bra, shorts, and a shirt. At trial, C.G. and M.T.S. offered very different accounts concerning the nature of their relationship and the events that occurred after C.G. had gone upstairs. The trial court did not credit fully either teenager's testimony.

C.G. stated that earlier in the day, M.T.S. had told her three or four times that he "was going to make a surprise visit up in her bedroom." She said that she had not taken M.T.S. seriously and considered his comments a joke because he frequently teased her. She testified that M.T.S. had attempted to kiss her on numerous other occasions and at least once had attempted to put his hands inside of her pants, but that she had rejected all of his previous advances.

C.G. testified that on May 22, at approximately 1:30 A.M., she awoke to use the bathroom. As she was getting out of bed, she said, she saw M.T.S., fully clothed, standing in her doorway. According to C.G., M.T.S. then said that "he was going to tease [her] a little bit." C.G. testified that she "didn't think anything of it"; she walked past him, used the bathroom, and then returned to bed, falling into a "heavy" sleep within fifteen minutes.

The next event C.G. claimed to recall of that morning was waking up with M.T.S. on top of her, her underpants and shorts removed. She said "his penis was into [her] vagina." As soon as C.G. realized what had happened, she said, she immediately slapped M.T.S. once in the face, then "told him to get off [her], and get out." She did not scream or cry out. She testified that M.T.S. complied in less than one minute after being struck; according to C.G., "he jumped right off of [her]." She said she did not know how long M.T.S. had been inside of her before she awoke.

C.G. said that after M.T.S. left the room, she "fell asleep crying" because "[she] couldn't believe that he did what he did to [her]." She explained that she did not immediately tell her mother or anyone else in the house of the events of that morning because she was "scared and in shock." According to C.G., M.T.S. engaged in intercourse with her "without [her] wanting it or telling him to come up [to her bedroom]." By her own account, C.G. was not otherwise harmed by M.T.S.

At about 7:00 A.M., C.G. went downstairs and told her mother about her encounter with M.T.S. earlier in the morning and said that they would have to "get [him] out of the house." While M.T.S. was out on an errand, C.G.'s mother gathered his clothes and put them outside in his car; when he returned, he was told that "[he] better not even get near the house." C.G. and her mother then filed a complaint with the police.

According to M.T.S., he and C.G. had been good friends for a long time, and their relationship "kept leading on to more and more." He had been living at C.G.'s home for about five days before the incident occurred; he testified that during the three days preceding the incident they had been "kissing and necking" and had discussed having sexual intercourse. The first time M.T.S. kissed C.G., he said, she "didn't want him to, but she did after that." He said C.G. repeatedly had encouraged him to "make a surprise visit up in her room."

M.T.S. testified that at exactly 1:15 A.M. on May 22, he entered C.G.'s bedroom as she was walking to the bathroom. He said C.G. soon returned from the bathroom, and the two began "kissing and all," eventually moving to the bed. Once they were in bed, he said, they undressed each other and continued to kiss and touch for about five minutes. M.T.S. and C.G. proceeded to engage in sexual intercourse. According to M.T.S., who was on top of C.G., he "stuck it in" and "did it [thrust] three times, and then the fourth time [he] stuck it in, that's when [she] pulled [him] off of her." M.T.S. said that as C.G. pushed him off, she said "stop, get off," and he "hopped off right away."

According to M.T.S., after about one minute, he asked C.G. what was wrong; she replied with a backhand to his face. He recalled asking C.G. what was wrong a second time, and her replying, "how can you take advantage of me or something like that." M.T.S. said that he proceeded to get dressed and told C.G. to calm down, but that she then told him to get away from her and began to cry. Before leaving the room, he told C.G., "I'm leaving...I'm going with my real girlfriend, don't talk to me...I don't want nothing to do with you or anything, stay out of my life... don't tell anybody about this...it would just screw everything up." He then walked downstairs and went to sleep.

On May 23, 1990, M.T.S. was charged with conduct that if engaged in by an adult would constitute second-degree sexual assault of the victim, contrary to N.J.S.A. 2C:142c(1)....

Following a two-day trial on the sexual assault charge, M.T.S. was adjudicated delinquent. After reviewing the testimony, the court concluded that the victim had consented to a session of kissing and heavy petting with M.T.S. The trial court did not find that C.G. had been sleeping at the time of penetration, but nevertheless found that she had not consented to the actual sexual act. Accordingly, the court concluded that the State had proven second-degree sexual assault beyond a reasonable doubt.

On appeal, following the imposition of suspended sentences on the sexual assault and the other remaining charges, the Appellate Division determined that the absence of force beyond that involved in the act of sexual penetration precluded a finding of second-degree sexual assault. It therefore reversed the juvenile's adjudication of delinquency for that offense.

OPINION

Under New Jersey law a person who commits an act of sexual penetration using physical force or coercion is guilty of second degree sexual assault. The sexual assault statute does not define the words "physical force." The question posed by this appeal is whether the element of "physical force" is met simply by an act of nonconsensual penetration involving no more force than necessary to accomplish that result.

That issue is presented in the context of what is often referred to as "acquaintance rape." The record in the case discloses that the juvenile, a seventeen-year-old boy, engaged in consensual kissing and heavy petting with a fifteen-year-old girl and thereafter engaged in actual sexual penetration of the girl to which she had not consented. There was no evidence or suggestion that the juvenile used any unusual or extra force or threats to accomplish the act of penetration.

The trial court determined that the juvenile was delinquent for committing a sexual assault. The Appellate Division reversed the disposition of delinquency, concluding that nonconsensual penetration does not constitute sexual

assault unless it is accompanied by some level of force more than that necessary to accomplish the penetration.

The New Jersey Code of Criminal Justice, N.J.S.A. 2C:142c(1), defines "sexual assault" as the commission "of sexual penetration" "with another person" with the use of "physical force or coercion." An unconstrained reading of the statutory language indicates that both the act of "sexual penetration" and the use of "physical force or coercion" are separate and distinct elements of the offense. Neither the definitions section of N.J.S.A. 2C:141 to 8, nor the remainder of the Code of Criminal Justice provides assistance in interpreting the words "physical force."

The initial inquiry is, therefore, whether the statutory words are unambiguous on their face and can be understood and applied in accordance with their plain meaning. The answer to that inquiry is revealed by the conflicting decisions of the lower courts and the arguments of the opposing parties. The trial court held that "physical force" had been established by the sexual penetration of the victim without her consent. The Appellate Division believed that the statute requires some amount of force more than that necessary to accomplish penetration.

The parties offer two alternative understandings of the concept of "physical force" as it is used in the statute. The State would read "physical force" to entail any amount of sexual touching brought about involuntarily. A showing of sexual penetration coupled with a lack of consent would satisfy the elements of the statute. The Public Defender urges an interpretation of "physical force" to mean force "used to overcome lack of consent." That definition equates force with violence and leads to the conclusion that sexual assault requires the application of some amount of force in addition to the act of penetration....

...Pre-reform rape law in New Jersey, with its insistence on resistance by the victim, greatly minimized the importance of the forcible and assaultive aspect of the defendant's conduct. Rape prosecutions turned then not so much on the forcible or assaultive character of the defendant's actions as on the nature of the victim's response.... That the law put the rape victim on trial was clear....

The New Jersey Code of Criminal Justice [reformed the law of rape in 1978].... The Code does not refer to force in relation to "overcoming the will" of the victim, or to the "physical overpowering" of the victim, or the "submission" of the victim. It does not require the demonstrated nonconsent of the victim.... In reforming the rape laws, the Legislature placed primary emphasis on the assaultive nature of the crime, altering its constituent elements so that they focus exclusively on the forceful or assaultive conduct of the defendant.

The Legislature's concept of sexual assault and the role of force was significantly colored by its understanding of the law of assault and battery. As a general matter, criminal battery is defined as "the unlawful application of force to the person of another." The application of force is criminal when it results in either (a) a physical injury or (b) an offensive touching. Any "unauthorized touching of another [is] a battery."

Thus, by eliminating all references to the victim's state of mind and conduct, and by broadening the definition of penetration to cover not only sexual intercourse between a man and a woman but a range of acts that invade another's body or compel intimate contact, the Legislature emphasized the affinity between sexual assault and other forms of assault and battery.... We are thus satisfied that an interpretation of the statutory crime of sexual assault to require physical force in addition to that entailed in an act of involuntary or unwanted sexual penetration would be fundamentally inconsistent with the legislative purpose to eliminate any consideration of whether the victim resisted or expressed nonconsent.

We note that the contrary interpretation of force—that the element of force need be extrinsic to the sexual act—would not only reintroduce a resistance requirement into the sexual assault law, but also would immunize many acts of criminal sexual contact short of penetration. The characteristics that make a sexual contact unlawful are the same as those that make a sexual penetration unlawful. An actor is guilty of criminal sexual contact if he or she commits an act of sexual contact with another using "physical force" or "coercion." N.J.S.A. 2C:143(b). That the Legislature would have wanted to decriminalize unauthorized sexual intrusions on the bodily integrity of a victim by requiring a showing of force in addition to that entailed in the sexual contact itself is hardly possible.

Because the statute eschews any reference to the victim's will or resistance, the standard defining the role of force in sexual penetration must prevent the possibility that the establishment of the crime will turn on the alleged victim's state of mind or responsive behavior. We conclude, therefore, that any act of sexual penetration engaged in by the defendant without the affirmative and freely given permission of the victim to the specific act of penetration constitutes the offense of sexual assault. Therefore, physical force in excess of that inherent in the act of sexual penetration is not required for such penetration to be unlawful. The definition of "physical force" is satisfied under N.J.S.A. 2C:142c(1) if the defendant applies any amount of force against another person in the absence of what a reasonable person would believe to be affirmative and freely-given permission to the act of sexual penetration....

Today the law of sexual assault is indispensable to the system of legal rules that assures each of us the right to decide who may touch our bodies, when, and under what circumstances. The decision to engage in sexual relations with another person is one of the most private and intimate decisions a person can make. Each person has the right not only to decide whether to engage in sexual contact with another, but also to control the circumstances and character of that contact. No one, neither a spouse, nor a friend, nor an acquaintance, nor a stranger, has the right or the privilege to force sexual contact. "Forcible rape is viewed as a heinous crime primarily because it is a violent assault on a person's bodily security, particularly degrading because that person is forced to submit to an act of the most intimate nature."

We emphasize as well that what is now referred to as "acquaintance rape" is not a new phenomenon. Nor was it a "futuristic" concept in 1978 when the sexual assault law was enacted. Current concern over the prevalence of forced sexual intercourse between persons who know one another reflects both greater awareness of the extent of such behavior and a growing appreciation of its gravity. Notwithstanding the stereotype of rape as a violent attack by a stranger, the vast majority of sexual assaults are perpetrated by someone known to the victim. One respected study indicates that more than half of all rapes are committed by male relatives, current or former husbands, boyfriends or lovers. Similarly, contrary to common myths, perpetrators generally do not use guns or knives and victims generally do not suffer external bruises or cuts. Acquaintance Rape, supra, at 10. Although this more realistic and accurate view of rape only recently has achieved widespread public circulation, it was a central concern of the proponents of reform in the 1970s.

The insight into rape as an assaultive crime is consistent with our evolving understanding of the wrong inherent in forced sexual intimacy. It is one that was appreciated by the Legislature when it reformed the rape laws, reflecting an emerging awareness that the definition of rape should correspond fully with the experiences and perspectives of rape victims. Although reformers focused primarily on the problems associated with convicting defendants accused of violent rape, the recognition that forced sexual intercourse often takes place between persons who know each other and often involves little or no violence comports with the understanding of the sexual assault law that was embraced by the Legislature. Any other interpretation of the law, particularly one that defined force in relation to the resistance or protest of the victim, would directly undermine the goals sought to be achieved by its reform....

We acknowledge that cases such as this are inherently fact sensitive and depend on the reasoned judgment and common sense of judges and juries. The trial court concluded that the victim had not expressed consent to the act of intercourse, either through her words or actions. We conclude that the record provides reasonable support for the trial court's disposition.

Accordingly, we REVERSE the judgment of the Appellate Division and reinstate the disposition of juvenile delinquency for the commission of second degree sexual assault.

Questions

1. List all of the evidence relevant to determining whether M.T.S.'s actions satisfied the intrinsic force element of the New Jersey sexual assault statute.

2. Summarize the reasons the court gives for adopting the intrinsic force standard.

3. Taking into account the evidence, decision, and reasoning of *Commonwealth v. Berkowitz,* which do you think is the better approach to the force requirement—intrinsic or extrinsic force? Defend your answer.

4. Should legislatures or courts decide whether to adopt the intrinsic or extrinsic force standard? Defend your answer.

Make sure you understand that the *actual* use of force isn't required to satisfy the force requirement. The *threat* of force is enough. To satisfy the threat-of-force requirement, the prosecution has to prove two things:

1. The victim honestly feared imminent and serious bodily harm.

2. The fear was reasonable under the circumstances.

Brandishing a weapon satisfies the requirement. So do verbal threats—like threats to kill, seriously injure, or kidnap. But the threat doesn't have to include showing weapons or specifically threatening words. Courts can consider all of the following in deciding whether the victim's fear was reasonable (Edwards 1996, 260–261):

- Respective ages of the perpetrator and the victim
- Physical sizes of the perpetrator and the victim
- Mental condition of the perpetrator and the victim
- Physical setting of the assault
- Position of authority, domination, or custodial control of the perpetrator over the victim.

Not even the threat of force is required in cases where perpetrators obtain consent fraudulently, or when a minor, a mentally deficient person, or an insane person consents. In these cases, the penetration alone is enough.

Rape *Mens Rea*

Most people think of rape as a **specific-intent crime,** meaning the rapist intended to use force for the purpose of having sexual intercourse. The leading case on the point is *Regina v. Morgan* (1975). In this widely publicized (and heavily criticized) case, Morgan and three companions were drinking in a bar. When they failed to "find some women," Morgan invited the other three to come home with him to have sexual intercourse with his wife. Morgan told the others not to worry if she struggled because she was "kinky"; the struggle "turned [her] on." The trial court convicted the men, and the intermediate appellate court upheld the conviction. But, the House of Lords (England's highest court) overturned the conviction because the defendants didn't specifically intend to have sexual intercourse by force and without consent. Why? Because they believed that Morgan's wife wanted the struggle.

Despite the storm of protest following the House of Lords ruling, England has stuck to the specific-intent requirement. But U.S. statutes and decisions barely mention intent, except in attempted rape, where intent is the essence of the crime. Where courts face the intent question, they vary in their response. At the other extreme from the English rule, the Maine Supreme Judicial Court, in *State v. Reed* 1984, ruled that rape is a strict liability crime:

> Certain crimes are defined to expressly include a culpable state of mind and others are not. The more forceful or egregious sexual conduct, including rape compelled by force, is defined without reference to the actor's state of mind. The legislature, by carefully defining the sex offenses in the criminal code, and by making no reference to a culpable mental state for rape, clearly indicated that rape compelled by force or threat requires no culpable state of mind. (1296)

Other courts stand between the English specific-intent rule and strict liability. These courts have adopted a reckless or negligent standard with regard to forcible sexual penetration, saying that rapists either have to be aware they are risking coerced sexual intercourse or should know that their victims haven't consented. Critics argue that rape is too serious a charge and the penalties are too severe to allow convictions on anything less than specific intent. Law professor Susan Estrich (1987), a rape law scholar and herself a rape victim, disagrees:

> If inaccuracy or indifference to consent is "the best that this man can do" because he lacks the capacity to act reasonably, then it might well be unjust and ineffective to punish him for it.... More common is the case of the man who could have done better but did not; heard her refusal or saw her tears, but decided to ignore them. The man who has the inherent capacity to act reasonably but fails to has, through that failure, made a blameworthy choice for which he can justly be punished. The law has long punished unreasonable action which leads to the loss of human life as manslaughter—a lesser crime than murder, but a crime nonetheless.... The injury of sexual violation is sufficiently great, the need to provide that additional incentive pressing enough, to justify negligence liability for rape as for killing. (97–98)

Can defendants' actions satisfy the *mens rea* requirement of sex offenses even if they didn't intend to sexually assault their victims? The Wisconsin Supreme Court answered this question in *State v. Bonds* (1991).

CASE | *Did He Intend to Rape Her?*

State v. Bonds
277 N.W.2d 265 (Wisc.1991)

Anthony Bonds, was found guilty of second-degree sexual assault in the Circuit Court, Milwaukee County. Bonds appealed. The Wisconsin Court of Appeals reversed. The Supreme Court reversed.

STEINMETZ, J.

FACTS

The victim was confronted by Bonds in the boarding house where she resided. Bonds had previously lived in the building but because of certain problems was told to move. When the victim saw Bonds, she told him that a guard was waiting for him downstairs. She then proceeded to return to her room. Bonds began to utter profanities and followed her back to her apartment. The victim could not recall exactly what was said; however, she considered the verbiage to be threatening. When the victim turned to confront Bonds, he reached out his hand, grabbed the nipple of her left breast, squeezed and pulled it, causing pain. She responded by knocking Bonds' hand away. Bonds then attempted to bring his fist toward her face. The victim grabbed Bonds' hand and bit it.

The defendant negotiated a guilty plea and was sentenced to six years in prison. The defendant claimed at the plea hearing that when he squeezed and pulled the victim's nipple he did so intending to hurt her, not to violate her sexually. On appeal, the court of appeals held that the defendant's actions did not constitute sexual contact "by use or threat of force or violence" and therefore did not fall under second-degree sexual assault. The court of appeals reversed Bonds' conviction and remanded the case to the trial court with specific directions. The directions were as follows: "First, Bonds is to be permitted to withdraw his guilty plea. Second, the felony-bind over is to be vacated...." This court concludes that the defendant's actions constitute second-degree sexual assault, and we thereby reverse the decision of the court of appeals.

OPINION

The issue in this case is whether a defendant's use of force in making sexual contact with his victim by forcibly grabbing her nipple and then squeezing and pulling it, constitutes the crime of second-degree sexual assault. Under § 940.225(2)(a), one is guilty of a Class C felony for second-degree sexual assault when an individual "has sexual contact or sexual intercourse with another person without consent of that person by use or threat of force or violence."

Bonds asserts that he should be charged with a misdemeanor rather than a felony. Bonds argues that he should have been charged with either the misdemeanor under sec. 940.225(3m), Stats., fourth-degree sexual assault, or under sec. 940.19(1), battery. Fourth-degree sexual assault does not require a showing of force, violence or injury. Second-degree sexual assault, however, is classified as a felony and requires a showing of force, violence or injury.

The defendant argues that the statutory element "by use or threat of force or violence" in sec. 940.225(2)(a), Stats., requires that a causal relationship exists between the "use or threat of force or violence" and the sexual contact or intercourse. He contends that the statutory requirement of sexual contact or intercourse "by use or threat of force or violence" is not satisfied where, as in the present situation, the force used is the force applied in the sexual contact. It is argued that the statutory element could be satisfied only where the force used or threatened was the means or

mechanism by which the sexual contact or intercourse was accomplished. The court of appeals agreed and reasoned:

> The legislature's use of the word "by" is not ambiguous. Rather, it clearly requires that there be a cause and effect relationship between the "use or threat of force or violence" and the prohibited sexual contact or intercourse. Simply put, it is not enough that the sexual contact or sexual intercourse be forceful or violent; the "use or threat of force or violence" must be the means by which the sexual assault is accomplished.

The court of appeals refers to *State v. Baldwin*, 304 N.W.2d 742 (1981), which states that the force threatened and force applied concept encompassed by the words "by use or threat of force or violence" means action that is "directed toward compelling the victim's submission." The court opined that the force applied by Bonds was not directed toward compelling her submission to the grabbing and pinching of her nipple. The court of appeals stated that: "it is not enough that the sexual contact...be forceful or violent; the 'use or threat of force or violence' must be the means by which the sexual assault is accomplished." We find no support for this conclusion and disagree with the court of appeals interpretation of sec. 940.225(2)(a), Stats.

In statutory construction, courts are to give effect to the intent of the legislature. This begins with the language of the statute itself. We give the language its ordinary and accepted meaning. By its very terms, § 940.225(2)(a), Stats. prohibits nonconsensual sexual contact "by use or threat of force or violence." Sexual contact under this section includes "actual or attempted battery." "Sexual contact" is defined in sec. 940.225(5)(b), Stats., as

> any intentional touching by the complainant or defendant, either directly or through clothing by the use of any body part or object, of the complainant's or defendant's intimate parts if that intentional touching is either for the purpose of sexually degrading or for the purpose of sexually humiliating the complainant or sexually arousing or gratifying the defendant or if the touching contains the elements of actual or attempted battery under s. 940.19(1).

"Intimate parts" is defined in sec. 939.22(19), Stats., and includes any of the following: "breast, buttock, anus, groin, scrotum, penis, vagina or pubic mound of a human being."

Battery occurs when one "causes bodily harm to another by an act done with intent to cause bodily harm to that person or another without the consent of the person so harmed...." See sec. 940.19(1), Stats.

The defendant admitted using force and conceded that he had intended to hurt his victim. Section 940.225(2)(a),

Stats., does not state that the force used or threatened may not be the force employed in the actual nonconsensual contact. Nor does it state that the force must be directed toward compelling the victim's submission. The phrase "by use of force" includes forcible contact or the force used as the means of making contact.

We recognize that the force element of sexual assault maintains the proscription against force or compulsion not as separate and distinct forms of conduct, but as a more generalized concept of conduct, including force threatened and force applied, directed toward compelling the victim's submission. Force used at the time of contact can compel submission as effectively as force or threat occurring before contact. Regardless of when the force is applied, the victim is forced to submit. When force is used at the time of contact, the victim has no choice at the moment of simultaneous use of force and making of contact. When force is used before contact, the choice is forced. In both cases, the victim does not consent to the contact. Consent under sec. 940.225(4), Stats., reads in part as: "words or overt actions by a person who is competent to give informed consent indicating a freely given agreement to have sexual intercourse or sexual contact...."

We conclude that based on the plain language of the statute, the defendant falls within second-degree sexual assault because he made sexual contact of a complainant's intimate part through the means of actual or attempted battery. The defendant's guilty plea for the crime of second-degree sexual assault is reinstated as is his conviction and sentence.

The decision of the court of appeals is REVERSED.

Questions

1. Based on the evidence in the case, what exactly was Anthony Bonds's intent in this case?

2. Explain the court's reasoning for deciding that Anthony Bonds committed second-degree sexual assault.

3. In your opinion, does the evidence in this case justify a conviction for sexual assault? Or should it be a case of nonsexual assault? Defend your answer.

 Go to Exercise 10-2 on the Criminal Law 8e CD to learn more about *State v. Bonds*.

◆   ◆   ◆

Nonconsent

According to the law, nonconsent by the victim is an element the prosecution has to prove beyond a reasonable doubt. Practically speaking, consent almost always arises as a defense to rape. In the typical case, defendants claim either that their victims consented, or that they mistakenly believed their victims consented. This doesn't mean defendants have to get their victims' consent in writing, or even that victims have to "announce their consent." Consent can be (and almost always *is*) indicated by actions, not words. No state has gone as far as the guidelines for student sexual conduct adopted by Antioch College. One critic (Crichton and others 1993) of the guidelines wrote:

> Deep among the cornfields and pig farms of central Ohio in the town of Yellow Springs, Antioch prides itself on being "A Laboratory for Democracy." The dress code is grunge and black; multiple nose rings are de rigueur, and green and blue hair are preferred (if you have hair). Seventy percent of the student body are womyn (for the uninitiated, that's women—without the dreaded m-e-n). And the purpose of the Sexual Offense Policy is to empower these students to become equal partners when it comes time to mate with males. The goal is 100 percent consensual sex, and it works like this: it isn't enough to ask someone if she'd like to have sex, as an Antioch women's center advocate told a group of incoming freshmen this fall. You must obtain consent every step of the way. "If you want to take her blouse off, you have to ask. If you want to touch her breast, you have to ask. If you want to move your hand down to her genitals, you have to ask. If you want to put your finger inside her, you have to ask" (52).
>
> How silly this all seems; how sad. It criminalizes the delicious unexpectedness of sex—a hand suddenly moves to here, a mouth to there. What is the purpose of sex if not to lose

control? (To be unconscious, no.) The advocates of sexual correctness are trying to take the danger out of sex, but sex is inherently dangerous. It leaves one exposed to everything from euphoria to crashing disappointment. That's its great unpredictability. But of course, that's sort of what we said when we were all made to use seat belts. What is implicit in the new sex guidelines is that it's the male who does the initiating and the woman who at any moment may bolt. Some young women rankle at that. "I think it encourages wimpy behavior by women and [the idea] that women need to be handled with kid gloves," says Hope Segal, 22, a fourth-year Antioch student. Beware those boys with their swords, made deaf by testosterone and, usually, blinded by drink. (54)

 Go to Exercise 10-3 on the Criminal Law 8e CD to learn more about "sexual correctness."

Statutory Rape

Statutory rape consists of having sex with minors. Statutory rapists don't have to use force; the victim's immaturity takes the place of force. Furthermore, nonconsent is not an element; nor is consent a defense because minors can't legally consent to sex. In other words, statutory rape is a strict liability crime. A few states, such as California and Alaska, however, do permit the **defense of reasonable mistake of age.** The defense applies if a man reasonably believes his victim is over the age of consent. In other words, negligence is the required *mens rea*. A divided Maryland supreme court refused to adopt the defense of mistake in statutory rape in *Garnett v. State* (1993).

CASE | *Did He Rape Her?*

Garnett v. State
632 A.2d 797 (Md. 1993)

Raymond Leonard Garnett, the defendant, was convicted in the Circuit Court, Montgomery County, of second-degree rape under the statute proscribing sexual intercourse between persons under 14 and another at least four years older than the victim. Garnett appealed. Maryland's supreme court, The Court of Appeals, granted certiorari prior to intermediate appellate review by the Court of Special Appeals to consider the important issue presented in the case. The Court of Appeals affirmed Garnett's conviction.

MURPHY, CJ.

FACTS

Raymond Lennard Garnett is a young retarded man. At the time of the incident in question he was 20 years old. He has an I.Q. of 52. His guidance counselor from the Montgomery County public school system, Cynthia Parker, described him as a mildly retarded person who read on the third-grade level, did arithmetic on the 5th-grade level, and interacted with others socially at school at the level of someone 11 or 12 years of age. Ms. Parker added that Raymond attended special education classes and for at least one period of time was educated at home when he was afraid to return to school due to his classmates' taunting. Because he could not understand the duties of the jobs given him, he failed to complete vocational assignments; he sometimes lost his way to work. As Raymond was unable to pass any of the State's functional tests required for graduation, he received only a certificate of attendance rather than a high-school diploma.

In November or December 1990, a friend introduced Raymond to Erica Frazier, then aged 13; the two subsequently talked occasionally by telephone. On February 28, 1991, Raymond, apparently wishing to call for a ride home, approached the girl's house at about nine o'clock in the evening. Erica opened her bedroom window, through which Raymond entered; he testified that "she just told me to get a ladder and climb up her window." The two talked, and later engaged in sexual intercourse. Raymond left at about 4:30 A.M. the following morning. On November 19, 1991, Erica gave birth to a baby, of which Raymond is the biological father.

Raymond was tried before the Circuit Court for Montgomery County (Miller, J.) on one count of second degree rape under § 463(a)(3) proscribing sexual intercourse between a person under 14 and another at least four years older than the complainant. At trial, the defense twice proffered evidence to the effect that Erica herself and her friends had previously told Raymond that she was 16 years old, and that he had acted with that belief. The trial court excluded such evidence as immaterial, explaining: Under 463, the only two requirements as relate to this case are that there was vaginal intercourse, and that...Ms. Frazier was under 14 years of age and that...Mr. Garnett was at least four years older than she. In the Court's opinion, consent is no defense to this charge. The victim's representation as to her age and the defendant's belief, if it existed, that she was not under age, what amounts to what otherwise might be termed a good faith defense, is in fact no defense to what amounts to statutory rape. It is in the Court's opinion a strict liability offense.

The court found Raymond guilty. It sentenced him to a term of five years in prison, suspended the sentence and imposed five years of probation, and ordered that he pay restitution to Erica and the Frazier family. Raymond noted an appeal; we granted certiorari prior to intermediate appellate review by the Court of Special Appeals to consider the important issue presented in the case.

OPINION

Maryland's "statutory rape" law prohibiting sexual intercourse with an underage person is codified in Maryland Code (1957, 1992 Repl.Vol.) Art. 27, § 463, which reads in full:

"Second degree rape.
(a) What constitutes.—A person is guilty of rape in the second degree if the person engages in vaginal intercourse with another person:
 (1) By force or threat of force against the will and without the consent of the other person; or
 (2) Who is mentally defective, mentally incapacitated, or physically helpless, and the person performing the act knows or should reasonably know the other person is mentally defective, mentally incapacitated, or physically helpless; or
 (3) Who is under 14 years of age and the person performing the act is at least four years older than the victim.
(b) Penalty.—Any person violating the provisions of this section is guilty of a felony and upon conviction is subject to imprisonment for a period of not more than 20 years."

...Now we consider whether under the present statute, the State must prove that a defendant knew the complaining witness was younger than 14 and, in a related question, whether it was error at trial to exclude evidence that he had been told, and believed, that she was 16 years old....

Section 463(a)(3) does not expressly set forth a requirement that the accused have acted with a criminal state of mind, or *mens rea*. The State insists that the statute, by design, defines a strict liability offense, and that its essential elements were met in the instant case when Raymond, age 20, engaged in vaginal intercourse with Erica, a girl under 14 and more than 4 years his junior. Raymond replies that the criminal law exists to assess and punish morally culpable behavior. He says such culpability was absent here. He asks us either to engraft onto subsection (a)(3) an implicit *mens rea* requirement, or to recognize an affirmative defense of reasonable mistake as to the complainant's age. Raymond argues that it is unjust, under the circumstances of this case which led him to think his conduct lawful, to brand him a felon and rapist.

Raymond asserts that the events of this case were inconsistent with the criminal sexual exploitation of a minor by an adult. As earlier observed, Raymond entered Erica's bedroom at the girl's invitation; she directed him to use a ladder to reach her window. They engaged voluntarily in sexual intercourse. They remained together in the room for more than seven hours before Raymond departed at dawn.

With an I.Q. of 52, Raymond functioned at approximately the same level as the 13-year-old Erica; he was mentally an adolescent in an adult's body. Arguably, had Raymond's chronological age, 20, matched his socio-intellectual age, about 12, he and Erica would have fallen well within the four-year age difference obviating a violation of the statute, and Raymond would not have been charged with any crime at all.

The precise legal issue here rests on Raymond's unsuccessful efforts to introduce into evidence testimony that Erica and her friends had told him she was 16 years old, the age of consent to sexual relations, and that he believed them. Thus the trial court did not permit him to raise a defense of reasonable mistake of Erica's age, by which defense Raymond would have asserted that he acted innocently without a criminal design.

At common law, a crime occurred only upon the concurrence of an individual's act and his guilty state of mind. In this regard, it is well understood that generally there are two components of every crime, the *actus reus* or guilty act and the *mens rea* or the guilty mind or mental state accompanying a forbidden act. The requirement that an accused have acted with a culpable mental state is an axiom of criminal jurisprudence.*...

To be sure, legislative bodies since the mid-19th century have created strict liability criminal offenses requiring no *mens rea*.** Almost all such statutes responded to the demands of public health and welfare arising from the complexities of society after the Industrial Revolution. Typically misdemeanors involving only fines or other light penalties, these strict liability laws regulated food, milk, liquor, medicines and drugs, securities, motor vehicles and traffic, the labeling of goods for sale, and the like. See Richard G. Singer, *The Resurgence of Mens Rea: III—The Rise and Fall of Strict Criminal Liability*, 30 B.C.L.Rev. 337, 340–373 (1989) (suggesting, however, that strict liability doctrine in the United States in the late 19th century was motivated largely by moralistic fervor, such as found in the prohibitionist movement).

Statutory rape, carrying the stigma of felony as well as a potential sentence of 20 years in prison, contrasts markedly with the other strict liability regulatory offenses and their light penalties. Modern scholars generally reject the concept of strict criminal liability.... The commentators similarly disapprove of statutory rape as a strict liability crime.... They observe that statutory rape prosecutions often proceed even when the defendant's judgment as to the age of the complainant is warranted by her appearance, her sexual sophistication, her verbal misrepresentations, and the defendant's careful attempts to ascertain her true age. Voluntary intercourse with a sexually mature teen-ager lacks the features of psychic abnormality, exploitation, or physical danger that accompanies such conduct with children....

We acknowledge here that it is uncertain to what extent Raymond's intellectual and social retardation may have impaired his ability to comprehend imperatives of sexual morality in any case.

The legislatures of 17 states have enacted laws permitting a mistake of age defense in some form in cases of sexual offenses with underage persons.... In the landmark case of *People v. Hernandez*, 393 P.2d 673 (1964), the California Supreme Court held that, absent a legislative directive to the contrary, a charge of statutory rape was defensible wherein a criminal intent was lacking; it reversed the trial court's refusal to permit the defendant to present evidence of his good faith, reasonable belief that the complaining witness had reached the age of consent. In so doing, the court first questioned the assumption that age alone confers a sophistication sufficient to create legitimate consent to sexual relations: "the sexually experienced 15-year-old may be far more acutely aware of the implications of sexual intercourse than her sheltered cousin who is beyond the age of consent." The court then rejected the traditional view that those who engage in sex with young persons do so at their peril, assuming the risk that their partners are underage:

> If [the perpetrator] participates in a mutual act of sexual intercourse, believing his partner to be beyond the age of consent, with reasonable grounds for such belief, where is his criminal intent? In such circumstances he has not consciously taken any risk. Instead he has subjectively eliminated the risk by satisfying himself on reasonable evidence that the crime cannot be committed. If it occurs that he has been misled, we cannot realistically conclude for such reason alone the intent with which he undertook the act suddenly becomes more heinous.... The courts have uniformly failed to satisfactorily explain the nature of the criminal intent present in the mind of one who in good faith believes he has obtained a lawful consent before engaging in the prohibited act....

We think it sufficiently clear, however, that Maryland's second-degree rape statute defines a strict liability offense that does not require the State to prove *mens rea*; it makes no allowance for a mistake-of-age defense. The plain language of § 463, viewed in its entirety, and the legislative history of its creation lead to this conclusion.... Section 463(a)(3) prohibiting sexual intercourse with underage persons makes no reference to the actor's knowledge, belief, or other state of mind. As we see it, this silence as to *mens rea* results from legislative design.... Second, an examination of the drafting history of § 463 during the 1976 revision of Maryland's sexual offense laws reveals that the statute was viewed as one of strict liability from its inception and throughout the amendment process.... The Legislature explicitly raised, considered, and then explicitly jettisoned any notion of a *mens rea* element with respect to the complainant's age in enacting the law.... In the light of such legislative action, we must inevitably conclude that the current law imposes strict liability on its violators.

This interpretation is consistent with the traditional view of statutory rape as a strict liability crime designed to protect young persons from the dangers of sexual exploitation by adults, loss of chastity, physical injury, and, in the case of girls, pregnancy. The majority of states retain statutes which impose strict liability for sexual acts with underage complainants....

Any new provision introducing an element of *mens rea*, or permitting a defense of reasonable mistake of age, with respect to the offense of sexual intercourse with a person less than 14, should properly result from an act of

---

*Chapters 3–4.

**Chapter 4.

the Legislature itself, rather than judicial fiat. Until then, defendants in extraordinary cases, like Raymond, will rely upon the tempering discretion of the trial court at sentencing.

Judgment AFFIRMED, with costs.

DISSENT

BELL, J.

... I do not dispute that the legislative history of Maryland Code (1957, 1992 Repl.Vol.), Art. 27, section 463 may be read to support the majority's interpretation that subsection (a)(3) was intended to be a strict liability statute. Nor do I disagree that it is in the public interest to protect the sexually naive child from the adverse physical, emotional, or psychological effects of sexual relations. I do not believe, however, that the General Assembly, in every case, whatever the nature of the crime and no matter how harsh the potential penalty, can subject a defendant to strict criminal liability. To hold, as a matter of law, that section 463(a)(3) does not require the State to prove that a defendant possessed the necessary mental state to commit the crime, i.e. knowingly engaged in sexual relations with a female under 14, or that the defendant may not litigate that issue in defense, "offends a principle of justice so rooted in the traditions of conscience of our people as to be ranked as fundamental" and is, therefore, inconsistent with due process.

In ... this case ..., according to the defendant, he intended to have sex with a 16-, not a 13-, year-old girl. This mistake of fact was prompted, he said, by the prosecutrix herself; she and her friends told him that she was 16 years old. Because he was mistaken as to the prosecutrix's age, he submits, he is certainly less culpable than the person who knows that the minor is 13 years old, but nonetheless engages in sexual relations with her. Notwithstanding, the majority has construed section 463(a)(3) to exclude any proof of knowledge or intent. ...

I would hold that the State is not relieved of its burden to prove the defendant's intent or knowledge in a statutory rape case and, therefore, that the defendant may defend on the basis that he was mistaken as to the age of the prosecutrix. Generally, a culpable mental state, often referred to as *mens rea*, or intent, is, and long has been, an essential element of a criminal offense. A crime ordinarily consists of prohibited conduct and a culpable mental state; a wrongful act and a wrongful intent must concur to constitute what the law deems a crime, the purpose being to avoid criminal liability for innocent or inadvertent conduct. Historically, therefore, unless the actor also harbored an evil, or otherwise culpable, mind, he or she was not guilty of any crime. ...

When a legislature wants to eliminate intent as an element of a particular crime, it should expressly so state in the statute. ... Strict liability crimes are recognized exceptions to the "guilty mind" rule in that they do not require the actor to possess a guilty mind, or the *mens rea*, to commit a crime. His or her state of mind being irrelevant, the actor is guilty of the crime at the moment that he or she does the prohibited act. ...

A man who engages in consensual intercourse in the reasonable belief that his partner has reached [the age of consent] evidences no abnormality, no willingness to take advantage of immaturity, no propensity to corruption of minors. In short, he has demonstrated neither intent nor inclination to violate any of the interests that the law of statutory rape seeks to protect. At most, he has disregarded religious precept or social convention. In terms of mental culpability, his conduct is indistinguishable from that of any other person who engages in fornication. Whether he should be punished at all depends on a judgment about continuing fornication as a criminal offense, but at least he should not be subject to felony sanctions for statutory rape. ...

In this case ... the defendant does not dispute that he had sexual relations with the 13-year-old prosecutrix. He seeks only to be able to defend himself against being labeled a rapist. He may only do so, however, if he is allowed to present evidence that he acted under a mistake of fact as to the prosecutrix's age, that he believed, and reasonably so, that she was above the age of consent. The proof he proposed to present to prove his defense was that the victim and her friends told him that the victim was 16 years old. He should have been allowed to show that he lacked the "guilty mind" to have sex with a 13-year-old. ...

I respectfully dissent.

Questions

1. List all the evidence relevant to determining both the *actus reus* and the *mens rea* of rape in this case.

2. Did Raymond Garnett intend to rape Erica Frazier? Did he rape her recklessly? Negligently? Back up your answer with facts from the case.

3. According to the majority, why is Raymond's intent irrelevant? According to the dissent, why is it relevant?

4. Should statutory rape be a strict liability crime? Defend your answer.

Grading the Seriousness of Rape

Most statutes divide rape into two degrees: **simple (second-degree) rape** and **aggravated (first-degree) rape.** *Aggravated rape* involves at least one of the following circumstances:

- The victim suffers serious bodily injury.
- A stranger commits the rape.
- The rape occurs in connection with another crime.
- The rapist is armed.
- The rapist has accomplices.
- The victim is a minor and the rapist is several years older.

All other rapes are "simple" rapes, for which the penalties are less severe. The criminal sexual conduct statutes comprise a broad range of criminal sexual penetrations and contacts that grades penetrations more seriously than contacts but also takes into account aggravating circumstances (see the bulleted list).

BODILY INJURY CRIMES

Assault and battery, although combined in most statutes, were distinct offenses at common law. A *battery* is unwanted and unjustified offensive touching. Body contact is central to the crime of battery. An **assault** is either an attempted or a threatened battery. The essential difference between assault and battery is that assault requires no physical contact; an assault is complete before the offender touches the victim.

In this section, we'll look at the elements of battery; how the law grades, or establishes, the seriousness of acts of battery; the elements of assault; and the *Model Penal Code* assault and battery statute.

The Elements of Battery

The *actus reus* of battery is unlawful touching, but, not every offensive physical contact is unlawful. Spanking children is offensive, at least to the children, but it's not battery. Why? Because the law recognizes it as a justified act of disciplining children. Unlawful touching includes a broad spectrum but usually means any unjustified touching without consent. Some courts have even included spitting in the face of someone you want to insult (*State v. Humphries* 1978).

Statutes don't always spell out the battery *mens rea*. At common law, battery was an intentionally inflicted injury. Modern courts and statutes extend battery *mens rea* to include reckless and negligent contacts. The *Model Penal Code* (American Law

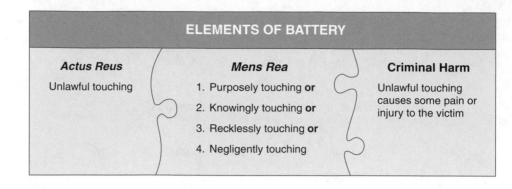

ELEMENTS OF BATTERY		
Actus Reus Unlawful touching	**Mens Rea** 1. Purposely touching **or** 2. Knowingly touching **or** 3. Recklessly touching **or** 4. Negligently touching	**Criminal Harm** Unlawful touching causes some pain or injury to the victim

Institute 1953, no.11) defines battery to include "purposely, recklessly, or negligently causing bodily injury," or "negligently causing bodily injury...with a deadly weapon." Some state statutes call this expanded offense by a different name. Louisiana (Louisiana Statutes Annotated 1974, 17-A, 14.39), for example, provides that "inflicting any injury upon the person of another by criminal negligence" is "negligent injuring."

Grading the Seriousness of Battery

Battery requires some injury. Batteries that cause minor physical injury or emotional injury are misdemeanors in most states. Batteries that cause serious bodily injury are felonies. Some code provisions are directed at injuries caused by special circumstances. For example, injuries caused by pit bulls prompted the Minnesota legislature (Minnesota Statutes Annotated 1989, § 609.26) to enact the following provision:

> Section 609.26. A person who causes great or substantial bodily harm to another by negligently or intentionally permitting any dog to run uncontrolled off the owner's premises, or negligently failing to keep it properly confined is guilty of a petty misdemeanor....
>
> Subd. 3. If proven by a preponderance of the evidence, it shall be an affirmative defense to liability under this section that the victim provoked the dog to cause the victim's bodily harm.

Injuries and deaths resulting from drug abuse led the same legislature to enact the following provision:

> 609.228 Whoever proximately causes great bodily harm by, directly or indirectly, unlawfully selling, giving away, bartering, delivering, exchanging, distributing, or administering a controlled substance...may be sentenced to imprisonment for not more than ten years or to payment of a fine of not more than $20,000, or both.

The *Model Penal Code* grades bodily harm offenses as follows:

§ 211.1

2. Bodily injury is a felony when
   a. such injury is inflicted purposely or knowingly with a deadly weapon; or
   b. serious bodily injury is inflicted purposely, or knowingly or recklessly under circumstances manifesting extreme indifference to the value of human life.

ELEMENTS OF ASSAULT		
Actus Reus	***Mens Rea***	**Criminal Harm (threatened battery only)**
1. Attempted battery **or**	1. Intent to injure in (attempted battery)	Fear in victim caused by defendant's acts
2. Threatened battery	2. Intent to put in fear of harm (threatened battery)	

c. except as provided in paragraph (2), bodily injury is a misdemeanor, unless it was caused in a fight or scuffle entered into by mutual consent, in which case it is a petty misdemeanor.

The Elements of Assault

Assaults are either attempted batteries or threatened batteries, depending on the state. (Notice both kinds are complete crimes without touching the victim.) **Attempted battery assault** consists of having the specific intent to commit a battery and taking substantial steps toward carrying it out without actually completing the attempt. **Threatened battery assault,** sometimes called the crime of **intentional scaring,** requires only that actors intend to frighten their victims, thus expanding assault beyond attempted battery. Threatened battery doesn't require having the intent to actually physically injure their victims; the intent to frighten victims into believing the actor will hurt them is enough.

Victims' awareness is critical to proving threatened battery assault. Specifically, victims have to reasonably fear an immediate battery. Words alone aren't assaults; threatening gestures have to accompany them. But, this requirement isn't always just. For example, what if an assailant approaches from behind a victim, saying, "Don't move, or I'll shoot!" These words obviously are grounds to reasonably fear imminent injury, but they aren't assault because they are, after all, *only* words.

Conditional threats aren't enough either, because they're not immediate. The conditional threat, "I'd punch you out if you weren't a kid," isn't immediate because it depends on the victim's age. In a few jurisdictions, a present ability to carry out the threat has to exist. But in most, even a person who approaches a victim with a gun she knows is unloaded, points the gun at the victim, and pulls the trigger (intending only to frighten her victim) has committed threatened battery (*Encyclopedia of Crime and Justice* 1983, 1:89).

Remember: attempted and threatened battery assaults address separate harms. Attempted battery assault deals with an incomplete physical injury (see Chapter 6). Threatened battery assault is directed at a present psychological or emotional harm— namely, putting a victim in fear. So, in attempted battery assault, a victim's awareness doesn't matter; in threatened battery assault, it's indispensable. **Stalking**—intentionally scaring a victim by following, tormenting, or harassing her—is an excellent example of the importance of victim awareness in threatened battery assault, as the case of *Simms v. State* (2003) illustrates.

Simms v. State
791 N.E.2d 225 (Ind.App. 2003)

Michael Anthony Simms, Defendant, was convicted in the Elkhart Circuit Court, of stalking as a class B felony. Defendant appealed. The Court of Appeals affirmed.

RILEY, J.

FACTS

Michael Anthony Simms (Simms) married Heather Simms (Heather) in 1997. The couple have two children, who were six and two at the time of trial. By March of 2001, Heather decided she wanted a divorce, due to Simms' violent outbursts towards Heather and the children. At that time, Heather informed Simms of her decision.

Subsequently, Heather began receiving threatening phone calls from Simms that frightened her. On March 29, 2001, Heather filed for divorce and obtained a temporary protective order against Simms. When Simms received the divorce papers, he became very angry and stated, "it wasn't happening" and that he was going to kill Heather.

On April 3, 2001, Heather returned home from work to find approximately forty-five messages from Simms on her telephone answering machine. In several of the messages, Simms threatened Heather and frightened her. For example, Heather testified that she was particularly frightened by the message in which Simms stated he was going to take Heather's severed head and set it on the front desk at the police station. In response to the messages, Heather immediately took her children to stay at her mother's house. From there, Heather took a tape recording of the threatening messages to the police station and then went to stay with a friend. Heather remained away from her home and left her children with her mother for the next several weeks.

In late April of 2001, Heather wanted to return to her normal life and decided to go back to her home. On Heather's second night back, Simms appeared at the house. As Simms approached the house, Heather's dog ran towards him and Simms punched the dog in the head. Heather told Simms to leave and started back into the house. Simms pushed his way into the house, began hitting Heather in the face and head, and broke her glasses. Simms stopped hitting Heather and left the house when an unidentified female, who was outside of the house, told Simms, "Come on, we gotta go."

Simms continued to leave threatening messages on Heather's telephone answering machine until June of 2001, when she obtained a new, unlisted phone number. Heather did not see Simms during the summer of 2001, with the exception of seeing him driving past her house on two different occasions sometime in August. Heather and her children continued to stay with a friend during this time.

On October 2, 2001, Heather drove to her mother's house to pick up some clothing for her children. As Heather was leaving, she saw Simms walking toward her. Heather told him to leave her alone and turned to get into her truck. Simms pulled a gun out of his pocket, pointed it toward Heather, and fired a shot just as Heather opened the door to get into her truck. Heather heard four or five other shots and the sound of the bullets hitting the truck as she was inside. Simms fled on foot. Heather pursued Simms in her truck and Simms fired three additional shots at her, two of which hit her truck.

…From May 6, 2002, to May 11, 2002, the matter was tried to a jury…. The jury … returned a verdict of guilty on the charge of stalking, a Class B felony. On June 6, 2002, Simms received the maximum sentence of ten years with an additional ten years for aggravating circumstances, for a total of twenty years to be served in the Department of Correction.

Simms now appeals….

OPINION

Simms contends that the State did not present sufficient evidence to support his conviction for stalking while armed with a deadly weapon, a Class B felony. In reviewing sufficiency of the evidence claims, this court does not reweigh the evidence or assess the credibility of witnesses. We consider only the evidence most favorable to the verdict, together with all reasonable and logical inferences to be drawn therefrom. The conviction will be affirmed if there is substantial evidence of probative value to support the conclusion of the trier-of-fact.

Indiana Code § 35-45-10-5 states, in pertinent part:

(a) A person who stalks another person commits stalking, a Class D felony.

….

(c) The offense is a Class B felony if:

(1) the act or acts were committed while the person was armed with a deadly weapon.

With regard to I.C. § 35-45-10-5, "stalk," "harassment," and "impermissible contact" are statutorily defined as follows

As used in this chapter, "stalk" means a knowing or an intentional course of conduct involving repeated or continuing harassment of another person that would cause a reasonable person to feel terrorized, frightened, intimidated, or threatened and that actually causes the victim to feel terrorized, frightened, intimidated, or threatened. The term does not include statutorily or constitutionally protected activity.

I.C. § 35-45-10-1

As used in this chapter, "harassment" means conduct directed toward a victim that includes but is not limited to repeated or continuing impermissible contact that would cause a reasonable person to suffer emotional distress and that actually causes the victim to suffer emotional distress. Harassment does not include statutorily or constitutionally protected activity, such as lawful picketing pursuant to labor disputes or lawful employer-related activities pursuant to labor disputes.

I.C. § 35-45-10-2

As used in this chapter, "impermissible contact" includes but is not limited to knowingly or intentionally following or pursuing the victim.

I.C. § 35-45-10-3

Thus, in order to convict Simms of stalking, as a Class B felony, the State was required to prove to the jury beyond a reasonable doubt that Simms:

(1) knowingly or intentionally;

(2) while armed with a deadly weapon;

(3) engaged in a course of conduct involving repeated or continuing harassment of Heather;

(4) that would cause a reasonable person to feel terrorized, frightened, intimidated, or threatened; and

(5) that actually caused Heather to feel terrorized, frightened, intimidated, or threatened.

Simms first argues that the State failed to prove that Heather was actually terrorized by Simms' conduct. Therefore, the State's failure to prove this essential element of stalking, as a Class B felony, requires reversal of his conviction. We disagree.

At trial, the State presented evidence that Simms left a multitude of vulgar and, often, violent messages on Heather's telephone answering machine subsequent to Heather filing for divorce. Over the course of several months, Heather collected nearly seven hours of messages on cassette tapes. Heather testified as to the content of some of the threatening messages and the fear she felt upon hearing them. For instance, when the State asked Heather which message scared her the most, she described one in which Simms told her he was going to take her severed head to the police station and set it on the front desk.

Further, Heather testified that she felt threatened, intimidated and harassed. Heather's actions in response to Simms' threats confirm her testimony. The record reveals that, when she filed for divorce in late March of 2001, Heather obtained a temporary protective order in an effort to stop Simms' harassing telephone calls and with the hope that he would leave her alone. The order was converted to a permanent protective order by the divorce court in late April of 2001. Simms threatened to take Heather's life on several occasions in telephone answering machine messages and in front of family members.

Heather testified that, as a result, she took her children to stay at her mother's house because, if something was going to happen to her, she did not want her kids to witness it. While her children stayed with her mother, Heather stayed with a friend for several weeks. She testified that she saw her children every day, but only briefly, because she feared that Simms was watching her—as he told her in the messages. Heather did not want Simms to know that she or the children were at her mother's.

The record further indicates that Heather bought a different car and obtained an unlisted phone number. Given this testimony, it was reasonable for the jury to infer that Heather felt terrorized, frightened, intimidated and threatened. Therefore, we find that the State carried its burden of proving this essential element of stalking, as a Class B felony.

Next, Simms challenges the sufficiency of the evidence in his conviction for stalking, as a Class B felony, by asserting an absence of harassing conduct. Specifically, Simms contends that the messages he left on the answering machine in Heather's house subsequent to April 3, 2001, should not qualify as harassment because Heather moved out of her house on April 3; therefore, she was not there to hear them. Simms' argument is wholly without merit.

. . . The record reveals that the reason Heather was not present in her house to receive Simms' threatening messages was precisely *because* of Simms' threatening messages. Thus, harassment, as defined in I.C. § 35-45-10-2, existed prior to Heather's leaving her home in an effort to hide from Simms. Further, even if the post-April 3, 2001 messages left by Simms on Heather's answering machine are disregarded, the evidence demonstrates several other examples of Simms' repeated and continuing harassment of Heather sufficient to support his conviction. Therefore,

Simms' argument on this issue fails. Accordingly, we conclude that the State presented sufficient evidence to support Simms' conviction for stalking, a Class B felony....

Simms asserts that the twenty-year prison sentence imposed by the trial court was manifestly unreasonable.... Specifically, Simms asserts that the trial court did not give enough weight to three mitigating factors, namely: (1) Simms' criminal history contains no felony convictions; (2) Simms' criminal history is not violent; and (3) Simms sustained a head injury "that may have well been a primary contributor to his anger-management problems and diagnosis of explosive disorder."...

In its sentencing statement, the trial court addressed Simms' criminal history. However, despite the lack of felony convictions, the trial court viewed Simms' criminal history as an aggravating factor, as follows: "The aggravating circumstances consist of the following: [f]our misdemeanor convictions that preceded this case. All of which indicate your unwillingness to abide by the laws of this state." The trial court did not specifically address Simms' assertion that his prior criminal history was non-violent. However, as stated above, the trial court is not required to accept as mitigating the circumstances proffered by the defendant. Thus, the trial court's decision to consider Simms' misdemeanor convictions as an aggravating factor is not an abuse of discretion.

Finally, in its sentencing statement, the trial court found the history of a head injury, the fact that Simms did not take his medication, and the fact that Simms was receiving therapy for explosive disorder as mitigating factors. Nevertheless, Simms contends that, "the suggestion is quite strong that an organic condition was influencing [his] behavior" and "constitutes a *significant* mitigator." (emphasis added). However, it is the sole discretion of the trial court to determine which aggravating and mitigating circumstances to consider, and to determine the weight accorded each of these factors. Therefore, we find no abuse of discretion with regard to the trial court's decision not to accord greater weight to this mitigating factor.

Next, Simms argues that the trial court failed to consider provocation when balancing the aggravating and mitigating factors. Specifically, Simms contends that Heather admittedly "knew how to make [Simms] angry" and "seemed to undertake some actions with no purpose other than to stir up trouble." However, Simms did not raise provocation as a mitigating factor to the trial court. If the defendant fails to advance a mitigating circumstance at sentencing, this court will presume that the circumstance is not significant and the defendant is precluded from advancing it as a mitigating circumstance for the first time on appeal. Consequently, Simms is precluded from raising provocation as a mitigating factor on appeal.

When reviewing whether a defendant was properly sentenced, we consider whether the sentence is appropriate in light of the nature of the offense and the character of the offender. In considering the appropriateness of the sentence for the crime committed, trial courts should initially focus upon the presumptive sentence.... Here, the jury convicted Simms of stalking, a Class B felony. The presumptive sentence for a Class B felony is ten years, with not more than ten years added for aggravating circumstances or not more than four years subtracted for mitigating circumstances. *See* I.C. § 35-50-2-5. The trial court sentenced Simms to the maximum sentence of twenty years—the ten-year presumptive with ten years added for aggravating circumstances. In support of its sentence, the trial court found several aggravating factors, some of which are summarized from the trial court's sentencing order as follows:

1. Simms' criminal history, which indicates his unwillingness to abide by the laws of the State.

2. Simms' numerous pending harassment cases also indicating Simms' unwillingness to abide by rules of law and court orders.

3. Simms violated a restraining order and made 40 to 50 phone calls including threats to place the severed head of the victim on the desk at the police station and other threats to kill the victim. Simms chose to use a handgun, and fired it multiple times creating a danger of injury to bystanders in the residential area.

4. The 40 to 50 threatening messages Simms left on Heather's answering machine were essential to the State's burden of proving stalking, as a Class B felony, and therefore cannot be used as an aggravating factor. However, the heinous nature of Simms' threat to place Heather's severed head on the front desk of the police station goes to the nature of the offense and is thus a proper aggravating factor.

5. Simms has violent tendencies and is in need of rehabilitation that can only be provided in a penal facility.

6. Simms injured the pet dog when he hit it.

As discussed above, the trial court found three mitigating circumstances. In balancing the mitigating circumstances with the aggravating circumstances, the trial court found that, "the aggravating circumstances in this case [ ] outweigh the mitigating circumstances substantially." Accordingly, the trial court enhanced Simms' sentence to the maximum of twenty years in the Department of Correction.

Simms contends that maximum sentences should be reserved for the worst offenders with the worst records, and that he does not qualify as a "worst offender." Therefore, Simms maintains that his sentence should be reduced to the presumptive sentence of ten years. However, after reviewing the record along with the sentencing statement and the aggravating and mitigating circumstances, we conclude that the trial court did not abuse its discretion in determining that the aggravating factors substantially outweigh the mitigating factors. Additionally, we do not find the sentence imposed inappropriate in light of the nature of the offense and the character of the offender. . . .

AFFIRMED.

Questions

1. State the elements of the Indiana stalking statute.

2. Collect all the evidence to support the elements of stalking.

3. Summarize the arguments and interpretation of the evidence that led the court to the conclusion that Simms was guilty of aggravated stalking.

4. In your opinion was Simms guilty of stalking or aggravated stalking? Back up your answer by applying the elements of the statute to the evidence.

5. Summarize the court's reason for imposing the 20-year sentence. Do you agree with the court's sentence? Explain your answer.

◆   ◆   ◆

The *Model Penal Code* deals with threatened and attempted battery assaults as follows:

§ 211.1 SIMPLE ASSAULT.

A person is guilty of assault if he:
   a. attempts to cause bodily injury to another; or
   b. attempts by physical menace to put another in fear of imminent serious bodily harm.

Simple assault is a misdemeanor unless committed in a fight or scuffle entered into by mutual consent, in which case the assault is a petty misdemeanor.

Historically, all assaults were misdemeanors. However, modern statutes have created several aggravated or felonious assaults. Most common are assaults with the intent to commit violent felonies (murder, rape, and robbery, for example), assaults with deadly weapons (such as guns and knives), and assaults on police officers. In *Harrod v. State* (1985), the Maryland Court of Appeals dealt with the *mens rea* of assault.

CASE | *Did He Intend to Assault?*

Harrod v. State
499 A.2d 959 (Md.App. 1985)

John Harrod, Defendant, was convicted in the Circuit Court, Carroll County, of two counts of assault, and he appealed. The Court of Special Appeals reversed.

ALPERT, J.
The common law crime of assault encompasses two definitions: (1) an attempt to commit a battery or (2) an unlawful intentional act which places another in reasonable apprehension of receiving an immediate battery. The facts in the instant case present this court with an excellent opportunity to explain the distinctions between these two different types of assault.

FACTS

The assault charges arose out of a confrontation among appellant (Harrod), his wife Cheryl, and her friend Calvin Crigger. The only two witnesses at trial were appellant and Cheryl Harrod.

Cheryl testified that on September 15, 1983, Calvin Crigger came over to visit when she thought Harrod had gone to work; that "all of a sudden Harrod came out of the bedroom with a hammer in his hand, swinging it around, coming after me and my friend [Calvin]"; that Calvin ran out of the house and down the steps; that Harrod "had thrown the hammer over top of [Christopher's (their son's)] port-a-crib in the living room, and it went into the wall"; that Harrod then reentered the bedroom and returned with a five-inch blade hunting knife; that Harrod told Cheryl that he was going to kill her and that, if she took his daughter away from him, he was going to kill Christopher; that Harrod put the knife into the bannister near Cheryl's arm; that Harrod followed Cheryl out to Calvin's car and "went after Calvin, going around and around the car."

Harrod testified that he missed his ride to work that day; that he came back home around 10:00 A.M. and went to sleep in a back room; that he was awakened by Calvin's deep voice; that Harrod picked up his hammer and, walking into the living room, told Calvin to leave; that Cheryl told Calvin he didn't have to leave; that he then told Calvin, "Buddy, if you want your head busted in, stand here; if you want to be healthy and leave, go." Harrod said that Calvin just stood there, so he swung the hammer, Calvin moved his head back, and the hammer struck the wall over Christopher's crib, which was near the door.

In rendering its verdict, the court stated:

And, the Court finds beyond a reasonable doubt and to a moral certainty that Mr. Harrod . . . came after [Cheryl] and . . . Calvin; and that Mr. Harrod came out of his room swinging a . . . hammer, and ultimately threw it, not too far from the child, Christopher, and that he went after both Cheryl and Calvin, down the steps with a knife, with a blade of about four to five inches. The Court finds that he is guilty of two counts of Carrying a Deadly Weapon; that is the knife and the hammer; and, also two counts of Assault; one against Cheryl and one against the minor child.

Defense counsel inquired of the court: ". . . Is the Court finding specific intent on behalf of the Defendant to injure his child?" The court responded, "Yes. Threw that hammer within a very short distance—sticking it—it was still sticking in the wall."

OPINION

Harrod contends that there was insufficient evidence to demonstrate that he harbored a specific intent to injure Christopher when he threw the hammer. Further, he notes that there was no evidence that Christopher was injured by

the hammer or that he was even aware that a hammer was thrown. Therefore, appellant claims that the trial court's finding that he committed a criminal assault upon Christopher was clearly erroneous. We agree. . . .

An assault "is committed when there is *either* an attempt to commit a battery *or* when, by an unlawful act, a person is placed in reasonable apprehension of receiving an immediate battery." (emphasis added). These two types of assaults—*attempted battery* and *putting another in fear*—are indeed two distinct crimes that have been inadvertently overlapped and confused. One commentator explained this confusion:

In the early law the word "assault" represented an entirely different concept in criminal law than it did in the law of torts. As an offense it was an attempt to commit a battery; as a basis for a civil action for damages it was an intentional act wrongfully placing another in apprehension of receiving an immediate battery. The distinction has frequently passed unnoticed because a misdeed involving either usually involves both. If, with the intention of hitting X, D wrongfully threw a stone that X barely managed to dodge, then D would have been guilty of a criminal assault because he had attempted to commit a battery, and he would also have been liable in a civil action of trespass for assault because he had wrongfully placed X in apprehension of physical harm.

Some commentators have been so imbued with the tort theory of assault that they have had difficulty in realizing that in the early law a criminal assault was an attempt to commit a battery and that only. Perkins and Boyce, *Criminal Law* 159

. . . In an attempted battery-type assault, the victim need not be aware of the perpetrator's intent or threat:

If a person be struck from behind, or by stealth or surprise, or while asleep, he is certainly the victim of a battery. But if we accept the oft-repeated statement that every battery included or is preceded by an assault, and if there could be no assault without premonitory apprehension in the victim, then it could be argued that there was no battery. That is not the law. In other words, because there may be committed a battery without the victim first being aware of the attack, an attempted battery-type assault cannot include a requirement that the victim be aware.

The facts in this case do not support a finding that Harrod committed an attempted battery towards the infant, Christopher. An attempt to commit any crime requires a specific intent to commit that crime. An attempted battery-type assault thus requires that the accused harbor a specific intent to cause physical injury to the victim, and take a substantial step towards causing that injury.

Nowhere does the record indicate that Harrod threw the hammer with the specific intent to injure Christopher. The court expressly stated that it found specific intent on behalf of appellant because he "threw that hammer within a very short distance" of the child. The court here is merely inferring a criminal intent from reckless or negligent acts of Harrod. This is not sufficient, especially where all of the evidence tends to the contrary: that Harrod's intent was to injure Calvin.

An additional question . . . is whether the necessary specific intent as against Christopher could derive from the specific intent toward Calvin; in other words, did the intent to injure Calvin *transfer* to Christopher? This doctrine of "transferred intent" was explained by the Court of Appeals in *Gladden v. State*, 330 A.2d 176 (1974):

> "If one intends injury to the person of another under circumstances in which such a mental element constitutes *mens rea*, and in the effort to accomplish this end he inflicts harm upon a person other than the one intended, he is guilty of the same kind of crime as if his aim had been more accurate." In such cases all the components of the crime are present. The psychical element which consists of a certain general mental pattern is not varied by the particular person who may be actually harmed.

Gladden, as well as all of the cases cited in that opinion, involved an attempt to kill one person, but resulted in the death or injury of another, unintended victim. In every case cited in *Gladden*, the third party to whom the intent was "transferred" was in fact injured. The Court of Appeals expressly held that, under the doctrine, "the *mens rea* of a defendant as to his intended victim will carry over and affix his culpability *when such criminal conduct causes the death of an unintended victim.*" (emphasis added).

. . . The closest case we have found to support the rule that the doctrine does not apply absent actual injury is *State v. Martin*, 119 S.W.2d 298 (1938). In *Martin*, the defendants were charged with assault upon Lloyd DeCasnett, with the intent to maim. The evidence in that case showed that the defendants threw a sulphuric acid–filled light bulb at a vehicle in which DeCasnett was a passenger. However, there was no evidence that the defendants knew that DeCasnett was in fact there, while there was ample evidence that they were aware of other persons in the target vehicle. The Missouri court considered the common law notion in homicide cases "that a constructive intent follows the bullet," but stated, "it cannot be the law in a case like this *where no one was hurt*, and the State's case rests solely on the overt act of throwing the acid-filled bulb and the felonious intent to be deduced therefrom." (emphasis added). The court went on to reverse the conviction for assault with intent to maim DeCasnett, because, although the record evidence demonstrated a felonious intent to injure a passenger in the car, it did not appear that DeCasnett was the object of that intent.

To extend the doctrine of transferred intent to cases where the intended victim is not harmed would be untenable. The absurd result would be to make one criminally culpable for each unintended victim who, although in harm's way, was in fact not harmed by a missed attempt towards a specific person. We refuse, therefore, to extend the doctrine of transferred intent to cases where a third person is not in fact harmed.

This is the situation before us in the instant case. The record indicates that Harrod swung a hammer which struck the wall "not too far from" Christopher. Significantly, there is no evidence that Christopher was harmed. Further, the weight of the evidence shows that appellant's specific intent, if any, was to injure Calvin, not Christopher. Why the State charged Harrod with assaulting Christopher, rather than Calvin, we will not speculate. There is clearly insufficient evidence to find that Harrod committed an attempted battery-type assault upon Christopher.

There is likewise insufficient evidence that Harrod, by an unlawful intentional act, placed Christopher in reasonable apprehension of receiving an immediate battery. By definition the victim must be aware of the impending contact. . . . There is no evidence in the record before us that Christopher was in fact aware of the occurrences in his home on the morning in question. Therefore, there was insufficient evidence to find appellant guilty of the putting victim in fear-type assault.

Because the trial court was clearly erroneous in finding appellant guilty of an assault on Christopher, we must REVERSE that conviction. . . .

Questions

1. How does the court define the two kinds of assault?

2. How does the court define the *mens rea* of assault?

3. List all of the evidence relevant to determining whether John Harrod satisfied the *mens rea* of both types of assault?

4. How would you define the *mens rea* of assault?

5. Should the state have prosecuted Calvin Crigger instead of Harrod? Neither? Both? Defend your answer.

The *Model* Assault and Battery Statute

The *Model Penal Code* includes a comprehensive assault and battery statute that integrates, rationalizes, and grades assault and battery. It takes into account *actus reus, mens rea,* circumstance elements, and intended harm. Note the careful attention paid to these elements:

§ 211.2

A person is guilty of aggravated assault if he:

a. attempts to cause serious bodily injury to another, or causes such injury purposely, knowingly or recklessly under circumstances manifesting extreme indifference to the value of human life; or

b. attempts to cause or purposely or knowingly causes bodily injury to another with a deadly weapon.

Aggravated assault under paragraph (a) is a felony of the second degree; aggravated assault under paragraph (b) is a felony of the third degree.

§ 211.3

A person commits a misdemeanor if he recklessly engages in conduct which places or may place another person in danger of death or serious bodily injury. Recklessness and danger shall be presumed where a person knowingly points a firearm at or in the direction of another, whether or not the actor believed the firearm to be loaded.

PERSONAL RESTRAINT CRIMES

One of the greatest things about living in a free society is the right to control our freedom of movement (even though we may not appreciate it until it's taken away from us). The eighteenth century called it the **right of locomotion,** meaning the right to come and go as we please; to stay if we don't want to move, and to move if we don't want to stay. I'm reminded of how precious this right is every time we get several inches of snow (which is pretty often here in Minnesota). My house has a long driveway that needs plowing before I can get out. As much as I love my house, I start feeling confined if the snowplow doesn't get there within an hour. This is a silly example, but it underscores the issues of the two crimes against personal liberty we'll look at in this section: kidnapping and false imprisonment.

Kidnapping

Kidnapping is an ancient offense that originally involved holding the kings' relatives for ransom. Of course, it was considered a serious offense because it interfered with the personal liberty of members of royal families. At common law, kidnapping consisted of six elements:

1. Seizing,

2. Carrying away (asportation of) and

3. Confining

4. Another person

5. By force, threat of force, fraud, or deception

6. With the intent to deprive the other person of his or her liberty.

In the 1900s, kidnapping came to be considered a very serious felony in the United States—even a capital offense in some states. And, the seriousness had nothing to do with royalty but a lot to do with events during the first half of the twentieth century. During Prohibition (1919 to 1933), kidnapping was prevalent in the organized crime world. One gang member might abduct a rival, "take him for a ride," and kill him. However, much more frequently, rivals were captured and held hostage for ransom. Before long, law-abiding citizens were being abducted, especially the spouses and children of wealthy and otherwise prominent citizens.

The most famous early case (*State v. Hauptmann* 1935) was the ransom kidnap and murder of Charles Lindbergh's son. Lindbergh was an aviator who captured Americans' hearts and imaginations when he flew solo across the Atlantic Ocean. Kidnapping was only a misdemeanor in New Jersey in 1932 when the crime occurred, but the tremendous sympathy that Lindbergh's popular hero status generated and the public outrage toward what was perceived as a rampant increase in random kidnappings of America's "pillars of wealth and virtue" led legislatures to enact harsh new kidnapping statutes. These statutes remain largely in force today, even though they were passed in an emotional overreaction to a few notorious cases.

In 1974, another widely publicized case breathed new life into these harsh statutes when Patricia Hearst, heiress to newspaper tycoon William Randolph Hearst, was kidnapped. The case met with public outrage, not only because of sympathy for the prominent Hearst family but also because of shock at the psychological and physical dimensions of the crime. The kidnappers were self-styled revolutionaries calling themselves the Symbionese Liberation Army (SLA). One of the SLA's first demands was that William Randolph Hearst distribute $1 million in food to the poor of California. Later on, much to her parents' and the public's horror, Patricia Hearst converted to the SLA, participating in bank robberies to raise money for the "revolution." This all happened during a time when radicalism and violence were much feared and when the Vietnam War protest and airline hijackings for terrorist political purposes were very much on the public's mind. Hence, the public saw not only Patty Hearst's capture and her family's deep trauma but also a threat to destroy American society.

The Hearst case focused attention on kidnapping's heinous side. It drew together in one story capture and detention, terror, violence, and political radicalism. The details were trumpeted every day in newspapers and on radio and television. Hope that existing harsh and sweeping kidnapping legislation would be calmly reassessed vanished in this inflamed, emotional atmosphere. President Nixon expressed his hope—a hope that many others shared—that the Supreme Court would not declare capital punishment for kidnapping to be unconstitutional. Then–California Governor Reagan reflected the deep public outrage against kidnapping when he wished aloud that the kidnappers' demand for a free food program would set off a botulism epidemic among the poor.

We'll look at the *actus reus* and *mens rea* elements of kidnapping and at how the law grades the seriousness of acts of kidnapping.

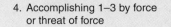

ELEMENTS OF KIDNAPPING

Actus Reus

1. Detention **and**
2. Moving (asportation) **or**
3. Hiding **and**
4. Accomplishing 1–3 by force or threat of force

Mens Rea

Intent to detain and take another person beyond the aid of family, friends, and the law

Kidnapping *Actus Reus*

The critical difference between false imprisonment and kidnapping is the *actus reus* of **asportation** (carrying away) of victims. Since at least the eighteenth century, carrying a victim into a foreign country where no friends or family could give aid and comfort, and the law could not protect the victim, added a particularly terrifying dimension to kidnapping. In the early days, the victim had to be carried at least as far as another county and usually across its border.

Modern interpretations have rendered the *asportation requirement* almost meaningless. The famous case of *People v. Chessman* (1951) is the best example. Caryl Chessman was a serial rapist who, in one instance, forced a young woman to leave her car and get into his, which was only 22 feet away. The court held that the mere fact of moving the victim, not how far she was moved, satisfied the asportation requirement. So, moving his victim 20 feet was enough to convict and sentence Chessman to the gas chamber.

The California Supreme Court dealt with the meaning of asportation in the carjacking case of *People v. Allen* (1997).

CASE | *Did He Move Her a "Substantial" Distance?*

People v. Allen
64 Cal.Rptr.2d 497 (1997)

Tyrone Allen was convicted in the Superior Court, City and County of San Francisco, of kidnapping of a person under the age of 14. He appealed. The Court of Appeal affirmed.

RUVOLO, J.

FACTS

On August 7, 1995, May SunYoung and her family lived at 2951 Treat Street in San Francisco. That morning, Ms. Sun-Young was on her way to take her 7-year-old daughter, Kirstie, to summer camp and stopped her automobile briefly in the driveway to close her garage door manually as she was backing out onto the street.

As Ms. SunYoung closed her garage door, a man approached her from behind and said, "Excuse me, can you do me a favor?" While turning around she saw the man later identified as the appellant Tyrone Allen getting into her vehicle, whose engine was still running. He then locked the car doors. Kirstie was still in the vehicle with her seatbelt on and began crying. Because the driver's side window was rolled down about seven inches, Ms. SunYoung put her arms through the window and struggled with appellant in an attempt to reach the ignition key and turn off the engine.

Allen then released the parking brake, put the vehicle in reverse, and backed out of the driveway with Kirstie inside and Ms. SunYoung running alongside the vehicle still attempting to reach the ignition key. The vehicle backed across Treat Street, which was a two-lane road with two parking lanes, until it hit the opposite curb and came to a stop. Allen estimated the vehicle movement was 30–40 feet. While Allen now claims this estimate to be "speculation," both sides at different times suggested that the distance moved was approximately 5 car lengths, or 50 feet.

Allen exited the vehicle, threw the car keys onto the ground, shoved Ms. SunYoung against a fence, and ran down the street carrying her purse which had been left in the vehicle. Shortly thereafter, a neighbor on Treat Street several blocks away saw a man run by. In response to the neighbor's attempts to stop the man, the fleeing suspect stated, "Stay back, I got a gun." After a brief struggle, the man ran off but was later apprehended by San Francisco police officers and identified as appellant.

The jury instruction given regarding the simple kidnapping count was CALJIC No. 9.52, which sets forth the elements of kidnapping of a person under 14 years of age as follows: "Every person who unlawfully and with physical force or by any other means of instilling fear moves any other person under 14 years of age without her consent for a substantial distance, that is, a distance more than slight or trivial, is guilty of the crime of kidnapping. . . ." (Pen. Code, § 208, subd. (b); all further statutory references are to the Penal Code unless otherwise indicated.)

OPINION

The only element of the crime for which appellant asserts there was insufficient evidence and inadequate jury instructions is asportation. For "simple" kidnapping, that is, a kidnapping not elevated to a statutory form of "aggravated" kidnapping, the movement needed must be "substantial," or a distance that is more than "trivial, slight, or insignificant."

Appellant Allen . . . argues that his conviction for simple kidnapping must be reversed because the minimum distance requirement for asportation is not met. He asserts the movement of Ms. Sun-Young's vehicle 30–50 feet down her driveway and across Treat Street with Kirstie inside as a matter of law cannot be "substantial," or a distance that is more than "trivial, slight or insignificant."

Allen is correct that under most cases decided pre-1981 which have examined only the actual distance involved, the movement here would not meet the legal test of substantiality. In *People v. Brown* (1974) 523 P.2d 226, after breaking into the victim's residence, Brown forced the victim to accompany him through a search of her house for

her husband. When the victim's husband was not found, the defendant moved the victim outside and along a passageway next to the house until a neighbor's intervention caused the defendant to abandon the victim and flee alone. The total distance the victim was moved was unascertained. The Supreme Court held the asportation of the victim was insufficient to satisfy the "substantial" requirement and was no more than trivial.

. . . Those cases which have considered the quality and character of the movement in addition to its absolute distance have weighed the purpose for the movement, whether it posed an increased risk of harm to the victim, and the "context of the environment in which the movement occurred." Purposes for movement found to be relevant have been those undertaken to facilitate the commission of a further crime, to aid in flight, or to prevent detection. We believe these factors are appropriate considerations. "Substantiality" implies something more than only measured distance. While "slight" is consistent with a quantitative analysis, the term "trivial" is a qualitative term suggestive of the conclusion that more is envisioned in determining whether a kidnapping occurs than simply how far the victim is moved. The legal requirement for asportation is satisfied by a finding of either. (CALJIC No. 9.52.)

In so holding, we conclude that while in absolute footage the distance moved here may have been empirically short, it was of a character sufficient to justify a finding of "substantiality" by the jury. The movement, in part, was plainly made to prevent Ms. SunYoung from regaining possession of her vehicle and to facilitate appellant's flight from the area with Kirstie. In addition to evasion of capture, the vehicle was moved from a position of relative safety onto a thoroughfare. The boundary crossed was significant because it placed Kirstie at greater risk of injury. We confirm these factors, coupled with the distance traveled, are sufficient to satisfy the "substantial movement" requirement for the crime of simple kidnapping. . . .

[AFFIRMED.]

DISSENT

KLINE, J.

. . . The majority essentially concedes the movement in this case does not meet the legal test of substantiality if only actual distance is considered. In light of this, I need not belabor the manifest insufficiency of the evidence to satisfy the asportation requirement properly applicable to simple kidnapping.

It deserves emphasis, however, that movement as short a distance as that shown here—30 to 40 feet—has never been held to satisfy the asportation requirement of kidnapping. Indeed, considerably greater distances have often been held insufficient. As the majority opinion points out, movement of 90 feet, nearly three times the distance the victim in this case was moved, was held insufficient in *People v. Green* (1980) 27 Cal.3d 1, 164 Cal.Rptr. 1, 609 P.2d 468, where the Supreme Court noted that "the shortest distance this court has ever held to be 'substantial' for this purpose was a full city block."

People v. Brown (1974) 523 P.2d 226 also dramatically demonstrates that the movement in the present case must be deemed trivial as a matter of law. The defendant in *Brown* had gone to the victim's residence in search of her husband, whose name he had discovered in the home of his estranged wife. He forced the victim to accompany him in a search of the house for her husband. When a neighbor who heard the victim scream telephoned and asked if she needed help, the defendant dragged her out of the house and along a narrow passageway between her house and the house next door. A neighbor then ordered the defendant to release the victim and told him the police were on their way. Defendant released her and fled. "All in all he had taken her approximately 40 to 75 feet from the back door of her house." A unanimous Supreme Court had little difficulty concluding that "the asportation of the victim within her house and for a brief distance outside the house must be regarded as trivial." "Under the particular facts of this case," the court said, "the movement of the victim did not constitute a forcible taking 'into another part of the same county' and . . . the conviction of simple kidnapping must be reversed."

The movement in the present case is about half the distance which in *Brown* was held "trivial." Further, the victim in *Brown* was moved out of one area, the house, into another; and the movement of the victim was much more clearly intentional than that here, as it is not even clear appellant knew a child was in the vehicle when he moved it across the street.

I think it unreasonable to conclude that, when it enacted Penal Code section 207, the Legislature contemplated that backing up a car 30 to 40 feet across a street constitutes asportation "into another part of the same county" within the meaning of that statute. It must be remembered that the only definition of kidnapping that appears in the California Penal Code is that which appears in section 207. As the Supreme Court has noted on several occasions, the verb "kidnaps" used in section 209 (as well as in other statutes prescribing increased punishments for aggravated kidnappings, such as section 208 and 209.5) means kidnapping as defined in section 207. When the

Legislature enacted section 209.5 in 1993 it not only adopted the section 207 definition of kidnapping, but explicitly incorporated into the new statute the "substantial distance" requirement imposed by the courts. (Pen.Code, § 209.5, subd. (b).) The Legislature must be deemed to have been aware of the distances considered by the courts too "slight" or "trivial" to satisfy this requirement. . . .

The fact that the Legislature punished aggravated kidnapping more severely than simple kidnapping has nothing to do with the distance the victim is moved but only to the greater harm to which the victim is exposed when a kidnapping is related to certain other serious offenses. If the Legislature felt aggravated kidnapping required movement over a greater distance than would suffice for simple kidnapping it would not have adopted the section 207 definition of kidnapping in an aggravated kidnapping statute, as it has, nor applied to aggravated kidnapping the same substantial distance requirement applicable to simple kidnapping, as it also has done. (Pen.Code, § 290.5, subd. (b).)

I agree that by moving the child in the vehicle across the street Allen committed a crime other than carjacking and the various other offenses of which he was properly convicted; that crime was not kidnapping, however, but false imprisonment (Pen.Code, § 236), which does not require any movement. . . . As the Supreme Court has repeatedly observed, "the Legislature did not intend to apply criminal sanctions [for any form of kidnapping] where the 'slightest movement' is involved."

Because the asportation in this case was trivial within the meaning of the applicable case law, I would reverse the judgment of conviction of simple kidnapping for lack of evidentiary support. I agree that in all other respects the judgment should be affirmed.

Questions

1. What test did the court establish to determine how far defendants have to move victims to satisfy the asportation element of kidnapping *actus reus*?

2. What reasons does the majority give to support its definition of asportation?

3. How does the dissent's definition of asportation differ from that of the majority?

4. What reasons does the dissent give for its definition?

5. Do you agree with the majority or the dissent's definition of asportation? Defend your answer.

◆   ◆   ◆

Kidnapping *Mens Rea*

The *mens rea* of kidnapping is usually stated as the specific intent to confine, significantly restrain, or hold victims in secret. The Wisconsin statute, for example, defines a kidnapper as one who "seizes or confines another without his consent and with intent to cause him to be secretly confined." Whatever the changes, the heart of the crime remains to "isolate the victim from prospect of release or friendly intervention."

Grading the Seriousness of Kidnapping

Kidnapping is usually divided into two degrees: simple and aggravated. The most common aggravating circumstances include kidnapping for the purpose of:

- Sexual invasions
- Obtaining a hostage
- Obtaining ransom
- Robbing the victim
- Murdering the victim
- Blackmail
- Terrorizing the victim
- Achieving political aims

The penalty for aggravated kidnapping is usually life imprisonment and, until recently, occasionally even death.

False Imprisonment

False imprisonment is a lesser form of personal restraint than kidnapping, but the heart of the crime remains depriving others of their personal liberty. It's been defined as compelling a person "to remain where he does not wish to remain or to go where he does not wish to go" (*McKendree v. Christy* 1961, 381). As with other felonies, prosecutors must prove the critical elements of *actus reus* and *mens rea* [Chapter 4] to convict those accused of false imprisonment.

False Imprisonment *Actus Reus*

Most forcible detentions or confinements satisfy the *actus reus* of false imprisonment. This doesn't include restraints authorized by law—like when parents restrict their children's activities or victims detain their victimizers.

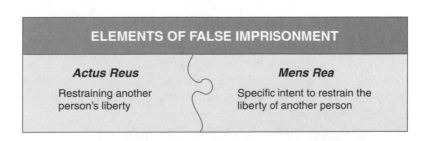

ELEMENTS OF FALSE IMPRISONMENT	
Actus Reus	*Mens Rea*
Restraining another person's liberty	Specific intent to restrain the liberty of another person

The *Model Penal Code* requires the restraint to "interfere *substantially* with the victim's liberty," but, in most state statutes, *any* interference with another person's liberty is enough. For example, here's the way the Florida statute defines the *actus reus* of false imprisonment:

> False imprisonment means forcibly, by threat, or secretly confining, abducting, imprisoning, or restraining another person without lawful authority and against her or his will. (Florida Criminal Code. 2003)

Although physical force often accomplishes the detention, it doesn't have to; threatened force is enough. So, the threat, "If you don't come with me, I'll drag you along," is enough. Even nonthreatening words can qualify, such as when a police officer who has no right to do so orders someone on the street into a squad car, asserting, "You're under arrest."

False Imprisonment *Mens Rea*

False imprisonment is a specific-intent crime. According to a typical statute:

> False imprisonment consists of intentionally confining or restraining another person without his consent.... (New Mexico Criminal Code 2003)

The motive for the detention doesn't matter. For example, if police officers make unlawful arrests, they can be prosecuted for false imprisonment even if they believed the arrests were lawful.

SUMMARY

I. Three kinds of crimes against persons (in this chapter):
   A. Sexual offenses
   B. Bodily injury crimes
   C. Personal restraint crimes

II. Sex offenses
   A. The history of rape law
      1. Originally, only narrowly defined rape and sodomy
         a. Rape—forced heterosexual vaginal penetration of women not married to the rapist
         b. Sodomy—anal intercourse between males
      2. The elements of common-law rape
         a. Intentional vaginal intercourse
         b. Between a man with a woman not his wife
         c. Achieved by force or threat of serious bodily harm
         d. Without the woman's consent
      3. Victims could testify against rapists, but the woman's credibility depended on three conditions that were difficult (if not impossible) to prove:
         a. Her chastity
         b. Whether she reported the rape promptly
         c. Whether the rape was corroborated by other testimony

4. Force and resistance standard—focused on the woman's consent
  a. Utmost resistance standard (1600s–1950s)—victims had to prove by resistance to the utmost they didn't consent
  b. Reasonable resistance standard (1950s–1970s)—amount of required resistance depended on the circumstances of each case
5. Rape and related sex offense law reforms (1970s–1980s)
  a. Changes in prosecution procedures
    (1) Abolished the corroboration rule
    (2) Relaxed the prompt reporting rule
    (3) Banned introduction of evidence of the victim's past sexual conduct through rape shield laws
  b. Changes in the definition of rape and related sex offenses
    (1) Marital rape exception (husbands can't rape wives) abolished in some states
    (2) Consolidated criminal sexual conduct statutes
      (a) All nonconsensual sexual penetrations and contacts included
      (b) Sex offenses made gender-neutral
      (c) Seriousness of offense divided into several degrees, graded by
        i. Penetration (more serious) and contact (less serious)
        ii. Use of force (more serious)
        iii. Physical injury aggravates crime

B. The elements of modern rape law
  1. Rape *actus reus,* two parts
    a. Sexual penetration, however slight
    b. By force or *threat* of force
      (1) "Intrinsic" in some jurisdictions—only the amount of physical exertion to achieve penetration in nonconsensual sex needed
      (2) "Extrinsic" in some jurisdictions—some force in addition to the amount of exertion to achieve nonconsensual penetration needed
    c. No force or threat required if victim is insane or tricked
  2. Rape *mens rea*
    a. English rule—specific intent to penetrate with force
    b. Maine rule—strict liability with respect to intent to use force
    c. Middle rule—recklessness or negligence regarding penetration by force
  3. Circumstance—nonconsent by the victim
    a. Formal law—state has to prove nonconsent beyond a reasonable doubt
    b. Informal practice—defendants raise consent by the victim as a defense
    c. Consent doesn't have to be in writing

C. Statutory rape
  1. Victim's immaturity substitutes for the element of consent
  2. Strict liability as to age in most states
  3. A few states allow a defense of reasonable mistake of age

III. Bodily injury crimes
  A. Battery is unwanted and unjustified offensive touching; assault is either an attempted or threatened battery

B. The elements of battery
  1. *Actus reus*
     a. Unlawful touching
     b. Only unauthorized offensive touching (parents and law enforcement officers are authorized)
  2. *Mens rea* varies as to whether it requires purposely, knowingly, recklessly, or negligently offensive touching
C. Grading the seriousness depends on
  1. The degree of injury—mere touching, minor injury, or serious injury
  2. The circumstances of the touching—like injuries caused by loose dogs or drug abuse
D. The elements of assault
  1. Assault requires no touching
  2. Kinds:
     a. Attempted battery elements—having the specific intent to commit battery and taking steps to complete it
     b. Threatened battery elements—intentionally scaring the victim
  3. Victim awareness
     a. Not important in attempted battery because the offense focuses on the physical injury
     b. Indispensable in threatened battery because the offense focuses on fear of the victim
E. The *Model* assault and battery statute
  1. Part of the *Model Penal Code*
  2. Integrates, rationalizes, and grades assault and battery
  3. Takes into account *actus reus, mens rea,* circumstance elements, and criminal harm

IV. Personal restraint crimes
  A. Laws protect the fundamental right of locomotion—the right to come and go as we please
  B. Kidnapping
    1. Elements of common-law kidnapping:
       a. Seizing, carrying away (asportation of), and confining another person
       b. By force or threat of force, fraud, or deception
       c. With the intent to deprive the other person of her or his liberty
    2. Elements of modern kidnapping law
       a. *Actus reus*—asportation requirement recognizes even practically no movement of the victim
       b. *Mens rea*—the specific intent to confine, significantly restrain, or hold victims in secret without the victim's consent
       c. Aggravating circumstances include kidnapping for the purpose of
          (1) Sexual invasion
          (2) Obtaining a hostage
          (3) Obtaining ransom
          (4) Robbing the victim
          (5) Murdering the victim
          (6) Blackmail

       (7) Terrorizing the victim

       (8) Achieving political aims

    3. Grading the seriousness of kidnapping

      a. Simple

      b. Aggravated

  C. False imprisonment

    1. *Actus reus*—keeping another person from moving freely (no asportation requirement)

    2. *Mens rea*—having the specific intent to confine or restrain another person without his consent

 Go to the Criminal Law 8e CD to download this summary outline. The outline has been formatted so that you can add notes to it during class lectures, or later create a customized chapter outline to use while reviewing. Either way, the summary outline will help you understand the "big picture" and fill in the details as you study.

REVIEW QUESTIONS

1. Describe the differences between aggravated and unarmed acquaintance rape.

2. According to Professor David Bryden, under what circumstances is an unarmed acquaintance rapist most likely to escape justice?

3. Identify in chronological order and then define the major definitions of the element of force in the history of rape law.

4. List and describe the main reforms in the procedures of rape prosecution adopted in statutes enacted in the 1970s and the 1980s.

5. List the changes in the definitions of sex offenses adopted in the criminal sexual conduct statutes enacted in the 1970s and the 1980s.

6. Identify three criteria used to grade the seriousness of sex offenses in the criminal conduct statutes of the 1970s and the 1980s.

7. Identify the four elements of modern rape law.

8. Explain the difference between the "extrinsic force" and "intrinsic force" standards in rape *actus reus*.

9. Identify the three different rules regarding the *mens rea* of rape: the English rule, the Maine rule, and the rule in between these two.

10. Explain Susan Estrich's position on the rape *mens rea* requirement.

11. What substitutes for the requirement of force in statutory rape?

12. List the circumstances that qualify rape for the grade of "aggravated rape."

13. Explain the difference between assault and battery.

14. Summarize the variety of definitions of the *actus reus* and *mens rea* of battery that appears in the statutes and court opinions.

15. What criteria determine the seriousness of battery?

16. Explain the difference between attempted battery and threatened battery assault.

17. Explain the difference between simple and aggravated assault.

18. What's the basic value the laws against crimes of kidnapping and false imprisonment are aimed at protecting?

19. How and why have the modern interpretations changed the asportation requirement in kidnapping? Be specific.

20. What's the difference between false imprisonment and kidnapping?

KEY TERMS

battery p. 333
common-law rape p. 333
common-law sodomy p. 334
criminal sexual conduct statutes
   p. 334
aggravated rape p. 334
unarmed acquaintance rape p. 334
element of consent p. 336
utmost resistance standard p. 336
reasonable resistance standard
   p. 337
corroboration rule p. 337
rape shield statutes p. 337

prompt reporting rule p. 337
marital rape exception p. 337
sexual penetration p. 338
criminal sexual contact p. 338
rape *actus reus* p. 339
extrinsic force standard p. 339
intrinsic force standard p. 339
specific-intent crime p. 345
statutory rape p. 349
defense of reasonable mistake of
   age p. 349
simple rape (second degree)
   p. 353

aggravated rape (first degree)
   p. 353
assault p. 353
attempted battery assault p. 355
threatened battery assault p. 355
intentional scaring p. 355
stalking p. 355
right of locomotion p. 362
kidnapping p. 362
asportation p. 364
false imprisonment p. 367

SUGGESTED READINGS

 Go the Criminal Law 8e CD for Suggested Readings for this chapter.

THE COMPANION WEB SITE
FOR *CRIMINAL LAW*, EIGHTH EDITION

http://cj.wadsworth.com/samaha/crim_law8e

 Supplement your review of this chapter by going to the companion Web site to take one of the Tutorial Quizzes, use the flash cards to test your knowledge of the elements of various crimes and defenses, and check out the many other study aids you'll find there. You'll find valuable data and resources at your fingertips to help you study for that big exam or write that important paper.

Crimes Against Property

Chapter Main Points

- Crimes against property are one of three types: taking it, damaging or destroying it, or invading it.
- "New" property crimes are really only new ways of committing the three original types of crimes; so computer and Internet crimes consist of taking, damaging or destroying, or invading other people's computers or information stored on them.
- Theft is a specific-intent crime; it requires the intent to keep other people's property permanently.
- Keeping property already stolen by someone else still is regarded as taking other people's property.
- Getting other people's money by making false documents (forgery) or uttering (passing) false documents is a crime.
- Robbery and extortion are crimes against persons *and* their property.
- Arson (damaging or destroying other people's buildings by fire, explosives, or other "dangerous means") is a felony; criminal mischief (destroying or tampering with other people's "stuff" or causing money loss by "expensive practical jokes" or false threats) is a misdemeanor.
- Unwanted presence is at the heart of crimes of invasion of property, even when there's no taking, damaging, or destroying other people's property.

Did He "Trespass" by Computer Hacking?

Cal Edwards, Director of Engineering at Telco, observed that Telco's general access number was being dialed at regular intervals of approximately 40 seconds. After each dialing, a different 6-digit number was entered, followed by a certain long distance number. Edwards observed similar activity on January 10, between 10 P.M. and 6 A.M. From his past experience, Edwards recognized this activity as characteristic of that of a "computer hacker" attempting to obtain the individualized 6-digit access codes of Telco's customers. Edwards surmised that the hacker was using a computer and modem to dial Telco's general access number, a randomly selected 6-digit number, and a long distance number. Then, by recording which 6-digit numbers enabled the long distance call to be put through successfully, the hacker was able to obtain the valid individual access codes of Telco's customers. The hacker could then use those codes fraudulently to make long distance calls that would be charged improperly to Telco's paying customers. ◆

THE THREE TYPES OF PROPERTY CRIMES

All specific property crimes are one of three types of offenses against other people's property:

1. Taking it

2. Damaging and/or destroying it

3. Invading it

The individual crimes discussed in the chapter are arranged according to these three types, so keep this big picture in mind as you read.

One other point before we start our journey through the vast land of property crimes. We often call identity theft, computer hacking, and Internet crimes "new crimes," but the chapter opener illustrates that they're really only variations (admittedly sometimes very complex variations) of one of these three ancient types of crimes against property. According to *The Electronic Frontier* (2000):

> Advances in technology—the advent of the automobile and the telephone for instance—have always given wrongdoers new means for engaging in unlawful conduct. The internet is no different: it is simply a new medium through which traditional crimes can now be committed....

TAKING OTHER PEOPLE'S PROPERTY

All crimes of taking someone else's property descend from **larceny**—the ancient crime of sneaking away with (stealing) someone else's property without their consent. Larceny was born as the common-law instrument to protect the Anglo-Saxons' most valuable possession—livestock. People who lived on the western frontier in the United States centuries later placed a similar value on cattle and horses. The disgrace attached to thieves of these valuable possessions still lingered when I was young, voiced in the epithet "horse thief," meaning a dishonest or untrustworthy person (LaFave and Scott 1986, chap. 8; Perkins and Boyce 1982, chap. 4).

"Larceny," however, left two big gaps in efforts to criminalize taking other people's property: taking it by force (as opposed to sneaking away with it) and keeping property an owner had voluntarily handed over to a caretaker. Larceny couldn't protect against the exploding range and quantities of valuable possessions (**tangible property**) and money, checks, and other paper (worth nothing by itself but it was proof of something of value—**intangible property**) that clever people could get their hands on.

Early in its history, taking property by force grew into the felony we still call **robbery**—a violent felony committed against individuals and their property (Hall 1952). The second gap, taking property voluntarily handed over to caretakers (embezzlement, false pretenses, fraud), grew into an enormous problem as society became more complex. These **abuse-of-trust crimes** by caretakers are the first examples of what eventually became **white-collar crimes**—crimes growing out of opportunities to get someone else's property provided by the perpetrator's occupation. Although the term was first used to refer only to business executives, it's now used to include property crimes that grow out of opportunities created by any lawful occupation. Statutes and courts are still creating new crimes to combat the same old evil of satisfying the excessive desire to get other people's property by the new methods of stealing their identities and using computers and the Internet.

In this section, we'll look more closely at the crimes of taking other people's property: larceny; white-collar crimes; theft, including identity theft and theft by computers and the Internet; receiving stolen property; forgery and uttering; robbery; and extortion.

Larceny

For 500 years, larceny has been defined as wrongfully taking (**trespassory taking**) and carrying away (**asportation**) someone else's property with the intent to permanently keep it. Let's look at the three elements this definition boils down to: *actus reus, mens rea,* and the circumstance elements related to the type and value of property involved.

Larceny *Actus Reus*

Larceny *actus reus* consists of two parts:

1. Taking

2. Carrying away (sometimes called asportation)

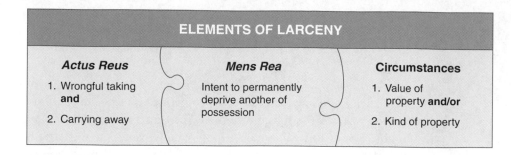

ELEMENTS OF LARCENY

Actus Reus	Mens Rea	Circumstances
1. Wrongful taking **and**	Intent to permanently deprive another of possession	1. Value of property **and/or**
2. Carrying away		2. Kind of property

Taking requires getting control—if only briefly—of someone else's property. Taking includes direct actions like picking a pocket, lifting objects from a shop, or stealing a car. But sometimes, indirect takings are enough. For example, suppose I see someone's unlocked bike parked outside a shop. I offer to sell the bicycle to an unsuspecting passerby for forty dollars. She accepts my offer, pays me the money, and gets on the bike. In most states, I've taken the bike as soon as she gets on the bicycle, even though I never touched it.

Carrying away means moving someone else's property from the place where it was taken. Carrying the property a short distance, even a few inches, is enough. All that's required is that the property actually be moved from the exact spot where it was taken. So, a pickpocket who got the money only partway out wasn't guilty, because he didn't move it from its original position. Another man who tried to steal a barrel wasn't guilty, because he'd only turned the barrel on its side so he could pick it up more easily. A woman who tried to walk off with a watch she didn't know was chained to the counter in a store took the watch, but she didn't "carry it away."

In *People v. Olivo* (1981), the New York Court of Appeals (New York state's highest court) dealt with the element of taking in larceny.

| *Did the Shoplifters Wrongfully Take the Property?*

People v. Olivo
420 N.E. 2d 40 (N.Y. 1981)

Ronald Olivo, Stefan Gasparik, and George Spatzier were convicted of petit larceny.* The N.Y. Supreme Court (New York's intermediate appellate court) affirmed. The New York Court of Appeals, New York's highest court, affirmed.

COOKE, CJ.

---

*Petit larceny refers to the amount of money—namely, a small amount—as opposed to grand larceny, or a larger amount. This is discussed in the "Circumstance Element: 'Property' and Its Value" section of Larceny.

FACTS

In *People v. Olivo*, the defendant was observed by a security guard in the hardware area of a department store. Initially conversing with another person, defendant began to look around furtively when his acquaintance departed. The security agent continued to observe and saw defendant assume a crouching position, take a set of wrenches and secret it in his clothes. After again looking around, defendant began walking toward an exit, passing a number of cash registers en route. When defendant did not stop to pay for the merchandise, the officer accosted him a few feet from the exit. In response to the guard's inquiry, he denied having the wrenches, but as he proceeded to the security office, defendant removed the wrenches and placed them under his jacket. At trial, defendant testified that he had placed the tools under his arm and was in line at a cashier when apprehended. The jury returned a verdict of guilty on the charge of petit larceny. The conviction was affirmed by Appellate Term.

In *People v. Gasparik*, defendant was in a department store trying on a leather jacket. Two store detectives observed him tear off the price tag and remove a "sensor-matic" device designed to set off an alarm if the jacket were carried through a detection machine. There was at least one such machine at the exit of each floor. Defendant placed the tag and the device in the pocket of another jacket on the merchandise rack. He took his own jacket, which he had been carrying with him, and placed it on a table. Leaving his own jacket, defendant put on the leather jacket and walked through the store, still on the same floor, bypassing several cash registers. When he headed for the exit from that floor, in the direction of the main floor, he was apprehended by security personnel. At trial, defendant denied removing the price tag and the sensormatic device from the jacket, and testified that he was looking for a cashier without a long line when he was stopped. The court, sitting without a jury, convicted defendant of petit larceny. Appellate Term affirmed.

In *People v. Spatzier*, defendant entered a bookstore on Fulton Street in Hempstead carrying an attaché case. The two co-owners of the store observed the defendant in a ceiling mirror as he browsed through the store. They watched defendant remove a book from the shelf, look up and down the aisle, and place the book in his case. He then placed the case at his feet and continued to browse. One of the owners approached defendant and accused him of stealing the book. An altercation ensued and when defendant allegedly struck the owner with the attaché case, the case opened and the book fell out. At trial, defendant denied secreting the book in his case and claimed that the owner had suddenly and unjustifiably accused him of stealing. The jury found defendant guilty of petit larceny, and the conviction was affirmed by the Appellate Term.

OPINION

These cases present a recurring question in this era of the self-service store which has never been resolved by this court: may a person be convicted of larceny for shoplifting if the person is caught with goods while still inside the store? For reasons outlined below, it is concluded that a larceny conviction may be sustained, in certain situations, even though the shoplifter was apprehended before leaving the store.

The primary issue in each case is whether the evidence, viewed in the light most favorable to the prosecution, was sufficient to establish the elements of larceny as defined by the Penal Law.*

... Larceny at common law was defined as a trespassory taking and carrying away of the property of another with intent to steal it. The early common-law courts apparently viewed larceny as defending society against breach of the peace, rather than protecting individual property rights, and therefore placed heavy emphasis upon the requirement of a trespassory taking. As the reach of larceny expanded, the intent element of the crime became of increasing importance, while the requirement of a trespassory taking became less significant.... During this evolutionary process, the purpose served by the crime of larceny obviously shifted from protecting society's peace to general protection of property rights....

This evolution is particularly relevant to thefts occurring in modern self-service stores. In stores of that type, customers are impliedly invited to examine, try on, and carry about the merchandise on display. Thus in a sense, the owner has consented to the customer's possession of the goods for a limited purpose. That the owner has consented to that possession does not, however, preclude a conviction for larceny. If the customer exercises dominion and control wholly inconsistent with the continued rights of the owner, and the other elements of the crime are present, a larceny has occurred.

Such conduct on the part of a customer satisfies the "taking" element of the crime. It is this element that forms the core of the controversy in these cases. The defendants argue, in essence, that the crime is not established, as a matter of law, unless there is evidence that the customer departed the shop without paying for the merchandise.

Although this court has not addressed the issue, case law from other jurisdictions seems unanimous in holding that a shoplifter need not leave the store to be guilty of larceny. This is because a shopper may treat merchandise in a manner inconsistent with the owner's continued rights—and in a manner not in accord with that of prospective purchaser—without actually walking out of the store.

Under these principles, there was ample evidence in each case to raise a factual question as to the defendants' guilt. In *People v. Olivo*, defendant not only concealed goods in his clothing, but he did so in a particularly suspicious manner. And, when defendant was stopped, he was moving towards the door, just three feet short of exiting the store.

---

*[§ 155.05 of New York Penal Law, subdivision 1, provides: "A person steals property and commits larceny when, with intent to deprive another of property or to appropriate the same to himself or to a third person, he wrongfully takes, obtains or withholds such property from an owner thereof."]

In *People v. Gasparik*, defendant removed the price tag and sensor device from a jacket, abandoned his own garment, put the jacket on and ultimately headed for the main floor of the store. Removal of the price tag and sensor device, and careful concealment of those items, is highly unusual and suspicious conduct for a shopper. Coupled with defendant's abandonment of his own coat and his attempt to leave the floor, those factors were sufficient to make out a prima facie case of taking.

In *People v. Spatzier*, defendant concealed a book in an attaché case. Unaware that he was being observed in an overhead mirror, defendant looked furtively up and down the aisle before secreting the book. In these circumstances, given the manner in which defendant concealed the book and his suspicious behavior, the evidence was not insufficient as a matter of law.

In sum, in view of the modern definition of the crime of larceny, and its purpose of protecting individual property rights, a taking of property in the self-service store context can be established by evidence that a customer exercised control over merchandise wholly inconsistent with the store's continued rights. Quite simply, a customer who crosses the line between the limited right he or she has to deal with merchandise and the store owner's rights may be subject to prosecution for larceny. Such a rule should foster the legitimate interests and continued operation of self-service shops, a convenience which most members of the society enjoy.

Accordingly, in each case, the order of the Appellate Term should be AFFIRMED.

Questions

1. Summarize the evidence relevant to deciding whether Olivo, Gasparik, and Spatzier "took" and "carried away" the stores' property.

2. Summarize the court's reasons for adopting the rule that shoplifters don't have to leave a store before they've "taken" property.

3. What rule would you adopt? Why?

◆   ◆   ◆

One final note on larceny *actus reus*. Larceny law doesn't follow the old rhyme, "Finders keepers, losers weepers." Lost property is still the owners.' So, those who take and carry away lost money or other property still satisfy the *actus reus* of larceny.

Larceny *Mens Rea*

Common-law larceny is a specific-intent crime. Thieves have to intend to *permanently* deprive someone of her property. So, intent to *temporarily* take someone else's property isn't larceny. Statutes make the intent to temporarily take someone else's property a lesser offense. **Joyriding** statutes are the typical example. It's a crime, although not as serious as larceny, to take a vehicle to drive around for a short while, fully intending to return it. The joyrider lacks the larceny *mens rea*—the intent to permanently deprive the owner of possession.

Circumstance Element: "Property" and Its Value

Common-law larceny applied only to tangible (property valuable in itself) personal property. So, you couldn't steal real estate or anything attached to it; intangible personal property (paper not valuable in itself but proof of something of value, like stocks and bonds and checks); services; or labor.

Modern statutes have greatly expanded the property you can steal. The Texas Penal Code (2003, § 31.01[5]), for example, includes:

- Land

- Anything severed from the land

- Documents, including money, that represent or embody anything of value

- Services, including labor or professional services; telecommunication, public utility, and transportation services; lodging, restaurant services, and entertainment; and the supply of a motor vehicle or other property for use

The value of the property stolen usually determines the seriousness of the crime: the higher the value, the more serious the larceny. **Grand larceny,** a felony punishable by one year or more in prison, includes property exceeding a dollar amount, typically between $100 and $400. Property worth less than the designated amount for grand larceny is usually included in the misdemeanor of **petty larceny,** which is punishable by less than one year in jail or a fine, or both. The dividing line between grand and petty larceny differs from state to state. In South Carolina, for example, the dividing line is $1,000 (South Carolina Code of Laws 2004 [16-13-30]); in Pennsylvania, it's $2,000 (Pennsylvania Criminal Code 2004, § 3903).

The line between grand and petty larceny isn't always drawn according to dollar amounts. Sometimes it's the kind of property taken. In Texas, for example, stealing natural oil, no matter what the value, is grand larceny. The California Penal Code (2004, § 487) provides that grand larceny is stealing property worth more than $400, but it's also grand larceny to steal avocados, olives, citrus or deciduous fruits, vegetables, artichokes, nuts, or other farm crops worth more than $100.

Larceny doesn't just protect property itself; it also protects who and where the property's taken from. So, taking property directly from a person (pickpocketing) and taking property from a home are always felonies. These cases reflect the high value we place not just on our property but on our bodies and homes.

White-Collar Crimes

Larceny is about taking someone else's property without their consent, but what about property taken by someone you handed it over to voluntarily—like when a bank clerk takes money out of your account, or an attendant takes the car you left for her to park? Until an English statute of 1799, neither the clerk nor the attendant committed larceny. Larceny's ancient origins explain why: There were no banks or parking lots.

The shift from rural, agrarian, sparsely populated communities to urban, commercial, and industrial society with its banks, businesses, services, and concentrated populations created the need to rely on others to conduct the daily business of ordinary life. Both those who owned and those who possessed property left it with caretakers for a number of purposes: safekeeping, shipping, repair, and storage. They trusted these caretakers to carry out the purpose for which the property was left with them. The common law and then increasingly statute law created new crimes—such as embezzlement, false pretenses, receiving stolen property, and forgery—to punish these new forms of taking other people's property by abuse of trust.

We'll look at embezzlement and false pretenses in this section. Later, we'll examine receiving stolen property and forgery after our discussion of theft.

Embezzlement

The English Parliament created embezzlement (the first "white-collar crime") during the period when temporary possessors (legally known as **bailees**) were becoming a huge part of an advancing commercial and industrial age. The crime of **embezzlement** brought larceny up to date by making it a crime for parking lot attendants, dry cleaners, auto repair people, bank tellers, and many others to take advantage of their job or profession lawfully to get possession of someone else's property and then keep it for (convert it to) their own use.

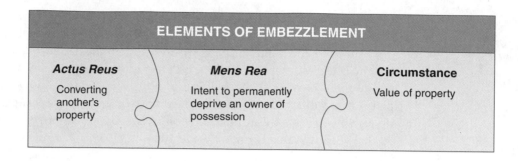

ELEMENTS OF EMBEZZLEMENT

Actus Reus	***Mens Rea***	**Circumstance**
Converting another's property	Intent to permanently deprive an owner of possession	Value of property

Legally, **conversion** of someone else's property in embezzlement substitutes for "taking" in larceny. Notice that conversion can only happen *after* possession is lawfully acquired. Embezzlers acquire possession for a specific purpose—to keep money, repair a car, dry-clean clothes, and so on—and then convert the property to their own use or profit. Conversion breaches the trust placed in caretakers. The breach of trust is just as bad, some say worse, as sneaking away with (taking) someone else's property.

False Pretenses

Larceny covers those who sneak away with someone else's property. Embezzlement covers those who keep permanently someone else's property that they have only a temporary right to possess. But, what about owners who are deceived into giving up possession or ownership? The deceivers haven't "taken" the property, because the owners have willingly given it to them. They haven't converted it either, because they didn't even have a temporary right to possess it. The crime of obtaining property by **false pretenses** (also called **theft by deceit**) fills the gap in criminally getting other people's property left by larceny and embezzlement.

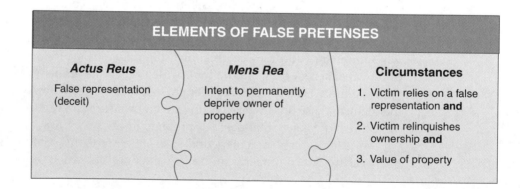

ELEMENTS OF FALSE PRETENSES

Actus Reus	***Mens Rea***	**Circumstances**
False representation (deceit)	Intent to permanently deprive owner of property	1. Victim relies on a false representation **and** 2. Victim relinquishes ownership **and** 3. Value of property

In the *actus reus* of getting someone else's property by false pretenses, *deceiving* replaces *taking* in larceny and *converting* in embezzlement. Deception requires a lie, like making a promise to deliver something when you can't or don't intend to keep the promise. Technically, the law often expresses the *actus reus* as falsely representing a past or existing fact. The false pretenses *mens rea* requires the purpose or specific intent to obtain property by deceit and lies. In addition to *actus reus* and *mens rea*, false pretenses includes three circumstance elements. Victims have to part with property; they have to part with it because they believed the lie, and the property they parted with has to be worth an amount named in the false pretenses statute.

Obtaining property by false pretenses is usually (but not always) a white-collar crime. In *State v. Watson* (1997), Watson took advantage of his job to get someone else's property.

Did He Attempt to Steal by Deceit?

State v. Watson
WL 342497 (Mo.App. W.D. 1997)

Following a jury trial before the Circuit Court, Clay County, Andre Watson was convicted of attempted stealing by deceit and was sentenced to one year in the county jail. He appealed. The Court of Appeals affirmed the conviction.

ULRICH, CJ.

FACTS

In June 1995, Andre Watson was employed by A.B. May Sales and Service Company, a heating and air retailer, as an installer's helper. A.B. May purchases furnaces, air conditioners, humidifiers, and other parts used to repair and maintain equipment from Comfort Products, a distributor in Missouri and Kansas for Carrier Heating and Air. A.B. May places its orders with Comfort Products over the telephone using a purchase order system. Purchase order numbers are generated by A.B. May at the time an order is placed.

Bobbie Brakenbury, an employee of Comfort Products, received an order by telephone from a man named "Brian" on June 6, 1995. The man said he worked for A.B. May. The man placed an order for six condensing units, six furnaces, six coils, and six humidifiers. The caller ascribed A.B. May purchase order number 9400 to the order. The cost of the order was approximately $12,000.

Later, Ms. Brakenbury discovered that the coils ordered by the man did not match the size of the furnaces. She called A.B. May and asked to speak with "Brian." There was no employee at A.B. May named "Brian," however, so Ms. Brakenbury spoke with Trent Bryant who normally places the equipment orders for A.B. May. Mr. Bryant informed her that purchase order number 9400 was assigned to Lennox, another vendor, and not Comfort Products. The

order was then "put on hold" until the validity of the order was determined.

Mr. Watson was working on an installation job in Prairie Village as an installer's helper on the same day. Just before lunch, the installer and Mr. Watson determined what additional parts they would need to complete the job. Mr. Watson was then sent to acquire the parts. During the lunch hour, Mr. Watson was involved in an automobile accident and did not return to work.

The next day, June 7, 1995, Mr. Watson arrived at Comfort Products requesting to pick up the six systems ordered by Brian. The warehouse manager, Thomas Dunmire, recognized Mr. Watson because he had been to Comfort Products on many occasions to get parts and equipment. Mr. Watson drove an A.B. May truck and was dressed in shorts and an A.B. May shirt with the name "Bill" printed on it.

Because the order was on hold, Mr. Dunmire informed Mr. Watson that there was a problem with the paper work and that he would have to wait a few minutes. Mr. Watson made a phone call, said he would be back in fifteen minutes, and departed. He did not return.

In the meantime, Ms. Brakenbury called Shane Coughlin, the chief financial officer at A.B. May, to confirm the order. Because the purchase order number was assigned to a different vendor and the cost of the order was approximately ten times larger than the normal $1500 order to Comfort Products, appropriate authority at Comfort Products concluded the order was not legitimate. Further inquiry at A.B. May disclosed that no one at the company was authorized to purchase six air conditioners and furnaces from Comfort Products on June 6 or 7, 1995.

Mr. Watson did not return to work at A.B. May except for part of a day on June 15, 1995. Attempts by A.B. May personnel to contact Mr. Watson by telephone failed. Ultimately, Mr. Watson was charged with attempted stealing

TAKING OTHER PEOPLE'S PROPERTY ◆ **381**

by deceit. At trial, Mr. Watson testified in his own defense. He claimed that on June 7, 1995, he was at home recuperating from the automobile accident that occurred the previous day.

OPINION

... Mr. Watson was convicted of attempted stealing by deceit. "A person is guilty of attempt to commit an offense when, with the purpose of committing the offense, he does any act which is a substantial step towards the commission of the offense." 564.011.1, RSMo 1994. The crime of stealing is committed if a person

> appropriates property or services of another with the purpose to deprive him thereof, either without his consent or by means of deceit or coercion. 570.030.1, RSMo 1994.

Deceit is defined as

> purposely making a representation which is false and which the actor does not believe to be true and upon which the victim relies, as to a matter of fact, law, value, intention or other state of mind. 570.010(6), RSMo 1994.

Mr. Watson contends that the evidence was insufficient to prove that he had the intent to deceive or that he knew or should have known that he did not have authority to pick up the furnaces and air conditioners. The subjective intent of a defendant to deceive may be proven by circumstantial evidence. The evidence presented in this case showed that an invalid order for six systems consisting of furnaces, air conditioners, coils, and humidifiers was placed with Comfort Products on June 6, 1995, by a man who identified himself as "Brian" from A.B. May. A.B. May did not have an employee named Brian on June 6, 1995, and no A.B. May employee had authority on June 6 or 7, 1995, to purchase six systems. The purchase order number provided was 9400, and the value of the six systems was about $12,000.00.

The evidence also established that Mr. Watson was working in Prairie Village for A.B. May on June 6 and was asked by his supervisor to order parts to complete the job and to get them. He did not return to work that day because he was involved in an automobile accident.

The next day, Mr. Watson arrived at Comfort Products to obtain six systems that included six furnaces, six coils and six air conditioners. He wore an A.B. May shirt with the name "Bill" printed on it and was not wearing the pants that are the normal uniform A.B. May employees wear. He was informed that the order was "on hold" because of a problem with the paper work. Mr. Watson left and did not return. Mr. Watson did not return to work at A.B. May except for part of June 15.

This evidence was sufficient for a reasonable juror to have concluded that Mr. Watson made a substantial act to steal six systems by deceit. From the evidence, a reasonable inference could have been drawn that Mr. Watson knowingly made a false representation that he had A.B. May's authorization to acquire the furnaces and air conditioners from Comfort Products. The trial court, therefore, did not err in overruling Mr. Watson's motion for judgment of acquittal at the close of all the evidence.

The judgment of conviction is AFFIRMED.

Questions

1. State the definitions of "stealing" and "deceit" as the Missouri statute defines them.

2. List all the evidence relevant to prove Watson attempted to "steal" by "deceit."

3. Assume you're the prosecutor, and argue there's proof a reasonable juror could find Watson attempted to steal by deceit under Missouri law.

4. Now, assume you're Watson's lawyer, and argue there's a reasonable doubt he stole by deceit.

◆   ◆   ◆

Theft

In most criminal codes, larceny, embezzlement, and obtaining property by false pretenses were distinct offenses until the 1970s. Although all three involved wrongfully getting other people's property (taking in larceny, converting in embezzlement, and deceiving in false pretenses), they were considered different enough to require separate provisions in criminal codes. The truth is, there's a lot more history than reason behind separating these three ways to get other people's property into different crimes. As we saw earlier, when society changed, embezzlement supplemented larceny, and then theft by deceit (false pretenses) supplemented both larceny and embezzlement to fight the new ways of unlawfully taking other people's money.

Most states have made some effort to turn away from classifying based on history toward logic by consolidating larceny, embezzlement, and false pretenses into one offense called **theft**. These consolidated theft statutes do away with the artificial need to decide whether property was "taken and carried away," "converted," or "swindled." They accept the social reality that they're all aimed at the same criminal offense—wrongfully getting someone else's property. Here's California's consolidated theft statute:

> [E]very person who shall feloniously steal the personal property of another, or who shall fraudulently appropriate property which has been entrusted to him, or who shall knowingly and designedly, by any false or fraudulent representation or pretense, defraud any other person of money, labor or real or personal property, shall be guilty of theft.
>
> California Penal Code 2004, § 484

The *Model Penal Code* (American Law Institute [ALI] 1985) theft provision is even more ambitious. It includes all nonviolent thefts: larceny, embezzlement, false pretenses, extortion, blackmail, receiving stolen property, keeping lost property, and temporarily using other people's property without consent. Only robbery—because it's a violent crime—has its own section.

Let's look at two "new" forms of theft that are growing at an alarming rate: identity theft and theft by the computer or the Internet.

Identify Theft

Identity theft means stealing someone else's property by first stealing their identity. There are plenty of indications that this new way to commit the ancient crime of getting other people's money is on the rise. California's attorney general Bill Lockyer (2001) reports that

> Despite historic lows in violent crime rates, Californians today are more at risk than ever of becoming a victim of crime. The fastest growing crime wave in our state and America today is the crime of identity theft. An estimated 750,000 Americans per year are victims of identity theft schemes, up from 40,000 in 1992—an 18-fold increase. (238)

The key to someone else getting your property is their getting your personal information (ID 2003), and that's easy to do according to Lockyer (2001):

> What makes identity theft so devastating is the ease with which criminals can perpetrate the offense and the enormous damage that can be inflicted upon its victims. Thieves can steal wallets, snatch your mail with your bank and credit card statements, complete a "change of address form" to divert your mail to another location, "dumpster dive" for personal data and access personal information you share on the Internet. Once in possession of your identifying details, scam artists can use your credit card or open up a new account. They can drain your bank account, establish phone or wireless service, file for bankruptcy, counterfeit checks or debit cards and take out loans—all in your name. For victims, the trauma and hassle associated with restoring your credit, clearing your name or, in some cases, escaping criminal prosecution can take an average of two years to complete. (238)

The Federal Trade Commission (2002) reported the following facts on how thieves steal others' property by stealing their identity (*percentage of victims reporting this type of identity theft):

TABLE 11.1	
Sources of Personal Information Used by Identity Thieves	
Source	**Percentage**
Strangers	80%
Family members	8%
Friends	3%
Neighbors	2%
Roommates	1%
Co-workers	1%

Source: Federal Trade Commission 2002

1. *Credit card.* Get a credit card in your name and charge stuff or services to it (42%*)

2. *Utility service.* Set up service in your name and run up bills before you find out (cell phone service theft reported by victims); regular telephone service (26%*); cable service (12%*)

3. *Bank account.* Open up a checking account in your name and write checks on it before you catch it (13%*)

4. *Loan.* Get a loan in your name for personal, student, or business loan (53%*) or auto loans (28%*)

Table 11.1 lists some of the most popular sources used by identity thieves to get your personal information.

Several states have adopted identity theft statutes. The Wisconsin Court of Appeals interpreted and applied the elements of the Wisconsin statute in *State v. Ramirez* (2001), a case of an illegal immigrant who stole someone else's Social Security number to get a job in a bike shop.

CASE | *Did He Steal the Identity to Get Something of Value?*

State v. Ramirez
633 N.W.2d 656 (Wis.App. 2001)

Alfredo Ramirez, Defendant, was convicted in the Walworth County Circuit Court on his guilty plea to misappropriating the personal identifying information of another person. Ramirez appealed. The Court of Appeals affirmed.

NETTESHEIM J.

FACTS

Ramirez was an illegal resident of the United States and did not have a social security number. On September 2, 1997, Ramirez obtained employment at Trek Bike in Wal-

worth county. On June 4, 1999, a human resources manager at Trek Bike reported to the police that a list of people with corresponding social security numbers had been discovered in the desk of a former employee who had been fired. One of the social security numbers was listed to a Jose Ramirez. A check with the social security administration revealed that this social security number was actually assigned to Benjamin Wulfenstein of Elko, Nevada. In an interview with the police, Ramirez stated that Jose Ramirez was his cousin and that Jose had sent him the social security card two years earlier. Ramirez admitted that he had used Wulfenstein's social security number when he applied for employment at Trek Bike. Trek Bike terminated Ramirez on July 6, 1999.

Based on this information, the State charged Ramirez with intentionally misappropriating the personal identifying information of an individual to obtain a thing of value without the individual's consent pursuant to Wis. Stat. § 943.201(2). Wisconsin Stat. § 943.201(2) reads as follows:

Whoever intentionally uses or attempts to use any personal identifying information or personal identification document of an individual to obtain credit, money, goods, services or anything else of value without the authorization or consent of the individual and by representing that he or she is the individual or is acting with the authorization or consent of the individual is guilty of a Class D felony.

The complaint and information alleged that the offense occurred between the dates of Ramirez's employment, September 2, 1997 to July 6, 1999.

OPINION

... We first determine whether Ramirez obtained a thing of value as the result of his unauthorized use of Wulfenstein's social security number. Ramirez contends that all he obtained was a job, which he describes as "the opportunity to work." He says, "A job has no intrinsic value if it is obtained and then the employee squanders the opportunity and never begins to work. What makes a job valuable is the opportunity to work hard and earn money." We think this is far too narrow a concept of the value of Ramirez's employment at Trek Bike. True, Ramirez obtained employment at Trek Bike. But what Ramirez ultimately sought and obtained was the compensation and other economic benefits that flowed from the employment. Obviously these were things of value within the meaning of § 943.201(2)....

Wisconsin Stat. § 943.201(2) makes it a crime to intentionally use the personal identifying information or document of another for purposes of obtaining "credit, money, goods, services or anything else of value" without the consent of the other person and by representing that the actor is the other person or is acting with the consent or authorization of such person. This crime has four elements:

(1) the defendant's intentional use of the personal identifying information or document;

(2) the defendant's use of such information to obtain credit, money, goods, services, or anything else of value;

(3) the defendant's use of such information without the authorization or consent of the other person; and

(4) the defendant's intentional representation that he or she was the other person or acted with such person's authorization or consent.

... Ramirez concedes that he intentionally used Wulfenstein's social security number to conceal his illegal resident status and his true identity in order to obtain employment at Trek Bike and that he did so without Wulfenstein's consent or authorization. Rather, it is the second element that lies at the heart of this case. This element requires that the defendant "obtain credit, money, goods, services or anything else of value."

While Wis. Stat. § 943.201(2) may be clear enough as to what it criminalizes, it is not so clear as to whether it creates a continuing offense. ... Wis. Stat. § 943.201(2) requires that as a consequence of the identity theft, the defendant must have obtained "credit, money, goods, services or anything else of value." Common sense would advise that in most cases of identify theft, that consequence will be a recurring, not an isolated, event. This suggests that the statute creates a continuing offense.

We therefore conclude that the statute is ambiguous as to whether it creates a continuing offense. In that situation, we must ascertain the legislative intent from the language of the statute in relation to its scope, history, context, subject matter and object intended to be accomplished. The legislative history of Wis. Stat. § 943.201(2) does not expressly speak to the issue of whether the legislation creates a continuous offense. However, the legislative history includes an article from the *Los Angeles Times* concerning proposed identify theft legislation in California. The article was made a part of the legislative history file of § 943.201(2) by the author of the proposed Wisconsin legislation. This article is informative because it speaks of the ongoing harm inflicted on victims of identify theft.

With just a few key information coordinates, a crook can start phone service in your name, open charge cards, take over your existing credit lines and change the address on hijacked accounts so statements go to a mail drop....

The actual number of consumers affected and volume of loss have increased, however, as the industry surges toward $2 trillion a year in transactions. Incidents of identity fraud—the kind that leaves consumers most helpless—were reported at one major company to have risen 540% in the U.S. during the first half of 1995, and industry wide it is estimated to account for as much as $90 million of the $1.5 billion written off as card fraud losses, according to various industry sources. Patric Hedlund, *Identity Crisis*, L.A. TIMES, Mar. 11, 1997.

This history reveals that Wis. Stat. § 943.201(2) was targeted at much more than the isolated act of misappropriating the personal identifying information of another or the initial receipt by the defendant of a thing of value as a result of the misappropriation. Rather, the legislation addressed a problem of much larger proportion with far greater consequences. Given this scope, history, context, and legislative objective of the statute, we conclude that the legislature envisioned that the theft of a person's identity would, in many instances, produce recurring episodes in which the defendant would obtain things of value as a result of the original act of identity theft. Hence, the statutory language, "to obtain credit, money, goods, services or anything else of value."

. . . As a result of his unauthorized use of Wulfenstein's social security number, Ramirez obtained money in the form of wages from Trek Bike over the course of his employment and after the effective date of the statute. Absent Ramirez's unauthorized use of Wulfenstein's social security number, Trek Bike could not have legally hired Ramirez. . . .

We hold that Ramirez obtained money in the form of wages, not merely the opportunity for employment, as the result of his unauthorized use of Wulfenstein's personal identifying information.

Judgment AFFIRMED.

Questions

1. Identify the four elements of the Wisconsin identity theft statute.

2. Summarize the court's reasons for concluding that Ramirez stole "something of value."

3. Summarize Ramirez's arguments claiming he didn't steal anything of value.

4. In your opinion, which argument is more persuasive? Defend your answer.

Theft by Computers and the Internet

The vast expansion of computers and the exponential growth of the Internet have created great opportunities for good, but, like all good things, they've created new opportunities for evil as well. These new opportunities are already making it difficult for the laws of privacy and copyrights and the relationship between states and the federal government to keep up with the real world. The same is true of the law of theft. Every day, new opportunities to take **intellectual property**—information and services stored in and transmitted to and from electronic data banks—show how far short even the most advanced theft laws fall.

Some states have attempted to deal with crimes by computers and the Internet by expanding the interpretation of the elements of the common-law crimes of larceny, embezzlement, and false pretenses. For example, in *Hancock v. Texas* (1966), the court ruled that computer programs are property for purposes of larceny.

Most states, however, have concluded that trying to shoehorn computer crimes into the law of theft isn't enough. So, most states have enacted specific **computer crimes statutes,** with parts specifically aimed at computer theft. The Arkansas legislature (Benson, Jablon, Kaplan, and Rosenthal 1997, 439) stated its purpose for enacting a specific computer crimes statute:

> It is found and determined that computer-related crime poses a major problem for business and government; that losses for each incident of computer-related crime are potentially astronomical; that the opportunities for computer-related crime in business and government through the introduction of fraudulent records into a computer system, the unauthorized use of computers, alteration or destruction of computerized information or files, and the stealing of financial instruments, data, and other assets, are great; that computer-related crime has a direct effect on state commerce; and that, while various forms of computer-related crime might possibly be the subject of criminal charges based on other provisions of law, it is appropriate and desirable that a statute be enacted which deals directly with computer-related crime. (n. 147)

The Kansas Supreme Court applied its computer crimes statute in *State v. Allen* (1996).

State v. Allen
917 P.2d 848 (Kans. 1996)

Anthony Allen, the defendant, was charged with felony computer crime. The Johnson District Court dismissed the complaint, and the state appealed. The Kansas Supreme Court affirmed.

LARSON, J.

FACTS

Allen admitted to Detective Kent Willnauer that he had used his computer, equipped with a modem, to call various Southwestern Bell computer modems. The telephone numbers for the modems were obtained by random dialing. If one of Allen's calls were completed, his computer determined if it had been answered by voice or another computer. These were curiosity calls of short duration.

The State presented no evidence which showed that Allen ever had entered any Southwestern Bell computer system. Detective Willnauer was unable to state that Allen had altered any programs, added anything to the system, used it to perform any functions, or interfered with its operation. Willnauer specifically stated he had no evidence that the Southwestern Bell computer system had been damaged.

Ronald W. Knisley, Southwestern Bell's Regional Security Director, testified Allen had called two different types of Southwestern Bell computer equipment—SLC-96 system environmental controls and SMS-800 database systems. The telephone numbers for the SLC-96 systems were thought to be known only to Southwestern Bell employees or agents on a need-to-know basis. Access to the SLC-96 systems required knowledge of a password. If one connected to the system it displayed "KEYWORD?" without any identification or warning. No evidence existed that Allen attempted to respond to the prompt.

Testimony confirmed Allen also called and connected 28 times with the SMS-800 systems at several different modem numbers. Each call but two was under 1 minute. Upon connection with this system, a person would see a log on request and a "banner." The banner identifies the system that has answered the incoming call and displays that it is Southwestern Bell property and that access is restricted. Entry into the system itself then requires both a user ID and a password which must agree with each other. No evidence indicated Allen went beyond this banner or even attempted to enter a user ID or password.

Knisley testified that if entry into an SMS-800 system were accomplished and proper commands were given, a PBX system could be located which would allow unlimited and nonchargeable long distance telephone calls. There was no evidence this occurred, nor was it shown that Allen had damaged, modified, destroyed, or copied any data.

James E. Robinson, Function Manager responsible for computer security, testified one call to an SMS-800 system lasted 6 minutes and 35 seconds. Although the system should have retained information about this call, it did not, leading to speculation the record-keeping system had been overridden. Robinson speculated Allen had gained entry into the system but admitted he had no evidence that Allen's computer had done anything more than sit idle for a few minutes after calling a Southwestern Bell modem number.

Robinson testified that Southwestern Bell was unable to document any damage to its computer equipment or software as a result of Allen's activities. However, as a result of its investigation, Southwestern Bell decided that prudence required it to upgrade its password security system to a more secure "token card" process. It was the cost of this investigation and upgrade that the State alleges comprises the damage caused by Allen's actions. Total investigative costs were estimated at $4,140. The cost of developing deterrents was estimated to be $1,656. The cost to distribute secure ID cards to employees totaled $18,000. Thus, the total estimated damage was $23,796.

In closing arguments, the State admitted Allen did not get into the computer system, nor did he modify, alter, destroy, copy, disclose, or take possession of anything. See K.S.A. 21-3755(b)(1). Instead, the State argued Allen's conduct in acquiring the unlisted numbers and calling them constituted an "approach" to the systems, within the meaning of K.S.A. 21-3755(a)(1), which questioned the integrity of the systems and resulted in the altered or added security precautions.

In its oral ruling, the trial court noted K.S.A. 21-3755 was unclear. The court then held the mere fact Allen made telephone calls, a legal activity, which resulted in the connection of two modems, was insufficient to prove he had "gained access" to Southwestern Bell's computer systems as the K.S.A. 21-3755(b)(1) charge required. In addition, the court held Southwestern Bell's investigative expenses and voluntary security upgrade costs did not constitute damage to the computer systems or other property as defined in the statute.

OPINION

In this first impression case, we are presented with the question of whether a person's telephonic connections that prompt a computer owner to change its security systems constitute felony computer crime in violation of K.S.A. 21-3755(b).

The charges against Anthony A. Allen arose from several telephonic connections he made with Southwestern Bell Telephone Company's computers in early 1995. After preliminary hearing, the trial court dismissed the complaint, finding no probable cause existed to believe Allen had committed any crime. The State has appealed pursuant to K.S.A. 22-3602(b)(1). We affirm the trial court....

Allen was charged under K.S.A. 21-3755, which in applicable part provides:

(a) As used in this section, the following words and phrases shall have the meanings respectively ascribed thereto:

(1) 'Access' means to approach, instruct, communicate with, store data in, retrieve data from, or otherwise make use of any resources of a computer, computer system or computer network.

(2) 'Computer' means an electronic device which performs work using programmed instruction and which has one or more of the capabilities of storage, logic, arithmetic or communication and includes all input, output, processing, storage, software or communication facilities which are connected or related to such a device in a system or network.

(3) 'Computer network' means the interconnection of communication lines, including microwave or other means of electronic communication, with a computer through remote terminals, or a complex consisting of two or more interconnected computers.

. . . .

(6) 'Computer system' means a set of related computer equipment or devices and computer software which may be connected or unconnected.

. . . .

(8) 'Property' includes, but is not limited to, financial instruments, information, electronically produced or stored data, supporting documentation and computer software in either machine or human readable form.

. . . .

(b) Computer crime is:

(1) Intentionally and without authorization gaining or attempting to gain access to and damaging, modifying, altering, destroying, copying, disclosing or taking possession of a computer, computer system, computer network or any other property;

. . . .

(c) . . .

(2 Computer crime which causes a loss of the value of at least $500 but less than $25,000 is a severity level 9, nonperson felony.

. . . .

(e) Criminal computer access is intentionally, fraudulently and without authorization gaining or attempting to gain access to any computer, computer system, computer network or to any computer software, program, documentation, data or property contained in any computer, computer system or computer network. Criminal computer access is a class A nonperson misdemeanor."

Allen was charged with a violation of K.S.A. 21-3755(b)(1), with the second amended complaint alleging that he

did then and there intentionally and without authorization gain access and damage a computer, computer system, computer network or other computer property which caused a loss of the value of at least $500.00 but less than $25,000.00, a severity level 9 non-person felony.

Felony computer crime as it is charged in this case under K.S.A. 21-3755(b)(1) required the State to prove three distinct elements: (1) intentional and unauthorized access to a computer, computer system, computer network, or any other property (as property is defined in K.S.A. 21-3755[a][8]); (2) damage to a computer, computer system, computer network, or any other property; and (3) a loss in value as a result of such crime of at least $500 but less than $25,000. The trial court found that the State failed to show probable cause as to each of these elements.

Did the trial court err in ruling there was insufficient evidence to show Allen gained "access" to Southwestern Bell's computers?

After finding the evidence showed Allen had done nothing more than use his computer to call unlisted telephone numbers, the trial court ruled there was insufficient evidence to show Allen had gained access to the computer systems. Although a telephone connection had been established, the evidence showed Allen had done nothing more. The trial court reasoned that unless and until Allen produced a password that permitted him to interact with the data in the computer system, he had not "gained access" as the complaint required.

The State argues the trial court's construction of the statute ignores the fact that "access" is defined in the statute, K.S.A. 21-3755(a)(1), as "to approach, instruct, communicate with, store data in, retrieve data from, or otherwise make use of any resources of a computer, computer system or computer network." By this definition, the State would lead us to believe that any kind of an "approach" is criminal behavior sufficient to satisfy a charge that Allen did in fact "gain access" to a computer system.

The problem with the State's analysis is that K.S.A. 21-3755(b)(1) does not criminalize "accessing" (and, thus, "approaching") but rather "gaining or attempting to gain access." If we were to read "access" in this context as the equivalent of "approach," the statute would criminalize the behavior of "attempting to gain approach" to a computer or computer system. This phrase is lacking in any common meaning such that an ordinary person would have great difficulty discerning what conduct was prohibited, leading to an effective argument that the statute was void for vagueness.

The United States Department of Justice has commented about the use of "approach" in a definition of "access" in this context: "The use of the word 'approach' in the definition of 'access,' if taken literally, could mean that any unauthorized physical proximity to a computer could constitute a crime." National Institute of Justice, Computer Crime: Criminal Justice Resource Manual, p. 84 (2d ed.1989).

We read certain conduct as outside a statute's scope rather than as proscribed by the statute if including it within the statute would render the statute unconstitutionally vague. Consequently, although K.S.A. 21-3755 defines "access," the plain and ordinary meaning should apply rather than a tortured translation of the definition that is provided. See *State Dept. of SRS v. Public Employee Relations Board*, 249 Kan. 163, 168, 815 P.2d 66 (1991) (statutory words presumed used in ordinary and common meanings).

In addition, K.S.A. 21-3755 is certainly rendered ambiguous by the inclusion of the definition of "access" as a verb when its only use in the statute is as a noun. As a criminal statute, any ambiguity is to be resolved in favor of the accused. See *State v. JC Sports Bar, Inc.*, 253 Kan. 815, 818, 861 P.2d 1334 (1993) (criminal statutes construed strictly against the State).

Webster's defines "access" as "freedom or ability to obtain or make use of." *Webster's New Collegiate Dictionary*, p. 7 (1977). This is similar to the construction used by the trial court to find that no evidence showed that Allen had gained access to Southwestern Bell's computers. Until Allen proceeded beyond the initial banner and entered appropriate passwords, he could not be said to have had the ability to make use of Southwestern Bell's computers or obtain anything. Therefore, he cannot be said to have gained access to Southwestern Bell's computer systems as gaining access is commonly understood. The trial court did not err in determining the State had failed to present evidence showing probable cause that Allen had gained access to Southwestern Bell's computer system.

Did the trial court err in ruling that no evidence showed Allen had damaged any computer, computer system, computer network, or any other property?

The State acknowledges it cannot meet the damage element of the crime it has charged by any means other than evidence showing Allen's actions resulted in expenditures of money by Southwestern Bell. It is crystal clear there is absolutely no evidence Allen modified, altered, destroyed, copied, disclosed, or took possession of anything. The State's evidence clearly shows Allen did not physically affect any piece of computer equipment or software by his telephone calls. All the State was able to show was that Southwestern Bell made an independent business judgment to upgrade its security at a cost of $23,796. The State argues this is sufficient.

The State's argument is clearly flawed. The trial court reasoned by a fitting analogy that the State is essentially saying that a person looking at a no trespassing sign on a gate causes damage to the owner of the gate if the owner decides as a result to add a new lock. The trial court has clearly and correctly pointed to the correct analysis of this issue.

The State's circular theory is that if someone incurs costs to investigate whether an activity is criminal, it becomes criminal because investigative costs were incurred. Although computer crime is not, for obvious reasons, a common-law crime, it nevertheless has a common-law predicate which helps us to understand the legislature's intent. K.S.A. 21-3755 was not designed to update criminal trespass or malicious mischief statutes to the computer age but "to address inadequacies in the present theft statute related to prosecution of computer related crimes. Specifically, present theft statutes make prosecution difficult among crimes in which the computer owner was not actually deprived of the computer or its software." Kansas Legislature Summary of Legislation 1985, p. 80.

Theft, as defined in K.S.A. 21-3701, is not concerned with mere occupation, detention, observation, or tampering, but rather requires permanent deprivation. The intent required for theft is an "intent to deprive the owner permanently of the possession, use, or benefit of the owner's property." K.S.A. 21-3701(a). One may have wrongful intent, such as intent to trespass, without having the intent required for a theft. In addition, at common law, the thing of which the victim was deprived had to be something of value. The second element of computer crime mirrors this common-law requirement of the deprivation of something of value in a larceny action. As in a larceny action, the extent of the deprivation determines the severity level of the crime. This element of computer crime, as with other theft statutes, cannot be satisfied where there is no deprivation as in this case.

The State argues that investigative costs qualify as damages under the statute because investigative costs may be recovered from the perpetrator of computer crime as restitution. In our case, the issue is whether Allen's conduct is rendered criminal because it was investigated, not whether restitution for conduct already determined to be criminal includes investigative costs. *Lindsly* has no application to the present case.

The degree of a theft crime is established by the value of the stolen property. Restitution, in contrast, can include not only the fair market value of the property lost, but other costs in connection with the theft as well. The amount of restitution can be greater than the damages used to classify the crime. It requires only a causal connection between the crime proved and the loss on which restitution is based. We will not utilize the State's "restitution" theory to determine if there is probable cause to determine that the damage elements of a crime have been shown.

Southwestern Bell's computer system was not "damaged" in the sense the statute requires. Southwestern Bell was not deprived of property in the manner required to support a criminal charge. The fact an independent business judgment that Southwestern Bell's computer systems might be accessible was made after Allen's conduct was discovered does not support the second and third elements of the crime charged. The trial court correctly determined the State failed to meet its probable cause burden on these issues as well.

AFFIRMED.

Questions

1. State the elements of the statute that relate to the facts of the case.

2. List all of the facts relevant to deciding whether Anthony Allen was guilty of computer crime.

3. Summarize the state's arguments in favor of Anthony Allen's guilt.

4. Do you agree with the supreme court's decision upholding the lower court's decision? Defend your answer.

5. Was Anthony Allen guilty of "criminal computer access"? Back up your answer by stating the elements of the crime and applying the facts of the case to the elements.

6. Why do you think the state didn't charge Anthony Allen with "criminal computer access"?

◆　　◆　　◆

Receiving Stolen Property

It's not only a crime to steal someone else's property, it's also a crime to "receive" (accept) property someone else has already stolen. Called **receiving stolen property**, the purpose of making this a crime is to prevent and to punish individuals who benefit from someone else's theft, even though they didn't have anything to do with the original theft. Although the crime is primarily directed at **fences** (professionals who sell stolen property for profit), it also targets people who should know they're buying stolen stuff because the prices are too low.

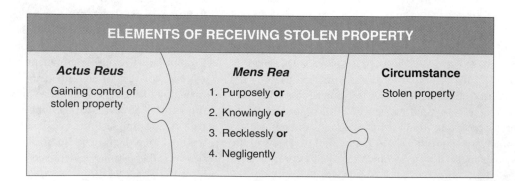

ELEMENTS OF RECEIVING STOLEN PROPERTY

Actus Reus	Mens Rea	Circumstance
Gaining control of stolen property	1. Purposely **or** 2. Knowingly **or** 3. Recklessly **or** 4. Negligently	Stolen property

Receiving Stolen Property *Actus Reus*

The *actus reus* of receiving stolen property is receiving the property. *Receiving* means the receiver has to control the property, at least briefly. Receiving doesn't mean the receiver has to *physically* possess the property. So, if I buy a stolen TiVO® from a fence for a friend and the fence hands it over directly to my friend, I've received the stolen TiVO, even though I've never seen or touched it. If my friend gives the TiVO to her friend, my friend also has received the stolen TiVO. Also, anyone who *temporarily* hides stolen goods for someone else has received the stolen goods.

Receiving Stolen Property *Mens Rea*

Receiving stolen property *mens rea* varies. Some states require actual knowledge that the goods are stolen. In others, honestly believing the goods are stolen is enough. In all jurisdictions, knowledge may be inferred from surrounding circumstances, like receiving goods from a known thief or buying goods at a fraction of their real value (like buying a top-of-the-line digital audio recording system for $75). Some jurisdictions require only that receivers were reckless or negligent about whether the property was stolen. Recklessness and negligence as to whether the property was stolen are often directed at likely fences, usually junk dealers and pawn shop operators.

Another aspect of the *mens rea* of receiving stolen property is that receivers have to intend to keep the property permanently. This means that police officers who knowingly accept stolen property and secretly place it in the hands of suspected fences to catch them haven't received stolen property because they don't intend to keep it.

The Georgia Court of Appeals dealt with receiving stolen property *actus reus* and *mens rea* in *Hurston v. State* (1991).

CASE | *Did He Receive the Stolen Car?*

Hurston v. State
414 S.E.2d 303 (Ga.App. 1991)

Illya Hurston and Demetrious Reese were convicted by a jury of theft by receiving stolen property before the Rockdale County Superior Court. Hurston appealed the denial of his motion for a new trial. The Court of Appeals affirmed.

ANDREWS, J.

FACTS

A silver 1986 Pontiac Fiero belonging to Stella Burns was stolen from a parking lot at Underground Atlanta on June 11, 1989, between 10:35 and 11:05 P.M. Two Rockdale County sheriff's deputies observed a silver Fiero at a convenience store later that night at approximately 1:20 A.M. Hurston's co-defendant, Reese, was driving the car and Hurston was slumped in the passenger seat. The deputies

became suspicious because of the late hour, the cautious manner in which Reese was walking after exiting the car, and the fact that Hurston appeared to be hiding, and decided to follow the Fiero.

When Reese drove away from the store with the deputies following in their marked car, he crossed the centerline of the highway. The deputies, who by this time had ascertained from computer records that the car was stolen, turned on the blue lights and siren of their automobile. Reese refused to stop, drove away from the deputies at a speed in excess of 100 miles per hour and attempted at one point to run the police vehicle into a wall. The deputies pursued the Fiero until Reese lost control and wrecked in a field. Reese ran from the scene and was pursued and apprehended by one deputy. Another officer apprehended Hurston, who had gotten out of the car immediately after the accident and appeared to be ready to run.

At trial, Hurston testified that he spent the day at his former girlfriend's home watching television with her and a friend of hers. Later in the day, the friend called her boyfriend, Reese, whom Hurston testified he had never met, to join them. Hurston testified Reese came to the house and stayed for awhile, left for several hours, and then returned and invited Hurston to ride in the Fiero with him to a relative's home. Hurston recalled that he was suspicious about the ownership of the vehicle because Reese, a teenager, seemed too young to own such a nice car, but that in response to his inquiry Reese stated that the car belonged to his cousin. Hurston testified that after they left the convenience store and Reese saw the deputies in pursuit, he began to speed, and admitted to Hurston for the first time that the car was stolen. Hurston's trial testimony differed somewhat from an earlier statement he gave regarding the evening's events.

Burns, the vehicle's owner, testified that the vehicle was driven without keys and that the steering wheel had been damaged, which was consistent with it having been stolen. She testified that various papers, including the car registration and business cards bearing the owner's name and address, had been removed from the glove compartment and were on the floor of the car; that grass, mud, food, drink and cigarettes were scattered in the car; and that a picture of her daughter was displayed on a visor. Hurston denied noticing the personal items or the damaged steering wheel.

OPINION

OCGA § 1687(a) provides:

> a person commits the offense of theft by receiving stolen property when he receives, disposes of, or retains stolen property which he knows or should know was stolen unless the property is received, disposed of, or retained with intent to restore it to the owner. 'Receiving' means acquiring possession or control....

Unexplained possession of recently stolen property, alone, is not sufficient to support a conviction for receiving stolen property but guilt may be inferred from possession in conjunction with other evidence of knowledge. Guilty knowledge may be inferred from circumstances which would excite suspicion in the mind of an "ordinary prudent man." "Possession, as we know it, is the right to exercise power over a corporeal thing...." Furthermore, "if there is any evidence of guilt, it is for the jury to decide whether that evidence, circumstantial though it may be, is sufficient to warrant a conviction."

Construed most favorably for the State, there was sufficient evidence for a jury to find Hurston guilty of receiving stolen property. First, there was sufficient evidence for a jury to find that Hurston knew, or should have known, that the vehicle was stolen. At trial, Hurston admitted that

he doubted that the vehicle belonged to Reese. There was evidence from which the jury could reasonably have concluded that Hurston was aware during the two hours that he spent in the small vehicle that it was stolen, in that the vehicle was being driven without keys, the steering wheel was damaged and the interior was disorderly, which was inconsistent both with Reese's ownership of the vehicle and with his explanation that he borrowed it from a relative. Hurston's suspicious behavior at the convenience store and his attempt to flee also indicated that he knew the vehicle was stolen.

There was also evidence from which the jury could conclude that Hurston possessed, controlled or retained the vehicle. Although Hurston was only a passenger in the vehicle, the inquiry does not end here, for in some circumstances, a passenger may possess, control or retain a vehicle for purposes of OCGA § 1687. Here, there was sufficient evidence that Hurston exerted the requisite control over the vehicle in that Reese left Hurston alone in the car with the vehicle running when he went into the convenience store.

"Questions as to reasonableness are generally to be decided by the jury which heard the evidence and where the jury is authorized to find that the evidence, though circumstantial, was sufficient to exclude every reasonable hypothesis save that of guilt, the appellate court will not disturb that finding, unless the verdict of guilty is unsupportable as a matter of law."

...Judgment AFFIRMED.

DISSENT

SOGNIER, C.J.

I respectfully dissent, for I find the evidence was insufficient to establish the essential element of "receiving" beyond a reasonable doubt. "A person commits the offense of theft by receiving stolen property when he receives, disposes of, or retains stolen property which he knows or should know was stolen.... 'Receiving' means acquiring possession or control...of the property." OCGA § 1687(a).

The record is devoid of evidence that Hurston exercised or intended to exercise any dominion or control over the car or that he ever acquired possession of it. The "mere presence" of a defendant in the vicinity of stolen goods "furnishes only a bare suspicion" of guilt, and thus is insufficient to establish possession of stolen property. Evidence that a defendant was present as a passenger in a stolen automobile, without more, is insufficient to establish possession or control. *Abner v. State*, 196 Ga.App. 752753, 397 S.E.2d 36 (1990) (conviction for theft by receiving automobile upheld where defendant was in actual possession of car).

I disagree with the majority that the circumstantial evidence that Hurston, the automobile passenger, was observed to be "slumped" in the seat while Reese parked the car and entered a store was sufficient to constitute the type of "other incriminating circumstances" that would authorize a rejection of the general principle that "the driver of the [stolen] automobile [is] held prima facie in exclusive possession thereof."...

Moreover, the evidence also did not meet the standard required for a conviction based on circumstantial evidence—i.e., that the evidence exclude every reasonable hypothesis except the guilt of the accused. The only evidence offered by the State to connect appellant to the stolen car was that he was a passenger in the car several hours after it was stolen. In response, appellant offered his explanation of his activities. "While neither the jury nor this court is required to accept these explanations, in the absence of any other valid explanation, we cannot ignore the only explanation offered. I conclude that there is no circumstantial evidence of guilt on which to base a conviction beyond a reasonable doubt." Accordingly, I would reverse....

Questions

1. Collect all the evidence relevant to determining whether Illya Hurston received stolen property.

2. State the elements of receiving stolen property according to the Georgia statute.

3. Summarize the court's opinion with respect to the elements you stated in (2).

4. Summarize the dissenting judge's reasons for dissenting.

5. Do you agree with the dissent or the majority? Defend your answer.

EXPLORING RECEIVING STOLEN PROPERTY FURTHER

 Go to the Criminal Law 8e CD to read the full text version of the case featured here.

Did He "Receive" the Stolen Astro by Sitting in It?

FACTS

A 1992 Chevrolet Astro van was stolen from a mobile home park in Spalding County. The van was subsequently utilized in a drive-by shooting on August 28, 1996. Later on the same day, Corporal Bradshaw of the Spalding

County Sheriff's Department observed the van and recognized it as being similar to one that was reported stolen, as well as one that was reported as being involved in a drive-by shooting a few hours earlier. Corporal Bradshaw followed the van and could see four to five black males inside; he couldn't determine who was driving. While Corporal Bradshaw was following the van, it abruptly turned into a driveway, where two or three men jumped out and ran from the scene. Without the driver, the van, which was left in the "drive" mode, rolled backward into the patrol car. Then, two young men, one of whom was the appellant, attempted to exit the van through the passenger door but were caught by Corporal Bradshaw before they could flee and were arrested at the scene.

The arresting officer was never able to determine who the driver had been or who had been in control of the stolen vehicle. The car keys were never found. When questioned by an investigator after receiving *Miranda* warnings, C.W. stated that he had only been along for a ride and didn't know that the van was stolen. At the hearing, the appellant's co-defendant, D.L.S., testified that C.W. had only gone for a ride in the van and didn't have control of the vehicle at any time.

The juveniles were charged with theft by receiving stolen property because they had been in the stolen vehicle. They were tried in Spalding County Juvenile Court on October 23, 1996. The juvenile court judge determined that C.W. was delinquent and sentenced him to 90 days in custody. The appellant timely appealed, asserting that the adjudication of delinquency was contrary to the law and to the evidence. Did C.W. receive the stolen van?

DECISION AND REASONS

No, according to the Georgia Court of Appeals:

Mere proximity to stolen property is insufficient to establish possession or control. In a similar vein, riding in a stolen van or automobile as a passenger does not support a conviction for theft by receiving unless the accused also, at some point, acquires possession of or controls the vehicle, i.e., has the right to exercise power over a corporeal thing. Therefore, one cannot be convicted of the crime of receiving stolen property absent exercise of control over the stolen goods, or if one is a passenger, intentionally aiding and abetting the commission of the crime.

...No evidence was presented by the state that the appellant ever retained, disposed of, acquired possession of, or controlled the stolen van, nor was any evidence presented of any affirmative act by the appellant that rose to the level of aiding and abetting the crime. The undisputed evidence indicates that the appellant got into the van while it was driven by an acquaintance, known as "Rat," and that Rat previously had acquired the van from a "Geek Monster," i.e., a crack addict, who apparently traded the van for cocaine.

Appellant denied ever driving the van, an assertion supported by his co-defendant, D.L.S. In addition, there was no evidence that appellant ever exercised control over the van, i.e., determined where it would go, who it would transport, etc., or that the appellant otherwise actively aided and abetted the crime. All evidence indi-cates that appellant was simply along for the ride. While appellant admitted being in the van while another passenger shot at an acquaintance in a drive by shooting, appellant was not charged with being an accessory to that offense. Therefore, lacking evidence that the appellant ever possessed or controlled the van under OCGA § 1687(A) or affirmatively acted as a party to the crime under OCGA § 16220(B), his adjudication of delinquency for the offense of theft by receiving stolen property must be reversed.

In the Interest of C.W., a child, 485 S.E.2d 561, (Ga.App. 1997)

Forgery and Uttering

Forgery consists of making false legal documents or altering existing ones—such as checks, deeds, stocks, bonds, and credit cards—for the purpose of getting someone else's property. **Uttering** means to pass false documents on to others. Forgery and uttering harm not only the individuals who lose their property but also society in general. Because the day-to-day business of life relies on legal instruments for smooth and efficient operation, damaging confidence in the genuineness of those instruments can lead to serious disruptions in business, commercial, and financial transactions. Let's look at forgery and uttering in more detail.

Forgery

Documents subject to forgery make up a long list, because the law defines fraudulent or false writings broadly. California's Penal Code (2004, § 470) is a good example of the broad reach of most forgery statutes.

> Every person who, with intent to defraud, signs the name of another person, or of a ficti-tious person, knowing that he has no authority so to do, or falsely makes, alters, forges, or counterfeits, any charter, letters patent, deed, lease, indenture, writing obligatory, will, testa-ment, codicil, bond, covenant, bank bill or note, post note, check, draft, bill of exchange, contract, promissory note, due bill for the payment of money or property, receipt for money or property, passage ticket, trading stamp, power of attorney, or any certificate of any share, right, or interest in the stock of any corporation or association, or any con-troller's warrant for the payment of money at the treasury, county order or warrant, or re-quest for the payment of money, or the delivery of goods or chattels of any kind, or for the delivery of any instrument of writing, or acquittance, release, or receipt for money or goods, or any acquittance, release, or discharge of any debt, account, suit, action, demand, or other thing, real or personal, or any transfer or assurance of money, certificates of shares of stock, goods, chattels, or other property whatever, or any letter of attorney, or other power to receive money, or to receive or transfer certificates of shares of stock or annuities, or to let, lease, dispose of, alien, or convey any goods, chattels, lands, or tenements, or other estate, real or personal, or any acceptance or endorsement of any bill of exchange, promissory note, draft, order, or any assignment of any bond, writing obligatory, promis-sory note, or other contract for money or other property; or counterfeits or forges the seal or handwriting of another; or utters, publishes, passes, or attempts to pass, as true and gen-uine, any of the above named false, altered, forged, or counterfeited matters, as above spec-

ELEMENTS OF FORGERY

Actus Reus	Mens Rea	Circumstance
1. Sign **or**	Intent to deceive	Document of legal significance
2. Alter **or**		
3. Make		

ified and described, knowing the same to be false, altered, forged, or counterfeited, with intent to prejudice, damage, or defraud any person; or who, with intent to defraud, alters, corrupts, or falsifies any record of any will, codicil, conveyance, or other instrument, the record of which is by law evidence, or any record of any judgment of a court or the return of any officer to any process of any court, is guilty of forgery.

Other states don't list documents by name; instead, they capture the breadth of the offense by using catchall phrases like "any writing," "any writing having legal efficacy or commonly relied on in business or commercial transactions," or "any written instrument to the prejudice of another's right." In addition to the writing, forgers have to intend to deceive their victims.

When the *Model Penal Code* (ALI 1960) drafters wrote a sweeping forgery definition, they aimed the code's forgery provision against three harms: direct property loss, damage to reputation, and impaired business and commercial confidence. Except in grading forgery, the *Model Penal Code* abandons a significant traditional circumstance element: that a forged document has to have legal or evidentiary significance. So, the *Model Code*'s provision includes doctors' prescriptions, identification cards, diaries, and letters, not just deeds, wills, contracts, stocks, and bonds. Also, forgery under the code isn't limited to making false *documents*; you can forge coins, tokens, paintings, and antiques. According to the code commentary, "Anything which could be falsified in respect of 'authenticity' can be the subject of forgery" (81–82). In *People v. Lawrence* (1996), the New York Supreme Court, Kings County, dealt with the problem of whether a cloned cell phone is a "written instrument."

CASE	*Was the Cell Phone a "Written Instrument"?*

People v. Lawrence
647 N.Y.S.2d 675 (Sup.Ct. Kings County, 1996)

Stephen Lawrence, Defendant, was charged with attempted criminal possession of a forged instrument, specifically, "cloned" cellular telephones. On a motion to dismiss the indictment, the Supreme Court sustained the indictment.

JUVILER, J.

...The question treated here is whether a computer program in a "cloned" cellular telephone is a "written instrument" within the meaning of Penal Law 170.00(1) and therefore is a "forged instrument" whose possession with intent to defraud is criminal. See Penal law 170.00(1), (7), 170.10(1), 170.25.

The question presented is of considerable importance because of the growing use of cloned cellular telephones in illegal enterprises, including trafficking in narcotics; and the widespread use of cloned cellular telephones to avoid paying for calls. According to a prominent police commander, because "cloned cellular phones are not registered to those people using them, investigators are often unable to obtain records such as subscriber information [and] toll and origination information and it often takes months for officers to trace back calls on a clone phone." The director of fraud management for the Cellular Telecommunications Industry Association has noted that this kind of fraud costs the industry "about 1.5 million a day."

FACTS

According to the testimony before the grand jury, the defendant, a police officer, was subjected to a Police Department "integrity test" administered by an undercover agent posing as a drug dealer. The defendant agreed to the agent's request that he act as a bodyguard in the transfer and sale to another purported drug dealer (played by a second undercover agent) of more than four ounces of cocaine and four cloned cellular telephones. The defendant accepted the agent's offer in exchange for a cut of the proceeds. He assisted the "selling" undercover agent in the transaction and took part in the negotiations with the "buyer."

OPINION

A person commits the underlying crime of criminal possession of a forged instrument in the third degree when with knowledge that it is forged and with intent to defraud, deceive or injure another, he utters or possesses any "forged instrument." Penal Law 170.20. A "forged instrument" is a defined term meaning a *written instrument* which has been falsely made, completed or altered." § 170.00(7) (*emphasis added*). A "written instrument," in turn, is "any instrument or article, including computer data or a computer program, containing written or printed matter or the equivalent thereof, used for the purpose of reciting, embodying, conveying or recording information, or constituting a symbol or evidence or value, right, privilege or identification, which is capable of being used to the advantage or disadvantage of some person." § 170.00(1).

The lesser crime is aggravated to criminal possession of a forged instrument in the second degree—the crime charged here—if the forged instrument is of a kind specified in section 170.10 of the Penal Law. Penal Law 170.25. This includes a forged instrument that "does or may evidence, create, transfer, terminate or otherwise affect a legal right, interest, obligation or status . . ." Penal Law 170.10(1).

Determining whether these statutes apply to cloned telephones requires an understanding of some of the technology behind the fraudulent use of cloned phones. Every cellular telephone has a unique electronic serial number (ESN) and a unique mobile identification number (MIN). When in use, the cellular telephone transmits a signal that identifies that telephone's MIN and ESN. The purposes of the signal are (1) to inform the cellular telephone carrier

where the telephone is located, so that the carrier may route transmissions to that telephone, and (2) to identify that telephone for billing. If the MIN and ESN numbers are intercepted, they can be programmed into other cellular telephones—"cloned" phones—to be used by a person who wishes to avoid paying for telephone service or avoid identification in a criminal investigation. This technology in cloned phones was explained in more abbreviated form by an expert witness in the presentation of this case to the grand jury.

The issue whether a cloned telephone is a "written instrument" as that term is defined in Penal Law 170.00(1) has been addressed in two recent well-reasoned opinions. See *People v. Pena, supra; People v. Morel, supra.* This court finds those opinions persuasive. In combination, they point out that the computer semiconductor chip in a cellular telephone contains encoded computer data. The definition of a written instrument in Penal Law 170.00(1), these opinions note, goes beyond writings on documents; it includes "computer data or a computer program." That computer program has been "falsely altered," as that term is used in § 170.00(6): It has been encoded without the authorization of the rightful owner. Further, both the user and carrier have a "legal interest" in the ESN and MIN codes, because the codes allow the carrier to bill the proper user. Hence, the unauthorized use of those codes "affects a legal . . . interest." § 170.10(1). Possession of a forged instrument of the kind that "affects . . . legal interests," with knowledge that it is forged and with intent to defraud, deceive or injure another constitutes the crime of criminal possession of a forged instrument in the second degree. § 170.25.

To this analysis in *Morel* and *Pena* this court respectfully adds the following history of section 170.00(1) of the Penal Law. When enacted as part of the revised Penal Law effective in 1967, section 170.00(1) contained its present language, except for the words "including computer data or a computer program," which were added in 1986. As the Staff Notes of the Commission on the Revision of the Penal Law disclose, the definition of "written instrument" in section 170.00(1) (in its unamended form) was meant to include "every kind of document *and other item* deemed susceptible of deceitful use in a forgery sense, the main requirement being only that it be capable of being used to the advantage or disadvantage of some person." (*emphasis added*) This statement of legislative purpose makes clear the broad coverage intended by the drafters of this statute.

To further this policy, section 170.00(1) of the Penal Law was amended in 1986 by the insertion of the phrase "including computer data or a computer program." This was done in acknowledgment of the "proliferation of computers and the technological advances of recent years [which] have left the State without adequate protection against the many insidious forms of computer crime." The amendment to include computer data and computer programs was designed to "fill the legal void by providing a comprehensive statutory framework for responding to the illegal and unethical use of computers."

One case cited in the Governor's Memorandum underscores the revision's broad intent to prevent fraudulent use of computer data in many forms. In that case, a group of computer hackers repeatedly used a commercial electronic message service without paying the required fee; to do so they had to overcome three separate security password codes, a scheme which contributed to the Governor's finding that the law was "woefully inadequate" to combat the "menacing threat" of computer and computer-related crime in its various forms. If the amendment was designed to cover that kind of scheme, clearly it was meant to cover the present case.

In sum, the original language and legislative history of section 170.00(1), the wording of the 1986 amendment,

and the accompanying legislative history of that amendment establish that section 170.00(1) in its present form, incorporated in section 170.25, forbids the duplication of data encoded on the computer chip in a cellular phone, or possession of such a cloned telephone, with intent to defraud.

Accordingly, counts 3, 4, 5, and 6 of the indictment are sustained.

Questions

1. State the definition of "written instrument" in the New York State forgery statute.

2. Summarize the arguments the court uses to back up its conclusion that the cell phone was a "written instrument" within the meaning of the statute.

3. Does applying the definition of forgery to the cell phone PIN and MIN achieve the purposes of the crime of forgery? Defend your answer with arguments from the court.

◆　　　◆　　　◆

The *actus reus* of forgery consists of creating a false document from scratch. So, just putting false information into an authentic document isn't forgery. And, if I change only the amount on a check made out and signed by the owner of the checking account, I haven't committed forgery because the check itself is genuine. Similarly, if a properly authorized payroll clerk alters payrolls by adding hours, it's not forgery because the payroll is still good. Checks drawn on insufficient funds aren't forgeries either. Why? First, the checks aren't false; second, unless the writer of the check doesn't intend to back up the checks with a later deposit, they lack the forgery *mens rea*.

Forgery is a specific-intent crime. The forger has to intend to defraud others with a false writing. It's not necessary to intend to defraud specific individuals; a general purpose to fraudulently use the falsified document is good enough. Furthermore, forgery doesn't require the falsifier to intend to obtain *money* fraudulently. Intending to secure any advantage will do. So, a false letter of recommendation intended to gain membership in a desirable professional organization satisfies the forgery *mens rea*. And, forgers don't have to actually gain from their falsifications and fraudulent intent. Why? The harm of forgery lies in undermining confidence in the authenticity of documents and the consequent disruption created by such undermined confidence. So, once documents are falsified or altered with proper fraudulent intent, the crime of forgery is complete.

Uttering

Forgery means making false documents with the intent to defraud, even if the forger never defrauds anyone. *Uttering* consists of the *actus reus* of passing or using forged documents—even if the utterer never altered anything on the documents—with the intent to defraud others. So, forgery and uttering are different offenses. Forgery is directed at making and altering documents in order to defraud. Uttering is directed at passing and using forged documents in order to defraud.

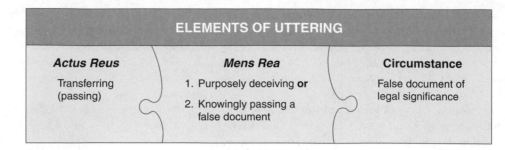

ELEMENTS OF UTTERING

Actus Reus	Mens Rea	Circumstance
Transferring (passing)	1. Purposely deceiving **or** 2. Knowingly passing a false document	False document of legal significance

Robbery

Robbery is a crime against persons *and* their property; it's taking someone else's property from their person by force or the threat of immediate force. Robbery consists of three elements:

1. Actus reus
   a. Taking and
   b. Carrying away
   c. By immediate force or the threat of immediate force
   d. From another person's property from his body or in his presence

2. Mens rea. The intent to permanently deprive someone else of her property by immediate force or the threat of immediate force

3. *Circumstance.* Property taken from the victim's person or in her presence

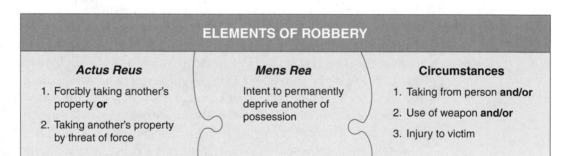

ELEMENTS OF ROBBERY

Actus Reus	Mens Rea	Circumstances
1. Forcibly taking another's property **or** 2. Taking another's property by threat of force	Intent to permanently deprive another of possession	1. Taking from person **and/or** 2. Use of weapon **and/or** 3. Injury to victim

Robbery *Actus Reus*

When you think of robbery, the image of thugs using guns and knives, seriously injuring or even killing to get their victims' money and other valuable stuff, probably comes to mind. Of course, these are robberies, but they're not typical. Most robbery victims are hardly touched, let alone *physically* injured or killed. But, they *have* lost their property, and as a victim of more than one mugging I can vouch for the fear, anger, and sense of violation that goes along with losing something valuable (like the watch my mother gave me as a graduation present).

The *actus reus* of robbery takes this combination of property loss *and* personal violation into account by not requiring actual violence and physical injury. Any force (or threat) beyond the amount needed to take and carry away someone else's property is enough. Picking a pocket isn't robbery because picking pockets requires only enough force to remove the contents of the pocket. But even slightly mishandling the victim (a push) turns the pickpocket into a robber. Robbery doesn't even require actual force; *threatened* force (a drawn gun or knife) is enough. Also, robbers don't have to threaten victims themselves; threats to family members will do. But, robbers *do* have to threaten their victims with death or great bodily injury. Threats to property aren't enough, although some cases have said threats to homes are.

Most statutes say robbers have to threaten to use force *immediately,* not in the future. Furthermore, victims have to give up their property because they honestly and reasonably feared the robbers' threats. The court in *State v. Curley* (1997) dealt with the element of force in robbery *actus reus.*

CASE | *Did He Take Property by Force?*

State v. Curley
WL 242286 (N.M.App. 1997)

Erwin Curley was convicted in the District Court of robbery. He appealed. The Court of Appeals reversed and remanded for new trial.

PICKARD, J.

FACTS

The victim was walking out of a mall with her daughter when Curley grabbed her purse and ran away. The victim described the incident as follows: "I had my purse on my left side . . . and I felt kind of a shove of my left shoulder where I had my purse strap with my thumb through it and I kind of leaned—was pushed—toward my daughter, and this person came and just grabbed the strap of my purse and continued to run." The victim used the words "grab" or "pull" to describe the actual taking of the purse and "shove" or "push" to describe what Curley did as he grabbed or "pulled [the purse] from her arm and hand."

However, there was also evidence that the victim's thumb was not through the strap of the purse, but was rather on the bottom of the purse. The purse strap was not broken, and the victim did not testify that she struggled with Curley for the purse in any way or that any part of her body offered any resistance or even moved when the purse was pulled from her arm and hand. Curley presented evidence that he was drunk and did not remember the incident at all.

OPINION

Robbery is theft by the use or threatened use of force or violence. Because the words "or violence" refer to the unwarranted exercise of force and do not substantively state an alternative means of committing the offense, we refer simply to "force" in this opinion. The force must be the lever by which the property is taken. Although we have cases saying . . . that even a slight amount of force, such as jostling the victim or snatching away the property, is sufficient, we also have cases in which a taking of property from the person of a victim has been held not to be robbery, see *State v. Sanchez,* 430 P.2d 781, 782 (Ct.App.1967) (wallet taken from victim's pocket while victim was aware that the defendant was taking the wallet).

A defendant is entitled to a lesser-included-offense instruction when there is some evidence to support it. There must be some view of the evidence pursuant to which the lesser offense is the highest degree of crime committed, and that view must be reasonable. Thus, in this case, to justify giving Curley's larceny instruction, there must be some view of the evidence pursuant to which force sufficient to constitute a robbery was not the lever by which Curley removed the victim's purse.

Curley contends that such evidence exists in that the jury could have found that Curley's shoving of the victim was part of his drunkenness, and then the purse was taken without force sufficient to constitute robbery. We agree. We are persuaded by an analysis of our own cases, as well as cases from other jurisdictions, that the applicable rule in this case is as follows:

> when property is attached to the person or clothing of a victim so as to cause resistance, any taking is a robbery, and not larceny, because the lever that causes the victim to part with the property is the force that is applied to break that resistance; however, when no more force is used than would be necessary to remove property from a person who does not resist, then the offense is larceny, and not robbery.

In our cases where we have not found sufficient force to be involved, the victim did not resist the property being taken from his person. See, e.g., *Sanchez*, 430 P.2d at 782 (defendant took wallet from victim's pants, but force was not lever by which wallet was taken); see also *State v. Aldershof*, 556 P.2d 371, 372, 376 (1976) (purse lifted from victim's lap while she sat at a table). . . .

The general rule from other jurisdictions is stated in 4 Charles E. Torcia, Wharton's Criminal Law Section 465, at 4749 (15th ed. 1996) that a mere snatching of property from a victim is not robbery unless the property is attached to the person or clothes of the owner so as to afford resistance. A minority position is represented by the analysis in *Commonwealth v. Jones*, 283 N.E.2d 840, 844 (1972). There, the court held that the values sought to be protected by the crime of robbery, as opposed to larceny, are equally present when any property is taken from a person as long as that person is aware of the application of force which relieves the person of property and the taking is therefore, at least to some degree, against the victim's will. See also *Commonwealth v. Ahart*, 641 N.E.2d 127, 131 (1994) (the snatching of a purse necessarily involves the use of force).

The minority rule adopted by Massachusetts, however, appears inconsistent with our earlier cases. Pursuant to the Massachusetts rule, any purse snatching not accomplished by stealth would be robbery. We are not inclined to overrule cases such as *Sanchez*, in which we held that the taking of a wallet accompanied by just so much force as is necessary to accomplish the taking from a person who was not resisting was not robbery. Rather, we adhere to what we perceive to be the majority rule.

According to the majority rule, robbery is committed when attached property is snatched or grabbed by sufficient force so as to overcome the resistance of attachment. In cases such as this one, where one view of the facts appears to put the case on the border between robbery and larceny, it is necessary to further explore what is meant by the concept of "the resistance of attachment." Our exploration is informed by the interests protected by the two crimes.

In *Fuentes*, 888 P.2d at 988, 990, we said that robbery is a crime "primarily" directed at protecting property interests. That statement, however, was made in the context of contrasting the crime of robbery with the crime of assault, which is directed exclusively toward protecting persons. In this case, contrasting the crime of robbery with the crime of larceny, we could similarly say that robbery is directed "primarily" at protecting persons inasmuch as larceny is directed exclusively at protecting property interests. In truth, it is probably inaccurate to say that the crime of robbery is directed "primarily" at either personal or property interests. That is because it is directed at both interests. It is the aspect of the offense that is directed against the person which distinguishes the crime of robbery from larceny and also justifies an increased punishment. Thus, "the resistance of at-

tachment" should be construed in light of the idea that robbery is an offense against the person, and something about that offense should reflect the increased danger to the person that robbery involves over the offense of larceny.

. . . We now apply these rules to the facts of this case. Although the facts in this case are simply stated, they are rich with conflicting inferences. Either robbery or larceny may be shown, depending on the jury's view of the facts and which inferences it chooses to draw.

In the light most favorable to the State, Curley shoved the victim to help himself relieve her of the purse, and the shove and Curley's other force in grabbing the purse had that effect. This view of the facts establishes robbery, and if the jury believed it, the jury would be bound to find Defendant guilty of robbery.

However, there is another view of the facts. Curley contends that the evidence that he was drunk allows the jury to infer that the shove was unintentional and that the remaining facts show the mere snatching of the purse, thereby establishing larceny. Two issues are raised by this contention that we must address:

(1) is there a reasonable view of the evidence pursuant to which the shove was not part of the robbery? and

(2) even disregarding the shove, does the remaining evidence show only robbery?

We agree with Curley that the jury could have inferred that the shove was an incidental touching due to Curley's drunkenness. Curley's testimony of his drunkenness and the lack of any testimony by the victim or any witness that the shove was necessarily a part of the robbery permitted the jury to draw this inference. Once the jury drew the inference that the shove was independent of the robbery, the jury could have found that Curley formed the intent to take the victim's purse after incidentally colliding with her. Alternatively, the jury could have found that Curley intended to snatch the purse without contacting the victim and that the contact (the shove) was not necessary to, or even a part of, the force that separated the victim from her purse. The victim's testimony (that she felt "kind of a shove" and then Defendant grabbed her purse) would allow this inference. Thus, the jury could have found that the shove did not necessarily create a robbery.

The question would then remain, however, whether the grabbing of the purse was still robbery because more force was used than would have been necessary to remove the purse if the victim had not resisted. Under the facts of this case, in which the victim did not testify that she held the strap tightly enough to resist and in which there was some evidence that she was not even holding the strap, we think that there was a legitimate, reasonable view of the evidence that, once the shove is eliminated from consideration,

Curley used only such force as was necessary to remove the purse from a person who was not resisting. Under this view of the facts, Curley took the purse by surprise from a person who was not resisting, and not by force necessary to overcome any resistance. Therefore, the trial court should have given Curley's tendered larceny instructions.

...Accordingly, Defendant's conviction is REVERSED and REMANDED for a new trial.

Questions

1. List all of the evidence relevant to determining whether the purse snatching was a robbery.

2. State both the majority and the minority rule regarding the element of force in purse snatching.

3. Summarize the evidence in favor of and against each rule.

4. In your opinion, which is the better rule? Defend your answer. See the Exploring Further case below.

EXPLORING ROBBERY FURTHER

 Go to the Criminal Law 8e CE to read the full text version of the case featured here.

Was the "Purse Snatching" Robbery?

FACTS

About 7:30 P.M., on June 10, 1994, two elderly women, Nancy Colantonio and Vera Croston, returned in Cros-ton's 1981 Chevrolet Citation automobile to their home at 36 Webster Street, Haverhill. Croston, upon entering the driveway, located by the side of the stairs leading to the porch and front door, stopped the car to let Colantonio out. As Colantonio walked up the stairs, she felt James Zingari snatch her purse from under her arm. She was stunned for a moment, then she turned around and saw Zingari running down Webster Street in the direction of Summer Street. She said she couldn't believe what she was seeing. Was Zingari guilty of purse snatching?

DECISION AND REASONS

Yes, according to the Appeals Court of Massachusetts:

Where the snatching or sudden taking of property from a victim is sufficient to produce awareness, there is sufficient evidence of force to permit a finding of robbery. In pickpocketing, which is accomplished by sleight of hand, such evidence is lacking. The difference accounts for the perceived greater severity of the offense of unarmed robbery in contrast with larceny. The [minority rule followed in Massachusetts]...was firmly adopted in the face of contrary authority in some States. It seems that a division continues to the present although, as usual, one can anticipate that a classification of jurisdictions may falter somewhat when the decisions are examined in detail. Judgment affirmed.

 Go to Exercise 11-1 on the Criminal Law 8e CD to learn more about purse snatching and robbery.

◆   ◆   ◆

Robbery *Mens Rea*

Robbery *mens rea* is the same as theft *mens rea* (the intent to take another person's property and keep it permanently) but with the additional intent to use immediate force, or the threat of immediate force, to get it. So, it's not robbery to take an MP3 player you honestly but mistakenly believe is yours. Of course, it's still a crime (battery if you use force or assault if you threaten to use it); it's just not robbery (LaFave and Scott 1986, 778–779).

The Degrees of Robbery

Most states have divided robbery into degrees according to whether robbers are armed and the injury they cause to their victims. New York's Penal Code (2003, §160.00) is typical. First-degree robbers (§160.15) carry deadly weapons (or "play weapons" that look real) and seriously injure their victims. Second-degree robbers (§160.10) have accomplices or display play weapons and inflict some injury on their victims. Third-degree robbers (§160.05) are unarmed, and they inflict no injury on their victims.

Extortion

Extortion (also called blackmail) is a crime against persons *and* their property. Theft by extortion is taking someone else's property by threats of *future* harm. *Time* separates extortion from robbery: robbery is a threat to hurt someone *right now* if they don't give up their property; extortion is a threat to hurt someone *later*.

The elements of extortion consist of:

1. Mens rea. The specific intent to take someone else's property by means of a variety of threats

2. Actus reus. A wide range of specific threats by which the taking of property is accomplished

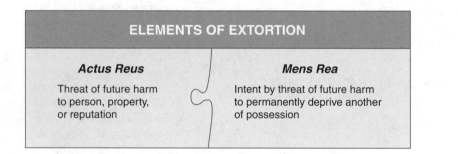

ELEMENTS OF EXTORTION

Actus Reus

Threat of future harm to person, property, or reputation

Mens Rea

Intent by threat of future harm to permanently deprive another of possession

The *Model Penal Code* "Theft by Extortion" (ALI 1985 2:2, 179) is an excellent example of a comprehensive statute based on existing state law:

§ 223.4 THEFT BY EXTORTION

A person is guilty of theft if he purposely obtains property of another by threatening to:
(1) inflict bodily injury on anyone or commit any other criminal offense; or
(2) accuse anyone of a criminal offense; or
(3) expose any secret tending to subject any person to hatred, contempt or ridicule, or to impair his credit or business repute; or
(4) take or withhold action as an official, or cause an official to take or withhold action; or
(5) bring about or continue a strike, boycott or other collective unofficial action, if the property is not demanded or received for the benefit of the group in whose interest the actor purports to act; or
(6) testify or provide information or withhold testimony or information with respect to another's legal claim or defense; or
(7) inflict any other harm which would not benefit the actor.

It is an affirmative defense to prosecution based on paragraphs (2), (3) or (4) that the property obtained by threat of accusation, exposure, lawsuit or other invocation of official action was honestly claimed as restitution or indemnification for harm done in the circumstances to which such accusation, exposure, lawsuit or other official action relates, or as compensation for property or lawful services.

Notice that threats don't have to be spelled out in detail; they can be indirect. The *Model Penal Code* (ALI 1985, 2:2) reporter puts it this way:

It is sufficient, for example, that the actor ask for money in exchange for "protection" from harms where the actor intends to convey the impression that he will in some fashion instigate the harm from which he proposes to "protect" the victims. (205–206)

Also, threats don't have to be directed at hurting the victim; threats to hurt anyone are good enough, according to the code.

DAMAGING AND DESTROYING OTHER PEOPLE'S PROPERTY

In this section, we'll discuss two crimes of destroying property: **arson** (damaging or destroying buildings by burning) and **criminal mischief** (damaging or destroying personal property).

Arson

In the 1700s, *arson* was defined as "the malicious and willful burning of the house or outhouses of another." Blackstone (1769) called it an "offense of very great malignity, and much more serious than simple theft." According to Blackstone, here's why:

> Because, first, it is an offence against that right, of habitation, which is acquired by the law of nature as well as the laws of society. Next, because of the terror and confusion that necessarily attends it. And, lastly, because in simple theft the thing stolen only changes its master, but still remains in essence for the benefit of the public, whereas by burning the very substance is absolutely destroyed. (220)

Arson has grown far beyond its origins in burning houses to include the burning of almost any kind of building, vessel, or vehicle. Also, the property burned doesn't have to be someone else's. Today, arson is a crime against possession and occupancy, not just against ownership. So, even where owners aren't in possession or don't occupy their own property, they still can commit arson against it. For example, if I lease my house and become its landlord, and I set fire to it to collect insurance on it, I've committed arson because I transferred occupancy to my tenant.

One thing hasn't changed; arson is still a very serious crime against property and persons. Arson kills hundreds and injures thousands of people every year. It damages and destroys more than a billion dollars worth of property and costs millions in lost

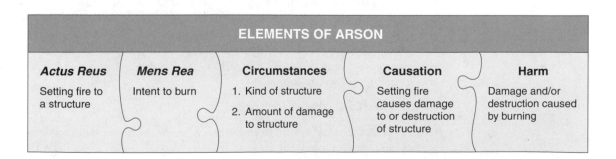

ELEMENTS OF ARSON				
Actus Reus	***Mens Rea***	**Circumstances**	**Causation**	**Harm**
Setting fire to a structure	Intent to burn	1. Kind of structure 2. Amount of damage to structure	Setting fire causes damage to or destruction of structure	Damage and/or destruction caused by burning

taxes and jobs. It's also significantly increased insurance rates. Most states prescribe harsh penalties for arson. For example, in Texas and Alabama, arson is punishable by life imprisonment.

Let's look further at the *actus reus*, *mens rea*, and degrees of arson.

Arson *Actus Reus:* Burning

At common law, **burning** had its obvious meaning—setting a building on fire. However, just setting the fire wasn't enough; the fire had to reach the structure and burn it. But, burning didn't mean burning to the ground. Once the building caught on fire, arson was complete, however slight the actual burning was. Modern statutes have adopted the common-law rule, and the cases pour great effort into deciding whether the smoke from the fire only blackened or discolored buildings, whether the fire scorched them, or whether the fire burned only the outside wall or the wood under it.

The *Model Penal Code* (ALI 1985, 2:2, 3) tries to clear up many of the technical questions in common-law arson by providing that burning means "starting a fire," even if the fire never touches the structure it was aimed at. The drafters justify this expansion of common-law burning on the ground that there's no meaningful difference between a fire that has already started but hasn't reached the structure and a fire that's reached the structure but hasn't done any real damage to it. Burning also includes explosions, even though the phrase "set on fire" doesn't usually mean "to explode."

In *Williams v. State* (1992), "the only physical damage caused by fire [set by Tonyia Williams, one of the guests at a New Year's Eve party] was smoke throughout the house and soot and smoke damage to one of the walls in the basement" (963). Indiana's arson statute defined arson as: "A person who, by means of fire or explosive, knowingly or intentionally damages: (1) a dwelling of another person without his consent" (964). Williams argued that the "soot and smoke damage to the wall of the basement do not constitute 'damages' within the meaning of the arson statute." She argued that arson "requires proof of burning or charring as was the case at common law" (964). The state argued that

> damages in our present statute is not tied to the common law definition of the word "burning" and should therefore be construed in its plain and ordinary sense. Any damage, even smoke damage, would therefore be enough to satisfy the requirements of the statute. (964)

Williams was convicted, and she appealed. According to the Indiana Appeals Court:

> Traditionally the common law rigidly required an actual burning. The fire must have been actually communicated to the object to such an extent as to have taken effect upon it. In general, any charring of the wood of a building, so that the fiber of the wood was destroyed, was enough to constitute a sufficient burning to complete the crime of arson. However, merely singeing, smoking, scorching, or discoloring by heat were not considered enough to support a conviction. (964)

The Appeals court agreed with the state:

> We find . . . that the smoke damage and the soot on the basement wall were enough to support a conviction for arson. (965)

Arson *Mens Rea*

Most arson statutes follow the common-law *mens rea* requirement that arsonists "maliciously and willfully" burn or set fire to buildings. Some courts call arson *mens rea* general intent. *State v. O'Farrell* (1976) is one example:

> Arson is a crime of general, rather than specific, criminal intent. The requirement that defendant act "willfully and maliciously" does not signify that defendant must have actual subjective purpose that the acts he does intentionally shall produce either (1) a setting afire or burning of any structure or (2) damage to or destruction of said structure. So long as defendant has actual subjective intention to do the act he does and does it in disregard of a conscious awareness that such conduct involves highly substantial risks that will be set afire, burned or caused to be burned—notwithstanding that defendant does not "intend" such consequences in the sense that he has no actual subjective purpose that his conduct produce them—defendant acts "willfully and maliciously." (398)

According to the general-intent standard, purpose refers to the act in arson (burning or setting fire to buildings), not to the resulting harm (damaging or destroying them). So, a prisoner who burned a hole in his cell to escape was guilty of arson because he purposely started the fire. So was a sailor who lit a match to find his way into a dark hold in a ship to steal rum. The criminal intent in arson is general—an intent to start a fire, even if there is no intent to burn a specific structure.

 Go to Exercise 11-2 on the Criminal Law 8e CD to learn more about arson statutes.

The Degrees of Arson

Typically, there are two degrees of arson. Most serious (first-degree arson) is burning homes or other occupied structures (such as schools, offices, and churches) where there's danger to human life. Second-degree arson includes burning unoccupied structures, vehicles, and boats.

The *Model Penal Code* divides arson into two degrees, according to defendants' blameworthiness. Most blameworthy are defendants who intend to destroy buildings and not merely to set fire to or burn them; these are first-degree arsonists. Second-degree arsonists are defendants who set buildings on fire for other purposes. For example, if I burn a wall with an acetylene torch because I want to steal valuable fixtures attached to the wall, I'm guilty of second-degree arson for "recklessly" exposing the building to destruction even though I meant only to steal fixtures.

Statutes don't grade arson according to motive, but it probably ought to play some part, if not in formal degrees, then in sentencing. Why? Because arsonists act for a variety of motives. Some are so consumed by rage they burn down their enemies' homes. Then there are the pyromaniacs, whose psychotic compulsion drives them to set buildings on fire for thrills. And there are the rational, but equally deadly, arsonists who burn down their own buildings or destroy their own property to collect insurance. Finally, and most deadly and difficult to catch, the professional torch commits arson for hire.

Criminal Mischief

Arson was (and still is) the serious common-law felony of intentionally burning occupied buildings. Criminal mischief descends from another common-law crime, the

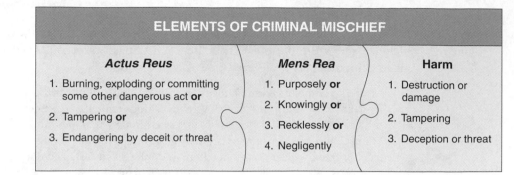

ELEMENTS OF CRIMINAL MISCHIEF

Actus Reus	*Mens Rea*	Harm
1. Burning, exploding or committing some other dangerous act **or**	1. Purposely **or**	1. Destruction or damage
2. Tampering **or**	2. Knowingly **or**	2. Tampering
3. Endangering by deceit or threat	3. Recklessly **or**	3. Deception or threat
	4. Negligently	

misdemeanor called *malicious mischief*. **Malicious mischief** consisted of destroying or damaging tangible property ("anything of value" that you can see, weigh, measure, or feel). The modern counterpart of malicious mischief (what the *Model Penal Code* calls *criminal mischief*) includes three types of harm to tangible property:

1. *Destruction or damage* by fire, explosives, or other "dangerous acts" (the original malicious mischief)

2. *Tampering* with tangible property so as to endanger property

3. *Deception or threat* that causes someone to suffer money loss

All three forms of damage and destruction are usually defined as felonies but less-serious felonies than the more-serious felony arson.

Criminal Mischief *Actus Reus*

The *actus reus* of criminal mischief mirrors the three types of criminal mischief. In "destruction or damage" criminal mischief, the *actus reus* is burning, exploding, flooding, or committing some other dangerous act. Tampering is any act that creates a danger to property, even if it doesn't actually cause any damage to the property. So, a cross burning on the lawn of an interracial couple's house wasn't tampering with the property, because the burning cross by itself created no damage and it didn't pose a threat of damage to the property (*Commonwealth v. Kozak* 1993). Deception or threat *actus reus* are usually "expensive practical jokes," like "sending a false telegram notifying the victim that his mother is dying so that he spends several hundred dollars on a vain trip," or "misinforming a neighboring farmer that local tests of a particular seed variety have been highly successful, so that he wastes money and a year's work planting that seed" (ALI 1985, 2:2, 49).

Criminal Mischief *Mens Rea*

Generalizations about criminal mischief *mens rea* are impossible because statutes are all over the place, including whether they contain all the mental states we've encountered throughout the book (purposely, knowingly, recklessly, and negligently). So, you need to check the malicious (or criminal) mischief statute of an individual state to find out how it defines the element of criminal intent.

We'll quote the *Model Penal Code* provision because its *actus reus* and *mens rea* requirements make sense, and they're comprehensive.

(1) *Offense Defined.* A person is guilty of criminal mischief if he:
  (a) damages tangible property of another purposely, recklessly, or by negligence in the employment of fire, explosives, or other dangerous means; or
  (b) purposely or recklessly tampers with tangible property of another so as to endanger person or property; or
  (c) purposely or recklessly causes another to suffer pecuniary loss by deception or threat.
(2) *Grading.* Criminal mischief is a felony of the third degree if the actor purposely causes pecuniary loss in excess of $5,000, or a substantial interruption or impairment of public communication, transportation, supply of water, gas or power, or other public service. It is a misdemeanor if the actor purposely causes pecuniary loss in excess of $100, or a petty misdemeanor if he purposely or recklessly causes pecuniary loss in excess of $25. Otherwise criminal mischief is a violation.

Pennsylvania's criminal mischief statute closely tracks the *Model Penal Code* provision. The Pennsylvania Superior Court applied the statute's *actus reus* and *mens rea* elements in *Commonwealth v. Mitchell* (1993).

CASE | *Was He Guilty of Malicious Mischief?*

Commonwealth v. Mitchell
WL 773785 (Pa. Com.Pl. 1993)

Following a non-jury trial, held on December 22, 1992, Duane Mitchell (defendant) was convicted of the criminal mischief…graded as a misdemeanor of the third degree. Defendant filed timely post-trial motions, which were denied, and the defendant was sentenced to pay a fine of $150. The defendant filed post trial motions which were denied. The Superior Court affirmed the trial court's denial of the motions.

CRONIN, JR., J.

FACTS

Following a report to the Upper Darby Police Department on Sunday, June 21, 1992 at 9:49 P.M., Lieutenant Michael Kenney and Officer Mark Manley of the Upper Darby Police Department, proceeded to 7142 Stockley Road Upper Darby, Pennsylvania. Upon arriving at the above location, both officers observed the following: painted on the front walk the word "nigger," the letters "KKK"; and a cross painted under three dark marks; on each of the steps leading to the house was spray painted the word "nigger"; the front screen door had a painted cross with three marks above it; the patio was painted with the word "nigger" and a cross with three dark marks; the front walk had the word

"nigger" and a cross with three dark marks; the front walk had the words "nigger get out" painted on it; the rear wall had painted the words "nigger get out or else" and a cross with the letters "KKK"; and, the rear door had the words "KKK Jungle Fever Death" and a cross painted on it.

The owners of 7142 Stockley Road, Upper Darby, Pennsylvania are James and Betty Jo Johnson, who had made settlement on the property on June 15, 1992, but had not occupied the home with their 7 year old daughter, Zena. The Johnsons are an interracial couple, James Johnson being Afro-American and Betty Jo Johnson being Caucasian. The Johnsons had not given the defendant nor any other person permission to spray paint on their property.

On June 25, 1992, defendant, Duane Mitchell, was taken into custody by the Upper Darby Police, the defendant voluntarily waived, in writing, his right to counsel and his right to remain silent and freely gave a statement to the police. The defendant told the Upper Darby Police that he, the defendant, alone spray painted the above-mentioned words and symbols on the Johnson property located at 7142 Stockley Road, Upper Darby, Pennsylvania; at the time that he did the spray painting, he had been drinking.

Following a non-jury trial, held on December 22, 1992, defendant was convicted of the summary offense of criminal mischief and the offense of ethnic intimidation, graded as a misdemeanor of the third degree in accordance with 18 Pa.C.S. § 2710(B). Defendant filed timely post-trial motions, which were denied by the order of trial court dated May 17, 1993.

OPINION

Criminal mischief is defined at 18 Pa.C.S. § 3304 as follows:

"SECTION 3304 CRIMINAL MISCHIEF

(A) Offense Defined—A person is guilty of criminal mischief if he:

(1) damages the tangible property of another intentionally, recklessly, or by negligence in the employment of fire, explosives, or other dangerous means listed in section 3302(A) of this title (relating to causing or risking catastrophe);

(2) intentionally or recklessly tampers with tangible property of another so as to endanger person or property; or

(3) intentionally or recklessly cause another to suffer pecuniary loss by deception or threat." 18 Pa.C.S. § 3304(A)

The defendant argues that the evidence was insufficient to prove that tangible property was damaged in the employment of fire, explosion, or other dangerous means. 1 Pa.C.S. § 1903 states that "(A) Words and phrases shall be construed according to rules of grammar and according to their common usage; . . ."

Section 1 of 18 Pa.C.S. § 3304 makes a person guilty of the crime of criminal mischief if that person either intentionally damages the tangible property of another; recklessly damages the tangible property of another; or negligently damages the tangible personal property of another in the employment of fire, explosives or other dangerous means listed in section 3302(A) of title 18.

In this case it is abundantly clear that the defendant spray painted the phrases and words mentioned herein on the Johnsons's home located at 7142 Stockley Road, Upper Darby, Pennsylvania and that the defendant did so without the permission of the Johnsons. Sufficient evidence exists to support a verdict if the evidence, when viewed in a light most favorable to the verdict winner along with all reasonable inferences drawn therefrom, allows a factfinder to find that all elements of a crime have been established beyond a reasonable doubt. The evidence was sufficient to prove beyond a reasonable doubt that the defendant intentionally damaged the tangible property of the Johnsons. A court must interpret a statute to ascertain the intent of the legislature. It is clear from the use of the conjunctive "or" in section 1 of 18 Pa.C.S. § 3304, that the legislature intended to punish either the intentional or the reckless or the negligent damaging of the tangible property of another person. The intentional spray painting of graffiti on the walls of a building is factually sufficient to support a conviction for criminal mischief.

It is equally clear that the commission of any of the other acts specified in either section 1 or section 2 or section 3 of 18 Pa.C.S. § 3304 is sufficient to support a conviction for criminal mischief since the conjunctive "or" is used between sections 2 and 3 of 18 Pa.C.S. § 3304 and the conjunctive "or" is to be given the same meaning and legislative intent as "or" is given with the states of mind (intent, reckless or negligent) in section 1 of 18 Pa.C.S. § 3304. See 1 Pa.C.S. § 1903(A), 1 Pa.C.S. § 1921(A)(B).

For the foregoing reasons the defendant's post-trial motions were denied.

Questions

1. State the elements of *actus reus* and *mens rea* as the Pennsylvania criminal mischief statute defines them.

2. List the facts relevant to each of the elements.

3. Assume you're Duane Mitchell's lawyer, and argue that the facts don't prove the elements beyond a reasonable doubt.

4. Assume you're the state's prosecutor, and argue that the facts prove the elements beyond a reasonable doubt.

◆   ◆   ◆

INVADING OTHER PEOPLE'S PROPERTY

The heart of burglary and criminal trespass is invading others' property, not taking, destroying, or damaging it. Invasion itself is the harm. So, the two main crimes of invading someone else's property, homes, and other occupied structures (**burglary**) or invading other property (**criminal trespass**) are crimes even if no property is taken, damaged, or destroyed during the invasion.

Burglary

> Burglary, or nighttime housebreaking...has always been looked upon as a very heinous offense, not only because of the abundant terror that it naturally carries with it, but also as it is a forcible invasion and disturbance of that right of habitation, which every individual might acquire in a state of nature....And the law of England has so particular and tender regard to the immunity of a man's house, that it styles it a castle and will never suffer it to be violated....
>
> Blackstone 1769, 223

Blackstone's definition of *burglary* just before the American Revolution emphasizes the special nature of homes. Why are they special? For many people, their homes are their most valuable if not their only material asset, but homes are more than property that's worth money. The novelist Sinclair Lewis described this difference between homes as things with money value and homes as special places ("castles") that can't be measured by money alone:

> The Babbitts' house was five years old....It had the best of taste, the best of inexpensive rugs, a simple and laudable architecture, and the latest conveniences. Throughout, electricity took the place of candles and slatternly hearth-fires. Along the bedroom baseboard were three plugs for electric lamps, concealed by little brass doors. In the halls were plugs for the vacuum cleaner, and in the living-room plugs for the piano lamp, for the electric fan. The trim dining-room (with its admirable oak buffet, its leaded-glass cupboard, its creamy plaster walls, its modest scene of a salmon expiring upon a pile of oysters) had plugs which supplied the electric percolator and the electric toaster.
>
> *In fact there was but one thing wrong with the Babbitt house: It was not a home* (Lewis 1922, chap. 2) (emphasis added).

Lewis means that a house is the material thing worth money, but a home is the haven of refuge where security and privacy from the outside world are possible.

The elements of common-law burglary from which our modern law of burglary descends included:

1. Breaking and entering (*actus reus*)

2. The dwelling of another (circumstance element)

3. In the nighttime (circumstance element)

4. With the intent to commit a felony inside (*mens rea*)

Modern burglary has outgrown its common-law origin of just protecting homes. Now, you can "burglarize" all kinds of **structures**, even vehicles, at any time of the day

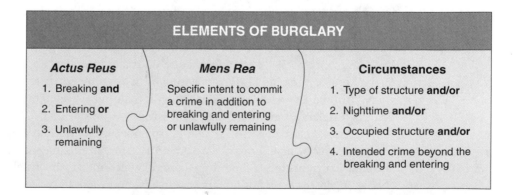

ELEMENTS OF BURGLARY

Actus Reus
1. Breaking **and**
2. Entering **or**
3. Unlawfully remaining

Mens Rea
Specific intent to commit a crime in addition to breaking and entering or unlawfully remaining

Circumstances
1. Type of structure **and/or**
2. Nighttime **and/or**
3. Occupied structure **and/or**
4. Intended crime beyond the breaking and entering

or night. Definitions such as "any structure" or "any building" are common in many statutes. One writer (Note 1951, 411) who surveyed the subject concluded that any structure with "four walls and a roof" was included.

Here's California's list of "structures" you can burglarize:

> Every person who enters any house, room, apartment, tenement, shop, warehouse, store, mill, barn, stable, outhouse or other building, tent, vessel, ... floating home...., locked or sealed cargo container, whether or not mounted on a vehicle, trailer coach..., any house car, inhabited camper..., vehicle..., when the doors are locked, aircraft..., or mine or any underground portion thereof....

California Penal Code 2003, §459

Let's look at the elements needed to prove burglary and the degrees of burglary.

Burglary *Actus Reus*

Until the 1900s, burglary *actus reus* consisted of two actions—*breaking* and *entering*. In the early days of common law, **breaking** meant a making violent entry, usually knocking down doors and smashing windows. By the 1700s, Blackstone (1769, 226) wrote that breaking included "picking a lock, or opening it with a key; nay, by lifting up the latch of a door, or unloosing any other fastening which the owner has provided." Even if an outer door wasn't locked, it was breaking if a felon had to loosen the door to get in. Only walking through a wide open door, or climbing through an open window, wasn't breaking. ("But if a person leaves his doors and windows open, it is his own folly and negligence, and if a man enters therein, it is no burglary.") By 1900, the common-law element of breaking had become a mere technicality, and most modern statutes have eliminated it entirely, leaving entering as the only element. A few states, like Massachusetts, have retained the ancient definition, "Whoever, in the night time, breaks and enters..." (Massachusetts Criminal Code 2003, Chap. 266 § 266).

Entering, like breaking, has a broad meaning in burglary law. From about 1650, partial entry was enough to satisfy burglary. One court (*Rex v. Bailey* 1818) ruled that a burglar "entered" a house because his finger was inside the windowsill when he was caught. In another case (Hale 1670, 553), an intruder who assaulted an owner on the owner's threshold "entered" the house because his pistol crossed over the doorway. In Texas (*Nalls v. State* 1920), a man who never got inside a building at all, but who fired a gun into it intending to injure an occupant, "entered" by means of the bullet.

Some statutes completely remove the entering element by providing that **remaining** in a structure lawfully entered is enough. So, it's burglary to go into a store during business hours and wait in a rest room until the store closes with the intent to steal. Some states don't even require burglars to get inside; it's enough if they *try* to get in. In *State v. Myrick* 1982, a man who got a door ajar but never set foot inside was convicted because the state's burglary statute didn't require entering or remaining. To some criminal law reformers, substituting remaining for breaking and entering badly distorts burglary's core idea—nighttime invasions into homes.

The *Model Penal Code* and several jurisdictions take a middle ground between the old common-law requirement of **actual entry** and eliminating entering. They've adopted a **surreptitious remaining** element, which means the burglar entered lawfully (like going into a bank during business hours) and waited inside to commit a crime.

Occupied Structures

The *Model Penal Code* (ALI 1985, 2:2, 60) definition limits burglary to *occupied structures,* because they're the "intrusions that are typically the most alarming and dangerous." According to the code, **occupied structure** means "any structure, vehicle, or place adapted for overnight accommodations of persons, or for carrying on business therein, whether or not a person is actually present" (72). Most states take occupancy into account either as an element or as part of grading burglary as "aggravated burglary." The Ohio Court of Appeals dealt with the problem of defining "occupied structure" in *State v. Burns* (1997).

CASE	*Did He Burglarize an "Occupied" Apartment?*

State v. Burns

WL 152074 (OhioApp. Dist. 6 1997)

Robert Burns was found guilty of aggravated burglary and other felonies. He appealed and the Ohio Court of Appeals affirmed.

RESNICK, J.

FACTS

On January 8, 1996, an apartment manager of a one hundred thirty-eight unit complex in Maumee, Ohio was visited by a man who said he was looking to rent a one-bedroom apartment. The manager showed the man the community room and the laundry facilities. She then took the man to a one-bedroom, upper level apartment that had been vacant for approximately one month. She unlocked the door with her master keys and walked into the kitchen. As she turned around to face the man she saw he had a gun pointed at her. The man instructed her to do as she was told. He ordered her to walk down a hallway into the bedroom. There, he pushed her down on the floor, tied a scarf around her mouth and placed her in handcuffs. He removed her boots, slacks and pantyhose. He then tied her ankles together with the pantyhose and fondled her. The man took her keys and asked for money. When she was sure he had left the apartment, the manager escaped to another apartment and called the police. The manager identified appellant as the man who had attacked her.

A jury found appellant guilty of aggravated burglary, aggravated robbery, kidnapping and gross sexual imposition. The jury further found that the state had proven the specification that appellant used a firearm in the commis-

sion of these offenses. The court sentenced appellant to twelve to twenty-five concurrent years for aggravated burglary, aggravated robbery and kidnapping. He received a consecutive three to five year term of imprisonment for the offense of gross sexual imposition and a three year term of imprisonment for the firearm specification. The firearm specification sentence was ordered to be served consecutively to all the other sentences. In total, appellant was sentenced to not less than eighteen years nor more than thirty-three years.

OPINION

...Appellant contends the state failed to prove the elements of aggravated burglary in that a vacant apartment is not an "occupied structure" pursuant to R.C. 2911.11. The elements of aggravated burglary, a violation of R.C. 2911.11 are as follows:

(A) No person, by force, stealth, or deception, shall trespass in an occupied structure, as defined in section 2909.01 of the Revised Code, or in a separately secured or separately occupied portion thereof, with purpose to commit therein any theft offense, as defined in section 2913.01 of the Revised Code, or any felony, when any of the following apply:
(1) The offender inflicts, or attempts or threatens to inflict physical harm on another;
(2) The offender has a deadly weapon or dangerous ordnance, as defined in section 2923.11 of the Revised Code, on or about his person or under his control;
(3) The occupied structure involved is the permanent or temporary habitation of any person, in

which at the time any person is present or likely to be present.

R.C. 2909.01(C) defines occupied structure as:

any house, building, outbuilding, watercraft, aircraft, railroad car, truck, trailer, tent, or other structure, vehicle, or shelter, or any portion thereof, to which any of the following applies:

(1) It is maintained as a permanent or temporary dwelling, even though it is temporarily unoccupied and whether or not any person is actually present.

The court's jury instruction regarding "occupied structure" mirrored the above definition.

The Tenth District Court of Appeals addressed a similar issue in *State v. Green* (1984), 18 Ohio App.3d 69. The court stated:

It is obvious that the General Assembly, in adopting the definition of 'occupied structure' found in R.C. 2909.01, intended to broaden the concept of the offense of burglary from one of an offense against the security of habitation, to one concerned with the serious risk of harm created by the actual or likely presence of a person in a structure of any nature. In that context, it is noteworthy that the General Assembly utilized the word 'maintained' in division (A), as opposed to 'occupied,' although it did use that latter word in division (B), which deals with structures other than dwellings. We believe that the distinction between 'maintained' and 'occupied' is significant, in the sense that the former alludes more to the character or type of use for which the dwelling is intended to be subjected, whereas the latter is more closely related to the actual use to which the structure is presently being subjected.

Thus, a structure which is dedicated and intended for residential use, and which is not presently occupied as a person's habitation, but, which has neither been permanently abandoned nor vacant for a prolonged period of time, can be regarded as a structure 'maintained' as a dwelling within the meaning of division (A). In this context, then, division (A) includes a dwelling whose usual occupant is absent on prolonged vacation, a dwelling whose usual occupant is receiving long-term care in a nursing home, a summer cottage, or a residential rental unit which is temporarily vacant. In all these examples, even though the dwelling is not being presently occupied as a place of habitation, that situation is temporary, and persons are likely to be present from time to time to look after the property to help 'maintain' its character as a dwelling.

Applying this analysis to the instant case, we conclude that there was sufficient evidence to support a finding that the apartment at issue was an "occupied structure" as that term is used in R.C. 2911.11. Accordingly, appellant's sole assignment of error is found not well-taken.

On consideration whereof, the court finds that appellant was not prejudiced or prevented from having a fair trial, and the judgment of the Lucas County Court of Common Pleas is AFFIRMED. It is ordered that appellant pay the court costs of this appeal.

Questions

1. List all of the facts relevant to deciding whether Robert Burns broke and entered an "occupied structure."

2. How did the Ohio Court of Appeals define *occupied structure*?

3. What policy interests does this definition promote?

4. Do you agree that Robert Burns committed burglary of an occupied structure? Explain your answer.

◆   ◆   ◆

"Of Another"

Another circumstance element of common-law burglary was that burglars had to break and enter the dwelling "of another." Modern law has expanded the common-law definition to include your own property; now, for example, landlords can burglarize their tenants' apartments. In *Jewell v. State* (1996), the court dealt with the problem of whether you can burglarize your own home.

Jewell v. State
672 N.E.2d 417 (Ind.App. 1996)

Barry L. Jewell, after a jury trial, was convicted of burglary with a deadly weapon resulting in serious bodily injury, a class A felony, and battery resulting in serious bodily injury, a class C felony. Jewell was sentenced to an aggregate term of 48 years imprisonment. After a re-trial Jewell appealed. The Indiana Court of Appeals affirmed.

ROBERTSON, J.

FACTS

In 1989, Bridget Fisher, who later married Jewell and changed her name to Bridget Jewell, purchased a home on contract in her maiden name from her relatives. Bridget and Jewell lived in the house together on and off before and after they married in 1990. Jewell helped fix the house up, and therefore, had some "sweat equity" in the house.

Jewell and Bridget experienced marital difficulties and dissolution proceedings were initiated. Jewell moved out of the house and Bridget changed the locks so that Jewell could not reenter. At a preliminary hearing in the dissolution proceedings, Bridget's attorney informed Jewell that Bridget wanted a divorce and wanted Jewell to stop coming by the house. Jewell moved into a friend's house, agreeing to pay him $100.00 per month in rent and to split the utility expenses.

Bridget resumed a romantic relationship with her former boyfriend, Chris Jones. Jewell told a friend that he wanted to get Jones in a dark place, hit him over the head with a 2 × 4 (a board), and cut his "dick" off. Jewell confronted Jones at his place of employment and threatened to kill him if he were to continue to see Bridget. Jewell was observed on numerous occasions watching Bridget's house. Jewell used a shortwave radio to intercept and listen to the phone conversations on Bridget's cordless phone.

At approximately 4:00 A.M. on the morning of June 13, 1991, Jewell gained entry to Bridget's house through the kitchen window after having removed a window screen. Bridget and Jones were inside sleeping. Jewell struck Jones over the head with a 2 × 4 until he was unconscious, amputated Jones' penis with a knife, and fed the severed penis to the dog. Bridget awoke and witnessed the attack, but she thought she was having a bad dream and went back to sleep. Bridget described the intruder as the same size and build as Jewell and as wearing a dark ski mask similar to one she had given Jewell. She observed the assailant hit Jones on the head with a board, and stab him in the lower part of his body.

A bloody 2 × 4 was found at the scene. The sheets on the bed where Bridget and Jones had been sleeping were covered in blood. Bridget discovered that one of her kitchen knives was missing. However, the police did not preserve the sheets or take blood samples and permitted Bridget to dispose of the sheets. A police officer involved explained that the possibility that any of the blood at the crime scene could have come from anyone other than Jones had not been considered.

Jones' severed penis was never found and he underwent reconstructive surgery. His physicians fashioned him a new penis made from tissue and bone taken from his leg. Jones experienced complications and the result was not entirely satisfactory.

OPINION

... Jewell attacks the sufficiency of evidence supporting his conviction of Burglary, which is defined as:

> A person who breaks and enters the building or structure of another person, with intent to commit a felony in it, commits burglary. Ind. Code 354321

Jewell argues he was improperly convicted of breaking into his own house. ...

The Burglary statute's requirement that the dwelling be that "of another person" is satisfied if the evidence demonstrates that the entry was unauthorized. *Ellyson v. State*, 603 N.E.2d 1369, 1373 (Ind. Ct.App.1992). In *Ellyson*, we held a husband was properly convicted of burglary for breaking into the house in which he and his estranged wife had lived previously with the intent of raping his wife. ... We upheld the husband's burglary conviction even though he may have had a right to possession of the house co-equal with his wife at the time of the breaking and entering.

In the present case, Bridget had purchased the house in her own name before the marriage. When she and Jewell experienced marital difficulties, Jewell moved out and Bridget changed the locks to prevent Jewell from reentering the house. Bridget alone controlled access to the house. Jewell entered the house at 4:00 A.M. through the kitchen window after having removed the screen.

The evidence supports the conclusion that the entry was unauthorized; and, therefore, we find no error. . . .

Judgment AFFIRMED.

Questions

1. List all of the facts relevant to determining whether Barry Jewell burglarized his own home.

2. How does the state of Indiana define the "of another" element?

3. How did the court arrive at the conclusion that Barry Jewell burglarized his own home?

4. What's the reason for the "unauthorized entry" requirement?

5. Do you agree with it? Defend your answer.

◆　　◆　　◆

"In the Nighttime"

At common law, another circumstance element was "in the nighttime." There were three reasons for the "nighttime" element. First, it's easier to commit crimes at night. Second, it's harder to identify suspects you've seen at night. Third, and probably most important, nighttime intrusions frighten victims more than daytime intrusions. At least eighteen states retain the nighttime requirement. Some do so by making nighttime an element of the crime. Others treat nighttime invasions as an aggravating circumstance. Some have eliminated the nighttime requirement entirely.

Burglary *Mens Rea*

Burglary is a specific-intent crime. The prosecution has to prove two *mens rea* elements:

1. The intent to commit the *actus reus* (breaking, entering, or remaining)

2. The intent to commit a crime once inside the structure broken into, entered, or remained in

The intended crime doesn't have to be serious. Intent to steal is usually good enough, but some states go further to include "any crime," "any misdemeanor," or even "any public offense" (Note 1951, 420).

Keep in mind another important point: It isn't necessary to complete or even attempt to commit the intended crime. Suppose I sneak into my rich former student Pat's luxurious condo in Kona while he's out making more money, intending to steal one of his three wireless notebook computers he doesn't need or use. Right after I get inside the front door and not even close to where the notebooks are, my conscience gets the better of me, and I say to myself, "I can't do this, even if Pat *does* have three notebook computers," and I slink back out the front door. I committed burglary, because the burglary was complete the moment I was inside with the intent to steal one of the notebooks.

The Degrees of Burglary

Because burglary is defined so broadly, many states divide it into several degrees. Alabama's burglary statute is typical:

§ 13A-7-5. BURGLARY IN THE FIRST DEGREE.

(a) A person commits the crime of burglary in the first degree if he knowingly and unlawfully enters or remains unlawfully in a dwelling with intent to commit a crime therein, and, if, in effecting entry or while in dwelling or in immediate flight therefrom, he or another participant in the crime:

(1) Is armed with explosives or a deadly weapon; or

(2) Causes physical injury to any person who is not a participant in the crime; or

(3) Uses or threatens the immediate use of a dangerous instrument.

Sentence: 10 years to life

§ 13A-7-6. BURGLARY IN THE SECOND DEGREE.

(a) A person commits the crime of burglary in the second degree if he knowingly enters or remains unlawfully in a building with intent to commit theft or a felony therein and, if in effecting entry or while in the building or in immediate flight therefrom, he or another participant in the crime:

(1) Is armed with explosives or a deadly weapon; or

(2) Causes physical injury to any person who is not a participant in the crime; or

(3) Uses or threatens the immediate use of a dangerous instrument.

(b) In the alternative to subsection (a) of this section, a person commits the crime of burglary in the second degree if he unlawfully enters a lawfully occupied dwelling-house with intent to commit a theft or a felony therein.

Sentence: 2–20 years

§ 13A-7-7. BURGLARY IN THE THIRD DEGREE.

(a) A person commits the crime of burglary in the third degree if he knowingly enters or remains unlawfully in a building with intent to commit a crime therein.

Sentence: 1–10 years

Despite efforts to grade burglary according to seriousness, the broad scope of the offense invites injustices in most statutes. This is true in large part because burglary punishes the invasion and not the **predicate crime**—namely, the crime the burglar entered to commit. In many cases, the penalty for burglary is a lot harsher than the penalty for the intended crime. The difference between a 5-year sentence and a 20-year sentence sometimes depends upon the largely philosophical question of whether a thief forms the intent to steal *before* or *after* entering a building.

 Go to Exercise 11-3 on the Criminal Law 8e CD to learn more about burglary statutes.

Criminal Trespass

Criminal trespass is a broader but less-serious crime than burglary. It's broader because it's not limited to invasions of occupied buildings and the trespasser doesn't have to intend to commit a crime in addition to the trespass. The heart of criminal trespass is unwanted presence. The ancient misdemeanor called trespass referred to unwanted presence on (invasion of) another person's land. Not all unwanted presence was (or is) criminal trespass; only *unauthorized* presence qualifies. So, of course law enforcement officers investigating a crime, or gas company employees reading the meter, no matter how unwanted they are, aren't trespassers because they're authorized to be there.

Trespass used to be limited to unauthorized invasions of **physical property.** At first, only entry onto land was included; then entering and remaining on land and buildings were added; and since the explosion of computers and the Internet, unauthorized access to electronic information systems has been included.

Let's look at the elements and degrees of criminal trespass and at the special trespassing offense of computer trespass.

ELEMENTS OF CRIMINAL TRESPASS	
Actus Reus	**Mens Rea**
1. Unauthorized entering **or**	1. Purposely **or**
2. Remaining on another's premises	2. Knowingly **or**
	3. Without any culpable state of mind

The Elements of Criminal Trespass

The *actus reus* of criminal trespass is the unauthorized entering of or remaining on the premises of another person (ALI 1985, 2:2, 87). The *mens rea* varies, including (88):

1. Knowingly enters or remains without authority or by invitation, license, privilege, or legality (most states)

2. Specific intent to enter or remain without authority for some unlawful purpose (a few states)

3. Strict liability (Missouri, enters "unlawfully")

The Degrees of Criminal Trespass

The *Model Penal Code* created three degrees of criminal trespass:

1. *Misdemeanor.* Entering or remaining in an occupied dwelling at night

2. *Petty misdemeanor.* Entering or remaining in any occupied building or structure

3. *Violation.* Entering or remaining in any place where a "no trespass" notice is given (warning to person, "no trespassing" sign, or fence)

Computer Trespass

The law of criminal trespass has provided another opportunity to use an ancient offense to respond to a new unwanted presence—*computer hackers* (Nimmer 2002, chap. 9). **Computer hackers** are unauthorized intruders on a protected environment, so the invasion itself is the crime, whether the invasion is intended to (or actually does) take, damage, or destroy someone else's property (in this case the information or information system). The modern laws criminalizing these trespasses are **computer trespass statutes** (in some states, they're called **unauthorized computer access statutes**).

The Washington State Supreme Court applied that state's computer trespass statute in *State v. Riley* (1993).

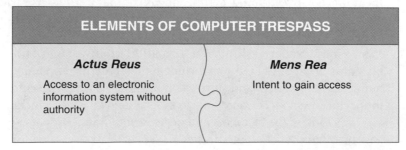

ELEMENTS OF COMPUTER TRESPASS	
Actus Reus	**Mens Rea**
Access to an electronic information system without authority	Intent to gain access

State v. Riley
846 P.2 1365 (Wash. 1993)

Joseph Riley, Defendant, was convicted in the Superior Court, Kitsap County of three counts of computer trespass... The Supreme Court affirmed.

GUY, J.

FACTS

Northwest Telco Corporation ("Telco") is a company that provides long distance telephone service. Telco's customers dial a publicly available general access number, then enter an individualized 6-digit access code and the long distance number they wish to call. A computer at Telco's central location then places the call and charges it to the account corresponding to the entered 6-digit code.

On January 9, 1990, Cal Edwards, Director of Engineering at Telco, observed that Telco's general access number was being dialed at regular intervals of approximately 40 seconds. After each dialing, a different 6-digit number was entered, followed by a certain long distance number. Edwards observed similar activity on January 10, between 10 P.M. and 6 A.M. From his past experience, Edwards recognized this activity as characteristic of that of a "computer hacker" attempting to obtain the individualized 6-digit access codes of Telco's customers. Edwards surmised that the hacker was using a computer and modem to dial Telco's general access number, a randomly selected 6-digit number, and a long distance number. Then, by recording which 6-digit numbers enabled the long distance call to be put through successfully, the hacker was able to obtain the valid individual access codes of Telco's customers. The hacker could then use those codes fraudulently to make long distance calls that would be charged improperly to Telco's paying customers.

On January 11, Edwards contacted Toni Ames, a U.S. West security investigator, and requested her assistance in exposing the hacker. In response, Ames established a line trap, which is a device that traces telephone calls to their source. By 3 P.M., Ames had traced the repeated dialing to the home of Joseph Riley in Silverdale, Washington. The dialing continued until 6 A.M. on January 12.

Ames contacted the Kitsap County Prosecutor's Office on January 12, 1990, and was directed to Investigator Richard Kitchen. Kitchen filed an affidavit for a search warrant after interviewing both Ames and Edwards. The affidavit stated that hackers program computers to conduct the repeated dialing of random numbers and, after discovering valid codes, often transfer them to notebooks, ledgers, or lists. Because the telephone company's system that processes long distance calls is a computer "switch," the crime listed in the affidavit was computer trespass....

OPINION

Riley... contends that his convictions of computer trespass against Telco must be reversed because his conduct—repeatedly dialing Telco's general access number and entering random 6-digit numbers in an attempt to discover access codes belonging to others—does not satisfy the statutory definition of computer trespass. We disagree.

RCW 9A.52.110 provides in relevant part that

> a person is guilty of computer trespass in the first degree if the person, without authorization, intentionally gains access to a computer system or electronic data base of another...

Riley contends the telephone company's long distance switch is not a "computer" under RCW 9A.52.110. We reject this contention. The trial court explicitly found that the switch is a computer. This finding was based on unrebutted expert testimony. A trial court's findings of fact will not be disturbed on appeal when they are supported by undisputed evidence. *Leonard v. Washington Employers, Inc.*, 77 Wash.2d 271, 272, 461 P.2d 538 (1969).

Riley also argues that acts accomplished by simply dialing the telephone are not encompassed within the statutorily defined crime of computer trespass, and are merely the equivalent of placing a telephone call. He contends he is not guilty of computer trespass because he did not enter, read, insert, or copy data from the telephone system's computer switch. Instead, he argues, RCW 9.26A.110, dealing with telephone fraud, is more appropriately applied.

Riley's acts were not equivalent to placing a telephone call. He used his home computer to dial Telco's general access number and enter random 6-digit numbers representing customer access codes every 40 seconds for several hours at a time. Moreover, RCW 9A.52.110 criminalizes the unauthorized, intentional "access" of a computer system. The term "access" is defined under RCW 9A.52.010(6) as "to approach...or otherwise make use of any resources of a computer, directly or by electronic means." Riley's repeated attempts to discover access codes by sequentially entering random 6-digit numbers constitute "approaching" or "otherwise making use of any resources of a computer."

The switch is a computer. Long distance calls are processed through the switch. Riley was approaching the switch each time he entered the general access number, followed by a random 6-digit number representing a customer access code, and a destination number. Therefore, Riley's conduct satisfied the statutory definition of "access" and so was properly treated as computer trespass.

Riley challenges three conditions of his sentence: the prohibitions against Riley owning a computer, associating with other computer hackers, and communicating with computer bulletin boards. He argues that these conditions are not directly crime related, in violation of RCW 9.94A.120(5) and RCW 9.94A.030(7), (11). We disagree and hold that all the conditions the trial court imposed are reasonably related to Riley's convictions of two counts of computer trespass against Telco.

Riley was sentenced pursuant to RCW 9.94A.120(5) which provides that a first-time offender may be sentenced to "up to two years of community supervision, which [includes the imposition of] crime-related prohibitions." Under RCW 9.94A.030(11), a crime-related prohibition is defined as "an order of a court prohibiting conduct that directly relates to the circumstances of the crime for which the offender has been convicted." The philosophy underlying the "crime-related" provision is that "persons may be punished for their crimes and they may be prohibited from doing things which are directly related to their crimes, but they may not be coerced into doing things which are believed will rehabilitate them."

The main concern that arises when reviewing crime-related prohibitions is thus the prevention of coerced rehabilitation. Otherwise, the assignment of crime-related prohibitions has traditionally been left to the discretion of the sentencing judge. Thus, a sentence will be reversed only if it is manifestly unreasonable such that no reasonable man would take the view adopted by the trial court.

Here, proscribing Riley from possessing a computer is clearly permissible under RCW 9.94A.030(7), (11). We find unpersuasive Riley's argument that this portion of his sentence is not crime related because he cannot commit computer trespass without a modem. Allowing Riley to possess a computer would facilitate his commission of computer trespass in the future. Further, given that punishment is a main goal of sentences imposed pursuant to RCW 9.94A.030(7), (11), prohibiting Riley from possessing a computer for the length of his sentence is a reasonable punishment for a self-proclaimed computer hacker.

Prohibiting Riley from associating with other computer hackers is also reasonable. Limitations upon fundamental rights are permissible, provided they are imposed sensitively. The convict's freedom of association may be restricted if reasonably necessary to accomplish the essential needs of the state and public order. The prohibition against Riley associating with other computer hackers is punitive and helps prevent Riley from further criminal conduct for the duration of his sentence. It is therefore not an unconstitutional restriction of Riley's freedom of association. The prohibition against Riley communicating with computer bulletin boards is also reasonably crime related as a means of discouraging his communication with other hackers.

We hold that the conditions of Riley's sentence were reasonably related to Riley's convictions of computer trespass. We therefore uphold the trial court's imposition of those conditions. . . .

Questions

1. State the elements of computer trespass as they're defined in the Washington statute.

2. Summarize Riley's arguments against applying the elements to his actions.

3. Summarize the court's reasons for rejecting Riley's arguments.

4. State the terms of Riley's sentence. Summarize the court's reasons for upholding the sentence. Do you agree? Explain your answer.

◆   ◆   ◆

SUMMARY

    I. Crimes against other people's property are one of three general types: taking it, damaging or destroying it, and invading it

    II. Taking other people's property

        A. History of taking other people's property

1. Simple rural, agricultural society needed protection against sneaking away with (larceny) someone else's property (mainly livestock, the most valuable possession in medieval England)
2. As society grew more complex and more personal property and more kinds of property appeared, other ways to "take" other people's property became serious problems
   a. Taking someone else's property by force
   b. Caretakers taking someone else's property that was handed over to them voluntarily
      (1) Abuse-of-trust crimes
      (2) White-collar crimes

B. Larceny
1. *Actus reus*—taking and carrying away
2. *Mens rea*—intent to permanently deprive someone else of their property
3. Circumstance element—property (something of value)
   a. Tangible personal property (property valuable itself like an MP3 player)
   b. Intangible personal property (paper that stands for something of value like checks, stocks, and bonds)
   c. Services (like cell phone service)
   d. Labor

C. White-collar (occupation-related) crimes
1. Embezzlement (the first white-collar crime)
   a. Keeping (converting) property lawfully obtained
   b. "Converting" substitutes for "taking" in larceny
2. False pretenses (theft by deceit)
   a. Tricking (deceiving) someone into giving up their property
   b. Deceiving substitutes for taking in larceny and converting in embezzlements

D. Theft
1. Consolidated theft statutes—turn away from history to logic in consolidating larceny, embezzlement, and false pretenses into one crime of theft: getting other people's money by taking, converting, or deceiving
2. Identity theft
   a. New way of committing an old crime—steal someone else's property by first stealing their identity
   b. Key to identity theft—get others' personal information
   c. Sources for stealing personal information—strangers, family members, friends, neighbors
   d. Sources for stealing other people's property—credit cards, utility services, bank accounts, and loans
3. Theft by computers and the Internet
   a. Computers and the Internet—created sources of great good but also great evil by creating new means to get other people's property
   b. Some states' response is to expand the definition of traditional theft law
   c. Most states have created specific statutes aimed at stealing by means of computers and the Internet

E. Receiving stolen property

1. It's a crime not only to take someone else's property but also to "receive" (accept) property already stolen
2. *Actus reus—receiving* means controlling (not necessarily physically) property
3. *Mens rea* varies from knowingly to recklessly to negligently, depending on the state
4. *Mens rea* also includes the intent to keep the property permanently

F. Forgery and uttering
   1. Forgery
      a. Elements
         (1) *Actus reus*—making a false document
         (2) *Mens rea*—intent to get someone else's property
      b. Document expanded in some statutes to "anything that can be falsified" (cloned cell phone, *People v. Lawrence*)
   2. Uttering
      a. Elements
         (1) *Actus reus*—passing or using a forged document
         (2) *Mens rea*—intent to defraud (get other people's property) by passing or using the forgery
      b. Utterer doesn't have to alter the document

G. Robbery
   1. Crimes against persons and their property
   2. Robbery elements
      a. *Actus reus*—taking and carrying away someone else's property by force or threat of immediate force
      b. *Mens rea*—intent to take property from another person by force or threat of immediate force
      c. Degrees measured by
         (1) Force (kind and degree) used
         (2) Injury (kind and degree) inflicted

H. Extortion (blackmail)
   1. Crimes against persons and their property
   2. Extortion elements
      a. *Actus reus*—taking someone else's property by threat of a variety of future harms
      b. *Mens rea*—intent to take someone else's property by threat of future harm

III. Damaging and destroying other people's property
   A. Crimes of damaging or destroying buildings (arson) and personal (tangible) property (criminal mischief)
   B. Arson elements
      1. *Actus reus*—"burning" building
      2. *Mens rea*—intent to commit the act of burning or setting fire to a building (not necessary to intend to damage or destroy the building)
      3. Degrees
         a. First degree—burning occupied buildings
         b. Second degree—burning unoccupied structures
   C. Criminal mischief
      1. Three kinds of harm to tangible property

a. Damage or destruction by fire, explosives, or "dangerous acts"

b. Tampering so as to endanger tangible property

c. Deception or threat that causes monetary loss

2. Other elements

a. *Actus reus*—burning, exploding, or other dangerous act

b. *Actus reus*—tampering or endangering by deceit or threat

c. *Mens rea*—purposely, knowingly, recklessly, or negligently doing any of the acts

IV. Invading other people's property

A. Invasion of property is the heart of burglary and criminal trespass

B. Burglary and criminal trespass are crimes even if someone else's property is not taken, damaged, or destroyed

C. Burglary

1. History

a. Originated as a crime of nighttime invasion of homes (regarded as castles deserving special protection, especially at night).

b. Grew to include invasions of all kinds of buildings and vessels at any time of day or night

2. Elements

a. *Actus reus*—entering or remaining in (and in a few states "breaking into") someone else's "structure"

b. *Mens rea*—intent to commit a crime once inside ("crime" intended varies widely from "felony" to "any violation of law")

3. Circumstance elements

a. Structure includes more than homes ("any structure," "any building," vessels, and vehicles)

b. Structure has to be someone else's

4. Degree (grading) depends on

a. What type of dwelling

b. Whether a weapon was used

c. Whether the dwelling was occupied

d. Whether the occupant was assaulted

e. Whether a crime was intended once inside

D. Criminal trespass

1. Essence of the offense—unwanted presence

2. Elements

a. *Actus reus*—unauthorized entering or remaining in someone else's premises (definition of premises differs from state to state)

b. *Mens rea* varies

(1) Knowledge of lack of authority (most states)

(2) Specific intent to enter or remain to commit a crime without authority

(3) Strict liability

3. Degrees (grading) depends on

a. Whether the trespass was of a home at night—misdemeanor

b. Whether the dwelling was an occupied structure—petty misdemeanor

c. Whether there was a "no trespass" notice—violation

4. Computer trespass
    a. An old response to unwanted presence (unauthorized access) by "hackers" to computer information systems
    b. No need to prove destruction or damage
    c. Invasion itself is the crime

 Go to the Criminal Law 8e CD to download this summary outline. The outline has been formatted so that you can add notes to it during class lectures, or later create a customized chapter outline to use while reviewing. Either way, the summary outline will help you understand the "big picture" and fill in the details as you study.

REVIEW QUESTIONS

1. Identify three types of property crimes, and give an example of a specific crime of each type.

2. Identify, describe, and give examples of each of the elements of larceny.

3. Explain the difference between the *actus reus* of larceny, embezzlement, and false pretenses.

4. What's the key to taking other's people's property by means of identity theft?

5. Describe the purpose of the consolidated theft statutes.

6. Identify and describe two ways states have responded to the effects of computers and the Internet on the law of theft.

7. State the *actus reus* and *mens rea* of receiving stolen property, and give an example of each.

8. State and give an example of forgery *actus reus*. What's the significance of actually profiting from forgery as an element of the crime?

9. How are robbery and extortion different from other crimes of taking other people's property?

10. Identify the elements in the *actus reus* and *mens rea* of robbery.

11. What's the difference between extortion and robbery?

12. State and give examples of arson *actus reus* and *mens rea*.

13. State the *actus reus* and *mens rea* criminal mischief, and give an example of each.

14. Identify the heart of burglary and criminal trespass.

15. What's the significance of the quotation from Sinclair Lewis's *Babbitt*?

16. Identify the elements of common-law burglary.

17. Identify the two elements in burglary *mens rea*.

18. What's the difference between burglary and criminal trespass?

19. State the *actus reus* and *mens rea* of criminal trespass, and give an example of each.

20. Describe how the law of criminal trespass applies to computer hackers.

KEY TERMS

larceny p. 375
tangible property p. 375
intangible property p. 375
robbery p. 375
abuse-of-trust crimes p. 375
white-collar crimes p. 375
trespassory taking p. 375
asportation p. 375
taking p. 376
carrying away p. 376
joyriding p. 378
grand larceny p. 379
petty larceny p. 379
bailee p. 379
embezzlement p. 379
conversion p. 380

false pretenses p. 380
theft by deceit p. 380
theft p. 383
identity theft p. 383
intellectual property p. 386
computer crimes statutes p. 386
receiving stolen property p. 390
fences p. 390
forgery p. 394
uttering p. 394
extortion p. 402
arson p. 403
criminal mischief p. 403
burning p. 404
malicious mischief p. 406
burglary p. 408

criminal trespass p. 408
structures p. 409
breaking p. 410
entering p. 410
remaining p. 410
actual entry p. 410
surreptitious remaining p. 410
occupied structure p. 411
predicate crime p. 415
physical property p. 415
computer hackers p. 416
computer trespass statutes p. 416
unauthorized computer access
    statutes p. 416

SUGGESTED READINGS

 Go to the Criminal Law 8e CD for Suggested Readings for this chapter.

THE COMPANION WEB SITE
FOR *CRIMINAL LAW,* EIGHTH EDITION

http://cj.wadsworth.com/samaha/crim_law8e

 Supplement your review of this chapter by going to the companion Web site to take one of the Tutorial Quizzes, use the flash cards to test your knowledge of the elements of various crimes and defenses, and check out the many other study aids you'll find there. You'll find valuable data and resources at your fingertips to help you study for that big exam or write that important paper.

12 Crimes Against Public Order and Morals

Chapter Main Points

- Modern disorderly conduct crimes have the same names as and similar meanings to their ancient ancestors: the misdemeanor of individual disorderly conduct and the felony of group disorderly conduct (riot).

- Some disorderly conduct crimes are now called "quality of life" crimes, but they're still aimed at the same conduct—"bad manners" in public.

- Efforts to control bad manners in public underscore the tension between order and liberty in constitutional democracies.

- Quality-of-life crimes are minor offenses, but the "broken windows" theory claims (based on mixed empirical results) they're linked to serious crime.

- There's widespread public support among all classes, races, and communities for controlling the bad behaviors of "street people" and "street gangs."

- Most people are more worried about bad public manners (loitering, panhandling, public drunkenness, and prostitution) than they are about serious crimes (rape, robbery, burglary, and assault).

- "Victimless" crimes (the ancient "crimes against public morals") are a "hot button" issue between those who believe the criminal law should enforce morality and those who believe the nonviolent behavior of competent adults is none of the law's business.

Can Criminal Law Enforce "Good Manners" and Good "Morals"?

Rocksprings is an urban war zone. The four-square-block neighborhood, claimed as the turf of a gang variously known as Varrio Sureno Town, Varrio Sureno Treces (VST), or Varrio Sureno Locos (VSL), is an occupied territory. Gang members, all of whom live elsewhere, congregate on lawns, on sidewalks, and in front of apartment complexes at all hours of the day and night. They display a casual contempt for notions of law, order, and decency— openly drinking, smoking dope, sniffing toluene, and even snorting cocaine laid out in neat lines on the hoods of residents' cars. The people who live in Rocksprings are subjected to loud talk, loud music, vulgarity, profanity, brutality, fistfights, and the sound of gunfire echoing in the streets. Gang members take over sidewalks, driveways, carports, and apartment parking areas, and impede traffic on the public thoroughfares to conduct their drive-up drug bazaar. Murder, attempted murder, drive-by shootings, assault and battery, vandalism, arson, and theft are commonplace. ◆

THE ISSUES OF PUBLIC ORDER

> The last species of offenses which especially affect the commonwealth are the due regulation and domestic order of the kingdom. The individuals of the state, like members of a well-governed family, are bound to conform their general behavior to the rules of propriety, good neighborhood, and good manners; and to be decent, industrious, and inoffensive . . . This head of offenses must therefore be very miscellaneous, as it comprises all such crimes as especially affect public society.
>
> Sir William Blackstone [1765]

In this chapter, we examine crimes against public order and morals, two vast areas of criminal law that involve mostly very minor crimes but, nonetheless, affect many more people than the crimes against persons and their property we've already discussed (Chapters 9–11) and the crimes against the state we'll discuss in Chapter 13. We'll first look at disorderly conduct crimes—the misdemeanor of individual disorderly conduct and the group disorderly conduct felony of riot. Next, we'll examine in depth the application of disorderly conduct laws to what are now called "quality of life" crimes. These are crimes directed at "bad manners" in public. Finally, we'll examine **"victimless" crimes** (crimes involving willing participants, or participants who don't see themselves as victims).

DISORDERLY CONDUCT CRIMES

Disorderly conduct crimes—except for riots—are minor crimes that legislators, judges, and scholars didn't pay much attention to until the 1950s when the *Model Penal Code* was drafted. Why the lack of attention? The punishment was minor (small fines or a few days in jail); most defendants were poor; and convictions were rarely appealed. But disorderly conduct offenses are an important part of the criminal justice system. Why? Three reasons: They "affect large numbers of defendants, involve a great proportion of public activity, and powerfully influence the view of public justice held by millions of people" (American Law Institute [ALI] 1985, 3:309).

We'll divide our discussion of these crimes into two sections: the minor offenses included in **individual disorderly conduct** statutes (fighting in public) and the felony of riot (**group disorderly conduct**).

Individual Disorderly Conduct

Disorderly conduct statutes grew out of the ancient common-law crime (Chapter 1, "Common-Law Origins" section) known as **breach of the peace.** It included both the misdemeanors of **actual disorderly conduct** (fighting in public, making unreasonable noise) and **constructive disorderly conduct,** which was conduct that "tends to provoke or excite others to break it [the peace]" (Blackstone 1769, 148).

Some statutes define disorderly conduct in general terms. Wisconsin's is a good example (Wisconsin Criminal Code 2003, § 947.01):

Whoever, in a public or private place, engages in violent, abusive, indecent, profane, boisterous, unreasonably loud or otherwise disorderly conduct under circumstances in which the conduct tends to cause or provoke a disturbance is guilty of a Class B misdemeanor.

Here's the other extreme, the frequently quoted Chicago disorderly conduct ordinance, which one court (*Landry v. Daley* 1968, 969) called "one of the most charming grab bags of criminal prohibitions ever assembled":

All persons who shall make, aid, countenance or assist in making any improper noise, riot, disturbance, breach of the peace or diversion tending to a breach of the peace, within the limits of the city; all persons who shall collect in bodies or crowds for unlawful purposes, or for any purpose, to the annoyance or disturbance of other persons; all persons who are idle or dissolute and go about begging; all persons who use or exercise any juggling or other unlawful games, all persons who are found in houses of ill-fame or gaming houses; all persons lodging in or found at any time in sheds, barns, stables, or unoccupied buildings, or lodging in the open air and not giving a good account of themselves; all persons who shall wilfully assault another in the city, or be engaged in, aid, abet in any fight, quarrel, or other disturbance in the city; all persons who stand, loiter, or stroll about in any place in the city, waiting or seeking to obtain money or other valuable things from others by trick or fraud, or to aid or assist therein; all persons that shall engage in any fraudulent scheme, device or trick to obtain money or other valuable thing in any place in the city, or who shall aid, abet, or in any manner be concerned therein; all touts, rapers, steerers, or cappers, so called, for any gambling room or house who shall ply or attempt to ply their calling on any public way in the city; all persons found loitering about any hotel, block barroom, dramshop, gambling house, or disorderly house, or wandering about the streets either by night or day without any known lawful means of support, or without being able to give a satisfactory account of themselves; all persons who shall have or carry any pistol, knife, dirk, knuckles, slingshot, or other dangerous weapon concealed on or about their persons; and all persons who are known to be narcotic addicts, thieves, burglars, pickpockets, robbers or confidence men, either by their own confession or otherwise, or by having been convicted of larceny, burglary, or other crime against the laws of the state, who are found lounging in, prowling, or loitering around any steamboat landing, railroad depot, banking institution, place of public amusement, auction room, hotel, store, shop, public way, public conveyance, public gathering, public assembly, court room, public building, private dwelling house, house of ill-fame, gambling house, or any public place, and who are unable to give a reasonable excuse for being so found, shall be deemed guilty of disorderly conduct, and upon conviction thereof, shall be severally fined not less than one dollar nor more than two hundred dollars for each offense.

ALI 1985, 3:326–327

Both types of statutes create two problems. They're too vague to give individuals and law enforcement officers notice of what the law prohibits (Chapter 2, "Void-for-Vagueness Doctrine" section) and neither requires *mens rea* (Chapter 4). The *Model Penal Code* (ALI 1985, 3:324–325) addresses both of these problems in Section 250.2:

§ 250.2 DISORDERLY CONDUCT

(1) Offense Defined. A person is guilty of disorderly conduct if, with purpose to cause public inconvenience, annoyance or alarm, or recklessly creating a risk thereof, he:
　(a) engages in fighting or threatening, or in violent or tumultuous behavior; or
　(b) makes unreasonable noise or offensively coarse utterance, gesture or display, or addresses abusive language to any person present; or
　(c) creates a hazardous or physically offensive condition by any act which serves no legitimate purpose of the actor.

"Public" means affecting or likely to affect persons in a place to which the public or a substantial group has access; among the places included are highways, transport facilities, schools, prisons, apartment houses, places of business or amusement, or any neighborhood.

(2) Grading. An offense under this section is a petty misdemeanor if the actor's purpose is to cause substantial harm or serious inconvenience, or if he persists in disorderly conduct after reasonable warning or request to desist. Otherwise disorderly conduct is a violation.

Notice that Section 250.2(1) requires a *mens rea* requirement of purpose or recklessness. So conscious risk creation is the minimum level of culpability; negligence isn't good enough (Chapter 4, "Recklessness" and "Negligence" sections).

Next, notice that the code limits conduct that qualifies as disorderly conduct *actus reus* to three kinds:

1. Fighting in public

2. Making "unreasonable noise" or using "abusive language" (Chapter 2, "Free Speech" section)

3. Creating a "hazardous or physically offensive condition" like strewing garbage, setting off "stink bombs," or turning off lights in crowded public places

In practice, the most common use of disorderly conduct statutes is against fighting in public. Fighting can cause two harms: disturbing community peace and quiet and disturbing or endangering innocent bystanders.

TABLE 12.1
Model Penal Code Special Disorderly Conduct Sections

Offense	Elements
False public alarms (250.3)	1. *Mens rea.* Knowingly 2. *Actus reus.* Initiating or circulating a report or warning of a bombing or a catastrophe 3. Harm. Likely to cause evacuation or public inconvenience or alarm
Public drunkenness (250.5)	1. *Actus reus.* Appearing in a public place "manifestly under the influence of alcohol, narcotics, or other drug, not therapeutically administered" 2. Harm. To the degree it may "endanger himself or other persons or property, or annoy persons in his vicinity"
Loitering or prowling (250.6)	1. *Actus reus.* Loitering or prowling 2. Circumstances. a. "In a place, at a time, or in a manner not usual for law-abiding individuals" b. Warrant "alarm for the safety of persons or property in the vicinity"
Obstructing highways or other public passages (250.7)	1. *Mens rea.* Purposely or recklessly 2. *Actus reus.* Obstructs highway or public passage (except if exercising lawful First Amendment rights) (Chapter 2)
Disrupting meetings and processions (250.8)	1. *Mens rea.* Purposely 2. *Actus reus.* Prevent or disrupt a lawful meeting, procession, or gathering either physically or by words, gestures, or displays designed to "outrage the sensibilities of the group"

The code also includes several "special" sections devoted to other specifically defined acts of disorderly conduct (see Table 12.1). A majority of states have adopted the *actus reus* and *mens rea* provisions of the *Model Penal Code*.

 Go to Exercise 12-1 on the Criminal Law 8e CD to learn more about disorderly conduct statutes.

Group Disorderly Conduct (Riot)

Group disorderly conduct consisted of three misdemeanors at the common law: unlawful assembly, rout, and riot. All three were aimed at preventing "the ultimate evil of open disorder and breach of the public peace" (ALI 1985, 3:313). **Unlawful assembly** was committed when a group of at least three persons joined together for the purpose of committing an unlawful act. If the three or more started toward achieving their purpose, they committed **rout.** If the group actually committed an unlawful *violent* act, or performed a lawful act in a "violent or tumultuous manner," they committed **riot.** Committing riot didn't require the group to plan their unlawful violent act before they got together; it was enough that once together they came up with the riotous plan of violence.

The Riot Act of 1714 turned the common-law misdemeanor of riot into a felony. The felony consisted of twelve or more persons who "being unlawfully, riotously, and tumultuously assembled together" stayed together for one hour after being warned to disperse by the reading of a proclamation. (Now you know the original meaning of "reading the riot act.") Here's Queen Victoria's version:

> Our sovereign lady the Queen chargeth and commandeth all persons being assembled immediately to disperse themselves and peaceably to depart to their habitations or to their

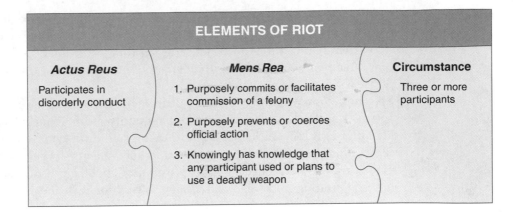

ELEMENTS OF RIOT		
Actus Reus	**Mens Rea**	**Circumstance**
Participates in disorderly conduct	1. Purposely commits or facilitates commission of a felony 2. Purposely prevents or coerces official action 3. Knowingly has knowledge that any participant used or plans to use a deadly weapon	Three or more participants

lawful business, upon the pains contained in the Act made in the first year of King George for preventing tumults and riotous assemblies. God Save the Queen.

ALI 1985, 3:314, n. 8

Modern riot law also makes riot a felony. Why? Two reasons:

1. To provide harsher penalties for disorderly conduct when group behavior gets "especially alarming or dangerous"
2. To punish persons in a disorderly crowd who disobey police orders to disperse (ALI 1985, 3:316–317)

Every state has some form of riot act; many have adopted the *Model Penal Code* provision:

RIOT §250.1(1)

(1) Riot. A person is guilty of riot, a felony of the third degree, if he participates with [two] or more others in a course of disorderly conduct:

> (a) with purpose to commit or facilitate the commission of a felony or misdemeanor;
> (b) with purpose to prevent or coerce official action; or
> (c) when the actor or any other participant to the knowledge of the actor uses or plans to use a firearm or other deadly weapon.

 Go to Exercise 12-2 on the Criminal Law 8e CD to learn more about riot.

"QUALITY-OF-LIFE" CRIMES

Significant numbers of people across the spectrums of age, sex, race, ethnicity, and class believe strongly that "bad manners" in public places create disorder and threaten the quality of life of ordinary people (Skogan 1990). Others believe just as strongly that making bad manners a crime denies individuals their liberty without due process of law (Fifth and Fourteenth Amendments to the U.S. Constitution; Chapter 2).

Constitutional democracy can't survive without order *and* liberty, but, there's a natural tension between them because they're values in conflict. The U.S. Supreme

Court has recognized the need to balance order and liberty by holding repeatedly that "ordered liberty" is a fundamental requirement of our constitutional system (Chapter 2). In this chapter, **order** refers to acting according to ordinary people's standard of "good manners." **Liberty** refers to the right of individuals to come and go as they please without government interference.

Throughout most of our history, **"bad manners" crimes** have been called **crimes against public order.** Today, we call them **quality-of-life crimes.** The list of quality-of-life offenses is long, including public drinking and drunkenness; begging and aggressive panhandlng; threatening behavior and harassment; blocking streets and public places; graffiti and vandalism; street prostitution; public urination and defecation; unlicensed vending; and even "squeegeeing"—washing the windshields of stopped cars and demanding money for the "service."

In the 1980s, two prominent scholars sensed a deep public yearning for what they called a lost sense of public "good manners," especially in our largest cities. Professors James Q. Wilson and George L. Kelling (1982) suggested that what were labeled "petty crimes" weren't just "bothering" law-abiding people; they were connected to serious crime. They called this connection between disorderly conduct and serious crime the **broken-windows theory.** According to Kelling, research conducted since the article was written in 1982 has demonstrated "a direct link between disorder and crime...." Wilson described the broken-windows theory in 1996 more cautiously. In the foreword to a book written by Kelling and Catherine M. Coles, *Fixing Broken Windows* (1996), Wilson wrote:

> We used the image of broken windows to explain how neighborhoods might decay into disorder and even crime if no one attends faithfully to their maintenance. If a factory or office window is broken, passersby observing it will conclude that no one cares or no one is in charge. In time, a few will begin throwing rocks to break more windows. Soon all the windows will be broken, and now passersby will think that, not only is no one in charge of the building no one is in charge of the street on which it faces. Only the young, the criminal, or the foolhardy have any business on an unprotected avenue, and so more and more citizens will abandon the street to those they assume prowl it. Small disorders lead to larger and larger ones, and perhaps even to crime. (xiv)

Professor Wesley G. Skogan (1990), the author of some of the research on which Kelling relies, has also characterized his and others' research more cautiously than Kelling:

> Our concern with common crime is limited to whether disorder is a cause of it.... Neighborhood levels of disorder are closely related to crime rates, to fear of crime, and the belief that serious crime is a neighborhood problem. *This relationship could reflect the fact that the link between crime and disorder is a causal one, or that both are dependent on some third set of factors (such as poverty or neighborhood instability).* (10) [italics added]

Despite the caution, Skogan still concluded that the data "support the proposition that disorder needs to be taken seriously in research on neighborhood crime, and that both directly and through crime, it plays an important role in neighborhood decline" (75).

Replications of Skogan's research have found little or no causal link between disorder and serious crime (Harcourt 2001, 8–9). What the best and most recent research suggests is that disorder and serious crime have *common* causes, but they don't cause each other, at least not directly (Sampson and Raudenbush 1999, 637–638).

Most of the national debate over crime, criminal law books (this one included), and criminal justice courses concentrate on the serious crimes we've analyzed (Chapters 9–11). But there's a disconnect between this focus on one side and local concern on the other. Mayors and local residents do worry about murder, rape, burglary, and theft, but they also care a lot about order on their streets, in their parks, and in other public places. In a careful and extensive survey of a representative sample of high- and low-crime neighborhoods in major cities, public drinking, followed closely by loitering youths, topped the list of worries among all classes, races, and ethnic groups, among both men and women. Survey participants also listed begging, street harassment, noisy neighbors, vandalism, street prostitution, and illegal vending (Skogan 1990, 2). Prosecutor Karen Hayter found this out when she created Kalamazoo, Michigan's Neighborhood Prosecutor Program. When Hayter "asked residents what crimes worried them the most, she thought it would be the big ones: murder, assault, breaking and entering," but that's not what she was told. Instead, said Hayter, "Loud noise, littering, loitering, curfew violations, junk autos, rundown houses—those are considered quality-of-life crimes, and they're very important to residents in an area" (National Public Radio 2003).

Any examination of criminal law has to recognize quality-of-life crimes as part of early twenty-first century life. Since the 1980s, state statutes and city ordinances have reinvigorated and molded the old crimes against public order and morals to fit the public's demand that criminal justice preserve, protect, and even restore the quality of life in their communities. The courts have assumed the burden of balancing the social interest in public order against the social interest in individual liberty and privacy (Skogan 1990, 21).

Next, we examine how states and localities have shaped traditional public order and morals laws to control the public behavior of two groups—"street people" and street gangs—and the quality-of-life crimes commonly associated with them: vagrancy, loitering, panhandling, and gang activity.

Vagrancy and Loitering

For at least 600 years, it's been a crime for poor people to *roam* around without visible means of support (**vagrancy**) or to *stand* around with no apparent purpose (**loitering**). The Articles of Confederation specifically denied to paupers the freedom to travel from state to state. In 1837, in *Mayor of New York v. Miln*, the U.S. Supreme Court approved the efforts by the state of New York to exclude paupers arriving by ship. According to the Court, it's

> as necessary for a state to provide precautionary measures against the moral pestilence of paupers, vagabonds, and possibly convicts as it is to guard against the physical pestilence, which may arise from unsound and infectious articles.

Every state in the union had and enforced vagrancy and loitering statutes that wrote the Court's view into law (Simon 1992, 631).

Vagrancy

Laws targeting poor people behavior, and the attitudes behind them, began to change during the Great Depression of the 1930s. In 1941, the U.S. Supreme Court struck down a vagrancy statute that prohibited the importation of paupers into California.

In response to the argument that the regulation of paupers enjoyed a long history, the Court dismissed the earlier decisions as out of date. According to the Court, "We do not think that it will now be seriously contended that because a person is without employment and without funds he constitutes a 'moral pestilence.'" In a concurring opinion, Justice Robert Jackson encouraged the Court to "say now, in no uncertain terms, that a mere property status, without more, cannot be used by a state to test, qualify, or limit his rights as a citizen of the United States" (*Edwards v. California* 1941, 184).

During the 1960s and 1970s, courts began to strike down vagrancy laws because they unfairly discriminated against the poor. The following excerpt from an opinion written by Chief Justice Thompson of the Nevada Supreme Court in *Parker v. Municipal Judge* (1967) reflects this trend:

> It is simply not a crime to be unemployed, without funds, and in a public place. To punish the unfortunate for this circumstance debases society. The comment of [U.S. Associate Supreme Court] Justice Douglas is relevant: "How can we hold our heads high and still confuse with crime the need for welfare or the need for work?"

In *Papichristou v. City of Jacksonville* (1972), the U.S. Court struck down the Jacksonville, Florida, vagrancy ordinance, which was nearly identical to virtually every other vagrancy law in the country. Writing for a unanimous Court, Justice Douglas declared the ordinance void for vagueness, because it both failed to give adequate notice to individuals and it encouraged arbitrary law enforcement (Chapter 2). The Court warned that criminal statutes aimed at the poor

> teach that the scales of justice are so tipped that even-handed administration of the law is not possible. The rule of law, evenly applied to minorities as well as majorities, to the poor as well as the rich, is the great mucilage that holds society together. (169)

Loitering

In *Kolender v. Lawson* (1983), the U.S. Supreme Court tightened the constitutional restrictions on loitering statutes. The counterpart to *vagrancy,* which means to roam about with no visible means of support, *loitering* means to "remain in one place with no apparent purpose." In *Kolender,* the Court struck down a California statute that combined ancient vagrancy and loitering into a new crime defined as "wandering the streets and failing to produce credible identification" when a police officer asked for it. As it did with the vagrancy statute in *Papichristou,* the Court ruled that the statute was void for vagueness.

According to Harry Simon (1992), staff attorney for the Legal Aid Society in Santa Ana, California:

> With the Supreme Court's decisions in *Papichristou* and *Kolender,* loitering and vagrancy laws ceased to be effective tools to punish and control the displaced poor. While judicial attitudes on vagrancy and loitering laws had changed, local officials perceived the invalidation of these laws as a dangerous assault on their authority to enforce social order. (645)

According to Robert C. Ellickson (1996), professor of Property and Urban Law at the Yale Law School:

> Many judges at the time seemed blind to the fact that their constitutional rulings might adversely affect the quality of urban life and the viability of city centers. It is one thing to protect unpopular persons from wrongful confinement; it is another to imply that these persons have no duty to behave themselves in public places. In addition, federal constitutional

rulings are one of the most centralized and inflexible forms of lawmaking. In a diverse and dynamic nation committed to separation of powers and federalism, there is much to be said for giving state and local legislative bodies substantial leeway to tailor street codes to city conditions, and for giving state judges ample scope to interpret the relevant provisions of state constitutions. (1213–1214)

At the same time these decisions were easing up on control over the behavior of poor people in public, other events were creating a rapidly—and to many a frightening—growth of an underclass. Mental institutions were in the midst of major deinstitutionalization of the mentally ill; family breakdowns and breakups were increasing steeply; crack cocaine was becoming more available on the streets; hard economic times were upon us; and budgets for social programs were tightening. By the late 1980s, this rising underclass and its public presence and behavior led many city dwellers to conclude that "things had gone too far." The liberal columnist Ellen Goodman, in "Swarms of Beggars Cause 'Compassion Fatigue,'" captured this attitude when she wrote, "Today at least, this tourist, walking from one block to another, one cup to another, one city to another, wants to join in a citizens' chorus: 'Enough's enough'" (Simon 1992, 1218). Municipal codes reflected this growing intolerance of street people's behavior. By the late 1990s, Juliette Smith (1996) found that "at least thirty-nine American cities had initiated or continued policies that criminalize activities associated with homelessness" (29).

Enforcing the laws regulating the behavior of homeless and other "street people" generates controversy because these laws seem to target the poorest and weakest members of the community in order to provide for the comfort and convenience of better-off residents. But James Q. Wilson defends these laws, noting that the special competence of courts lies in defining and applying rights; courts typically hear the cases of "an individual beggar, sleeper, or solicitor." Such an individual rarely poses a threat to anyone, "and so the claims of communal order often seem, in the particular case, to be suspect or overdrawn."

> But the effects on a community of many such individuals taking advantage of the rights granted to an individual (or often, as the court sees it, an abstract depersonalized individual) are qualitatively different from the effects of a single person. A public space—a bus stop, a market square, a subway entrance—is more than the sum of its parts; it is a complex pattern of interactions that can become dramatically more threatening as the scale and frequency of those interactions increase. As the number of unconventional individuals increases arithmetically, the number of worrisome behaviors increases geometrically.
>
> Kelling and Coles 1996, xiv

San Francisco is one of many cities whose officials enforced the "quality of life" laws against the "bad public manners" of street people, but, it's also a city where a few individuals turned to the courts to fight for the constitutional rights of homeless people. In *Joyce v. City and County of San Francisco* (1994), Federal District Judge Lowell Jensen heard a motion to grant a **preliminary injunction** (a temporary court order to do or to stop doing something) to stop the city of San Francisco from continuing its Matrix Program, which was designed to preserve the quality of life on San Francisco streets and other public places. (Granting a preliminary injunction isn't a decision that the plaintiff is right; it only means the plaintiff has enough of a case to justify a temporary freeze to give the court time to decide whether to decide the case in the plaintiff's favor.)

Joyce v. City and County of San Francisco
846 F.Supp. 843 (N.D.Cal. 1994)

Bobby Joe Joyce, Timothy E. Smith, Thomas O'Halloran, and Jim Tullah, homeless persons, brought an action against the city seeking a preliminary injunction against the Matrix Program which targeted violation of certain ordinances and thus allegedly penalized homeless persons for engaging in life sustaining activities. U.S. District Judge Lowell Jensen denied the plaintiffs' motion for a preliminary injunction.

JENSEN, J.

FACTS

Plaintiffs to this action seek preliminary injunctive relief on behalf of themselves and a class of homeless individuals alleged to be adversely affected by the City and County of San Francisco's (the "City's") "Matrix Program." While encompassing a wide range of services to the City's homeless, the Program simultaneously contemplates a rigorous law enforcement component aimed at those violations of state and municipal law which arguably are committed predominantly by the homeless. Plaintiffs endorse much of the Program, challenging it not in its entirety, but only insofar as it specifically penalizes certain "life sustaining activities" engaged in by the homeless.

Institution of the Matrix Program followed the issuance of a report in April of 1992 by the San Francisco Mayor's Office of Economic Planning and Development, which attributed to homelessness a $173 million drain on sales in the City. In August of 1993, the City announced commencement of the Matrix Program, and the San Francisco Police Department began stringently enforcing a number of criminal laws.

The City describes the Program as "initiated to address citizen complaints about a broad range of offenses occurring on the streets and in parks and neighborhoods. . . . [The Matrix Program is] a directed effort to end street crimes of all kinds." The program addresses offenses including public drinking and inebriation, obstruction of sidewalks, lodging, camping or sleeping in public parks, littering, public urination and defecation, aggressive panhandling, dumping of refuse, graffiti, vandalism, street prostitution, and street sales of narcotics, among others.

An illustration of the enforcement efforts characteristic of the Program can be found in a four-page intradepartmental memorandum addressed to the Police Department's Southern Station Personnel. That memorandum, dated August 10, 1993 and signed by acting Police Captain Barry Johnson, defines "Quality of Life" violations and establishes a concomitant enforcement policy. Condemning a "type of behavior [which] tends to make San Francisco a less desirable place in which to live, work or visit," the memorandum directs the vigorous enforcement of eighteen specified code sections, including prohibitions against trespassing, public inebriation, urinating or defecating in public, removal and possession of shopping carts, solicitation on or near a highway, erection of tents or structures in parks, obstruction and aggressive panhandling.

Pursuant to the memorandum,

All station personnel shall, when not otherwise engaged, pay special attention and enforce observed "Quality of Life" violations. . . . One Officer . . . shall, daily, be assigned specifically to enforce all "Quality of Life" violations. . . .

Officers are to stop and advise all individuals pushing shopping carts that said carts are the property of local stores (Grocery/Drug etc.) and that these carts are never sold: Therefore the carts will, in the near future, be confiscated for return to their rightful owner or otherwise disposed of by the police. . . . Note: This phase of the "Quality of Life" operation will be implemented when appropriate containers, for the contents of the shopping carts, are available. . . .

In a Police Department Bulletin entitled "Update on Matrix Quality of Life Program," dated September 17, 1993, Deputy Chief Thomas Petrini paraphrased General Order D6, the source of the intended nondiscriminatory policy of the Program's enforcement measures:

All persons have the right to use the public streets and places so long as they are not engaged in specific criminal activity. Factors such as race, sex, sexual preference, age, dress, unusual or disheveled or impoverished appearance do not alone justify enforcement action. Nor can generalized complaints by residents or merchants or others justify detention of any person absent such individualized suspicion.

The memorandum stated that the "rights of the homeless must be preserved," and included as an attachment a Department Bulletin on "Rights of the Homeless," which stated that:

[All members of the Department] are obligated to treat all persons equally, regardless of their economic or living conditions. The homeless enjoy the same legal and individual rights afforded to others. Members shall at all times respect these rights. . . .

The Police Department has, during the pendency of the Matrix Program, conducted continuing education for officers regarding nondiscriminatory enforcement of the Program. When, in mid-August of 1993, concerns were raised by interests outside the Department about proper enforcement of the ordinances prohibiting lodging and sleeping in public parks, the Department issued a clarification of its policies. Again, in mid-November of 1993, inquiries were made of the Police Department concerning the confiscation of grocery store shopping carts. Police Chief Anthony Ribera responded with the issuance of a Department Bulletin establishing topical guidelines.

Since implementation of the Matrix Program, the City estimates that "according to unverified statistics kept by the Department," approximately sixty percent of enforcement actions have involved public inebriation and public drinking, and that other "significant categories" include felony arrests for narcotics and other offenses, and arrests for street sales without a permit. Together, enforcement actions concerning camping in the park . . . , sleeping in the park during prohibited hours . . . , and lodging . . . have constituted only approximately 10% of the total.

Plaintiffs, pointing to the discretion inherent in policing the law enforcement measures of the Matrix Program, allege certain actions taken by police to be "calculated to punish the homeless." As a general practice, the Program is depicted by plaintiffs as "targeting hundreds of homeless persons who are guilty of nothing more than sitting on a park bench or on the ground with their possessions, or lying or sleeping on the ground covered by or on top of a blanket or cardboard carton." On one specific occasion, according to plaintiffs, police "cited and detained more than a dozen homeless people, and confiscated and destroyed their possessions, leaving them without medication, blankets or belongings to cope with the winter cold."

The City contests the depiction of Matrix as a singularly focused, punitive effort designed to move "an untidy problem out of sight and out of mind." Instead, the City characterizes the Matrix Program as

an interdepartmental effort . . . [utilizing] social workers and health workers . . . and offering shelter, medical care, information about services and general assistance. Many of those on the street refuse those services, as is their right; but Matrix makes the choice available. . . .

The City emphasizes its history as one of the largest public providers of assistance to the homeless in the State, asserting that "individuals on general assistance in San Francisco are eligible for larger monthly grants than are available almost anywhere else in California." Homeless persons within the City are entitled to a maximum general assistance of $345 per month—an amount exceeding the grant provided by any of the surrounding counties. General assistance recipients are also eligible for up to $109 per month in food stamps. According to the City, some 15,000 City residents are on general assistance, of whom 3,000 claim to be homeless.

The City's Department of Social Services encourages participation in a Modified Payments Program offered by the Tenderloin Housing Clinic. Through this program, a recipient's general assistance check is paid to the Clinic, which in turn pays the recipient's rent and remits the balance to the recipient. The Clinic then negotiates with landlords of residential hotels to accept general assistance recipients at rents not exceeding $280 per month.

By its own estimate, the City will spend $46.4 million for services to the homeless for 1993–94. Of that amount, over $8 million is specifically earmarked to provide housing, and is spent primarily on emergency shelter beds for adults, families, battered women and youths. An additional $12 million in general assistance grants is provided to those describing themselves as homeless, and free health care is provided by the City to the homeless at a cost of approximately $3 million.

The City contends that "few of the Matrix-related offenses involve arrest." Those persons found publicly inebriated, according to the City, are taken to the City's detoxification center or district stations until sober. "Most of the other violations result in an admonishment or a citation."

Since its implementation, the Matrix Program has resulted in the issuance of over 3,000 citations to homeless persons. Plaintiffs contend these citations have resulted in a cost to the City of over $500,000. Citations issued for encampment and sleeping infractions are in the amount of $76, according to Alissa Riker, Director of the Supervised Citation Release Program ("SCRP") with the Center for Juvenile and Criminal Justice. Those cited must pay or contest the citation within twenty-one days; failure to do so results in a $180 warrant for the individual's arrest, which is issued approximately two months after citation of the infraction. Upon the accrual of $1,000 in warrants, which equates roughly to the receipt of six citations, an individual becomes ineligible for citation release and may be placed in custody. The typical practice, however, is that those arrested for Matrix-related offenses are released on their own recognizance or with "credit for time served" on the day following arrest. [Seventeen homeless persons were held in custody as a result of high bail amounts accruing from Matrix-identified infraction warrants.] In each instance, the individual was released after being sentenced to "credit for time served." Plaintiffs characterize the system as one in which "homeless people are cycled through the criminal justice system and released to continue their lives in the same manner, except now doing so as 'criminals.'"

According to plaintiffs, the City has conceded the inadequacy of shelter for its homeless. Plaintiffs have cited as supporting evidence an application made to the State Department of Housing and Community Development in which the City's Director of Homeless Services described an "emergency situation" created by the closure of the Transbay Terminal, which had served as "the largest de facto shelter for homeless individuals."

Plaintiffs have proffered estimates as to the number of homeless individuals unable to find nightly housing. Plaintiffs cite a survey conducted by Independent Housing Services, a nonprofit agency which among its aims seeks the improvement of access to affordable housing for the homeless. Begun in July of 1990 and conducted most recently in August of 1993, the survey tracks the number of homeless individuals turned away each night from shelters in the San Francisco area due to a lack of available bed space. Based on the data of that survey, plaintiffs contend that from January to July of 1993, an average of 500 homeless persons was turned away nightly from homeless shelters. That number, according to plaintiffs, increased to 600 upon the closing of the Transbay Terminal. . . .

OPINION

. . . The Court is called upon to decide whether to grant a preliminary injunction. . . . Such relief constitutes an extraordinary use of the Court's powers, and is to be granted sparingly and with the ultimate aim of preserving the status quo pending trial on the merits. . . . The decision whether to grant preliminary injunctive relief is largely left to its discretion. However, this discretion has been circumscribed by the presence or not of various factors, notably, the likelihood that the moving party will prevail on the merits and the likelihood of harm to the parties from granting or denying the injunctive relief. . . .

The injunction sought by plaintiffs at this juncture of the litigation must be denied for each of two independent reasons. First, the proposed injunction lacks the necessary specificity to be enforceable, and would give rise to enforcement problems sufficiently inherent as to be incurable by modification of the proposal. Second, those legal theories upon which plaintiffs rely are not plainly applicable to the grievances sought to be vindicated, with the effect that the Court cannot find at this time that, upon conducting the required balance of harm and merit, plaintiffs have established a sufficient probability of success on the merits to warrant injunctive relief. . . .

. . . Equal Protection Clause

[Preliminary] . . . to an equal protection clause violation is a finding of governmental action undertaken with an intent to discriminate against a particular individual or class of individuals. Such intent may be evinced by statutory language, or in instances where an impact which cannot be explained on a neutral ground unmasks an invidious discrimination. Under the latter approach, a neutral law found to have a disproportionately adverse effect upon a minority classification will be deemed unconstitutional only if that impact can be traced to a discriminatory purpose.

In the present case, plaintiffs have not at this time demonstrated a likelihood of success on the merits of the equal protection claim, since the City's action has not been taken with an evinced intent to discriminate against an identifiable group. . . . Various directives issued within the Police Department mandate the nondiscriminatory enforcement of Matrix. Further, the Police Department has, during the pendency of the Matrix Program, conducted continuing education for officers regarding nondiscriminatory enforcement of the Program. It has not been proven at this time that Matrix was implemented with the aim of discriminating against the homeless. That enforcement of Matrix will, de facto, fall predominantly on the homeless does not in itself effect an equal protection clause violation. . . .

Even were plaintiffs able at this time to prove an intent to discriminate against the homeless, the challenged sections of the Program might nonetheless survive constitutional scrutiny. Only in cases where the challenged action is aimed at a suspect classification, such as race or gender, or premised upon the exercise of a fundamental right, will the governmental action be subjected to a heightened scrutiny.

Counsel for plaintiff proposed at the hearing that this Court should be the first to recognize as a fundamental right the "right to sleep." This is an invitation the Court, in its exercise of judicial restraint, must decline. Despite the seeming innocence of a right so defined, the natural corollary to recognition of a right is an obligation to enforce it. The discovery of a right to sleep concomitantly requires prohibition of the government's interference with that right. This endeavor, aside from creating a jurisprudential morass, would involve this unelected branch of government in a legislative role for which it is neither fit, nor easily divested once established. . . .

Due Process of Law

Plaintiffs contend the Matrix Program has been enforced in violation of the due process clause . . . of the United

States...Constitution....Plaintiffs specifically argue that due process has been violated by employing punitive policing measures against the homeless for sleeping in public parks; plaintiffs also argue that certain state codes are unconstitutionally vague.

1. *Punishing the Homeless for Sitting or Sleeping in Parks*
   Plaintiffs claim that San Francisco Park Code section 3.12 has been applied by police in an unconstitutional manner. That section provides,

   > No person shall construct or maintain any building, structure, tent or any other thing in any park that may be used for housing accommodations or camping, except by permission from the Recreation and Park Commission.

   Plaintiffs contend the Police Department has impermissibly construed this provision to justify citing, arresting, threatening and "moving along" those "persons guilty of nothing more than sitting on park benches with their personal possessions or lying on or under blankets on the ground." Plaintiffs have submitted declarations of various homeless persons supporting the asserted application of the San Francisco Park Code section. It appears, if plaintiffs have accurately depicted the manner in which the section is enforced, that the section may have been applied to conduct not covered by the section and may have been enforced unconstitutionally....

2. *...Vagueness Challenges to Enforcement Measures*
   Plaintiffs also contend that San Francisco Park Code section 3.12...and California Penal Code Section 647(i)* are unconstitutionally overbroad and vague....

   The possible success of the vagueness challenge is... as it seems readily apparent the measure is not "impermissibly vague in all of its applications...." This likely failing follows from plaintiffs' inability to prove at this stage that police have been granted an excess of discretion pursuant to the statute. Plaintiffs assert vagueness in the San Francisco Park Code prohibition against maintaining "any other thing" that "may be used for... camping," and in enforcing the Penal Code prohibition against one "who lodges in...public," claiming "the vagueness of these [Park Code] terms has apparently allowed San Francisco police officers to determine that blankets or possessions in carts are sufficiently connected to 'camping' to violate the ordinance." Plaintiffs

have also submitted declarations of homeless persons supporting these assertions, and a concession by Assistant District Attorney Paul Cummins to the effect that the standards for enforcement are vague....

Similarly, the challenged Penal Code section cannot be concluded by the Court at this time to be unconstitutionally vague. Read in conjunction with supplemental memoranda, the challenged measures appear, as a constitutional matter, sufficiently specific. Police officers were specifically cautioned in a September 17, 1993 memorandum that "the mere lying or sleeping on or in a bedroll of and in itself does not constitute a violation." While plaintiffs argue the additional memoranda were circulated too late to save the enforcement measures from vagueness, and also that they do not eliminate the confusion, it is far from clear that plaintiffs could meet the requisite showing that the measure was impermissibly vague in all its applications. Accordingly, even if the limits of permissible enforcement of these sections have not been perfectly elucidated, preliminary injunctive relief is inappropriate at this stage of the litigation.

Conclusion

In common with many communities across the country, the City is faced with a homeless population of tragic dimension. Today, plaintiffs have brought that societal problem before the Court, seeking a legal judgment on the efforts adopted by the City in response to this problem.

The role of the Court is limited structurally by the fact that it may exercise only judicial power, and technically by the fact that plaintiffs seek extraordinary pretrial relief. The Court does not find that plaintiffs have made a showing at this time that constitutional barriers exist which preclude that effort. Accordingly, the Court's judgment at this stage of the litigation is to permit the City to continue enforcing those aspects of the Matrix Program now challenged by plaintiffs.

The Court therefore concludes that the injunction sought, both as it stands now and as plaintiffs have proposed to modify it, is not sufficiently specific to be enforceable. Further, upon conducting the required balance of harm and merit, the Court finds that plaintiffs have failed to establish a sufficient probability of success on the merits to warrant injunctive relief. Accordingly, plaintiffs' motion for a preliminary injunction is DENIED.

IT IS SO ORDERED.

Questions

1. Describe the main elements of the Matrix Program.
2. Why did San Francisco adopt the Matrix Program?

---

*Every person who commits any of the following acts is guilty of disorderly conduct, a misdemeanor: ... Who lodges in any building, structure, vehicle, or place, whether public or private, without the permission of the owner or person entitled to the possession or in control thereof. Cal. Penal Code § 647(i).

3. What are the plaintiffs' objections to the Matrix Program?

4. Assume you're the attorney for San Francisco, and argue that the court should deny the injunction.

5. Assume you're the attorney for the homeless people, and argue that the court should issue the injunction.

6. If you could, what terms would you include in an injunction in this case?

Panhandling

On the concrete plaza outside [San Francisco] City Hall here, day or night, dozens of homeless men and women shuffle from bench to grate dragging blankets or pushing shopping carts stuffed with all they own. They beg, they bicker, they sleep. It is a ragged, aimless procession that never ends. It is also a sight that this ever-tolerant city is tired of seeing. Frustrated by how difficult it is to end homelessness even in robust economic times, and facing pressure to make neighborhoods and business centers safe and clean, San Francisco has become the latest in a growing number of cities deciding that it is time to get tougher. (A3)

So wrote *Washington Post* reporter Renee Sanchez (1998) about the continuing backlash against the so-called rights revolution of the 1960s and 1970s. According to Robert Tier (1993), General Counsel of the American Alliance for Rights and Responsibilities:

Many City Councils have been convinced to adopt new and innovative controls on antisocial behavior to maintain minimal standards of public conduct and to keep public spaces safe and attractive.... One of the most common examples of these efforts are ordinances aimed at aggressive begging. (286)

These "new and innovative controls" rely on ancient laws against begging. At the outset, keep in mind that these new anti-begging ordinances don't apply to organized charities. So, although it's a crime for a private beggar to panhandle for money, it's legal for the Salvation Army to ring their bells to get contributions. Why the distinction? Supporters of the distinction say the rights revolution has simply gone too far. It's reached the point, they say, where the rights of a minority of offensive individuals trump the quality of life of the whole community. Associate Supreme Court Justice Clarence Thomas (1996), commenting on "how judicial interpretations of the First Amendment and of 'unenumerated' constitutional rights have affected the ability of urban communities to deal with crime, disorder, and incivility on their public streets," told the Federalist Society:

Vagrancy, loitering, and panhandling laws were challenged [during the rights revolution] because the poor and minorities could be victims of discrimination under the guise of broad discretion to ensure public safety. Moreover, as a consequence of the modern tendency to challenge society's authority to dictate social norms, the legal system began to prefer the ideal of self-expression without much attention to self-discipline or self-control. What resulted was a culture that declined to curb the excesses of self-indulgence—vagrants and others who regularly roamed the streets had rights that could not be circumscribed by the community's sense of decency or decorum. (269)

"Hey, buddy, can you spare some change?" is clearly speech. And, of course the First Amendment guarantees individuals freedom of speech. But, free speech doesn't mean you can say anything you want anywhere at anytime (Chapter 2). The U.S. Supreme Court has "rejected the notion that a city is powerless to protect its citizens from unwanted exposure to certain methods of expression which may legitimately be deemed a public nuisance" (Scheidegger 1993, 7).

The Court has established a number of tests to determine whether ordinances violate the First Amendment guarantee of free speech. One is to look at the place where the speech takes place. In traditional public forums—streets, sidewalks, and parks—where people have since ancient times expressed their views, the freedom to solicit is virtually unrestricted. In designated public forums—places the government chooses to make available to the public—the government has more leeway to regulate solicitation. In nonpublic forums—airports, bus stations, railroad stations, subways, and shopping malls—the government has broad power to restrict and even prohibit solicitation (Scheidegger 1993, 7–9).

Second, the First Amendment free speech clause permits **time, place, and manner regulations.** According to the U.S. Supreme Court (*R.A.V. v. City of St. Paul* 1992), to be constitutional, restrictions have to satisfy three elements of a time, place, and manner test:

1. They aren't based on the *content* of the speech.

2. They serve a significant government interest, like maintaining the free flow of pedestrian traffic.

3. They leave open other channels of expression.

The first element in the test bars the use of the regulation to suppress any message about social conditions that panhandlers are trying to convey. The second element is often hotly debated. Advocates for panhandlers argue that the regulation of panhandling is really a government policy of removing "unsightly" poor people from public view. Others maintain that the "purpose is to permit people to use the streets, sidewalks, and public transportation free from the borderline robbery and pervasive fraud which characterizes so much of today's panhandling" (Scheidegger 1993, 10–11). The third element requires the regulation to allow panhandlers to beg in other ways. So, a panhandling ordinance that prohibits *"aggressive* panhandling" leaves panhandlers free to beg peaceably. So do bans on fraudulent panhandling or panhandling in subways. Panhandlers can beg honestly or on streets and in parks (10–11).

In addition to forum and time, place, and manner restrictions, the First Amendment gives the government considerable leeway to regulate nonverbal expression (**expressive conduct**; Chapter 2). This would allow direct efforts to stop panhandlers from approaching people or blocking the sidewalk to beg or receiving the money they solicited.

Finally, the First Amendment grants **commercial speech** (advertising and other means of "asking for" money) less protection than other types of speech. Since begging relies on talking listeners into handing over their money, panhandling is commercial speech. The U.S. Court of Appeals for the Seventh Circuit decided whether an Indianapolis ordinance restricting panhandling violated the First Amendment right to free speech in *Gresham v. Peterson* (2000).

Gresham v. Peterson
225 F.3d 899 (7th Cir. 2000)

Jimmy Gresham challenged an Indianapolis ordinance that limits street begging in public places and prohibits entirely activities defined as "aggressive panhandling." Gresham believes that the ordinance infringes his First Amendment right to free speech and his Fourteenth Amendment right to due process. The city considers the ordinance a reasonable response to the public safety threat posed by panhandlers. The district court found that a state court could construe the ordinance in such a way to render it sufficiently clear and specific and granted the city summary judgment on Gresham's request for a permanent injunction. The U.S. Circuit Court affirmed.

KANNE, J.

FACTS

In June 1999, the City of Indianapolis amended an ordinance regarding solicitation in public places. The ordinance, which became effective on July 6, 1999, reads as follows:

(a) As used in this section, panhandling means any solicitation made in person upon any street, public place or park in the city, in which a person requests an immediate donation of money or other gratuity from another person, and includes but is not limited to seeking donations:

(1) By vocal appeal or for music, singing, or other street performance; and,

(2) Where the person being solicited receives an item of little or no monetary value in exchange for a donation, under circumstances where a reasonable person would understand that the transaction is in substance a donation.

However, panhandling shall not include the act of passively standing or sitting nor performing music, singing or other street performance with a sign or other indication that a donation is being sought, without any vocal request other than in response to an inquiry by another person.

(b) It shall be unlawful to engage in an act of panhandling on any day after sunset, or before sunrise.

(c) It shall be unlawful to engage in an act of panhandling when either the panhandler or the person being solicited is located at any of the following locations; at a bus stop; in any public transportation vehicle or public transportation facility; in a vehicle which is parked or stopped on a public street or alley; in a sidewalk cafe; or within twenty (20) feet in any direction from an automatic teller machine or entrance to a bank.

(d) It shall be unlawful to engage in an act of panhandling in an aggressive manner, including any of the following actions:

(1) Touching the solicited person without the solicited person's consent.

(2) Panhandling a person while such person is standing in line and waiting to be admitted to a commercial establishment;

(3) Blocking the path of a person being solicited, or the entrance to any building or vehicle;

(4) Following behind, ahead or alongside a person who walks away from the panhandler after being solicited;

(5) Using profane or abusive language, either during the solicitation or following a refusal to make a donation, or making any statement, gesture, or other communication which would cause a reasonable person to be fearful or feel compelled; or,

(6) Panhandling in a group of two (2) or more persons.

(e) Each act of panhandling prohibited by this section shall constitute a public nuisance and a separate violation of this Code. Each violation shall be punishable as provided in section 103-3 of the Code, and the court shall enjoin any such violator from committing further violations of this section.

City-County General Ordinance No. 78 (1999), Revised Code of Indianapolis and Marion County § 407-102.

Section 103-3 provides that a person convicted of violating the ordinance will be fined not more than $2,500 for each violation. The ordinance does not provide for imprisonment of violators, except, of course, a past offender who violates the mandatory injunction provided in Paragraph (e) could be jailed for contempt.

Jimmy Gresham is a homeless person who lives in Indianapolis on Social Security disability benefits of $417 per month. He supplements this income by begging, using the money to buy food. He begs during both the daytime and nighttime in downtown Indianapolis. Because different people visit downtown at night than during the day, it is important to him that he be able to beg at night. Gresham approaches people on the street, tells them he is homeless and asks for money to buy food. Gresham has not been cited for panhandling under the new ordinance, but he fears being cited for panhandling at night or if an officer interprets his requests for money to be "aggressive" as defined by the law.

Gresham filed this class action shortly after the ordinance took effect, requesting injunctive and declaratory relief. Gresham moved for a preliminary injunction barring enforcement of the ordinance on the grounds that it was unconstitutionally vague and violated his right to free speech. The district court, after hearing oral argument... entered a final order denying the motion for preliminary injunction and dismissing the case.

In the order, the district court construed the list of six actions that constitute aggressive panhandling as exclusive, eliminating the danger that someone could be cited for other, unenumerated acts. The court further ruled that the proscription in Paragraph (d)(5) against actions that make a person "fearful or feel compelled" was not unconstitutionally vague because it could be interpreted to mean "fear for his safety or feel compelled to donate." The court held that because the ordinance was civil in nature and the actions prohibited under aggressive panhandling were not related to speech interests, no intent element was necessary. Finally, the court found the ordinance to be a valid content-neutral regulation.... ["Content neutral" means that the government regulation isn't an excuse to censor the message of the speech.]

OPINION

On appeal, Gresham raises two principal arguments. First, he contends that the provisions defining aggressive panhandling are vague because they fail to provide clear criteria to alert panhandlers and authorities of what constitutes a violation and because they fail to include an intent element. Second, he argues that the statute fails the test for content neutral time, place and manner restrictions on protected speech. We review de novo* the question of whether a state law violates the Constitution.

A. The First Amendment

Laws targeting street begging have been around for many years, but in the last twenty years, local communities have breathed new life into old laws or passed new ones. Cities, such as Indianapolis, have tried to narrowly draw the ordinances to target the most bothersome types of street solici-

---

*A review without deference to the trial court's ruling on the ordinance's constitutionality.

tations and give police another tool in the effort to make public areas, particularly downtown areas, safe and inviting.

While the plaintiff here has focused the inquiry on the effects of the ordinance on the poor and homeless, the ordinance itself is not so limited. It applies with equal force to anyone who would solicit a charitable contribution, whether for a recognized charity, a religious group, a political candidate or organization, or for an individual. It would punish street people as well as Salvation Army bell ringers outside stores at Christmas, so long as the appeal involved a vocal request for an immediate donation.

The ordinance bans panhandling by beggars or charities citywide on any "street, public place or park" in three circumstances. First, it would prohibit any nighttime panhandling. § 407-102(b). Second, it would prohibit at all times—day or night—panhandling in specified areas. § 407-102(c). Third, it would prohibit "aggressive panhandling" at all times. § 407-102(d)(1)-(6). The defendants emphatically point out that the ordinance allows a great deal of solicitation, including "passive" panhandling, which does not include a vocal appeal, street performances, legitimate sales transactions and requests for donations over the telephone or any other means that is not "in person" or does not involve an "immediate donation." Under the ordinance, one could lawfully hold up a sign that says "give me money" and sing "I am cold and starving," so long as one does not voice words to the effect of "give me money."

Several courts before us, as well as many commentators, have grappled with understanding panhandling laws in light of the First Amendment guarantee of free speech and the constitutional right to due process. See, e.g., *Smith v. City of Fort Lauderdale*, 177 F.3d 954 (11th Cir.1999); *Loper v. New York City Police Dep't*, 999 F.2d 699 (2d Cir.1993). To this point, the Supreme Court has not resolved directly the constitutional limitations on such laws as they apply to individual beggars, but has provided clear direction on how they apply to organized charities, not-for-profits and political groups.

To the extent the Indianapolis ordinance could be enforced against organized charities, such as the United Way, Salvation Army or others, the Supreme Court's holding in *Schaumburg* would control resolution of the case.... The Court placed charitable solicitations by organizations in a category of speech close to the heart of the First Amendment, and distinguished it from "purely commercial speech" which is "primarily concerned with providing information about the characteristics and costs of goods and services." Commercial speech, on the other hand, has been placed lower in the First Amendment food chain, somewhere between political speech and pornography. It deserves protection, but authorities are more free to regulate commercial speech than core-value speech....

Similarly, the Indianapolis ordinance protects the communication of ideas by solicitors and limits only the bare request for cash. Yet the two can be closely intertwined. Beggars at times may communicate important political or social messages in their appeals for money, explaining their conditions related to veteran status, homelessness, unemployment and disability, to name a few. Like the organized charities, their messages cannot always be easily separated from their need for money. While some communities might wish all solicitors, beggars and advocates of various causes be banished from the streets, the First Amendment guarantees their right to be there, deliver their pitch and ask for support....

After recognizing a First Amendment right to solicit money in public places, the *Schaumburg* Court held that a government may enact "reasonable regulations" so long as they reflect "due regard" for the constitutional interests at stake. The parties assume that the proper analysis to determine whether the Indianapolis ordinance is one such reasonable regulation is that set out for "time, place and manner" restrictions.... Because the Indianapolis ordinance does not ban all panhandling, we agree that the law could be understood as a time, place or manner regulation.... Governments may "enforce regulations of the time, place and manner of expression which are content neutral, are narrowly tailored to serve a significant government interest, and leave open ample alternative channels of communication."...

Because the parties here agree that the regulations are content neutral..., the Indianapolis ordinance should be upheld if it is narrowly tailored to achieve a significant governmental purpose and leaves open alternate channels of communication.

The city has a legitimate interest in promoting the safety and convenience of its citizens on public streets. The plaintiff concedes this much, but argues that a total nighttime ban on verbal requests for alms is substantially broader than necessary and therefore cannot be considered narrowly tailored. However, a government regulation can be considered narrowly tailored "so long as the... regulation promotes a substantial government interest that would be achieved less effectively absent the regulation." This means the regulation need not be a perfect fit for the government's needs, but cannot burden substantially more speech than necessary. Furthermore, a time, place or manner restriction need not be the least restrictive means of achieving the government purpose, so long as it can be considered narrowly tailored to that purpose.

The city determined that vocal requests for money create a threatening environment or at least a nuisance for some citizens. Rather than ban all panhandling, however, the city chose to restrict it only in those circumstances where it is considered especially unwanted or bothersome—at night,

around banks and sidewalk cafes, and so forth. These represent situations in which people most likely would feel a heightened sense of fear or alarm, or might wish especially to be left alone. By limiting the ordinance's restrictions to only those certain times and places where citizens naturally would feel most insecure in their surroundings, the city has effectively narrowed the application of the law to what is necessary to promote its legitimate interest.

Finally, the plaintiff contends that the statute fails to provide ample alternative channels of communication. We disagree. An adequate alternative does not have to be the speaker's first or best choice, or one that provides the same audience or impact for the speech. However, the Court has "shown special solicitude for forms of expression that are much less expensive than feasible alternatives," and so an alternative must be more than merely theoretically available. It must be realistic as well. Furthermore, an adequate alternative cannot totally foreclose a speaker's ability to reach one audience even if it allows the speaker to reach other groups.

The Indianapolis ordinance allows many feasible alternatives to reach both the daytime and nighttime downtown Indianapolis crowds. Under the ordinance, panhandlers may ply their craft vocally or in any manner they deem fit (except for those involving conduct defined as aggressive) during all the daylight hours on all of the city's public streets. Gresham contends that soliciting at night is vital to his survival, a fact we do not dispute, but the ordinance leaves open many reasonable ways for him to reach the nighttime downtown crowd. He may solicit at night, so long as he does not vocally request money. He may hold up signs requesting money or engage in street performances, such as playing music, with an implicit appeal for support. Although perhaps not relevant to street beggars, the ordinance also permits telephone and door-to-door solicitation at night. Thus to the extent that "give me money" conveys an idea the expression of which is protected by the First Amendment, solicitors may express themselves vocally all day, and in writing, by telephone or by other non-vocal means all night. Furthermore, they may solicit in public places on all 396.4 square miles of the city, except those parts occupied by sidewalk cafes, banks, ATMs and bus stops. This is a far cry from the total citywide ban on panhandling overturned by the court in *Loper*, 999 F.2d at 705 ("A statute that totally prohibits begging in all public places cannot be considered 'narrowly tailored.'"), or the total ban on panhandling in a five-mile area of public beach upheld by the court in *Smith*, 177 F.3d at 956.

B. Vagueness

Gresham next challenges certain provisions of the ordinance as unconstitutionally vague. Specifically, he contends that the definition[s] of aggressive panhandling in sections (d)(4) and (d)(5) are not sufficiently clear to direct authorities on the enforcement of the law, nor to allow panhandlers such as Gresham to avoid violating the law. Section (d)(4) prohibits "following behind, ahead or alongside a person who walks away from the panhandler after being solicited."* Gresham argues hypothetically that police could cite a person for inadvertently violating this section merely by walking in the same direction as the solicited person, without intending to engage in "aggressive panhandling." Also, section (d)(5) refers to making a person "fearful or feel compelled" without defining what the terms mean in relation to panhandling. A generalized guilt at economic inequality might make one "feel compelled" even by the meekest request for money.

The void-for-vagueness doctrine forbids the enforcement of a law that contains "terms so vague that [persons] of common intelligence must necessarily guess at its meaning and differ as to its application." Legislative enactments must articulate terms "with a reasonable degree of clarity" to reduce the risk of arbitrary enforcement and allow individuals to conform their behavior to the requirements of the law. A statute that "vests virtually complete discretion in the hands of the police" fails to provide the minimal guidelines required for due process.

In assessing the constitutionality of an allegedly vague state law or ordinance, "a federal court must, of course, consider any limiting construction that a state court or enforcement agency has proffered." In this case, the Indiana courts have not yet had an opportunity to interpret the terms of the Indianapolis ordinance, and so we have no authoritative judicial construction of its terms. However, the rule that federal courts should defer to state court interpretations of state laws, also discourages federal courts from enjoining statutes that could be easily narrowed by a state court to avoid constitutional problems. Therefore, we will not hold a vague statute unconstitutional if a reasonable interpretation by a state court could render it constitutional in some application.

Laws must contain a "reasonable degree of clarity" so that people of "common intelligence" can understand their meaning. Furthermore, because the penalties for noncompliance are less severe, laws imposing civil rather than criminal penalties do not demand the same high level of clarity. Like the civil sanction at issue in Hoffman Estates, Gresham faces only a fine for noncompliance with the Indianapolis law. However, this lowered burden is mitigated by the fact that the Indianapolis ordinance potentially interferes with the right of free speech, suggesting that a "more stringent vagueness test should apply."

The challenged provisions in this case define what the City Council meant by the term "aggressive panhandling"

---

*Chapter 2, "Void for Vagueness Doctrine" section.

and must be read in that context. The district court was rightly concerned that Paragraph (d) could be construed as offering an incomplete list of examples of prohibited behavior, leaving open the possibility that other unspecified actions might also be considered illegal, which would raise serious due process concerns. The district court suggested that the list might be exclusive rather than illustrative, a reasonable interpretation which, if adopted by the Indiana courts, would save it from a vagueness challenge.

Likewise, Paragraphs (d)(4) and (d)(5) are subject to reasonable interpretations that answer the vagueness challenge. A state court interpreting Paragraph (d)(4) may read it to prohibit "following" only in the context of a continued request for money such that the victim reasonably interprets the behavior as a threat. A continuing request for a donation coupled with "following" would be prohibited, but walking in the same direction as the solicited person would not be against the law if the walking were divorced from the request. Construed this way, the statute would prohibit the type of harassing behavior that governments routinely outlaw. See, e.g., Ind.Code § 35-45-2-1 (prohibiting as intimidation a threat by words or action that forces a person to engage in conduct against their will); Ind.Code § 35-45-10-1 (prohibiting as stalking a "course of conduct involving repeated or continuing harassment of another person that would cause a reasonable person to feel terrorized, frightened, intimidated, or threatened").

Numerous cases hold that governments may proscribe threats, extortion, blackmail and the like, "despite the fact that they criminalize utterances because of their expressive content." See, e.g., Watts v. United States, 394 U.S. 705, 707 (1969) (upholding constitutionality of law against threatening life of the President); United States v. Velasquez, 772 F.2d 1348, 1357 (7th Cir. 1985) (holding that threats of physical violence are not protected by First Amendment); see also R.A.V. v. City of St. Paul, 505 U.S. 377, 420, (1992) (Stevens, J., concurring) (quoting Frederick Schauer, Categories and the First Amendment: A Play in Three Acts, 34 Vand. L.Rev. 265, 270 (1981)) ("Although the First Amendment broadly protects 'speech,' it does not protect the right to 'fix prices, breach contracts, make false warranties, place bets with bookies, threaten, or extort.'").

Paragraph (d)(5) could be construed to prohibit "any statement, gesture, or other communication" that makes a reasonable person feel they face danger if they refuse to donate, that they are being compelled out of physical fear. The possibility that a polite request for a donation might be heard as a threatening demand by an unusually sensitive or timid person is eliminated by the "reasonable person" standard included in the ordinance. A statement that makes a reasonable person feel compelled to donate out of physical fear amounts to a prohibition on robbery or extortion, which of course would be constitutional. While it is not a certainty that the state courts would adopt constitutional interpretations of the panhandling provisions, they are entitled to the opportunity to do so, and we will not interfere with that right. The district court did not err in refusing to enjoin the ordinance based on the vagueness concerns.

Conclusion

For the foregoing reasons, we AFFIRM the district court's denial of a permanent injunction and dismissal of Gresham's complaint.

Questions

1. State the main elements in Indianapolis's panhandling ordinance.

2. Summarize the positions of the city of Indianapolis and Jimmy Gresham regarding the ordinance.

3. Should there be a distinction between organized charities and individual beggars when it comes to asking for money in this ordinance? Explain your answer.

4. According to the court, what's the difference between solicitation and commercial speech? What's the significance of distinguishing between them?

5. According to the court, why doesn't the ordinance violate the free speech clause of the First Amendment?

6. Should panhandling be considered speech? Defend your answer.

7. Assuming that panhandling is speech, is this ordinance a reasonable "time, place, and manner" regulation of free speech?

8. Summarize the arguments the court gives for ruling that the ordinance is not unconstitutionally vague. Do you agree? Defend your answer.

EXPLORING PANHANDLING FURTHER

Go to the Criminal Law 8e CD to read the full text version of the case featured here.

Did the City of Chicago's Panhandling Ordinance Violate the First Amendment?

FACTS

Section 8-4-010(f) of the Chicago Municipal Code, which states that "a person commits disorderly conduct when he knowingly: ...(f) Goes about begging or soliciting funds on the public ways, except as provided in Chapter 10-8, Sections 10-8-110 through 10-8-170." Chapter 10-8 allows individuals to solicit charitable donations provided they have a permit. Jesse Thompson is a homeless person who panhandles money from pedestrians on the public sidewalks in the City. Thompson and other homeless people sued the City of Chicago for violating their First Amendment rights. They alleged that the City has repeatedly ticketed and arrested them, pursuant to section 8-4-010(f), for panhandling on public sidewalks. On October 30, 2001, the City sent a facsimile to the various police districts instructing the police not to enforce the ordinance. Despite this alleged change in policy, Plaintiffs contend that the City has maintained a policy of arresting and harassing them for panhandling on public sidewalks. The City has moved to dismiss.

DECISION AND REASONS

The U.S. Court of Appeals (7th Cir.) denied the motion:

To plead a claim for a violation of the First Amendment against a municipality, plaintiffs must allege that they sustained or are immediately in danger of sustaining a specific, direct injury from a government policy that chills the exercise of their First Amendment rights. The government policy, however, must present an objective harm or threat to the plaintiffs; allegations of a subjective "chill" are not sufficient.

Section 8-4-010(f) prohibits panhandling on any of the City's "public ways." Although neither the Supreme Court nor the Seventh Circuit has addressed the issue, in *Loper v. New York Police Department*, 999 F.2d 699, 709 (2d Cir. 1993), the Second Circuit held that a similar panhandling statute, which broadly prohibited all panhandling on city streets, violated the First Amendment. In *Gresham v. Peterson*, 225 F.3d 899 (7th Cir. 2000), the Seventh Circuit rejected a constitutional challenge to an Indianapolis panhandling ordinance that prohibited "aggressive panhandling," but permitted peaceful panhandling at certain times and in certain locations. The Seventh Circuit, however, noted that the ordinance was a "far cry from the total citywide ban on panhandling overturned by the court in *Loper*."

Here, the City has not at this time challenged [the plaintiffs' allegations]...that section 8-4-010(f)'s broad prohibition on panhandling violated Plaintiffs' First Amendment rights. On October 30, 2001, after this suit was filed, the City sent a facsimile to each police district stating that the police were no longer to enforce the panhandling ordinance. Plaintiffs, however, allege...

that, despite the patently illegal nature of section 8-4-101(f) and the October 30 facsimile, the City, nevertheless, has a policy of harassing and reprimanding persons who panhandle on public sidewalks in Chicago. Consequently, construing the allegations as true, this Court finds that Plaintiffs have sufficiently alleged that the City has a custom and practice that presents a sufficiently objective barrier to Plaintiffs' First Amendment right to panhandle on public sidewalks.

Thompson and others v. City of Chicago,
WL 31115578 (N.D.Ill. 2002)

◆ ◆ ◆

Gang Activity

"Bands of loitering youth" seriously threaten their quality of life, say many city residents (Skogan 1990, 23). Gangs can include everything from casual groups of kids who are just hanging out drinking a little bit all the way to "organized fighting squads" who terrorize neighborhoods. The casual groups do little more than "bother" residents. According to one observer, "They are neighborhood kids, and they sometimes make a nuisance of themselves. Actually they stand there because they have no place to go" (23). Gangs composed of older, rowdier members are more threatening. According to a resident in a neighborhood with one of these gangs:

> Sometimes I walk out of my house and start to try to walk down the street, and a gang will cross the street and try to scare me and my mother. A gang used to sit and drink beer and smoke pot in front of our stairs. My mom used to come out and tell them to get off; they would, and then when she would go into the house they'd come back, sit down, and look at us. Actually we're afraid to walk around in the neighborhood after it gets dark. I stay right in front of the house where my mom can see me. (24)

A number of state and city governments have passed criminal laws to regulate gang behavior. In some places, it's a crime to participate in a gang. Some statutes and ordinances have stiffened the penalties for crimes committed by gang members. Others make it a crime to encourage minors to participate in gangs. Some have applied organized crime statutes to gangs. A few have punished parents for their children's gang activities. Cities have also passed ordinances banning gang members from certain public places, particularly city parks.

In addition to criminal penalties, cities have also turned to civil remedies to control gang activity. For example, in the ancient civil remedy **injunction to abate public nuisances,** which is still used,, city attorneys ask courts to declare gang activities and gang members public nuisances and to issue injunctions (court orders) to abate (eliminate) the public nuisance. According to the California Supreme Court, in *People ex rel. Gallo v. Acuna* (1997), a public nuisance may be any act

> which alternatively is injurious to health or is indecent, or offensive to the senses; the result of the act must interfere with the comfortable enjoyment of life or property; and those affected by the act may be an entire neighborhood or a considerable number of people.

The city attorney of Santa Clara in *Acuna* asked for an injunction ordering gang members to stop doing all of the following:

"(a) Standing, sitting, walking, driving, gathering or appearing anywhere in public view with any other defendant herein, or with any other known 'VST' (Varrio Sureno Town or Varrio Sureno Locos) member;

(b) Drinking alcoholic beverages in public excepting consumption on properly licensed premises or using drugs;

(c) Possessing any weapons including but not limited to knives, dirks, daggers, clubs, nunchukas, BB guns, concealed or loaded firearms, and any other illegal weapons as defined in the California Penal Code, and any object capable of inflicting serious bodily injury including but not limited to the following: metal pipes or rods, glass bottles, rocks, bricks, chains, tire irons, screwdrivers, hammers, crowbars, bumper jacks, spikes, razor blades, razors, sling shots, marbles, ball bearings;

(d) Engaging in fighting in the public streets, alleys, and/or public and private property;

(e) Using or possessing marker pens, spray paint cans, nails, razor blades, screwdrivers, or other sharp objects capable of defacing private or public property;

(f) Spray painting or otherwise applying graffiti on any public or private property, including but not limited to the street, alley, residences, block walls, vehicles and/or any other real or personal property;

(g) Trespassing on or encouraging others to trespass on any private property;

(h) Blocking free ingress and egress to the public sidewalks or street, or any driveways leading or appurtenant thereto in 'Rocksprings';

(i) Approaching vehicles, engaging in conversation, or otherwise communicating with the occupants of any vehicle or doing anything to obstruct or delay the free flow of vehicular or pedestrian traffic;

(j) Discharging any firearms;

(k) In any manner confronting, intimidating, annoying, harassing, threatening, challenging, provoking, assaulting and/or battering any residents or patrons, or visitors to 'Rocksprings,' or any other persons who are known to have complained about gang activities, including any persons who have provided information in support of this Complaint and requests for Temporary Restraining Order, Preliminary Injunction and Permanent Injunction;

(l) Causing, encouraging, or participating in the use, possession and/or sale of narcotics;

(m) Owning, possessing or driving a vehicle found to have any contraband, narcotics, or illegal or deadly weapons;

(n) Using or possessing pagers or beepers in any public space;

(o) Possessing channel lock pliers, picks, wire cutters, dent pullers, sling shots, marbles, steel shot, spark plugs, rocks, screwdrivers, 'slim jims' and other devices capable of being used to break into locked vehicles;

(p) Demanding entry into another person's residence at any time of the day or night;

(q) Sheltering, concealing or permitting another person to enter into a residence not their own when said person appears to be running, hiding, or otherwise evading a law enforcement officer;

(r) Signaling to or acting as a lookout for other persons to warn of the approach of police officers and soliciting, encouraging, employing or offering payment to others to do the same;

(s) Climbing any tree, wall, or fence, or passing through any wall or fence by using tunnels or other holes in such structures;

(t) Littering in any public place or place open to public view;

(u) Urinating or defecating in any public place or place open to public view;

(v) Using words, phrases, physical gestures, or symbols commonly known as hand signs or engaging in other forms of communication which describe or refer to the gang known as 'VST' or 'VSL' as described in this Complaint or any of the accompanying pleadings or declarations;

(w) Wearing clothing which bears the name or letters of the gang known as 'VST' or 'VSL';

(x) Making, causing, or encouraging others to make loud noise of any kind, including but not limited to yelling and loud music at any time of the day or night."

The California trial court issued the injunction, and the California Supreme Court upheld the injunction against challenges that it both violated freedom of association and was void for vagueness. Injunctions, like crimes that outlaw gang activities, call for balancing community and individual rights. The community interest in the quality of life requires peace, quiet, order, and a sense of security. At the same time, even members of street gangs have the right to associate, express themselves, travel freely, and be free from vague laws (see Chapter 2, "Void for Vagueness Doctrine" section).

In 1992, Chicago was facing a skyrocketing increase in crime rates that many outspoken people blamed on street gangs. But, unlike the sweeping injunction approved in California, the Chicago City Council passed a modern version of the ancient loitering ordinances (discussed in the "Loitering" section). Chicago's ordinance gave its police the power to order groups of loiterers (people who "remain in one place with no apparent purpose") to disperse or face arrest if officers reasonably believed that one of the loiterers was a gang member (Poulos 1995, 379–381).

No one was surprised when the ordinance set off an angry debate. Mayor Richard Daley, Jr. expressed one view, "In some areas of the city, street gangs are terrorizing residents and laying claim to whole communities." Bobbie Crawford, a waitress, expressed another view, "When kids reach a certain age they hang around on street corners. I sure wouldn't like my children taken to a police station for hanging around." And Joan Suglich, mother of six, asked, "What if somebody asks his boys to walk him home so gang members don't jump him. Are police going to arrest them?" Nor was anyone surprised when the debate ended up in the U.S. Supreme Court. A divided Court decided the constitutionality of the ordinance in *City of Chicago v. Morales* (1999).

CASE | *Was the Loitering Ordinance Void for Vagueness?*

City of Chicago v. Morales
527 U.S. 41 (1999)

After they were charged with violating the city's gang loitering ordinance, Jesus Morales moved to dismiss the actions. The Circuit Court, Cook County, granted the motion. The City appealed. The Appellate Court affirmed, and granted the city's subsequent request for a certificate of importance. After the defendants in another set of actions were charged with violating the ordinance, the Circuit Court dismissed the charges. On review, the Appellate Court affirmed. The City petitioned for a leave to appeal. In a further set of actions, the defendants were convicted in the Circuit Court of violating the ordinance and were sentenced to jail terms. The defendants appealed. The Appellate Court reversed. The City petitioned for leave to appeal. After granting the petitions and consolidating the cases, the Supreme Court of Illinois affirmed. Granting certiorari, the United States Supreme Court affirmed the judgment of the Illinois Supreme Court.

STEVENS, J. announced the judgment of the Court and delivered the following opinion.

FACTS

In 1992, the Chicago City Council enacted the Gang Congregation Ordinance, which prohibits "criminal street gang members" from "loitering" with one another or with other persons in any public place. The question presented is whether the Supreme Court of Illinois correctly held that the ordinance violates the Due Process Clause of the Fourteenth Amendment to the Federal Constitution.

. . .

Before the ordinance was adopted, the city council's Committee on Police and Fire conducted hearings to explore the problems created by the city's street gangs, and more particularly, the consequences of public loitering by gang members. Witnesses included residents of the neighborhoods where gang members are most active, as well as some of the aldermen who represent those areas. Based on that evidence, the council made a series of findings that are included in the text of the ordinance and explain the reasons for its enactment.

The council found that a continuing increase in criminal street gang activity was largely responsible for the city's rising murder rate, as well as an escalation of violent and drug related crimes. It noted that in many neighborhoods throughout the city, "the burgeoning presence of street gang members in public places has intimidated many law abiding citizens." Furthermore, the council stated that gang members "establish control over identifiable areas . . . by loitering in those areas and intimidating others from entering those areas; and . . . members of criminal street gangs avoid arrest by committing no offense punishable under existing laws when they know the police are present. . . ." It further found that "loitering in public places by criminal street gang members creates a justifiable fear for the safety of persons and property in the area" and that "aggressive action is necessary to preserve the city's streets and other public places so that the public may use such places without fear." Moreover, the council concluded that the city "has an interest in discouraging all persons from loitering in public places with criminal gang members."

The ordinance creates a criminal offense punishable by a fine of up to $500, imprisonment for not more than six months, and a requirement to perform up to 120 hours of community service. Commission of the offense involves four predicates. First, the police officer must reasonably believe that at least one of the two or more persons present in a "public place" is a "criminal street gang member." Second, the persons must be "loitering," which the ordinance defines as "remain[ing] in any one place with no apparent purpose." Third, the officer must then order "all" of the persons to disperse and remove themselves "from the area." Fourth, a person must disobey the officer's order. If any person, whether a gang member or not, disobeys the officer's order, that person is guilty of violating the ordinance. The ordinance states in pertinent part:

(a) Whenever a police officer observes a person whom he reasonably believes to be a criminal street gang member loitering in any public place with one or more other persons, he shall order all such persons to disperse and remove themselves from the area. Any person who does not promptly obey such an order is in violation of this section.
(b) It shall be an affirmative defense to an alleged violation of this section that no person who was observed loitering was in fact a member of a criminal street gang.
(c) As used in this section:
(1) 'Loiter' means to remain in any one place with no apparent purpose.
(2) 'Criminal street gang' means any ongoing organization, association in fact or group of three or more persons, whether formal or informal, having as one of its substantial activities the commission of one or more of the criminal acts enumerated in paragraph (3) and whose members individually or collectively engage in or have engaged in a pattern of criminal gang activity. . . .
(5) 'Public place' means the public way and any other location open to the public, whether publicly or privately owned.

. . .

(e) Any person who violates this Section is subject to a fine of not less than $100 and not more than $500 for each offense, or imprisonment for not more than six months, or both. In addition to or instead of the above penalties, any person who violates this section may be required to perform up to 120 hours of community service pursuant to section 1-4-120 of this Code. Chicago Municipal Code § 8-4-015 (added June 17, 1992).

Two months after the ordinance was adopted, the Chicago Police Department promulgated General Order 92-4 to provide guidelines to govern its enforcement. That order purported to establish limitations on the enforcement discretion of police officers "to ensure that the anti-gang loitering ordinance is not enforced in an arbitrary or discriminatory way." The limitations confine the authority to arrest gang members who violate the ordinance to sworn "members of the Gang Crime Section" and certain other designated officers, and establish detailed criteria for defining street gangs and membership in such gangs. In addition, the order directs district commanders to "designate areas in which the presence of gang members has a demonstrable effect on the activities of law abiding persons in the surrounding community," and provides that the ordinance "will be enforced only within the designated areas." The city, however, does not release the locations of these "designated areas" to the public.

...

During the three years of its enforcement, the police issued over 89,000 dispersal orders and arrested over 42,000 people for violating the ordinance. In the ensuing enforcement proceedings, two trial judges upheld the constitutionality of the ordinance, but eleven others ruled that it was invalid. In respondent Youkhana's case, the trial judge held that the "ordinance fails to notify individuals what conduct is prohibited, and it encourages arbitrary and capricious enforcement by police."

The city believes that the ordinance resulted in a significant decline in gang-related homicides. It notes that in 1995, the last year the ordinance was enforced, the gang-related homicide rate fell by 26%. In 1996, after the ordinance had been held invalid, the gang-related homicide rate rose 11%. However, gang-related homicides fell by 19% in 1997, over a year after the suspension of the ordinance. Given the myriad factors that influence levels of violence, it is difficult to evaluate the probative value of this statistical evidence, or to reach any firm conclusion about the ordinance's efficacy. Cf. Harcourt, "Reflecting on the Subject: A Critique of the Social Influence Conception of Deterrence, the Broken Windows Theory, and Order-Maintenance Policing New York Style," 97 Mich. L.Rev. 291, 296 (1998) (describing the "hotly contested debate raging among...experts over the causes of the decline in crime in New York City and nationally")....

OPINION

The basic factual predicate for the city's ordinance is not in dispute. As the city argues in its brief,

> the very presence of a large collection of obviously brazen, insistent, and lawless gang members and hangers-on on the public ways intimidates residents, who become afraid even to leave their homes and go about their business. That, in turn, imperils community residents' sense of safety and security, detracts from property values, and can ultimately destabilize entire neighborhoods.

The findings in the ordinance explain that it was motivated by these concerns. We have no doubt that a law that directly prohibited such intimidating conduct would be constitutional, but this ordinance broadly covers a significant amount of additional activity. Uncertainty about the scope of that additional coverage provides the basis for respondents' claim that the ordinance is too vague.

In fact the city already has several laws that serve this purpose. See, e.g., Ill. Comp. Stat. ch. 720 §§ 5/12-6 (1998) (Intimidation); 570/405.2 (Streetgang criminal drug conspiracy); 147/1 et seq. (Illinois Streetgang Terrorism Omnibus Prevention Act); 5/25-1 (Mob action). Deputy Superintendent Cooper, the only representative of the police department at the Committee on Police and Fire hearing on the ordinance, testified that, of the kinds of behavior people had discussed at the hearing, "90 percent of those instances are actually criminal offenses where people, in fact, can be arrested."

We are confronted at the outset with the city's claim that it was improper for the state courts to conclude that the ordinance is invalid on its face. The city correctly points out that imprecise laws can be attacked on their face...[if they fail] to establish standards for the police and public that are sufficient to guard against the arbitrary deprivation of liberty interests.* The freedom to loiter for innocent purposes is part of the "liberty" protected by the Due Process Clause of the Fourteenth Amendment. We have expressly identified this "right to remove from one place to another according to inclination" as "an attribute of personal liberty" protected by the Constitution. Indeed, it is apparent that an individual's decision to remain in a public place of his choice is as much a part of his liberty as the freedom of movement inside frontiers that is "a part of our heritage" or the right to move "to whatsoever place one's own inclination may direct" identified in Blackstone's *Commentaries*....

Vagueness may invalidate a criminal law for either of two independent reasons. First, it may fail to provide the kind of notice that will enable ordinary people to understand what conduct it prohibits; second, it may authorize and even encourage arbitrary and discriminatory enforcement. Accordingly, we first consider whether the ordinance provides fair notice to the citizen and then discuss its potential for arbitrary enforcement.

"It is established that a law fails to meet the requirements of the Due Process Clause if it is so vague and standardless that it leaves the public uncertain as to the conduct it prohibits...." The Illinois Supreme Court recognized that the term "loiter" may have a common and accepted meaning, but the definition of that term in this ordinance—"to remain in any one place with no apparent purpose"—does not. It is difficult to imagine how any citizen of the city of Chicago standing in a public place with

---

*Chapter 2, "Void for Vagueness Doctrine" section.

a group of people would know if he or she had an "apparent purpose." If she were talking to another person, would she have an apparent purpose? If she were frequently checking her watch and looking expectantly down the street, would she have an apparent purpose?

Since the city cannot conceivably have meant to criminalize each instance a citizen stands in public with a gang member, the vagueness that dooms this ordinance is not the product of uncertainty about the normal meaning of "loitering," but rather about what loitering is covered by the ordinance and what is not.

The Illinois Supreme Court emphasized the law's failure to distinguish between innocent conduct and conduct threatening harm. . . . Its decision followed the precedent set by a number of state courts that have upheld ordinances that criminalize loitering combined with some other overt act or evidence of criminal intent (ordinance criminalizing loitering with purpose to engage in drug-related activities; ordinance criminalizing loitering for the purpose of engaging in or soliciting lewd act). However, state courts have uniformly invalidated laws that do not join the term "loitering" with a second specific element of the crime (statute that made it unlawful "for any person to loiter or prowl upon the property of another without lawful business with the owner or occupant thereof").

The city's principal response to this concern about adequate notice is that loiterers are not subject to sanction until after they have failed to comply with an officer's order to disperse. "Whatever problem is created by a law that criminalizes conduct people normally believe to be innocent is solved when persons receive actual notice from a police order of what they are expected to do." We find this response unpersuasive for at least two reasons.

First, the purpose of the fair notice requirement is to enable the ordinary citizen to conform his or her conduct to the law. "No one may be required at peril of life, liberty or property to speculate as to the meaning of penal statutes." Although it is true that a loiterer is not subject to criminal sanctions unless he or she disobeys a dispersal order, the loitering is the conduct that the ordinance is designed to prohibit. . . . Because an officer may issue an order only after prohibited conduct has already occurred, it cannot provide the kind of advance notice that will protect the putative loiterer from being ordered to disperse. Such an order cannot retroactively give adequate warning of the boundary between the permissible and the impermissible applications of the law.

Second, the terms of the dispersal order compound the inadequacy of the notice afforded by the ordinance. It provides that the officer "shall order all such persons to disperse and remove themselves from the area." This vague phrasing raises a host of questions. After such an order issues, how long must the loiterers remain apart? How far must they move? If each loiterer walks around the block and they meet again at the same location, are they subject to arrest or merely to being ordered to disperse again? As we do here, we have found vagueness in a criminal statute exacerbated by the use of the standards of "neighborhood" and "locality.". . . Both terms are elastic and, dependent upon circumstances, may be equally satisfied by areas measured by rods or by miles.

Lack of clarity in the description of the loiterer's duty to obey a dispersal order might not render the ordinance unconstitutionally vague if the definition of the forbidden conduct were clear, but it does buttress our conclusion that the entire ordinance fails to give the ordinary citizen adequate notice of what is forbidden and what is permitted. The Constitution does not permit a legislature to "set a net large enough to catch all possible offenders, and leave it to the courts to step inside and say who could be rightfully detained, and who should be set at large." This ordinance is therefore vague "not in the sense that it requires a person to conform his conduct to an imprecise but comprehensible normative standard, but rather in the sense that no standard of conduct is specified at all."

The broad sweep of the ordinance also violates the requirement that a legislature establish minimal guidelines to govern law enforcement. There are no such guidelines in the ordinance. In any public place in the city of Chicago, persons who stand or sit in the company of a gang member may be ordered to disperse unless their purpose is apparent. The mandatory language in the enactment directs the police to issue an order without first making any inquiry about their possible purposes. It matters not whether the reason that a gang member and his father, for example, might loiter near Wrigley Field is to rob an unsuspecting fan or just to get a glimpse of Sammy Sosa leaving the ballpark; in either event, if their purpose is not apparent to a nearby police officer, she may—indeed, she "shall"—order them to disperse.

Recognizing that the ordinance does reach a substantial amount of innocent conduct, we turn, then, to its language to determine if it "necessarily entrusts lawmaking to the moment-to-moment judgment of the policeman on his beat." As we discussed in the context of fair notice, the principal source of the vast discretion conferred on the police in this case is the definition of loitering as "to remain in any one place with no apparent purpose."

As the Illinois Supreme Court interprets that definition, it "provides absolute discretion to police officers to determine what activities constitute loitering." We have no authority to construe the language of a state statute more narrowly than the construction given by that State's highest court. "The power to determine the meaning of a statute carries with it the power to prescribe its extent and limitations as well as the method by which they shall be determined."

Nevertheless, the city disputes the Illinois Supreme Court's interpretation, arguing that the text of the ordinance limits the officer's discretion in three ways. First, it does not permit the officer to issue a dispersal order to anyone who is moving along or who has an apparent purpose. Second, it does not permit an arrest if individuals obey a dispersal order. Third, no order can issue unless the officer reasonably believes that one of the loiterers is a member of a criminal street gang.

Even putting to one side our duty to defer to a state court's construction of the scope of a local enactment, we find each of these limitations insufficient. That the ordinance does not apply to people who are moving—that is, to activity that would not constitute loitering under any possible definition of the term—does not even address the question of how much discretion the police enjoy in deciding which stationary persons to disperse under the ordinance. Similarly, that the ordinance does not permit an arrest until after a dispersal order has been disobeyed does not provide any guidance to the officer deciding whether such an order should issue. The "no apparent purpose" standard for making that decision is inherently subjective because its application depends on whether some purpose is "apparent" to the officer on the scene.

Presumably an officer would have discretion to treat some purposes—perhaps a purpose to engage in idle conversation or simply to enjoy a cool breeze on a warm evening—as too frivolous to be apparent if he suspected a different ulterior motive. Moreover, an officer conscious of the city council's reasons for enacting the ordinance might well ignore its text and issue a dispersal order, even though an illicit purpose is actually apparent.

It is true, as the city argues, that the requirement that the officer reasonably believe that a group of loiterers contains a gang member does place a limit on the authority to order dispersal. That limitation would no doubt be sufficient if the ordinance only applied to loitering that had an apparently harmful purpose or effect, or possibly if it only applied to loitering by persons reasonably believed to be criminal gang members. Not all of the respondents in this case, for example, are gang members. The city admits that it was unable to prove that Morales is a gang member but justifies his arrest and conviction by the fact that Morales admitted "that he knew he was with criminal street gang members." But this ordinance, for reasons that are not explained in the findings of the city council, requires no harmful purpose and applies to non-gang members as well

as suspected gang members. It applies to everyone in the city who may remain in one place with one suspected gang member as long as their purpose is not apparent to an officer observing them. Friends, relatives, teachers, counselors, or even total strangers might unwittingly engage in forbidden loitering if they happen to engage in idle conversation with a gang member.

Ironically, the definition of loitering in the Chicago ordinance not only extends its scope to encompass harmless conduct, but also has the perverse consequence of excluding from its coverage much of the intimidating conduct that motivated its enactment. As the city council's findings demonstrate, the most harmful gang loitering is motivated either by an apparent purpose to publicize the gang's dominance of certain territory, thereby intimidating nonmembers, or by an equally apparent purpose to conceal ongoing commerce in illegal drugs. As the Illinois Supreme Court has not placed any limiting construction on the language in the ordinance, we must assume that the ordinance means what it says and that it has no application to loiterers whose purpose is apparent. The relative importance of its application to harmless loitering is magnified by its inapplicability to loitering that has an obviously threatening or illicit purpose.

Finally, in its opinion striking down the ordinance, the Illinois Supreme Court refused to accept the general order issued by the police department as a sufficient limitation on the "vast amount of discretion" granted to the police in its enforcement. We agree. That the police have adopted internal rules limiting their enforcement to certain designated areas in the city would not provide a defense to a loiterer who might be arrested elsewhere. Nor could a person who knowingly loitered with a well-known gang member anywhere in the city safely assume that they would not be ordered to disperse no matter how innocent and harmless their loitering might be.

In our judgment, the Illinois Supreme Court correctly concluded that the ordinance does not provide sufficiently specific limits on the enforcement discretion of the police "to meet constitutional standards for definiteness and clarity." We recognize the serious and difficult problems testified to by the citizens of Chicago that led to the enactment of this ordinance. "We are mindful that the preservation of liberty depends in part on the maintenance of social order." However, in this instance the city has enacted an ordinance that affords too much discretion to the police and too little notice to citizens who wish to use the public streets.

Accordingly, the judgment of the Supreme
Court of Illinois is AFFIRMED.

DISSENT

SCALIA, J.

The citizens of Chicago were once free to drive about the city at whatever speed they wished. At some point Chicagoans (or perhaps Illinoisans) decided this would not do, and imposed prophylactic speed limits designed to assure safe operation by the average (or perhaps even sub-average) driver with the average (or perhaps even subaverage) vehicle. This infringed upon the "freedom" of all citizens, but was not unconstitutional.

Similarly, the citizens of Chicago were once free to stand around and gawk at the scene of an accident. At some point Chicagoans discovered that this obstructed traffic and caused more accidents. They did not make the practice unlawful, but they did authorize police officers to order the crowd to disperse, and imposed penalties for refusal to obey such an order. Again, this prophylactic measure infringed upon the "freedom" of all citizens, but was not unconstitutional.

Until the ordinance that is before us today was adopted, the citizens of Chicago were free to stand about in public places with no apparent purpose—to engage, that is, in conduct that appeared to be loitering. In recent years, however, the city has been afflicted with criminal street gangs. As reflected in the record before us, these gangs congregated in public places to deal in drugs, and to terrorize the neighborhoods by demonstrating control over their "turf." Many residents of the inner city felt that they were prisoners in their own homes. Once again, Chicagoans decided that to eliminate the problem it was worth restricting some of the freedom that they once enjoyed. The means they took was similar to the second, and more mild, example given above rather than the first: Loitering was not made unlawful, but when a group of people occupied a public place without an apparent purpose and in the company of a known gang member, police officers were authorized to order them to disperse, and the failure to obey such an order was made unlawful. The minor limitation upon the free state of nature that this prophylactic arrangement imposed upon all Chicagoans seemed to them (and it seems to me) a small price to pay for liberation of their streets.

The majority today invalidates this perfectly reasonable measure by...elevating loitering to a constitutionally guaranteed right, and by discerning vagueness where, according to our usual standards, none exists....The fact is that the present ordinance is entirely clear in its application, cannot be violated except with full knowledge and intent, and vests no more discretion in the police than innumerable other measures authorizing police orders to preserve the public peace and safety. As suggested by their tortured analyses, and by their suggested solutions that bear no relation to the identified constitutional problem, the majority's real quarrel with the Chicago Ordinance is simply that it permits (or indeed requires) too much harmless conduct by innocent citizens to be proscribed.

...Justice O'CONNOR's concurrence says with disapprobation, "the ordinance applies to hundreds of thousands of persons who are not gang members, standing on any sidewalk or in any park, coffee shop, bar, or other location open to the public." But in our democratic system, how much harmless conduct to proscribe is not a judgment to be made by the courts. So long as constitutionally guaranteed rights are not affected, and so long as the proscription has a rational basis, all sorts of perfectly harmless activity by millions of perfectly innocent people can be forbidden—riding a motorcycle without a safety helmet, for example, starting a campfire in a national forest, or selling a safe and effective drug not yet approved by the FDA. All of these acts are entirely innocent and harmless in themselves, but because of the risk of harm that they entail, the freedom to engage in them has been abridged. The citizens of Chicago have decided that depriving themselves of the freedom to "hang out" with a gang member is necessary to eliminate pervasive gang crime and intimidation—and that the elimination of the one is worth the deprivation of the other. This Court has no business second-guessing either the degree of necessity or the fairness of the trade.

I dissent from the judgment of the Court.

THOMAS, J. joined by REHNQUIST, CJ. and SCALIA, J.
The duly elected members of the Chicago City Council enacted the ordinance at issue as part of a larger effort to prevent gangs from establishing dominion over the public streets. By invalidating Chicago's ordinance, I fear that the Court has unnecessarily sentenced law-abiding citizens to lives of terror and misery. The ordinance is not vague. Any fool would know that a particular category of conduct would be within its reach. Nor does it violate the Due Process Clause. The asserted "freedom to loiter for innocent purposes," is in no way "deeply rooted in this Nation's history and tradition," I dissent.

The human costs exacted by criminal street gangs are inestimable. In many of our Nation's cities, gangs have "virtually overtaken certain neighborhoods, contributing to the economic and social decline of these areas and causing fear and lifestyle changes among law-abiding residents." Gangs fill the daily lives of many of our poorest and most vulnerable citizens with a terror that the Court does not give sufficient consideration, often relegating them to the status of prisoners in their own homes. "From the small business owner who is literally crippled because he refuses to pay 'protection' money to the neighborhood gang, to the families who are hostages within their homes, living in neighborhoods ruled by predatory drug trafficking gangs, the harmful impact of gang violence...is both physically and psychologically debilitating."...

Before enacting its ordinance, the Chicago City Council held extensive hearings on the problems of gang loitering. Concerned citizens appeared to testify poignantly as to how gangs disrupt their daily lives. Ordinary citizens like Ms. D'Ivory Gordon explained that she struggled just to walk to work:

> When I walk out my door, these guys are out there.... They watch you....They know where you live. They know what time you leave, what time you come home. I am afraid of them. I have even come to the point now that I carry a meat cleaver to work with me....I don't want to hurt anyone, and I don't want to be hurt. We need to clean these corners up. Clean these communities up and take it back from them.

Eighty-eight-year-old Susan Mary Jackson echoed her sentiments, testifying, "We used to have a nice neighborhood. We don't have it anymore....I am scared to go out in the daytime...you can't pass because they are standing. I am afraid to go to the store. I don't go to the store because I am afraid. At my age if they look at me real hard, I be ready to holler." Another long-time resident testified:

> I have never had the terror that I feel everyday when I walk down the streets of Chicago....I have had my windows broken out. I have had guns pulled on me. I have been threatened. I get intimidated on a daily basis, and it's come to the point where I say, well, do I go out today. Do I put my ax in my briefcase. Do I walk around dressed like a bum so I am not looking rich or got any money or anything like that.

Following these hearings, the council found that "criminal street gangs establish control over identifiable areas... by loitering in those areas and intimidating others from entering those areas." It further found that the mere presence of gang members "intimidates many law abiding citizens" and "creates a justifiable fear for the safety of persons and property in the area." It is the product of this democratic process—the council's attempt to address these social ills—that we are asked to pass judgment upon today....

We recently reconfirmed that "our Nation's history, legal traditions, and practices...provide the crucial 'guideposts for responsible decisionmaking' that direct and restrain our exposition of the Due Process Clause." Only laws that infringe "those fundamental rights and liberties which are, objectively, 'deeply rooted in this Nation's history and tradition'" offend the Due Process Clause. The plurality asserts that "the freedom to loiter for innocent purposes is part of the 'liberty' protected by the Due Process Clause of the Fourteenth Amendment." Yet it acknowledges—as it must—that "antiloitering ordinances have long existed in this country."

Loitering and vagrancy statutes have been utilized throughout American history in an attempt to prevent crime by removing 'undesirable persons' from public before they have the opportunity to engage in criminal activity....The plurality's sweeping conclusion that this ordinance infringes upon a liberty interest protected by the Fourteenth Amendment's Due Process Clause withers when exposed to the relevant history: Laws prohibiting loitering and vagrancy have been a fixture of Anglo-American law at least since the time of the Norman Conquest. The American colonists enacted laws modeled upon the English vagrancy laws, and at the time of the founding, state and local governments customarily criminalized loitering and other forms of vagrancy. Vagrancy laws were common in the decades preceding the ratification of the Fourteenth Amendment, and remained on the books long after....

The Court concludes that the ordinance is also unconstitutionally vague because it fails to provide adequate standards to guide police discretion and because, in the plurality's view, it does not give residents adequate notice of how to conform their conduct to the confines of the law. I disagree on both counts. At the outset, it is important to note that the ordinance does not criminalize loitering per se. Rather, it penalizes loiterers' failure to obey a police officer's order to move along. A majority of the Court believes that this scheme vests too much discretion in police officers. Nothing could be further from the truth. Far from according officers too much discretion, the ordinance merely enables police officers to fulfill one of their traditional functions. Police officers are not, and have never been, simply enforcers of the criminal law. They wear other hats—importantly, they have long been vested with the responsibility for preserving the public peace. Nor is the idea that the police are also peace officers simply a quaint anachronism. In most American jurisdictions, police officers continue to be obligated, by law, to maintain the public peace....

In concluding that the ordinance adequately channels police discretion, I do not suggest that a police officer enforcing the Gang Congregation Ordinance will never make a mistake. Nor do I overlook the possibility that a police officer, acting in bad faith, might enforce the ordinance in an arbitrary or discriminatory way. But our decisions should not turn on the proposition that such an event will be anything but rare. Instances of arbitrary or discriminatory enforcement of the ordinance, like any other law, are best addressed when (and if) they arise, rather than prophylactically through the disfavored mechanism of a facial challenge on vagueness grounds.

The plurality's conclusion that the ordinance "fails to give the ordinary citizen adequate notice of what is forbidden and what is permitted," is similarly untenable. There is nothing "vague" about an order to disperse. While "we can never expect mathematical certainty from our language," it is safe to assume that the vast majority of people who are ordered by the police to "disperse and remove themselves from the area" will have little difficulty understanding how to comply.

Assuming that we are also obligated to consider whether the ordinance places individuals on notice of what conduct might subject them to such an order...I subscribe to the view of retired Justice White—"If any fool would know that a particular category of conduct would be within the reach of the statute, if there is an unmistakable core that a reasonable person would know is forbidden by the law, the enactment is not unconstitutional on its face." This is certainly such a case. As the Illinois Supreme Court recognized, "persons of ordinary intelligence may maintain a common and accepted meaning of the word 'loiter.'"...

Today, the Court focuses extensively on the "rights" of gang members and their companions. It can safely do so— the people who will have to live with the consequences of today's opinion do not live in our neighborhoods. Rather, the people who will suffer from our lofty pronouncements are people like Ms. Susan Mary Jackson; people who have seen their neighborhoods literally destroyed by gangs and violence and drugs. They are good, decent people who must struggle to overcome their desperate situation, against all odds, in order to raise their families, earn a living, and remain good citizens. As one resident described,

"There is only about maybe one or two percent of the people in the city causing these problems maybe, but it's keeping 98 percent of us in our houses and off the streets and afraid to shop." By focusing exclusively on the imagined "rights" of the two percent, the Court today has denied our most vulnerable citizens the very thing that Justice STEVENS, elevates above all else—the "freedom of movement." And that is a shame.

Questions

1. List the four elements in the Chicago gang loitering ordinance.

2. List the specific arguments the majority gave to support its conclusion that the ordinance was vague.

3. Explain specifically all of the reasons why the dissenting judges disagreed.

4. Would "any fool know" what conduct this ordinance prohibited? Defend your answer.

5. Did the majority properly balance the interest in community order with the individual liberty? Explain your answer.

6. If the majority didn't properly strike the balance, how would you do it differently? Explain your answer.

 Go to Exercise 12-2 on the Criminal Law 8e CD to learn more about gangs, *Chicago v. Morales*, and the Constitution.

◆　　◆　　◆

"VICTIMLESS" CRIMES

Right at the start, let's be clear about how we're going to use the term *victimless* in this section. First, "victimless crime" applies only to *adults,* not *minors.* Second, it refers to crimes committed by *adults* who don't see themselves as victims of their behavior. Let's look at the crimes that are generally considered victimless and then more specifically at prostitution and solicitation.

Controversial Victimless Crimes

Referring to many crimes in which the perpetrators don't see themselves as victimized as "victimless" crimes is controversial; Table 12.2 lists some of these crimes. We've already examined the question of adult drug use in a constitutional democracy (Chapters 2 and 3, *Robinson v. California* and *Powell v. Texas*). And, we've discussed the application of the principles of *actus reus* and *mens rea* to drug crimes (Chapters 3 and 4).

TABLE 12.2
"Victimless" Crimes

Substance abuse (Chapters 2 and 3)

Internet censorship

Loitering

Prostitution

Sodomy (*Lawrence v. Texas*, Chapter 2)

Seat belt law violations

Helmet law violations

Violating bans on bungee jumping

Assisted suicide

Let's take a little closer look at a few of the offenses that involve *consensual* adult sexual conduct. First a little history: In medieval days, when the Church was more powerful than kings and queens, ecclesiastical courts had total power to try and punish crimes against "family and morals," including all nonviolent sexual behavior and marital relations breaches. As monarchs grew stronger, royal courts eventually gained control over most of these offenses. Once the monarch's courts took them over they became the **crimes against public morals,** most of which would be on the list of anyone who subscribes to the idea of victimless crimes (Morris and Hawkins 1970, chap. 1).

Controversy makes it tough to balance public good and individual privacy in these cases. There's broad agreement that the crimes against persons and property you read about in Chapters 9 through 11 deserve punishment. However, no such agreement exists when it comes to whether those listed in Table 12.2 should be crimes. In fact, there's a deep rift between those who believe criminal law should enforce morals to "purify" society and those who just as deeply believe that consenting adults' nonviolent sexual conduct is none of the criminal law's business (Morris and Hawkins 1970).

Perhaps no issue in criminal policy has caused more acrimonious debate over a longer time than that of the role law should play in enforcing public morals. Two English Victorian scholars, the philosopher John Stuart Mill and the historian Sir James F. Stephen, started the debate. Its two major positions were summed up in the **Wolfendon Report,** an English document recommending the decriminalization of private sexual conduct between adult consenting male homosexuals and prostitution. Here's the summary of the majority of the commission's position:

> There remains one additional argument which we believe to be decisive, namely, the importance which society and the law ought to give to individual freedom of choice and action in matters of private morality. Unless a deliberate attempt is to be made by society, acting through the agency of the law, to equate the sphere of crime with that of sin, there must remain a realm of private morality and immorality which is, in brief and crude terms, not the law's business. To say this is not to condone or encourage private immorality. On the contrary, to emphasize the personal private nature of moral or immoral conduct is to emphasize the personal and private responsibility of the individual for his own actions, and that is a responsibility which a mature agent can properly be expected to carry for himself without the threat of punishment from the law.
>
> Wolfendon Report 1957, 20–21

TABLE 12.3
Prostitution and Related Offenses

Fornication

Prostitution and solicitation of prostitution ("pimping")

Adult consensual sex

Adultery

And here's English jurist Sir Patrick Devlin's rebuttal to the majority position:

> I think, therefore, that it is not possible to set theoretical limits to the power of the State to legislate against immorality. It is not possible to settle in advance exceptions to the general rule or to define inflexibly areas of morality into which the law is in no circumstances to be allowed to enter. Society is entitled by means of its laws to protect itself from dangers, whether from within or without. Here again I think that the political parallel is legitimate. The law of treason is directed against aiding the king's enemies and against sedition from within. The justification for this is that established government is necessary for the existence of society and therefore its safety against violent overthrow must be secured. But an established morality is as necessary as good government to the welfare of society. Societies disintegrate from within more frequently than they are broken up by external pressures. There is disintegration when no common morality is observed and history shows that the loosening of moral bonds is often the first state of disintegration, so that society is justified in taking the same steps to preserve its moral code as it does to preserve its government and other essential institutions. The suppression of vice is as much the law's business as the suppression of subversive activities; it is no more possible to define a sphere of private morality than it is to define one of private subversive activity.
>
> Wolfendon Report 1957, 48

Nonviolent sex offenses cover a broad spectrum (Table 12.3) Let's look at a few of these crimes related to prostitution.

Prostitution and Solicitation

Prostitution is an ancient business, prospering in all cultures at all times no matter what the condemnation of religion and morals. It's also a crime nearly everywhere in the United States, persisting no matter how severe the laws or how tough the efforts of police to enforce them. **Prostitution** used to be reserved for describing the act of selling sexual intercourse for money—and, only selling, not buying, sex was included. Now it means all contacts and penetrations (Chapter 10 defines these terms) as long as they're done with the intent to gratify sexual appetite. And, both **patrons** (buyers) and **prostitutes** (sellers) can commit prostitution. In the past, the law recognized only women as prostitutes. Now both men and women who sell sex are prostitutes.

It's a crime not only to buy and sell sex but also to **solicit prostitution** (sometimes called **promoting prostitution**, or "pimping," or "pandering"). Soliciting prostitution means getting customers for prostitutes and/or providing a place for prostitutes and customers to engage in sex for money.

Prostitution and promoting prostitution are misdemeanors in most states, but it's a serious felony when circumstances like minors, violence, and weapons are involved.

Here's an edited version of Minnesota's elaborate and detailed statute on prostitution, promotion, and aggravating circumstances:

609.324 PROSTITUTION

Subdivision 1. Engaging in, hiring, or agreeing to hire a minor to engage in prostitution; penalties.

(a) Whoever intentionally does any of the following may be sentenced to imprisonment for not more than 20 years or to payment of a fine of not more than $40,000, or both:

(1) engages in prostitution with an individual under the age of 13 years; or

(2) hires or offers or agrees to hire an individual under the age of 13 years to engage in sexual penetration or sexual contact.

(b) Whoever intentionally does any of the following may be sentenced to imprisonment for not more than ten years or to payment of a fine of not more than $20,000, or both:

(1) engages in prostitution with an individual under the age of 16 years but at least 13 years; or

(2) hires or offers or agrees to hire an individual under the age of 16 years but at least 13 years to engage in sexual penetration or sexual contact.

(c) Whoever intentionally does any of the following may be sentenced to imprisonment for not more than five years or to payment of a fine of not more than $10,000, or both:

(1) engages in prostitution with an individual under the age of 18 years but at least 16 years; or

(2) hires or offers or agrees to hire an individual under the age of 18 years but at least 16 years to engage in sexual penetration or sexual contact.

Subd. 2. Solicitation or acceptance of solicitation to engage in prostitution; penalty.

Whoever solicits or accepts a solicitation to engage for hire in sexual penetration or sexual contact while in a public place may be sentenced to imprisonment for not more than one year or to payment of a fine of not more than $3,000 or both. Except as otherwise provided in subdivision 4, a person who is convicted of violating this subdivision while acting as a patron must, at a minimum, be sentenced to pay a fine of at least $1,500.

Subd. 3. Engaging in, hiring, or agreeing to hire an adult to engage in prostitution; penalties.

Whoever intentionally does any of the following may be sentenced to imprisonment for not more than 90 days or to payment of a fine of not more than $700, or both:

(1) engages in prostitution with an individual 18 years of age or above; or

(2) hires or offers or agrees to hire an individual 18 years of age or above to engage in sexual penetration or sexual contact.

Except as otherwise provided in subdivision 4, a person who is convicted of violating clause (1) or (2) while acting as a patron must, at a minimum, be sentenced to pay a fine of at least $500.

Whoever violates the provisions of this subdivision within two years of a previous conviction may be sentenced to imprisonment for not more than one year or to payment of a fine of not more than $3,000, or both.

Except as otherwise provided in subdivision 4, a person who is convicted of a gross misdemeanor violation of this subdivision while acting as a patron, must, at a minimum, be sentenced as follows:

(1) to pay a fine of at least $1,500; and

(2) to serve 20 hours of community work service.

The court may waive the mandatory community work service if it makes specific, written findings that the community work service is not feasible or appropriate under the circumstances of the case.

Subd. 4. Community service in lieu of minimum fine.

The court may order a person convicted of violating subdivision 2 or 3 to perform community work service in lieu of all or a portion of the minimum fine required under those subdivisions if the court makes specific, written findings that the convicted person is indigent or that payment of the fine would create undue hardship for the convicted person or that person's immediate family. Community work service ordered under this subdivision is in addition to any mandatory community work service ordered under subdivision 3.

Subd. 5. Use of motor vehicle to patronize prostitutes; driving record notation.

When a court sentences a person convicted of violating this section while acting as a patron, the court shall determine whether the person used a motor vehicle during the commission of the offense. If the court finds that the person used a motor vehicle during the commission of the offense, it shall forward its finding to the commissioner of public safety who shall record the finding on the person's driving record. . . .

SUMMARY

I. Issues of public order include
   A. Disorderly conduct crimes
   B. Quality-of-life crimes
   C. Victimless crimes

II. Disorderly conduct crimes
   A. Historically, these were largely ignored misdemeanors
   B. Purposes for *Model Penal Code* provision
      1. Define *actus reus* more precisely than "disorderly conduct"
      2. Add a *mens rea* element to what used to be strict liability offenses
   C. Individual disorderly conduct in *Model Penal Code*
      1. *Actus reus*—three kinds
         a. Fighting
         b. Making unreasonable noise, using offensive language
         c. Creating hazardous or offensive conditions
      2. *Mens rea*—acting purposely, knowingly, or recklessly
      3. Special individual disorderly conduct sections in *Model Penal Code*
         a. Knowingly spreading false alarms
         b. Appearing drunk in public (no *mens rea* requirement)
         c. Loitering or prowling (no *mens rea* requirement)
         d. Purposely or recklessly obstructing highways or other public passages
         e. Purposely disrupting lawful meetings, processions, or gatherings
   D. Group disorderly conduct ("riot")
      1. Background
         a. Three ancient misdemeanor crimes (unlawful assembly, rout, riot)
         b. Riot Act of 1714—made riot a felony
         c. "Reading the riot act" comes from this act
      2. Elements
         a. *Actus reus*—participate in disorderly conduct
         b. *Mens rea*

        (1) Have specific intent or purpose to commit or facilitate the commission of a felony

        (2) Have the purpose to prevent or coerce an official action

        (3) Have knowledge that any participant used or plans to use a deadly weapon

III. "Quality-of-life" crimes

  A. Control "bad manners" in public places (sidewalks, streets, parks)

  B. Ancient offenses (crimes against public order) applied to new situations ("street people" and "gangs") called by a new name (quality-of-life crimes)

  C. They underscore the tension between liberty and order in a constitutional democracy

  D. Are the application of due process of liberty (Chapter 2) to maintaining order in public

  E. "Broken windows" theory

    1. Theory—There's a link between "minor" quality-of-life offenses (public drunkenness, panhandling, graffiti, vandalism, prostitution, loitering) and serious crimes (rape, robbery, burglary)

    2. Reality

      a. National debate concentrates on serious crime; local officials and public more worried about quality-of-life offenses

      b. Empirical findings mixed as to link between serious crime and disorder

        (1) Some find a causal relationship (Kelling, Skogan)

        (2) Others find common origins but not a causal link (Sampson and Radenbush)

  F. Wide public agreement on what "bad public manners" consists of

  G. Vagrancy and loitering

    1. Two ancient offenses aimed at roaming around (vagrancy) with no visible means of support and at standing around (loitering)

    2. Vagrancy and loitering have been tailored to meet modern problems of "bad public manners" of street people and gangs

    3. Due process (void-for-vagueness) restricts power to criminalize vagrancy (*Papichristou v. City of Jacksonville* 1972) and loitering (*Kolender v. Lawson* 1983)

    4. Vagrancy and loitering can overcome the vagueness objection if they're defined to include more than just roaming around or standing around

II. Panhandling

    1. Panhandling statutes call the ancient crime of public begging into service to control "aggressive" begging by "street people"

    2. Bans on panhandling don't apply to "organized charities" (Salvation Army)

    3. Panhandling is "speech" protected by the First Amendment

      a. Right to panhandle is "commercial speech," and so it's less protected than other types of speech

      b. States can control time, place (subways), and manner ("aggressive") of panhandling

      c. States can't control the *content* of panhandling (the right to ask for money)

I. Street gangs
   1. "Bands of loitering youth" scare ordinary people
   2. Anti-gang ordinances raise due process questions (liberty and void-for-vagueness)
   3. Anti-gang ordinances meet due process and liberty requirements if they define loitering more specifically than "hanging out with no apparent purpose" (OK to ban loitering "for the purpose of committing a crime")
IV. "Victimless" crimes
   A. Applies only to adults
   B. Refers to crimes committed by adults who don't see themselves as victims
   C. Referring to these crimes as "victimless" is controversial
   D. The Wolfendon Report in 1950s England recommended decriminalizing private sexual conduct between consenting adults with regard to homosexuality and prostitution
   E. Today, both patrons and prostitutes (male or female) commit prostitution

 Go to the Criminal Law 8e CD to download this summary outline. The outline has been formatted so that you can add notes to it during class lectures, or later create a customized chapter outline to use while reviewing. Either way, the summary outline will help you understand the "big picture" and fill in the details as you study.

REVIEW QUESTIONS

1. Why is there a natural tension between order and liberty in a constitutional democracy?

2. Explain the difference between individual and group disorderly conduct, and give an example of each.

3. Summarize public opinion regarding quality-of-life crimes.

4. Describe the disconnect between the national crime debate and the attitude of local officials and the public.

5. Describe the "broken windows" theory.

6. Summarize the empirical findings regarding the validity of the broken-windows theory.

7. What's the difference between loitering and vagrancy?

8. Trace the constitutional history of vagrancy statutes.

9. What's the significance of the *Papichristou v. City of Jacksonville* case?

10. What's the significance of the *Kolender v. Lawson* case?

11. What was the columnist Ellen Goodman referring to by her comment, "Enough's enough"?

12. Summarize James Q. Wilson's defense of laws targeting "street people."

13. Describe and explain the distinction between panhandling and organized charities in panhandling ordinances.

14. What's the difference between "commercial" and other speech, and why is the distinction constitutionally important?

15. Describe the spectrum of groups included within the meaning of "gang."

16. Describe the behavior included in criminal laws regulating gangs.

17. Describe the gang activities that fall within the definition of "public nuisance" in the injunction asked for by the Santa Clara, California, city attorney.

18. Summarize the California Supreme Court decision in *People ex rel. Gallo v. Acuna.*

19. Summarize the Chicago ordinance and the debate over it that finally reached the U.S. Supreme Court in *Chicago v. Morales.*

20. Summarize the controversy over victimless crimes.

KEY TERMS

"victimless" crimes p. 425
individual disorderly conduct p. 426
group disorderly conduct p. 426
breach of the peace p. 426
actual disorderly conduct p. 426
constructive disorderly conduct p. 426
unlawful assembly p. 428
rout p. 428
riot p. 428
order p. 430

liberty p. 430
"bad manners" crimes p. 430
crimes against public order p. 430
quality-of-life crimes p. 430
broken-windows theory p. 430
vagrancy p. 431
loitering p. 431
preliminary injunction p. 433
time, place, and manner regulations p. 439
expressive conduct p. 439
commercial speech p. 439

injunction to abate public nuisances p. 445
crimes against public morals p. 455
Wolfendon Report p. 455
prostitution p. 456
patrons p. 456
prostitutes p. 456
solicit prostitution p. 456
promoting prostitution p. 456

SUGGESTED READINGS

 Go to the Criminal Law 8e CD for Suggested Readings for this chapter.

THE COMPANION WEB SITE FOR *CRIMINAL LAW,* EIGHTH EDITION

http://cj.wadsworth.com/samaha/crim_law8e

 Supplement your review of this chapter by going to the companion Web site to take one of the Tutorial Quizzes, use the flash cards to test your knowledge of the elements of various crimes and defenses, and check out the many other study aids you'll find there. You'll find valuable data and resources at your fingertips to help you study for that big exam or write that important paper.

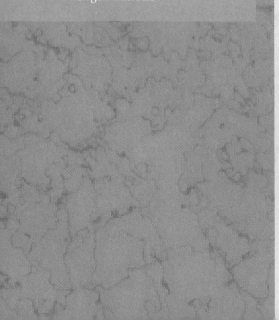

13

Crimes Against the State

Chapter Main Points

- To survive, governments everywhere have always had to rely on protection against foreign enemies and the allegiance and loyalty of the people at home.

- Allegiance, loyalty, and protection are never more important than during times of threats to national security from hidden enemies inside and outside the country.

- This chapter is about applying the enduring idea of balancing security and freedom during wartime when our constitutional democracy is threatened by hidden enemies.

- A fundamental weapon against disloyalty to the homeland and allegiance to enemies is the crime of treason, which strikes at acts of fighting for or giving aid to enemies of the United States.

- Other crimes punish *potential* harms against the state because we can't wait until "the fuse is being lit" before striking at those who want to kill us.

- Crimes aimed at the potential harm of terrorist attack are still subject to the limits placed on criminal law—specifically, the principle of *actus reus;* the constitutional ban on vague laws; and the First Amendment rights of speech and association.

- The most commonly prosecuted crime against the state since September 11, 2001, is "providing material support or resources" to terrorists or terrorist organizations.

Whoever, within the United States or subject to the jurisdiction of the United States, knowingly provides material support or resources to a foreign terrorist organization, or attempts or conspires to do so, shall be fined under this title or imprisoned not more than 10 years, or both.

USA Patriot Act (2001)

"You don't have to wait until the fuse is being lit. If that were the standard, a lot of bombs would go off and a lot of people would lose their lives" (Anderson, 2003). This is how Michael Chertoff, former head of the U.S. Department of Justice's criminal division (and now a judge on the Third Circuit U.S. Court of Appeals), defended the tough anti-terrorism provisions in the USA Patriot Act. But, this is how Neal Sonnett, a past president of the National Association of Criminal Defense Lawyers, put the case for the critics of the Patriot Act: "If you cast too wide a net and you don't use appropriate discretion to limit these prosecutions, you risk ensnaring innocent people and you demean the entire process of prosecuting terror" (Anderson 2003). You can see in these different views of the Patriot Act the tension between two core values in our constitutional democracy—the need for safety and security and the desire for privacy and liberty.

The **USA Patriot Act** is an acronym for "Uniting and Strengthening America by Providing Appropriate Tools Required to Intercept and Obstruct Terrorism." Aimed at fighting and preventing *international* terrorism, it was passed and signed into law on October 16, 2001, after the September 11 attacks on the World Trade Center and the Pentagon.

This chapter is about how we apply the enduring principles of criminal law (Chapters 1–4) to protect the core values of security and freedom in a time of great testing by threats from terrorist groups who are prepared to kill innocent Americans both in the United States and around the world. Grave as the threat may be today, we should remember our Constitution was adopted during a time of similar major threats to our nation's security.

We'll examine the history and modern law of treason, the other ancient crimes of disloyalty (sedition, sabotage, and espionage), and the specific crimes against domestic and international terrorism enacted after the Oklahoma City bombing in 1993 and the attacks on the World Trade Center and the Pentagon on September 11, 2001.

TREASON

Treason is the only crime defined in the U.S. Constitution. This is how Article III, Section 3 defines this most heinous of all crimes against the state:

> Treason against the United States, shall consist only in levying War against them, or, in adhering to their Enemies, giving them Aid and Comfort. No Person shall be convicted of

Treason unless on the Testimony of two Witnesses to the same overt Act, or on Confession in open Court.

There's also a U.S. Code treason statute that includes the constitutional definition and adds a penalty:

> Whoever, owing allegiance to the United States, levies war against them or adheres to their enemies, giving them aid and comfort within the United States or elsewhere, is guilty of treason and shall suffer death, or shall be imprisoned not less than five years and fined under this title but not less than $10,000; and shall be incapable of holding any office under the United States. (Title 18, Part I, Chapter 115, Section 2381)

Let's look at how treason laws were viewed during both the pre– and post–American Revolution periods.

Distrust of Treason Laws and the American Revolution

The revolutionaries who wrote the U.S. Constitution knew very well the new government they were about to create couldn't survive without the active support (or at least the passive submission) of most of the people. They also realized it was going to be some time before this new republican form of government took hold among the people.

The people's allegiance to the new government would be especially important to the newborn nation's survival in the early years following the Revolution, a time of gigantic threats from enemies inside and outside the new country. Benedict Arnold's betrayal of General Washington was fresh in their minds, and English royalists remained deeply loyal to King George III. Unfriendly countries had designs on the new country's territory. To the north in Canada, England was hovering, smarting from the loss of the American colonies, and looking for payback. Spain to the south had just taken back Florida and claimed the whole Mississippi Valley. And, France had only recently been thrown out of the Ohio Valley. These unfriendly nations formed alliances with Native American nations by taking advantage of deep injustices the Americans continued to inflict on the tribes.

These threats led the authors of the Constitution to take a tough stand against individuals who broke their allegiance in the face of these dangers. But, there was a flip side to their stand. Many of the drafters' ancestors had fled to the colonies to escape persecution for heresy and prosecution for treason. And more to the point, almost all were traitors themselves under British law. *Treason* consisted either of levying war against the king or giving aid and comfort to the king's enemies. They'd done both. They'd levied war against the King of England by fighting the Revolutionary War, and they'd given aid and comfort to England's bitter enemy France. Everything they did to further the interests of the colonies was done under threat of prosecution for treason.

And, English prosecutions for treason weren't pretty. Thomas Jefferson referred to the English law of treason as a "deadly weapon" in the hands of "tyrannical kings" and "weak and wicked Ministers which had drawn the blood of the best and honestest men in the kingdom" (Jefferson 1853, 1:215). Treason prosecutions were probably on Benjamin Franklin's mind when he quipped at the signing of the Declaration of Independence, "We must all hang together, or most assuredly we shall all hang separately" (Lederer 1988, 27).

What were they worried about? The existing law of treason in England defined treason as "**adherence to the enemy.**" *Adherence* here means breaking allegiance to your own country by forming an attachment to the enemy. Criminalizing attachment—joining the enemy's military forces—wasn't an issue; they all thought that was treason. But, what about "**giving aid and comfort to the enemy**"? With this loose phrase, "attachment" could lead to attacks on thoughts and feelings. Suppose "disloyalty" took the forms of sympathy for our enemies or even apathy toward our own cause. Were they treason, too? (They were in England.) And, would zealous patriotism so needed in troubled times tempt the government to bend the rules in their attempt to protect the country? (They did in England.) So, the worries that treason law would be abused boiled down to two concerns:

1. That *peaceful* opposition to the government, not just rebellion, would be repressed

2. That innocent people might be convicted of treason because of perjury, passion, and/or insufficient evidence

The authors of the Constitution were determined that disloyal *feelings* or *opinions* (or lack of them) and the passions of the time wouldn't be a part of the law of treason. So, as much as they recognized the need for allegiance to the new government, their fear of abusive prosecutions for treason led them to adopt "every limitation that the practice of governments had evolved or that politico-legal philosophy to that time had advanced" (*Cramer v. U.S.* 1945, 23–24). By the time the Constitution was adopted, government and philosophy had come to accept two limits on disloyal behaviors:

1. Levying war against your own country

2. Giving aid and comfort to the enemy

Then, the authors of the Constitution added two of their own limits:

1. They banned legislatures *and* courts from creating new treasons.

2. They required two witnesses to at least one overt (unconcealed) act of treason or a confession in open court.

They wrote these limits into the body of the U.S. Constitution, where it would be very tough to tamper with them because of the intentionally cumbersome constitutional amendment process:

> Treason against the United States, shall consist only in levying War against them, or in adhering to their Enemies, giving them Aid and Comfort. No Person shall be convicted of Treason unless on the Testimony of two Witnesses to the same overt Act, or on Confession in open Court. (Article III, § 3)

According to Article III, § 3, treason has three elements. First, treason requires the *actus reus* of either levying war against the United States or giving aid and comfort to the enemies of the United States. Second, the act of giving aid and comfort has to be intentional and for the very purpose of betraying the United States by means of this act. Third, proof of treason requires either two witnesses to the *actus reus* or confession in open court.

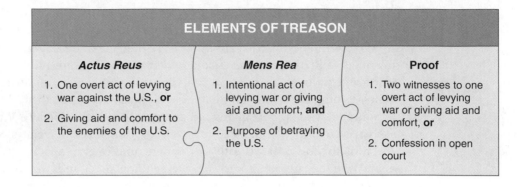

ELEMENTS OF TREASON		
Actus Reus	**Mens Rea**	**Proof**
1. One overt act of levying war against the U.S., **or**	1. Intentional act of levying war or giving aid and comfort, **and**	1. Two witnesses to one overt act of levying war or giving aid and comfort, **or**
2. Giving aid and comfort to the enemies of the U.S.	2. Purpose of betraying the U.S.	2. Confession in open court

Associate U.S. Supreme Court Robert Jackson, whose words in *Cramer v. U.S.* (1945) I can't (and wouldn't even try to) improve on, had this to say about the elements of treason:

> The crime of treason consists of two elements: adherence to the enemy; and rendering him aid and comfort. A citizen intellectually or emotionally may favor the enemy and harbor sympathies or convictions disloyal to this country's policy or interest, but so long as he commits no act of aid and comfort to the enemy, there is no treason. On the other hand, a citizen may take actions, which do aid and comfort the enemy—making a speech critical of the government or opposing its measures, profiteering, striking in defense plants or essential work, and the hundred other things which impair our cohesion and diminish our strength—but if there is no adherence to the enemy in this, if there is no intent to betray, there is no treason. (29)

Treason Law Since the Adoption of the U.S. Constitution

Distrust of treason prosecutions didn't end with the adoption of the Constitution. Throughout U.S. history, the government has prosecuted only a handful of people for treason, and presidents have pardoned or at least mitigated death sentences of those few who've been found guilty. The only exception was President Eisenhower's refusal to stop the execution of Ethel Rosenberg, convicted of conspiring to give atomic bomb secrets to the Soviet Union. She and her husband Julius were executed in 1951. (And, there's still plenty of controversy surrounding their execution [Meerpol 2003].)

In 1945, six years before the Rosenbergs' execution, the U.S. Supreme Court dealt with disloyalty—giving aid and comfort to Nazi Germany for the purpose of betraying the United States—and *proving* it, in *Cramer v. U.S.* This case was part of the fallout from the darkest days of World War II. Early in June 1942, when the war was going badly for the Allies, two German submarines were able to get close enough to the East Coast of the United States to get eight Nazi saboteurs ashore, four on Long Island and four in Florida. They managed to also get ashore several crates of dynamite and lots of cash. The plan was to blow up bridges, factories, and maybe a department store owned by Jews. The object of the plan was, first, to sabotage the war effort by destroying strategic places. Second, they planned to demoralize the American public by terror—namely, by the brazen act of coming right onto U.S. soil and blowing up our places of defense and business.

The saboteurs never committed sabotage. Within days of their landing, they turned themselves in to the FBI. The reason they went to the FBI isn't clear. They may have had a change of heart, feared getting caught, or perhaps never were really saboteurs, only disloyal Germans disillusioned with Hitler hoping to escape to the United States (Nazi Saboteur Case 1942, Transcript of Military Commission). Whatever the reason, the eight saboteurs were immediately tried by a secret military commission and convicted. Six were quickly executed; two were sentenced to life in prison.

Before the saboteurs were caught, Anthony Cramer got together with two of them, Werner Thiel and Edward Kerling, at the Lexington Inn in New York City. Later that day, Cramer had dinner with Werner Thiel at Thompson's Cafeteria in New York City. In 1943, Cramer was arrested and charged with treason based on his meetings with the by-then executed Thiel and Kerling. At Cramer's treason trial, two FBI agents testified they had witnessed his meetings with Thiel and Kerling, and that the three ate, drank, and "engaged long and earnestly in conversation." The government claimed these acts amounted to "giving aid and comfort to the enemy," and that the FBI agents' testimony satisfied the constitutional requirement of two witnesses. The trial judge and jury agreed; Cramer was convicted (*Cramer v. U.S.*, 1945). However, the U.S. Supreme Court, by a vote of 5–4, disagreed and reversed Cramer's conviction. According to Justice Jackson, writing for the majority, two witnesses to the dinner wasn't good enough to prove treason:

> The whole purpose of the constitutional [two witness] provision is to make sure that a treason conviction shall rest on direct proof of two witnesses and not even a little on imagination. And without the use of some imagination it is difficult to perceive any advantage which this meeting afforded to Thiel and Kerling as enemies or how it strengthened Germany or weakened the United States in any way whatever. It may be true that the saboteurs were cultivating Cramer as a potential "source of information and an avenue for contact." But there is no proof either by two witnesses or by even one witness or by any circumstance that Cramer gave them information.... Meeting with Cramer in public drinking places to tipple and trifle was no part of the saboteurs' mission and did not advance it. It may well have been a digression which jeopardized its success. (38)

 Go to Exercise 13-1 on the Criminal Law 8e CD for a full report of *Cramer v. U.S.*

MORE CRIMES AGAINST DISLOYALTY: SEDITION, SABOTAGE, AND ESPIONAGE

The lesson of *Cramer v. U.S.* is clear: It's very hard to convict someone of treason—and it's supposed to be. But, treason isn't the only crime aimed at combating disloyalty and keeping the allegiance of our citizens. Let's look at three of these crimes, which are very much like ancient crimes with the same names:

1. Sedition
2. Sabotage
3. Espionage

Then, we'll examine some specific anti-terrorism laws borrowed from these three ancient crimes.

Sedition

For centuries, it's been a crime against the state not only to commit treason but also to "stir up" others to overthrow the government by violence. Advocating the violent overthrow of the government was called **sedition.** The "stirring up" could be done by speeches **(seditious speech),** writings **(seditious libel),** or agreement **(seditious conspiracy).** In 1798, in the wake of the French Revolution and impending war with France, the U.S. Congress enacted the country's first sedition act. Banning a lot more than stirring up the violent overthrow of the government, it made it a crime to

> unlawfully combine or conspire together with intent to oppose any measure or measures of the government of the United States..., or to impede the operation of any law of the United States, or to intimidate or prevent any [official]...from undertaking, performing, or executing his...duty.
>
> Urofsky and Finkelman 2002a, I:141

It also made it a crime to

> "write, print, utter, or publish any...false, scandalous and malicious writing or writings..." with intent to "defame" the U.S. Government...or excite the hatred of the good people [against the U.S. Government]. (142)

The U.S. Criminal Code (2003) definition of seditious conspiracy sticks to conspiracies that advocate violence. It provides:

> If two or more persons in any State or Territory, or in any place subject to the jurisdiction of the United States, conspire to overthrow, put down, or to destroy by force the Government of the United States, or to levy war against them, or to oppose by force the authority thereof, or by force to prevent, hinder, or delay the execution of any law of the United States, or by force to seize, take, or possess any property of the United States contrary to the authority thereof, they shall each be fined under this title or imprisoned not more than twenty years, or both. (§ 2384)

In the **Smith Act of 1940,** Congress made it a crime to conspire to *teach* or *advocate* overthrowing the government by force, or to be a *member* of a *group* that advocated the violent overthrow of the government. In 1948, a federal grand jury indicted twelve national leaders of the U.S. Communist Party. After an often-explosive trial that lasted nine months, the leaders were convicted in 1949 (Urofsky and Finkelman 2002b, II: 758–759). In *Dennis v. U.S.* (1951), the U.S. Supreme Court upheld the convictions of the Communist Party leaders against a challenge that the Smith Act violated the First Amendment's ban on laws that "abridge" free speech and association.

| CASE | *Did They Have a Right to Teach and Advocate the Violent Overthrow of the Government?* |

Dennis v. U.S.
341 U.S. 494 (1951)

Eugene Dennis and others were convicted in the U.S. District Court for the Southern District of New York on an indictment for violation of Section 3 of the Smith Act (18 U.S.C.A. § 2385) for conspiring to organize the Communist Party of the U.S. as a group to teach and advocate the overthrow of the Government of the United States by force and violence. They appealed. The U.S. Court of Appeals,

2nd Circuit affirmed. The U.S. Supreme Court granted certiorari, and affirmed.

VINSON, CJ.

FACTS

Sections 2 and 3 of the Smith Act, 54 Stat. 671, 18 U.S.C. (1946 ed.) ss 10, 11 (see present 18 U.S.C. § 2385), provide as follows:

SEC. 2.

(a) It shall be unlawful for any person—

(1) to knowingly or willfully advocate, abet, advise, or teach the duty, necessity, desirability, or propriety of overthrowing or destroying any government in the United States by force or violence, or by the assassination of any officer of any such government;

(2) with intent to cause the overthrow or destruction of any government in the United States, to print, publish, edit, issue, circulate, sell, distribute, or publicly display any written or printed matter advocating, advising, or teaching the duty, necessity, desirability, or propriety of overthrowing or destroying any government in the United States by force or violence;

(3) to organize or help to organize any society, group, or assembly of persons who teach, advocate, or encourage the overthrow or destruction of any government in the United States by force or violence; or to be or become a member of, or affiliate with, any such society, group, or assembly of persons, knowing the purposes thereof.

(b) For the purposes of this section, the term 'government in the United States' means the Government of the United States, the government of any State, Territory, or possession of the United States, the government of the District of Columbia, or the government of any political subdivision of any of them.

SEC 3. It shall be unlawful for any person to attempt to commit, or to conspire to commit, any of the acts prohibited by the provisions of . . . this title.

The indictment charged the petitioners with wilfully and knowingly conspiring

(1) to organize as the Communist Party of the United States of America a society, group and assembly of persons who teach and advocate the overthrow and destruction of the Government of the United States by force and violence, and

(2) knowingly and wilfully to advocate and teach the duty and necessity of overthrowing and destroying the Government of the United States by force and violence.

The indictment further alleged that § 2 of the Smith Act proscribes these acts and that any conspiracy to take such action is a violation of § 3 of the Act.

[This section of the Facts is taken from the Court of Appeals opinion, *U.S. v. Dennis*, 183 F.2d (1950)]

There was abundant evidence, if believed, to show that they were all engaged in an extensive concerted action to teach what indeed they do not disavow—the doctrines of Marxism-Leninism. These doctrines were set forth in many pamphlets put in evidence at the trial, the upshot of which is—indeed an honest jury could scarcely have found otherwise—that capitalism inescapably rests upon, and must perpetuate, the oppression of those who do not own the means of production; that to it in time there must and will succeed a 'classless' society, which will finally make unnecessary most of the paraphernalia of government; but that there must be an intermediate and transitional period of the 'dictatorship, of the proletariat,' which can be established only by the violent overthrow of any existing government, if that be capitalistic.

No entrenched bourgeoisie, having everything to lose and nothing to gain by the abolition of capitalism, by which alone it can continue to enjoy its privileged position, will ever permit itself to be superseded by the means which it may have itself provided for constitutional change: e.g., by the ballot. No matter how solemnly it may profess its readiness to abide the result, and no matter how honestly and literally the accredit processes of amendment may in fact be followed, it is absurd to expect that a bourgeoisie will yield; and indeed to rely upon such a possibility is to range oneself among the enemies of Marxist-Leninist principles. Therefore the transition period involves the use of 'force and violence,' temporary it is true, but inescapable; and, although it is impossible to predict when a propitious occasion will arise, one certainly will arise: as, for example, by financial crisis or other internal division. When the time comes the proletariat will find it necessary to establish its 'dictatorship' by violence.

The defendants protest against this interpretation of their teaching and advocacy. They say that the use of 'force and violence' is no part of their program, except as it may become necessary after the proletariat has succeeded in securing power by constitutional processes. Thereafter, being itself the lawful government, it will of course resist any attempt of the ousted bourgeoisie to regain its position; it will meet force with force as all governments may, and must. If the defendants had in fact so confined their teaching and advocacy, the First Amendment would indubitably protect them, for it protects all utterances, individual or concerted, seeking constitutional changes, however revolutionary, by the processes which the Constitution provides....

It is unnecessary to quote in detail the many passages in the pamphlets and books, published and disseminated by the defendants, which flatly contradict their declarations that they mean to confine the use of 'force or violence' to the protection of political power, once lawfully obtained. The prosecution proved this part of its case quite independently of the testimony of its witnesses, though the jury might have relied upon that, had it stood alone. The sufficiency of the evidence therefore comes down to whether it is a crime to form a conspiracy to advocate or teach the duty and necessity of overthrowing the government by violence, and to organize the Community Party as a group so to teach and to advocate.

OPINION

The trial of the case extended over nine months, six of which were devoted to the taking of evidence, resulting in a record of 16,000 pages. Our limited grant of the writ of certiorari has removed from our consideration any question as to the sufficiency of the evidence to support the jury's determination that petitioners are guilty of the offense charged....

[The Court of Appeals]...held that the record in this case amply supports the necessary finding of the jury that petitioners, the leaders of the Communist Party in this country, were unwilling to work within our framework of democracy, but intended to initiate a violent revolution whenever the propitious occasion appeared. Petitioners dispute the meaning to be drawn from the evidence, contending that the Marxist-Leninist doctrine they advocated taught that force and violence to achieve a Communist form of government in an existing democratic state would be necessary only because the ruling classes of that state would never permit the transformation to be accomplished peacefully, but would use force and violence to defeat any peaceful political and economic gain the Communists could achieve.

But the Court of Appeals held that the record supports the following broad conclusions: By virtue of their control over the political apparatus of the Communist Political Association, petitioners were able to transform that organization into the Communist Party; that the policies of the Association were changed from peaceful cooperation with the United States and its economic and political structure to a policy which had existed before the United States and the Soviet Union were fighting a common enemy, namely, a policy which worked for the overthrow of the Government by force and violence; that the Communist Party is a highly disciplined organization, adept at infiltration into strategic positions, use of aliases, and double-meaning language; that the Party is rigidly controlled; that Communists, unlike other political parties, tolerate no dissension from the policy laid down by the guiding forces, but that the approved program is slavishly followed by the members of the Party; that the literature of the Party and the statements and activities of its leaders, petitioners here, advocate, and the general goal of the Party, was, during the period in question, to achieve a successful overthrow of the existing order by force and violence....

Section 2(a)(1) makes it unlawful "to knowingly or willfully advocate...or teach the duty, necessity, desirability, or propriety of overthrowing or destroying any government in the United States by force or violence..."; Section 2(a)(3), "to organize or help to organize any society, group, or assembly of persons who teach, advocate or encourage the overthrow...." Because of the fact that § 2(a)(2) expressly requires a specific intent to overthrow the Government, and because of the absence of precise language in the foregoing subsections, it is claimed that Congress deliberately omitted any such requirement.

We do not agree. It would require a far greater indication or congressional desire that intent not be made an element of the crime than the use of the disjunctive 'knowingly or willfully' in § 2(a)(1), or the omission of exact language in § 2(a)(3). The structure and purpose of the statute demand the inclusion of intent as an element of the crime. Congress was concerned with those who advocate and organize for the overthrow of the Government. Certainly those who recruit and combine for the purpose of advocating overthrow intend to bring about that overthrow. We hold that the statute requires as an essential element of the crime proof of the intent of those who are charged with its violation to overthrow the Government by force and violence....

The obvious purpose of the statute is to protect existing Government, not from change by peaceable, lawful and constitutional means, but from change by violence, revolution and terrorism. That it is within the power of the Congress to protect the Government of the United States from armed rebellion is a proposition which requires little discussion. Whatever theoretical merit there may be to the argument that there is a 'right' to rebellion against dictatorial governments is without force where the existing structure of the government provides for peaceful and orderly change. We reject any principle of governmental helplessness in the face of preparation for revolution, which principle, carried to its logical conclusion, must lead to anarchy. No one could conceive that it is not within the power of Congress to prohibit acts intended to overthrow the Government by force and violence. The question with which we are concerned here is not whether Congress has such power, but whether the means which it has employed conflict with the First and Fifth Amendments to the Constitution....

...The basis of the First Amendment is the hypothesis that speech can rebut speech, propaganda will answer propaganda, free debate of ideas will result in the wisest governmental policies. It is for this reason that this Court has recognized the inherent value of free discourse. An analysis of the leading cases in this Court which have involved direct limitations on speech, however, will demonstrate that both the majority of the Court and the dissenters in particular cases have recognized that this is not an unlimited, unqualified right, but that the societal value of speech must, on occasion, be subordinated to other values and considerations.

No important case involving free speech was decided by this Court prior to *Schenck v. United States,* 1919, 249 U.S. 47....That case involved a conviction under the Criminal Espionage Act, 40 Stat. 217. The question the Court faced was whether the evidence was sufficient to sustain the conviction. Writing for a unanimous Court, Justice Holmes stated that the 'question in every case is whether the words used are used in such circumstances and are of such a nature as to create a clear and present danger that they will bring about the substantive evils that Congress has a right to prevent.' But the force of even this expression is considerably weakened by the reference at the end of the opinion to *Goldman v. United States,* 1918, 245 U.S. 474, a prosecution under the same statute. Said Justice Holmes..., The fact is inescapable...that the phrase bore no connotation that the danger was to be any threat to the safety of the Republic. The charge was causing and attempting to cause insubordination in the military forces and obstruct recruiting. The objectionable document denounced conscription and its most inciting sentence was, 'You must do your share to maintain, support and uphold the rights of the people of this country.' Fifteen thousand copies were printed and some circulated. This insubstantial gesture toward insubordination in 1917 during war was held to be a clear and present danger of bringing about the evil of military insubordination.

In several later cases involving convictions under the Criminal Espionage Act, the nub of the evidence the Court held sufficient to meet the 'clear and present danger' test enunciated in Schenck was as follows: *Frohwerk v. United States,* 1919, 249 U.S. 204—publication of twelve newspaper articles attacking the war; *Debs v. United States,* 1919, 249 U.S. 211—one speech attacking United States' participation in the war; *Abrams v. United States,* 1920, 250 U.S. 616—circulation of copies of two different socialist circulars attacking the war; *Schaefer v. United States,* 1920, 251 U.S. 466—publication of a German language newspaper with allegedly false articles, critical of capitalism and the war; *Pierce v. United States,* 1920, 252 U.S. 239—circulation of copies of a four-page pamphlet written by a clergyman, attacking the purposes of the war and United States' participation therein.

Justice Holmes wrote the opinions for a unanimous Court in *Schenck, Frohwerk* and *Debs.* He and Justice Brandeis dissented in *Abrams, Schaefer* and *Pierce.* The basis of these dissents was that, because of the protection which the First Amendment gives to speech, the evidence in each case was insufficient to show that the defendants had created the requisite danger under *Schenck.* But these dissents did not mark a change of principle. The dissenters doubted only the probable effectiveness of the puny efforts toward subversion. In *Abrams,* they wrote, 'I do not doubt for a moment that by the same reasoning that would justify punishing persuasion to murder, the United States constitutionally may punish speech that produces or is intended to produce a clear and imminent danger that it will bring about forthwith certain substantive evils that the United States constitutionally may seek to prevent.' And in *Schaefer* the test was said to be 'one of degree,' although it is not clear whether 'degree' refers to clear and present danger or evil. Perhaps both were meant.

The rule we deduce from these cases is that where an offense is specified by a statute in nonspeech or nonpress terms, a conviction relying upon speech or press as evidence of violation may be sustained only when the speech or publication created a 'clear and present danger' of attempting or accomplishing the prohibited crime, e.g., interference with enlistment. The dissents, we repeat, in emphasizing the value of speech, were addressed to the argument of the sufficiency of the evidence....

In this case we are squarely presented with the application of the 'clear and present danger' test, and must decide what that phrase imports. We first note that many of the cases in which this Court has reversed convictions by use of this or similar tests have been based on the fact that the interest which the State was attempting to protect was itself too insubstantial to warrant restriction of speech. Overthrow of the Government by force and violence is certainly a substantial enough interest for the Government to limit speech. Indeed, this is the ultimate value of any society, for if a society cannot protect its very structure from armed internal attack, it must follow that no subordinate value can be protected. If, then, this interest may be protected, the literal problem which is presented is what has been meant by the use of the phrase 'clear and present danger' of the utterances bringing about the evil within the power of Congress to punish.

Obviously, the words cannot mean that before the Government may act, it must wait until the putsch is about to be executed, the plans have been laid and the signal is awaited. If Government is aware that a group aiming at its overthrow is attempting to indoctrinate its members and to commit them to a course whereby they will strike when the leaders feel the circumstances permit, action by the Government is required. The argument that there is no need for Government to concern itself, for Government is strong, it possesses ample powers to put down a rebellion, it may defeat the revolution with ease needs no answer. For that is not the question. Certainly an attempt to overthrow the Government by force, even though doomed from the outset because of inadequate numbers or power of the revolutionists, is a sufficient evil for Congress to prevent....

The damage which such attempts create both physically and politically to a nation makes it impossible to measure the validity in terms of the probability of success, or the immediacy of a successful attempt. In the instant case the trial judge charged the jury that they could not convict unless they found that petitioners intended to overthrow the Government 'as speedily as circumstances would permit.' This does not mean, and could not properly mean, that they would not strike until there was certainty of success. What was meant was that the revolutionists would strike when they thought the time was ripe. We must therefore reject the contention that success or probability of success is the criterion....

Chief Judge Learned Hand, writing for the majority below, interpreted the phrase as follows: 'In each case (courts) must ask whether the gravity of the 'evil,' discounted by its improbability, justifies such invasion of free speech as is necessary to avoid the danger.' We adopt this statement of the rule. As articulated by Chief Judge Hand, it is as succinct and inclusive as any other we might devise at this time. It takes into consideration those factors which we deem relevant, and relates their significances. More we cannot expect from words.

Likewise, we are in accord with the court below, which affirmed the trial court's finding that the requisite danger existed. The mere fact that from the period 1945 to 1948 petitioners' activities did not result in an attempt to overthrow the Government by force and violence is of course no answer to the fact that there was a group that was ready to make the attempt. The formation by petitioners of such a highly organized conspiracy, with rigidly disciplined members subject to call when the leaders, these petitioners, felt that the time had come for action, coupled with the inflammable nature of world conditions, similar uprisings in other countries, and the touch-and-go nature of our relations with countries with whom petitioners were in the very least ideologically attuned, convince us that their convictions were justified on this score.

And this analysis disposes of the contention that a conspiracy to advocate, as distinguished from the advocacy itself, cannot be constitutionally restrained, because it comprises only the preparation. It is the existence of the conspiracy which creates the danger. If the ingredients of the reaction are present, we cannot bind the Government to wait until the catalyst is added.

Although we have concluded that the finding that there was a sufficient danger to warrant the application of the statute was justified on the merits, there remains the problem of whether the trial judge's treatment of the issue was correct. He charged the jury, in relevant part, as follows:

> In further construction and interpretation of the statute I charge you that it is not the abstract doctrine of overthrowing or destroying organized government by unlawful means which is denounced by this law, but the teaching and advocacy of action for the accomplishment of that purpose, by language reasonably and ordinarily calculated to incite persons to such action. Accordingly, you cannot find the defendants or any of them guilty of the crime charged unless you are satisfied beyond a reasonable doubt that they conspired to organize a society, group and assembly of persons who teach and advocate the overthrow or destruction of the Government of the United States by force and violence and to advocate and teach the duty and necessity of overthrowing or destroying the Government of the United States by force and violence, with the intent that such teaching and advocacy be of a rule or principle of action and by language reasonably and ordinarily calculated to incite persons to such action, all with the intent to cause the overthrow or destruction of the Government of the United States by force and violence as speedily as circumstances would permit.

If you are satisfied that the evidence establishes beyond a reasonable doubt that the defendants, or any of them, are guilty of a violation of the statute, as I have interpreted it to you, I find as a matter of law that there is sufficient danger of a substantive evil that the Congress has a right to prevent to justify the application of the statute under the First Amendment of the Constitution.

> This is a matter of law about which you have no concern. It is a finding on a matter of law which I deem essential to support my ruling that the case should be submitted to you to pass upon the guilt or innocence of the defendants....

It is thus clear that he reserved the question of the existence of the danger for his own determination, and the question becomes whether the issue is of such a nature that it should have been submitted to the jury.

The first paragraph of the quoted instructions calls for the jury to find the facts essential to establish the substantive crime, violation of §§ 2(a)(1) and 2(a)(3) of the Smith Act, involved in the conspiracy charge. There can be no doubt that if the jury found those facts against the petitioners violation of the Act would be established. The argument that the action of the trial court is erroneous, in declaring as a matter of law that such violation shows sufficient danger to justify the punishment despite the First Amendment, rests on the theory that a jury must decide a question of the application of the First Amendment. We do not agree.

When facts are found that establish the violation of a statute, the protection against conviction afforded by the First Amendment is a matter of law. The doctrine that there must be a clear and present danger of a substantive evil that Congress has a right to prevent is a judicial rule to be applied as a matter of law by the courts. The guilt is established by proof of facts. Whether the First Amendment protects the activity which constitutes the violation of the statute must depend upon a judicial determination of the scope of the First Amendment applied to the circumstances of the case. . . .

There remains to be discussed the question of vagueness—whether the statute as we have interpreted it is too vague, not sufficiently advising those who would speak of the limitations upon their activity. It is urged that such vagueness contravenes the First and Fifth Amendments. This argument is particularly nonpersuasive when presented by petitioners, who, the jury found, intended to overthrow the Government as speedily as circumstances would permit. A claim of guilelessness ill becomes those with evil intent.

We agree that the standard as defined is not a neat, mathematical formulary. Like all verbalizations it is subject to criticism on the score of indefiniteness. But petitioners themselves contend that the verbalization, 'clear and present danger' is the proper standard. We see no difference, from the standpoint of vagueness, whether the standard of 'clear and present danger' is one contained in haec verba within the statute, or whether it is the judicial measure of constitutional applicability.

We have shown the indeterminate standard the phrase necessarily connotes. We do not think we have rendered that standard any more indefinite by our attempt to sum up the factors which are included within its scope. We think it well serves to indicate to those who would advocate constitutionally prohibited conduct that there is a line beyond which they may not go—a line which they, in full knowledge of what they intend and the circumstances in which their activity takes place, will well appreciate and understand. Where there is doubt as to the intent of the defendants, the nature of their activities, or their power to bring about the evil, this Court will review the convictions

with the scrupulous care demanded by our Constitution. But we are not convinced that because there may be borderline cases at some time in the future, these convictions should be reversed because of the argument that these petitioners could not know that their activities were constitutionally proscribed by the statute. . . .

We hold that § § 2(a)(1), 2(a)(3) and 3 of the Smith Act, do not inherently, or as construed or applied in the instant case, violate the First Amendment and other provisions of the Bill of Rights, or the First and Fifth Amendments because of indefiniteness. Petitioners intended to overthrow the Government of the United States as speedily as the circumstances would permit. Their conspiracy to organize the Communist Party and to teach and advocate the overthrow of the Government of the United States by force and violence created a 'clear and present danger' of an attempt to overthrow the Government by force and violence. They were properly and constitutionally convicted for violation of the Smith Act. The judgments of conviction are affirmed.

CONCURRING OPINIONS*

JACKSON, J.

This prosecution is the latest of never ending, because never successful, quests for some legal formula that will secure an existing order against revolutionary radicalism. It requires us to reappraise, in the light of our own times and conditions, constitutional doctrines devised under other circumstances to strike a balance between authority and liberty.

[The] Activity here charged to be criminal is conspiracy—that defendants conspired to teach and advocate, and to organize the Communist Party to teach and advocate, overthrow and destruction of the Government by force and violence. There is no charge of actual violence or attempt at overthrow. The principal reliance of the defense in this Court is that the conviction cannot stand under the Constitution because the conspiracy of these defendants presents no 'clear and present danger' of imminent or foreseeable overthrow.

The statute before us repeats a pattern, originally devised to combat the wave of anarchistic terrorism that plagued this country about the turn of the century, which lags at least two generations behind Communist Party techniques. Anarchism taught a philosophy of extreme individualism and hostility to government and property. Its avowed aim was a more just order, to be achieved by violent destruction of all government. Anarchism's sporadic

---

*Justice Frankfurter's concurring opinion is omitted.

and uncoordinated acts of terror were not integrated with an effective revolutionary machine, but the Chicago Haymarket riots of 1886, attempted murder of the industrialist Frick, attacks on state officials, and assassination of President McKinley in 1901, were fruits of its preaching....

The Communist Party...does not seek its strength primarily in numbers. Its aim is a relatively small party whose strength is in selected, dedicated, indoctrinated, and rigidly disciplined members. From established policy it tolerates no deviation and no debate. It seeks members that are, or may be, secreted in strategic posts in transportation, communications, industry, government, and especially in labor unions where it can compel employers to accept and retain its members. It also seeks to infiltrate and control organizations of professional and other groups. Through these placements in positions of power it seeks a leverage over society that will make up in power of coercion what it lacks in power of persuasion.

The Communists have no scruples against sabotage, terrorism, assassination, or mob disorder; but violence is not with them, as with the anarchists, an end in itself. The Communist Party advocates force only when prudent and profitable. Their strategy of stealth precludes premature or uncoordinated outbursts of violence, except, of course, when the blame will be placed on shoulders other than their own. They resort to violence as to truth, not as a principle but as an expedient. Force or violence, as they would resort to it, may never be necessary, because infiltration and deception may be enough....

The 'clear and present danger' test was an innovation by Mr. Justice Holmes in the *Schenck* case, reiterated and refined by him and Mr. Justice Brandeis in later cases, all arising before the era of World War II revealed the subtlety and efficacy of modernized revolutionary techniques used by totalitarian parties. In those cases, they were faced with convictions under so-called criminal syndicalism statutes aimed at anarchists but which, loosely construed, had been applied to punish socialism, pacifism, and left-wing ideologies, the charges often resting on far-fetched inferences which, if true, would establish only technical or trivial violations. They proposed 'clear and present danger' as a test for the sufficiency of evidence in particular cases.

I would save it, unmodified, for application...in the kind of case for which it was devised. When the issue is criminality of a hot-headed speech on a street corner, or circulation of a few incendiary pamphlets, or parading by some zealots behind a red flag, or refusal of a handful of school children to salute our flag, it is not beyond the capacity of the judicial process to gather, comprehend, and weigh the necessary materials for decision whether it is a clear and present danger of substantive evil or a harmless letting off of steam.

It is not a prophecy, for the danger in such cases has matured by the time of trial or it was never present....

The formula in such cases favors freedoms that are vital to our society, and, even if sometimes applied too generously, the consequences cannot be grave. But its recent expansion has extended, in particular to Communists, unprecedented immunities. Unless we are to hold our Government captive in a judge-made verbal trap, we must approach the problem of a well-organized, nation-wide conspiracy, such as I have described, as realistically as our predecessors faced the trivialities that were being prosecuted until they were checked with a rule of reason. I think reason is lacking for applying that test to this case.

If we must decide that this Act and its application are constitutional only if we are convinced that petitioner's conduct creates a 'clear and present danger' of violent overthrow, we must appraise imponderables, including international and national phenomena which baffle the best informed foreign offices and our most experienced politicians. We would have to foresee and predict the effectiveness of Communist propaganda, opportunities for infiltration, whether, and when, a time will come that they consider propitious for action, and whether and how fast our existing government will deteriorate. And we would have to speculate as to whether an approaching Communist coup would not be anticipated by a nationalistic fascist movement. No doctrine can be sound whose application requires us to make a prophecy of that sort in the guise of a legal decision. The judicial process simply is not adequate to a trial of such far-flung issues. The answers given would reflect our own political predilections and nothing more.

The authors of the clear and present danger test never applied it to a case like this, nor would I. If applied as it is proposed here, it means that the Communist plotting is protected during its period of incubation; its preliminary stages of organization and preparation are immune from the law; the Government can move only after imminent action is manifest, when it would, of course, be too late.

The highest degree of constitutional protection is due to the individual acting without conspiracy. But even an individual cannot claim that the Constitution protects him in advocating or teaching overthrow of government by force or violence. I should suppose no one would doubt that Congress has power to make such attempted overthrow a crime. But the contention is that one has the constitutional right to work up a public desire and will to do what it is a crime to attempt. I think direct incitement by speech or writing can be made a crime, and I think there can be a conviction without also proving that the odds favored its success by 99 to 1, or some other extremely high ratio.

The names of Mr. Justice Holmes and Mr. Justice Brandeis cannot be associated with such a doctrine of governmental disability. After the *Schenck* case, in which they set forth the clear and present danger test, they joined in these words of Mr. Justice Holmes, spoken for a unanimous Court:

...The First Amendment while prohibiting legislation against free speech as such cannot have been, and obviously was not, intended to give immunity for every possible use of language. We venture to believe that neither Hamilton nor Madison, nor any other competent person then or later, ever supposed that to make criminal the counselling of a murder within the jurisdiction of Congress would be an unconstitutional interference with free speech.

...As aptly stated by Judge Learned Hand in *Masses Publishing Co. v. Patten*, D.C., 244 F. 535, 540: 'One may not counsel or advise others to violate the law as it stands. Words are not only the keys of persuasion, but the triggers of action, and those which have no purport but to counsel the violation of law cannot by any latitude of interpretation be a part of that public opinion which is the final source of government in a democratic state.'

Of course, it is not always easy to distinguish teaching or advocacy in the sense of incitement from teaching or advocacy in the sense of exposition or explanation. It is a question of fact in each case.

What really is under review here is a conviction of conspiracy, after a trial for conspiracy, on an indictment charging conspiracy, brought under a statute outlawing conspiracy. With due respect to my colleagues, they seem to me to discuss anything under the sun except the law of conspiracy. One of the dissenting opinions even appears to chide me for 'invoking the law of conspiracy.' As that is the case before us, it may be more amazing that its reversal can be proposed without even considering the law of conspiracy.

The Constitution does not make conspiracy a civil right. The Court has never before done so and I think it should not do so now. Conspiracies of labor unions, trade associations, and news agencies have been condemned, although accomplished, evidenced and carried out, like the conspiracy here, chiefly by letter-writing, meetings, speeches and organization. Indeed, this Court seems, particularly in cases where the conspiracy has economic ends, to be applying its doctrines with increasing severity. While I consider criminal conspiracy a dragnet device capable of perversion into an instrument of injustice in the hands of a partisan or complacent judiciary, it has an established place in our system of law, and no reason appears for applying it only to concerted action claimed to disturb interstate commerce and withholding it from those claimed to undermine our whole Government....

The basic rationale of the law of conspiracy is that a conspiracy may be an evil in itself, independently of any other

evil it seeks to accomplish....The reasons underlying the doctrine that conspiracy may be a substantive evil in itself, apart from any evil it may threaten, attempt or accomplish, are peculiarly appropriate to conspiratorial Communism.

'The reason for finding criminal liability in case of a combination to effect an unlawful end or to use unlawful means, where none would exist, even though the act contemplated were actually committed by an individual, is that a combination of persons to commit a wrong, either as an end or as a means to an end, is so much more dangerous, because of its increased power to do wrong, because it is more difficult to guard against and prevent the evil designs of a group of persons than of a single person, and because of the terror which fear of such a combination tends to create in the minds of people.'

There is lamentation in the dissents about the injustice of conviction in the absence of some overt act. Of course, there has been no general uprising against the Government, but the record is replete with acts to carry out the conspiracy alleged, acts such as always are held sufficient to consummate the crime where the statute requires an overt act. But the shorter answer is that no overt act is or need be required. The Court, in antitrust cases, early upheld the power of Congress to adopt the ancient common law that makes conspiracy itself a crime. Through Mr. Justice Holmes, it said: 'Coming next to the objection that no overt act is laid, the answer is that the Sherman act punishes the conspiracies at which it is aimed on the common law footing—that is to say, it does not make the doing of any act other than the act of conspiring a condition of liability.' It is not to be supposed that the power of Congress to protect the Nation's existence is more limited than its power to protect interstate commerce....

I do not suggest that Congress could punish conspiracy to advocate something, the doing of which it may not punish. Advocacy or exposition of the doctrine of communal property ownership, or any political philosophy unassociated with advocacy of its imposition by force or seizure of government by unlawful means could not be reached through conspiracy prosecution. But it is not forbidden to put down force or violence, it is not forbidden to punish its teaching or advocacy, and the end being punishable, there is no doubt of the power to punish conspiracy for the purpose....

Having held that a conspiracy alone is a crime and its consummation is another, it would be weird legal reasoning to hold that Congress could punish the one only if there was 'clear and present danger' of the second. This would compel the Government to prove two crimes in order to convict for one.

When our constitutional provisions were written, the chief forces recognized as antagonists in the struggle between authority and liberty were the Government on the one hand and the individual citizen on the other. It was thought that if the state could be kept in its place the individual could take care of himself.

In more recent times these problems have been complicated by the intervention between the state and the citizen of permanently organized, well-financed, semisecret and highly disciplined political organizations. Totalitarian groups here and abroad perfected the technique of creating private paramilitary organizations to coerce both the public government and its citizens. These organizations assert as against our Government all of the constitutional rights and immunities of individuals and at the same time exercise over their followers much of the authority which they deny to the Government. The Communist Party realistically is a state within a state, an authoritarian dictatorship within a republic. It demands these freedoms, not for its members, but for the organized party. It denies to its own members at the same time the freedom to dissent, to debate, to deviate from the party line, and enforces its authoritarian rule by crude purges, if nothing more violent.

The law of conspiracy has been the chief means at the Government's disposal to deal with the growing problems created by such organizations. I happen to think it is an awkward and inept remedy, but I find no constitutional authority for taking this weapon from the Government. There is no constitutional right to 'gang up' on the Government.

While I think there was power in Congress to enact this statute and that, as applied in this case, it cannot be held unconstitutional, I add that I have little faith in the long-range effectiveness of this conviction to stop the rise of the Communist movement. Communism will not go to jail with these Communists. No decision by this Court can forestall revolution whenever the existing government fails to command the respect and loyalty of the people and sufficient distress and discontent is allowed to grow up among the masses.

Many failures by fallen governments attest that no government can long prevent revolution by outlawry. Corruption, ineptitude, inflation, oppressive taxation, militarization, injustice, and loss of leadership capable of intellectual initiative in domestic or foreign affairs are allies on which the Communists count to bring opportunity knocking to their door. Sometimes I think they may be mistaken. But the Communists are not building just for today—the rest of us might profit by their example. . . .

DISSENTS

BLACK, J.
. . . These petitioners were not charged with an attempt to overthrow the Government. They were not charged with overt acts of any kind designed to overthrow the Government. They were not even charged with saying anything or writing anything designed to overthrow the Government. The charge was that they agreed to assemble and to talk and publish certain ideas at a later date: The indictment is that they conspired to organize the Communist Party and to use speech or newspapers and other publications in the future to teach and advocate the forcible overthrow of the Government. No matter how it is worded, this is a virulent form of prior censorship of speech and press, which I believe the First Amendment forbids. I would hold § 3 of the Smith Act authorizing this prior restraint unconstitutional on its face and as applied.

So long as this Court exercises the power of judicial review of legislation, I cannot agree that the First Amendment permits us to sustain laws suppressing freedom of speech and press on the basis of Congress' or our own notions of mere 'reasonableness.' Such a doctrine waters down the First Amendment so that it amounts to little more than an admonition to Congress. The Amendment as so construed is not likely to protect any but those 'safe' or orthodox views which rarely need its protection. I must also express my objection to the holding because, as Mr. Justice Douglas' dissent shows, it sanctions the determination of a crucial issue of fact by the judge rather than by the jury. . . .

Public opinion being what it now is, few will protest the conviction of these Communist petitioners. There is hope, however, that in calmer times, when present pressures, passions and fears subside, this or some later Court will restore the First Amendment liberties to the high preferred place where they belong in a free society.

DOUGLAS, J.
If this were a case where those who claimed protection under the First Amendment were teaching the techniques of sabotage, the assassination of the President, the filching of documents from public files, the planting of bombs, the art of street warfare, and the like, I would have no doubts. The freedom to speak is not absolute; the teaching of methods of terror and other seditious conduct should be beyond the pale along with obscenity and immorality. This case was argued as if those were the facts. The argument imported much seditious conduct into the record. That is easy and it has popular appeal, for the activities of Communists in plotting and scheming against the free world are common knowledge. But the fact is that no such evidence was introduced at the trial. There is a statute which makes a seditious conspiracy unlawful. Petitioners, however, were not charged with a 'conspiracy to overthrow' the Government. They were charged with a conspiracy to form a party and groups and assemblies of people who teach and advocate the overthrow of our Government by force or violence

and with a conspiracy to advocate and teach its overthrow by force and violence. It may well be that indoctrination in the techniques of terror to destroy the Government would be indictable under either statute. But the teaching which is condemned here is of a different character.

So far as the present record is concerned, what petitioners did was to organize people to teach and themselves teach the Marxist-Leninist doctrine contained chiefly in four books: *Foundations of Leninism* by Stalin (1924); *The Communist Manifesto* by Marx and Engels (1848); *State and Revolution* by Lenin (1917); *History of the Communist Party of the Soviet Union* (B.) (1939).

Those books are to Soviet Communism what *Mein Kampf* was to Nazism. If they are understood, the ugliness of Communism is revealed, its deceit and cunning are exposed, the nature of its activities becomes apparent, and the chances of its success less likely. That is not, of course, the reason why petitioners chose these books for their classrooms. They are fervent Communists to whom these volumes are gospel. They preached the creed with the hope that some day it would be acted upon.

The opinion of the Court does not outlaw these texts nor condemn them to the fire, as the Communists do literature offensive to their creed. But if the books themselves are not outlawed, if they can lawfully remain on library shelves, by what reasoning does their use in a classroom become a crime? It would not be a crime under the Act to introduce these books to a class, though that would be teaching what the creed of violent overthrow of the Government is. The Act, as construed, requires the element of intent—that those who teach the creed believe in it. The crime then depends not on what is taught but on who the teacher is. That is to make freedom of speech turn not on what is said, but on the intent with which it is said. Once we start down that road we enter territory dangerous to the liberties of every citizen. . . .

Free speech has occupied an exalted position because of the high service it has given our society. Its protection is essential to the very existence of a democracy. The airing of ideas releases pressures which otherwise might become destructive. When ideas compete in the market for acceptance, full and free discussion exposes the false and they gain few adherents. Full and free discussion even of ideas we hate encourages the testing of our own prejudices and preconceptions. Full and free discussion keeps a society from becoming stagnant and unprepared for the stresses and strains that work to tear all civilizations apart.

Full and free discussion has indeed been the first article of our faith. We have founded our political system on it. It has been the safeguard of every religious, political, philosophical, economic, and racial group amongst us. We have counted on it to keep us from embracing what is cheap and false; we have trusted the common sense of our people to choose the doctrine true to our genius and to reject the rest. This has been the one single outstanding tenet that has made our institutions the symbol of freedom and equality. We have deemed it more costly to liberty to suppress a despised minority than to let them vent their spleen. We have above all else feared the political censor. We have wanted a land where our people can be exposed to all the diverse creeds and cultures of the world.

There comes a time when even speech loses its constitutional immunity. Speech innocuous one year may at another time fan such destructive flames that it must be halted in the interests of the safety of the Republic. That is the meaning of the clear and present danger test. When conditions are so critical that there will be no time to avoid the evil that the speech threatens, it is time to call a halt. Otherwise, free speech which is the strength of the Nation will be the cause of its destruction.

Yet free speech is the rule, not the exception. The restraint to be constitutional must be based on more than fear, on more than passionate opposition against the speech, on more than a revolted dislike for its contents. There must be some immediate injury to society that is likely if speech is allowed. The classic statement of these conditions was made by Mr. Justice Brandeis in his concurring opinion in *Whitney v. People of State of California*, 274 U.S. 357.

Fear of serious injury cannot alone justify suppression of free speech and assembly. Men feared witches and burnt women. It is the function of speech to free men from the bondage of irrational fears. To justify suppression of free speech there must be reasonable ground to fear that serious evil will result if free speech is practiced. There must be reasonable ground to believe that the danger apprehended is imminent. There must be reasonable ground to believe that the evil to be prevented is a serious one. Every denunciation of existing law tends in some measure to increase the probability that there will be violation of it. Condonation of a breach enhances the probability. Expressions of approval add to the probability. Propagation of the criminal state of mind by teaching syndicalism increases it. Advocacy of law-breaking heightens it still further. But even advocacy of violation, however reprehensible morally, is not a justification for denying free speech where the advocacy falls short of incitement and there is nothing to indicate that the advocacy would be immediately acted on. The wide difference between advocacy and incitement, between preparation and attempt, between assembling and conspiracy, must be borne in mind. In order to support a finding of clear and present danger it must be shown either that immediate serious violence was to be expected or was advocated, or that the past conduct furnished reason to believe that such advocacy was then contemplated.

Those who won our independence by revolution were not cowards. They did not fear political change. They did not exalt order at the cost of liberty. To courageous, self-reliant men, with confidence in the power of free and fearless reasoning applied through the processes of popular government, no danger flowing from speech can be deemed clear and present, unless the incidence of the evil apprehended is so imminent that it may befall before there is opportunity for full discussion. If there be time to expose through discussion the falsehood and fallacies, to avert the evil by the processes of education, the remedy to be applied is more speech, not enforced silence.

... The nature of Communism as a force on the world scene would, of course, be relevant to the issue of clear and present danger of petitioners' advocacy within the United States. But the primary consideration is the strength and tactical position of petitioners and their converts in this country. On that there is no evidence in the record.

If we are to take judicial notice of the threat of Communists within the nation, it should not be difficult to conclude that as a political party they are of little consequence. Communists in this country have never made a respectable or serious showing in any election. I would doubt that there is a village, let alone a city or county or state, which the Communists could carry. Communism in the world scene is no bogey-man; but Communism as a political faction or party in this country plainly is. Communism has been so thoroughly exposed in this country that it has been crippled as a political force.

Free speech has destroyed it as an effective political party. It is inconceivable that those who went up and down this country preaching the doctrine of revolution which petitioners espouse would have any success. In days of trouble and confusion, when bread lines were long, when the unemployed walked the streets, when people were starving, the advocates of a short-cut by revolution might have a chance to gain adherents. But today there are no such conditions. The country is not in despair; the people know Soviet Communism; the doctrine of Soviet revolution is exposed in all of its ugliness and the American people want none of it.

How it can be said that there is a clear and present danger that this advocacy will succeed is, therefore, a mystery. Some nations less resilient than the United States, where illiteracy is high and where democratic traditions are only budding, might have to take drastic steps and jail these men for merely speaking their creed. But in America they are miserable merchants of unwanted ideas; their wares remain unsold. The fact that their ideas are abhorrent does not make them powerful.

The political impotence of the Communists in this country does not, of course, dispose of the problem. Their numbers; their positions in industry and government; the extent to which they have in fact infiltrated the police, the armed services, transportation, stevedoring, power plants, munitions works, and other critical places—these facts all bear on the likelihood that their advocacy of the Soviet theory of revolution will endanger the Republic. But the record is silent on these facts.

If we are to proceed on the basis of judicial notice, it is impossible for me to say that the Communists in this country are so potent or so strategically deployed that they must be suppressed for their speech. I could not so hold unless I were willing to conclude that the activities in recent years of committees of Congress, of the Attorney General, of labor unions, of state legislatures, and of Loyalty Boards were so futile as to leave the country on the edge of grave peril. To believe that petitioners and their following are placed in such critical positions as to endanger the Nation is to believe the incredible. It is safe to say that the followers of the creed of Soviet Communism are known to the F.B.I.; that in case of war with Russia they will be picked up overnight as were all prospective saboteurs at the commencement of World War II; that the invisible army of petitioners is the best known, the most beset, and the least thriving of any fifth column in history. Only those held by fear and panic could think otherwise.

This is my view if we are to act on the basis of judicial notice. But the mere statement of the opposing views indicates how important it is that we know the facts before we act. Neither prejudice nor hate nor senseless fear should be the basis of this solemn act. Free speech—the glory of our system of government—should not be sacrificed on anything less than plain and objective proof of danger that the evil advocated is imminent. On this record no one can say that petitioners and their converts are in such a strategic position as to have even the slightest chance of achieving their aims.

The First Amendment provides that 'Congress shall make no law ... abridging the freedom of speech.' The Constitution provides no exception. This does not mean, however, that the Nation need hold its hand until it is in such weakened condition that there is no time to protect itself from incitement to revolution. Seditious conduct can always be punished. But the command of the First Amendment is so clear that we should not allow Congress to call a halt to free speech except in the extreme case of peril from the speech itself.

The First Amendment makes confidence in the common sense of our people and in their maturity of judgment the great postulate of our democracy. Its philosophy is that violence is rarely, if ever, stopped by denying civil liberties to those advocating resort to force. The First Amendment reflects the philosophy of Jefferson 'that it is time enough for the rightful purposes of civil government, for its officers to interfere when principles break out into overt acts against peace and good order.' The political censor has no place in our public debates. Unless and until extreme and necessitous circumstances are shown our aim should be to keep speech unfettered and to allow the processes of law to be invoked only when the provocateurs among us move from speech to action.

Vishinsky wrote in 1938 in *The Law of the Soviet State,* 'In our state, naturally, there is and can be no place for freedom of speech, press, and so on for the foes of socialism.' Our concern should be that we accept no such standard for the United States. Our faith should be that our people will never give support to these advocates of revolution, so long as we remain loyal to the purposes for which our Nation was founded.

Questions

1. State the *mens rea* and *actus reus* elements of Sections 1, 2, and 3 of the Smith Act.

2. List the relevant facts for deciding whether the defendants violated the Smith Act.

3. Summarize the conclusions reached by the Court of Appeals.

4. According to Chief Justice Vinson's opinion, what is the "obvious purpose" of the Smith Act?

5. Define the "clear and present danger" test to decide when limits on speech don't violate the First Amendment.

6. According to Chief Justice Vinson's opinion, how does the "clear and present danger" test apply to the facts of the case?

7. According to Chief Justice Vinson's opinion, why is the Smith Act *not* void for vagueness?

8. Summarize the "never ending quest" Justice Jackson refers to in his concurring opinion.

9. Summarize Justice Jackson's arguments supporting his conclusion that this case is about a criminal conspiracy.

10. According to Justice Jackson, what characteristics of the Communist Party make the "clear and present danger" test too strict for deciding whether the Smith Act violates the First Amendment ban on free speech and association?

11. Summarize Justice Black's reasons for dissenting from the Court's judgment.

12. Summarize Justice Douglas's reasons for dissenting from the Court's judgment.

Go to Exercise 13-2 on the Criminal Law 8e CD to read the full version of *Dennis v. U.S.*

Sabotage

Sabotage is the crime of damaging or destroying property for the purpose of interfering with and hindering preparations for war and defense during national emergencies. Here's how the U.S. Criminal Code (2003, Title 18, Part I, Chapter 105, § 2153) defines sabotage of war and defense materials, buildings, and utilities:

> Whoever, when the United States is at war, or in times of national emergency . . . with intent to injure, interfere with, or obstruct the United States or any associate nation in preparing for or carrying on the war or defense activities, or, with reason to believe that his act may injure, interfere with, or obstruct the United States or any associate nation in preparing for or carrying on the war or defense activities, willfully injures, destroys, contaminates or infects, or attempts to so injure, destroy, contaminate or infect any war material, war premises, or war utilities, shall be fined under this title or imprisoned not more than thirty years, or both.

Other sections of Chapter 105 apply to similar acts against forts, harbors, and sea areas (§ 2152); production of defective war (§ 2154) or national defense (§ 2155) material, premises, and utilities; and destruction of national defense materials, premises, and utilities. Utilities include

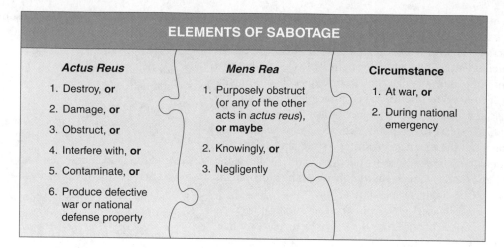

ELEMENTS OF SABOTAGE

Actus Reus

1. Destroy, **or**
2. Damage, **or**
3. Obstruct, **or**
4. Interfere with, **or**
5. Contaminate, **or**
6. Produce defective war or national defense property

Mens Rea

1. Purposely obstruct (or any of the other acts in *actus reus*), **or maybe**
2. Knowingly, **or**
3. Negligently

Circumstance

1. At war, **or**
2. During national emergency

railroads, railways, electric lines, roads of whatever description, any railroad or railway fixture, canal, lock, dam, wharf, pier, dock, bridge, building, structure, engine, machine, mechanical contrivance, car, vehicle, boat, aircraft, airfields, air lanes, and fixtures or appurtenances thereof, or any other means of transportation whatsoever, whereon or whereby such war material or any troops of the United States, or of any associate nation, are being or may be transported either within the limits of the United States or upon the high seas or elsewhere; and all air-conditioning systems, dams, reservoirs, aqueducts, water and gas mains and pipes, structures and buildings, whereby or in connection with which air, water or gas is being furnished, or may be furnished, to any war premises or to the Armed Forces of the United States, or any associate nation, and all electric light and power, steam or pneumatic power, telephone and telegraph plants, poles, wires, and fixtures, and wireless stations, and the buildings connected with the maintenance and operation thereof used to supply air, water, light, heat, power, or facilities of communication to any war premises or to the Armed Forces of the United States, or any associate nation. (§ 2151)

The code isn't completely clear as to the required *mens rea*. Most of the time, it is expressed using the word "willfully," sometimes "with intent to," and at least once "with reason to believe." But, the *mens rea* is probably closest to the highest level of culpability—purpose (Chapter 4).

Espionage

We know **espionage** by its more common name *spying*. Merriam-Webster (2003) defines espionage as

> the systematic secret observation of words and conduct . . . by special agents upon people of a foreign country or upon their activities or enterprises (for example, war production or scientific advancement in military fields) and the accumulation of information **(intelligence gathering)** about such people, activities, and enterprises for political or military uses.

The U.S. Criminal Code (2003, Title 18, Chapter 37, § 794) separates spying into two crimes: espionage during peace and espionage during war. The code defines espionage during peace as turning or attempting to turn over information about national defense to any foreign country with "intent or with reason to believe" the information is "to be used" to either hurt the United States or help any foreign country. The

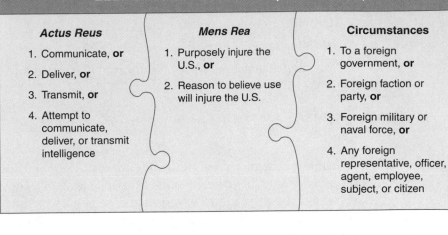

ELEMENTS OF ESPIONAGE (AT ANY TIME)

Actus Reus	*Mens Rea*	**Circumstances**
1. Communicate, **or**	1. Purposely injure the U.S., **or**	1. To a foreign government, **or**
2. Deliver, **or**	2. Reason to believe use will injure the U.S.	2. Foreign faction or party, **or**
3. Transmit, **or**		3. Foreign military or naval force, **or**
4. Attempt to communicate, deliver, or transmit intelligence		4. Any foreign representative, officer, agent, employee, subject, or citizen

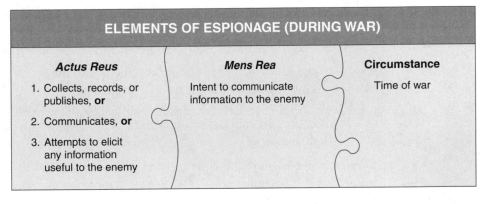

ELEMENTS OF ESPIONAGE (DURING WAR)

Actus Reus	*Mens Rea*	**Circumstance**
1. Collects, records, or publishes, **or**	Intent to communicate information to the enemy	Time of war
2. Communicates, **or**		
3. Attempts to elicit any information useful to the enemy		

penalty is any term of imprisonment up to life or, if someone died as a result of the espionage, death (§ 794[a]).

The crime of espionage during war consists of collecting, recording, publishing, or communicating (or attempting to do any of these) "any information" about troop movements, ships, aircraft, or war materials and any other information "which might be useful to the enemy." The penalty is death or any term of imprisonment up to life (§794[b]).

ANTI-TERRORISM CRIMES

A number of sections of the U.S. Code are available for prosecuting crimes related to terrorists and terrorist organizations. These include the crimes we've already discussed—treason, sedition, sabotage, and espionage. The murder, attempted murder, and conspiracy to murder provisions in the code are also available. Then, there are some specific anti-terrorism crimes— mainly, U.S. Code Chapter 113B, "Terrorism" (Title 18), the **Anti-Terrorism and Effective Death Penalty Act (AEDPA)** (1996), and the USA Patriot Act (2001). These acts include the following crimes:

1. Use of certain weapons of mass destruction (§ 2332a)

2. Acts of terrorism transcending national boundaries (§ 2332b)

3. Harboring or concealing terrorists (§ 2339)

4. Providing material support to terrorists (§ 2339A)

5. Providing material support or resources to designated foreign terrorist organizations (§ 2339B)

 Go to Exercise 13-3 on the Criminal Law 8e CD to read the full text of terrorism sections in the U.S. Code.

Before we examine these crimes, it's important that you know the official definition of terrorism as it's defined in the U.S. Code (§ 2331). The code divides terrorism into two kinds: international terrorism and domestic terrorism. According to the code, **international terrorism** (§ 2331[1]) consists of violent acts or acts dangerous to human life that

1. Are committed outside the United States

2. Would be crimes if they were committed inside the United States

3. Are committed, or appear to be committed, with the intent
   (a) To intimidate or coerce a civilian population;
   (b) To influence the policy of a government by intimidation or coercion; or
   (c) To affect the conduct of a government by mass destruction, assassination, or kidnapping

Domestic terrorism (§ 2331[5]) consists of the same elements, but the acts are committed inside the United States. OK, now let's look at some specific terrorist crimes included in the U.S. Code.

Use of Weapons of Mass Destruction

According to the U.S. Code (2003), it's a felony punishable by up to life imprisonment (or execution if anyone dies) to threaten to use, or attempt or conspire to use, a **weapon of mass destruction** against a U.S. citizen *outside* the United States (Title 18, Chapter 113B, § 2332a[a]), any person *inside* the United States (§ 2332a[b]), or any *property* inside or outside the United States (§ 2332a[c]). "Weapons of mass destruction" means "any **destructive device**," including any:

• Explosive, incendiary, or poison gas

• Bomb

• Grenade

• Rocket that has a propellant charge over 4 ounces

• Missile that has an explosive or incendiary charge over ¼ ounce

• Mine

• Device similar to the devices listed in (1)–(6) (U.S. Code, Title 18, Ch. 44, § 921)

The following are also defined as weapons of mass destruction:

- Any weapon intended to cause death or serious bodily injury by poisonous chemicals, or their precursors
- Any weapon involving a disease mechanism
- Any weapon designed to release radiation or radioactivity at a level dangerous to human life (§ 2332[c][2]).

Acts of Terrorism Transcending National Boundaries

According to Section 2332b, it's a felony for anyone whose **"conduct transcends national boundaries"** (*actus reus* of conduct occurring partly *outside* and partly *inside* the U.S.) to

1. Kill, kidnap, maim, assault resulting in serious bodily injury, or assault with a deadly weapon any person within the United States; or
2. "Create a substantial risk of serious bodily injury to any other person" by destroying or damaging any structure, conveyance, or other property within the United States; or
3. Threaten, or attempt, or conspire to commit (1) or (2)

if (circumstance elements)

1. The victim, or intended victim is the U.S. government, a member of the uniformed services, or any official, officer, employee, or agent of the legislative, executive, or judicial branches, or of any department or agency, of the United States
2. The structure, conveyance, or other property is owned by or leased by the United States

The penalties are

1. Death or up to life imprisonment for killing or for death resulting from the conduct
2. Up to life imprisonment for kidnapping
3. Up to 35 years for maiming
4. Up to 30 years for assault with a deadly weapon or assault resulting in serious bodily injury
5. Up to 25 years for damaging or destroying property

Harboring or Concealing Terrorists

Section 2339 of the U.S. Code provides:

Whoever harbors or conceals any person who he knows, or has reasonable grounds to believe, has committed, or is about to commit, an offense under section 32 (relating to destruction of aircraft or aircraft facilities), section 175 (relating to biological weapons), section 229 (relating to chemical weapons), section 831 (relating to nuclear materials), paragraph (2) or (3) of section 844(f) (relating to arson and bombing of government property risking or causing injury or death), section 1366(a) (relating to the destruction of an energy facility), section 2280 (relating to violence against maritime navigation),

TABLE 13.1		
Types of "Material Support"		
Currency or monetary instruments or financial securities		Communications equipment
		Facilities
Financial services		Weapons, lethal substances, explosives
Lodging		Personnel
Training		Transportation
Expert advice or assistance		Other physical assets, except medicine or religious materials
Safehouses		
False documentation or identification		

section 2332a (relating to weapons of mass destruction), or section 2332b (relating to acts of terrorism transcending national boundaries) of this title, section 236(a) (relating to sabotage of nuclear facilities or fuel) of the Atomic Energy Act of 1954 (42 U.S.C. 2284(a)), or section 46502 (relating to aircraft piracy) of title 49, shall be fined under this title or imprisoned not more than ten years, or both.

The *actus reus* is harboring or concealing persons who have committed or are about to commit a list of terrorist-related crimes. The *mens rea* requires knowing (or that a reasonable person should have known) the *actus reus* was about to be committed. The penalty is a fine or up to 10 years imprisonment.

Providing "Material Support" to Terrorists and/or Terrorist Organizations

All of the crimes we've covered so far in this chapter are available to the U.S. government for prosecuting suspected terrorists and convicting guilty ones. Still (so far anyway), the government hasn't used them in terrorism cases since September 11. In the more than thirty cases prosecuted since 9/11 (Roth 2003), the government's charge of choice has been "providing **material support** or resources to individual terrorists (U.S. Code 2003, Title 18, §§ 2339A) and/or terrorist organizations" (§ 2339B) (Table 13.1).

The felony of providing material support was first created in the 1996 Anti-Terrorism and Effective Death Penalty Act (AEDPA) (§ 323), which was aimed at *domestic* terrorist acts. It was passed after Timothy McVeigh bombed the federal building in Oklahoma City, Oklahoma. The AEDPA felony (with ratcheted-up penalties) became §§ 2339A and B of the 2001 USA Patriot Act.*

According to Section 2339B of the Patriot Act, it's a crime not only to *provide* material support to terrorist organizations but also to attempt, or conspire, to provide it. So, the crime of material support to terrorist organizations relies heavily on the traditional inchoate crimes of attempt, conspiracy, and solicitation (Chapter 6) and accom-

---

*The Patriot Act is a huge law (300+ pages long) passed with lightning speed only six weeks after the September 11 attacks. Most of the act deals with criminal procedure (surveillance and intelligence, law enforcement information sharing, search and seizure, interrogation, and detention). Of course, these are extremely important, but they're subjects for criminal *procedure,* not criminal law.

ELEMENTS OF MATERIAL SUPPORT TO TERRORISTS

Actus Reus

1. Provides material support to individual terrorists, **or**

2. Conceals or disguises the nature, location, source, or ownership of material support or resources

Mens Rea

Knowing or intending that support or resources are to be used in preparation for, or in carrying out, a long list of crimes in the U.S. Code that are helpful to terrorists

ELEMENTS OF MATERIAL SUPPORT TO TERRORIST ORGANIZATIONS

Actus Reus

Provides material support or resources to a foreign terrorist organization, or attempts or conspires to do so

Mens Rea

Knowingly

plices, accessories, and vicarious liability (Chapter 5). In fact, criminalizing the providing of support is directed at "nipping terrorism in the bud." It tries to prevent what we most want to prevent—killing and destruction by terrorist acts.

Here's how the law defines providing support for individual terrorists (§ 2339A) and terrorist organizations (§ 2339B):

SEC. 2339A. — PROVIDING MATERIAL SUPPORT TO TERRORISTS

(a) *Offense.* — Whoever provides material support or resources or conceals or disguises the nature, location, source, or ownership of material support or resources, knowing or intending that they are to be used in preparation for, or in carrying out, a violation of [a list of provisions related to terrorist acts in the U.S. Code] or in preparation for, or in carrying out, the concealment or an escape from the commission of any such violation, or attempts or conspires to do such an act, shall be fined under this title, imprisoned not more than 15 years, or both, and, if the death of any person results, shall be imprisoned for any term of years or for life. . . .

(b) *Definition.* — In this section, the term "material support or resources" means currency or monetary instruments or financial securities, financial services, lodging, training, expert advice or assistance, safehouses, false documentation or identification, communications equipment, facilities, weapons, lethal substances, explosives, personnel, transportation, and other physical assets, except medicine or religious materials.

SEC. 2339B. — PROVIDING MATERIAL SUPPORT OR RESOURCES TO DESIGNATED FOREIGN TERRORIST ORGANIZATIONS

(a) Prohibited Activities. —

(1) Unlawful conduct. — Whoever, within the United States or subject to the jurisdiction of the United States, knowingly provides material support or resources to a foreign

terrorist organization, or attempts or conspires to do so, shall be fined under this title or imprisoned not more than 15 years, or both, and, if the death of any person results, shall be imprisoned for any term of years or for life.

The most-argued issues in the cases now in the court system are two constitutional questions:

1. Is the term "providing material support" void for vagueness because it violates due process? (Chapter 2)

2. Does the provision violate the First Amendment rights of speech and association?

None of the cases has reached the U.S. Supreme Court, but a few have reached and been decided in the U.S. District Courts and the U.S. Courts of Appeals. One of these cases was the prosecution of John Walker Lindh, the "American Taliban." Lindh attended a military training camp in Pakistan run by Harakut ul-Mujahideen, whose followers had been designated by the U.S. Secretary of State as a "terrorist group dedicated to an extremist view of Islam"; traveled to Afghanistan; and joined the Taliban. There, he informed Taliban personnel "that he was an American and that he wanted to go to the front lines to fight." Lindh was captured by the Northern Alliance, an ally of the United States in the War in Afghanistan. Later, he was indicted for providing and conspiring to provide material support to Harakut ul-Mujahideen.

In *U.S. v. Lindh*, Lindh tried to get the indictment dismissed on vagueness and First Amendment grounds. Here's an excerpt from the U.S. District Court, Eastern District of Virginia's opinion.

| CASE | *Is the "Material Support" Statute Unconstitutional?* |

U.S. v. Lindh
212 F. Supp.2d 541 (E.D. Virginia, 2002)

John Phillip Walker Lindh was indicted under anti-terrorism laws, stemming from his alleged involvement with the al Qaeda organization and the Taliban government in Afghanistan. The U.S. District Court, Eastern District of Virginia, denied Lindh's motions to dismiss the indictment.

ELLIS, J.

FACTS

The Indictment's allegations may be succinctly summarized. In mid-2001, Lindh attended a military training camp in Pakistan run by Harakat ul-Mujahideen ("HUM"), a terrorist group dedicated to an extremist view of Islam. After receiving several weeks of training, Lindh informed

HUM officials that "he wished to fight with the Taliban* in Afghanistan." Thus, in May or June 2001, he traveled from Pakistan into Afghanistan "for the purpose of taking up arms with the Taliban," eventually arriving at a Taliban recruiting center in Kabul, Afghanistan—the Dar ul-Anan Headquarters of the Mujahideen. On his arrival, Lindh presented a letter of introduction from HUM and advised Taliban personnel "that he was an American and that he wanted to go to the front lines to fight."

---

*According to the indictment, the Taliban is Afghanistan's dominant political force and its members, like the members of HUM, practice an extremist form of Islam. Specifically, members of the Taliban believe in conducting "jihad," or holy war, against those whom they believe threaten their form of Islam, including the United States.

While at the Dar ul-Anan Headquarters, Lindh agreed to receive additional and extensive military training at an al Qaeda* training camp. He made this decision "knowing that America and its citizens were the enemies of Bin Laden and al-Qaeda and that a principal purpose of al-Qaeda was to fight and kill Americans." In late May or June 2001, Lindh traveled to a bin Laden guest house in Kandahar, Afghanistan, where he stayed for several days, and then traveled to the al Farooq training camp, "an al Qaeda facility located several hours west of Kandahar." He reported to the camp with approximately twenty other trainees, mostly Saudis, and remained there throughout June and July.

During this period, he participated fully in the camp's training activities, despite being told early in his stay that "Bin Laden had sent forth some fifty people to carry out twenty suicide terrorist operations against the United States and Israel." As part of his al Qaeda training, Lindh participated in "terrorist training courses in, among other things, weapons, orienteering, navigation, explosives and battlefield combat." This training included the use of "shoulder weapons, pistols and rocket-propelled grenades, and the construction of Molotov cocktails."

During his stay at al Farooq, Lindh met personally with bin Laden, "who thanked him and other trainees for taking part in jihad." He also met with a senior al Qaeda official, Abu Mohammad Al-Masri, who inquired whether Lindh was interested in traveling outside Afghanistan to conduct operations against the United States and Israel. Lindh declined Al-Masri's offer in favor of going to the front lines to fight. It is specifically alleged that Lindh swore allegiance to jihad in June or July 2001.

When Lindh completed his training at al Farooq in July or August 2001, he traveled to Kabul, Afghanistan, where he was issued an AKM rifle "with a barrel suitable for long range shooting." Armed with this rifle, Lindh, together with approximately 150 non-Afghani fighters, traveled from Kabul to the front line at Takhar, located in Northeastern Afghanistan, where the entire unit was placed under the command of an Iraqi named Abdul Hady. Lindh's group was eventually divided into smaller groups that fought in shifts against Northern Alliance troops in the Takhar trenches, rotating every one to two weeks. During this period, Lindh "carried various weapons with him,

including the AKM rifle, an RPK rifle he was issued after the AKM rifle malfunctioned, and at least two grenades."

He remained with his fighting group following the September 11, 2001 terrorist attacks, "despite having been told that Bin Laden had ordered the [September 11] attacks, that additional terrorist attacks were planned, and that additional al Qaeda personnel were being sent from the front lines to protect Bin Laden and defend against an anticipated military response from the United States." Indeed, it is specifically alleged that Lindh remained with his fighting group from October to December 2001, "after learning that United States military forces and United States nationals had become directly engaged in support of the Northern Alliance in its military conflict with Taliban and al Qaeda forces."

In November 2001, Lindh and his fighting group retreated from Takhar to the area of Kunduz, Afghanistan, where they ultimately surrendered to Northern Alliance troops. On November 24, 2001, he and the other captured Taliban fighters were transported to Mazar-e-Sharif, and then to the nearby Qala-i-Janghi (QIJ) prison compound. The following day, November 25, Lindh was interviewed by two Americans—Agent Johnny Michael Spann from the Central Intelligence Agency (CIA) and another government employee. Later that day, it is alleged that Taliban detainees in the QIJ compound attacked Spann and the other employee, overpowered the guards, and armed themselves. Spann was shot and killed in the course of the uprising and Lindh, after being wounded, retreated with other detainees to a basement area of the QIJ compound. The uprising at QIJ was eventually suppressed on December 1, 2001, at which time Lindh and other Taliban and al Qaeda fighters were taken into custody by Northern Alliance and American forces.

Following his capture, Lindh was interrogated, transported to the United States, and ultimately charged in this district with the following offenses in a ten-count Indictment:

(i) conspiracy to murder nationals of the United States, including American military personnel and other governmental employees serving in Afghanistan following the September 11, 2001 terrorist attacks, in violation of 18 U.S.C. § 2332(b)(2) (Count One);

(ii) conspiracy to provide material support and resources to HUM, a foreign terrorist organization, in violation of 18 U.S.C. § 2339B (Count Two);

(iii) providing material support and resources to HUM, in violation of 18 U.S.C. § 2339B and 2 (Count Three);

(iv) conspiracy to provide material support and resources to al Qaeda, a foreign terrorist organization, in violation of 18 U.S.C. § 2339B (Count Four);

(v) providing material support and resources to al Qaeda, in violation of 18 U.S.C. § 2339B and 2 (Count Five);

---

*The indictment alleges that al Qaeda is an organization, founded by Osama bin Laden and others, that is dedicated to opposing non-Islamic governments with force and violence. On October 8, 1999, al Qaeda was designated by the Secretary of State as a foreign terrorist organization, pursuant to Section 219 of the Immigration and Nationality Act. See 64 Fed.Reg. 55112 (1999). The Secretary of State has also declared al Qaeda a "specially designated terrorist," pursuant to the International Emergency Economic Powers Act. See 66 Fed.Reg. 54404 (2001).

(vi)   conspiracy to contribute services to al Qaeda, in violation of 31 § § C.F.R. 595.205 and 595.204 and 50 U.S.C. § 1705(b) (Count Six);

(vii) contributing services to al Qaeda, in violation of 31 C.F.R. § § 595.204 595.204 and 595.205 and 50 U.S.C. § 1705(b) and 18 U.S.C. § 2 (Count Seven);

(viii) conspiracy to supply services to the Taliban, in violation of 31 C.F.R. § § 545.206(b) and 545.204 and 50 U.S.C. § 1705(b) (Count Eight);

(ix)   supplying services to the Taliban, in violation of 31 C.F.R. § § 545.204 and 545.206(a) and 50 U.S.C. § 1705(b) and 18 U.S.C. § 2 (Count Nine); and

(x)   using and carrying firearms and destructive devices during crimes of violence, in violation of 18 U.S.C. § § 924(c)(1)(A), 924(c)(1)(B)(ii) and 2 (Count Ten)....

Lindh ... seeks dismissal of Counts Two through Nine of the Indictment on freedom of association, overbreadth, and vagueness grounds. Counts Two through Five charge Lindh with conspiracy to provide and providing material support and resources to foreign terrorist organizations, namely HUM (Counts Two and Three) and al Qaeda (Counts Four and Five), in violation of 18 U.S.C. § 2339B.* Counts Six and Seven charge conspiracy to contribute and contributing services to al Qaeda, in violation of 50 U.S.C. § 1705(b).** And, Counts Eight and Nine charge conspiracy to supply and supplying services to the Taliban.

Each count of the Indictment also alleges that Lindh committed specific overt acts. Those acts include that Lindh crossed from Pakistan into Afghanistan for the purpose of taking up arms with the Taliban; that he reported to a Taliban recruiting center in Kabul; that he attended al Qaeda's al-Farooq training camp for military training and

participated in a terrorist training course; that after completing his training he was issued rifles and grenades; that he traveled with other combatants to the front line in Takhar, in northeastern Afghanistan, where he opposed Northern Alliance forces; that he remained with his fighting group after the entry of the United States into the conflict and until he surrendered at Konduz; and that he was among a group of Taliban prisoners who staged a violent uprising at the QIJ prison that resulted in the death of an American intelligence agent.

OPINION

Lindh's First Amendment argument, distilled to its essence, is that he has a constitutional right to associate with foreign individuals and groups and that Counts Two through Nine impermissibly infringe this right by criminalizing this association. The statutes and regulations on which the Counts rest amount, in his view, to the government's attempt to impose on him guilt by association.

This argument is specious. Lindh is not accused of merely associating with a disfavored or subversive group whose activities are limited to circulating inflammatory political or religious material exhorting opposition to the government. Far from this, Lindh is accused of joining groups that do not merely advocate terror, violence, and murder of innocents; these groups actually carry out what they advocate and those who join them, at whatever level, participate in the groups' acts of terror, violence, and murder. There is, in other words, a clear line between First Amendment protected activity and criminal conduct for which there is no constitutional protection. Justice Douglas understood this clear distinction; he put this point well in *Dennis v. United States*, 341 U.S. 494, 581(1951),[†] where, dissenting from a conviction of members of the Communist Party of the United States, he noted that

> if this were a case where those who claimed protection under the First Amendment were teaching the techniques of sabotage, the assassination of the President, the filching of documents from public files, the planting of bombs, the art of street warfare, and the like, I would have no doubts. The freedom to speak is not absolute; the teaching of methods of terror and other seditious conduct should be beyond the pale along with obscenity and immorality.

... The most apposite authority on the issue is *Humanitarian Law Project v. Reno*, 205 F.3d 1130, 1133–34 (9th Cir. 2000), where a Ninth Circuit panel squarely rejected a constitutional challenge to the "material support or resources"

---

*Section 2339B provides that any person within the United States or subject to its jurisdiction who "knowingly provides material support or resources to a foreign terrorist organization, or attempts or conspires to do so," commits a felony. A "terrorist organization" means an organization designated as such under 8 U.S.C. § 1189. *See* 18 U.S.C. § 2339B(g)(6). Both al Qaeda and HUM have been designated as foreign terrorist organizations by the Secretary of State. *See supra* Part I n. 2 and n. 4. The phrase "material support or resources" is defined as including currency or monetary instruments or financial securities, financial services, lodging, training, expert advice or assistance, safehouses, false documentation or identification, communications equipment, facilities, weapons, lethal substances, explosives, personnel, transportation, and other physical assets, except medicine or religious materials. 18 U.S.C. § 2339A(b).

**Section 1705(b) of Title 50, part of IEEPA, provides that whoever "willfully violates, or willfully attempts to violate, any license, order, or regulation issued under this chapter" commits a felony.

[†]Excerpted earlier in this chapter under the Smith Act, p. 469.

prohibition of Section 2339B. There, the court resisted any analogy to cases based on association alone, noting that Section 2339B and related laws do "not prohibit being a member of one of the designated groups or vigorously promoting and supporting the political goals of the group." *Id.* at 1133. Rather, "[p]laintiffs are even free to praise the groups for using terrorism as a means of achieving their ends." *Id.* What is prohibited by the statute is, in the court's words, "the act of giving material support." *Id.* For this act, the court went on,

> there is no constitutional right to facilitate terrorism by giving terrorists the weapons and explosives with which to carry out their grisly missions. Nor, of course, is there a right to provide resources with which terrorists can buy weapons and explosives.

Lindh also argues that Section 2339B . . . [is] unconstitutionally vague. The vagueness doctrine, which protects both free speech and due process values, is "concerned with clarity"; it "requires that a penal statute define the criminal offense with sufficient definiteness that ordinary people can understand what conduct is prohibited and in a manner that does not encourage arbitrary and discriminatory enforcement." Of course, the Constitution does not impose "impossible standards of clarity" on Congress or the regulatory agencies. . . .

In support of his vagueness argument, Lindh relies principally on the Ninth Circuit's decision in *Humanitarian Law Project*, 205 F.3d at 1137–38, where the Ninth Circuit concluded that the district court did not abuse its discretion in issuing a limited preliminary injunction on vagueness grounds regarding the term "personnel." The Ninth Circuit stated, "[i]t is easy to see how someone could be unsure about what [Section 2339B] prohibits with the use of the term 'personnel,' as it blurs the line between protected expression and unprotected conduct." The court observed that someone who advocates the cause of a terrorist organization "could be seen as supplying them with personnel," particularly since "having an independent advocate frees up members to engage in terrorist activities instead of advocacy." In response to the government's argument that "personnel" should be construed to extend only to a person's service "under the direction or control" of the terrorist organization, the Ninth Circuit declined to do so on the ground that it was "not authorized to rewrite the law so it will pass constitutional muster," and upheld the preliminary injunction in issue.

. . . The plain meaning of "personnel" is such that it requires, in the context of Section 2339B, an employment or employment-like relationship between the persons in question and the terrorist organization. The Ninth Circuit's

vagueness holding in *Humanitarian Law Project* is neither persuasive nor controlling. The term is aimed at denying the provision of human resources to proscribed terrorist organizations, and not at the mere *independent* advocacy of an organization's interests or agenda. Thus, the term "personnel" in Section 2339B gives fair notice to the public of what is prohibited and the provision is therefore not unconstitutionally vague.

Lindh's final vagueness argument focuses on the Regulations' prohibition on providing "services" to terrorist organizations. This argument also fails because the prohibition is set forth "with sufficient definiteness that an ordinary person could understand what conduct was prohibited." The obvious scope and purpose of the Regulations is to ban most transactions between U.S. persons and al Qaeda and the Taliban, with certain limited exceptions. . . .*

Questions

1. List and summarize the counts in the indictment that Lindh challenges.

2. List and summarize Lindh's arguments that he had a First Amendment right to do what he did in Counts 2 through 9.

3. Summarize the court's responses to Lindh's First Amendment arguments.

4. In your opinion, does the indictment violate Lindh's First Amendment rights? Back up your answer with facts and arguments from the excerpt.

5. State the court's formulation of the vagueness doctrine as it relates to the First Amendment.

6. What words in Section 2339B does Lindh claim are vague?

7. Summarize Lindh's arguments that Section 2339B is void for vagueness.

8. Summarize the court's responses to Lindh's vagueness claims.

9. In your opinion, is Section 2339B void for vagueness? Back up your answer with facts and arguments from the excerpt.

Go to Exercise 13-4 on the Criminal Law 8e CD to learn more about *U.S. v. Lindh*.

---

*The court denied all motions to dismiss the indictment.

The case never went to trial because Lindh signed a plea bargain with the United States. According to the terms of the agreement, Lindh pleaded guilty to two crimes ("supplying services to the Taliban" and "carrying an explosive during the commission of a felony") in exchange for receiving less than a life sentence. He was sentenced to 10 years for each offense, to be served consecutively (one after the other), and fined $250,000 for each offense and three years of supervised release following his 20 years in prison (*U.S. v. Lindh* 2002).

John Walker Lindh's acts were clearly within the *actus reus* of "providing material support" to al Qaeda and the Taliban—he trained, carried a weapon and a grenade, and fought on their side. And, the First Amendment clearly didn't protect his association with them. Other cases aren't so clear; *U.S. v. Sattar* (2003) is one of them.

CASE | *Did They Provide "Material Support" to a Terrorist Group?*

U.S. v. Sattar and others
02-Cr.-395 (SDNY 2003)

Ahmed Abdel Sattar ("Sattar") and Lynne Stewart ("Stewart") were indicted in a five-count indictment on April 8, 2002. Count One charges Sattar and Stewart with conspiring to provide material support and resources to a foreign terrorist organization ("FTO") in violation of 18 U.S.C. § 2339B. Count Two charges them with providing and attempting to provide material support and resources to an FTO in violation of 18 U.S.C. §§ 2339B. The defendants now move to dismiss the Indictment.

KOELTL, J.

FACTS

The Indictment alleges the following facts. At all relevant times, the Islamic Group ("IG"), existed as an international terrorist group dedicated to opposing nations, governments, institutions, and individuals that did not share IG's radical interpretation of Islamic law. IG considered such parties "infidels" and interpreted the concept of "jihad" as waging opposition against infidels by whatever means necessary, including force and violence....

According to the Indictment, IG's objectives in the United States include (1) the establishment of the United States as a staging ground for violent acts against targets in the United States and abroad; (2) the recruitment and training of members; and (3) fundraising for jihad actions in the United States and overseas. Since Sheikh Abdel Rahman's imprisonment, the Indictment alleges that IG members in the United States have also functioned as a worldwide communications hub for the group....IG was designated as a foreign terrorist organization by the Secretary of State on October 8, 1997..., and was redesignated as such on October 8, 1999 and again on October 5, 2001.

The Indictment alleges that Sheikh Abdel Rahman has been one of IG's principal leaders and a high-ranking member of jihad organizations based in Egypt and elsewhere since the early 1990s....Under his leadership, IG subordinates carried out the details of specific jihad operations while shielding Sheikh Abdel Rahman from prosecution. The Indictment charges that Sheik Abdel Rahman, among other things, provided guidance about what actions, including acts of terrorism, were permissible or forbidden under his interpretation of Islamic law; gave strategic advice on how to achieve IG's goals; recruited persons and solicited them to commit violent jihad acts; and sought to protect IG from infiltration by law enforcement.

Sheikh Abdel Rahman was convicted in October 1995 of engaging in a seditious conspiracy to wage a war of urban terrorism against the United States, including the 1993 World Trade Center bombing and a plot to bomb New York City landmarks. He was also found guilty of soliciting crimes of violence against the United States military and Egyptian President Hosni Mubarak. In January 1996 Sheik Abdel Rahman was sentenced to life imprisonment plus 65 years. His conviction was affirmed on appeal and, on January 10, 2000, the United States Supreme Court denied his petition for a writ of certiorari.

Sheikh Abdel Rahman has been incarcerated at the Federal Medical Center in Rochester, Minnesota since in or about 1997. IG has allegedly taken repeated steps to win

Sheikh Abdel Rahman's release. Such steps include the issuance of a statement in response to Sheikh Abdel Rahman's life sentence that warned that "all American interests will be legitimate targets for our struggle until the release of Sheikh Omar Abdel Rahman and his brothers" and that IG "swears by God to its irreversible vow to take an eye for an eye." Also, on or about November 17, 1997, six assassins shot and stabbed a group of tourists at an archeological site in Luxor, Egypt killing fifty-eight tourists and four Egyptians. Before exiting, the Indictment charges, the assassins scattered leaflets calling for Sheikh Abdel Rahman's release and inserted one such leaflet into the slit torso of one victim....

Defendant Stewart was Sheikh Abdel Rahman's counsel during his 1995 criminal trial and has continued to represent him since his conviction. The Indictment alleges that over the past several years, Stewart has facilitated and concealed messages between her client and IG leaders around the world....

During a May 2000 visit to Sheikh Abdel Rahman in prison, Stewart allegedly allowed defendant Yousry, who acted as the Arabic interpreter between Sheikh Abdel Rahman and his attorneys, to read letters from defendant Sattar and others regarding IG matters and to discuss with her client whether IG should continue to comply with a cease-fire that had been supported by factions within IG since in or about 1998.

According to the Indictment, Yousry provided material support and resources to IG by covertly passing messages between IG representatives and Sheik Abdel Rahman regarding IG's activities. The Indictment alleges that Stewart took affirmative steps to conceal the May 2000 discussions from prison guards and subsequently, in violation of the SAMs, announced to the media that Sheikh Abdel Rahman had withdrawn his support for the cease-fire....

The Indictment also charges that Sattar is an active IG leader who serves as a vital link between Sheik Abdel Rahman and the worldwide IG membership. The Indictment contends that Sattar operates as a communications center for IG from New York City through frequent telephonic contact with IG leaders around the world. More specifically, the Indictment alleges that Sattar provides material support and resources to IG by relaying messages between IG leaders abroad and Sheik Abdel Rahman through visits and phone calls by Sheikh Abdel Rahman's interpreter and attorneys; arranging and participating in three-way phone calls connecting IG leaders around the world to facilitate discussion and coordination of IG activities; passing messages and information from one IG leader and to other group leaders and members; and by providing financial support....

Sattar and Stewart move to dismiss Counts One and Two of the indictment on the ground that 18 U.S.C. § 2339B is unconstitutionally vague and overbroad....

OPINION

A foreign "terrorist organization" is defined as "an organization designated" under 8 U.S.C. § 1189 as a foreign "terrorist organization." 18 U.S.C. § 2339B(g)(6)....

The Indictment alleges that the defendants conspired to provide and provided communications equipment, personnel, currency, financial securities and financial services (currency, financial securities, and financial services hereinafter "currency"), and transportation to IG [designated as a terrorist organization].

The defendants argue that 18 U.S.C. § 2339B is unconstitutionally vague specifically with regard to the statute's prohibition on "providing" material support or resources in the form of "communications equipment" and "personnel."...The Government has argued that the defendants provided a communications pipeline by which they transmitted messages from Sheikh Abdel Rahman in prison to IG leaders and members throughout the world. Among the specific instances of the use of communications equipment, the Indictment points to the fact that Sattar had telephone conversations with IG leaders in which he related Sheikh Abdel Rahman's instructions to IG leaders and Stewart released Sheikh Abdel Rahman's statement to the press in which Sheikh Abdel Rahman withdrew his support from the then-existing cease-fire.

With respect to the provision of personnel, the Indictment alleges that "the defendants and the unindicted co-conspirators provided personnel, including themselves, to IG, in order to assist IG leaders and members in the United States and elsewhere around the world, in communicating with each other...."

The defendants argue that the statute fails to provide fair notice of what acts are prohibited by the prohibition against the provision of "communications equipment" and "personnel." A criminal statute implicating First Amendment rights "must 'define the criminal offense with sufficient definiteness that ordinary people can understand what conduct is prohibited and in a manner that does not encourage arbitrary and discriminatory enforcement.' In short, the statute must give notice of the forbidden conduct and set boundaries to prosecutorial discretion."

When analyzing a vagueness challenge, "a court must first determine whether the statute gives the person of ordinary intelligence a reasonable opportunity to know what is prohibited and then consider whether the law provides explicit standards for those who apply it." A "void for vagueness" challenge does not necessarily mean that the statute could not be applied in some cases but rather that, as applied to the conduct at issue in the criminal case, a reasonable person would not have notice that the conduct was unlawful and there are no explicit standards to determine that the specific conduct was unlawful.

First, with regard to the "provision" of "communications equipment," Sattar and Stewart argue that the Indictment charges them with merely talking and that the acts alleged in the Indictment constitute nothing more than using communications equipment rather than providing such equipment to IG. For example, the Indictment charges Sattar with participating in and arranging numerous telephone calls between IG leaders in which IG business was discussed, including the need for "a second Luxor." The Indictment describes numerous other telephone calls in which Sattar participated. Stewart is charged with, among other things, providing communications equipment to IG by announcing Sheikh Abdel Rahman's withdrawal of support for the cease-fire in Egypt and thereby making the statements of the otherwise isolated leader available to the media.

The defendants look to the legislative history of the statute as evidence that Congress did not intend § 2339B to criminalize the mere use of communications equipment, rather than the actual giving of such equipment to IG. The legislative history states:

> The ban does not restrict an organization's or an individual's ability to freely express a particular ideology or political philosophy. Those inside the United States will continue to be free to advocate, think and profess the attitudes and philosophies of the foreign organizations. They are simply not allowed to send material support or resources to those groups, or their subsidiary groups, overseas.*

The defendants are correct and by criminalizing the mere use of phones and other means of communication the statute provides neither notice nor standards for its application such that it is unconstitutionally vague as applied.... The Government...stated at oral argument that the mere use of one's telephone constitutes criminal behavior under the statute and that, in fact, "use equals provision." The Government also argued that using the conference call feature on a person's phone in furtherance of an FTO was prohibited....A criminal defendant simply could not be expected to know that the conduct alleged was prohibited

by the statute. A penal statute must speak for itself so that a lay person can understand the prohibition.

The defendants were not put on notice that merely using communications equipment in furtherance of an FTO's goals constituted criminal conduct....§ 2339B is void for vagueness as applied to the allegations in the Indictment.

Second, the defendants argue, § 2339B is unconstitutionally vague as applied to the allegations in the Indictment relating to the "provision" of "personnel." The defendants urge the Court to follow the Ninth Circuit Court of Appeals' decision in *Humanitarian Law Project v. Reno*, 205 F.3d 1130, 1137 (9th Cir. 2000), which found that "it is easy to see how someone could be unsure about what [§ 2339B] prohibits with the use of the term 'personnel,' as it blurs the line between protected expression and unprotected conduct." The Court of Appeals affirmed the district court's finding that the use of the term "personnel" in § 2339B was unconstitutionally vague.

The Government relies on *United States v. Lindh*, 212 F. Supp. 2d 541, 574 (E.D. Va. 2002), which rejected *Humanitarian Law Project* and found that the alleged plain meaning of personnel—"an employment or employment-like relationship between the persons in question and the terrorist organization"—gave fair notice of what conduct is prohibited under the statute and thus was not unconstitutionally vague. In that case, the court rejected a vagueness challenge in the context of a person who joined certain foreign terrorist organizations in combat against American forces. In defining the reach of the term personnel, the court found that it was not vague because it applied to "employees" or "employee-like operatives" or "quasi-employees" who work under the "direction and control" of the FTO.

Whatever the merits of *Lindh* as applied to a person who provides himself or herself as a soldier in the army of an FTO, the standards set out there are not found in the statute, do not respond to the concerns of the Court of Appeals in *Humanitarian Law Project*, and do not provide standards to save the "provision" of "personnel" from being unconstitutionally vague as applied to the facts alleged in the Indictment. The fact that the "hard core" conduct in *Lindh* fell within the plain meaning of providing personnel yields no standards that can be applied to the conduct by alleged "quasi-employees" in this case. It is not clear from § 2339B what behavior constitutes an impermissible provision of personnel to an FTO. Indeed, as the Ninth Circuit Court of Appeals stated in *Humanitarian Law Project*, "Someone who advocates the cause of the [FTO] could be seen as supplying them with personnel."

The Government accuses Stewart of providing personnel, including herself, to IG. In so doing, however, the Government fails to explain how a lawyer, acting as an agent of

---

*H.R. Rep. 104-383 at 45. Thus, the defendants argue, simply making a phone call or similarly communicating one's thoughts does not fall within the ambit of § 2339B.

her client, an alleged leader of an FTO, could avoid being subject to criminal prosecution as a "quasi-employee" allegedly covered by the statute....The Government attempts to distinguish the provision of "personnel" by arguing that it applies only to providing "employees" or "quasi-employees" and those acting under the "direction and control" of the FTO. But the terms "quasi-employee" or "employee-like operative" or "acting at the direction and control of the organization" are terms that are nowhere found in the statute or reasonably inferable from it.

Moreover, these terms and concepts applied to the prohibited provision of personnel provide no notice to persons of ordinary intelligence and leave the standards for enforcement to be developed by the Government. When asked at oral argument how to distinguish being a member of an organization from being a quasi-employee, the Government initially responded "You know it when you see it."...Such a standard...is an insufficient guide by which a person can predict the legality of that person's conduct.

The Government argues, moreover, that the Court should construe the statute to avoid constitutional questions. However, the Court "is not authorized to rewrite the law so it will pass constitutional muster." *Humanitarian Law Project*, 205 F.3d at 1137–38 (rejecting Government's suggestion to construe "personnel" as used in § 2339B as "under the direction or control" of an FTO)....

The statute's vagueness as applied to the allegations in the Indictment concerning the provision of personnel is a fatal flaw that the Court cannot cure by reading into the statute a stricter definition of the material support provision than the statute itself provides....The motions to dismiss Counts One and Two as void for vagueness are granted....

SO ORDERED.

Questions

1. State the specific charges against Sattar and Stewart in counts 1 and 2 of the indictment.

2. List all the facts the government argues prove that Stewart and Sattar provided "material support" to IG.

3. State specifically the terms in the statute that the defense claims are void for vagueness.

4. List and summarize the defense arguments that the terms make the statute void for vaguensss.

5. List and summarize the arguments that the statute is constitutional.

6. Summarize the court's arguments for dismissing counts 1 and 2 in the indictment.

SUMMARY

    I. The criminal law during national emergencies
        A. The USA Patriot Act and conflicting values in our constitutional democracy
            1. Need for public safety and security
            2. Desire for privacy and freedom
        B. Problem: how to apply enduring principles of criminal law when terrorists and terrorist groups have killed and are still trying to kill Americans at home and around the world
        C. Allegiance and loyalty are especially critical during national emergencies
        D. The Constitution was written during times of emergency

   II. Treason
        A. The only crime defined in the Constitution
        B. After the Revolution, the new government was fragile because it was so new and needed time for loyalty and allegiance to take hold
            1. England, Spain, France, and Native American nations threatened from all directions

2. Traitors, spies, and other disloyal individuals and groups threatened from within
C. Authors of the Constitution had mixed feelings about treason
   1. They were tough on traitors who broke allegiance and were disloyal
   2. Their own ancestors had fled from religious persecution and prosecution for treason
   3. Treason was broadly defined in England to include thoughts and feelings that led to prosecution of innocent people
   4. Two worries
      a. Repression of *peaceful* opposition to government
      b. Conviction of the innocent because of perjury, passion, and/or insufficient evidence
D. Treason is defined in the body of the Constitution, where it's tough to change
E. Elements
   1. *Actus reus*
      a. Levying war against the U.S.
      b. Giving aid and comfort to enemies of the U.S.
   2. *Mens rea*
      a. Intent to give aid and comfort
      b. For the very purpose of betraying the U.S. by means of the aid and comfort
   3. Proof
      a. Two witnesses to *actus reus*
      b. Confession in open court

III. More crimes against disloyalty
A. Sedition
   1. Ancient crime of "stirring up" treason (advocate violent overthrow of government) by
      a. Speeches
      b. Writing (libel)
      c. Conspiracy
   2. In the U.S. Code, sedition includes only advocating the *violent* overthrow of the government
B. Sabotage
   1. Damaging and/or destroying property related to war and defense material, buildings, and utilities (which includes transportation and harbors)
   2. Producing defective property related to war and defense
   3. Elements
      a. *Actus reus*
         (1) Destroy
         (2) Damage
         (3) Obstruct
         (4) Interfere
         (5) Contaminate
         (6) Produce defective war or national defense materials
      b. *Mens rea*
         (1) Purposely obstruct (or any other acts in *actus reus*)

        (2) Knowingly obstruct (or any other acts in *actus reus*)

        (3) Negligently obstruct (or any other acts in *actus reus*)

    c. Circumstance

        (1) At war

        (2) During national emergency

C. Espionage (spying)

  1. Definition of espionage—secret intelligence gathering by spies about foreign people, activities, and enterprises for political and military uses

  2. U.S. Code espionage elements (at *any time*)

    a. *Actus reus*

        (1) Communicate

        (2) Deliver

        (3) Transmit

        (4) Attempt to (1), (2), or (3) intelligence (information harmful to the U.S.)

    b. *Mens rea*

        (1) Purposely injure

        (2) Reason to believe use of intelligence will injure

    c. Circumstances

        (1) Intelligence provided to foreign government

        (2) Foreign faction or party

        (3) Foreign military or naval force

        (4) Foreign representative, officer, agent, employee, subject, or citizen

  3. U.S. Code espionage elements (*during war*)

    a. *Actus reus*

        (1) Collect any intelligence useful to the enemy

        (2) Publish it

        (3) Communicate it

        (4) Attempt to do so

    b. *Mens rea*—intent to communicate information to enemy

    c. Circumstance—time of war

IV. Anti-terrorism crimes

  A. General crimes applicable to terrorist acts

    1. Treason, sedition, sabotage, and espionage

    2. Murder, attempted murder, and conspiracy to murder also apply

  B. Use of weapons of mass destruction

    1. Elements

      a. *actus reus*

        (1) Use

        (2) Threaten to use

        (3) Attempt or conspire to use

      b. *Mens rea*—without lawful authority (voluntarily)

      c. Circumstance(s)

        (1) Against a U.S. "national" outside the U.S.

        (2) Against any "person" inside the U.S.

        (3) Against any property inside or outside the U.S.

    2. Definition of "weapon of mass destruction"

a. "Any destructive device"—explosive, incendiary, poison gas; bomb; grenade; rocket; missile; mine; or similar device

b. Any weapon intended to cause death or serious bodily injury by poisonous chemicals or precursor

c. Any weapon involving a disease mechanism

d. Any weapon designed to release radiation or radioactivity at levels dangerous to human life

C. Acts of terrorism transcending national boundaries

1. Definition—conduct occurring partly inside and partly outside the U.S.

2. Types of conduct (*actus reus*)

   a. Commit violent crimes against any person inside the U.S.

   b. Create a substantial risk of serious bodily injury by destroying or damaging property within the U.S.

   c. Threatening, or attempting, or conspiring to commit (a) or (b)

3. Circumstances

   a. Victims—U.S. government; members of uniformed services; officials, employees, and agents of the U.S.

   b. Property owned or leased by the U.S.

4. Penalties

   a. Death for killing or death resulting from the act

   b. Up to life for kidnapping

   c. Up to 35 years for maiming

   d. Up to 30 years for assault

   e. Up to 25 years for damaging or destroying property

D. Harboring or concealing terrorists

1. *Actus reus*—harboring or concealing persons who have committed or are about to commit a list of terrorist-related crimes

2. *Mens rea*—knowing (or a reasonable person should have known) the crimes in (1) were going to be committed

3. Penalty—fine or up to 10 years imprisonment

E. Providing material support to terrorists (§ 2339A) and terrorist organizations (§ 2339B)

1. Prosecutions for violating Section 2339B most frequent in practice

2. Material support crimes created after Oklahoma City bombing in the Anti-Terrorism and Effective Death Penalty Act (AEDPA) of 1996

3. Amendment increased the AEDPA penalty in the USA Patriot Act (Uniting and Strengthening America by Providing Appropriate Tools Required to Intercept and Obstruct Terrorism) of 2001

4. The 300+-page Patriot Act is devoted mainly to criminal *procedure*—surveillance and intelligence, law enforcement information sharing, search and seizure, detention, and interrogation

5. Definition—material support includes

   a. Currency or monetary instruments or financial securities

   b. Financial services

   c. Lodging

   d. Training

   e. Expert advice or assistance

f. Safehouses

g. False documentation or identification

h. Communications equipment

i. Facilities

j. Weapons, lethal substances, explosives

k. Personnel

l. Transportation

m. Other physical assets, except medicine or religious materials

6. Material support to *individual* terrorists

a. *Actus reus*

(1) Provide material support to individual terrorist

(2) Conceal or disguise nature, location, source, or ownership of material support or resources

b. *Mens rea*—intending or knowing support or resources are to be used in preparing or committing list of crimes helpful to terrorists

7. Material support to terrorist organizations

a. *Actus reus*—provides material support or resources to terrorist organizations

b. *Mens rea*—knowingly provides material support

8. Most-argued issues in material support cases are constitutional

a. Due process—term "material support" is void for vagueness

b. First Amendment—providing material support violates right to free speech and association

 Go to the Criminal Law 8e CD to download this summary outline. The outline has been formatted so that you can add notes to it during class lectures, or later create a customized chapter outline to use while reviewing. Either way, the summary outline will help you understand the "big picture" and fill in the details as you study.

REVIEW QUESTIONS

1. Why did the authors of the U.S. Constitution define treason in the body of the U.S. Constitution?

2. State the elements of the constitutional crime of treason.

3. State the two worries the authors of the Constitution had about the abuse of treason law.

4. According to the authors of the Constitution, what place do feelings, opinions, and passions have in the law of treason, and why?

5. By the time the authors defined treason in the Constitution, what were the two limits government and philosophy had come to accept? What two limits of their own did the authors add?

6. Identify and explain the three elements of treason as it's defined in Article III, § 3 of the U.S. Constitution.

7. Why is it so hard to convict individuals for treason in the United States?

8. What did Justice Jackson point out with respect to combating disloyalty and the law of treason?

9. Identify and distinguish among the three forms of sedition.

10. How does the U.S. Code define seditious conspiracy, and how does the crime contrast with the first sedition law?

11. State the elements of sabotage as it's defined in the U.S. Code.

12. State the elements of espionage during war and at other times as it's defined in the U.S. Code.

13. How does the U.S. Code define domestic and international terrorism?

14. How does the U.S. Code define the crime of "use of weapons of mass destruction"?

15. List the kinds of "destructive devices" included within the meaning of "weapons of mass destruction."

16. List the kinds of weapons of mass destruction that aren't included within the meaning of "destructive devices."

17. How does the U.S. Code define "harboring or concealing terrorists"?

18. What's the most frequently prosecuted anti-terrorism crime?

19. Identify and state the elements of the crime of providing material support to individual terrorists, and compare them with providing material support to terrorist organizations.

20. Identify the two most common issues raised in prosecutions for providing material assistance to terrorists and terrorist organizations.

KEY TERMS

USA Patriot Act p. 463
treason p. 463
adherence to the enemy p. 465
giving aid and comfort to the
 enemy p. 465
sedition p. 468
seditious speech p. 468
seditious libel p. 468

seditious conspiracy p. 468
Smith Act of 1940 p. 468
sabotage p. 479
espionage p. 480
intelligence gathering p. 480
Anti-Terrorism and Effective
 Death Penalty Act (AEDPA)
 p. 481

international terrorism p. 482
domestic terrorism p. 482
weapon of mass destruction
 p. 482
destructive device p. 482
conduct transcending national
 boundaries p. 483
material support p. 484

SUGGESTED READINGS

Go the Criminal Law 8e CD for Suggested Readings for this chapter.

THE COMPANION WEB SITE
FOR *CRIMINAL LAW,* EIGHTH EDITION

http://cj.wadsworth.com/samaha/crim_law8e

 Supplement your review of this chapter by going to the companion Web site to take one of the Tutorial Quizzes, use the flash cards to test your knowledge of the elements of various crimes and defenses, and check out the many other study aids you'll find there. You'll find valuable data and resources at your fingertips to help you study for that big exam or write that important paper.

APPENDIX
Selected Amendments of the Constitution of the United States

Amendment I [1791]

Congress shall make no law respecting an establishment of religion, or prohibiting the free exercise thereof; or abridging the freedom of speech, or of the press; or the right of the people peaceably to assemble, and to petition the Government for a redress of grievances.

Amendment VIII [1791]

Excessive bail shall not be required, nor excessive fines imposed, nor cruel and unusual punishments inflicted.

Amendment XIV [1868]

Section 1 All persons born or naturalized in the United States, and subject to the jurisdiction thereof, are citizens of the United States and of the State wherein they reside. No State shall make or enforce any law which shall abridge the privileges or immunities of citizens of the United States; nor shall any State deprive any person of life, liberty, or property, without due process of law; nor deny to any person within its jurisdiction the equal protection of the laws.

Section 2 Representatives shall be apportioned among the several States according to their respective numbers, counting the whole number of persons in each State, excluding Indians not taxed. But when the right to vote at any election for the choice of electors for President and Vice President of the United States, Representatives in Congress, the Executive and Judicial officers of a State, or the members of the Legislature thereof, is denied to any of the male inhabitants of such State, being twenty-one years of age, and citizens of the United States, or in any way abridged, except for participation in rebellion, or other crime, the basis of representation therein shall be reduced in the proportion which the number of such male citizens shall bear to the whole number of male citizens twenty-one years of age in such State.

Section 3 No person shall be a Senator or Representative in Congress, or elector of President and Vice-President, or hold any office, civil or military, under the United States, or under any State, who having previously taken an oath, as a member of Congress, or as an officer of the United States, or as a member of any State legislature, or as an executive or judicial officer of any State, to support the Constitution of the United States, shall have engaged in insurrection or rebellion against the same, or given aid or comfort to the enemies thereof. But Congress may by a vote of two thirds of each House, remove such disability.

Section 4 The validity of the public debt of the United States, authorized by law, including debts incurred for payment of pensions and bounties for services in suppressing insurrection or rebellion, shall not be questioned. But neither the United States nor any State shall assume or pay any debt or obligation incurred in aid of insurrection or rebellion against the United States, or any claim for the loss or emancipation of any slave; but all such debts, obligations and claims shall be held illegal and void.

Section 5 The Congress shall have power to enforce, by appropriate legislation, the provisions of this article.

 Go to the Criminal Law 8e CD for the full text of the Constitution of the United States.

Glossary

abnormal (in defense of insanity) mental disease or defect.

abuse-of-trust crimes (in property crime) crimes committed by caretakers.

accessories the parties liable for separate, lesser offenses following a crime.

accessories after the fact persons who help after crimes are committed (for example, harboring a fugitive).

accessories before the fact persons not present when crimes are committed who helped before the crimes were committed (for example, someone who provided a weapon used in a murder).

accomplice *actus reus* person who took some positive action to aid in the commission of a crime.

accomplices the parties liable as principals before and during a crime.

actual disorderly conduct completed disorderly conduct (fighting).

actual entry (in burglary) physical entry into a structure in burglary.

actual possession physical possession; on the possessor's person.

actus reus the criminal act or the physical element in criminal liability.

adequate provocation acts that qualify as reducing murder to manslaughter.

adherence to the enemy (in treason) breaking allegiance to your own country.

affirmative defense defense in which the defendant bears the burden of production.

affirmative defense of voluntary abandonment (in criminal attempt) defense that the defendant vol-untarily gave up the attempt to commit a crime before it was completed.

affirmed when a trial court's decision is upheld.

aforethought planned in advance.

aggravated rape (first degree) rape committed with a weapon, or by more than one person, or causing serious physical injury to the victim.

alibi a defense that places defendants in a different place from the scene at the time of the crime.

American bystander rule there's no legal duty to rescue or call for help to aid someone who's in danger even if helping poses no risk whatsoever to the potential rescuer.

Anti-Terrorism and Effective Death Penalty Act (AEDPA) law defining new crimes of domestic terrorism and increasing the penalties for domestic terrorism crimes.

appellant a party who appeals a lower court decision.

appellate cases cases heard and decided by appeals courts.

appellee the party against whom an appeal is filed.

arbitrary action (in void-for-vagueness rulings) law enforcement officers acted without standards or reasons.

arson intentionally burning a house or other structure.

asportation the carrying away of another's property.

assault an attempt to commit a battery or intentionally putting another in fear.

attempt *actus reus* steps taken to complete a crime that never gets completed.

attempt *mens rea* specific intent to commit a crime that never gets completed.

attempted battery the crime of assault that focuses on *actus reus*.

authorized consent legal authority to consent for another person.

automatism acts committed while unconscious.

"bad manners" crimes modern form of disorderly conduct, sometimes called quality-of-life crimes.

bailee a temporary possessor who had control over others' property (a term operative when the English Parliament created "embezzlement").

barbaric punishments punishment considered no longer acceptable.

battery offensive bodily contact.

blameworthiness (also called culpability) idea that we can only punish people that we can blame, and we can only blame people that are responsible for what they do.

brain death no brain activity or heartbeat and breathing is sustained by artificial means.

breach of peace disorderly conduct or acts that tend to lead to disorderly conduct.

breaking (in burglary) *actus reus* of common-law burglary requiring an unlawful entry into someone else's building.

"broken windows" theory theory that minor offenses can lead to a rise in serious crime.

burden of persuasion the responsibility to convince the fact finder of the truth of the defense.

burden of production the responsibility to introduce initial evidence to support a defense.

burden of proof the affirmative duty to prove a point in dispute; the responsibility to produce the evidence to persuade the fact finder.

burglary breaking and entering a building with intent to commit a crime inside the building.

burning (in arson) part of the *actus reus* of arson, consisting of setting a building on fire and where the fire actually reached the structure.

"but for" cause cause in fact (also called *sine qua non* cause); the actor's conduct sets in motion a chain of events that, sooner or later, leads to a result.

capital felony a felony punishable by death or life imprisonment without parole.

carrying away part of the *actus reus* of common law larceny.

case history steps in the procedure of a case.

castle exception the principle stating that defenders have no need to retreat when attacked in their homes.

chain conspiracies participants at one end of the chain may know nothing of those at the other end, but every participant handles the same commodity at different points, such as manufacture, distribution, and sale.

choice-of-evils defense defense of making the right choice—namely, choosing the lesser of two evils.

circumstance element element of crime other than *actus reus*, *mens rea*, concurrence, causation, and resulting harm.

circumstantial evidence indirect evidence.

citation source reference to a case or other legal authority.

civil commitment involuntary confinement not based on criminal conviction.

clear and present danger test of whether a law limiting free speech violates the First Amendment.

clear and present danger doctrine (free speech) only speech that creates a risk of causing serious harm that's close to happening can be banned.

code jurisdictions states where crimes are defined by statutes.

cognition (insanity defense) mental capacity to reason sufficiently to know what you're doing and/or know the difference between right and wrong.

coincidental intervening act acts by *defendants* that "merely put the victim in a certain place at a certain time" that made it possible for the intervening cause to kill or hurt the victim.

collateral attack a proceeding asking an appellate court to rule against the trial court's jurisdiction to decide a question or case.

commercial speech advertising as a form of First Amendment speech.

common-law crimes crimes originating in the English common law.

common-law felonies felonies defined by the common law, not by statute.

common-law jurisdictions jurisdictions that still recognize the common-law crimes.

common-law misdemeanors misdemeanors defined by common law, not by statute.

common-law paramour rule defense to murder that a husband found his wife in the act of adultery.

common-law rape intentional forced heterosexual vaginal penetration by a man with a woman not his wife.

common-law sodomy anal intercourse between two males.

complicity (doctrine of) when one person is liable for another person's crime.

computer crime statutes state statutes defining the elements of crimes related to computers.

computer hackers unauthorized intruders into a "protected electronic environment."

computer trespass statutes statutes making it a crime to enter other people's computers without their consent.

concurrence the requirement that *actus reus* must join with *mens rea* to produce criminal conduct or that conduct must cause a harmful result.

concurring opinion an opinion that supports the court's result but not its reasoning.

conduct transcending national boundaries (in terrorist crimes) element in new anti-terrorism crime statute.

conspiracy agreeing to commit a crime.

conspiracy *actus reus* the act of agreeing to commit a crime.

conspiracy *mens rea* the intent to make an agreement to commit a crime.

constitutional democracy form of government where the majority is limited by constitutional rights.

constructive disorderly conduct acts that tend toward causing others to breach the peace.

constructive intent intent in which the actors didn't intend any harm but should have known that their behavior created a high risk of injury.

constructive possession legal possession or custody of an item or substance.

conversion illegal use of another's property.

corroboration rule element in rape that prosecution had to prove rape by the testimony of witnesses other than the victim.

crimes against persons crimes that harm persons (criminal homicide).

crimes against property crimes that harm persons' property (theft).

crimes against public morals crimes that harm the public morals generally (for example, prostitution).

crimes against public order crimes that harm the public peace generally (for example, disorderly conduct).

crimes against the administration of justice crimes that harm the operation of government (for example, obstruction of justice).

crimes against the state crimes that harm the existence of the state (for example, treason).

crimes of criminal conduct acts triggered by criminal intent.

crimes of criminal conduct causing a criminal harm crimes requiring *actus reus* + *mens rea* + causation of a criminal harm.

criminal attempt intending to commit a crime and taking steps to complete it but something interrupts the completion of the crime's commission.

criminal codes definitions of crimes and punishments by elected legislatures.

criminal conspiracy agreement between two or more persons to commit a crime.

criminal homicide a homicide that's neither justified nor excused.

criminal homicide *mens rea* can include purposeful, knowing, reckless, and negligent killing.

criminal mischief (in property crimes) misdemeanor of damaging or destroying other people's property.

criminal negligence creating a *substantial* and *unjustifiable* risk the defendant *should've* been, but in fact wasn't, aware of.

criminal objective the criminal goal of an agreement to commit a crime.

criminal omission two forms: (1) mere failure to act or (2) failure to intervene in order to prevent a serious harm.

criminal punishment punishments prescribed by legislatures.

criminal recklessness conscious awareness of a *substantial* and *unjustifiable* risk.

criminal sexual conduct statutes expanded the definition of sex offenses to embrace a wide range of nonconsensual penetrations and contact.

criminal sexual contact unlawful touching for sexual gratification.

criminal solicitation urging another person to commit a crime even though the person doesn't respond to the urging.

criminal trespass (in property crimes) the crime of invading another person's property.

cruel and unusual punishment punishments banned by the Eighth Amendment to the U.S. Constitution.

culpability blameworthiness based on *mens rea;* deserving of punishment because of individual responsibility for actions.

curtilage area immediately surrounding a dwelling.

dangerous conduct rationale (in attempt law) looking at how closely a defendant came to completing a crime.

dangerous person rationale (attempt law) looking at how fully a defendant developed a criminal purpose to commit a crime.

dangerous proximity test (attempt law) looking at the seriousness of the offense intended; the closeness to completion of the crime; and the probability the conduct would actually have resulted in completion of the crime.

deep coma enough brain functions to sustain breathing and a heartbeat but nothing more.

defense of excuse defenses based on the idea that what defendants did was a crime but under the circumstances they weren't responsible for what they did (insanity).

defense of justification defenses based on the idea that what defendants did was a crime but under the circumstances they were right to do it (self-defense).

defense of reasonable mistake of age defense to rape if a man reasonably believed his victim was over the age of consent.

depraved-heart murder cause death by criminally reckless risk conduct.

destructive device (in terrorist crimes) device used to commit terrorist acts (for example, bombs, poison gas).

determinism actions beyond the control of free will.

diminished capacity mental capacity less than "normal" but more than "insane."

dissenting opinion the opinion of the minority of justices.

distinguishing cases finding that facts differ enough from those in a prior case to release judges from the precedent of the decision in that case.

doctrine of complicity the principle regarding parties to crime that establishes the conditions under which more than one person incurs liability before, during, and after committing crimes.

doctrine of vicarious liability see vicarious liability.

domestic terrorism terrorist crimes committed inside the United States.

due process of law fair procedures guaranteed by the U.S. Constitution, Amendments V and XIV.

duress (defense of) excuse of being forced to commit a crime.

Durham **rule, or product test of insanity** an insanity test to determine whether a crime was a product of mental disease or defect.

element of consent requirement that women had to prove lack of consent in rape.

elements of a crime the parts of a crime that the prosecution must prove beyond a reasonable doubt, such as *actus reus, mens rea,* concurrence, causation, and harmful result.

ellipses editing mark (...) indicating omitted text from a quote.

embezzlement crime of lawfully gaining possession of someone else's property and later converting it to one's own use.

entering (in burglary) part of the *actus reus* of burglary.

entrapment government actions that induce individuals to commit crimes that they otherwise wouldn't commit.

equal protection of the law protection guaranteed by the U.S. Constitution, Amendment XIV.

espionage the crime of spying for the enemy.

excerpts parts of cases and/or quotations from the referenced text.

excusable homicide accidental killing and killing while insane.

excuse see principle of excuse.

ex post facto laws laws passed after the occurrence of the conduct constituting the crime.

expressive conduct conduct that communicates an idea or emotion without using words.

express or implied malice aforethought *mens rea* in common-law murder.

extortion misappropriation of another's property by means of threats to inflict bodily harm in the future.

extraneous factor a condition beyond the attempter's control.

extrinsic force standard requires some force in addition to the amount needed to accomplish the penetration.

factual cause conduct that in fact leads to a harmful result.

factual impossibility the defense that some extraneous factor made it impossible to complete a crime.

failure to intervene (criminal omission) one type of omission *actus reus*.

failure to report (criminal omission) one type of omission *actus reus*.

false imprisonment the crime of depriving others of their right of locomotion.

false pretenses in modern law often called "theft by deceit."

federal system structure of U.S. government divided into federal and state governments.

felony a serious crime generally punishable by one year or more in prison.

felony murder deaths occurring during the commission of felonies.

fences those who sell stolen merchandise for profit.

fetal death statute law defining when life begins for purposes of the law of criminal homicide.

fighting words words likely to provoke the average person to breach the peace by retaliation.

first-degree murder premeditated, deliberate killings and other particularly heinous capital murders.

forgery making false writings or materially altering authentic writings.

fundamental right preferred rights guaranteed in the Bill of Rights that require a compelling state interest to justify legislation restricting them.

general attempt statute statutes that define the elements of attempt that apply to all crimes.

general deterrence (also called general prevention) aims by threat of punishment to deter criminal behavior in the general population.

general intent intent to commit the *actus reus*—the act required in the definition of the crime.

general part of criminal law principles that apply to all crimes.

general prevention the purpose of punishment based on the idea that punishment of one person will deter others who are thinking of committing a crime.

general principle of necessity (defense to crime) the justification of committing a lesser crime to avoid the imminent danger of a greater crime.

giving aid and comfort to the enemy (in treason) giving physical (not just intellectual or emotional) support to the enemy.

Good Samaritan doctrine doctrine that imposes a legal duty to render or summon aid for imperiled strangers.

government regulation using a tax or a license instead of criminal punishment to regulate behavior.

grand larceny the severest form of stealing another person's property.

gross criminal negligence very great negligence; actions without even slight care but not amounting to intentional or conscious wrongdoing.

gross misdemeanor offense with a maximum penalty of close to one year in jail.

group disorderly conduct committing breaches of the peace in groups (for example, riot).

habeas corpus a civil action challenging the legality of a prisoner's detention.

heightened scrutiny increased level of court review of legislation raising issues of equal protection of the laws.

holding the legal principle or rule that a case enunciates.

homicide *actus reus* the act of taking the life of another person.

identity theft stealing another person's identity for the purpose of getting something of value.

imminent danger element in self-defense that injury or death is going to happen right now.

imperfect defenses defenses reducing but not eliminating criminal liability.

incapacitation punishment by imprisonment, mutilation, and even death.

inchoate offenses offenses based on crimes not yet completed.

indispensable element test (attempt law) asks whether defendants have gotten control of everything they need to complete the crime.

individual disorderly conduct disorderly conduct committed by one person (contrasted with riot).

information an official document charging a person with a crime on the authority of the prosecutor without the participation of a grand jury.

initial aggressor person who begins a fight can't claim the right to self-defense.

injunction an action in which city attorneys ask the courts to declare gang activities and gang members public nuisances and to issue injunctions to abate the public nuisance.

insanity legal term for a person who is excused from criminal liability because a mental disease or defect impairs his *mens rea*.

intangible property property that lacks a physical existence (examples include stock options or "goodwill" in a business).

intellectual property information and services stored in and transmitted to and from electronic data banks; a rapidly developing area of property crimes.

intelligence gathering accumulation of information about terrorist suspects and groups and their activities.

intentional scaring *mens rea* of intending to frighten victims in assault.

international terrorism terrorist acts dangerous to U.S. citizens committed outside the United States.

intervening cause the cause that either interrupts a chain of events or substantially contributes to a result.

intrinsic force standard requires only the amount of force necessary to accomplish the penetration.

involuntary intoxication excuse based on the impairment of *actus reus* or *mens rea* caused by coerced or tricked intoxication of the defendant (for example, slipping crystal meth into the defendant's drink).

involuntary manslaughter criminal homicides caused either by recklessness or gross criminal negligence.

irrebuttable presumption a conclusive assumption that requires a finding of a presumed fact once the fact is introduced into evidence.

irresistible impulse impairment of the will that makes it impossible to control the impulse to do wrong.

joyriding (in property crime) temporarily taking and carrying away another person's property without the intent to keep it permanently.

judgment court's decision in a case (for example, affirmed).

justifiable homicide killing in self-defense, capital punishment, and police use of deadly force.

justification see principle of justification.

kidnapping taking and carrying away another person with intent to deprive the other person of personal liberty.

knowing consent (in defense of consent) the person consenting knows what she's consenting to.

knowing possession awareness of physical possession.

knowledge (in *mens rea*) consciously acting or causing a result.

larceny taking and carrying away another person's property with the intent to permanently deprive its owner of possession.

legal cause cause recognized by law to impose criminal liability.

legal duty (in criminal omission) liability only for duties imposed by contract, statute, or "special relationships."

legal fiction (in *actus reus*) treating as a fact something that's not a fact if there's a good reason for doing so.

legal impossibility the defense that what the actor attempted was not a "crime."

libel defamation expressed in print.

liberty the right of individuals to go about in public free of undue interference.

loitering remaining in one place with no apparent purpose.

majority opinion the opinion of the majority of justices.

malice *mens rea* of common-law homicide.

malicious mischief damaging or destroying another person's property.

malum in se a crime inherently bad or evil.

malum prohibitum a crime not inherently bad or evil but merely prohibited.

manifest criminality the requirement in law that intentions have to turn into criminal deeds to be punishable.

manslaughter unlawful killing of another person.

marital rape exception husbands can't rape their wives.

material support (in terrorist crimes) element in terrorist crimes that consists of helping terrorists or terrorist organizations.

mens rea see principle of *mens rea*.

mental defect (in insanity defense) retardation affecting *mens rea* (cognition) and/or *actus reus* (will).

mental disease (in insanity defense) psychoses affecting cognition (*mens rea*) or will (*actus reus*).

mere possession physical possession.

mere presence rule a person's presence at the scene of a crime doesn't by itself satisfy the *actus reus* requirement of accomplice liability.

misdemeanor a minor crime for which the penalty is usually less than one year in jail or a fine.

misdemeanor manslaughter deaths occurring during the commissions of misdemeanors.

mitigating circumstances facts that reduce but don't eliminate culpability.

Model Penal Code the code developed by the American Law Institute to guide reform in criminal law.

Model Penal Code and Commentaries the American Law Institute's model code and commentary, or the extent to which it had been enacted by the states as of 1985.

***Model Penal Code* standard (in insanity defense)** test of insanity based on the lack of substantial capacity either to appreciate the wrongfulness (criminality) of conduct or the capacity to conform conduct to the dictates of the law.

Model Penal Code* test of attempt *actus reus the requirement that substantial steps strongly corroborate the actor's purpose.

moral duty (in criminal omission) duty imposed by moral law but not sufficient to impose legal duty to report or intervene.

motive the reason why a defendant commits a crime.

murder intentionally causing the death of another person without adequate provocation.

nature and quality of the act (in insanity defense) mental disease affecting the capacity to know what you're doing.

necessity general principle of an honest and reasonable belief it's necessary to commit a lesser crime (evil) to avoid the imminent necessity of a greater crime (evil).

negligence the unconscious creation of substantial and unjustifiable risks.

negligent manslaughter negligently causing the death of another person.

objective test of cooling-off-time in voluntary manslaughter, the element of whether in similar circumstances a reasonable person would've had time to cool off.

objective test of entrapment focuses on the actions that government agents take to induce individuals to commit crimes.

obscenity material whose predominant appeal is to nudity, sex, or excretion.

occupied structures (in burglary and arson) an aggravated form of burglary and arson based on the presence of people inside when the crimes are committed.

order behavior in public that comports with minimum community standards of civility.

ordinary misdemeanor minor crime with a penalty of a fine or 90 days to 6 months jail time.

overt act (in conspiracy) requirement of conspiracy *actus reus* of some act toward completing the crime in addition to the agreement.

parental responsibility laws statutes that make parents liable for their children's crimes.

parties to crime those who are criminally liable for another person's crimes.

patrons (in prostitution) persons who pay for sex.

perfect defenses defenses that lead to outright acquittal.

petty larceny minor form of larceny based on the low value of items stolen.

petty misdemeanor offense punishable by a jail sentence of up to thirty days.

physical property (in trespass) originally trespass could only be committed against land, then it was extended to buildings, and now includes computers.

physical proximity test the principle that the number of remaining acts in attempt determines attempt *actus reus.*

Pinkerton **rule** the rule that conspiracy and the underlying crime are separate offenses.

plurality opinion an opinion that announces the result of the case but whose reasoning doesn't command a majority of the court.

precedent prior court decision that guides judges in deciding future cases.

predicate crime crime another crime is based on (for example, the crime a burglar entered to commit).

preliminary injunction a temporary order issued by a court after giving notice and holding a hearing.

premeditation planned in advance.

preparation acts amounting to just getting ready to commit a crime (attempt law).

preponderance of the evidence more than 50 percent of the evidence proves justification or excuse.

present danger danger that's probably going to happen some time in the future but not right now (self defense).

prevention punishing offenders to prevent crimes in the future.

prima facie criminal liability proven unless it's rebutted by evidence submitted by defendant.

principals in the first degree persons who actually commit the crime.

principals in the second degree persons who are present when crimes are committed and participate in the crime (for example, drive getaway car).

principle of *actus reus* see *actus reus.*

principle of causation requirement that criminal conduct cause a harm defined in the criminal code.

principle of concurrence see concurrence.

principle of excuse it's wrong to punish someone who's not responsible.

principle of harmful result requirement that criminal conduct result in harm defined as a crime.

principle of justification a defense deeming acceptable under the circumstances what is otherwise criminal conduct.

principle of legality a principle stating that there can be no crime or punishment if there are no specific laws forewarning citizens that certain specific conduct will result in a particular punishment.

principle of limited methods criminal law is the last resort of social control.

principle of *mens rea* the mental element in crime, including purpose, knowledge, recklessness, and negligence.

principle of proportionality a principle of law stating that the punishment must be proportionate to the crime committed.

principles of criminal liability the principles of *actus reus*, *mens rea*, concurrence, causation, and harmful result, which are the basis for the elements of crime the prosecution has to prove beyond a reasonable doubt.

private lawsuits suing another person to recover money damages for a harm caused by the defendant.

product test (insanity defense) an insanity test to determine whether a crime was a product of mental disease or defect.

profanity irreverence toward sacred things.

promoting prostitution the crime of soliciting customers for prostitutes ("pimping").

prompt reporting rule rape victims have to report the rape soon after it occurs.

prostitutes persons who "buy" and who "sell" sex.

prostitution the crime of "buying" or "selling" sex.

proximate cause the main cause of the result of criminal conduct.

purpose (in *mens rea***)** the specific intent to act and/or cause a criminal harm.

quality-of-life crimes breaches of minimum standards of decent behavior in public.

rape *actus reus* the act of sexual penetration.

rape shield statutes statutes that prohibit introducing evidence of victims' past sexual conduct.

rational basis (in equal protection cases) the standard for deciding whether treating people differently in a statute isn't completely irrational.

reason (in insanity defense) the mental capacity to distinguish right from wrong.

reasonable force (in defense of self-defense) amount of force necessary to repel an attacker in self defense.

reasonable provocation (in voluntary manslaughter) a provocation to kill in the heat of passion that's recognized by law and that will reduce murder to manslaughter.

reasonable resistance standard (in rape) amount of force required to repel rapist to show nonconsent in rape prosecution.

reasoning the reasons a court gives to support its holding.

receiving stolen property benefiting from someone else's property without having participated in the wrongful acquisition in the first place.

reckless manslaughter criminal homicides that aren't murder.

recklessness the conscious creation of substantial and unjustifiable risk.

rehabilitation prevention of crime by treatment.

remaining (in burglary) part of the *actus reus* consisting of illegally staying in a building lawfully entered (for example, entering a store during business hours and hiding until the store closes).

remanded sent a case back to a trial court for further proceedings consistent with the reviewing court's decision.

res ipsa loquitur **test** examines whether an ordinary person who saw the defendants' acts without knowing their intent would guess that they were determined to commit a crime (attempt law).

resisting-victim exception exception to the third-party exception to felony murder.

responsive intervening act (in causation) reactions to conditions created by defendants' triggering acts.

retreat rule you have to retreat, but only if you reasonably believe that backing off won't unreasonably put you in danger of death or serious bodily harm.

retribution punishment based on just deserts.

reversed set aside the decision of the trial court and substituted a different decision.

reversed and remanded appeals court overturns the judgment of a lower court and sends the case back to the lower court for a decision consistent with the appeals court decision.

right of locomotion the right to come and go without restraint.

right-wrong test (in insanity defense) (*M'Naghten* rule) capacity to either know right from wrong or to know the act is against the law.

riot disorderly conduct committed by more than three persons.

robbery taking and carrying away another's property by force or threat of force with the intent to permanently deprive the owner of possession.

rout three or more people moving toward the commission of a riot.

rule of law the principles that require that established written rules and procedures define, prohibit, and prescribe punishments for crimes.

sabotage damaging or destroying property for the purpose of hindering preparations for war and national defense during national emergencies.

second-degree murder a catchall offense including killings that are neither manslaughter nor first-degree murder.

sedition the crime of "stirring up" treason by words.

seditious conspiracy agreement to "stir up" treason.

seditious libel writings aimed at "stirring up" treason.

seditious speech "stirring up" treason by means of the spoken word.

serious (grievous) bodily injury injury serious enough to require medical treatment in a hospital.

sexual penetration element of unlawfully inserting something into body openings for sexual gratification.

simple rape (second degree) rape without aggravated circumstances.

slander defamation by the spoken word.

Smith Act of 1940 U.S. statute aimed at Communists who advocated the violent overthrow of the government.

social condemnation leave sanctions to the disapproval of friends and others.

solicitation trying to get someone to commit a crime.

solicitation *actus reus* urging another person to commit a crime.

solicitation *mens rea* intent to get another person to commit a crime.

solicit prostitution procuring customers for prostitutes ("pimping").

somnambulism sleepwalking.

special deterrence the threat of punishment aimed at individual offenders in the hope of deterring future criminal conduct.

special part of criminal law defines the elements of specific crimes.

specific attempt statute separate statute for each crime attempted (attempted murder).

specific intent the intent to do something beyond the *actus reus*.

specific-intent crime a crime done with the very purpose of either engaging in criminal conduct or causing a criminal result.

stalking intentionally scaring another person by following, tormenting, or harassing.

stand-your-ground rule says that if you didn't start the fight, you can stand your ground and kill.

stare decisis the principle that binds courts to stand by prior decisions and to leave undisturbed settled points of law.

status (as *actus reus*) who we are as opposed to what we do; a condition that's not an action can't substitute for action as an element in crime.

statutory rape to have carnal knowledge of a person under the age of consent whether or not accomplished by force.

strict liability liability without fault, or in the absence of *mens rea*.

strict liability offenses criminal liability without fault.

strict scrutiny statutory classifications that require proof that they further a compelling state interest.

structures (in burglary and arson) buildings capable of being burglarized or set on fire.

subjective provocation provocation that in fact drives someone to kill another person.

subjective test of entrapment focuses on the predisposition of defendants to commit crimes.

substantial capacity test insanity due to mental disease or defect impairing the substantial capacity either to appreciate the wrongfulness of conduct or to conform behavior to the law.

"substantial steps" test (in attempt *actus reus*) in the *Model Penal Code,* substantial acts toward completion of a crime and that strongly corroborate the actor's intent to commit the crime.

surreptitious remaining entering a structure lawfully with the intent to commit a crime inside.

syndromes (defense of) novel defenses of excuse based on symptoms of conditions like being a Vietnam vet suffering from post-traumatic stress disorder or having premenstrual symptoms.

taking (in larceny) element of getting control of another person's property.

tangible property personal property (not real estate).

text-case book book based on text and case excerpts.

theft consolidated crimes of larceny, embezzlement, and false pretenses.

theft by deceit (larceny by trick) trick or lie to get possession of someone else's property (substitutes for physically taking someone else's property).

third-party exception defense to felony murder that someone other than the felon caused death during the commission of a felony.

threatened battery assault the crime of assault that focuses on the *mens rea.*

time, place, and manner regulations legitimate limits on the First Amendment right of free speech.

torture murder acts intended to cause lingering death.

transferred intent actor intends to harm one victim but instead harms another.

treason crime of levying war against the United States or of giving aid and comfort to its enemies.

trespassory taking (in larceny) *actus reus* consisting of getting possession of another person's property without consent.

unarmed acquaintance rape nonconsensual sex between people who know each other; rape involv-

ing dates, lovers, neighbors, co-workers, employers, and so on.

unauthorized computer access statutes statutes defining the crime of accessing another person's computer without permission.

unequivocality test examines the likelihood the defendant won't complete the crime (attempt law).

unilateral approach not all the conspirators need to agree to commit a crime to impose criminal liability (conspiracy *actus reus*).

unlawful act manslaughter involuntary manslaughter based on deaths that take place during the commission of another crime.

unlawful assembly ancient crime of three or more persons gathering together to commit an unlawful act.

unprovoked attack (in self defense) those who claim self-defense can't have started the fight that required force to prevent further harm.

USA Patriot Act act passed by Congress following September 11, creating some new (and enhancing the penalties for existing) crimes of domestic and international terrorism.

utmost resistance standard the requirement that rape victims must use all the physical strength they have to prevent penetration.

uttering knowing or conscious use or transfer of false documents.

vagrancy ancient crime of poor people wandering around with no visible means of support.

vicarious liability the principle of liability for another based on relationship.

"victimless" crimes crimes without complaining victims (for example, recreational illegal drug users).

violation a minor legal infraction subject to a small fine.

void-for-overbreadth doctrine the principle that a statute is unconstitutional if it includes in its definition of undesirable behavior conduct protected under the U.S. Constitution.

void-for-vagueness doctrine the principle that statutes violate due process if they don't clearly define crime and punishment in advance.

volition (in defense of insanity) mental disease or defect impairs will (capacity to control actions).

voluntary consent (in consent of defense) victim consented to defendants' actions without coercion.

voluntary manslaughter intentional killings committed in the sudden heat of passion upon adequate provocation.

weapon of mass destruction (in terrorist crimes) any destructive device used to commit acts of terror.

wheel conspiracies one or more defendants participate in every transaction.

white-collar crimes crimes growing out of opportunities to get someone else's property provided by the perpetrator's occupation.

withdrawal exception (self-defense) if initial aggressors completely withdraw from fights they provoke, they can claim the defense of self-defense.

Wolfendon Report English document recommending the decriminalization of private sexual conduct between adult consenting male homosexuals and prostitution.

wrong (in insanity defense) lack of capacity to know right from wrong can mean either "against the law" or against the moral code.

Bibliography

Alaska Criminal Code. 2003. Second-degree murder. http://www.touchngo.com/lglcntr/akstats/Statutes/Title11/Chapter41/Section110.htm.

Allam v. State. 1992. 830 P.2d 435 (AlaskaApp.).

American Jurisprudence. 2003. "Constitutional Law." Rochester, N.Y.: Lawyers Corporation Publishing.

American Law Institute (ALI). 1953. *Model Penal Code, Tentative Draft 1.* Philadelphia: ALI.

American Law Institute (ALI). 1960. *Model Penal Code, Tentative Drafts 11, 12, 13.* Philadelphia: ALI.

American Law Institute (ALI). 1985. *Model Penal Code and Commentaries.* Philadelphia: ALI.

American Psychiatric Association. 2003. "Don't Many Criminals Try to Use the Insanity Defense to Escape Severe Punishment?" http://www.psych.org/public_info/insanity.cfm.

Anderson v. State. 1997. 562 P.2d 351, 358–359 (Alaska).

Anderson, Curt. 2003. "'Material Support' Charge Under Legal Eye." *Associated Press,* 13 August.

Arizona Criminal Code. 2003. http://www.azleg.state.az.us/ars/13/00503.htm.

Arizona Criminal Code. 2003. Second-degree murder. http://www.azleg.state.az.us/ars/13/01104.htm.

Associated Press. 1990. "Gunman Tells Story of Shooting on Subway." *Toronto Star,* 27 September.

Bachun v. U.S. 1940. 112 F.2d 635 (4th Cir.).

Bailey v. U.S. 1969. 416 F.2d 1110 (D.C. Cir.).

Barnes v. Glen Theatre, Inc., et al. 1991. 501 U.S. 560.

Beasley v. State. 1886. 8 So. 234. (Miss.).

Benson, Carl, Andrew J. Jablon, Paul J. Kaplan, and Mara Elena Rosenthal. 1997. "Computer Crimes." *American Criminal Law Review* 34:409.

Blackstone, Sir William. 1769. *Commentaries on the Laws of England.* IV. Oxford: Clarendon Press.

Blakely, Richard, and Mark Gettings. 1980. "Racketeer Influenced and Corrupt Organizations (RICO): Basic Concepts—Criminal and Civil Remedies." *Temple Law Quarterly* 53.

Board of Commissioners v. Backus. 1864. 29 How. Pr. 33.

Bond, Julian P., ed. 1950. *Papers of Thomas Jefferson.* Vol. 2. Princeton N.J.: Princeton University Press.

Bowers v. Hardwick. 1986. 478 U.S. 186.

Boy Scouts of America v. Dale. 2000. 530 U.S. 640.

Bradley v. Ward. 1955. N.Z.L.R. 471.

Brodie, Kyle S. 1995. "The Obviously Impossible Attempt: A Proposed Revision to the *Model Penal Code. Northern Illinois University Law Review* 15:237.

Brown v. State. 1906. 106 N.W. 536 (Wis.).

Brown v. United States. 1921. 256 U.S. 335, 343.

Bryden, David P. 2000. "Redefining Rape." *Buffalo Criminal Law Review* 3:318.

Buck v. Bell. 1927. 274 U.S. 200.

Burnett v. State. 1999. 807 So.2d 573 (Ala.App.).

Burrows v. State. 1931. 297 P. 1029.

Butler, Samuel. 1927. *Erehwon.* New York: Modern Library.

California Penal Code. 2003. http://www.leginfo.ca.gov/.html/pen_table_of_contents.html.

California Penal Code. 2004. http://www.leginfo.ca.gov/cgi-bin/calawquery?codesection=pen&codebody=&hits=20.

Campbell v. State. 1982. 444 A.2d 1034.

Cardozo, Benjamin. 1921. *The Nature of the Judicial Process.* New Haven Conn.: Yale University Press.

Carey v. Population Services International. 1977. 431 U.S. 678.

Carlson, Jonathan C. 1987. "The Act Requirement and the Foundations of the Entrapment Defense." *Virginia Law Review* 73:1011.

Carney, Robert Mark, and Brian D. Williams. 1983. "Premenstrual Syndrome: A Criminal Defense." *Notre Dame Law Review* 59:263–269.

Casico v. State. 1947. 25 N.W.2d 897 (Neb.).

Chaplinsky v. New Hampshire. 1942. 315 U.S. 568.

City of Chicago v. Morales. 1999. 527 U.S. 41.

Code of Alabama. 1975. Chapter 4: Inchoate Offenses, Section 13A-4-2. http://www.legislature.state.al.us/CodeofAlabama/1975/13A-4-2.htm.

Cohen, Fred. 1985. "Old Age Defense." *Criminal Law Bulletin* 21.

Coker v. Georgia. 1977. 433 U.S. 584.

Commonwealth v. Barnette. 1998. 699 N.E.2d, 1230 (Mass.App.).

Commonwealth v. Berkowitz. 1994. 641 A.2d 1161 (Pa.).

Commonwealth v. Gilliam. 1980. 417 A.2d 1203 (Pa.Sup.).

Commonwealth v. Golston. 1977. 249, 366 N.E.2d 744 (Mass.).

Commonwealth v. Kozak. 1993. WL 768932 (Pa.Com.Pl.).

Commonwealth v. Mitchell. 1993. WL 773785 (Pa.Com.Pl.).

Commonwealth v. Mlinarich. 1988. 542 A.2d 1335 (Pa.).

Commonwealth v. Peaslee. 1901. 59 N.E. 55 (Mass.).

Commonwealth v. Schnopps. 1983. 459 N.E.2d 98 (Mass.).

Cramer v. U.S. 1945. 325 U.S. 1.

Crichton, Sarah, Debra Rosenberg, Stanley Holmes, Martha Brant, Donna Foote, and Nina Biddle. 1993. "Sexual Correctness: Has It Gone Too Far?" *Newsweek*, 25 October. pp. 52–54.

Cullen, Francis T., William J. Maakestad, and Gray Cavender. 1987. *Corporate Crime Under Attack: The Ford Pinto Case and Beyond.* Cincinnati: Anderson.

Dawkins v. State. 1988. 313 Md. 638, 547 A.2d 1041.

Dennis v. U.S. 1951. 341 U.S. 494.

DePasquale v. State. 1988. 757 P.2d 367.

Dershowitz, Alan. 1994. *The Abuse Excuse and Other Cop-Outs, Sob Stories, and Evasions of Responsibility.* Boston: Little, Brown.

Dial v. State. 2003. WL 352982 (Wash.App.).

Diamond, John L. 1996. "The Myth of Morality and Fault in Criminal Law." *American Criminal Law* 34.

DiFonzo, James. 2001. "Parental Responsibility for Juvenile Crime." *Oregon Law Review* 80:1.

Direct Sales Co. v. U.S. 1943. 319 U.S. 703.

D. P. v. State. 1998. 705 So.2d 593 (Fla.App.).

Dubber, Markus D. 2002. *Criminal Law: Model Penal Code.* New York: Foundation Press.

Duest v. State. 1985. 462 So.2d 446 (Fla.).

Dunn v. Commonwealth. 1997. WL 147448 (Va.App.).

Durham v. U.S. 1954. 214 F.2d 862 (D.C. Cir.).

Dutile, Ferdinand, and Harold F. Moore. 1979. "Mistake and Impossibility: Arranging a Marriage Between Two Difficult Partners." *Northwestern University Law Review* 74.

Edwards v. California. 1941. 314 U.S. 162.

Edwards, Daphne. 1996. "Acquaintance Rape and the 'Force' Element: When 'No' is Not Enough." *Golden Gate Law Review* 26:241.

Eisenstadt v. Baird. 1972. 405 U.S. 438.

Electronic Frontier. 2000. http://www.usdoj.gov/criminal/cybercrime/unlawful.htm.

Ellickson, Robert C. 1996. "Controlling Chronic Misconduct in City Spaces: Of Panhandlers, Skid Rows, and Public-Space Zoning." *Yale Law Journal* 105.

Elton, Geoffrey R. 1972. *The Tudor Constitution.* Cambridge, UK: Cambridge University Press.

Encyclopedia of Crime and Justice. 1983. Vol. 1. New York: Free Press.

Enker, Arnold. 1977. "*Mens Rea* in Criminal Attempt." *American Bar Foundation Research Journal.*

Estrich, Susan. 1987. *Real Rape.* Cambridge, Mass.: Harvard University Press.

Farnsworth, Clyde. 1994. "Mercy Killing in Canada Stirs Calls for Changes in Law." *New York Times,* 21 November.

Farrand, Max, ed. 1929. Introduction to *The Laws and Liberties of Massachusetts.* Cambridge, Mass.: Harvard University Press.

Federal Criminal Code and Rules. 1988. St. Paul, Minn.: West.

Federal Trade Commission. 2002 (March 20). "Identity Theft: The FTC's Response." http://www.ftc.gov/os/2002/03/idthefttest.htm.

Fisse, Brian. 1986. "Sanctions Against Corporations: Economic Efficiency?" In *Punishment and Privilege.* Edited by W. Byron Groves and Graeme Newman. Albany, N.Y.: Harrow and Heston.

Fletcher, George. 1978. *Rethinking Criminal Law.* Boston: Little, Brown.

Fletcher, George. 1988. *A Crime of Self-Defense: Bernhard Goetz and the Law on Trial.* New York: Free Press.

Fletcher, George. 1996. "Justice for All, Twice." *New York Times,* 24 April.

Florida Constitution. 1998. http://www.flsenate.gov/Statutes/index.cfm?Mode=Constitution&Submenu=3&Tab=statutes#A01S23.

Florida Criminal Code. 2003. § 787.02. http://www.flsenate.gov/statutes/index.cfm?App_mode=Display_Statute&Search_String=&URL=Ch0787/SEC02.HTM&Title=->2002->Ch0787->Section%2002.

Foreman, Judy. 1986. "Most Rape Victims Know Assailant, Don't Report to Police, Police Report Says." *Boston Globe,* 16 April.

Fried, Joshua Mark. 1996. "Forcing the Issue: An Analysis of the Various Standards of Forcible Compulsion in Rape." *Pepperdine Law Review* 23:120.

Ganeson v. State. 2001. 45 S.W.3d 197 (Tex.).

Garnett v. State. 1993. 632 A.2d 797 (Md.).

Gaylin, Willard. 1982. *The Killing of Bonnie Garland.* New York: Simon and Schuster.

George v. State. 1984. 681 S.W.2d 43 (Tex.Crim.App.).

Gibeaut, John. 1997. "Sobering Thoughts." *American Bar Association Journal* 83.

Gitlow v. New York. 1925. 268 U.S. 652.

Goldstein, Joseph, Alan Dershowitz, and Richard D. Schwartz. 1974. *Criminal Law: Theory and Process.* New York: Free Press.

Goodman v. State. 1977. 573 P.2d 400 (Wyo.).

Gray v. State. 1979. 403 A.2d 853.

Greenhouse, Steven. 1985. "Three Executives Convicted of Murder for Unsafe Workplace Conditions." *New York Times,* 15 June.

Gresham v. Peterson. 2000. 225 F.3d 899 (7th Cir.).

Griswold v. Connecticut. 1965. 381 U.S. 479.

Gross, Hyman. 1978. *A Theory of Criminal Justice.* New York: Oxford University Press.

Hale, Matthew. 1670. *Pleas of the Crown*. London: W. Shrowsbery.

Hall, Jerome. 1952. *Theft, Law, and Society*. 2nd ed. Indianapolis: Bobbs-Merrill.

Hall, Jerome. 1960. *The General Principles of Criminal Law*. 2nd ed. Indianapolis: Bobbs-Merrill.

Hall, John Wesley, Jr. 1993. *Search and Seizure*. 2nd ed. New York: Clark, Boardman, and Callaghan.

Hanby v. State. 1970. 479 P.2d 486, 498 (Alaska).

Hancock v. Texas. 1966. 402 S.W.2d 906.

Harcourt, Bernard E. 2001. *Illusions of Order*. Cambridge, Mass.: Harvard University Press.

Harmelin v. Michigan. 1991. 501 U.S. 957.

Harrod v. State. 1985. 499 A.2d 959 (Md.App.).

Haupt v. U.S. 1947. 330 U.S. 631.

Henyard v. State. 1996. 689 So.2d 239 (Fla.).

Holmes, Oliver Wendell. 1963. *The Common Law*. Boston: Little, Brown.

Holy Bible: King James Version. 2000. http://www.bartleby.com/108/03/24.html.

Home Office. 1957. *Scottish Home Department Report of the Committee on Homosexual Offenses and Prostitution*. London: Her Majesty's Stationery Office.

Hurston v. State. 1991 414 S.E.2d 303 (Ga.App.).

Hyde v. U.S. 1912. 225 U.S. 347.

ID. 2003. http://www.consumer.gov/idtheft/index.html.

Idaho State Historical Society. n.d. Ray Snowden File. Boise: Idaho State Historical Society Library and Archives.

Illinois Criminal Law and Procedure. 1988. St. Paul, Minn.: West.

In re Kemmler. 1890. 136 U.S. 436.

In the Interest of C.W., a Child. 1997. 485 S.E.2d 561 (Ga.App.).

Jefferson, Thomas. 1853. *The Writings of Thomas Jefferson*. Edited by Albert Ellery Bergh. Washington, D.C.: U.S. Government.

Jewell v. State. 1996. 672 N.E.2d 417 (Ind.App.).

Joyce v. City and County of San Francisco. 1994. 846 F.Supp. 843 (N.D.Cal.).

Keeler v. Superior Court. 1970. 470 P.2d 617 (Cal.).

Kelling, George L., and Catherine M. Coles. 1996. *Fixing Broken Windows*. New York: Free Press.

King v. Cogdon. Reported in Morris 1951, 29.

Kolender v. Lawson. 1983. 461 U.S. 352.

Koppersmith v. State. 1999. 742 So.2d 206 (Ala.App.).

Krulewitch v. U.S. 1949. 336 U.S. 440.

LaFave, Wayne, and Jerold Israel. 1984. *Criminal Procedure*. Vol. 1. St. Paul, Minn.: West.

LaFave, Wayne, and Austen Scott. 1986. *Criminal Law*. 2nd ed. St. Paul, Minn.: West.

Landry v. Daley. 1968. 280 F.Supp. 968 (N.D.Ill.).

Lanzetta v. New Jersey. 1939. 306 U.S. 451.

Law v. State. 1974. 318 A.2d 859 (Md.App.).

Law v. State. 1975. 349 A.2d 295 (Md.App.).

Lawrence v. Texas. 2003. 123 S.Ct. 2472.

Le Barron v. State. 1966. 145 N.W.2d 79 (Wis.).

Lederer, Richard. 1988. *Get Thee to a Punnery*. New York: Bantam Doubleday.

Lewin, Tamar. 1985. "Criminal Onus on Executives." *New York Times*, 5 March.

Lewis et al. v. State. 1952. 251 S.W.2d 490 (Ark.).

Lewis, Sinclair. 1922. *Babbitt*. New York: Harcourt Brace.

Livermore, Joseph, and Paul Meehl. 1967. "The Virtues of M'Naghten." *Minnesota Law Review* 51:800.

Lockyer, Bill. 2001. "California's New Crime Wave." http://www.safestate.org/index.cfm?navid=238.

Loewy, Arnold. *Criminal Law*. 1987. St. Paul, Minn.: West.

Louisiana Statutes Annotated. 1974. Rev. Stat. tit. 17–A.

Low, Peter. 1990. *Criminal Law*. St. Paul, Minn.: West.

M'Naghten's Case. 1843. 8 Eng.Rep. 718.

Macias v. State. 1929. 283 P. 711.

Madison, James. 1961. "The Federalist No. 51." In *The Federalist*. Edited by Jacob E. Cooke. Middletown, Conn.: Wesleyan University Press.

Marcus, Paul. 1986. "The Development of Entrapment Law." *Wayne Law Review* 33:5.

Maryland Code. 1957. Repl. Vol. Art. 27.

Massachusetts Criminal Code. 2003. http://www.state.ma.us/legis/laws/mgl/gl-pt4-toc.htm.

Mayer, Andre, and Michael Wheeler. 1982. *The Crocodile Man: A Case of Brain Chemistry and Criminal Violence*. Boston: Houghton Mifflin.

Mayor of New York v. Miln. 1837. 36 U.S. (11 Pet.) 102.

McClain v. State. 1997. 678 N.E.2d 104 (Ind.).

McDonald, Forrest. 1982. *A Constitutional History of the United States*. Malibar, Fla.: Robert E. Krieger.

McKendree v. Christy. 1961. 172 N.E.2d 380.

McMullen, Richie. 1990. *Male Rape: Breaking the Silence on the Last Taboo*. London: Gay Men Press.

Medea, Anra, and Kathleen Thompson. 1974. *Against Rape*. New York: Farrar, Straus and Giroux.

Merriam-Webster. *The Unabridged Dictionary*. 2003. http://unabridged.merriam-webster.com.

Meerpol, Robert. 2003. *An Execution in the Family: One Son's Journey*. New York: St. Martin's Press.

Michael M. v. Superior Court of Sonoma County. 1981. 450 U.S. 464.

Michigan Criminal Code. 1974. http://www.michiganlegislature.org/mileg.asp?page=getObject&objName=mcl-328-1931-LXXVI&highlight=750.520.

Michigan Criminal Code. 2003. Second-degree murder. http://www.michiganlegislature.org/law/mileg.asp?page=getObject&objName=mcl-750-317&queryid=4296620&highlight=750.317.

Miller v. State. 1999. 6 S.W.3d 812 (Ark.App.).

Minnesota Criminal Code. 2003. http://www.revisor.leg.state.mn.us/stats/609/341.html.

Minnesota Identity Theft Statute. 2003. http://www.revisor.leg.state.mn.us/stats/609/527.html.

Minnesota Statutes Annotated. 1989. Cumulative Supplement.

Mitford, Jessica. 1969. *The Trial of Dr. Spock*. New York: Knopf.

Moran v. People. 1872. 25 Mich. 356.

Moriarty, Daniel G. 1989. "Extending the Defense of Renunciation." *Temple Law Review* 62.

Morris, Herbert. 1976. *On Guilt and Innocence*. Los Angeles: University of California Press.

Morris, Norval. 1951. "Somnambulistic Homicide: Ghosts, Spiders, and North Koreans." *Res Judicata* 5.

Morris, Norval, and Gordon Hawkins. 1970. *An Honest Politician's Guide to Crime Control*. Chicago: University of Chicago Press.

Nalls v. State. 1920. 219 S.W. 473 (Tex. Crim. App.).

National Public Radio. 2003. 18 September. Morning Edition.

Nazi Saboteur Case. 1942. Transcript (copy owned by author). Washington, D.C.: National Archives.

Nesson, Charles. 1982. *New York Times*, 1 July.

New Mexico Criminal Code. 2003. § 30-4-3. http://198.187.128.12/newmexico/lpext.dll?f= templates&fn=fs-main.htm&2.0.

Newsweek. 1982. "Not Guilty Because of PMS?" 8 November.

New York Penal Code. 2003. http://assembly.state.ny. us/leg/?cl=82.

New York Times. 1977. 16 April. p. 25.

New York Times. 1995. 5 August. p. 4.

New York Times. 1995. 25 July. p. B-1.

Nimmer, Raymond T. 2002. *Information Law*. St. Paul, Minn.: West.

Note. 1951. "Statutory Burglary: The Magic of Four Walls and a Roof." *University of Pennsylvania Law Review* 100:411.

Oliver v. State. 1985. 703 P.2d 869.

Olmeda Rafael, Virginia Breen, and Jane Purse. 1996. "From First Vote Jurors Knew." *New York Daily News*, 24 April.

Papichristou v. City of Jacksonville. 1972. 405 U.S. 156.

Parker v. Municipal Judge. 1967. 427 P.2d 642 (Nev.).

Parsons v. State. 1877. 2 So. 854 (Ala.).

Pennsylvania Criminal Code. 2004. http://members. aol.com/StatutesPA/18.html.

Pennsylvania Laws. 1794. Ch. 257, §§ 1–2.

People ex rel. Gallo v. Acuna. 1997. 929 P.2d 596.

People v. Allen. 1997. 64 Cal.Rptr.2d 497.

People v. Armitage. 1987. 239 Cal.Rptr. 515 (Cal.App.).

People v. Bowie. 2002. WL 1072088 (Cal.App. 4 Dist.).

People v. Burroughs. 1984. 678 P.2d 894 (Cal.).

People v. Chessman. 1951. 238 P.2d 1001 (Cal.).

People v. Datema. 1995. 533 N.W.2d 272 (Mich.).

People v. Davis. 1994. 872 P.2d 591 (Cal.).

People v. Decima. 1956. 138 N.E.2d 799 (N.Y.).

People v. Dover. 1990. 790 P.2d 834 (Colo.).

People v. Goetz. 1986. 497 N.E.2d 41 (N.Y.).

People v. Guenther. 1987. 740 P.2d 971 (Colo.).

People v. Hernandez. 2002. 774 N.E.2d 198 (N.Y.).

People v. Howell. 2002. WL 126056 (Cal.App. 2 Dist.).

People v. Kibbe. 1974. 362 N.Y.S.2d 848.

People v. Kimball. 1981. 311 N.W.2d 343 (Mich).

People v. Lawrence. 1996. 647 N.Y.S2d 675 (Sup.Ct. King's County).

People v. Mills. 1904. 70 N.E. 786.

People v. Moreland. 2002. WL 459026. (Cal.App. 2 Dist.).

People v. Moseley. Reported in Rosenthal 1999.

People v. Muñoz. 1960. 200 N.Y.S.2d 957.

People v. Nitz. 1996. 674 N.E.2d 802.

People v. Oliver. 1989. 258 Cal.Rptr. 138.

People v. Olivo. 1981. 420 N.E.2d 40 (N.Y.).

People v. O'Neil. 1990. 550 N.E.2d 1090 (Ill.App.).

People v. Penman. 1915. 110 N.E. 894.

People v. Phillips. 1966. 414 P.2d 353 (Cal.).

People v. Poplar. 1970. 173 N.W.2d 732.

People v. Rizzo. 1927. 158 N.E. 888 (N.Y.App.).

People v. Rokicki. 1999. 718 N.E.2d 333 (Ill.App.).

People v. Schmidt. 1915. 216 N.Y.S.2d 324.

People v. Stark. 1965. 400 P.2d 923.

People v. Thomas. 1978. 85 Mich.App. 618, 272 N.W.2d 157.

People v. Velez. 1986. 221 Cal.Rptr. 631 (Cal.App.).

People v. Washington. 1976. 130 Cal.Rptr. 96.

People v. Williams. 1965. 205 N.E.2d 749 (Ill.).

Perkins, Rollin M., and Ronald N. Boyce. 1982. *Criminal Law*. 3rd ed. Mineola, N.Y.: Foundation Press.

Phipps v. State. 1994. 883 S.W.2d 138 (Tenn.App.).

Pinkerton v. U.S. 1946. 328 U.S. 640.

Planned Parenthood of Southeastern Pennyslvania v. Casey. 1992. 505 U.S. 833.

Plato. 1975. *Laws*. Translated by Trevor J. Saunders. Middlesex, England: Penguin Books.

Porter v. State. 2003. WL 1919477 (Ark.App.).

Poulos, Peter W. 1995. "Chicago's Ban on Gang Loitering: Making Sense Out of Vagueness and Overbreadth in Loitering Laws." *California Law Review* 83:379.

Powell v. Texas. 1968. 392 U.S. 514.

Preyer, Kathryn. 1983. "Crime, the Criminal Law and Reform in Post-Revolutionary Virginia." *Law and History Review* 1.

Queen v. Dudley & Stephens. 1884. 14 Q. B. 273.

R.A.V. v. City of St. Paul. 1992. 505 U.S. 377, 112 S.Ct. 2538.

Ravin v. State. 1977. 537 P.2d 494, 511 & n. 69 (Alaska).

Regina v. Morgan. 1975. 2. W.L.R. 923 (H.L.).

Reinhold, Robert. 1985. "Trial Opens in Death at Texas Nursing Home." *New York Times*, 1 October.

Remick, Lani Anne. 1993. "Read Her Lips: An Argument for a Verbal Consent Standard in Rape." *University of Pennsylvania Law Review* 141:1103.

Rex v. Bailey. 1818. *Crown Cases Reserved*.

Rex v. Scofield. 1784. Cald. 397.

Reynolds v. State. 1889. 42 N.W. 903.

Robinson v. California. 1962. 370 U.S. 660.

Rochman, Sue. n.d. "Silent Victims: Bring Male Rape Out of the Closet." http://www.interactivetheatre.org/resc/ silent.html.

Roe v. Wade. 1973. 410 U.S. 113.

Rosenthal, Abe M. 1999. *Thirty-Eight Witnesses.* Berkeley: University of California Press.

Roth, Siobahn. 2003. "Material Support Law: Weapon in the War on Terror." *Legal Times,* 9 May.

Rubenfeld, Jed. 1989. "The Right to Privacy." *Harvard Law Review* 102:737–807.

Russell, Diana. 1975. *The Politics of Rape: The Victim's Perspective.* New York: Stein and Day.

Safire, William. 1989. "The End of RICO." *New York Times,* 30 January.

Samaha, Joel. 1974. *Law and Order in Historical Perspective.* New York: Academic Press.

Samaha, Joel. 1981. "The Recognizance in Elizabethan Law Enforcement." *American Journal of Legal History* 25.

Sampson, Robert J., and Stephen W. Raudenbush. 1999. "Deterrent Effect of the Police on Crime." *American Journal of Sociology* 105:163–189.

Sanchez, Renee. 1998. "City of Tolerance Tires of Homeless: San Francisco Aims to Roust Street Dwellers." *Washington Post,* 28 November.

Satterwhite v. Commonwealth. 1960. 111 S.E.2d 820 (Va.).

Scheidegger, Kent S. 1993. *A Guide to Regulating Panhandling.* Sacramento: Criminal Justice Legal Foundation.

Schenck v. U.S. 1919. 249 U.S. 47.

Schopp, Robert F. 1988. "Returning to *M'Naghten* to Avoid Moral Mistakes: One Step Forward, or Two Steps Backward for the Insanity Defense?" *Arizona Law Review* 30:135.

Schur, Edwin M., and Hugo Adam Bedau. 1974. *Victimless Crimes: Two Sides of a Controversy.* Englewood Cliffs, N.J.: Prentice-Hall.

Seattle v. Stone. 1966. 410 P.2d 583 (Wash.).

Serritt v. State. 2003. WL 21182608 (Ga.App.).

Shenon, Philip. 1985. "Dispute Over Intent in Drug Cases Divided F.D.A. and Justice Department." *New York Times,* 19 September.

Sherman v. U.S. 1958. 356 U.S. 369.

Sherman, Rorie. 1994. "Insanity Defense: A New Challenge." *National Law Journal,* 28 March.

Siegel, Barry. 1996. "Held Accountable for Son's Burglaries." *Los Angeles Times,* 10 May.

Simms v. State. 2003. 791 N.E.2d 225 (Ind.App.).

Simon, Harry. 1992. "Towns Without Pity: A Constitutional and Historical Analysis of Official Efforts to Drive Homeless Persons from American Cities." *Tulane Law Review* 66.

Skogan, Wesley G. 1990. *Disorder and Decline.* New York: Free Press.

Smith, Juliette. 1996. "Arresting the Homeless for Sleeping in Public: A Paradigm for Expanding the Robinson Doctrine." *Columbia Journal of Law and Social Problems* 29.

Solem v. Helm. 1983. 463 U.S. 277.

South Carolina Code of Laws. 2004. http://www.scstatehouse.net/code/titl16.htm.

Stanley v. Georgia. 1969. 394 U.S. 557.

State in the Interest of M.T.S. 1992. 609 A.2d 1335 (Pa.).

State v. Aguillard. 1990. 567 So.2d 674 (La.).

State v. Akers. 1979. 400 A.2d 38 (N.H.).

State v. Allen. 1996. 917 P.2d 848 (Kan.).

State v. Anderson. 1991. 566 N.E.2d 1224 (Ohio).

State v. Barnes. 1997. 945 P.2d 627 (Ore.App.).

State v. Beaudry. 1985. 365 N.W.2d 593 (Wis.).

State v. Bethley. 1996. 685 So.2d 1063.

State v. Bonds. 1991. 477 N.W.2d 265 (Wis.).

State v. Brown. 1976. 364 A.2d 27 (N.J.).

State v. Burns. 1997. WL 152074 (OhioApp. Dist. 6).

State v. Celli. 1978. 263 N.W.2d 145 (S.D.).

State v. Chism. 1983. 436 So.2d 464 (La.).

State v. Clark. 1990. 236 Neb. 475, 461 N.W.2d 576.

State v. Coulverson. 2002. WL 433633 (OhioApp. 10 Dist.).

State v. Cramer. 1993. 841 P.2d 1111 (Kan.App.).

State v. Crane. 1981. 279 S.E.2d 695.

State v. Curley. 1997. WL 242286 (N.Mex.App.).

State v. Damms. 1960. 100 N.W.2d 592 (Wis.).

State v. Dial. 2003. WL 352982 (Wash.App. Div. 2).

State v. Elder. 1991. 579 N.E.2d 420 (Ill.App.).

State v. Ely. 1921. 194 P. 988 (Wash.).

State v. Fiero. 1979. 603 P.2d 74.

State v. Flory. 1929. 276 P. 458 (Wyo.).

State v. Foster. 1987. 522 A.2d 277 (Conn.).

State v. Fransua. 1973. 510 P.2d 106 (N.Mex.App.).

State v. Friedman. 1997. 697 A.2d 947 (N.J. Sup.Ct.).

State v. Good. 1917. 195 S.W. 1006.

State v. Hall. 1932. 13 P.2d 624 (Nev.).

State v. Hall. 1974. 214 N.W.2d 205.

State v. Harrell. 2002. 811 So.2d 1015 (La.App.).

State v. Hartfiel. 1869. 24 Wis. 60, 62.

State v. Hatfield. 2002. 639 N.W.2d 372 (Minn.).

State v. Hauptmann. 1935. 180 A.2d 809 (N.J.).

State v. Herron. 1996. WL 715445 (OhioApp. 2 Dist.).

State v. Hiott. 1999. 987 P.2d 135 (Wash.App.).

State v. Humphries. 1978. 586 P.2d 130 (Wash.App.).

State v. Jantzi. 1982. 56, 57, 641 P.2d 62 (Ore.App.).

State v. Jerrett. 1983. 307 S.E.2d 339.

State v. Kennamore. 1980. 604 S.W.2d 856 (Tenn.).

State v. King. 2002. 293 A.D.2d 815 (N.Y. Sup.Ct.).

State v. Kordas. 1995. 528 N.W.2d 483 (Wis.).

State v. K.R.L. 1992. 840 P.2d 210 (Wash.App.).

State v. Kuntz. 2000. 995 P.2d 951 (Mt.).

State v. Loge. 2000. 608 N.W.2d 152 (Minn.).

State v. Mays. 2000. WL 1033098 (OhioApp. Dist. 1).

State v. Metzger. 1982. 319 N.W.2d 459 (Neb.).

State v. Michaud. 1998. 724 A.2d 1222.

State v. Mitcheson. 1977. 560 P.2d 1120 (Utah).

State v. Myrick. 1982. 291 S.E.2d 577.

State v. Nesbitt. 2001. 550 S.E.2d 864 (S.C.App.).

State v. Noren. 1985. 371 N.W.2d 381 (Wis.).

State v. O'Dell. 1984. 684 S.W.2d 453.

State v. O'Farrell. 1976. 355 A.2d 396 (Me.).

State v. Ownbey. 2000. 996 P.2d 510 (Ore.App.).

State v. Phillips. 1966. 414 P.2d 353.

State v. Pranckus. 2003. 815 A.2d 678 (Conn.App.).

State v. Quinet. 2000. 752 A.2d 490 (Conn.).

State v. Ramirez. 2001. 633 N.W.2d 656 (Wis.App.).

State v. Reed. 1984. 479 A.2d 1291 (Me.).

State v. Riley. 1993. 846 P.2d 1365 (Wash.).

State v. Robins. 2002. 647 N.W.2d 287 (Wis.).

State v. Sanders. 1978. 245 S.E.2d 397.

State v. Schleifer. 1923. 432, 121 A. 805.

State v. Shamp. 1988. 422 N.W.2d 520 (Minn.).

State v. Shelley. 1997. 929 P.2d 489 (Wash.App.).

State v. Snowden. 1957. 313 P.2d 706 (Idaho).

State v. Stark. 1992. 832 P.2d 109 (Wash.App.).

State v. Stewart. 1988. 763 P.2d 572 (Kan.).

State v. Stewart. 1995. 663 A.2d 912 (R.I.).

State. v. Ulvinen. 1981. 313 N.W.2d 425 (Minn.).

State v. Vargas. 2003. 812 A.2d. 205.

State v. Wagner. 1995. Nos. 94-0978-CR and 94-1980-CR, Court of Appeals (Wis.).

State v. Walden. 1982. 293 S.E.2d 780.

State v. Watson. 1975. 214 S.E.2d 85 (N.C.).

State v. Watson. 1997. WL 342497 (Mo.App. W.D.).

State v. Wilson. 1996. 685 So.2d 1063.

Stephen, Sir James F. 1883 (1). *A History of the Criminal Law of England.* Vol. 2. London: Macmillan.

Stephen, Sir James F. 1883. *A History of the Criminal Law of England.* Vol. 3. London: Macmillan.

Texas v. Johnson. 1989. 491 U.S. 397.

Texas Penal Code. 2003. http://www.capitol.state.tx.us/statutes/petoc.html.

Texas Penal Code Annotated. 2003. § 21.06a.

Thomas, Clarence. 1996. "Federalist Society Symposium: The Rights Revolution." *Michigan Law and Policy Review* 1:269.

Thompson and others v. City of Chicago. 2002. WL 31115578 (N.D.Ill.).

Tier, Robert. 1993. "Maintaining Safety and Civility in Public Spaces: A Constitutional Approach to Aggressive Begging." *Lousiana Law Review* 54:285.

Urofsky, Melvin, and Paul Finkelman. 2002a. *Documents of American Constitutional and Legal History.* New York: Oxford University Press.

Urofsky, Melvin, and Paul Finkelman. 2002b. *A March of Liberty.* New York: Oxford University Press.

U.S. v. Bruno. 1939. 105 F.2d 921.

U.S. v. Jenrette. 1984. 744 F.2d 817 (D.C. Cir.).

U.S. v. Lindh. 2002. "Plea Agreement." U.S. District Court, E.D. Virginia, Crim. No. 02-37A.

U.S. v. Mandujano. 1974. 499 F.2d 370 (5th Cir.).

U.S. v. Peoni. 1938. 100 F.2d 401 (2nd Cir.).

U.S. v. Peterson. 1973. 483 F.2d 1222 (2nd. Cir.).

U.S. v. Sattar and others. 2003. 02-Cr.-395 (S.D.N.Y.)

U.S. v. Simpson. 1987. 813. F.2d 1462.

U.S. v. Whitney. 2000. 229 F.3d 1296 (10th Cir.).

U.S.A. Patriot Act. 2001. http://frwebgate.access.gpo.gov/cgi-bin/getdoc.cgi?dbname=107_cong_bills&docid=f:h3162enr.txt.pdf.

U.S. Code. 2003. 18 U.S.C.A. § 17.

U.S. Criminal Code. 2003. http://www4.law.cornell.edu/uscode/.

Velazquez v. State. 1990. 561 So.2d 347 (Fla.App.).

Virginia Criminal Code 2003. http://leg1.state.va.us/cgi-bin/legp504.exe?000+cod+TOC1802000.

Weems v. U.S. 1910. 217 U.S. 349.

Weihofen, Henry E. 1960. "Retribution Is Obsolete." In *Responsibility.* Edited by C. Friedrich, *Nomos* series, no. 3. New York: Lieber-Atherton.

Weiss, Baruch. 2002. "What Were They Thinking? The Mental States of Aider and Abettor, and the Causer Under Federal Law." *Fordham Law Review*: 70:1341.

West's California Penal Code. 1988. St. Paul, Minn.: West.

West's Criminal Code of Alabama. 1975. § 13A-1-4. St. Paul, Minn.: West.

West's Florida Statutes Annotated. 1991. Title XLVI, § 775.01.

Whaley v. State. 1946. 26 So.2d 656 (Fla.).

Williams v. State. 1992. 600 N.E.2d 962 (Ind.App.).

Williams, Glanville. 1961. *Criminal Law.* 2nd ed. London: Stevens and Sons.

Williams, Linda. 1984. "The Classic Rape: When Do Victims Report?" *Social Problems* 31:464.

Wilson, James Q., and George L. Kelling. 1982 (March). "Broken Windows." *Atlantic Monthly.*

Wilson, James Q., and Richard Herrnstein. 1985. *Crime and Human Nature.* New York: Simon and Schuster.

Wisconsin Criminal Code. 2003. Wisconsin Statutes and Annotations. http://www.legis.state.wi.us/rsb/Statutes.html.

Wolfendon Report. 1957. Report of Committee on Homosexual Offenses and Prostitution. London: Stationer's Office.

Young v. New York City Transit Authority. 1990. 903 F.2d 146 (2nd Cir.).

Case Index

A

Aaron, State v., 327
Abner v. State, 392
Abrams v. United States, 471
Acuna, People ex rel. Gallo v., 445–447
Aguillard, State v., 217
Ahart, Commonwealth v., 400
Akers, State v., 139, 140–141
Aldershof, State v., 400
Allam v. State, 32–34, 258
Allen, People v., 364–366
Allen, State v., 386, 387–390
Anderson v. State, 33
Anderson, State v., 29—Ohio Supreme
 Court, 1991
Anthony Wilson, State v., 49–50
Armitage, People v., 107, 108–109

B

Backun v. United States, 122
Backus, Board of Commissioners v., 267
Bailey v. United States, 117
Bailey, Rex v., 410
Baird, Eisenstadt v., 43
Baldwin, State v., 347
Barnes v. Glen Theatre, Inc. et al., 39,
 CD-ROM
Barnes, State v., 94, 95–96
Barnette, Commonwealth v., 92–94
Beard v. United States, 221
Beardsley, People v., 69–70
Beasley v. State, 315
Beaudry, State v., 130–135, 136
Bell, Buck v., 32
Berkowitz, Commonwealth v., 333, 339,
 340–341
Board of Commissioners v. Backus, 267
Bonds, State v., 346–348, CD-ROM
Bowers v. Hardwick, 42, 43, 44, 45
Bowie, People v., 260–261
Boy Scouts of America v. Dale, 46
Bradley v. Ward, 157
Brown v. State, 336–337
Brown v. United States, 109
Brown, Commonwealth v., 91
Brown, People v., 365, 366

Brown, State v., 233–234, CD-ROM
Bruno, United States v., 179
Buck v. Bell, 32
Burnett v. State, 87
Burns, State v., 411–412
Burrows v. State, 262–263

C

Cabey v. Goetz, 204–205
Caffero, People v., 307
California, Edwards v., 432
California, Robinson v., 49, 63, 65, 66,
 454, CD-ROM
Campbell v. State, 305
Carey v. Population Service Int'l, 43
Carlo, People v., 266
Casey, Planned Parenthood of
 Southeastern Pa. v., 45
Casico v. State, 337
Celli, State v., 228, CD-ROM
Chaplinsky v. New Hampshire, 35–36
Chessman, People v., 364
Chism, State v., 125–128
Christy, McKendree v., 367
City and County of San Francisco, Joyce
 v., 433, 434–438
City of Chicago v. Morales, 447–454,
 CD-ROM
City of Chicago, Thompson and others v.,
 444–445, CD-ROM
City of Fort Lauderdale, Smith v., 441
City of Jacksonville, Papichristou v., 432
City of St. Paul, R.A.V. v., 37, 38, 439,
 443
Clark, State v., 80–81, CD-ROM
Clowes, State v., 226
Cogdon, King v., 55, 59–60
Coker v. Georgia, 49, 50
Cole, State v., 227
Commonwealth v. Ahart, 400
Commonwealth v. Barnette, 92–94
Commonwealth v. Berkowitz, 333, 339,
 340–341
Commonwealth v. Brown, 91
Commonwealth v. Gilliam, 161, CD-ROM
Commonwealth v. Golston, 301

Commonwealth v. Jones, 400
Commonwealth v. Kozak, 406
Commonwealth v. McAlister, 266
Commonwealth v. Mitchell, 407–408
Commonwealth v. Mlinarich, 338, 341
Commonwealth v. Peaslee, 162, CD-ROM
Commonwealth v. Schnopps, 282, 319–321
Commonwealth, Dunn v., 128,
 CD-ROM
Commonwealth, Satterwhite v., 337
Connecticut, Griswold v., 41–42, 43, 47
Coulverson, State v., 149, 150–152
Cramer v. United States, 465, 466–467,
 CD-ROM
Cramer, State v., 211–214
Crane, State v., 305
Crawford v. State, 220
Curley, State v., 399–401

D

D. P. v. State, 256–258
Dale, Boy Scouts of America v., 46
Daley, Landry v., 426–427
Damms, State v., 146, 162, 163–167, 172
Datema, People v., 326–328
Davis, People v., 285–290
Dawkins v. State, 81, CD-ROM
Debs v. United States, 471
Decina, People v., 60, CD-ROM
Dennis v. United States, 468–479, 488
DePasquale v. State, 270–271
Dewayne Bethley, State v., 49–50
Dial v. State, 253
Direct Sales Co. v. United States., 179
Dover, People v., 227–228, CD-ROM
Dudley & Stephens, The Queen v., 224
Duest v. State, 301
Dunn v. Commonwealth, 128, CD-ROM
Durham v. United States, 244

E

Edwards v. California, 432
Eisenstadt v. Baird, 43
Elder, State v., 322, CD-ROM
Ellyson v. State, 413
Ely, State v., 337

Index

void-for-vagueness and, 28
Fighting words, 35, 507
First Amendment, 501, CD-ROM
   free speech and, 35
   free speech, time, place and manner
      regulation, 439
   right to privacy and, 41
   Smith Act of 1940 and, 468–479,
      CD-ROM
   text of, 501, CD-ROM
First degree murder, 283, 292–295,
      298–301507
   actus reus of, 298–301
   elements of, 293
   mens rea of, 293–295
Fixing Broken Windows, 430
Flag burning, as free speech, 39, CD-ROM
Fletcher, George P., 58, 59, 67, 192, 201,
      205, 262, 282
Florida reception statute, 13
Force
   rape and, 339–340
   reasonable, 194, 196–201, 511
"Force and resistance" standard, 336–337
Forgery, 394–397, 507
Foster, Jodie, 246
Fourteenth Amendment, 501–502,
      CD-ROM
   age classifications and, 31–34,
      CD-ROM
   drug classifications and, 34, CD-ROM
   equal protection and, 31–32
   quality of life crimes and, 429
   right to privacy and, 41
   text of, 501–502
   void-for-vagueness and, 28
Franklin, Benjamin, 464–465
Fraud, as an inherently dangerous felony,
      309–310, CD-ROM
Free speech, 35–41
   content discrimination and, 38
   expressive conduct, 35
   as fundamental right, 26, 35
   infringement upon, 37–38
   time, place and manner regulations,
      439
Free will, 59
   retribution and, 7, 8
Fundamental fairness, vicarious liability
      and, 129–130
Fundamental right, 507
   constitutional democracy and, 26
   free speech as, 26,35
   privacy as, 41

G
Gangs, 28, 445–454, CD-ROM
Gaylin, Willard, 7
Gender classifications, equal protection
      and, 32
General attempt statutes, 149, 507,
      CD-ROM

General deterrence, 8, 507
General intent, 88, 507
General part of criminal law, 9, 507
General prevention, 8, 507
General principles of liability, 55–57
   of liability, homicide and, 57
   state codes and, CD-ROM
Genovese, Kitty, 74–75, 76
Getaway drivers, 116
Gibeaut, John, 262
Giuliani, Rudolf, 181
Giving aid and comfort to the enemy,
      465, 507
Gladstone, William, 267
Goetz, Bernard, 201–205
Good Samaritan doctrine, 68, 507
Goodman, Ellen, 433
Government, levels of, 11
Government actions, entrapment and
      271–272
Government regulation, 2, 507
Grading, 8. *See also specific crimes*
   crimes 8–11
   by punishment, 9–10
   schemes, 9–11, CD-ROM
   by subject, 10–11
Grading schemes, 9–11, CD-ROM
Grand larceny, 379, 507
Grievous bodily injury, 196
Gross, Hyman, 258–259
Gross criminal negligence, 323, 507
Gross misdemeanor, 10, 508
Group disorderly conduct, 426, 428–429,
      508
Guilty but mentally ill, 240

H
Habeas corpus, 16, 508
Hadley Jr., Joseph E., 313
Hale, Lord, 335
Hale, Matthew, 223
Hall, Jerome, 259
Harboring a fugitive, 116
Harboring or concealing terrorists,
      483–484
Harm, arson and, 403
Harmful result, principle of, 57, 510
Hate crimes, free speech and, 36–39
Hayter, Karen, 431
Hearst, Patricia, 363
Hearst, William Randolph, 363
Heightened scrutiny, 32, 508
Herrnstein, Richard, 7
Hinckley, Jr., John, 246, 252
Hire, 117
HIV exposure, purpose and, 90–92
Holding, 17, 508
Holmes, Oliver Wendell, 35–36, 59
   attempt and, 149
   mens rea and, 87
   overt act and, 175
Home, defense of 218–233, CD-ROM

Homeless
   due process of law and, 436–437
   equal protection and, 436
   Matrix program and, 433–438
   rights of, 433–438
Homicide, 282. *See also* Murder
   actus reus, 284, 508
   causation and, 284
   elements of, 284–292
   general principles of liability and, 57
   law, history of, 283
   mens rea, 291, 505
   principles of, 57
   result, 284
   state classifications, CD-ROM
Hughes, Graham, 70
Hypnotism, voluntary acts and, 61,
      CD-ROM

I
Identity theft, 383–386, 508
Illness, as an act, 63, CD-ROM
Immaturity, 253
Imminent danger, 194, 196–201,
      206–211, 508
Imperfect defenses, 192, 508
"In the nighttime," 414
Incapacitation, prevention and, 8, 508
Inchoate offenses, 146, 508
Incomplete criminal conduct, 146
Indirect evidence, *mens rea* and, 88
Indispensable element test, 156, 508
Individual conscience, 3
Individual disorderly conduct, 426–428,
      508
Individual liberty, 5
Individual rights, 5
Induce, 117
Inferring participation, 118
Information, 508
Inherently dangerous felony, 306–310,
      CD-ROM
Initial aggressor, 194–196, 508
Injunction, 508
   to abate public nuisance, 445
Insanity, 240, 508
   affirmative defense and, 252
   blameworthiness and, 246
   criminal liability 240–252
   culpability, 246
   defense of, 240–252, CD-ROM
   tests, 241–252
Intangible property, 375, 378, 508
Intellectual property, 386, 508
Intelligence gathering, 480, 508
Intent. *See Mens rea*
   attempt and, 148
   punishing, 58
Intentional scaring, 355, 508
Interfering with prosecution, 125
International terrorism, 482, 508
Intervene, failure to, 67, 507